THE CAMBRIDGE COMPANION TO

ANCIENT ROME

Rome was the largest city in the ancient world. As the capital of the
Roman empire, it was clearly an exceptional city in terms of size,
diversity and complexity. While the Colosseum, imperial palaces and
Pantheon are among its most famous features, this volume explores
Rome primarily as a city in which many thousands of men and women
were born, lived and died. The thirty-one chapters by leading historians, classicists and archaeologists discuss issues ranging from the
monuments and the games to the food and water supply, from policing
and riots to domestic housing, from death and disease to pagan cults
and the impact of Christianity. Richly illustrated, the volume introduces groundbreaking new research against the background of current
debates and is designed as a readable survey accessible in particular to
undergraduates and non-specialists.

PAUL ERDKAMP is Professor of Ancient History at the Free University
of Brussels (VUB). Previously, he was Research Fellow at the University
of Leiden. He has published two monographs, *Hunger and the Sword:
Warfare and Food Supply in Roman Republican Wars* (1998) and *The Grain
Market in the Roman Empire* (2005), and is editor of *The Roman Army
and the Economy* (2002), *A Companion to the Roman Army* (2007) and
A Cultural History of Food in Antiquity (2012). His research interests
include the ancient economy, army and warfare, ancient historiography,
in particular Polybius and Livy, and social and cultural aspects of food
in classical antiquity. Professor Erdkamp is currently co-chair of the
Roman Society Research Centre, in which various departments of
ancient history and archaeology at European universities participate.

THE CAMBRIDGE COMPANION TO

ANCIENT ROME

Edited by

PAUL ERDKAMP

CAMBRIDGE
UNIVERSITY PRESS

University Printing House, Cambridge CB2 8BS, United Kingdom

Published in the United States of America by Cambridge University Press, New York

Cambridge University Press is part of the University of Cambridge.

It furthers the University's mission by disseminating knowledge in the pursuit of education, learning and research at the highest international levels of excellence.

www.cambridge.org
Information on this title: www.cambridge.org/9780521896290

© Cambridge University Press 2013

First published 2013

Printed and bound in the United Kingdom by Bell & Bain Ltd

A catalogue record for this publication is available from the British Library

Library of Congress Cataloguing in Publication data
The Cambridge companion to ancient Rome / edited by Paul Erdkamp.
p.   cm.
Includes bibliographical references and index.
ISBN 978-0-521-89629-0 (hardback) – ISBN 978-0-521-72078-6 (pbk.)
1. Rome (Italy) – History – To 476.   2. Rome – Social conditions.
3. Rome – Social life and customs.   I. Erdkamp, Paul.
II. Title: Companion to ancient Rome.
DG63.C284   2012
937 – dc23   2012027120

ISBN 978-0-521-89629-0 Hardback
ISBN 978-0-521-72078-6 Paperback

CONTENTS

v

CONTENTS

CONTENTS

FIGURES

TABLE

∽

Maps

⅋

CONTRIBUTORS

GREGORY S. ALDRETE is Professor of History and Humanistic Studies at the University of Wisconsin-Green Bay. He is the author of a number of books including *Floods of the Tiber in Ancient Rome*, *Gestures and Acclamations in Ancient Rome*, and *Daily Life in the Roman City: Rome, Pompeii, and Ostia*, and is currently directing a project reconstructing and testing ancient linen armour. For more information, visit his website: <www.uwgb.edu/aldreteg/>.

ANDREAS BENDLIN is Associate Professor of Roman History at the University of Toronto. His research focuses on religion in Graeco-Roman antiquity, with a particular emphasis on the materiality of religion, the variety of religious practices and beliefs, and the many competing discourses about religion in the city of Rome and the Roman Empire. Other research interests include Roman social, cultural and literary history.

WIM BROEKAERT recently finished a PhD on Roman merchants and the organization of Mediterranean trade. He is currently working as a Postdoctoral research assistant at Ghent University on a structural and comparative study of Roman trading practice. His publications focus on Roman economic policies, commercial inscriptions on amphorae, and professional organizations of traders and shippers.

CHRISTER BRUUN is Professor of Classics at the University of Toronto, where he teaches Roman history and Latin literature. He has lived several years in Rome, as a student and scholar at the Finnish Institute, and in 1997–2000 as Director of the Institutum Romanum Finlandiae. He has published extensively on the water supply of Rome and on the topography and epigraphy of the city.

ELISHA ANN DUMSER is an Assistant Professor at the University of Akron. She was a contributing author and editor of *Mapping Augustan Rome* (2002) and is currently writing a monograph on the architectural patronage of Maxentius in Rome.

CATHARINE EDWARDS is Professor of Classics and Ancient History at Birkbeck, University of London and has a long-standing interest in the city of Rome and its receptions in literature ancient and modern. She is the author of, among other things, *Writing Rome: Textual Approaches to the City* (1996). She edited, with Greg Woolf, *Rome the Cosmopolis* (2003).

PAUL ERDKAMP is Professor of Ancient History at the Flemish Free University of Brussels. He is the author of *Hunger and the Sword: Warfare and Food Supply in Roman Republican Wars* (1998) and *The Grain Market in the Roman Empire* (2005). He has edited *A Companion to the Roman Army* (2007). His other research interests include Polybius and Livy and social and cultural aspects of food and dining.

SHAWN GRAHAM is Assistant Professor of Digital Humanities in the History Department at Carleton University in Ottawa, Canada. He is currently applying agent-based modelling approaches to various questions of Roman archaeology, including the emergence of social networks over space, the diffusion of information through social space, and the evolution of social networks in the extractive economy of the Roman world.

ALEXANDRE GRANDAZZI is a Professor at the Sorbonne University (Paris IV), who specializes in the origins of Rome. He is the author of numerous scholarly articles on archaic Rome. His publications include *The Foundation of Rome: Myth and History* (1997). His most recent book is entitled *Alba Longa, histoire d'une légende: Recherches sur l'archéologie, la religion, les traditions de l'ancien Latium*, 2 vols. (2008).

CAMERON HAWKINS is an Assistant Professor in the History Department at the University of Chicago. He has published studies on the organization of manufacturing in the Roman world and on the economics of manumission, and is currently working on a book about artisans and the urban economy in the late Republic and early Roman empire.

ELISABETH HERRMANN-OTTO has been Professor in Ancient History at the University of Trier since 2000. She is co-editor of the concise dictionary of ancient slavery. She has published *Ex ancilla natus: Untersuchungen zu den 'hausgeborenen' Sklaven und Sklavinnen im Westen des römischen Kaiserreiches* (1994); (in collaboration with J. Michael Rainer) *Corpus der Römischen Rechtsquellen zur Antiken Sklaverei* (1999); *Sklaverei und Freilassung in der griechisch-römischen Welt* (2009).

BENJAMIN KELLY is an Associate Professor in the History Department at York University, Toronto. He was previously a Lecturer in the History Program at the Australian National University. He is the author of *Petitions, Litigation and Social Control in Roman Egypt* (2011).

RAY LAURENCE is Professor of Roman History and Archaeology at the University of Kent (UK). He is the author of *Roman Pompeii: Space and Society* (2nd edn, 2007) and *The Roads of Roman Italy: Mobility and Cultural Change* (1999), as well as co-author of *The City in the Roman West* (2011) and co-editor of *Rome, Pompeii and Ostia: Movement and Space* (2011).

A. D. LEE is Professor of Ancient History in the Department of Classics at the University of Nottingham, where he teaches Roman history. He is the author of a number of books on aspects of the late Roman world, including *Pagans and Christians in Late Antiquity* (2000) and *War in Late Antiquity: A Social History* (2007).

JINYU LIU is Associate Professor of Classical Studies at DePauw University. She is the author of *Collegia Centonariorum: The Guilds of Textile Dealers in the Roman West* (2009). Her research interests include social relations in Roman cities, the non-elite in the Roman empire, Latin epigraphy, as well as the reception of Graeco-Roman classics in China.

J. BERT LOTT is Professor of Greek and Roman Studies at Vassar College in Poughkeepsie, New York. He is the author of *Neighbours of Augustan Rome* (2004).

THOMAS A. J. MCGINN is Professor of Classical Studies at Vanderbilt University. He is the author of numerous books and articles on prostitution, marriage and concubinage in ancient Rome. His books include

Widows and Patriarchy: Ancient and Modern, which was published in 2008.

MICHAEL MACKINNON is Associate Professor in the Department of Classics at the University of Winnipeg. As a zooarchaeologist who specializes in the archaeology of the ancient Greek and Roman worlds, he has worked for more than fifty different projects at sites in the Mediterranean area. He is the author of *Production and Consumption of Animals in Roman Italy: Integrating the Zooarchaeological and Textual Evidence* (2004).

R. DON MILLER is a Teaching Fellow in Greek and Roman history at Newcastle University. His research interests include the origins of Rome, the history of the Republic, and the topography and monuments of the city. His monograph, *Monuments, Memory, and Myth: The Arts of Public Commemoration in Republican Rome*, is forthcoming.

CLAUDIA MOATTI is a Professor at Paris VIII University and at the University of Southern California. Her research centres on the intellectual history of Roman politics (*La Raison de Rome*, 1997), as well as on the administrative capacity of the ancient states to control human mobility and territories. Her two current projects examine the concept of *res publica* and the 'cosmopolitization' of the Roman empire.

NEVILLE MORLEY is Professor of Ancient History at the University of Bristol. His recent publications include *Trade in Classical Antiquity* (2007), *Antiquity and Modernity* (2008) and *The Roman Empire: Roots of Imperialism* (2010).

NICHOLAS PURCELL has been Fellow and Tutor in Ancient History at St John's College, Oxford and a lecturer in Ancient History at Oxford University since 1979. He has been interested in the history and archaeology of the city of Rome and its neighbourhood throughout his career, and composed chapters on the *plebs urbana* and related topics in several volumes of the *Cambridge Ancient History*.

BERYL RAWSON was Professor Emerita and Adjunct Professor in Classics and Ancient History at the Australian National University. She has written on the social, political and cultural history of Rome. Her publications include *The Family in Ancient Rome* (1986), *Marriage,*

Divorce and Children in Ancient Rome (1991), *The Roman Family in Italy* (with Paul Weaver, 1997), and *Children and Childhood in Roman Italy* (2003).

INGRID ROWLAND lives in Rome, where she is a Professor at the University of Notre Dame School of Architecture and writes for both scholarly and general readers. Her books include *The Culture of the High Renaissance*, *The Scarith of Scornello* and *Giordano Bruno*. She has translated Vitruvius and Giordano Bruno's dialogue *De gli Heroici Furori*.

LEONARD V. RUTGERS is Professor of Late Antiquity at Utrecht University, the Netherlands. His area of expertise is late antique archaeology and Jewish–Christian relations. His latest book is entitled *Making Myths: Jews in Early Christian Identity Formation* (2009).

MICHELE RENEE SALZMAN is Professor of History at the University of California at Riverside. She is the author of several books, including *On Roman Time: The Codex-Calendar of 354 and the Rhythms of Urban Life in Late Antiquity* (1990) and *The Making of a Christian Aristocracy: Religious and Social Change in the Western Roman Empire* (2002). She is the translator (with Michael Roberts) and author of a commentary on *The Letters of Symmachus. Book 1* (2011). Her research focuses on the religious and social history of the Roman empire.

WALTER SCHEIDEL is Dickason Professor in the Humanities and Professor of Classics and History at Stanford University. His research focuses on ancient social and economic history, pre-modern demography, and comparative and transdisciplinary approaches to the past.

GLENN R. STOREY has a BA from Columbia University, New York, an Honours BA and MA in Classics from Trinity College, Oxford, and an MA and PhD in Anthropology from the Pennsylvania State University. He is currently Associate Professor of Classics and Anthropology at the University of Iowa.

STEVEN L. TUCK is Professor in Classics and the History of Art at Miami University. He received his PhD in Classical Art and Archaeology from the University of Michigan. His publications include articles on the spectacle schedule at Pompeii, the decorative programme of the amphitheatre at Capua, and triumphal imagery across the ancient

Roman world. He is the author of *Latin Inscriptions in the Kelsey Museum* (2006).

ROBERT WITCHER is Senior Lecturer in the Department of Archaeology, Durham University. His research concerns the theory and method of landscape archaeology with a particular focus on the Roman period. He is involved in archaeological research projects in Italy and Britain. His publications include studies of phenomenology and globalization as methods to interpret the Roman past. Most recently, he has published articles on the cultural value of Hadrian's Wall.

ADAM ZIOLKOWSKI is Professor of Ancient History at the University of Warsaw. His publications include *The Temples of Mid-Republican Rome and their Historical and Topographical Context* (1992), *Storia di Roma* (2000) and *Sacra Via: Twenty Years After* (2004).

ARJAN ZUIDERHOEK is a lecturer in ancient history at Ghent University. His research focuses on the social, political and economic history of the Roman empire, mainly the east, and on urban history. He is author of *The Politics of Munificence in the Roman Empire: Citizens, Elites and Benefactors in Asia Minor* (2009).

ABBREVIATIONS

∽

AE	*L'Année épigraphique*. Revue des publications épigraphiques relatives à l'antiquité romaine. Published in Revue Archéologique and separately. Paris, 1888–
CCSL	Corpus Christianorum, Series Latina. Turnhout, 1967–
CIL	Corpus Inscriptionum Latinarum. Berlin, 1862–
CSEL	Corpus Scriptorum Ecclesiasticorum Latinorum. Vienna, 1866–
FIRA	*Fontes Iuris Romani Antejustiniani*, ed. S. Riccobono et al. 3 vols. Florence, 1940
Hunt–Edgar	*Select papyri*, ed. and trans. A. S. Hunt and C. C. Edgar. Vol. 1: *Non-literary papyri. Private affairs*. Cambridge, MA, 1932. Vol. 2: *Official documents*. Cambridge, MA, 1934. Vol. 3: *Literary papyri: poetry*. Cambridge, MA, 1941
IGUR	*Inscriptiones Graecae Urbis Romae*, ed. L. Moretti. 4 vols. Rome, 1968–90
ILCV	*Inscriptiones Latinae Christianae Veteres*, ed. E. Diehl. Berlin, 1925–31
ILS	*Inscriptiones Latinae Selectae*, ed. H. Dessau. Berlin, 1856–1931
Insc. Ital.	*Inscriptiones Italiae*. Rome, 1931
LTUR	*Lexicon Topographicum Urbis Romae*, ed. E. M. Steinby. 6 vols. Rome, 1993–2000
LTURS	*Lexicon Topographicum Urbis Romae – Suburbium*, ed. A. La Regina. 4 vols. Rome, 2001–8
OGIS	*Orientis Graeci Inscriptiones Selectae*, ed. W. Dittenberger. Leipzig, 1903–5
RDGE	*Roman Documents from the Greek East*, ed. R. K. Sherk. Baltimore, 1969

INTRODUCTION

Paul Erdkamp

∽

At the time when Rome first began to rise into a position of worldwide splendour, destined to live so long as men shall exist, in order that she might grow to a towering stature, Virtue and Fortune [. . .] formed a pact of eternal peace. For if either one of them had failed her, Rome would not have attained complete supremacy. Her people, from the very cradle to the end of their childhood, a period of about 300 years, carried on wars about her walls. Then, entering upon adult life, after many toilsome wars, they crossed the Alps and the sea. Grown to youth and manhood, from every region which the vast globe includes, they brought back laurels and triumphs. And now, declining into old age, and often owing victory to its name alone, she has come to a quieter period of life. Thus the respected city, after humbling the proud necks of savage nations, and making laws, the everlasting foundations of liberty, like a careful parent, wise and wealthy, has entrusted the management of her inheritance to the Caesars, as to her children. [. . .] Throughout all regions and parts of the earth she is accepted as mistress and queen. Everywhere the white hair of the senators and their authority are honoured and the name of the Roman people is respected.

(*Ammianus Marcellinus* 14.6.3–6)

In the second half of the fourth century AD, the historian Ammianus Marcellinus – who was born in Syrian Antioch, but as an officer in the Roman army had seen much of the empire in east and west, including the city of Rome – compared the stages in her history to the phases in a person's life. In her young years, the settlement of farmers on the lower course of the Tiber had conquered its Italian neighbours. Rome reached adulthood, in Ammianus' view, when she began to expand her power across the Alps and overseas in the aftermath of the Punic Wars. It is at this stage that Rome emerged as the capital of the civilized world.

In Ammianus' days, however, the capital had grown old and had wisely handed over government to younger forces – the Caesars, her children as it were. It was a diplomatic way of saying that power had shifted to cities like York, Milan, Antioch – and above all Constantinople. Already in the early third century AD, Herodian (1.6) – historian and administrator – could write that Rome was where the emperor was, a process that had been finalized when Ammianus wrote the words quoted above. Rome had become peripheral, as the political and military gravity had shifted towards the war zones in the north and east. Fewer and fewer emperors found occasion to visit Rome. When Constantine founded Constantinople, Rome had long lost its position at the heart of the empire, although its high standing is reflected in the fact that the emperor deliberately reproduced the senate, the dole and games in his new capital.

Many studies of ancient Rome focus on its physical remains and monuments: even robbed of most of their marble, the fora, baths, temples, theatres and amphitheatres, arches and columns are still able to reflect some of the splendour and majesty of the city in former days. This is the aspect of ancient Rome that is most visible nowadays. Many people know the city through its ancient monuments. Ironically, after having been a quarry for building material and a citadel of noble families during the Middle Ages, the Colosseum today draws almost as many visitors as it did during the first centuries of its existence. Of course, much of this is part of the cliché of ancient Rome: gladiators, bread and circuses – one of the things that every tourist goes to see when in Rome. The crowds at the Ara Pacis or the Baths of Caracalla are significantly smaller.

The monuments are an important part of ancient Rome, but they do not provide the focal point of this companion. Martial (*Epigr.* 7.61) presents us with the following image of Rome in his day:

> The audacious shopkeepers had appropriated to themselves
> the whole city, and a man's own threshold was not his own.
> You, Germanicus [Domitian], bade the narrow streets
> grow wide; and what but just before was a pathway became
> a highway. No column is now girt at the bottom with
> chained wine-flagons; nor is the Praetor compelled to walk
> in the midst of the mud. Nor, again, is the barber's razor
> drawn blindly in the middle of a crowd, nor does the

smutty cookshop project over every street. The barber, the
vintner, the cook, the butcher, keep their own places. The
city is now Rome; recently it was a great shop.

According to modern estimates, Rome was home to roughly a million inhabitants, making it not only the largest city of Antiquity by
far, but probably also the most densely populated one. The passage
from Martial reveals a certain tension, as even in Antiquity the emperor
Domitian wanted to free the monuments from the rabble that lived
among them. His view, at least according to our hostile sources, was
the same as Nero's, who welcomed the fact that the Great Fire of
AD 64 created space for his new palace complex. However, Vespasian
gave the area back to the populace, not least in the form of the
Colosseum.

In a sense, we too want to give back Rome to its inhabitants.
Rome is addressed in this volume primarily as a city in which many
thousands of men and women were born, lived and died. While it may
seem at first sight no more than a curious fact that Rome was the first
city to have grown to such a size (reached by London only *c.* 1800), it is
worthwhile to ask how such an enormous metropolis operated. A city
in general is a complex phenomenon, characterized by the multifarious
social relations among its inhabitants (and the people beyond), their
economic functioning, the determinants governing the distribution of
political influence and their cultural diversity. Ancient Rome clearly
was an exceptional city in terms of size, diversity and complexity, and
it is this fact that provides the focal point of this volume. The guiding
principle that is intended to tie together the various approaches to the
city of ancient Rome in this volume is provided by the question of how
its exceptional position and status influenced and determined ancient
Rome as a city, in other words as a living organism consisting of many
thousands of people.

Most of the chapters will concentrate on the roughly 500 years of
what Ammianus called Rome's adulthood: its years of splendour and
power, when the city was still very much at the heart of the empire.
The centuries up to and including the first phase of Rome's expansion
overseas are dealt with in an opening chapter on the emergence of
Rome as a city-state and the development of the city as its power
expanded (Grandazzi, Chapter 1). Financed by the booty taken from
vanquished enemies, successful generals built monuments within the
urban space of Rome that expressed the link between military victory
and communal identity.

Part I of the companion deals with the size, composition and formation of the city's population. One of the exceptional features of Rome was its size, and the Part begins with an analysis of the evidence on population size, which is indissolubly linked to the question of the social make-up of the city, as the few figures we possess can only be interpreted in relation to the city's social structure (Morley, Chapter 2). The size and social fabric of the city's populace are determined by various demographic forces. The physical and biological conditions of a mega-city in Mediterranean surroundings shaped the mortality regime of Rome (Scheidel, Chapter 3). In view of the high levels of mortality, Rome's growth was clearly due to immigration, which not only determined the demography of Rome, but also its ethnic and cultural diversity (Moatti, Chapter 5). Another important aspect of human mobility in the Roman world was the trade in slaves. As slaves, either imported from overseas or born in servitude, and as freedmen they became a vital part of the populace of the Roman capital (Herrmann-Otto, Chapter 4). The smallest, but at the same time most important, unit of the city's populace was the family. One's social place and identity in Rome was very much determined by which family one belonged to and which position one had in that family (Rawson, Chapter 6). Finally, an aspect of Rome that has been too much neglected is that it was not only inhabited by people, but by numerous animals as well, who were either welcomed as pets or as working animals necessary for the city's logistics, or worsened living conditions by exacerbating disease transmission in the city (MacKinnon, Chapter 7).

Part II addresses the urban fabric of Rome, starting with an outline of the developments of the city's topography from the mid-republic to late imperial times (Dumser, Chapter 8). The smallest unit within the urban fabric consists of the inhabitants' dwellings, ranging from wealthy mansions to apartments in the infamous *insulae* (Storey, Chapter 9). Evidence on the streets, districts and neighbourhoods reflects higher levels of organization and administration (Lott, Chapter 10). A significant part of the city's space was devoted to various types of monuments. The development of these monuments and the shift in types of monument in republican and imperial times mirror changes in the political structure of Rome (Miller, Chapter 11). Analysis of the urban fabric inevitably leads to the question of where Rome exactly ended. In fact, urban Rome merged with its rural surroundings, as on its borders the city gradually evolved into countryside (Witcher, Chapter 12).

Shawn Graham (Chapter 16) compares the city of Rome to a living organism, and this image is at the heart of Part III. Not only the human and non-human inhabitants of the city, but also the buildings, monuments and infrastructure required sustenance in the form of food and fodder, building material, fuel and water. In view of the city's size, in combination with a transport system that depended on human, animal and wind energy, the logistics of the city may justly be characterized as a nightmare. The main arteries of Rome's logistical system consisted of the Tiber and of the roads. The Tiber and the transportation it offered were important factors in the location and urban development of Rome (Tuck, Chapter 13). Enormous quantities of goods needed to be brought into and distributed within the city, and the nature of transportation and traffic, exacerbated by the movement of the city's numerous inhabitants, constitutes an important aspect of the workings of the city (Laurence, Chapter 14). Rome's food supply operated on the margins of the logistically possible, and its functioning depended very much on the intense involvement of the authorities. What the inhabitants of Rome ate and how they received it reflects the city's exceptional position as imperial capital (Erdkamp, Chapter 15). The same applies to the supply of non-edible goods. Estimating the volumes of building material and fuel gives us an idea of the enormous volumes involved and shows the necessity to understand the nature of the networks involved (Graham, Chapter 16). Finally, Rome is famous for its water supply. The building and maintenance of the aqueducts and the organization of the distribution of water again reflect the choices made by the city's rulers (Bruun, Chapter 17).

In contrast to a widespread misconception, most of Rome's inhabitants had to work to sustain their accustomed way of life. The economic activities and the nature of the labour employed are the subject of Part IV. Not only the rich, but also the mass of common inhabitants of Rome together constituted an enormous market for goods and services. What does the evidence tell us about the size and nature of the economic activities in Rome (Broekaert and Zuiderhoek, Chapter 18)? Economic and social factors determine the nature of the labour involved, whether servile or free, whether male or female, and whether permanent or temporary (Hawkins, Chapter 19). The professional organizations clarify the workings of the urban community, as they were not only geared to the professional requirements of their members, but also fulfilled other needs (Liu, Chapter 20). One line of work within the city was built upon the sexual needs of part of the populace. This activity may be said to have taken place on the margins of society socially, but not topographically (McGinn, Chapter 21).

Part v discusses the various relationships between the rulers of Rome and the ruled. During the Republic the body of citizens developed civic rituals that strengthened and expressed the political community. As the nature of the rulers, but also of the political significance of the population of Rome changed, so did the nature of the civic rituals within the city (Ziolkowski, Chapter 22). Part of the process of state formation was the development of instruments to control the urban population. While the authorities expressed responsibility for maintaining order in Rome, the extent to which they actually undertook and succeeded in offering a secure environment to their citizens was fairly limited (Kelly, Chapter 23). The inhabitants of Rome were not passive subjects, even beyond the increasingly limited range of influence that the political constitution allowed them. Protests frequently turned into riots, as parts of the populace communicated their displeasure with current affairs or even tried to enforce their desires (Aldrete, Chapter 24). Apart from the food supply, the games were already denounced by contemporary observers as bribes directed by the emperors at a politically disempowered citizenry. What role did the games play in the relations between rulers and the ruled (Purcell, Chapter 25)?

Buildings and objects that testified to the various beliefs and ideas about the relationship between mortals and the gods were manifest throughout the city, as were religious activities within both the private and public domain (Bendlin, Chapter 26). The calendar, festivals and various ways in which time was structured in Rome also reveal the link between political and religious life within the city (Salzman, Chapter 27). The Romans commemorated their dead in various ways, but as the burial or cremation of the dead was prohibited within the city itself, this aspect of urban life was concentrated beyond the city's borders. The monuments and graves of the dead, including Christian catacombs, replicate their wealth and social status (Rutgers, Chapter 28). The number of Christians in Rome steadily grew, and as Rome became less and less an imperial capital, it became more and more a Christian city. The impact of Christianity on late-antique Rome is mirrored in the shift of the urban topography towards churches, the make-up and role of the urban aristocracy and the role of the bishop (Lee, Chapter 29).

The chapters in the Epilogue do not so much address Rome as a thriving community of men and women, citizens and slaves, rulers and the ruled, but rather as an idea. Edwards (Chapter 30) explores the thinking about Rome throughout the ages by investigating the image of Rome in ruins in the works of several Greek and Roman authors, Virgil and Tacitus in particular. Rowland (Chapter 31) discusses the image and symbolic power of Rome in the Middle Ages, the Renaissance and modern times. The Popes emphasized their position as heirs to Rome, but so did such revolutionaries as the fourteenth-century Roman Cola di Rienzo, who named himself Tribune, or Mussolini, whose symbols and themes were inspired by imperial Rome.

Numerous approaches to ancient Rome are possible and it would have been easier to fill two volumes under the heading 'Companion to Ancient Rome' than one. Many readers will undoubtedly prefer the book to have included chapters on topics that are now only touched upon in several chapters or, even worse, will consider them not to have been dealt with adequately at all. Such topics as politics and administration, Roman law, art history and architecture are only dealt with in relation to the perspective on the city of Rome outlined above. For example, several aspects of politics in Rome are dealt with in Chapter 22 (Ziolkowski) on civic rituals and political spaces in republican and imperial Rome, but no attempt is made to cover the entire subject of politics in ancient Rome. Hence, the debate about the nature of political decision-making and the workings of the popular assemblies in republican times has no place in this volume. Elements of Roman law may be found in Chapter 23 (Kelly) on policing Rome, of art history in Chapter 11 (Miller) on the monuments, of architecture in Chapter 9 (Storey) on housing, but these topics are not dealt with in their own right. Inevitably, some criticism of the book will be based on the feeling that this is not the companion that the reader himself or herself would have designed or desired. Fortunately, many general books on the city of Rome have been and will be published, and these may be more to his or her liking. I can only hope that the volume as it is succeeds in providing a clear and coherent outline of Rome as a city, and thus of the ways in which the lives of its inhabitants were determined by the fact that they lived in the capital of the Roman empire.

1: THE EMERGENCE OF
THE CITY

Alexandre Grandazzi

AN EXCEPTIONAL SITE

Before being a town, Rome occupied an exceptional site. Recent research makes it possible to understand how the Roman territory looked at the time when human communities, still small, began to visit it regularly and even live there temporarily. This happened in the mid-Bronze Age, roughly three and a half millennia ago. The Ancients sought the secret of the city's predominance in its beginnings. Moderns, using a different temporal scale, do so with the help of earth sciences. Neither geography nor even geology explains history. Rather, they make it possible.[1] Without taking into account the natural factors at work within the space that would become that of the largest town in the ancient world, we could understand neither the emergence of Rome in this precise spot nor many of its future developments.

The site of the city was produced by the interaction between a very ancient and originally maritime sedimentary substratum and the deposits, between 600,000 and 300,000 years ago, of two neighbouring volcanic systems, the Sabatini mountains to the north-east and the Alban mountains to the south-east. Another determining factor was a river, the valley of which was the widest in the whole peninsula and which, with its 400 km-long course and its forty or so tributaries, came to form a natural axis of communications.

The famous Roman hills were grouped around the river at a point where, checked by the mass of volcanic deposits, it bent sharply towards the south-west. In the centre of its meandering course, an island, formed as early as the Pleistocene, made it easier to cross the water. Two lines of ridges came to a halt at the left bank; one ran from the Quirinal to the Capitol, the other from the Esquiline to the Palatine, while the Caelian and the Aventine stood further back. Between these lay a wide

---

[1] For an analysis of the geology of the site of Rome, see Funiciello et al. 2006.

depression that used to be criss-crossed by watercourses and was liable to form marshland, as also happened around the Velabrum river. Further to the north, the alluvial plain within the river's wide western curve, which was frequently flooded, presented a huge open space. The hills, many of which were linked, were divided into secondary promontories. Thus the Capitol was made up of two peaks; the Palatine joined up with the Velia; the Quirinal had several peaks. We should imagine slopes many of which were steeper than they are today, the difference of altitude between the summits and the valley floor being *c.* 40 m. After twenty-seven centuries of urban life producing earthworks and fill-ins of many kinds, that distance of 40 m has been diminished.

Another particular feature is the abundance of fresh water, due to the presence of many springs. In a climate rather colder than that of today, these springs favoured the development of dense vegetation, as is reflected in place-names such as Querquetulanus mons, the hill of oaks (formerly the name of the Caelius), the Viminal and the Fagutal, names that indicate the presence of willows and beech trees.

With its hills, springs, river and island, the site of Rome at the dawn of its human history was clearly exceptional. Elsewhere, most of the places destined to become the sites of cities constituted naturally unified structures. The Etruscan cities of Veii, Tarquinia, Volsinies and Vulci each developed on a large plateau, isolated from their surroundings by a belt of waterways. In contrast, the hills alongside the Tiber presented a much more diverse framework.

Rome was by no means positioned at the centre of the region to which it belongs, namely Latium. Situated on the banks of the river that was to mark the boundary with Etruria, it was a frontier-town, an outpost facing foreign land. It was also to be the point at which the river could be bridged: a city that offered anyone arriving from the sea their first chance to cross the river. The coast was no more than *c.* 20 km away. Set behind the numerous coastal lagoons and thus protected against surprise incursions from the sea, Rome lay close enough to the shore to benefit from the civilizing inputs of Phoenicians, Greeks and Etruscans. As the Romans of the Republic liked to declare, geography itself showed that Rome, by virtue of its situation, was a town oriented towards the sea.

Nevertheless, the geological and geographical balance sheet remained mixed, for the advantages of the site were offset by obvious disadvantages, in particular the compartmentalized nature of the various districts. A site of such a nature could only be transformed into a unified whole by dint of collective human efforts. Nor did primitive

Latium possess the metal-bearing and agricultural riches that abounded in neighbouring Etruria. On the other hand, the configuration of the site of Rome did enable it to open up to the world beyond. Two axes crossed here, the one running from north-east to south-west, along the Tiber valley, the other, thanks to the island and the natural ford downstream from it, from north-west to south-east. Where these two axes intersected, the hills close to the river provided incomparable opportunities for defence and development.

We should also note the twofold centrality of the territory in which Rome would be founded and would develop: it was situated right in the middle of a peninsula that was itself at the centre of the world then constituted by the Mediterranean Sea.

A CHALLENGE FOR RESEARCH

Recent excavations have brought to light copious data, many still unpublished. Researchers compare these archaeological finds with the ancient texts. The exploration of Rome's origins began with Giacomo Boni's excavations in the Forum at the beginning of the twentieth century. Meanwhile, among the texts, apart from poetic works such as Virgil's *Aeneid*, we have a historiographical tradition, sometimes described as annalistic, that was exemplified in the first century BC by Livy and Dionysius of Halicarnassus; and also a learned tradition sometimes called 'antiquarian': here our principal representative is Varro. The epistemological problem for researchers stems from the basic disparity, both in nature and dates, that separates the archaeological data and the literary sources.[2] The archaeological evidence, contemporary with the past of which it constitutes a direct trace, is lacunose; and the literary sources go back no further than the third century BC and mostly date from the end of the first century BC. These texts recount a partly fabulous history, passed down through centuries in the city of Rome, in which authentic information concerning, for example, place-names and religious rites is intermingled with the myths and beliefs of the various generations through which the tradition passed. Among modern specialists, there are two schools of thought as to how to solve the methodological difficulties that arise from this documentary duality. For one of those schools of thought, which we may call sceptical rather than

[2] For a general presentation of questions of methodology and historiography, see Grandazzi 1997 and Grandazzi 2007.

hyper-critical, the ancient traditions on the origins of Rome contain no or very little historical truth. For the other school of thought (let us call it 'trustful'), that tradition, over and above the obviously mythical features that themselves testify to its authenticity, does possess considerable informative value for an understanding of the beginnings of the city of Rome. By and large, the sceptical trend is uppermost in English-speaking countries, while the 'trustful' interpretation prevails mainly in Italy and France.

A TOWN BEFORE THE CITY?

The new discoveries presented hermeneutic challenges for both schools of thought. Recent excavations on the Capitol have revealed that the earliest stable occupation of the site of Rome can be dated back to seventeen or sixteen centuries BC, when an 'Apennine' village was perched at the top of the hill. Earthworks designed to extend the available surfaces and rough fortifications were now set in place. There were traces of the presence – not necessarily permanent – of groups, still semi-nomadic, that came to live there in the summer, so as to control the ford at the bottom of the hill. Later, the Capitol's summit seems to have been reserved for activities linked with metalwork and also for a necropolis, where both inhumations and incinerations are attested. Other discoveries had already shown that the zone to which these small Bronze Age communities were most attracted lay within the space that later came to be known as the Forum Boarium, 'the cattle market'; and it was to this spot, flanked by the river and the slopes of three hills – the Capitol, the Palatine and the Aventine – that a path led, a path that bore an equally telling name: the *via Salaria*. The flocks brought by shepherds from the mountains of the interior were bartered here for salt (*sal*) which, for pre-industrial societies, constituted a veritable white gold. Once over the Tiber, this path was known as the *via Campana*, which suggests that the salt came from the coastal salt marshes, the *campus salinarum*, and that these were controlled by people installed at the foot of the Tiberian hills, whose earliest successes were founded upon that trade.

In those days, however, the centre of the region was not the future site of Rome, but the Alban mountain range.[3] This was to become the cradle of Latium culture, which began to spread in the eleventh

[3] See Grandazzi 2008.

century BC, in the shelter of Monte Cavo (949 m), the religious centre of Latium. The Alban mountains and the territory that separated them from the Tiber were then inhabited by small communities gathered around leaders whose role may have been as much religious as military. Here archaeology has identified a funerary rite quite distinct from those practised on the other side of the Tiber: its most manifest signs are miniature pieces of funerary furniture and the use of urns formed in the shape of huts. On the Roman site, a scattering of tombs testifies to the presence of hamlets composed of huts: they were found on the Capitol, on what was to become the Forum, close to the Arch of Augustus, on the Forum of Augustus and, most recently, at the lower level of the Forum of Caesar. These two groups of tombs may have served villages situated on the Quirinal. On the other side of the valley, the Palatine was occupied, in sporadic fashion at least, and possessed a necropolis datable to the Latian phase II A, that is to say the ninth or even the tenth century BC, traceable to the south-west side of the hill, just above the Forum Boarium. There, at the foot of the hill, stood the Lupercal, the sanctuary linked with purification and fertility, which was to be taken over by the legend of Romulus. The principal necropolis was the one said to belong to the temple of Antoninus and Faustina, on the Forum, which contained twenty or so tombs dating from this phase. Later it spread westward and seems to have served a village on the neighbouring Velia hill. Not far from this, the republican Regia was built on top of a few tombs of the same period. A very ancient document transmitted by ancient scholarship (Pliny the Elder, *Historia Naturalis*, 3.69) testifies to this scattered human presence all over the future site of Rome. It contains a list of the *populi Albenses*, whose name suggests that they would go to perform sacrifices in a place known as Alba, the modern Monte Cavo. Several of the groups included in this list can be traced within this space that did not yet bear the name Rome: the *Uelienses* are the best known, but mention should also be made of the *Latinienses* on the Parioli hills, the *Querquetulani* and possibly also the *Sacranes* and even the *Uiminitellarii*.

The potentialities of the terrain continued to be exploited. For the little Bronze Age villages that sought security above all else, the Capitol, with its steep slopes, was the most suitable spot. Now though, with its surface area of no more than 3 hectares, it was no longer large enough for communities that were more numerous and more self-confident. The Palatine, which likewise formed an autonomous hill, stood alongside the river and was easy to defend; and this was much larger. So this was where, from phase II B onward (the ninth century), a larger village, or possibly several, developed, mostly on the south-western side of the hill, for the northern slopes, above the valley separating the Palatine from the Velia, were reserved for craft activities.[4] Other hamlets were also growing, so much so that the necropolis of the temple of Antoninus and Faustina seems to have been abandoned in favour of a new area for tombs, on the Esquiline. On the other side, on the Quirinal, several dozen tombs have been identified alongside the Via Salaria, a fact that suggests the existence of at least one village here or even several.

By the ninth century BC, throughout the site of Rome we find evidence of hamlets perched on the hilltops and across the slopes. But archaeology is unable to tell us any more than that. Was this a dispersed habitat or a unified one? In other words, did Rome already exist or not? Modern specialists are divided on this question. Some are impressed by the chronological uniformity of the archaeological remains; others are more conscious of their spatial dispersal. The example of the large Etruscan villages, which were certainly unified by this period, suggests to some researchers that a similar evolution took place on the Roman site. They thus picture a large 'proto-Rome', covering over 150 hectares, within which several hundreds of huts were already gathered, the inhabitants of which might have been called, for example, *Uelienses*.[5] But that is an uncertain or even improbable reconstruction. The Roman geomorphology is different from that of the Etruscan sites: the depression that was to be occupied by the Forum constituted a break in the hills surrounding it and it seems unlikely that this plain, at that time frequently flooded by the waters of the adjacent Tiber, would have been inhabited. Furthermore, the necropolises had not yet been relegated to beyond the site. Besides, a document transmitted by Roman scholarship suggests widely dispersed habitats concentrated on the hilltops and their slopes. On the occasion of an annual festival called the *septimontium*, the inhabitants of eight hilltops or *montes* each celebrated a sacrifice. On the list of these habitats what is striking is first that the Palatine and the Velia occupy the first two places, but also that the Quirinal is not mentioned at all. Later, at the hands of Varro, the list was reduced to seven toponyms. So it would appear that Rome did not yet exist as a unit, but the villages scattered throughout its site had – at least in the central area – already established stable relations with one another and, with the sanction of religion, the glimmerings of a common identity.

---

[4] See the *Bollettino di Archeologia*, 31–4, 1995 (2000) and Pensabene and Falzone 2001.
[5] This is the position of Carandini 1997.

THE FOUNDATION OF ROME

Was Rome just formed or was it founded? Around 1950, a lively debate arose around these alternatives. The theory of a formation, a progressive urban development of the entity that was Rome (called a *Stadtwerdung*, after the works of H. Müller-Karpe[6]) was widely accepted. The idea of a foundation, locatable in both time and space, seemed to stem from ancient ideology, not from historically and archaeologically verifiable facts. Furthermore, scholarship had modernized the idea, replacing it with the concept of a synoecism, taken over from Greek studies. Gradually, researchers reached a compromise between the two models. By the 1970s many of them assumed that a long, indeed very long, phase of proto-urban formation had eventually, in the sixth century BC, resulted in the emergence of the city of Rome. The archaeological signs indicating this included an early level of paving for the *comitium* and the beginning of the construction of the Sanctuary of Vesta. While not excluding the possibility of an interruption in this development, this modern theory shifted the chronology to a relatively recent period. It was generally thought that the Tarquins were responsible for crossing this decisive threshold (in the past, the old concept of positivist historiography had attributed Rome's transformation into a town, *urbs*, to the Etruscans). This phase was now considered to be the outcome of a lengthy process, as it were a formation that had speeded up in its final phase, rather than a foundation in the ancient sense of the term. In these circumstances, a discovery made in the late 1980s came like a clap of thunder in a relatively serene sky.[7] Archaeologists found the remains of a wall at the foot of the northern slope of the Palatine. It was about 10 m long and, in its original state, was dateable to the mid-eighth century BC. These findings strengthen the rehabilitation of the legend of Romulus and the ancient tradition of the foundation of Rome on the Palatine. After all, a wall constitutes a relic far more significant than a mere shard. For the very first time, archaeology had revealed the tangible result of a public initiative, which, through its dating and location, corresponded exactly to what the ancient tradition confirmed. Even if that tradition, mistakenly described as 'literary', is set aside, the sacred nature of the boundary constituted by this wall – identifiable with the *pomerium* – is confirmed by the four restorations that were effected before its destruction in the sixth century. Others indications too, not all of them of an

---

[6] Müller-Karpe 1956 and Müller-Karpe 1962.   [7] See Carandini 2006a.

archaeological nature, have more recently come to light: toponomy, for example, such as the old name for the Palatine Gate, which was known as *Romanula* or *Romana*, evokes a Rome still limited to this one hill, on which a sanctuary positioned on the north-eastern edge is identified with the *curiae ueteres*: a fact that suggests that unification took place at an early date. Furthermore, comparative linguistics now indicates an Indo-European, rather than an Etruscan, origin for the word *urbs*. Nor should we regard as Etruscan the names of the three tribes – the Tities, the Ramnes and the Luceres – into which Romulus is believed to have divided the Roman population. This was an act of distribution that certainly took place prior to the sixth century, as did the introduction of the system, both territorial and civic, of the thirty *curiae*. Elsewhere in Latium, archaeology shows that the eighth century BC (that is to say the Latian phase III B/IV A) was precisely the period when a number of settlements were fortified. Thus, through its very excesses, the legend of the foundation of Rome celebrates a reality the importance of which it aims to underline.

The presence of relics earlier than the eighth century is often interpreted as proving the falsity of the legend of Romulus. But however numerous those remains may be, they do not prove that the future site of Rome formed a single, united whole as early as the ninth century. What is in question is not the reality of a proto-urban habitat, but rather its unity. Archaeology shows that the foundation cannot have been a creation *e nihilo*; the legend reveals that, of all the successive stages in the development of the site of Rome ever since its first stable occupation in the Bronze Age, it was the stage when a wall was built around the Palatine, to indicate a boundary with a sacred importance, that the Romans wished to mark as truly decisive and to commemorate as such. Archaeology shows that, ever since phase II B, that is to say the ninth century BC, the Palatine had been the most densely populated part of the site of Rome, with its necropolises on the hillside relegated to an area beyond the people's dwellings. The event of the foundation of Rome had thus been prepared for by a lengthy process to which it provided an eventual and religious conclusion. So formation and foundation are not mutually exclusive; and the foundation was a beginning that constituted a re-beginning for 'political' ends (in the precise meaning of that term) and for identificatory purposes. It was a beginning at once artificial and authentic, whose significance and efficacy were celebrated each year.

Curiously enough, the current rehabilitation of the legend of the founding of Rome ignores a theme that, in truth, is part of it.

Contemporary research, with few exceptions, neglects the Sabines, despite the fact that their presence on the Quirinal, emphasized by the ancient tradition, could well explain the absence of this name in the *Septimontium* list. It was probably only after their inclusion in the new Roman community, but at a much earlier date than had been believed, that a residential and sacred complex was set up in the Forum valley. This may have constituted the first Regia (royal palace) and the first sanctuary of Vesta. In fact, recent excavations beneath the republican dwelling of the Vestals uncovered the remains of a palatial edifice that had undergone repeated restorations.[8] The dates of these works of restoration correspond to those of the Romulean wall and all testify to a growing movement of monumentalization and a progression from simple adobe huts to edifices with stone foundations and tiled roofs and boasting inner courtyards and porticos. Meanwhile, a hut dating from the late eighth century BC was identified close to the sanctuary of Vesta erected in the republican period. So the Regia that Brown excavated years ago must have belonged to the last stage in the construction of a vaster monumental complex. Furthermore, ancient tradition attributed the royal palace to King Numa and emphasized its Sabine origins. This would seem to imply that, already in this period, the valley of the Forum no longer impeded communications between the two mountain systems of the site of Rome. Literary – or rather religious – tradition had retained the memory of topographical boundaries that may have been those of this Rome that extended beyond the Palatine but had not yet become the town of the sixth century:[9] the Tigillum Sororium Gate and the Janus Gate and the fortification of the *murus Carinarum* may date back to this intermediary phase, around the early seventh century BC. It is true that the theory of a large proto-Rome suggests that those boundaries should be dated to two centuries earlier: given that they did not encompass the Quirinal, said to have been part of that first Roman unit, the assumption might seem to be that the urban area had shrunk, then expanded later to its earlier boundaries. But it is more logical to think that a progressive and irreversible expansion of the civic Roman space would not have begun until the two poles of the left bank had been unified.

---

[8] See the file entitled 'Il progetto della prima Roma', in *Workshop di Archeologia Classica*, 12–2 (2004–5).

[9] On this, see Ziolkowski 2008.

THE GREAT ROME OF THE TARQUINS

In a pioneering article published in 1936, the philologist Giorgio Pasquali wrote of 'the great Rome of the Tarquins'. This phrase was for long rejected but today archaeological discoveries confirm its validity.[10] Ancient tradition mentions two kings of Rome called Tarquin, who were said to have reigned before and after another king, named Servius Tullius. Researchers today reckon those reigns to have corresponded at least partially to historical reality, provided they are not confused with the very earliest period of Roman monarchy, which is now generally relegated to the oblivion of fable. The importance of what was taking place within the Roman space at this time is incontestable. The first flooring of the *comitium*, composed of beaten earth, is believed to date back to 650, although earlier construction works going back to the eighth century cannot be ruled out. In subsequent years this public space was repeatedly redeveloped, a fact that indicates the major role that it played for the Roman civic community (see also Chapter 22). A paved floor was repaired in about 630 and one century later was replaced by a third one, along with the installation of a holy place known as the *Lapis niger*, the Black Stone. This was followed, right at the end of the sixth century and at the start of the fifth, by two new phases, both of which involved new paving. So the Forum had become Romanum, in virtue of its occupying the centre of the city, in the place known as the *comitium* (the etymology, *cum-ire*, indicates that it was the meeting place where all citizens gathered). It was here, in front of the *Curia Hostilia*, the seat of the senate, that the king would administer justice. The topography, with a senate, the people's assembly and a royal palace, preserves, as if fossilized, the ancient relations of power and reflects an unequal trinity in which the people did no more than voice their opinion in a roar (*fragor*) of approval (*suffragium*) for whatever the king proposed, on the advice of the Council of Elders (*senes*), which constituted the senate.

Archaeologically, the same stages are detectable at the Regia in the sixth century and at the foot of the Capitol. According to tradition, Servius Tullius constructed two temples here, the one dedicated to Fortuna, the other to Mater Matuta, although only one has been identified for the most ancient phase. Such recurrent and simultaneous reconstructions in several spots in an urban centre that

---

[10] See Cristofani 1990.

was becoming increasingly monumental no doubt indicate forceful movements of public intervention, possibly linked to political upheavals such as changing reigns or even regimes, in particular when the Tarquinian dynasty was replaced by the Republic.

To the east, the Esquiline necropolis by now extended beyond the *agger*, the powerful defensive trench that protected the town on this side that lacked any natural protective features. This indicates that demographic growth was definitely producing profound changes in the Roman city. In this pre-industrial society, such demographic growth is not likely to have resulted from an internal increase in the population already installed on the Roman site. For that reason, we may justify the ancient tradition that emphatically links the expansion of the town of Rome to the conquest of neighbouring towns, whose populations were then forcibly transferred to the city. Every king thus increased the Roman space. The ancient tradition constitutes a believable antecedent to a later regulation that stipulated that only rulers who had increased the territory of the *imperium* had the right to extend the *pomerium*.

Up until the reign of Sulla, Rome's *pomerium* remained the one that Servius Tullius had extended. It lay beyond the old boundary marked by the Palatine that had been established under Romulus and now coincided with a fortification that, with but one exception, surrounded the entire site on the left bank of the Tiber. The exception was the Aventine, which remained outside the *pomerium* but was integrated within the wall. The existence of a continuous rampart as early as the sixth century has now been confirmed.[11] In the late seventh century, on the hill overlooking the entire site, the royal authorities began to construct a temple which, by virtue of the god to whom it was consecrated, its situation, its size and its permanence, seems to have constituted Rome's poliad sanctuary. This was the temple of Jupiter Optimus Maximus, the great god of sovereignty who brought the Roman community power (*opes*) and dominion (*maximus*), thanks to what had now become an uninterrupted territorial expansion. The hill upon which this sanctuary was built was given the name Capitolium. Recent discoveries have confirmed the dating of the temple to the sixth century, although the exact dimensions of the edifice have yet to be calculated precisely.

Huts were now replaced by more elaborate constructions. On the Palatine, the slopes of which, like those of the Capitol, were now

---

[11] See Cifani 2008.

provided with strong retaining walls, temples with tall podiums shot up, topped by tiled roofs adorned by painted statues and architectural terracotta features. But there were palaces too, also highly decorated, for the aristocracy, which now laid claim to official magistracies and priesthoods. Access to some of these buildings made it necessary to widen and pave the streets. Cisterns, hollowed out from the rock, made it possible to trap the necessary water supplies. In the late 1980s, excavations at the foot of the northern part of the Palatine revealed large dwellings with atriums and gardens of a degree of luxury that indicates the presence of a confident ruling class. These discoveries showed that houses of the 'Italic' type, known from the excavations at Pompeii, had extremely ancient antecedents.

Rome was now a large and powerful town, and archaeology continues to provide further proofs of the city's power. Initially, the paths linking the various hills had followed the numerous watercourses that irrigated the site. From the end of the seventh century onward, those watercourses were either filled in or transformed into underground channels, and the paths became streets with artificially levelled surfaces. Tradition associates this Rome of the Tarquins with a number of huge official constructions: the great Circus, the Circus Maximus, and the main drainage system, the Cloaca Maxima. In both cases, the use of the superlative, *maximus*, testifies to a taste for gigantism: in other words, as early as this period, there was a tangible link between the successes of external Roman imperialism and the embellishment of Rome, the town. We lack archaeological confirmation for both the Circus and the Cloaca, but this is because the wooden stands of the former vanished, leaving no trace, and incessant reconstruction work on the latter obliterated the most ancient phase which may, however, be closely compared to important remains recently identified close to the *Meta Sudans*.[12]

Rome was thus now a great town, whose site had been improved by dint of the major construction works that the royal authorities imposed upon the population. The urban space thus regularized and unified was given a new configuration. Four 'regions', named Suburana, Esquilina, Collina and Palatina, replaced the old tripartite division of the population: blood-rights were thus replaced by land-rights, since hereditary membership of one or other of the thirty Romulean *curiae* now counted for less than one's place of residence and the size of one's fortune, both of which were regularly assessed by censuses. In this way,

[12] See Panella 1996.

Rome managed to disengage itself from the ethnic exclusivism that was favoured by Greek cities and was in a position to absorb new-comers. For their assemblies, significantly enough known by a name that also meant 'army' (*exercitus*), the soldier citizens who made up the population would now foregather on the Field of Mars, thereby respecting the *pomerium*'s exclusion of the military. Religion, which in Rome constituted an expression of the community's identity, was likewise affected by this act of urban unification: the list of the Argei comprised twenty-seven chapels, situated at various points in the four main quarters of a town that by now extended as far as the Quirinal and the Esquiline. Each year, on 17 March, a procession visited all these small sanctuaries and there deposited little puppets made from willow, which a second procession, led by the Grand Pontiff and Vestals, came to collect on 14 May and then took to the Sublicius Bridge, where they were hurled into the Tiber. In this ritual in two stages, which seems unlikely to have been performed solely in the proto-urban period, it is possible, at the level of religious symbolism, to detect a gathering, followed by an evacuation, of all the immaterial – that is, moral – impurities that defiled the urban space. The second phase of this rit-ual took place, significantly enough, opposite the outlet of the Cloaca Maxima which, for its part, ensured the evacuation of all material rubbish.[13]

By comparing contemporary Etruscan necropolises and by deduc-tion from the effective military forces, it is possible to estimate that this sixth-century Rome, which covered an area of close on 285 hectares, was composed of at least 30,000 inhabitants. They would gather regu-larly at grandiose religious ceremonies, which provided the city with opportunities to strengthen its sense of community solidarity: on the Field of Mars, which was then royal property, chariot races took place; in the Circus, yearly *ludi Romani*, great games in honour of Jupiter, were held; on the Capitol, the people foregathered to admire the triumph of the king who, thanks to his ceremonial chariot and costume seemed, for the duration of the procession, the very incarnation of Jupiter.[14] In this way, the authorities found in the newly refurbished urban space sufficient room and also the means to express a popular consensus over which the gods presided.

---

[13] This was the interpretation of G. Frazer, readopted by Ziolkowski 1999.
[14] On these ceremonies, probably of eastern origin, see Coarelli 1988.

THE BEGINNINGS OF THE REPUBLIC

When the monarchy came to an end, the city was governed by an oligarchy. The edifice consecrated to Capitoline Jupiter, which had taken over a century to build and was too firmly linked with the very identity of Rome to be abandoned, remained the poliad sanctuary. However, in Year One of the new regime, it was rededicated. Other temples, over-reminiscent of the monarchy, such as that of Fortuna, on the Forum Boarium, were either abandoned or lost their importance. However, the Republic did not neglect the gods. At the beginning of the fifth century, temples on the Forum were dedicated to Saturn, Mercury and the Castores, the latter expressing the influence of the elite cavalry.[15] The terracotta slabs that protected the cornices of buildings were no longer decorated by representations of banquets and chariot races, but instead by simple geometric figures. In a city now inspired by an *odium regni*, this was a sign of the dwindling popularity of the heroizing imagery of the past. Meanwhile, the hereditary monopoly over power appropriated by the ruling class was to provoke a reaction among the rest of the Roman population and, very soon, introduced a new balance within the civic space. A secession – that is to say a temporary exodus from the city limits – brought into being the plebs, which was the scornful name that the nobles gave to the soldiers who, by refusing to fight, forced them to recognize the plebeian tribunate, an institution with authority that extended exclusively to the urban territory. Because it was situated alongside the great commercial centre constituted by the Forum Boarium, the temple of the deities Ceres, Liber and Libera, at the foot of the Aventine, soon became the spot most favoured by the plebs, despite the fact that it had been dedicated by an aristocracy.[16] The plebs now adopted the custom of gathering close to this sanctuary and obtained the right to store the archives recording its decisions there – decisions that were eventually recognized by the Roman state as a whole. As a consequence of this quasi-revolution, in 456 BC the Aventine, a large hill with room to accommodate many new constructions, was shared out among the plebs, as decreed by the *lex Icilia de Aventino publicando*. Both this conflict and also the reconciliation that followed it, in the form of a compromise reached between the

---

[15] On the results of recent excavations of the temple of the Castores, see Poulson et al. 1992–2008.

[16] On the conflicts between the plebs and the patricians, see Raaflaub 2005.

diverse citizens of Rome, were thus both immediately reflected in the topography of the city. In 450, after the Decemvirate episode, during which ten nobles were appointed to codify Roman law, but gradually seized tyrannical powers, a text for all to see was posted up at the heart of the public space and it was this that made the return to harmony possible: the twelve measures (one of which concerned the prevention of city fires) that constituted this law, known as 'the XII Tables' because its text was engraved on twelve sheets of bronze, could thus be read by all and sundry and thereby guaranteed a law that would be equal for everyone.

In 435 BC, on the Field of Mars, the city presented itself with a *uilla publica*, a place for public representation and gatherings. It was used in particular for census-taking; and close by, the restoration of the Saepta, the booths where the citizens could go to vote, made it possible for the populace to exercise its sovereign right to elect its magistrates. Thus reconciled within itself, Rome was now to find a solution to its internal tensions in external expansion. In 395 BC, after a lengthy siege, it vanquished its neighbour and long-standing enemy, the Etruscan city of Veii. With the integration of the lands of Veii which, following an invasion from Gaul, were divided up among the Roman peasant-soldiers, the city, in the space of one generation, recovered its demographic vitality. The construction, on the Aventine, of a large temple dedicated to Juno the Queen, the goddess of the conquered town, commemorated this victory for all eternity within the city: this may have been the moment when, with Camillus, the ancient royal ritual of the triumph was reintroduced and the temples in the Sant'Omobono area were rebuilt.

Catastrophic though it may have seemed at the time, Rome's capture by the Gauls, in 390, did not check the city's irresistible rise: true, the city was taken, and taken in its entirety, including the Capitol, despite claims later made by the Roman tradition, but it was neither ravaged nor burned down. At the time of Livy, the centre of the city was still an inextricable tangle of tiny streets, but this was not, as the historian believed, a sign of the haste with which the city was assumed to have been reconstructed after the catastrophe; rather, it constituted proof that it had not been destroyed at the time of the victory of the Gauls! Significantly enough, archaeology has discovered no traces of any major fire in this period. On the other hand, it has had no difficulty in recognizing at least one visible consequence of this capture of the city: namely, the strong town wall that replaced the wall of the royal period.[17] The wall, 11 km in length, encompassed an area of close on 470 hectares and, even though not all of that land was built up, it testified to the power of a city which, though smaller than Syracuse, was at this point certainly larger than Athens.

A NEW DIMENSION

On the hills, in the valleys and on the outskirts of Rome, a burgeoning mass of temples[18] now marked a renaissance in the city. These, dedicated to Mars just outside the Capena Gate, to Juno Lucina, the goddess of births, on the Esquiline, and to Concordia in the Forum, expressed the confidence inspired by Rome's military forces, its demographic vitality and its political harmony. On the Forum, the orators' tribune, in front of the *comitium*, adorned with the rams of the ships of the Antium fleet, was now given the name *rostra*. By the third century BC, Rome had built itself a naval port, which extended for close on a kilometre along the left bank of the Tiber, from the Tiber island all the way along the Field of Mars. The construction may have been an extension of an earlier one dating back to the royal period. Moreover, this was not just a river port: given the conditions of ancient navigation, it also served as a maritime one. The subjection of Latium soon resulted in a constant influx of people to the city. Within the space of a few decades it led to a very definite growth in the urban population, which had swollen to about 90,000 inhabitants by 274 BC.

In the sanctuaries, the first colossal statues expressed the grandeur of the city that had just conquered the Samnites and now set its sights on Magna Graecia. The statues of Hercules and Jupiter, erected in 305 and 293, were the first of a series destined to a long future. The installation, in 296, in front of the *comitium*, of a sculpted group representing the she-wolf and the twins reflected the founding legend's great identificatory importance for the entire population, the plebs included. Likewise in that year, the same magistrates oversaw the paving of a first segment of the Via Appia, a fact that indicates that some of the major streets of the city itself were already paved.

Following the religious tension caused by the hazards of the Second Punic War, this was the spot where, in 205 BC, the Roman state

---

[17] See Säflund 1932.   [18] See Ziolkowski 1992.

decided to place the great goddess from the east, in the shape of a black stone, and to erect the temple of Magna Mater for her. First in 226, then in 216, and again in 113, right in the middle of the Forum, two couples, one Gallic and one Greek, were said to have been buried alive, as the masses looked on: this public human sacrifice, performed at the very heart of the city, testified to the gravity of the crisis. Not long before the Punic crisis arose, one of its future protagonists, Flaminius, had presented the city with a recreational space: this Circus Flaminius, bordering the Tiber, was for several centuries to be one of the plebs's favourite meeting-places. This was the point at which triumphal processions would set out. It was a ceremonial itinerary that was to assume a decisive importance in the urban refurbishment of Rome that began in the third century. From then on, victorious generals would insist that it be along this route that temples were created to commemorate their victories and to prolong the prestige of their respective families (*gens*). Many of the temples were indeed financed by wealth from the booty seized from the enemy. It was in this manner that the link between military victory, memorials and the communal identity was eternalized within the urban space of Rome. More than fifty temples were built during the fourth and third centuries BC, but only thirty or so more in the course of the next two centuries. The city treated itself to the spectacle of its own grandeur and, in the contemplation of these civic and religious monuments, the people of Rome kept alive its sense of superiority and destiny. However, in the absence of any overall plan, it can hardly be claimed that this republican Rome engaged in any real town-planning, except in the case of the Field of Mars, where the augural orientation of the Saepta, in accordance with the four cardinal points, was for several centuries emulated by all public buildings. Many temples were situated at points where the deities to which they had been consecrated had been the objects of an open-air cult ever since the archaic period. That is no doubt why many of them form part of two great topographical complexes, the one surrounding the Palatine, the other the Quirinal – in other words, the two primordial poles of the Roman site. At the beginning of the second century BC, the city boasted close on 100 sanctuaries, the number and positioning of which, first in the centre, later near the gates of the Servian Wall, and eventually even beyond, testify to the city's onward expansion. Rome, with over 100,000 inhabitants, despite the losses incurred in its wars, was now the greatest town of its time: half a millennium of world supremacy lay before it.

FURTHER READING

On the geological aspect of the Roman site, see Funiciello et al. 2006.
The archaeological remains of the Iron Age identified in Rome up until
the early 1970s have been catalogued by Gjerstadt 1953–73. No publication of this type for more recent discoveries yet exists. Discoveries
relating to eighth-century Rome are analysed by Carandini 2006a and a
preliminary approach to the city of the seventh and sixth centuries BC is
provided by Cristofani 1990, Holloway 1994 and Smith 1996. Accounts
of the historiographical debate provoked by these discoveries are provided principally by Grandazzi 1997 and Poucet 2000. The works of
Coarelli 1983, 1988 and 1997 have shed new light on the topography
of Rome. Cornell 1995, Raaflaub 2005 and Forsythe 2005 provide an
overall historical framework.

PART I

❧

INHABITANTS

2: POPULATION SIZE AND SOCIAL STRUCTURE

Neville Morley

> He used to play jokes on his slaves, even ordering them to bring him a thousand pounds of cobwebs and offering them a prize; and it is said that he collected ten thousand pounds' worth, and then remarked that one could realize from that how great a city Rome was.
>
> *Historia Augusta, Elagabalus 26*

Rome was exceptionally large for a pre-modern, pre-industrial city. The widely accepted estimate that its population at the time of Augustus was around 800,000–1,000,000 implies that it had only a handful of rivals for size, all in China, before the nineteenth century. Since 1800, dramatic improvements in technology and far-reaching changes in the organization of society and economy as a whole have meant that cities of several million are scarcely rare across the globe. For such a city to develop and thrive under far more restrictive conditions was a remarkable achievement, a reflection above all – as ancient commentators recognized – of the power and wealth of the Roman empire.

The size of Rome is not merely a symbol of greatness or a trump card in inter-cultural rivalry; it is directly significant for understanding the dynamics of Roman society. The fact that the city could grow so large, despite all the practical, ecological and technological impediments, provides a sense of the capacities of the Roman economy; scarcely comparable with modern economic performance, of course, but to be ranked highly among pre-industrial societies. Moreover, the growth of the city was itself one of the major sources of change, as its demands for people and raw materials transformed economic and social structures throughout its Mediterranean-wide hinterland. Rome's role as the capital of the empire constituted the main basis for its growth, as the ruling elite invested the spoils of imperialism in the urban environment and migrants flocked to service their needs and gain a share of the empire's wealth; but the elite made this investment precisely because of the importance of the city in establishing and maintaining their power – Rome's greatness was itself a crucial element of the ideology that sustained Roman rule. Further, the size of the city shaped the nature of urban life, politics and society. As will be discussed in later chapters, the concentration of a large population in a limited area gave rise to a distinctive demographic regime, leaving the city heavily dependent on inward migration just to maintain its size and so creating a society dominated by change, fluidity, insecurity and the interaction of many different cultures. In contrast to the relatively face-to-face social relations of the countryside or the small town, social interaction in the metropolis was largely impersonal and anonymous, with a gaping divide between the political elite and the masses. The maintenance of social order depended not on personal relationships between patron and client but on large-scale rituals, ceremonies and grand public occasions, and on the power of public architecture and imagery, to maintain the symbolic order as a means of binding society together.

It is clear from the ancient sources, from Latin poets to Greek orators, that Rome was far larger than any other city in the ancient Mediterranean; as Pliny the Elder concluded from his brief comments on the physical size of the city, 'a very fair estimate would be formed that would bring us to admit that there has been no city in the whole world that could be compared to Rome in magnitude' (*Historia Naturalis* 3.5.67). For many historical purposes, that general impression of exceptional size may be sufficient. However, in order to grasp properly the crucial issues of Rome's demographic regime and its demand for food and other resources, we need a more specific idea of the size of its population. This is particularly important if we wish to compare Rome with other great pre-industrial cities, in order to gain a broader understanding of the nature and impact of urbanization. In some historical contexts, such as western Europe in the Middle Ages, a 'primate' city might eclipse its rivals and dominate its society with a population of a few tens of thousands; the fact that it was, from a comparative perspective, relatively small might not lessen its political and cultural significance in that context, but it suggests that the city's potential impact on economy and society might be limited. If, on the other hand, Rome did indeed reach 1 million or more inhabitants, as many historians have argued, then its impact on the empire must have been significantly greater.

The problem is that there is no direct evidence for the size of the urban population; the figure of a million people is a widely accepted hypothesis, not a well-established fact. Historians find themselves in a similar position to the emperor Elagabalus, seeking to extrapolate from 'proxy' evidence, and returning time and again to debate the possible interpretations of the few figures (often of doubtful reliability) and measurable attributes at their disposal. One consequence has been the enormous range of estimates for the size of Rome developed over the last few centuries, from a mere 150,000 (still impressive compared with the cities of medieval Europe, admittedly) to a truly extraordinary 4 million, three or four times the size of any city known before the nineteenth century. Ten thousand pounds' worth of cobwebs is undoubtedly a very large quantity, the harvest of a great many rooms and buildings; but in the absence of reliable information about, for example, the typical number of spiders in each apartment block and their average productivity, deriving a sense of the size of the population from such data will always be a matter of fierce debate.

THE PHYSICAL CITY

Ancient sources rarely make direct reference to the size of the urban population. One exception was Cassiodorus, looking back at the city's past greatness from the sixth century:

> The vast numbers of the Roman people in the past are
> evidenced by the extensive provinces from which their
> food supply was drawn, as well as by the wide circuit of
> their walls, the massive structure of their amphitheatre, the
> marvellous size of their public baths, and the enormous
> multitude of mills, which could only have been made for
> use, not ornament.
>
> (*Varia* 11.39)

Earlier commentators eulogized Rome's greatness in more general terms, rather than focusing on the size of the population, but they considered similar themes: the city's physical extent, both in area and height, the magnificence and size of its principal monuments, and the sheer number of other, more mundane buildings. The Greek orator Aelius Aristides claimed that it might be considered presumptuous to attempt to praise the city; Rome was too great to be taken in by the eyes – only all-seeing Argus could adequately survey its extent – let alone to be encompassed in words.

> Like the snow, she covers mountain peaks, she covers the
> land intervening, and she goes down to the sea . . . And
> indeed she is poured out, not just over the level ground,
> but in a manner with which the simile cannot begin to
> keep pace she rises great distances into the air, so that her
> height is not to be compared to a covering of snow but to
> the peaks themselves.
>
> (*Oration* 26.6–8)

Other ancient writers celebrated the size and wealth of the city through
the enumeration of its public buildings, especially the 'veritable rivers' of
its aqueducts. Rome simply contained more of everything. According
to one of the texts collected in the Talmud, 'the great city of Rome has
365 streets, and in each street there are 365 palaces. Each palace has 365
stories, and each story contains enough food to feed the whole world'
(*Pesahim* 118b). Fourth-century descriptions of the city, known as the
Notitia and the *Curiosum* or the *Regionary Catalogues*, set out in great
detail the different buildings to be found in each of the fourteen regions
of the city, not only the temples and monuments known by name
but the total numbers of bath houses, warehouses, bakeries, fountains,
domus and *insulae*. These documents have been described as 'panegyrics
in statistics', designed to impress the reader through sheer weight of
numbers.[1]

It is understandable, therefore, that some historians have sought
to estimate the population of Rome on the basis of evidence for its
physical size and the number of residential buildings. The Regionary
Catalogues, which differ slightly in their figures, give a total of around
1,800 *domus*, the familiar town houses of the Roman elite, and around
46,500 *insulae*, clearly defined in legal sources as self-contained, independent buildings divided into separate apartments or *coenacula* and well
known as a result of the excavations at Ostia.[2] If one assumes that the
typical elite *familia* contained around thirty persons, including slaves
(though the richest senators might have several hundred of those), and
that the typical *insula* had three floors, each containing a number of
apartments inhabited by individual families, giving perhaps thirty to

---

[1] The text of these documents is in Nordh (1949); the best discussion of their date
and purpose, and the problems involved in using them to reconstruct the urban
population, as discussed in the following paragraphs, is Hermansen 1978.

[2] See Chapter 9 for a more detailed discussion of the nature of Roman residences.

thirty-six persons in each building, then the population of Rome in the fourth century was around 1.5–1.7 million, along with an unknown number of soldiers, the slaves and freedmen of the imperial household and other public buildings, and the homeless, perhaps another 80,000–100,000 individuals in total. Different estimates for average household size will push the figure up or down, but the sheer number of *insulae* means that the total is invariably well over a million.

The obvious problem with this calculation is highlighted when it is related to the physical area of Rome, the 13.86 km² that lay within the third-century Aurelian Wall, which may be rounded up to 15 km² to take account of the fact that the fourteen regions established by Augustus covered a larger area. If the population of the city was at least 1.5 million, this implies an average population density of 100,000 persons per km², a figure which is higher than any known historical example besides a few specific localities within proverbially crowded modern cities like Mumbai or Hong Kong. It seems scarcely conceivable that this could be a realistic average density for the entire city, given the amount of land taken up by public monuments, some of them – like the Circus Maximus – covering very large areas. Further, if only half of the total area of Rome was occupied by residential buildings, and the average *domus* is estimated to have occupied 600 m², then the ground area of the average *insula* was barely 150 m², hardly compatible with the remains of the *insulae* known from Ostia. This raises serious doubts about the credibility of the figure of 46,500 *insulae*.

One way of dealing with this problem and rescuing the credibility of the source is to conclude that the *insulae* listed in the Regionary Catalogues are not separate buildings, as the term is used in the legal texts, but the different floors of those buildings. If only ten to twelve people lived in each of these 'insulae', the fourth-century population would be a much more reasonable 580,000–680,000. A more extreme interpretation, put forward on the basis that the contemporaneous *Notitia* of Constantinople does not list *insulae* at all, is that the entire population of Rome was accommodated within the 1,790 *domus*, while the numbers given for *insulae* represent the number of door openings of these residences; that brings the population down to barely 150,000 all told, with a population density of only 10,000 per km². However, there is no evidence at all to support the interpretation of *insula* as either 'floor' or 'apartment', or as anything other than a self-contained block of flats, even if not necessarily identical to those found in Ostia. The absence of *insulae* from the Regionary Catalogue for

Constantinople may be explained by changes in residential fashion in the fourth century, but is more likely to be a simple omission; it certainly does not support the idea that the *insulae* of Rome were merely door openings.

The final attempt at saving the testimony of the Regionary Catalogues has been to recalculate how much of Rome's total area may have been taken up by monuments, producing a higher estimate of the space occupied by residential buildings; this in turn allows a new calculation of the average size of each *insula*, which then implies a different estimate for the inhabitants of each building and a new population total – around 1.2–1.3 million. The problem is that this new calculation works only by ignoring the detail of the Regionary Catalogues' description of each region; it may be possible to accommodate 45,000 *insulae* within the total area of the city, but it is impossible to accommodate the numbers specified by the texts as belonging to particular regions, especially in the highly monumentalized centre of the city. The only possible conclusion is that the numbers in the text are grossly inflated if not simply corrupt; the purpose of the Catalogues is not to provide an accurate description of the city but to represent and celebrate its greatness through the power of number. The statements about the numbers of residential buildings offer no secure basis for estimating the population; indeed, the way in which some historians have desperately sought to redefine the *insula* in order to find space for 45,000 of them within the city shows that the argument has shifted from attempting to estimate the population to attempting simply to defend the credibility of the figures.

If the figures for the number of *insulae* are set aside, there remains the possibility of deriving a more plausible estimate from the evidence of archaeology and the *Forma Urbis Romae*, the Severan marble plan of the city.[3] One reconstruction of the buildings identified as residential on fragments of the *Forma Urbis* suggests that the average *domus* covered 675 m^2 and the average *insula* 250 m^2. If half the city's built-up area was occupied by housing, 1,790 *domus* (the figure from the Regionary Catalogues, though why this should be considered more reliable than that for *insulae* is unclear) occupied 1.2 km^2 and the *insulae* covered the remaining 6.25 km^2; that suggests a total of about 25,000 *insulae* at 250 m^2 each, and a total population of around 880,000 to one million. This implies an average population density of about

---

[3] Developed by Hermansen 1978 and, drawing on more recent archaeological work at Pompeii and Ostia, Storey 1997. On the Severan marble plan, cf. Chapter 10.

60,000–70,000 people per km², still considerably higher than the average for cities like Mumbai or Hong Kong but considered by many to be credible. Studies of housing in Pompeii and Ostia, however, suggest that the figure is much too high; house-by-house counts from these sites, with computer-aided reconstructions of the unexcavated areas, produce estimates of population densities of 16,615 persons per km² and 31,700 persons per km² respectively, figures which imply much smaller household sizes and a total population for Rome of 250,000 or 475,000.

These population totals for Pompeii and Ostia tally well with recent estimates for those cities derived by other means, and that seems to confirm the validity of the figures used in the calculation for household size (3 to 6 individuals for each apartment, 13 to 17 for each *domus*). The crucial question is whether such household sizes were also typical of Rome, which was manifestly a very different sort of city from either Pompeii or Ostia, or whether a higher multiplier, yielding a higher population total and a higher density, should be used. The same issue is raised by cross-cultural comparisons; the rejection of estimates of a million on the grounds that they imply higher population densities than those known from other cities begs the question as to whether Rome should be assumed to be comparable to those other cities, or whether it might have been very different. The risk of circularity is clear; in order to obtain a sense of the overall population size to inform their understanding of the city and urban life, historians evaluate different estimates according to their preconceptions of what the city was like. Thus, those who see Rome as an over-crowded slum, the Calcutta of the ancient Mediterranean, are happy to accept exceptionally high estimates of average population density, whereas those who see it as a more pleasant and civilized place seek to reinterpret the meaning of *insula* or to draw on what they see as more appropriate comparative evidence.[4] Different interpretations rest on quite different assumptions, and so cannot be directly compared.

Consideration of the physical city does at least establish plausible maxima and minima for the urban population and exclude the most extreme estimates. An average density across the whole 15 km² of more than 80,000 persons per km², as high a figure as found in some of the most densely settled districts of more modern cities, is entirely implausible; older estimates of a total urban population of 1.5–2 million

---

[4] Compare Laurence 1997 and Morley 2005 on different traditions of interpretation of the healthfulness or otherwise of the Roman city.

can thus be rejected, and a figure of just over a million taken as a likely maximum. At the other end of the scale, it is difficult to imagine that Rome was less crowded than Pompeii, so it must have contained at least 250,000 people; given that we are dealing with the capital of the empire rather than a regional centre, the estimated population density for Ostia might seem a more likely comparison, implying a total of just under half a million inhabitants. We may then consider reasons why Rome may have been more crowded than Ostia: a greater capacity for drawing in migrants and keeping them, despite crowded living conditions, combined with a reduced scope for the city to spread further outwards because of the ring of gardens and the estates of the rich around it, so that a growing population could be accommodated only by increasing building height and population density. More importantly, we need to compare these arguments with the estimates obtained by looking at alternative sources of evidence.

FOOD SUPPLY AND DISTRIBUTION

The alternative set of proxy data for urban population relates to the city's imports of grain from the provinces and the distributions to recipients of the *annona*, the corn dole.[5] Several ancient sources make reference to the size of Rome's imports from Africa and Egypt or to the volume of its total consumption; unfortunately, the figures are not compatible with one another. Two schools of thought have developed; the combination of two of the four relevant sources produces an estimate of 60 million modii of imported grain per year, the combination of the other two suggests only 27 million. Quite apart from the risks of relying on any figures in a literary source, given the strong possibility of them being miscopied in the process of transcription and transmission, the procedure of combining figures from quite different dates and contexts is dubious at best. Further, even if one of these estimates is chosen, there is no certainty as to what size of population such levels of food imports might represent; as in the argument over likely population density, it depends on our assumptions about ancient living conditions. An optimistic estimate of how much grain each individual would receive,

---

[5] Oates 1934 develops an estimate of the population on the basis of the food supply; Garnsey 1983 and 1988 offer the best and most detailed discussions of grain supply and *annona*, along with the papers in Giovannini 1991, and see Chapter 15.

which also effectively makes allowance for the fact that some recipients of state grain like soldiers or officials would have received more than a basic ration, is 4 modii per month per head; the two estimates for supply then imply total populations of 1.25 million and 560,000 respectively. On a more pessimistic view of the nutritional status of the mass of the population, in which 2.5 modii of grain per month per head provided 75 per cent of individuals' calorific requirements, the same amount of grain supports many more people and the population totals are 2 million and 900,000. A further ground for scepticism is that we have no reason to imagine that any record was kept of Rome's total food imports or consumption, in which case any figure in an ancient source can only be a guess on the part of the author. It can be assumed that the state would have kept records of its own imports, excluding private trade, and that might be a reasonable interpretation of the figure of 27 million modii described in the *Scriptores Historiae Augustae* passage as the *canon frumentarius*. In that case, this lower figure represents a minimum level of import and consumption in the city, yielding a figure for the population of 560,000–900,000 that is not incompatible with the range of estimates derived from the density of settlement.

If we turn to the numbers of recipients of the grain distributed every month by the state, recorded not only in literary sources like Suetonius but in Augustus' *Res Gestae*, inscribed in stone, we are at least dealing with agreed and reliable figures, albeit ones which change over time.[6] Julius Caesar reduced the total number eligible for the dole to 150,000, from more than double that, by carrying out a special census of the urban population. Augustus reduced the lists to 200,000, after they had swollen yet again during the civil wars; at various points during his reign he distributed money and other largesse to the plebs, sometimes explicitly described as 'those in receipt of public grain', with 200,000 individuals benefiting on some occasions and 250,000 on others. Only 150,000 received largesse under Augustus' will, which might imply that the list had been reduced again, if we accept the idea that it would have suited the Roman state to use the records relating to the regular corn dole as a means of determining who should receive sporadic handouts as well.

The question is then what these figures represent, since that will determine how we can use them to produce an estimate of the size

---

[6] For a detailed discussion of the corn dole, especially the *recensus* carried out by Caesar, and its implications for the overall population, see Lo Cascio 1997.

of Rome; above all, it is a matter of what proportion of the urban population was in receipt of state grain. The size of the changes in the totals, from 320,000 to 150,000 in the case of Caesar's *recensus*, seems to rule out the idea that the changing numbers simply reflect changes in the size of the actual population of the city; rather, they result from changes in the criteria of eligibility and in the administration of the *annona*, as the emperors sought to keep the scale of the distributions manageable and to restrict the benefits to those deemed worthy of the state's largesse. There is no evidence that the corn dole was ever conceived as a form of poverty relief, nor that recipients were ever subjected to a means test; eligibility was determined by status, not need. It was certainly necessary to be a Roman citizen in order to receive the dole, and an adult male (though the precise age of eligibility is in dispute; perhaps 10, having been reduced by Clodius at the same time as he had made the distributions free of charge). However, it seems unlikely that in the course of the civil wars over 100,000 non-citizens could have managed to get themselves entered onto the lists; it is more plausible that Caesar and Augustus, in order to reduce the numbers receiving the dole, drew distinctions between different categories of citizens. The *plebs frumentaria* was therefore a privileged subset of the *plebs urbana*; the recorded numbers offer a basis for a minimum estimate of population, whereby the possible inclusion in the total of a certain number of individuals who lived outside the city but could afford to travel in to collect their monthly dole and to transport it home is more than compensated for by the number of urban residents who were not eligible for the corn dole.

As to what categories of citizens might have been excluded by the emperors' reforms, once again the argument becomes a matter of historians' preconceptions, this time about the character of the urban population as a whole. If, for example, we believe in the existence of a large core population of individuals of direct Roman descent, then we might interpret the trimming of the lists as the exclusion of Italians and other non-Romans, who possessed full citizenship but lacked Roman *origo*.[7] It should be noted that the concept of *origo* was relatively recent, developed after the extension of citizenship to the Italian allies after the Social War, and all the evidence for its legal codification and importance comes from the second century AD and later.

---

[7] Van Berchem 1939, 34–45; contrary arguments are to be found in Virlouvet 1991 and Purcell 1994.

Augustus' policies seem generally to aim to promote Italian integration, so that the exclusion of Italians from benefits enjoyed by 'proper' Roman citizens would be anomalous; our sources make no mention of the sort of popular outcry that might have been expected against such a measure. Finally, recent studies of the demography of the Roman population argue that it had been heavily dependent on migrants for centuries, so that the number whose ancestry was fully Roman over more than a generation or two must have been fairly small. An alternative explanation of the reforms identifies a group with citizen rights – and so at least a basic case for eligibility – whose exclusion would have caused no such outcry: the freedmen, former slaves whose rights were already inferior to those of the freeborn. Slaves who had been manumitted informally, rather than following the full legal procedures, would certainly have been considered ineligible for the dole, but the numbers involved suggest that freedmen manumitted *optimo iure* were also excluded.Certainly this is not incompatible with the emperors' recorded concerns with the health and strength of the body of Roman citizens, and the anecdote, recorded by Suetonius, that Augustus was on one occasion dismayed by the presence of freedmen at one of his distributions of coins to the plebs (Suetonius, *Augustus* 42.2).

THE NATURE AND DEVELOPMENT OF THE URBAN POPULATION

According to this interpretation, it was necessary to be freeborn, *ingenuus*, to keep one's place on the dole lists when Caesar and Augustus sought to trim their numbers. Once the lists had been finalized, it was then necessary to wait, either to inherit a vacancy or to compete for one, probably through a system of lots. New migrants to the city would have to wait their turn, perhaps for years; the *plebs frumentaria* was a privileged subsection of the urban masses. This implies, therefore, that in addition to a core group of 200,000–250,000 dole recipients there were significant numbers both of freedmen and of citizens who had not yet gained access to the full privileges of the *plebs frumentaria*, not to mention an unknown number of slaves – the only direct evidence is the unreliable paranoia of elite literary sources that slaves outnumbered free men, and the passing comment of the medical writer Galen that, in second-century Pergamum, there was one slave to every free man – and perhaps 20,000 soldiers and members of the upper classes. Once again, estimates – which can really be no more than guesses – for the number of slaves and recent migrants depend heavily on prior expectations of the nature of Roman society: was it dominated by foreign migrants, as sources like Juvenal tend to suggest, or is its apparent heterogeneity and alien, un-Roman nature the product of a small but visible group of foreigners and ex-slaves and of the prejudices of sources like Juvenal?[8] Were slaves and former slaves numerically dominant, or, as recent studies of the dynamics of the slave trade have suggested, were they prominent because of their location and roles in society rather than their numbers?

The *plebs frumentaria* can, as suggested above, be seen as a privileged group, sufficiently settled in Rome to have gained access to the corn dole and thus assured of a regular income: did they constitute the majority of the population of Rome, alongside a relatively small number of recent migrants and the very poor, or were they the upper layer of a more elaborate social hierarchy, set against large numbers of the less privileged? Roman sources tend to treat everyone outside the tiny wealthy elite as 'poor', an undifferentiated mass, which is little help in determining how far social and economic divisions may have existed within the group that comprised, at the most conservative estimates, at least 95 per cent of the urban population, and more like 98–99 per cent. Comparative evidence from medieval and early modern Europe suggests that in a typical city 4–8 per cent of the population was entirely incapable of earning a living and 20 per cent was permanently in crisis and falling below standard levels of subsistence (one of the most common definitions of poverty).[9] The corn dole was insufficient to cover all the subsistence needs of an entire family, so some members of the *plebs frumentaria* certainly fell into temporary or permanent poverty; but, as long as access to the dole was restricted, a significant number of urban inhabitants – at least 10 per cent, one might imagine – were in still more desperate straits. During periods of rapid urban expansion and large-scale immigration, such as in the last century of the Republic, the numbers involved must have been still greater, with serious implications for the social order.

We are clearly still dealing with approximations and plausible ranges: 200,000–250,000 recipients of the corn dole, perhaps 100,000 freedmen (the numbers removed from the lists by Augustus), perhaps 50,000 poor and recent migrants or perhaps 150,000 or more, and anything between 50,000 and 200,000 slaves. Further, the only certain figure, the 200,000–250,000 in the *plebs frumentaria*, represents adult

---

[8] See also Edwards and Woolf 2003.   [9] See Whittaker 1993 and Morley 2006.

males only; we need to multiply this figure, and the others, to obtain an estimate for the overall population. Model life tables, derived from data relating to populations with different levels of life expectancy and other demographic characteristics, offer an indication of the proportions of different age groups within a given population.[10] There are of course many inherent problems in applying such tables to the Roman world, not least that of deciding which table is most appropriate (a decision which once again rests on assumptions about living conditions in antiquity, in this case relating to what we conceive to be the most plausible level of life expectancy); however, for the purposes of this calculation we need only an approximation. If the age of eligibility was 10, and the age structure of the population was stable, a figure of 200,000 dole recipients represents roughly 260,000 males; if the sex ratio was balanced, a total population of around 520,000 freeborn citizens. These assumptions are undoubtedly problematic: comparative evidence from other pre-industrial societies strongly suggests that the proportion of children and women in large cities is often significantly lower than in the population at large, above all because of the importance of migration in supporting urban growth. On the other hand, members of the *plebs frumentaria* had been resident long enough to gain access to the lists and were as a result in a stronger position than other city dwellers to support a family; it seems reasonable to treat them as a 'core' population with an age structure and sex ratio not too different from that of Roman society at large, and so to assume that the 200,000–250,000 adult male dole recipients represented a freeborn population of 500,000–625,000, the vast majority of whom, if not all of them, lived in or very close to the city.

Arguments about uneven sex ratios and other demographic characteristics apply still more strongly to other groups within the population. Freedmen were less likely to marry and, because of their likely age at manumission, less likely to have children (one explanation for the predominance of inscriptions erected by former slaves and the scarcity of inscriptions erected by their freeborn offspring): 100,000–120,000 freedmen may therefore represent a total of no more than 150,000–200,000 former slaves and their families. Migrants, similarly, if only because of their exclusion from the dole, were less likely to be able to marry and reproduce. In some early modern cities, women made up a significant proportion of migrants to the cities, but that reflected

---

[10] See Chapter 3 on the problems of establishing the age structure and mortality rates of ancient populations.

the availability of work in domestic service and the like; Rome offered far fewer such opportunities, so we might imagine that the migrant population was weighted towards men in early and middle adulthood, with women constituting less than a third of the total. Arguably, urban life may be influenced adversely by the predominance of young men, uprooted from their original communities and insufficiently integrated into their new society.

From these figures, we can suggest a range of possibilities for the total population of the city of Rome at the time of Augustus, from around 650,000 (400,000 dole recipients and their families, 100,000 freedmen and their dependents, 80,000 migrants and poor, 50,000 slaves, 20,000 soldiers, officials and members of the elite) to well over a million. These estimates fall into the same general area as the figures implied by minimum annual grain imports of 27 million modii; the implied average population density, at $c.$ 45,000–65,000 per km^2, is high but not impossibly so, which might incline us towards the lower end of the range.

Charting the development of this population before and after the reign of Augustus is a still more uncertain procedure. For the earlier period, the only proxy evidence comes from the growth of the city's water supply. On the basis of the figures provided by Frontinus, who wrote a treatise on the subject at the beginning of the second century AD, the various aqueducts built under Augustus doubled the volume of water supplied to the city compared with 125 BC. It is clearly dangerous to take an emperor's perception of a problem as a clear indication of the reality of the situation, and equally dangerous to assume that aqueduct construction was a purely pragmatic activity – studies of other Roman cities make it clear that the prestige of the man responsible, the adornment of the city with fountains and the provision of bathing facilities were at least as significant motives as the supply of drinking water. However, unlike smaller cities, a significant proportion of Rome's population must have been dependent on the aqueducts for their water supply, and the scale of Augustan construction must imply significant growth from the earlier period, with the population more than doubling from somewhere around 200,000 to 400,000 (still, by comparative standards, an exceptionally large city).[11] Water capacity in 125 BC was in turn roughly double that of 270, but, given the size of Roman territory at that date, the population must have been far less than the 100,000–200,000 which might be inferred from the rate

---

[11] Brunt 1971, 383–4.

of increase of the volume of the water supply. A better guide to the chronology of Rome's growth might be the expansion of its overseas territories, since it is clear that the city's attraction to migrants was based above all on the flow of wealth from the empire to its centre. Historians who identify the major source of migrants as peasant farmers displaced by the introduction of slave-run villas into Italy might seek to correlate urban growth with the chronology of changes in the countryside, as revealed by literary accounts of the Gracchan crisis and the findings of archaeology; however, the traditional picture of rural development and its implications for the rest of Italy is increasingly under dispute, and migrants are seen to be impelled to Rome at least as much by its positive attractions as by any 'push' factors at their place of origin.[12]

New aqueducts continued to be built until the early third century, under such emperors as Claudius and Trajan; this might indicate a further (though much less dramatic) increase in population, or changes in the pattern of demand, or it might be a matter of improving the system (water quality and its capacity to cope with leaks and other problems) and enhancing the reputation of those emperors.[13] The increase in the number of *vici* at some time between the end of the first and the beginning of the fourth century could equally be a response to actual growth or an attempt at improving the administration of the existing urban area. Certainly the Aurelian Wall constructed in the third century enclosed a smaller area than the fourteen regions of Augustus' reign; the *annona* lists in the fourth century still contained 150,000–200,000 names, but if the levels of migration had slowed by this time, it is entirely possible that more or less the entire free population was now in receipt of the *annona*, rather than the *plebs frumentaria* being a privileged group. If the city did grow in the course of the first and second centuries, in response to the establishment of peace and prosperity across the empire, it must have been relatively marginal, up to just over a million people, in contrast to the astonishing rate of growth seen under the Republic.

FURTHER READING

The debate about the size of Rome and its implications is summarized in Hopkins 1978a and Morley 1996. Hermansen 1978 discusses the

---

[12] See De Ligt and Northwood 2008.   [13] See Durliat 1989 and Lançon 2000.

problematic evidence of the *Regionary Catalogues*; Storey 1997 offers a critique of higher estimates on the basis of archaeological work at Pompeii and Ostia; Lo Cascio 1997 offers, for readers of Italian, the most detailed discussion of the figures for the grain dole. Useful introductions to the study of Roman population history in general are to be found in Parkin 1992 and Scheidel 2001.

3: DISEASE AND DEATH

Walter Scheidel

IN SEARCH OF FUNDAMENTALS

Despite the city's prominence in our sources, its demographic conditions are remarkably poorly known. The size of Rome's population is never properly reported and modern estimates rely on inferences from the scale of public grain distribution schemes (Chapter 2). The geographical and social provenance of its inhabitants is likewise largely a matter of conjecture (Chapter 5). Marriage practice and household structure may well have been peculiar to the city's exceptional environment but are difficult to derive from epigraphic documents (Chapter 6). Overall fertility rates necessarily remain unknown. Metropolitan patterns of morbidity and mortality, however, are more amenable to empirical and even quantitative inquiry, and will therefore be the main concern of this chapter.

As always in demography, a field that is built on counting and measuring, pride of place belongs to large bodies of quantifiable data. Provided by funerary inscriptions, they record two vital features, the monthly distribution of deaths and age at death. Though very similar in character, these two datasets nevertheless lead us in opposite directions: whereas evidence of seasonal mortality has greatly improved our understanding of the impact of infectious disease on life in the city of Rome, demographic analysis of reported ages at death has remained a dead end.

SEASONAL MORTALITY AND CAUSES OF DEATH

Epitaphs that record the day or at least the month of death enable us to track variations in the mortality rate across the year. In Rome, relevant information is furnished in the first instance by early Christian commemorations from the fourth and fifth centuries AD which have survived

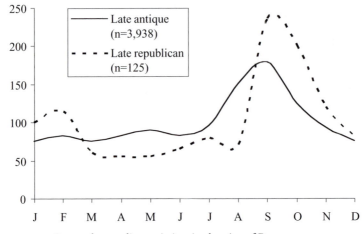

FIGURE 3.1 Seasonal mortality variation in the city of Rome
(100 = annual mean)
Source: Shaw 1996a, 115 and 2006, 100 (adjusted).

in large numbers in the catacombs that ring the city. A sample of nearly 4,000 dates of death gathered by Brent Shaw provides a solid basis for demographic investigation. In addition, Shaw has drawn attention to a much smaller but also much earlier body of corresponding records on inscribed cinerary urns dating from the first half of the first century BC that were found at a site on the Via Appia just outside Rome. Whilst separated by approximately half a millennium, both datasets reveal a comparable concentration of mortality in the late summer and early autumn (Fig. 3.1).[1]

There is no obvious way in which these profiles could be a mere artefact of biased recording practices. The much larger late antique sample allows differentiation according to age. It shows that the observed seasonal profile applies to most age groups: men and women up to the age of fifty, who represented the large majority of the population, disproportionately often died in August, September and October, whereas only the elderly − although they also appear to have suffered in this period − were similarly likely to die in the late autumn, winter and early spring (Fig. 3.2).

The latter observation is consistent with evidence from nineteenth-century Italy that shows a similar pattern at elevated ages and indicates increased susceptibility to pulmonary afflictions in the cool

[1] Shaw 1996a, esp. 115–21; Shaw 2006, 93–101.

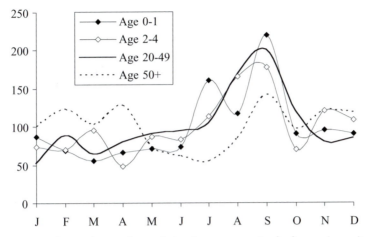

FIGURE 3.2 Seasonal mortality variation by age group in the late antique city of Rome
(100 = annual mean)
Source: Shaw 1996a, 118, 120.

and wet part of the year. From a comparative demographic perspective, it is the high degree of consistency across most age cohorts that requires explanation. In the more recent past, even though mortality among children, adolescents and young and middle-aged adults would often spike at the same time of the year, such spikes were usually much more pronounced among infants and small children, who are generally more vulnerable to infection. An environment in which young adults – the most resilient element of any given population – succumbed to seasonal diseases at the same rate as the very young is therefore highly exceptional. Moreover, added mortality in the cold and wet season probably conceals the extent to which even the elderly remained at risk in the late summer and early autumn. All this raises the question why adults failed to acquire some measure of immunity to seasonal diseases that carried off many children.

On a previous occasion I suggested that this unusual pattern might have been caused by a combination of two factors, a strong seasonal presence of the most pernicious strains of malaria and a high rate of immigration from healthier regions at mature ages. In the city of Rome in the nineteenth century, malaria infection peaked from August to October and overall death rates rose accordingly, a pattern that is fully consistent with that found in the late antique epitaphs. Various types of malaria, from comparatively mild benign tertian fever (caused by *Plasmodium vivax*) and quartan fever (*P. malariae*) to the more lethal malignant tertian fever (*P. falciparum*) and complications such as 'semitertian fever', are documented for the capital of the empire. As early as the first century BC, the physician Asclepiades of Bithynia described 'quotidian' fever (typical of primary falciparian infection) as being common there. Some 250 years later his more famous colleague Galen observed that physicians practising in Rome had no need to consult medical texts for descriptions of semitertian fever (related to the same infection) simply because its symptoms could not be observed better anywhere else: 'just as other diseases thrive in other places, this one abounds in that city'. Several literary sources likewise reflect the likely impact of malaria in the late summer and early autumn.[2]

If they do indeed refer to Rome proper, some of Galen's more specific references to the age-specific incidence of particular mani-festations of malaria may even allow the inference that falciparian malaria had attained what is known as hyperendemicity, creating an environment in which a majority of the population carried the par-asites in their blood but survivors gradually developed immunity in response to repeated infection. This suggests that persistently high sea-sonal death rates among adults may have been sustained by immigration from healthier – malaria-free – locales that were likely to generate net population growth for which the capital provided an attractive outlet. Comparative evidence from later periods of Italian history lends support to this conjecture.[3]

While falciparian malaria in particular was certainly capable of killing on its own, its lethality would have been greatly magnified by its synergistic interaction with other seasonal infections, such as gastro-intestinal disorders and respiratory diseases. In this connection, it is worth noting that some of these conditions – including typhoid and tuberculosis – tend to be more common among adolescents and even adults than among the very young. This, too, may help explain the striking persistence of high seasonal death rates well beyond early childhood that is documented in the epigraphic record.

It is true that seasonality profiles do not reveal either the actual scale of mortality, in the sense of the proportion of the population which died in a given year, or mean life expectancy, which is derived

---

[2] For the connection with malaria, see Scheidel 1994, 157–65; Scheidel 2003, 162–3. Medical observations: Asclepiades in Caelius Aurelianus 2.63–4, ed. Drabkin; Galen 7.135, 7.465, 17A.121–2 Kühn, with Sallares 2002, 220–3. The literary allusions are discussed in Scheidel 2003, 165–7; but cf. Lo Cascio 2001b, 191–2.

[3] Sallares 2002, 223–4 and Scheidel 2003, 164 on Galen 7.468, 11.23 Kühn.

from that measure. It is also true that epigraphic profiles from late antique southern Italy and Roman and early Arabic Egypt echo the metropolitan Roman pattern. Even so, comparison with later historical datasets suggests that the sheer scale of the endemic seasonal mortality surge beyond childhood that we find in the ancient city of Rome far exceeded anything that can be observed in the more recent past, except in years marred by major epidemics. This alone points to extremely high levels of mortality overall.

MORTALITY RATES, AGE STRUCTURE AND LIFE EXPECTANCY

One might think that ages recorded on Roman tombstones might be able to shed some light on this question. If the distribution of ages at death in these documents faithfully reflected actual conditions it could be used to reconstruct the age structure and hence the life expectancy of the metropolitan population. Unfortunately, as has long been recognized and frequently (and compellingly) reiterated, this is not the case. The frequency of funerary commemoration varied hugely according to sex and age as well as other factors, even including the language in which these texts were recorded. Looking beyond the city of Rome, we encounter tremendous diversity, from locations where death in childhood was frequently commemorated to others where almost everyone seems to have lived to a ripe old age, a situation unknown before our own time. This shows that these data are not representative of actual conditions and cannot be used to reconstruct demographic profiles.[4]

More specifically, comparison between the attested distribution of ages at death in the city of Rome and that predicted by a plausible high-mortality model life table suggests that the epigraphic record underreports the loss of life at very young ages; vastly privileges deaths among older children, adolescents and young adults; and equally vastly neglects death in old age (Fig. 3.3).

Somewhat desperate attempts to salvage some demographic credibility by attributing the attested profile to the effects of epidemic or otherwise 'catastrophic' mortality that might have shaped the city's population structure in unusual ways have signally failed to reconcile the observed pattern with any demographically plausible model. We must acknowledge that the real value of these texts lies in their capacity to

---

[4] Clauss 1973 is the best survey of epigraphic diversity.

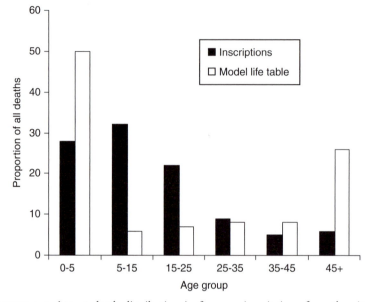

FIGURE 3.3 Age-at-death distribution in funerary inscriptions from the city of Rome and in a plausible model life table
Source: Paine and Storey 2006, 72.

elucidate cultural preferences such as the differential valuation of the sexes at specific ages and its change over time. Relevant as this is for the purposes of social and cultural history, it does not answer demographic questions.[5]

Skeletal remains are similarly unhelpful. Not only does palaeo-demographic analysis in general continue to suffer from a variety of technical and methodological problems – from difficulties in accurately ageing adult bones to the lack of information about the effect of in- and out-migration on local age structure – this approach is even less promising in a place like imperial Rome whose population may well have been mobile and unstable in unpredictable ways (Chapter 5 and below). This makes it impossible to apply the principles of stable pop-ulation analysis – that is, to derive mortality and fertility rates from an observed age distribution.[6] Thus, even if the correct age at death of all

[5] Paine and Storey 2006, esp. 82–5 (failure to explain observed pattern); Shaw 1991 (cultural preferences).

[6] A misguided attempt to undertake stable population analysis of what must have been an even more exceptional population – at Roman Portus – illustrates the pitfalls of this approach: Sperduti 1995.

available skeletons could eventually be ascertained, this would not necessarily tell us much about mortality rates and life expectancy beyond
broad outlines – life was short – that may readily be accepted on *a priori*
grounds.

DISEASES

In the face of these forbidding uncertainties, it is particularly important to complement quantitative study with consideration of qualita-
tive evidence. It is worth appreciating the range of diseases that were
experienced in the city even if their prevalence and demographic consequences remain unknown. Galen called Rome 'this populous city,
where daily ten thousand people can be discovered suffering from jaun-
dice, and ten thousand from dropsy' (11.328 ed. Kühn). Many of the
case histories he described in his works must have occurred there.[7] His
own and earlier medical references to malaria in the city have already
been mentioned. A century before Galen, Pliny the Elder devoted a
section of his *Historia Naturalis* (26.1–9) to 'novel diseases' that had been
introduced to Rome and Italy in the recent past. *Lichen* or *mentagra*,
a pustulous lichen on the chin transmitted by kissing and supposedly
confined to the upper classes, was one of them; *elephantiasis*, safely
identifiable as lepromatous leprosy, was another. While the ubiquity of
gastrointestinal infections – much endured yet rarely mentioned – may
be taken for granted, a reliable assessment of the prevalence and impact
of pulmonary tuberculosis, potentially a major killer, would require
empirical data that we do not currently possess. One can only hope
that future analysis of skeletal remains will shed more light on this issue
(see the final section of this chapter below).

Epidemic outbreaks added to the disease burden but tangible
information is scarce. The late republican and imperial periods are
not as well covered in our sources as earlier centuries. The annalistic tradition preserved by Livy reports numerous epidemics – usually
though not always in the city of Rome – between 490 and 292 BC and
especially from 212 to 174 BC: in the latter period, a mortality crisis is
mentioned on average every 4.3 years. By contrast, authors covering
the following centuries paid less attention to inauspicious events and
are often unspecific as to the location of reported epidemics. Thus,
from the mid-second century BC to the end of the second century AD,
epidemic outbreaks in the city of Rome itself are mentioned on only

---

[7] Mattern 2008, 173–202 lists all cases.

five occasions, for 142 BC, 23–22 BC, AD 65, AD 79/80 (?), and AD 189. The record is only marginally better for Late Antiquity, when epidemics are expressly placed in Rome on a further ten occasions between AD 284 and 750.[8] This paucity is undoubtedly a function of the nature of the evidence rather than a reflection of dramatic improvement: the ongoing Tiber floods alone, discussed in the next section, would have made that impossible.

The most dramatic mortality crisis in imperial Rome may well have been the so-called 'Antonine Plague', probably smallpox, that swept across the empire from AD 165 and continued into the 170s and perhaps into the late 180s AD or even later. If this epidemic was indeed a case of smallpox striking a 'virgin' (i.e. previously unexposed) population, it could in theory have killed a sizeable proportion of the metropolitan population (a third?), with a death toll in the hundreds of thousands. Yet we will never know, and sporadically proffered numbers are notoriously unreliable. Cassius Dio (72.14.3) refers to 2,000 fatalities a day during an epidemic in Rome in AD 189, possibly a resurgence of the 'Antonine Plague', a figure that has the dubious merit of being at least theoretically possible for the very large capital. Other tallies give the appearance of rounding or stylization and are probably merely symbolic, such as the 30,000 residents supposedly killed by an epidemic under Nero or, far less credibly, 10,000 per day under Titus or 5,000 per day under Gallienus.[9]

In any event, the size, density and connectedness of the city must have invited microbial onslaughts. This combination of risk factors was not lost on ancient observers: as Herodian noted, when an epidemic struck Italy in the late 180s AD – probably the same event mentioned by Cassius Dio – 'it was most severe in Rome, which, apart from being normally overcrowded, was still getting immigrants from all over the world' (1.12.1). We cannot tell if the thousands of bodies deposited in the ditch of the 'Servian' *agger* on the Esquiline that were reportedly found in 1876 were at least in part hastily discarded victims of epidemics. Yet the recent discovery (atop the later catacombs of St Peter and Marcellinus 3 km south-east of Rome) of a series of rooms filled

---

[8] For the earlier periods, see Duncan-Jones 1996, 111. Epidemics in Rome: Orosius 5.4.8; Cassius Dio 53.33.4, 54.1.3; Tacitus, *Annales* 16.13; Suetonius, *Nero* 39; Jerome, *Chronica* 188 Helm (with Suetonius, *Titus* 8.3 for the correct date); Cassius Dio 72.14.3. For Late Antiquity, see Stathakopoulos 2004, 175–386 (*pace* 30).

[9] Duncan-Jones 1996 (Antonine Plague); Scheidel 2003, 171–2 (outbreaks in Rome).

with large numbers of tightly stacked corpses that had been deposited
at the same time and clad in garments decorated with gold threads
and amber points to a sudden event that required the unceremoni-
ous disposal of numerous deceased individuals of not inconsiderable
standing, quite possibly an epidemic in the late second or early third
century AD that might even have been a resurgence of the 'Antonine
Plague'.[10]

ENVIRONMENT AND INFRASTRUCTURE

Throughout the Roman period the Tiber remained prone to flooding.
A new estimate based on over 2,000 years of records reckons with significant flooding every few years and massive inundations a few times per
century. The relationship between floods and spikes in infectious disease
is well established; malaria in particular would have been exacerbated
by these incidents. In this respect but also more generally, topography
played an important role in determining health conditions: Livy once
called the hills of Rome 'most healthy' (5.54.4), and data from later
periods suggest that they were indeed healthier than low-lying areas.
Among other things, locations even at moderately elevated altitudes are
less exposed to malaria infection.[11]

Even as the size of the city's population and hence its settlement
density remain uncertain, there can be little doubt that many of its
residents lived in crowded conditions that were conducive to unsan-
itary practices and infection (Chapter 9). As already noted, Rome's
nodal position encouraged the introduction of new strains of disease
while its exceptionally large population would have made it easier for
such arrivals to become endemic and contribute permanently to the
metropolitan disease pool. At the same time, we must ask which factors
that were peculiar to Rome might have mitigated health hazards.

The role of Roman urban infrastructure in particular merits consideration. From a public health perspective, this infrastructure's capacity
to provide clean water and dispose of human and animal waste must be
regarded as its most significant features (Chapter 17). The potential of
the city's sewer system to prevent disease was diminished to the extent to
which it served to provide street drainage rather than to remove sewage

---

[10] Graham 2006, 67, 73, 80–1 (ditch); Blanchard et al. 2007 (catacomb). Here and in
the following, all distances are from the Aurelian Wall.

[11] For flooding and its health consequences, see Aldrete 2007, 81, 141–54; and cf. also
Chapter 13. Malaria and altitude: Sallares 2002, 206–9, and cf. 331 s.v. 'altitude'.

from the source. Rome's costly network of aqueducts delivered clean water on a scale that would have been the envy of other pre-modern cities and could in principle have made a massive contribution to public health. However, once again the system was set up in a way that is likely to have reduced its actual benefits. Most residents obtained water from public basins and fountains, a practice that created several problems. The accumulation of garbage and excrement (and the occasional corpse and carcass) in the streets combined with the overflow from these water outlets to contaminate street surfaces, creating an environment that was conducive to the spread of gastroenteritis, typhoid, diarrhoea, salmonellosis and worm infection.[12]

It is true that the continual flow of water would have flushed out contaminants that reached these outlets, preventing them from being compromised for longer than in the very short term. Nevertheless, the availability of fresh water at these facilities, in relative abundance and free of charge, did not automatically translate to sanitary storage and consumption. Studies conducted in contemporary developing countries highlight the great importance of contamination between source and point-of-use: safe water drawn from improved sources frequently shows unsafe levels of *E. coli* upon consumption. A variety of factors are responsible, from bacterial regrowth in stored water and recontamination through dipping with unclean hands and cups to the presence of biofilms on the inner surfaces of containers. This is a phenomenon that historians need to keep in mind whenever they consider the actual health benefits of the generous public provision of clean water in the imperial city of Rome.[13]

The Roman culture of public bathing is another example of unexpected consequences. Immersion in unchlorinated water posed its own health hazards, especially when it was heated and thus triggered bacterial growth. Authorities such as Celsus and Pliny the Elder leave no doubt that 'medicinal bathing' was supposed to take place in public baths: as a matter of fact, the former advises patients with bowel troubles to bathe their anuses in the hot pools located at these venues but (not unreasonably) warns those with infected wounds not to expose them to the filthy contents of these facilities.[14]

---

[12] Scobie 1986, 407–22; Aldrete 2007, 142–5. Cf. also Dupré Raventós and Remolà 2000, 63–73, 95–105, 123–7.
[13] Aldrete 2007, 152–4 (overflow); Clasen and Bastable 2003; Wright et al. 2004; Gundry et al. 2006 (secondary contamination).
[14] Scobie 1986, 425–7; Fagan 2006, 191–4; Celsus, *De medicina* 4.25.3, 5.26.28c.

A 'POPULATION SINK'?

What this all means for the demographic 'balance sheet' of the city remains profoundly unclear. Large pre-modern cities in general were unhealthy places that tended to suffer from excess mortality or even an excess of deaths over births. The scale and especially the causes of these phenomena continue to be debated: a variety of factors from elevated levels of density-dependent morbidity and mortality to the effects of immigrants' age distribution and of urban labour markets on marriage and reproduction appear to have played a role. A very rough estimate for the early modern city of London envisioning an annual excess of deaths over births equivalent to 1 per cent of the total size of the population has repeatedly been acknowledged by Roman historians, yet its relevance is doubtful: it might equally well be too pessimistic (because imperial Rome enjoyed better infrastructure and welfare provisions) as too optimistic (because London was free from falciparian malaria).[15]

It is important to remember that not all pre-modern metropolises were equally deadly, and that in so far as they *were* deadly this was not necessarily so for the same reasons. On the one hand, the medical and demographic impact of the aqueducts and free food distributions of imperial Rome must not be overrated: while the benefits produced by the former would in part have been undone by the adverse consequences of overflow and secondary contamination, the significance of the latter is called into question by the observation that in pre-modern societies location and population density were generally more potent determinants of health and life expectancy than food intake. On the other hand, it would surely be unwise to throw the baby out with Celsus' soiled bathwater: a counterfactual city of Rome that had to rely on wells and the water of the Tiber, or one that had lacked a state-backed food supply, would almost certainly have been a worse place than the historical city actually was – smaller, perhaps, but also (even) less healthy.

To complicate matters further, Rome's inhabitants faced problems that were uncommon in other very large pre-modern cities, most notably endemic malaria. Comparative historians are left speculating that they might be dealing with a zero-sum game: although in the case of Rome, certain hazards that were more common elsewhere (primarily water contamination and food shortages) were mitigated by public provisions, their place may have been taken by others (such as malaria)

[15] See Woods 2003 for the debate. For London, see Wrigley 1987, 135.

that were less common elsewhere. The scope of modern guesswork is therefore only feebly constrained by comparative historical reasoning and the weighing of different factors. This leaves margins of uncertainty that are wide enough to accommodate quite diverse scenarios of metropolitan demography, from a city with a stable core population that was able to reproduce itself to one that relied on continuous massive immigration merely to maintain its size.[16]

THE WAY FORWARD

These uncertainties do not mean that there is no hope of progress. Science holds very considerable promise in expanding our empirical knowledge of Roman health. The best source of information on this topic is necessarily the Roman body itself, represented by large numbers of skeletons that have come to light near the city or are yet to be discovered. However, although it has long been possible to study dental, cranial, and other skeletal anomalies that are indicative of stress and disease, and analyses of ancient DNA that reveal the presence of a variety of pathogens have now also begun to appear, relevant work that focuses on the city of Rome and its *suburbium* has remained relatively rare. Skeletal material retrieved from the suburban catacombs has suffered the largest degree of neglect. Excavations prompted by construction work continue to expand the available evidence: by now over 5,000 Roman skeletons are said to have come to light in this way and mostly still await detailed study.[17]

The most telling skeletal features are two kinds of lesions that are often described as porotic hyperostosis but may actually have different aitiologies – namely orbital lesions (*cribra orbitalia*) that are associated with chronic iron-deficiency anaemia and other disorders, and porotic lesions of the cranial vault (*cribra cranii*) – as well as enamel hypoplasia, a dental condition resulting from the temporary arrest of enamel matrix growth caused by infection, parasitism or vitamin D deficiency. While these markers do not enable us to identify specific diseases, their

---

[16] While Morley 1996, 39–54 as well as Scheidel 2003, 175–6 and 2004, 15–19 argue for the need for massive immigration, Lo Cascio 2001a, 2001b and 2006 assumes greater stability. Skeletal isotope analysis can be expected finally to shed light on the actual scale of immigration: for now, see Prowse et al. 2007, on Portus near Rome; cf. also Killgrove 2010 and more generally the following section.

[17] Van der Linde 2009 (catacombs); Catalano 2008 (number of recent finds). Donoghue and Spigelman 2006 summarize references to pertinent DNA studies.

prevalence and distribution are indicative of the overall health status of affected populations.

Preliminary reports on a large imperial cemetery near the ancient Via Collatina, about 2 km east-north-east of the Porta Praenestina, refer to extremely high levels of enamel hypoplasia (80–92 per cent) and porotic hyperostosis (50–77 per cent). This is consistent with findings from more fully published suburban sites. In a sample from Lucus Feroniae, some 30 km north-east of Rome, at least 80 per cent suffered from enamel hypoplasia and a third – and two-thirds of pre-adults – exhibited advanced *cribra orbitalia*. At Vallerano, about 10 km south of the ancient city, 69 per cent had (mostly advanced) *cribra orbitalia* and the incidence of enamel hypoplasia was also very high. In a sample from the large cemetery on the Isola Sacra near Portus, the main port of imperial Rome, 80 per cent suffered from enamel hypoplasia. Signs of poor health have likewise been reported for a cemetery at Casale Capobianco near the Via Nomentana about 8 km north-east of Rome. All these datasets document high levels of ill-health and stress. However, preliminary investigation has revealed significantly higher well-being among skeletons unearthed at Casal Bertone, a Roman industrial site less than 2 km east of the Porta Maggiore: one in five people suffered from enamel hypoplasia and only one in six from *cribra orbitalia*. Similar conditions have been observed in a sample from yet another suburban site, Castellaccio Europarco 8 km south of Rome. This points to a considerable amount of local variation and should caution us against sweeping generalizations. Above all, it shows how much work remains to be done.[18]

Although malaria may induce anaemias that lead to porotic lesions, many other causes produce the same outcome; the presence of malaria must therefore be established in other ways. DNA of *Plasmodium falciparum*, responsible for the deadliest form of malaria, has been extracted from a late Roman child skeleton in Umbria, but comparable genetic evidence from the region of Rome itself is still lacking. The identification of tuberculosis poses its own problems. Only a very small proportion of modern tuberculosis sufferers develop visible bone lesions. For this reason alone, evidence of a healing tuberculous spinal infection in a skeleton from an early imperial suburban necropolis close to the Via Nomentana contributes little to our understanding of the weight of

---

[18] Buccellato et al. 2003, 346–8; Buccellato et al. 2008; Manzi et al. 1999, 338–9; Salvadei et al. 2001, 711; Cucina et al. 2006, 107; Nencioni et al. 2001; Killgrove 2010 (and cf. Ottini et al. 2001, 365).

this disease. Its actual prevalence can only be traced through biomolecular analysis. It is encouraging that DNA of *Mycobacterium tuberculosis* (as well as *M. leprae*, responsible for leprosy) has repeatedly been found in (provincial) Roman-period skeletons, and that the same is now also true of the *Yersinia pestis* bacterium that causes bubonic, pneumonic and septicemic plague. This suggests that similar discoveries may eventually be made on the outskirts of Rome.[19]

Weaning represented a considerable health hazard for small children and it is therefore important to be able to derive its timing from the study of dental remains: this task has already been accomplished for skeletons from Portus. Metropolitan air pollution also contributed to ill-health: the mummified body of a child from the second century AD found at Grottarossa, 7 km north of Rome, exhibits severe anthracosis, a lung disease caused by the inhalation of particulate pollutants. However, further investigation of this phenomenon may not be feasible for the city of Rome. For instance, the detection of pleurisy in several bodies from Herculaneum, a disorder associated with indoor pollution from lighting, cooking and heating, cannot readily be replicated elsewhere because it depends on exceptionally good skeletal preservation. Moreover, the DNA of pathogens that trigger intestinal diseases, which must have accounted for a large share of all deaths in Rome, cannot be recovered unless soft colonic tissue survives, which is not normally the case. To give another example of unique circumstances, carbonized foodstuffs from Herculaneum show high rates of microbial contamination, something that presumably also happened in Rome but cannot be empirically established. The same is true of lesser conditions such as pediculosis (lice infestation), which has been shown to have been common in Herculaneum.[20]

Despite these and other limitations, this line of research can hardly fail to put our understanding of Roman living conditions on a much more solid footing: we will know much more about what people ate, how healthy they were, and even where they came from. This information will reduce at least some of the uncertainties that I have highlighted throughout this chapter. In this respect, after generations of scholarship, we have the good fortune to be standing very much at the beginning.

[19] Sallares 2002, 67–8 (malaria); Canci et al. 2005 (osseous TB); Donoghue and Spigelman 2006 (DNA).
[20] FitzGerald et al. 2006; Prowse et al. 2008 (weaning); Ascensi et al. 1996 (mummy); Capasso 2000 and 2007 (Herculaneum). For soot from cooking in the capital, cf. Seneca, *Epistulae* 104.6.

Further reading

Scobie 1986 remains the classic survey of living conditions in Rome (and other Roman cities). While deliberately focusing on the bleak side and thereby inviting allegations of bias, it has generally weathered well. Lo Cascio 2006 seeks to make the case for a more optimistic perspective, arguably with rather limited success. Scheidel 2003 surveys the disease environment in the imperial city of Rome. The epigraphic evidence for seasonal mortality is most fully set out by Shaw 1996a and 2006 and was first associated with malaria by Scheidel 1994. Sallares 2002, 201–34 gives the best account of malaria in ancient Rome. Scheidel 2001 surveys the general demographic background. The invaluable scientific work introduced in the final section still awaits synoptic treatment.

4: SLAVES AND FREEDMEN*

Elisabeth Herrmann-Otto

No work concerning the inhabitants of ancient Rome could afford not to make mention of slaves and freedmen. The existence of slaves in the city can be traced back to the period of the Twelve Tables, to approximately 450 BC. A Romano-Carthaginian treaty dating from a century later, 348 BC, implies Roman involvement in the Punic slave trade. If we are to believe the annalistic tradition found in Livy, slaves, led by their aristocratic masters, have played an important part in the political struggles in the city as far back as the fifth century BC. Slavery itself was an ancient institution in the city of Rome. The first question that needs answering is:

HOW DID YOU BECOME A SLAVE IN ANCIENT ROME?

The oldest sources of slave labour are debt slavery, chattel slavery and slavery from captivity in war. Debt slavery was abolished quite early in Roman history. Since it was not permitted for Romans to sell their fellow citizens into slavery, insolvent debtors had to be sold *trans Tiberim*, i.e. beyond the borders of the city-state. This practice was prohibited at the latest by the *lex Poetelia Papiria* of 326 BC. Even earlier, debtors had delivered themselves into the hands of their creditors as serfs (*nexi*), to work off their debts as manual labourers.

The slaves mentioned in the Twelve Tables arrived at Rome probably through the Punic slave trade. Especially during the early period of the Republic, Carthaginian ships raided the coastal towns of Italy, pillaged and carried off their inhabitants into slavery, to be sold off to their trading partners, among which was early republican Rome itself. It was a profitable business, sustained by piracy on the seas, assaulting

---

* Translation by Christian Rollinger MA (Trier).

travelling parties on the overland trade routes and hit-and-run raids on coastal and/or trading towns. Incursions such as these lasted well into empire and even Late Antiquity. During the middle and late Republic, the slave trade in Italy itself was internationalized: slaves from the whole Mediterranean world were captured, brought in and sold on Italian slave markets. Even if Roman territory itself was less threatened by such attacks, there were among her slaves those who had been kidnapped as free citizens and sold and sold again on different slave markets until they reached Rome. It was rare for these unfortunates to be recognized as freeborn and have their freedom returned to them in a *causa liberalis*. Happy endings such as these are only attested in the comedies of Plautus and Terence. Their fictitious nature notwithstanding, these plays show that kidnappings and enslavements were a common occurrence that affected not only adult males, but especially women and children.

The international slave trade also played an important role in the treatment of conquered enemies. Florentinus, a lawyer of the second century AD, writes:

> Slaves are so called because commanders generally sell the
> people they capture and thereby save them instead of
> killing them. The word for property in slaves (*mancipia*) is
> derived from the fact that they are captured from the
> enemy by force of arms.[1]

Until the fifth century BC at the latest (probably earlier), it was common Roman practice to execute male prisoners of war. Later, it became accepted custom either to trade foreign captives for Roman ones, to enslave and divide them between general and troops, or, if the enemy had been vanquished completely, to absorb them into the Roman citizenry. Selling them off to be traded on one of the many slave markets was infrequent and the continuing expansion of Roman power into central Italy led to a marked change in the Roman attitude towards prisoners of war. Since the occupied territory needed labourers to cultivate it, captives were used either as slaves or *dediticii* to cultivate it. On those occasions however, when Rome waged a particularly savage form of warfare striving not only for victory on the battlefield, but aiming for the virtual annihilation of their enemies, mass enslavement was common. In the Third Samnite War of 298–290 BC nearly 55,000 Samnite

---

[1] *Digesta* 1.5.4.2–3. Translation: Wiedemann 1981, no. 1.

and Gallic captives were sold off on slave markets.[2] Italian agriculture seemed to need such quantities of forced labour although the grain supply of the city of Rome and the soldiers was aided by contributions from the *provinciae frumentariae* of Sicily and Sardinia since the Second Punic War (218–201 BC).[3]

Through Rome's wars in both the eastern and western Mediterranean and her rise to world-power status in the third and second centuries BC a steady and growing influx of slaves, both soldiers and civilians, men, women and children, reached Italy as enslaved people. Not all of them were employed in the agricultural sector, though: there were slaves in private households, in trade and commerce, in the 'entertainment' sector, medicine and intellectual professions. Slaves, particularly Greek slaves, were part of the luxuries that had flooded the city early in the second century. Wars of conquest and annexation, with their great quantities of prisoners of war, remained a principal source of fresh slaves throughout the whole period of Roman rule, even if the levels of Rome's expansionist era were never quite matched during the Principate, while the *Pax Augusta* held sway throughout the empire. Still, even then, the increasingly frequent wars against Dacians and Marcomanni provided for new prisoners of war to be sold at slave markets in Rome and the provinces. The ongoing pacification of the borders, agreements and treaties with foreign peoples soon dried up this source of slaves.

There were others, however, such as children born as and of slaves. Attested as early as the republican era, they became increasingly important during the Principate and well into Late Antiquity. Justinian's lawyers defined slave birth thus: 'Either one is born as a slave, or one becomes a slave later. Born as slaves are those who are born from our female slaves.'[4] A child was slave-born if its mother was a slave. The civic status of the father was inconsequential. Romans soon discovered that this principle of the *ius gentium* ('common law of peoples') presented some difficulties. Free women occasionally consorted with slaves of other households. Since the women were Roman citizens, the offspring of these unions were also considered to be freeborn Roman citizens. The slaves' virility benefited other families, and not their owners since they had no legal recourse to claim the child. In AD 54 the senate decided to intervene on behalf of the slave owners and decreed that a free woman who had consorted with a slave could herself be forced into slavery by the owner, if he had any objections to their union. If

---

[2] Welwei 2000, 39–49.   [3] Erdkamp 2005, 209–18.   [4] Justinian, *Institutiones* 1.3.4.

the woman did not break off the relationship after three warnings, she, and consequently her children, became slaves. This *Senatus Consultum Claudianum* seems to imply that slave owners were very much interested in the natural procreation of their slaves. A number of legal provisions concerning slave birth, sale, inheritance or forfeiting of unborn children (*partus ancillae*) seem to confirm this, as do the many funeral inscriptions, dedicated by the owners or parents of deceased slave children. This has been used as evidence by scholars to ascertain the dominant position of domestic breeding as the principal source of slaves in the Principate.

Using modern demographic models, and depending on how high they suppose the percentage of slaves among the general population to be (ranging from 5 per cent, 10 per cent to 30–40 per cent), scholars have estimated that around 160,000, 250,000 or 320,000 slave births per annum were necessary, to keep the numbers of slaves in the city constant.[5] There is some ancient evidence to dispute this. The balance between male and female slaves in Rome was very much in favour of male slaves. Slavery itself is a manifestation of a constant demand for a labour force and there were traditionally only few professions suited to women, such as wet nurses (*nutrices*), hairdressers (*ornatrices*) and walking companions (*pedisequae*). Even in personal households, cooks (*coci*), attendants (*pueri*), chamberlains (*cubicularii*) and dressers (*a veste, vestiarii*) were all male. The same can be said for the leading positions in the textile industries (*lanipendi*, sometimes *lanipendae*), even though the lower ranks were composed of a predominantly female labour force (*textrices, textriculae*). Consequently, the demand for male slaves was great and the available sources reflect this. It has been argued that in funeral inscriptions, for instance, women are underrepresented in consequence of the epigraphic habit and that this must not necessarily be a reflection on their true numbers. However, if women and children were really as essential to their masters and the maintenance of slave numbers, as some scholars have made them out to be, there should surely be a much greater number of memorial inscriptions than has been found hitherto. Furthermore, if domestic breeding really was an all-important source of slaves, it would have been patently absurd to manumit female slaves during their fecund age. There are, however, many known instances of early-age manumissions, of owners marrying their former slaves shortly after their manumission, or of slaves being rewarded with their freedom, after the birth of one (sic!) son. To fit into the reconstructed

---

[5] Scheidel 1997, 156–69; Andreau and Descat 2007, 74–85, 94–101.

demographic models mentioned above, the average female slave would on the contrary have to produce four healthy children at the least – this is irreconcilable with the available evidence. It also has to be mentioned that an owner relying solely on natural domestic breeding for his supply of slaves would be running very great economic risks: in the ancient world, mortality rates during birth and among infants were shockingly high (see Chapters 3 and 6). No wonder then, from the point of view of a slave owner, that obstacles were raised to sexual intercourse among slaves, that forced abortions or the immediate sale of a newborn slave were common practice. They are documented in the ancient sources and must be interpreted as a sort of knee-jerk reaction to the risks and vagaries of giving birth to a healthy child and raising it to be a productive slave. They are irreconcilable with the thought of slave owners systematically breeding new slaves. On the contrary, slave owners approached births very ambivalently. Some tried to prevent pregnancies among their slaves, others encouraged it. Some tolerated it and chose the most profitable solution for themselves. In any case, the natural procreation of slaves in slavery was but one source for slaves. It was never the only, or even dominant, one.[6]

That is not to say that the raising of slave children from an early age in the *familia* could not be a profitable undertaking. But not all slave owners were willing to risk the lives of their own slaves in birth. Foundling children played a not insubstantial part in the context of maintaining slave numbers. The exposing of unwanted children was the most widely practised method of birth control in antiquity. Even the political philosophers of Greece were loath to recommend it. If a Roman parent (the paterfamilias) had reached the conclusion that his family was large enough and did not want to reduce the inheritances of his sons (or indeed of his single daughter) further, all he needed to do was not to acknowledge the child and to leave it to its wet nurse or his slaves to expose. Slave merchants or owners with an eye for business opportunities literally picked the children out of rubbish heaps, public places or busy crossroads and had them raised as slaves. For this, a wet nurse was needed. If there was none in the household of the child's new owner, employed to raise the family's as well as the slaves' children (as attested in the household of Livia Augusta, or the aristocratic families of the Statilii or the Volusii), there was always the possibility of hiring one, which, in Rome, was exceedingly simple. One simply had to go to the *columna lactaria* in the Forum Olitorium, where women offered

---

[6] Herrmann-Otto 1994, 231–87.

their services as wet nurses. There was even a free trial included. A contract was concluded, which determined the salary, the length of the engagement, where and how the baby was to be cared for and which accoutrements (i.e. nappies, oils, etc.) the master would provide. The wet nurse herself, or as the case may be, her legal guardian or owner, if she was a slave, was responsible for the health and welfare of the child. In the case of the child's death, the consequences could be severe: in Egypt the wet nurse was under an obligation either to substitute her own child or to find another foundling. This way, the risk involved for the slave owner could be kept to a minimum, which might explain the large body of evidence for foundlings (*expositi, alumni*). If such a child was raised by a slave merchant, he could choose to educate the child, to train it in a craft or a trade, and then later sell it off for a high price, or just see to it that it survived into adulthood and still fetch a fair price for an able-bodied yet unqualified slave. By that stage it would be impossible to reconstruct the original status – whether freeborn or of slave descent – of the child. This source of new slaves was legally practised far into Late Antiquity. There was a short-lived and ineffective attempt under Constantine to restrict this practice by allowing parents to sell their newborns, but the exposing of young and very young children continued unabated. It was only under Justinian that all exposed children, whether they were of slave descent or not, were declared to be free.[7]

An important factor of slavery was poverty. It is for a very good reason that the self-sale of impoverished citizens into slavery is named first among the different ways of enslavement in Roman civil law. The burden of mounting debts and the risk of starving to death must have been great enough to prefer a life in slavery to a free existence below the margin of subsistence. There were no homeless shelters or soup kitchens in ancient Rome. The basic unit of society was the *familia*. Without a *familia* to support him, an impoverished Roman might well have chosen to sell himself into someone else's *familia*. It is difficult to say how many such former citizens were among the various slaves in the households throughout the city. What is known is that many of them ended up in the financial sector, as *procuratores, dispensatores, actores* or *arcarii*.[8]

A final source of new slave labour was enslavement as a form of legal punishment. It was routinely and systematically applied to members of the lower strata of society (*humiliores*), specifically as a

---

[7] Herrmann-Otto 2006, 86–8. [8] Herrmann-Otto 2001, 171–84.

punishment for capital offences. Whereas the higher classes were granted the privilege of being executed by the sword, the *humiliores* were often condemned *ad ludos* (to fight as gladiators) or *ad venationes*, to fight in the great animal hunts that took place in the Colosseum. Although by no means all the gladiators or hunters were convicted criminals – they included a fair number of prisoners of war and even free Roman citizens – for them, this was a comparatively mild form of punishment: there remained, at least in theory, the possibility of a victory in the arena and a subsequent reprieve combined with manumission. Gladiators often had regular supporters and admirers, particularly among the women of the city. Compared to those criminals condemned to spend the rest of their lives literally slaving in the mines, gladiators led a privileged life. The mining slaves, in contrast, faced certain death. Only an imperial pardon could save them.[9]

If even criminals condemned to fight in the gladiatorial games could hope to be freed, it is clear that freedmen and the act of manumission deserve special attention. It is this complex that we now must turn to.

HOW DID YOU BECOME A FREEDMAN IN ROME?

The Roman jurist Ulpian writes:

> Manumissions are also an institution of the common law of peoples (*ius gentium*). Manumission is the release from the 'hand', meaning the granting of freedom. Because so long as someone is in servitude, he is in the hand (*manus*) and under the power of his master and becomes free of this power upon release from the hand (*manumission*). This is an institution of the *ius gentium*, since according to natural law (*ius naturale*) everyone is born free and manumission was still unknown when slavery was unknown. But after slavery had spread through the common law of peoples, it was followed by the benefit of manumission.[10]

---

[9] Wiedemann 1992, ch. 5. For the amnestied mining slave named Callistus, later bishop of Rome, see Gülzow 1969, 142–72.
[10] *Digesta* 1.1.4.

One might suppose that the simultaneous appearance of slavery and manumission is an elegant invention by lawyers of the Principate. However, there is some evidence for manumission as early as the Twelve Tables, who mention manumission by will after the owner's death:

> If one has liberated (his slave) under the following
> condition: 'if he has paid 10,000 to the heir', then (the
> slave), even if he is sold on by the heir, will become free, if
> he pays the sum to his buyer (i.e. his new master): thus
> rules the Law of the Twelve Tables.[11]

The laws of the kings (*leges regiae*) seem to point towards the inclusion of freedmen into the four urban tribes under the mythical king Servius Tullius. Furthermore, Livy mentions the introduction of a tax on manumission (*vicesima manumissionum*) by the year 357 BC. The slave master must thereby pay 5 per cent of his slave's worth to the treasury.[12]

The accounts from the Principate are generally trustworthy as far as their contents go. The chronology is another matter. There is a certain tendency in the sources to ascribe an equally long tradition to manumission as to slavery itself, and to demonstrate that even in the earliest days, the Roman state itself practised a generous policy of manumitting prisoners of war. It seems certain, however, that the enfranchisement of freedmen, their inclusion into the urban tribes, goes back no further than the fourth century BC. This seems to have been part of a process to standardize the practice. For a short time, beginning in 312 BC, freedmen were also admitted into the rural tribes. There seems to have been considerable resistance to admitting former slaves into all thirty-six tribes, though, and this practice was abandoned eight years later. The allocation to the urban tribes was probably altogether more fitting, as most of the freedmen would have been tradesmen rather than farmers.[13] The introduction of a tax on manumission was probably a reaction to the events of the Second Punic War and an attempt to replenish the public treasury that had been bled dry by war. In 209 BC, profits from this tax amounted to 4,000,000 *denarii*, or, in other words, 10,000 manumissions (at 400 *denarii per capita*) had taken place.

---

[11] 7.12 Ulpian, *Fragmenta* 2.4.
[12] Servius Tullius VI.3 = Dionysius of Halicarnassus, *Antiquitates Romanae* 4.22 = *FIRA* I.17; Livy 27.10.12.
[13] Kolb 1995, 156–7; Weiler 2003, 191; Schumacher 2001, 292.

A century earlier, a tax such as this one would have been unthinkable for practical purposes alone: before the introduction of the silver *denarius* as standard currency, the tax would have to have been paid in *aes grave*, a heavy type of coin made from cast copper.[14]

Manumissions in the Principate were so common – about 16,000 a year[15] – that restrictions had to be introduced. With the *lex Fufia Caninia* of 2 BC, Augustus limited the maximum number of slaves that could be freed by will to 100, regardless of the size of the deceased's slave *familia*. He also introduced age limits for manumission: 20 years of age for the owner, 30 for the slave. Given that the hygienic and climatic conditions of the city left something to be desired (see Chapter 3), the average life expectancy can be assumed to have ranged somewhere between 25 and 30 years, possibly a bit longer (33 years) for imperial slaves.[16] This low figure is due to a high mortality rate among children and infants, as well as among women in childbirth, particularly during their early fertile period of approximately 12–22 years of age. It has to be said, though, that if a slave was raised as a foundling by slave merchants and survived childhood to be sold off by his owner, his own personal life expectancy might well change for the better, depending on the circumstances of his position. In such cases, slaves might well achieve between 40 and 60 years of age. However, many of them will not have reached the minimum age for manumissions. It should be noted, however, that Augustus introduced age limits only for complete manumissions that led to Roman citizenship for the freedman. He also allowed for a number of exceptions: wet nurses, pedagogues, parents or sibling slaves could all be freed without restrictions by a panel of dignitaries. If a slave owner wanted to free one of his slaves in order to marry her, there were conditions: if he did not honour his intentions within six months, the woman and her offspring, if there had been any, were relegated to slavery.[17]

It seems remarkable, that in a society so dependent on slave labour as the Romans, the act of manumission enjoyed a popularity so great that it had to be restricted. The benefits of manumission were great, both for the slave and for the master.

---

[14] Welwei 2000, 36–7.
[15] Kolb 1995, 197–8. Kolb extrapolates his number from the yearly tax on manumission.
[16] Herrmann-Otto 1994, 246–8 with footnotes 39–42 for a detailed analysis of prior research about life expectancy, age structure and mortality rates in ancient Rome.
[17] Wacke 2001, 133–58.

The Roman practice of freeing slaves and granting them citizenship upon their release was widely known throughout the ancient world and was either praised or criticized for its generosity. King Philip V of Macedon emphasized the advantages of the Roman way of manumission to the inhabitants of the Greek city of Larissa. 'The Romans', he proclaimed in 214 BC, 'accept former slaves into the citizenry by granting them citizenship upon release.'[18] Philip was mistaken, though, when he said that freedmen had the right to hold public office. It is true that freedmen were allowed to vote in the tribal assembly (*comitia tributa*), to marry, to enter into legally binding contracts and testaments, and to engage in business on their own. They were, however, barred from public and military service. There were no such restrictions placed on their freeborn children, who were accepted as full Roman citizens. Not everyone approved of this attitude to manumission: particularly in Greece there were voices that called it a debasement of citizenship to grant it to slaves.

The slaves themselves, understandably, had a different view. Even if they had to buy their freedom themselves with their own *peculium*, they were afterwards Roman citizens with almost all of the privileges and duties that this entailed. The *peculium*, the property in money, movable objects or sometimes even land, that a slave had managed to accumulate and which his owner mostly left him to do with as he pleased, could, with any luck be great enough not only to buy his own freedom, but also that of his slave 'wive' (*contubernalis*) or children. Often, the *peculium* also served as seed money for a new, free existence, perhaps as a shop owner, a merchant or a physician. The freedman had obligations to his former master, now his patron, to be sure: they consisted mostly of contractually defined labour (*operae*) that had to be performed daily for a limited time. There was also a moral obligation (*obsequium*) if needs be to support his former master and his family. Gratitude and moral obligations were, however, hard to quantify.[19] Under the emperor Nero, the senate debated whether or not to re-enslave (*revocatio in servitutem*) those freedmen who had proved to be ungrateful or failed in their obligation of *obsequium*. The emperor, however, waved aside these proposals and referred the senators to tradition (*mos maiorum*): since freedmen were, after all, Roman citizens and had certain inalienable rights, each case must be individually tried before court.[20]

---

[18] *ILS* 8763; Klees 2002, 91–7.   [19] Waldstein 1986, 162.
[20] Tacitus, *Annales* 13.26–7.

Manumission was for the greatest part of the slave population something earnestly to strive for, particularly during the prosperous years of the early empire. There were some voices, to be sure, that preferred the relative security of being a slave in the household of a wealthy master to the uncertainties of trying to make it on their own as freedmen.[21] It was not uncommon, particularly in the late Republic, for old or sickly slaves to be manumitted by their masters in order to cut the cost of a workforce that could no longer work to its full capabilities. These freedmen then formed part of the *plebs frumentaria*, which since the tribunate of Clodius Pulcher 58 BC was entitled to distributions of free grain. Conditions were exacerbated in Late Antiquity, by which time freedmen often preferred to remain in the household of their patron. The *patroni* were also charged with schooling and training their slaves before manumission, so that they would not add to the numbers of beggars and mendicants. There are even some documented cases of slaves protesting against their own manumission: social security was paramount to personal liberty.[22]

Let us return to the early Principate. Manumission was practised widely and regularly. Great numbers of slaves were freed and then obliged to render the requisite *operae* to their patrons (see Chapter 19). In many cases business partnerships between freedman and patron developed and the former slave took personal responsibility for his own business. Irrespective of economic aspects, there were other considerations. A Roman nobleman never walked the city streets alone: slaves accompanied him everywhere as attendants (*pedisequi*) or as litter-bearers (*lecticarii*). A great mass of clients – the greater the better – followed him wherever he went, with his freedmen also among them. The greater this appendage, the greater the patron's prestige and lustre: it demonstrated his wealth, his influence and his power to the world. The same principle was behind the endless *salutationes* that the patron had to endure each morning: ritual greetings by his clients in his house, petitions and pleas for help. Freedmen were obliged to attend. In modern parlance, freedmen formed part of a patron's social network and could either be draped representatively about him or used for palpable gains. The importance of freedmen for the interlinkage of the aristocratic class must not be underestimated, particularly in its contact with the emperor himself. When direct contact was impossible,

---

[21] Epictetus, *Diatribai* 4.1.33–7.
[22] Paulinus of Nola, *Carmina* 21.239–65 CSEL 30² 166.

communications between nobleman and emperor could easily happen through the influential freedmen of the *familia Caesaris*.

Even if Augustus restricted the number of formal manumissions by law, this need not present insurmountable obstacles. If testamentary manumission (*manumissio testamento*), manumission by the magistrate's rod (*manumissio vindicta*) or – during the Republic – the manumission by entering the slave on the censor's roll (*manumissio censu*) were impossible, the master would simply free his slaves in a more private environment. This could take place at a banquet (*in convivio, per mensam*), among friends (*inter amicos*) or through a written letter (*per epistulam*). Public gathering in theatres or the circus were also possible. All these forms of manumission lacked the necessary formalities that a Roman magistrate or the executor of wills would perform. They did not lead to full Roman citizenship, but only the Latin right (*ius Latii*), a lesser form of franchise (*lex Iunia Norbana*, AD 19). Freedmen of this kind, the so-called *Latini Iuniani*, were nevertheless to a certain extent protected by Roman law. The praetors protected their freedom against encroachment by their former masters or third parties and consequently the act by which these freedmen had gained their freedom was called praetorian manumission. During his lifetime, there was little difference between such a freedman and a Roman citizen (*libertus civis Romanus*). On his death, however, he reverted to the status of slave and his patron, who was still (or again) his master, inherited all of his possessions. The deceased's family was not entitled to anything. It was, however, possible to perform the formal manumission at a later date, when the prerequisites were met.[23] The epigraphic record shows no real difference between one form of manumission and another. Considering the low age of many of the people mentioned in inscriptions one may assume nevertheless that most of them were either *Latini Iuniani* or belonged to one of the categories of slave exempted from restrictions by Augustus' laws.[24]

It is exceedingly difficult to make assertions about the ratio between freedmen and slaves. In the past, some scholars have thought that practically every slave would have been manumitted at the age of 30 at the latest.[25] The epigraphic record contradicts this. There were a number of occupations that required an intimate trust between slave and master, primarily in the financial sector where the master must have had absolute confidence in the trustworthiness, loyalty and integrity of his trustee or procurator. Loyalty and integrity could to a certain degree be forced by denying the slave his freedom until very late or possibly

[23] Sirks 1983.   [24] Weiler 2003, 189–205.   [25] Alföldy 1988; cf. Wiedemann 1985.

not manumitting him at all. The advantage of retaining the master–slave relationship was that the master preserved his right to castigate or even kill the slave in the case of infidelity or embezzlement. As a compensation for his protracted servitude, the slave could be rewarded with money, land or free women with whom he could produce free children. But it was not only in the financial sector that the idea of a quasi-automatic manumission at a certain age loses its appeal: slaves employed as herdsmen, in agricultural businesses or in mining works were hardly, if ever, liberated.[26] The nomenclature of freedmen is a further obstacle to determining an exact ratio. The primary goal of freed slaves was mostly assimilation to their Roman masters and integration into Roman society. During the Republic and the early Principate, a number of freedmen tried to achieve this by erecting tombs along the Via Appia, where they are depicted in the dress of freeborn Roman citizens. The only distinguishing mark was the accompanying inscription, which declared them to be of slave descent. Later funeral inscriptions refrain from giving any mention of status. The omission of any status nomenclature means a perfect assimilation into the Roman society.[27]

THE DEMOGRAPHIC AND SOCIAL IMPORTANCE OF SLAVES AND FREEDMEN

At the end of the third century BC at the latest, Rome had become a truly multicultural city. In this melting pot of different peoples, cultures and religions, slaves and freedmen were not likely to stand out.[28] A well-known proposal during the reign of Nero intended to distinguish freedmen by forcing them to wear special clothing but was defeated. It was generally felt, even if there were no reliable numbers available, that the number of *libertini* within the city walls must have been substantial. It was also probably widely known that many of the aristocratic families had had servile ancestors – the Roman society was remarkably upwardly mobile (see Chapter 6).[29] Seneca supposed that the number of slaves living in Rome was threateningly high.[30] Augustus' manumission laws assumed that there were slave masters with more than 500 slaves. When the urban prefect Lucius Pedanius Secundus was murdered in his city home in AD 61, his more than 400 slaves were executed as accessories and authors! It is not at all clear how such a large household should have

---

[26] Herrmann-Otto 1994, 369–98; Schumacher 2001, 292–3.
[27] Fabre 1981; von Hesberg and Zanker 1987.   [28] See also Chapter 5.
[29] Tacitus, *Ann.* 13.27.   [30] Seneca, *De clementia* 1.24.1.

lived in a single home. If one supposes Rome's population to be around a million people, of whom 200,000 were privileged with free grain distributions, it is perhaps reasonable to assume a total number of around 100,000 slaves (10 per cent) in the city itself and maybe 50,000–70,000 freedmen. The next one and a half centuries will have seen another, albeit slight, increase in population. The figures argued by Morley (Chapter 2) are slightly smaller for the general population and slightly larger for the servile part of it. Since there is no statistical evidence whatsoever, these figures can be no more than mere approximations. As Frank Kolb puts it: 'The only thing we know, is that there were *many* slaves in the city of Rome.'[31] The reason that my own estimates for the slave population are lower is the substantial but unknown quantity of freeborn wage labour that – although it has left no traces in the epigraphic record – was probably dominant in all sectors of professional life with the exception of housekeeping and domestic servants (see Chapter 19). Labour in Rome does not automatically mean slave labour.

The emperors themselves followed a systematic demographic policy that included freedmen. Augustus may have restricted the number of formal manumissions principally in order to keep the number of people on the grain dole constant. He also took pains to assimilate freedmen as part of the free Roman population, for instance by strengthening the rights of freedwomen and annulling restrictions on marriage and procreation that may have been included in manumission contracts and by creating an equivalent of the *ius trium liberorum* for freedwomen (*ius quattuorum liberorum*). To further their assimilation, freedmen and freedwomen were allowed to marry Roman citizens of all social orders except the senatorial one (*lex Iulia de maritandis ordinibus* of 18 BC).[32] The slaves themselves were also included in imperial population policy: under the emperor Claudius old and sickly slaves that their masters had abandoned at the temple of Asclepius on the Tiber island were automatically declared free and impossible to re-enslave, their masters as having renounced all rights of patronage. If owners sought to get rid of unwanted slaves by killing them, they were to be charged with murder. They had broken their duty of familial care. Even then, humanitarian concerns hardly came into play. The real crime in murdering one's own slave was not a moral but a pragmatic one: it conflicted with public utility (*utilitas publica*).[33]

---

[31] Kolb 1995, 461: 'Wir wissen nur, dass es in der Stadt Rom *viele* Sklaven gab.'
[32] Treggiari 1991.   [33] More details in Knoch 2005.

Imperial slaves and freedmen presented a particular challenge: over time the emperors had created a new managing elite that far surpassed the competence of the old elites. Augustus had managed to embark on the necessary transformation of the Roman state by relying heavily on his own *familia* of slaves and freedmen. His successors, most notably Claudius, continued his work. The greatest problems were the inconsistencies between the power, prestige and influence of the servile or freedmen officials on the one side, and their social status and personal esteem on the other (i.e. status dissonance). The old aristocracy could only retaliate with derision and malice, especially the literary elites that wrote the greatest part of the surviving source material. There is hardly any defamatory allegation that is not at one point levied against the social upstarts in the imperial government. The modern picture of them is warped by the fear, conceitedness and unacknowledged sense of inferiority of bruised aristocratic egos. In their lurid description of prominent freedmen, one learns more about the slanderers than their victims.[34] It may be that this continued and persistent opposition by the old elites eventually led to success: beginning with the emperor Hadrian, freedmen were barred from the highest offices in the imperial administration, the only exception being if they acted in substitution of an official: *vice praefecti, procuratoris*, etc.

But it was not solely the emperor and the imperial women who disposed of large slave and freedmen *familiae* with secretaries, procurators, gardeners and domestics. The great noble families of the Statilii and the Volusii, the households of Maecenas and of Agrippa, to name but a few, commanded a vast number of slaves and freedmen who have left traces within the city.[35] First and foremost, they were an important factor in the economic life of the city. Like their masters and patrons, they themselves had to be clothed and fed. The surrounding *villae* in the countryside had adapted to this need and produced fresh fruit, vegetables and poultry daily (see Chapter 15). Wealthy imperial slaves and freedmen acted as benefactors (*euergetai*) to the *collegiae* of the city by erecting statues and altars and by dispensing money and financing public banquets (see Chapter 20). In this context, the importance of slaves and freedmen through their interaction with the freeborn population and the many aliens (*peregrini*) was particularly noticeable for the city itself.

With the rise of Christianity within the city walls during the first three centuries AD, its influence among the slave population extended steadily. Slave masters may not have been asked to release their slaves,

---

[34] Gonzales 2007.   [35] Treggiari 1975a.

but they were nevertheless invited to treat them in a Christian and brotherly way. The notion that all men were equal before God even allowed an amnestied mining slave named Callistus to become bishop of Rome. Influenced perhaps by his own humble past, he sought to make it easier for noble Christian women to find Christian spouses by allowing them to marry (Christian) slaves. This was soon abandoned, however. Even as Christianity was officially outlawed, there were many Christians among the slaves and freedmen of the emperors. The religious persecutions of the third century AD were mostly targeted at them. After Constantine had first legalized and then privileged Christianity, manumissions were regularly conducted in churches on Sunday (*manumissio in ecclesia*). Ironically, after the church itself had become the largest slaveholder after the emperors, the bishops of Rome – the Popes, as we may now call them – tried to restrict the manumission of slaves by their own clergy and finally forbade it.[36]

In conclusion, it may be worth pointing out that slaves and freedmen always played an important part in the life of Rome, without however ever reaching a dominant position. It is only with the demise of the Republic at the end of the first century BC that different groups of slaves and freedmen rose to greater prominence. In the new order of the empire, the members of the *familia Caesaris* competed with the old senatorial and equestrian orders for influence and power. They were the greatest pool of educated, trained and highly competent administrative specialists. In their own personal networks, they established both horizontal and vertical social connections that would otherwise not have existed.[37] Slaves and freedmen served as demographic stopgaps, keeping constant or increasing a population that, for various reasons in various localities, would otherwise have stagnated and declined. Especially in the city of Rome itself, freedmen and slaves were fully assimilated, along with other population groups, into a multicultural and multiethnic urban society.

FURTHER READING

For an overview of slaves and freedmen in Rome in general, see Wiedemann 1997, Schumacher 2001, Andreau and Descat 2007 and Herrmann-Otto 2009. The importance of ancient slavery for western culture from the Middle Ages to modern times is covered by Davis

---

[36] Harrill 1995; Herrmann-Otto 2008; Grieser 1997.   [37] Herrmann-Otto 2009.

1966. Moses Finley 1980 analyses Rome as one of five slave-holding societies and is commented on by Shaw et al. in the 1998 reprint. The idea of slavery as social death was originally formulated by Orlando Patterson 1982. Concerning possible passive opposition of slaves against their masters and the perennial fear of slave revolts of the masters, see Bradley 1994. On the continuity of slavery throughout Late Antiquity, see MacMullen 1990. Harris 1999a concerns himself with the sources of Roman slavery and a critical overview of the latest research and the main international controversies regarding ancient slavery is given by McKeown 2007.

5: IMMIGRATION AND COSMOPOLITANIZATION

Claudia Moatti

The importance of mobility in early societies now no longer needs demonstration. Research work over the last few decades has rendered obsolete the image of populations which are for the most part immobile that demographers have sought to purvey. Within the Mediterranean area, throughout a very long period lasting from Antiquity down to modern times, the circulation of human beings constitutes a fact that is both structural and structuring, an element of continuity that forms the very basis of the Mediterranean network.

Rome, according to legend a city of immigrants, is no more an exception than other Italian cities are. As early as the archaic period, great families of foreign origin were welcomed there, thanks to their links with the Roman *gentes*, and obtained positions of the highest responsibility. Subsequently, the city granted privileged conditions of access to the urban area on the basis of treaties such as those agreed with Carthage (Polybius 3.22–6) or the *foedus Cassianum* in the early fifth century BC, which guaranteed contracts drawn up between Romans and Latins and recognized the possibility of a changing citizen body (*mutatio civitatis*) as a result of immigration (*mutatio solis*). Such alliances, which testify to a desire to encourage the mobility of elite groups and also to promote the existence of a real Mediterranean market, created a certain fluidity within the Italian space, while at the same time strictly defining the conditions for legal immigration.

Later, hospitality both private and public, which provided for legal defence for 'guests', or even asylum, and the subsequent *ius gentium* favoured protection for foreigners and their inclusion in the city, at a time when mobility could create a situation that was, in truth, precarious. The sources certainly emphasize the extreme fragility of the position of an 'absolute', i.e. unknown, foreigner whose possessions or very person could be seized. The right of seizure, which still had not lapsed everywhere, even at the beginning of the early modern period, in Rome only disappeared under the empire: by granting the status of *peregrini* ('relative' foreigners) to increasingly numerous foreigners, the Romans had transformed the imperial territory into a legal and, hence, protected space.

Physically, Rome itself was an open city. Under the Republic, the town gates do not appear to have played a filtering role except in times of war, while elsewhere in the Mediterranean foreign merchants were no doubt checked when entering ports.[1] After the reforms of Augustus, which integrated the *continentia* (the ancient suburb) into the new fourteen regions, thereby distinguishing between the city (the part that lay within the town walls and the *pomerium*) and Roma (the territory as a whole, by which Roman birth and domicile were defined),[2] the fourth-century wall found itself located within the urban boundaries and its gates may only have recovered a role when the toll barrier was created in the late first or second century AD. As the jurist Paul (*Digesta* 33.9.4.4–5) wrote, 'Of course most towns are bounded by a wall, but the boundary of Rome is constituted by its suburbs.' Clearly, these formed a fluid kind of boundary since they expanded outward as urban development increased (see Chapter 12).

Our sources describe the growing density of the Roman population due to the influx of foreigners and their influence on not only *mores* but also the development of the *ius gentium*; and they show how the rules covering citizens' mobility were changing in the imperial period; in short, they describe Rome as a cosmopolitan town. Up to the empire, most of the immigrants to Rome probably came from other parts of Italy, although there is also evidence for the arrival of non-Italic populations (Carthaginians among others). But already by the end of the Republic, other groups were certainly present: Jews, whose political impact in the early 50s is noted by Cicero (*Pro Flacco* 68); Phrygians associated with the cult of Magna Mater on the Palatine Hill; Greeks from mainland Greece, who started arriving in the second century; and Egyptians, who are reported to have created disturbances when, on several occasions, in 59 (Tertullian, *Ad nationes* 1.10), in 50 (Valerius Maximus 1.3.4) and in 47 (Cassius Dio 42.26.2), the altars to Isis, located on the Capitol, were threatened with demolition. So numerous were these foreign communities, Suetonius tells us, that first Caesar and, later, Augustus laid on public entertainments in many

---

[1] Rickman 1980b; Nörr 2007.   [2] *Dig.* 50.16.147; 139.

different languages (Suetonius, *Caesar* 39). Who were these immigrants? Some were merchants, teachers, doctors, astrologers, actors, workers or craftsmen, all of whom had come of their own accord; but others were hostages or slaves, whose way of life in the city however was in some cases so free that 'it was hard to tell a free man from a slave'.[3] In the course of the empire, many other groups of foreigners arrived (Germans, Syrians, Africans, Thracians, Spaniards, Gauls, etc.) since, for them as for the Roman citizens of Italy and the provinces, reasons for making their way to the capital continued to multiply.

Despite all these data, the historians of the Roman world consider mobility to have been a marginal phenomenon. Even those who recognize its effects on demographic renewal tend to give a low estimate of its extent, placing it at around 5 per cent or less.[4] Admittedly, it is not possible to deduce precise numbers from the information provided by the sources. However, one can identify highs (periods of conquest or of major construction in the city) and lows (the period following Alaric's sack of Rome in 410, for example). This suggests that we should distinguish not only between seasonal, temporary and permanent immigration, but also between structural and cyclical immigration, even if partial estimates also show that Rome absorbed a continuous flow of immigrants right down to the end of Antiquity.[5] The number of Jews, for example (between 20,000 and 40,000 in the first century AD),[6] consisting of both citizens and *peregrini*, was constantly being increased by the waves of prisoners brought back by Pompey in 61 BC and by Titus between AD 66 and 70, and also by the arrival of free immigrants both before 19 and between 19 and 49: this may be one of the reasons for their expulsion first by Tiberius, then by Claudius. In the second century AD, there was a further influx of Jews, as is attested by the increase in the number of synagogues and catacombs.

Without venturing into that demographic debate, the present chapter will focus on the evolution of policies concerning immigrants, on the modes of regulating their flow and on the ways in which that mobility affected Roman society. But let us first define the different categories with which we are concerned.

---

[3] *Dig.* 18.1.5, *ad. Sab.* 5: *difficile dinosci potest liber homo a servo*, confirmed by Labeo in his account of a provincial who sent a slave to manage a shop in Rome (*Dig.* 5.1.19.3).
[4] Morley 1996; Scheidel 2005; Kolb 1995; Noy 2000a.   [5] Noy 2000b.
[6] MacMullen 1993; Solin 1983 suggests the figure 60,000.

MIGRANT CATEGORIES

Prior to the second century, when citizenship was linked to residence, a migrant was almost always identified as a non-citizen, whether he settled in Rome (and there, if he was a Latin, subsequently acquired rights of citizenship) or was simply passing through. In the Twelve Tables, he was called a *hostis*, and then, later, he took the name of *peregrinus*.[7] Then, when citizenship started to be granted to *peregrini* without *mutatio soli* and when the notion of residence (*domicilium*) entered into juridical vocabulary, mobility also became an internal phenomenon covered by Roman law. Immigrants now included, alongside foreigners, new domiciled citizens (*incolae*) and Roman citizens with neither a Roman *origo* nor a legal domicile in Rome, but who were running shops or other businesses. Throughout the imperial period, the definition of legal residence gave rise to endless controversy among jurists: could one have a domicile outside one's homeland? Was it conceivable to have several domiciles or to have none at all? What were the criteria for distinguishing between temporary mobility and permanent mobility? The scope of these arguments testifies to the fact that the city-state was being transformed into an empire in which mobility became a permanent aspect of city life.

While those granted Roman domicile formed a special category, other immigrants can be identified by a number of other terms: *adventor* or *advena* identified an immigrant at the point when he settled in a city, designating him as 'one who came from elsewhere', or 'a man who had fled his homeland and whom the Greeks called *apoikos*', as Pomponius put it in the second century (*Digesta* 50.16.239.1). Those who lived for long periods in the city without being domiciled there were called *consistentes* or *qui commorantur, qui morantur, qui consistunt* and *qui sunt* (*Dig.* 4.6.28.4): such people might be *negotiatores*, craftsmen,[8] athletes, actors,[9] or even students (*Codex Justinianus* 10.40(39)2). Finally, there were also travellers just passing through: these were *hospites*, a

---

[7] In particular, Cicero, *De officiis* 1.37; Festus 414–16 L.

[8] *Cod. Just.* 10.66.1 (2 August 337).

[9] On the status of actors and mimes, see Shaw 2000, 390f. The expression *qui commorantur* reoccurs in, for example, Justinian's constitution (edict) (*Novella* 80.9) in which the emperor expresses concern about the arrival of too many people with nothing useful to do in Constantinople: *qui hic vane commorantur*. On this period, see the remarks of Baccari 1996, 111ff.

term which, in inscriptions, may also designate public guests,[10] or *viatores*.

This vocabulary remained relatively constant throughout the duration of the empire. Only *peregrinus* acquired a wider application following Caracalla's edict. Although it never quite lost its original meaning, the word came to apply in particular to any Roman citizen in a situation of mobility: one who found himself in Rome but had not been born there, as opposed to the *indigeni* (*Codex Theodosianus* 6.37.1; AD 364), one who found himself in a province that was not his usual place of residence (*Cod. Theod.* 8.1.9; AD 365), or one who found himself in Rome but was not legally domiciled there: these were probably the Roman 'immigrants' whom Symmachus, the urban prefect, expelled at the time of the famine of 384.[11] *Peregrinus* thus became the most precise Latin word to designate a migrant and, later, a pilgrim, the migrant *par excellence*. In contrast, during roughly the same period, *civis romanus* took on the meaning of 'one who is resident in Rome' (*Cod. Just.* 6.24.7; Basilicus 35.13.17), while *provincialis*, which before 212 was used to designate a *peregrinus* from the provinces (Festus, *Epitome* 253 L), now referred principally to Roman citizens who were legally domiciled in a Roman province. From the third century onward, these *provinciales* thus made up a large proportion of the people passing through Rome.

WERE IMMIGRANTS REGISTERED?

Many cities in the Mediterranean area kept registers of foreigners.[12] What was the situation in Rome? Did the immigrants constitute an indistinct floating population, while being allowed to rent or subrent a dwelling or a shop, or sometimes even being encouraged to buy or build properties in Rome?[13]

Officially, Roman residence was reserved for Roman citizens and census specialists are all in agreement, following Suetonius, when they

---

[10] See *Dig.* 9.3.1.9, Ulpian *Lib.* 23 *ad edictum*; Petronius, *Satyricon*, 95b; Martial, *Epigr.* 3.5; Apuleius, *Metamorphoses* 1.17. See also *CIL* 6.2357.

[11] Cracco Ruggini 1976; against Kübler, *RE*, col. 655, who thinks these were *incolae*. On the evolution of the term *peregrinus*, see Baccari 1996, 117ff. On the date of the expulsion, see now Kelly 2008, 133ff.

[12] For example, in Pergamum, *OGIS* 338 (133 BC).

[13] Gaius notes that 'Nero decreed that if a Latin with a fortune of at least 200,000 sesterces built in Rome, investing more than half of his patrimony, he would acquire quiritary rights' (*Institutiones* 1.33).

say that the first official list of citizens who enjoyed this status (*cives Romani domo Roma*) was created by Caesar, who ordered a census of a new kind (*recensus*) centred on each city quarter (*vicatim*) and based on information given by the landlords of the *insulae* there.[14] Such a census would therefore, on the one hand, have excluded not only non-citizens but also their dependents and the tenants of a *domus*;[15] on the other hand, it would have made the landlords of *insulae* responsible for guaranteeing the legality of the residence and civic identity of their tenants. In these circumstances, the scope of the new Caesarian census would have been very different from that of the Egyptian censuses to which it has often been compared, the *kat'oikian apographai* set up by Augustus, in the course of which all the inhabitants of units of accommodation were declared.

Is it not reasonable however, to suppose that in fact the landlords of Roman *insulae* and *domus* may have declared *all* those living in the units of accommodation that they owned, leaving it up to the Roman authorities, for their part, to refer to the general census in order to pick out those who were legally domiciled Roman citizens? That would have constituted a *revision* of the census lists (which is, indeed, the most precise meaning of the term *recensus*). This hypothesis would explain, for example, how it was that in 68 Nero was able to demand from all tenants of *domus* and *insulae* (*inquilinos privatarum aedium et insularum*), without distinction of status, the equivalent of an annual rent (*pensionem annuam*), so as to finance his campaign against Vindex (Suetonius, *Nero* 44.11). In fact, such an idea was not new in Rome, for an earlier register of *peregrini* had already been established in 89 BC, when the purpose was to grant them citizenship according to the terms of the Lex Plautia Papiria (Cicero, *Pro Archia poeta* 7). This hypothesis, which supposes that Suetonius, then interested only in grain distributions, described only part of the reform, does not exclude the possibility that some groups were the object of partial registration: for example, the Jews, for the payment of taxes from AD 72 onward and, in the fourth century,

---

[14] Suetonius, *Caesar* 41: 'he submitted people to a census not in the usual manner or in the usual place, but in each city quarter, according to the reports of the proprietors of rented blocks of accommodation.' See Suetonius, *Aug.* 40; Livy *Periochae* 115. Before this reform, censuses related solely to tribes, so at that time residents in Rome belonged to urban tribes (as Lo Cascio 1997 explains). An *insula* is defined in the juridical texts as an independent unit of accommodation designed to be leased out, as in the case of a block of apartments, as has been shown by Hermansen 1973.

[15] Another hypothesis is that, in these texts, an *insula* had the wider meaning of 'a building', as Lo Cascio 1997, 58-9 tries to show.

the students. In parallel, other measures were introduced to control immigration, although how they were applied is not always clear.

IMMIGRATION POLICIES IN THE REPUBLICAN PERIOD

It was in the second century BC, following the first expulsions of Latins demanded by their cities,[16] that Roman immigration policies hardened. Not only did the authorities take measures to eject those who were getting themselves illegally listed on the census registers (the *lex Junia* in 126; the *lex Licinia Mucia* in 95; the *lex Papia* in 65), but they also transformed their integration strategies by particularly favouring elite figures in such a way as to allow them to obtain citizenship without *mutatio soli*. It is in this context that it becomes possible partially to understand the law of 125, which offered citizenship to Latins who had served as magistrates in their own cities, and likewise the law of 122, which offered it to anyone Latin or Italian who had won a *de repetundis* lawsuit against a Roman magistrate. In the first century BC, when Italy was unified by the concession of citizenship, other measures in effect limited Italian mobility: one example is the decentralization of the procedures for taking a census that is attested by the Table of Heraclea; another, the decentralization, under Augustus, of certain voting procedures.

Whether these measures actually proved to be an inhibiting factor is not certain. Sallust implies that 'young men who had endured their poverty by working in the fields were attracted by private and public distributions and had come to prefer leisure in the city to their thankless labour' (*Bellum Catilinae* 37.7) and the sources available to us testify to the arrival of numerous Italians in Rome, in particular during the 50s. It was, in truth, only under the empire that regular rules were introduced to regulate people passing through the city.

REGULATIONS COVERING RESIDENCE IN THE CITY: BANS, RESTRICTIONS, EXPULSIONS

Entry into the city seems to have been mostly unrestricted, but that absence of restrictions was offset by the social controls imposed by the

---

[16] Broadhead 2004.

vici, colleges and sanctuaries,[17] and also by various measures designed to keep under surveillance, not the town territory, but certain categories of people, as was also the practice at the empire's frontiers.[18] Bans, limited residence permits and expulsions were the three means of controlling immigrants.

The ban on residence depended on the *princeps* himself, but ever since Nero it had in practice been administered by the urban prefect who, under Alexander Severus, was put in charge of the *tutela urbis*.[19] According to the terms of the *lex Aelia Sentia* of AD 4, those affected by it were slaves who, although guilty of depravity, had been emancipated (Gaius, *Institutiones* I, 27; I, 160), Roman citizens who had been refused residence permits in a Roman province or in their city, along with their freedmen (Suetonius, *Claudius* 23.4–5; Paul, *Digesta* 48.22.13), and soldiers who had been dismissed with ignominy (*Dig.* 3.2.2.5). The efficacy of these measures seems to have depended on the self-censoring of the categories concerned.

Control could also be exercised by limiting residence permits, the best documented case being that of the students, from the second century onward. For this group, reputed generally to be disruptive (Petronius, *Satyricon* 6), the purpose of such limitations was twofold: on the one hand to define a particular status of residence that might turn out to be prolonged over several years and hence also to specify the conditions of exemption from municipal duties, the *munera* that citizens were obliged to fulfil in local cities; on the other hand, they were also designed to prevent the students from profiting from privileges accruing to Roman domicile. From the fourth century onward, measures of control became more precise, as can be seen from the constitution (edict) of March 370 that Valentinian I, Valens and Gratian addressed to the urban prefect, Olybrius (*Cod. Theod.* 14.9. 1). Not only was a young student obliged, upon arrival, to present himself before the *censuales*, clearly stating his address in Rome, but he also had to produce letters of recommendation from the governor of his province of origin, attesting to his merits. The constitution even specified that the *censuales* could expel students who were refractory: 'In the case of a student who does not behave in the town as is dictated by the dignity of liberal

---

[17] Much is known, for example, about the organization of the association of the sacred victors in athletic games and ecumenical athletes, an association which, like the association of actors, from the second century onward, had at its disposal a permanent headquarters in Rome: see Amelotti 1955.

[18] Moatti 2006.   [19] Seneca, *Epistulae* 83.14; *Dig.* 1.12.13; 1.12.1.

studies, we grant them the power to beat him publicly with switches, put him on a ship and forthwith send him away from the town and back to his province' (*ibid.*).

In Rome, expulsion had always been one of the principal means of regulating the flow of migrants, but for a long time it remained a selective public order measure targeted at particular groups for a predetermined period: such were the expulsions of *histriones* and Jews under Tiberius, of Jews under Claudius in 49, of *pantomimi* under Nero, of astrologers and philosophers under Nero and Domitian, etc. It was not until the fourth century that some expulsions, such as that of 384, targeted all *peregrini*, that is to say, at this time, all those without a Roman domicile.

THE EJECTION OF THE USELESS

The above measures indicate the moralizing and utilitarian ideology that underpinned the concept of legal immigration from the end of the Republic onward. It was an ideology that may be detected behind many policies designed to encourage 'good' immigration: that of intellectuals, for example. Thus, Caesar granted citizenship to 'all those who practised medicine in Rome or who were scholars of the liberal arts', 'so that they should be more inclined to take up Roman residence and others should seek to obtain it' (Suetonius, *Caesar* 42). After Caesar, and likewise with a view to attract such people, Augustus granted them privileges and excepted doctors and teachers (Suetonius, *Aug.* 42) from the expulsion of *peregrini*, gladiators and slaves in AD 6; Vespasian created chairs of Greek and Latin rhetoric and grammar (Suetonius, *Vespasian* 18); and Hadrian founded the Athenaeum (Cassius Dio 73.17; Aurelius Victor, *De Caesaribus* 14.3). In this way, Rome became an intellectual centre, as is attested by the constant arrival of intellectuals and the presence of private schools that attracted students from many parts of the world.[20]

---

[20] Thus, in the first century AD, Q. Remmius Palaemon had over 200 pupils, one of whom was perhaps Quintilian (*Inst. Or.* 1.4.20), who had come to his school from Caligurri, in Spain. The school run by Justin, a native of Flavia Neapolis, which opened in the reign of Antoninus Pius, also included many immigrants among its pupils: Tatian from Nisibis in Assyria, Irenaeus from Smyrna and Theophilus from the Euphrates region. In 245, Plotinus (205–70), a native of Egypt, likewise opened a school in Rome that attracted many students, including Porphyry, who was born in Tyre and had first gone to Athens to study, and many others. No full study has been written on Rome's role as an intellectual capital.

In the imperial period this selective policy is attested both in Rome and in the provinces, and in many different contexts.[21] It was a far cry from the days when Cicero declared that 'to deny residence in any town to foreigners is truly inhumane', that is to say contrary to *ius gentium* (Cicero, *De officiis* 3.11.47). Now it was pragmatism that in equal prevailed.[22]

The late empire confirms this trend. It was surely in the name of utility, rather than any sense of hospitality, that Ambrose protested against Symmachus' expulsion of *peregrini* from Rome (Ambrose, *De officiis ministrorum* 1.7.44–52). In this period, imperial policy where mobility was concerned likewise hardened, with the introduction of new measures designed permanently to prevent the mobility of the useless and so to repress 'laziness', a concept which, since the third century, had been reflected in legal vocabulary by terms such as *ignavia*, *desidia*, *pigritia*, *neglegentia*, and *inertia* (*Dig.* 9.4.26.6; 17.2.72. *pr.*; *Dig.* 48.3.12. *pr.*). A constitution introduced by Gratian in 382 ordered that the bodies of beggars should be carefully examined and that, in cases where they were found to be in good health, they should be forced to work as colonists.[23] This law, designed to prevent the depopulation of land and cities in the provinces and to compensate for deficiencies in the urban labour force and the shortage of soldiers, was evidently aimed against those unable to contribute to the state taxes.[24] It is clear that a distinction was drawn between 'good' and 'bad' beggars, classifying the former as legitimate and the latter as illegitimate, and it is also clear that the Roman administration delegated control in this area to private individuals, namely property owners. Bruno Pottier, whom I am following here, has shown that the law passed by Gratian was no innovation: in 303, Galerius had organized the expulsion of all beggars from Nicomedia, which was then one of the empire's capitals.[25] Similarly, in 397 or 399 a law was passed exiling anyone who constructed a hut on the Field of Mars, the effect of which was to clear beggars from the centre of Rome (*Cod. Theod.*, 14.14.1). Ambrose of Milan

---

[21] P. Geissen 40; P. Lond. 904, II, 18–38 (in Hunt–Edgar, II, 215; 220).

[22] As is shown by the policy followed with regard to colleges, from the time of Caesar's law and particularly that of Augustus onward. See Perry 2006.

[23] *Cod. Theod.* 14.18.1: the constitution of Gratian, Valentinian and Theodosius, addressed to the urban prefect, Severus, in 382. See the commentaries of Grey and Parkin 2003.

[24] On fiscal matters, see Grey and Parkin 2003; see also *Cod. Theod.* 14.18; *Cod. Just.* 11.25; 12.45.1–3.

[25] Lactantius, *De mortibus persecutorum*, 23, 7–9. See Grey and Parkin 2003; Pottier 2009.

gave his approval to the law that Gratian passed in 382,[26] in the name of drawing a distinction between beggars who were in good health and were consequently liars, and true beggars (widows, the sick and the infirm), who did deserve to receive help from the Church. The general consensus among Christians and pagans alike was that the population needed to be as active and numerous as possible but also useful in service to the state. This same idea found expression in Valentinian's constitution relating to students. It was primarily on the grounds of their future service to the state that, provided they behaved themselves, they were tolerated.

This was an idea that became prevalent in the society of the late empire and, two centuries later, in 539, it found expression in the New Decree (*Novella*) 80 passed by Justinian. The emperor decided to create in Constantinople a new magistrate, the *quaesitor*, whose function was to stem the influx into the capital of a mass of men who were of no use to it. The *quaesitor's* job was to investigate people passing through the city (monks, lawyers, *agricolae*, and so on), to ascertain their names, origins and the reasons for their presence in Constantinople, and to expel them if their presence was unjustifiable, or even to force them to work. The creation of the *quaesitor* followed on smoothly from the fourth-century measures, but the emperor now went a step further by declaring all unjustifiable immigration to be an offence (albeit quite a slight one: *mediocre delictum*).

Whether this constitution was long-lived or short-lived is not certain. Nevertheless, the very idea of creating a special magistracy to control, not particular categories of people, but the capital's territory, indicates an important change. Entry to the town by people just passing through had to be justified or else cut short. Leaving one's legal residence without good reason could thus be subject to penalties. In the late empire, regular means of control over the mobile sector of the population, the establishment of which was obviously prompted by fiscal reasons, became an essential part of 'the government of the people'.

THE COSMOPOLITANIZATION OF
THE EMPIRE

One of the essential questions raised by a study of the circulation of human beings is that of their integration into the host society. For many

---

[26] Ambrose, *De officiis ministrorum* 1.159; 2.76–7.

years this question has been approached from the angle of acculturation: we speak today of cultural transfers, a concept that assumes a reciprocal relationship between two identifiable poles, but does not take into account the full complexity of the subject.

In the first place, in Rome neither the 'Romans' nor the immigrants constituted homogeneous groups, even if the satirists, prompted by hostility, portrayed them as such by constructing imaginary communities. Even if immigrants sometimes referred to themselves with an ethnic identity, as the Syrians did, individuals felt primarily linked to some small homeland (a city or even a *vicus*). Not until the second century AD did regions or even provinces also become identifying labels.[27] Similarly, some quarters of Rome such as the Trastevere harboured more foreigners than others, but there were no such things as quarters set aside for particular communities.

Within what we might call an ethnic group, but one that was actually composed of a number of different communities, relations with external cultures might therefore vary considerably, as is attested by the choice of the language used in inscriptions, the names given to children, and also the artistic symbols and motifs that adorn tombs. Seen from this point of view, social status constituted an important factor of differentiation. Soldiers, for example, who kept themselves apart from the town, tended to preserve their own cults and traditions, whereas slaves were more open to influences, since the *familiae* were ethnically heterogeneous and the slaves did not constitute a separate and closed world: they lived alongside free men, for they could be accepted into colleges of humble folk (*collegia tenuiorum*) (*Dig.* 47.22.3 = Marcianus *libro 2 iudiciorum publicorum*) and some pursued activities closely associated with the plebs, with the possibility of eventually becoming Roman citizens. One other group that was similarly open to cultural contacts was that of hostages: members of foreign elite groups, who were expected to stand as guarantors for treaties concluded between Rome and their own countries. The size of some of these groups was considerable and their members might well spend many years in Rome where, living unrestricted lives, they were likely to adopt local *mores*. The hundred Carthaginian hostages brought to Rome in 202 BC were still there in 168; some of the thousand Achaeans who arrived in Italy at the same time as Polybius in 167 remained there beyond 150 BC. There were thus many young nobles living in Rome with their retinues, some of whom even pursued their studies there before returning to their own

---

[27] Noy 2000a, 222ff.

homelands. The cultural consequences of such protracted stays were quite clear to ancient authors and they constituted a by no means negligible aspect of the history of Roman immigration.[28]

Nevertheless, studies of the integration of foreigners via purely cultural exchanges raise delicate problems of interpretation. Was the diffusion of new customs seen as borrowing from another culture or as a response to new problems?[29] Did that diffusion result from urban (local) immigration or from global contacts with provincial worlds far from Rome? There is a continuous link between those two kinds of mobility that suggests that we should likewise take into account the impact of mobility on the cultures of migrants. For example, Christianity spread thanks to mobility and to its own networks, but it was also transformed in the course of its geographical and linguistic expansion. As can be seen, the notion of a cultural transfer suffers from limitations in any analysis of the processes of transformation. Perhaps it is preferable to use the expression 'cultural circulation'.

The Syrian cult of Jupiter Dolichenas presents an interesting example of the diverse problems that arise. Inscriptions show that from the second and third centuries onward, the Aventine sanctuary was also home to other gods: Apollo, Heracles, Artemis, Venus, Isis and others, and furthermore displayed Mithraic bas-reliefs.[30] Such cohabitation no doubt resulted from the very nature of polytheism. The faithful truly believed that they could honour all these gods at the same time and in the same place, just as a single individual could officiate for more than one deity. But, this may also be regarded as a manifestation of what I shall call the 'cosmopolitanization' of the empire.

By this, we should understand a process through which an individual's identity was thought of no longer in terms of an exclusion, but rather in terms of an accumulation. Cosmopolitanization was engendered by the accumulation of spatio-temporal experiences that resulted from a situation of mobility: it produced a global effect thanks to the links that the circulation of human beings forged between different parts of the world and those that immigrants from different regions forged in one particular place, links that then affected their identities, their language and their practices. All the actors in this process, including those from the 'host' society, were involved in equal measure.

[28] On soldiers, see Speidel 1994, 132; 144–5; on slaves, Noy 2000a, 11.
[29] Matthews 1989.
[30] Leon 1960 and Williams 1994 on the use of catacombs by Jews, which ran contrary to their traditions.

In order to describe this phenomenon, we need to distinguish between membership, identity and culture. For example, a Roman citizen felt linked to the city of Rome, to his *origo* (his local homeland) and, later on, likewise not only to the province of his birth but also to various other communities (colleges, professional groups and so on): these were different memberships. He could also claim an identity for example, by stating his origin (*natione, natus*) as a Parthian, a Thracian, a Palmyrene, to which, from the fourth century onward, he could add a religious identity; finally, he could even do this in several languages, thereby defining his cultures. The same applied to *peregrini*, who would state their membership (of such or such a village or city), their identity (Syrian, for example) and their culture (in Greek or Aramaic).

It is hard to estimate the proportion of people who felt themselves to be involved in this way, but it seems fair to say that such involvement was at least a good possibility. In the third century, for example, the jurist Paul explained how it was that senators who had to adopt a Roman *origo* and residence could at the same time remain linked with their respective homelands:

> Although senators are deemed to have their domicile in the city, nevertheless they are also considered as having a domicile in the place from which they originated. For their rank is seen to have given them an additional domicile rather than a change of domicile.
>
> (*Dig.* 1.9.11)

The term *adiectio* (addition) is of fundamental importance: senators could consider themselves to belong, so to speak, to two places. Indeed, by recognizing their double domicile, Caracalla acknowledged their right not only to mobility but also to a double identity, whereas previous emperors had done their utmost to wrest them from their local homeland and settle them down in the capital. Moreover, this idea of an additional identity was, in principle, valid for all citizens. The concept of *Roma patria communis*, which implied that even while living in Rome, citizens were not, on that account, absent from their local homeland, acknowledged that they possessed a kind of ubiquity. Yan Thomas has considered all the juridical effects of this idea.[31]

---

[31] Thomas 1996.

The multilingual inscriptions of Rome reveal the existence of varying degrees of cosmopolitanization among immigrants.[32] Take, for instance, the famous dedications in Latin and Greek (*IGUR* 117 = *CIL* 6.50–1) to the Palmyrene deities Belus and Malachbelus, seeking the well-being of the emperor: they were set up by two individuals, C. Licinius and Heliodorus, in one or several temples in the Trastevere quarter. Heliodorus indicates his identity: he is Palmyrene; possibly, like Licinius, he is a Roman citizen (if so he is a freedman). His inscriptions are written in two languages (i.e. cultures): Greek (which was one of the languages in Palmyra) and Latin (which he learnt in Rome).

Here is another example: a bilingual inscription, in Latin and Palmyrene Aramaic, by T. Claudius Felix (*CIL* 6.710 = *ILS* 4337), a Roman citizen who is both a freedman and a Palmyrene. The Latin version states that, together with his wife and son, he has fulfilled his promise to the Sun god, and it indicates their profession: *Galbienses de coh. III*, which shows that they worked in the *horrea Galbana*, close to the Emporium, and probably lived in the Trastevere quarter. The Palmyrean version records that, together with other Palmyrenes in Rome, he has dedicated an altar to the god Malachbel and the gods of Palmyra, but it adds nothing about the Roman side of his life: two lives, two juxtaposed, cumulative identities.

In the following century (February 236), their compatriot Heliodorus presents a rather different case: he had dedicated an altar to the gods of the Aglibol Moon and the Malachbel Sun and records this in a bilingual inscription (Greek and Palmyrene) (*IGUR* 119). Here again, we find a man living in two worlds: in the Greek version he identifies himself as Iulius Aurelius Heliodorus Hadrianus, the son of Antiochos, and a Palmyrene; but in the Palmyrean version, he uses his former name (*IGUR* 119): Iarhai, son of Haliphi, son of Iarhai, son of Li^{u}samus^u, son of Soadu. This Roman citizen, a freedman, combines two group memberships and identities, but retains his original culture (Greek and Palmyrene).

What is the explanation for the differences between the above three cases, all of which show that in the second and third centuries AD, there was in Rome a community of Palmyrenes who had probably retained links with Palmyra? Were those who used no Latinisms first-generation immigrants – as were two Greek individuals who gave their children Latin names: *Picen<ti>nus et Panteris i pace Doulkitiou ke Mellisses tekna* (*ILCV* 2534) – or did they constitute a particularly closed

---

[32] Price 2000, 298.

group? How long did it take for a foreigner to feel assimilated? The senator Fronto, who came from Numidia, was showered with honours by the imperial family, becoming the tutor of Marcus Aurelius and Lucius Verus. But he always felt himself to be a foreigner in Rome, even a barbarian, comparing himself to the Scythian Anacharsis (Fronto, *Epistle to Marcus Aurelius* 1.20). Plenty of other new senators hailing from the provinces may well have shared those feelings. Suetonius relates that, when Caesar admitted Gauls to the senate, inscriptions were displayed all over Rome, asking citizens not to show them the way to the Curia: *ne quis senatori nouo curiam mostrare uelit!* (Suetonius, *Caes.* 80). The anecdote certainly conveys the ambivalence of this society that was at once open yet scornful, arrogant yet also fearful of newcomers, whether foreigners or citizens:[33] as if the conquerors were doomed to fear that the conquered might one day conquer the conquerors themselves.

FURTHER READING

Studies of the immigration to Rome from a demographical point of view have multiplied since Brunt 1971: see mostly Morley 1996, Scheidel 2004 and Lo Cascio (1997; 2001b; 2003). Patterson 2006 and Noy (2000a and 2000b) have followed, developing also the social and economical conditions of the foreigners at Rome. The political and institutional conditions of mobility have been little studied: see Ampolo 1988 and Nörr 2007 for the archaic and early republican periods; Moatti for the later periods and for a comparative approach (2000; 2004; 2006; 2009). On the conditions of life of the foreigners, Noy 2000a proposes an important synthesis; see also Purcell 1999. On cultural contacts, besides Adams 1998, Palmer 1981 and Price 2000, different case studies are available: Rutgers 1995; Turcan 1996; Edwards and Woolf 2003. For a theoretical and broader approach of cultural contacts and mobility in the Mediterranean, see Horden and Purcell 2000.

---

[33] Adams 2003, 248ff.; see also MacMullen 1993.

6: MARRIAGES, FAMILIES, HOUSEHOLDS

Beryl Rawson

FAMILY AND IDENTITY

The Roman name advertised more than personal identity: it advertised family, an essential ingredient – perhaps *the* essential ingredient – in identity. For freeborn male citizens, father and grandfather were included in the most detailed form of nomenclature, so Julius Caesar was Gaius Iulius Caesar, son of Gaius, grandson of Gaius, expressed in succinct abbreviation as C. Iulius C. f. C. n. Caesar. The very succinctness added to the impact: this was a label immediately recognizable. The label proclaimed to the world that this man was of citizen family for at least three generations. He had roots in the Roman polity and culture. And, for the few hundred senatorial families, if the name was familiar, if it struck echoes of previous generations of high achievers, it was a powerful weapon in commanding respect and all kinds of influence, especially access to high office in the republican period when electoral competition was fierce. In the late Republic, the production of genealogies was an active industry, and sometimes divine ancestors were claimed. Julius Caesar's family connection with Venus was taken up by his heir Octavian/Augustus and built into the very fabric of his power and image.

Female citizens had a simpler form of nomenclature, but 'filiation' was an essential element, so Caesar's daughter was Iulia C. f., and she remained a member of her father's family even after marriage, so as Pompey's wife she remained a Julian. In those cases (rare by the late Republic) where a woman formally entered her husband's family (contracting a *manus* marriage), it could be indicated in her name that she belonged to her husband, as for Caecilia Metella Crassi, whose large circular tomb still stands along the Appian Way: she was 'of Crassus', probably a son of the triumvir Crassus at the end of the Republic. That form of name was parallel with that of slaves. A slave of M(arcus) Crassus was M(arci) ser(uus), or simply Marci. They belonged to the *familia*, the household, of the *paterfamilias* M. Crassus and came under his power, his *patria potestas*.

As Rome grew in size and power, her population grew in numbers and diversity. The growth of the city of Rome was fuelled by free immigrants, visitors, traders, and especially slaves (see Chapter 5). Much of the evidence available for Roman history, especially literary sources, tells us more about the upper-class, citizen components of society than about these groups. But, as detailed below, slaves were increasingly becoming part of Roman citizenry in the first century BC and the first two centuries AD, and evidence for slaves and freed slaves can be drawn from their inscriptions and tombs, from parts of Roman law, from domestic housing, from art, and from analyses of demography and disease, all of which have helped build up greater understanding, in recent decades, of the lower classes of Rome. The evidence is more helpful for urban society than for rural. Slaves and ex-slaves were part of Roman households in some significant ways, and those who assimilated shared in some of the upper-class values and identity being discussed here.

Slaves legally had no family, but they were in some sense members of their owner's family, in that they belonged to that *familia*. They belonged, as property, to a master or mistress, and their names showed such ownership rather than filiation. Even when freed, as many slaves were in the city of Rome, they could not claim the filiation of free birth, but their names reflected the surrogate father role of their ex-master: in place of C. f. they showed C. l(ibertus), so Tiro, the loyal slave of M. Tullius Cicero, became M. Tullius M. l. Tiro, whereas Cicero's son was M. Tullius M. f. Cicero. Now patron of Tiro, Cicero had obligations to his freedman (as did Tiro to Cicero). He was patron too to a flock of 'clients', dependants of lower social status, either residents of Rome or residents of his local region of Italy who visited Rome from time to time. These were not formally part of his *familia*, but they shared in the life of the *familia* in various ways, attending the household for special ceremonies and especially for the *salutatio*, the early morning ceremony to greet the head of household and to join his retinue when he started out on his daily public duties.

In the 'familial' context of a distinguished patron's home, especially in the public reception area of the *atrium*, were displayed the *imagines* of ancestors and the trappings of public life, especially the spoils of military victories won by republican generals. The *imagines* were realistic portrait masks of forebears which were kept in cupboards opened on ceremonial occasions and which were worn or carried in funeral processions when a prominent member died. A public funeral was one way in which family and wider public life interacted (see below).

A patron's retinue participated in, or observed, the city's ritual – political, religious, social – all in the physical context of buildings and other monuments which resonated with Roman history. For the elite families of the Republic, the city was their theatre. They paraded on the stage of the Forum and the Capitoline, as magistrates and priests and conquering generals, surrounded by increasingly splendid public works, many of which had intimate connections with their family name. Sons were inducted into this when fathers took them to the Forum for their *rite de passage*, the taking on of the adult garb, the *toga virilis*. Wives and daughters shared in the public esteem due to such families as they moved around the city, taking part in religious ceremonies and social events.

A specially privileged category of girls and women was that of the Vestals, the priestesses of Vesta, recruited as children (between six and ten years of age) from the most distinguished and unblemished families. These six females had significant religious responsibilities, protecting the welfare of Rome, and considerable public freedom and prestige. Although they took a vow of celibacy (as the 'Vestal Virgins') for their thirty-year term of service, they moved freely in society and exercised considerable political influence, partly through their powerful family connections.

The public importance of family marriages and other alliances in the republican period was highlighted by F. Münzer nearly a century ago (1920), when he identified patterns in office-holding which seemed to be connected with such alliances. Like any methodology, Münzer's could be carried to extremes and applied rigidly and mechanically, and such misuse led this approach into some disrepute. But even when this 'prosopographical' method, i.e. the study of biographies and family relationships, appeared to be losing its impact as the best explanation for republican political life, the great prosopographical works of scholarship continued and have endured as indispensable foundations for any study of public life.[1] The importance of these reference works underlines the centrality of families in many aspects of Roman political and social life, from early Republic to late empire.

---

[1] Most notable have been, in German, Pauly-Wissowa-Kroll (1893–1967), the multi-volume work to which Münzer made such a huge contribution, and, in English, Broughton (1951–86) for the republican period, Groag and Stein (1933–) for the 'high' empire and Jones et al. (1971) for the later empire.

After 31 BC, power and prestige were increasingly drawn into Augustus' own hands and focused on his own family. But he had to maintain a fine balance between autocracy and respect for old traditions. The role of the great families was part of Roman culture, and although their direct political influence declined under the Principate their family strategies and alliances continued to control much of Roman economic, social, and intellectual life. Elite families, especially those with long family histories linked to Roman public life, continued to take their self-importance seriously well into the Principate. The poet Juvenal in the early second century satirized their pretensions, contrasting the honour claimed for their ancestry with the alleged morals of their present lives:

> Genealogies: what use are they? What good does it do you, Ponticus, to be valued by the length of your pedigree, to display painted busts of ancestors, . . . ? . . . Who will call a man noble who is unworthy of his noble breeding and is distinguished only for a famous name?
>
> (*Satires* 8.1–3, 30–1)

Perpetuating a family and passing on a family name were fraught with difficulties, especially those of demography. Mortality rates were high: a high proportion of children did not survive to adulthood, and men did not always survive long enough to marry and procreate.[2] Most men at Rome probably did not marry until they were in their mid to late twenties (early twenties for elite families), about ten years older than their spouses. It might take a couple six successful pregnancies to achieve three live children who would survive beyond early childhood. Wives could die in childbirth, and remarriage for the widowed husband would not have been easy if, as is often claimed, the proportion of females in the population was reduced by the practice of abandoning ('exposing', the practice of *expositio*) more female babies than males. Reasons given for such a practice include the lesser economic value of females, the cost of providing dowries for the marriage of daughters, and the desire not to fragment inheritances. There is little explicit expression of low esteem or lack of affection for female children, and females' interests were given considerable protection in Roman law, but the proportion

---

[2] See Saller 1994 for details of a computer simulation which provides probabilities of the survival of children and parents at various ages.

of girls commemorated in epitaphs or art is indeed much lower than that of boys.

The question of the sex ratio in Rome's population is the subject of lively debate.[3] It affects questions of widow(er)hood and remarriage.[4] If there really was a deficit of females in the population of Rome, many men must have remained single or widowers. But in the absence of hard evidence for such men in sub-elite classes we can only speculate. In families of some standing, marriage and remarriage seem to have been the norm.

Divorce was easy procedurally, for both husband and wife, but women may well have been reluctant to divorce because children of the marriage remained legally in the custody of their father. Residential arrangements, however, could be worked out on an individual basis. The frequent remarriage after a divorce or a spouse's death (for the families for whom we have such records) led often to step-relationships. But to have had only one husband could be claimed as a mark of honour, or good luck, for some women: the term *uniuira* marked these women out.

Women did not pass on their family name to their children. In a few elite families, women of distinguished lineage did have their *nomen* added to the one which children inherited from their fathers. So Poppaea Sabina, who became wife of Nero, used only her maternal *nomen*, derived from her mother's famous father C. Poppaeus Sabinus, who was consul in AD 9, although she herself was daughter of T. Ollius. But in this case Poppaea was the end of her line. Her son by her first husband, Rufrius Crispinus, took the Rufrius name (and did not survive, killed by Nero); and any child which she might have produced with Nero would have taken the imperial Claudian family name.

Strategies used to perpetuate a family and a family name, when a male heir was lacking, included formal adoption or bequeathing an inheritance to an heir on condition that he take on the testator's family name. It is generally thought that this latter manoeuvre was how Octavian became Julius Caesar's heir and took on the name of C. Iulius Caesar with the *agnomen* Octavianus available to signal his family of birth. (He seems, however, not to have used that *agnomen*: the Julian name was to be the basis of his future.) His sister continued to be Octavia.

Formal adoption was a complex legal process and was used for young adult men, not for infants or young children as is often the practice in many modern societies. Women could not adopt, as they

---

[3] e.g. Scheidel 2007.   [4] See Krause 1994–5.

FIGURE 6.1 The *columbarium* of Pomponius, near Porta San Sebastiano.

did not have *potestas*, the full legal power of a head of household, to transfer someone from membership of one household to another. A simpler method of transmitting a family name, open to men and women, developed as slaves won freedom, took on the *nomen* of master or mistress, and thus became members of their *familia*, as we saw above for Cicero's slave Tiro. In the absence of biological children, slave owners thus obtained potential heirs, and, most important of all, successors who would see to their funeral and burial and maintenance of their tomb. Ex-slaves, as *liberti* or *libertae*, often had a vested interest in maintaining the familial tomb as they themselves had been given access to burial space there.

If freedmen were specified as heirs of a patron, they could not decline this role, as could other named heirs. They had to accept the responsibility of seeing to the patron's funeral. Many epitaphs end with the formula LIBERTIS LIBERTABVSQVE, sometimes expanded by POSTERISQVE EORVM: 'for (my) freedmen and freedwomen (and their descendants)'. This share of a family tomb was a significant benefit, as obtaining a proper burial and tomb was important in Roman society. Other organizations, such as *collegia* (largely trade-based guilds), could perform this service for members, but tombs belonging to a *familia*

FIGURE 6.2 Relief of the Servilii family, 30–20 BC.

were the most common burial site for commemorated ex-slaves (even if not necessarily commemorated individually by name). They were thus saved from the 'pits' (*puticuli*) dug for mass burials of the poor – slaves, ex-slaves and freeborn alike.

Funerary monuments for the large retinues maintained by wealthy households could be imposing constructions. These *columbaria*, 'dove-cots', consisting of niches for cremation pots and epitaphs, belong largely to imperial times. Family tombs of a similar kind can be seen in some modern cemeteries, often for Italian families (Fig. 6.1). One of the earliest of the imperial *columbaria* is that of the household of Marcella, a member of the imperial family, of the early first century AD. Along the roads leading out of the city were tombs of great and humble. It is a puzzle that comparatively few tombs of aristocratic families have been found near Rome. It seems that, as these families were increasingly squeezed out of the monumental urban space of Rome in imperial times, their funerary monuments also retreated to the country towns and estates where families had connections. Overwhelmingly, the funerary monuments on the outskirts of Rome belong to slaves and ex-slaves. This probably reflects the proportion of such status groups in Rome under the Principate as well as fashion and political pressure. An early epitaph of a family advertising movement from slavery to free-born from one generation to the next is that of the Servilii (30–20 BC) (Fig. 6.2), where the freeborn son P. Servilius Q. f. Globulus is differentiated on the stone in placement, dress and nomenclature from his ex-slave father Q. Servilius Q. l. Hilarus and Hilarus' wife, the ex-slave Sempronia C. l. Eune.

The epitaphs surviving from Rome (at least 75 per cent of more than 40,000 inscriptions) are brief and concise but yield valuable family information. This arises from the form of the Roman name as well as from explicit terms of relationship. In a marriage of two people of free status (freeborn or freed), children took the father's family name. When we find a different name we can detect an 'irregular' union. The father might have been precluded from giving a child his name because of his status, such as being a slave at the time of the child's birth (and thus having no legal right of marriage). Or, if the mother was a slave at the time of the child's birth, her child was of slave status, irrespective of the father's status, and any *nomen* which the child later bore must have been that of manumission. If the child remained in the mother's household, it belonged to her master or mistress and may have been freed later by that owner and thus taken the owner-patron's family name. If the child were sold or given into another household, any family name would derive from the new owner in that household.

The father of a slave woman's child must sometimes have been her master. The law recognized that a master might wish to have a formal marriage with his slave woman (pregnant or not), in order to have legitimate, freeborn children, and to facilitate this there were legal exceptions to the normal minimum age for a master to manumit (20) or for a slave to be freed (30).

In any 'irregular' union (a union which was not recognized as *matrimonium iustum*), the child was not the legitimate child of its father and had no legal claim on him. In some later European societies, illegitimate sons were sometimes recognized by their fathers and given positions of influence and favour, but in Rome there is no sign of this. In the upper classes, illegitimates are virtually absent from the record. In 1960, Ronald Syme wrote an article on 'Bastards in the Roman aristocracy' and speculated on Romans' stratagems for suppressing such births or suppressing evidence of them. Children born to free mothers were freeborn, irrespective of their father's status, and in some sub-elite families this was advertised in the child's name with the formula Sp. f. (for '*Spurii filius*', the son of a not-genuine father), using the filiation of free birth but with no (legally) recognizable father. What was lacking was *patria potestas*: there was no male figure responsible for the child.[5] But the willingness to advertise this status, either by this form of filiation or by displaying a name different from that of the father, reflects the prestige of free birth, or at least free status, and a lack of stigma associated with illegitimacy. 'Illegitimacy' was a consequence of one of the forms of legal restriction on marriage, rather than a wilful refusal to marry. Marriage seems to have been the expectation of all in Rome who were eligible and could find a partner.

[5] Rawson 1989.

What was the motivation for so many of the sub-elite in Rome to leave simple commemorations of themselves and their families, when they had little to advertise beyond their names and their relationships? They had few of the trappings of public achievement such as high office, military victory, or other contribution to the state. Some had a trade or occupation to advertise. But by the mid-first century BC, and especially in the first two centuries AD, there were increasing numbers of people of humble origin who were claiming a place for themselves in Rome's expanding economy and society, and who could see their children doing even better. Many of slave origin won for themselves freedom, and perhaps Roman citizenship, and produced freeborn Roman citizen children. These were the things advertised by the upwardly mobile and aspirational inhabitants of Rome, and it was often the names on the epitaphs which were the key to these stories. The epitaphs, alas, were not infrequently those of the very children for whom there had been hopes of a better future and continuation of the family. It was *mors immatura*, premature death, which was what was commemorated.

HOUSEHOLD STRUCTURE AND FAMILY BONDS

In a landmark analysis of all the epitaphs of Rome and most of the western empire, in 1984 Saller and Shaw revealed that overwhelmingly the relationships commemorated were those of the close biological family, what we call the 'nuclear family'. The bond most often recorded in the epitaphs is that of spouses and of parents and children. This does not tell the whole story of household structure, or other personal relationships, as we shall see below, but it tells a story of what relationships commemorators wished to record and leave for posterity. These were surely their closest affective relationships. The pattern of recorded family sentiment across the western empire is so consistent in its general features, and the numbers of commemorations available for such study so comparatively large, that these epitaph-erecting people are unlikely to be an aberrant sector of the total population. The sentiments attested must be at least a recognizable ideal of wider Roman society, and must reflect sentiments actually experienced by many, in spite of the comparative absence of records from rural and very poor elements. Literary and legal sources add to this general picture.

Discussion of such matters has continued to be lively, and the development of more sophisticated demographic methods and insights has helped refine our understanding. Some of the dissension about what can validly be deduced from epitaphs has been owing to a confusion between 'family' and 'household'. The co-resident group often included more than the nuclear family. Slaves were present in all but the most impoverished households, but we have seen that they could be envisaged as part of the *familia*. Others who might be present, but who were less likely to be considered part of the *familia*, included more remote kin, visitors or lodgers. There is evidence of such members of households – probably both short-term and long-term – and the term 'housefuls' is sometimes applied.[6]

Such evidence comes from the larger residential establishments (*domus*), and these survive more from a place like Pompeii than from Rome. It is more difficult to see how the small households in multi-unit buildings (*insulae*) so frequent in the big city of Rome could have accommodated more than close family and a slave or two, even under the crowded conditions endured by the poor (see Chapter 9). It is possible that over the life-cycle of a family, as one or more members departed, there was scope for others to be brought in, but in the *insulae* these must have been few. In the countryside there may have been more incentive for a household to be larger and to cooperate to work available land. In the city, with a more diversified economy and greater contiguity of residents, economic cooperation did not require co-residence. As Erdkamp notes, in his discussion of complex households in rural areas, 'When the economy offered many employment opportunities outside the family farm, the urge to form complex households was small. With the development of flexible labour markets, the proportion of complex households tended to decrease. Therefore, towns and cities may have shown a very small degree of household complexity.'[7]

One way of identifying 'the family' within larger residential groups might be to consider those who normally ate together. This is complicated by the fact that Romans frequently ate out, at public food counters and taverns. The poor had inadequate cooking facilities at home, and Rome in general was an outdoor culture. Nevertheless, there is evidence of what might be called 'family meals'. Even if children sat on chairs, perhaps a little apart from the adults who reclined on couches, there was scope for them to observe one another and to interact, and there was a tradition of using mealtime to share entertainment and 'improving' activities. But there is too little detail of specific dining groups to help us identify specific families. One instance recorded is

[6] Wallace-Hadrill 1994.   [7] Erdkamp 2005, 69.

that of Britannicus, son of the emperor Claudius (fourteen years old but held back socially to advantage his slightly older stepbrother Nero), who was sitting at a table with other young people near his family when he died of poison (Tacitus, *Annales* 13. 16).

In every situation and setting, slaves were ubiquitous. The evidence for them provides a picture not only of close family bonds but also of status differential within families, of social mobility, and of personal links not only within one household but also between households. Those with special skills (such as secretarial, accounting, teaching, nursing) might be lent on a short-term or long-term basis. This circulation of slaves (and, sometimes, freedmen) offers further glimpses of family and friendship connections in the society of Rome.[8]

MARRIAGE

As slaves obtained freedom and their unions became marriages, they themselves and the freeborn children whom they produced became part of the mass of free Roman society. Even when only the female partner obtained freedom, her subsequent children were freeborn, as such children took the status which their mother had at their birth. Tacitus (*Annales* 13. 27) gives us a glimpse of the widespread element of slave origin in Roman families by the middle of the first century AD. In a senatorial debate of AD 56, it is argued that, if *libertini* were to be distinguished from the freeborn, it would show up how few were the latter. The freed were spread widely through society (*late fusum id corpus*). During Augustus' reign legislation was introduced to try to impose some order on the rapid social changes occurring. Regulation of marriage, including marriage with ex-slaves, was part of this.

The procreation and status of children are central to the legislation of 18 BC and AD 9, although these laws ranged widely over marital matters, general morality and property. The importance of the identity and status of children is reflected in the introduction of birth registers. Augustus' own record in his *Res Gestae* (8.5) claimed that by his legislation he revived many ancestral traditions which were dying out in his own day and that he provided models of behaviour for posterity (*multa exempla maiorum exolescentia iam ex nostro saeculo reduxi et . . . exempla imitanda posteris tradidi*). Suetonius (*Augustus* 34) summarized Augustus' legislation as covering 'extravagance, adultery and chastity, bribery, and

---

[8] See Rawson 2011.

marriage between social classes'. The legislation of 18 BC, in Augustus' own name, the *lex Iulia de maritandis ordinibus*, met with resistance from the upper classes, and new legislation, with some modifications, was introduced by consuls in AD 9, the *lex Papia Poppaea*. These laws came to be cited by later sources as one set, the *lex Iulia et Papia*.

These laws recognized the reality and validity of intermarriage between freeborn citizens and ex-slaves (although marriage with prostitutes and other disreputable women was banned). Restrictions, however, were placed on those whom senators and members of their families could marry. For them, marriages with ex-slaves and actors (as well as with the disreputable women in the more general ban) were not recognized, a reflection of Augustus' concern to protect and promote the dignity of senatorial families.

Rewards were enacted for those who married and produced children, and there were corresponding penalties or disadvantages for others. These provisions applied to men between 25 and 60 and to women between 20 and 50. They were largely economic and political in their application, so these aspects would have concerned the upper classes rather than the general masses. The importance of the privileges associated with having three children, the *ius trium liberorum*, is reflected in the value attached to its honorary conferral on some who could not achieve real parenthood. Pliny the Younger received these privileges from the emperor Trajan in the early second century and supported Suetonius' request for them (Pliny the Younger, *Epistulae* 10.2 and 94).

The Augustan legislation remained in force until at least the early third century, with constant attention from emperors and jurists during this period. In summary, for our purposes here, we can say that at least from the time of Augustus (and probably for some time before) formal Roman marriage (*matrimonium iustum*) was a union between two Roman citizens who fulfilled a range of conditions of eligibility. Essential too was marital intention (*affectio maritalis*). A formal wedding ceremony, although not of the essence, could attest to this and could be an elaborate ritual. Catullus' lively poem (61), celebrating a friend's wedding in the late Republic, focused on the hoped-for formation of a new family. Dowry arrangements could also provide evidence of marriage. Marriage was for the purpose of producing children (*liberorum quaerendum gratia* was the ritual phrase often used). The type of marriage determined the status of children, and there were many consequences of this, especially in the matter of heirship. Romans had considerable flexibility in making wills, but legitimate freeborn children had certain rights to claim inheritance irrespective of what was in a parent's will.[9]

Those ineligible for full Roman marriage included those who were under age (12 for girls, 14 for boys), of close kin, rank-and-file soldiers (for at least the first two centuries AD), people of disreputable professions as noted above, and all non-citizens (except those from communities which had been granted intermarriage rights). Archaeological evidence provides some evidence for soldiers' family arrangements. Sites of forts and garrison posts have yielded signs of the presence of women and children inside their quarters, and epitaphs record some of these relationships. Many soldiers stayed on in the provinces after discharge, but, irrespective of their subsequent place of residence, at the end of the second century their 'marriages' were finally recognized on discharge and citizenship granted to their current spouses and the children of these unions.

The question of affections, even 'love', in any of these families is difficult to answer. Among the propertied classes, marriages were arranged by parents or persons in parental roles, and girls married young – in their early teens, younger than in the general population. For subsequent marriages women probably played a more active role in choice of partner. Marriage was monogamous (which did not preclude extramarital affairs in Rome, as it has not in any other society) and wives could share in much of a husband's social life. Concubinage was a marital-type relationship for those whose status prevented full Roman marriage.[10] The age gap of about ten years, or more, between spouses had implications for relationships between spouses and between father and child. Did it have a distancing effect? Probably; but in matters of emotions much depends on the normal expectations in a society.

There are glimpses of spouses' concern for each other in literary sources. The correspondence between Fronto and Marcus Aurelius reflects this, and Fronto expresses deep grief for the death of his young, 'very dear' (*carissima*) wife Gratia. In the political repression of the later Julio-Claudian period, some wives wished to share their husbands' suicides, and Arria senior even gave the lead to her husband Caecina Paetus (Pliny, *Epistulae* 3.16). Epithets in inscriptions commemorated wives in terms such as 'very dear' (*carissima*) and 'the sweetest' (*dulcissima*), and husbands as 'very dear' (*carissimus*) and 'the best' (*optimus*). Even slaves, who had no legal right to marriage or to the production of free, legitimate children, commemorated their *de facto*, biological families in the

---

[9] See Champlin 1991.   [10] Rawson 1974.

terminology of married partners and family values. There was no guarantee that slave spouses would be allowed to remain together or that
slave parents and children could remain together. As property, they were
subject to the commercial or other needs of their owners. They could
be sold or lent or given away. It is striking how many of them either
remained together or retained links, leaving a record of themselves as a
family.

The epitaphs may be largely formulaic, but spouse-to-spouse is
the most frequently commemorated relationship, which is some measure of the value attached to this relationship. In the hierarchy of natural
affection put forward by Cicero (*De officiis* 1. 54), the primary bond is
between spouses, followed by that with their children. Literature and
epitaphs provide copious evidence for affection and care for children,
and grief at their loss. At the very least, these are the ideals for relationships between spouses and parents and children.

Other members of family (blood relations and marriage relations)
are considered by Cicero, in the above passage, as beyond the household
but bound together by goodwill and affection (*benevolentia, caritas*).
These, however, figure less in our sources. Grandparents, aunts and
uncles, even siblings are a small minority compared with spouses and
children. The elderly in general do not have high visibility. This must
be due largely to demographic reasons, but there was no public system
for the support of the elderly. Individual wealth or poverty, and the
sense of duty of available family members, will have been major factors
in their welfare.[11]

Fatherless children were technically orphans in Roman society,[12]
but if there were mothers present they might rear and support such
children. The welfare of 'real' orphans (as in the modern sense of the
term) will have depended on material resources and surviving family in
the same way as for the elderly, except that there were more roles for
young children in the labour force of Rome. Children who lost their
families, or were 'lost' by them, will have had a variety of fates. Many
were taken into slavery; others eked out survival only as 'street children'.
Children who were abandoned at birth did not all die, and technically
those who were freeborn never lost that status: they could reclaim it at
any time if they could produce proof. But how few could? Those who
were rescued and raised in other households might have some kind of
foster-child status (such as that of *alumni*), but these seem to have been
a minority. *Alumni* could be slave or free, foundlings or kin.

---

[11] See Parkin 2003.   [12] See most recently Hübner and Ratzan 2009.

Marriage continued in its traditional Roman form well into early Christianity.[13] *Affectio maritalis* was still the basic principle cited. The concept of an indissoluble bond was late in being formalized: divorce was still recognized in Justinian's day in the sixth century.[14] There may have been a growing tendency in some Christian thinking to place a wife in an inferior and dependent position, and this eventually became formalized in Church law and writing, but for centuries after Augustus Roman law protected a wife's independence in property and other matters. Praise of asceticism and virginity seems not to have seriously undermined the institution of marriage. Christian clergy continued to marry for many centuries before a vow of celibacy became obligatory.

EDUCATION AND UPBRINGING

The traditional classical education also continued to be what formed young Romans.[15] The materials used, for both elementary and higher (rhetorical) education, remained largely unchanged for centuries. There was some debate by some Christian writers about the appropriateness of pagan literature, but this continued to be the basis of education, and rhetoric served successive generations of Roman youths well in a variety of careers, including the Church.

For more modest vocational training, many small businesses and workshops must have been family-based. The little evidence which we have for formal apprenticeships identifies the relationship as being with teacher or trade-master rather than with fathers. But Treggiari uses the evidence of women in trades to sketch a picture of family activity.[16]

This was the framework within which identities were formed: family and education. But education, or, more broadly, socialization, went beyond a formal curriculum. The physical context in which lives were lived played a major role. The city remained the same in some basic ways: its contours, its ritual, the public life of the streets, the baths, theatres, amphitheatres and circus.

The urban fabric and layout and ceremonial life provided the opportunities for families to participate – often only as observers, but in ways that enabled them to share an image of Rome and to develop

---

[13] See Cooper 2007. [14] Evans Grubbs 2002, 202–10.
[15] Morgan 1998, 146–7. [16] Treggiari 1979, 76–7.

a Roman identity together. They could gather to cheer on a military triumph, or join in prayers at a religious festival and then share in feasts following a sacrifice, or sit together to watch the chariot and horse racing in the Circus. Apart from the grand occasions in the central city, the local neighbourhood (the *vicus*) provided a more intimate setting for family and other relationships.

Families could share in a wide range of public activities in Rome. And yet the situations in which families participated, but on a basis other than family, bear scrutiny. As permanent theatres and amphitheatres developed, a hierarchy of seating was established, based on criteria such as rank, marital status, citizenship, gender and age. So doing things 'as a family' was not the only basis for learning to be a Roman, or a man, or a woman.

One of the most striking occasions for displaying and instilling civic and family values was the public funeral of distinguished citizens. Imperial family funerals increasingly dominated, but others' funerals were a significant part of public life from Republic through at least the first two centuries AD. The impact of such funerals derived largely from the display of family tradition and Roman history and the praise of the deceased's achievements. The procession from the deceased's home included family members and friends, ex-slaves of the family who had been given their freedom in the deceased's will, and actors wearing the family's ancestor masks (the *imagines*). Children within the procession advertised to observers the continuity of the family line, and they themselves internalized Roman history and their family's place in it. And as it wound through the Forum, past historic buildings, to the official speaking platform (the Rostra), observers saw a spectacle of Romanness. We cannot tell to what extent the diverse population of Rome identified with the values and history of such a spectacle, but this was an occasion to display the symbiotic bond of family and city, past and present, like perhaps no other.

FURTHER READING

Studies of 'The Roman Family' have multiplied and diversified since the 1980s. The study of Roman tombstones by Saller and Shaw 1984 provided extensive material for the first time for the discussion of lower-class family relationships. They drew some of their inspiration from the comparative work being done by the Cambridge Group for the History of Population and Social Structure. That approach, and further statistical and demographic expertise, has been used by Parkin and by Scheidel. Amongst the works of these scholars, note Saller 1994, Shaw 1991, Parkin 1992 and Scheidel 2007. A series of international conferences has been held on 'The Roman Family' since 1981, resulting in multi-authored volumes edited by Rawson (most recently 1997), George 2005, and Dasen and Späth 2011. Rawson 2003 provides greater detail on aspects of childhood and family raised above.

The large study of Roman marriage by Treggiari 1991 is the most important reference work on that topic. Dixon 1988 provided the first extensive study of Roman mothers and motherhood, and in 1992 she published *The Roman Family*. In the previous year 1991 Bradley raised methodological problems, reflected in the title *Discovering the Roman Family*. For legal aspects, Crook 1967 and Gardner 1998 are recommended.

New work on domestic space has helped illuminate the interaction of architecture, urban structure and family life. Wallace-Hadrill 1994 has been one of the leaders in this approach.

7: PACK ANIMALS, PETS, PESTS, AND OTHER NON-HUMAN BEINGS

Michael MacKinnon

INTRODUCTION

L iving cities require both human and non-human occupants. Indeed, animals form an integral component of urban life. Sometimes in their capacity as pack animals, pets or providers of various consumable and/or non-consumable resources they are purposeful additions to this context. At other times they are unwelcome pests.

Animals were certainly essential to ancient Roman life. They factored in aspects such as transport, food supply, dress and adornment, agriculture and husbandry, hunting, war, religion, pets, pleasure and scientific interest and entertainment. Moreover, their contributions within these domains altered as Rome developed and changed, with resultant impact on city life in general. Nevertheless, while animals were clearly important and omnipresent in ancient Rome, their analysis has traditionally received little attention by classical historians and archaeologists, who have focused more intently on the people and monuments of this impressive city. This imbalance highlights the need to assess, in greater detail, the role of non-human beings to the urban fabric of Rome. How many animals populated the city, and what were the consequences for the human inhabitants? What types of animals were around? Where did they live? How were they treated? These are key questions to investigate.

SOURCES OF DATA

Archaeologists and historians generally consult three key lines of evidence to reconstruct the role of animals in ancient Rome. First, inscriptions and other ancient texts – whether agricultural treatises, commodity price lists, pastoral poems, fictional or mythological tales, legal transactions or other forms of surviving script – reference animals or their products. Second, images of animals survive in ancient sculpture, mosaic, painting and other iconographical media. Finally, bones and other remains excavated from archaeological sites provide important data about the actual animals themselves, and their roles in antiquity. Each source has its strengths and weaknesses, making their combination integral for holistic reconstruction. Considerable ancient textual and iconographical evidence for Roman animals exists, but effective use of these sources requires a thorough understanding of the temporal and social context surrounding the creation and purpose of each written reference or visual representation. Details about the author's or artist's intentions, his experiences, skills and knowledge, and the demands and expectations of his audience are essential to contextualize and assess the value, role and purpose of such works. Similarly, animal bones collected from archaeological sites yield data about many topics – species and elements represented; age, sex and size differences; pathological conditions; butchery and burial circumstances; among others – to facilitate reconstructions of past animal use. However, samples analysed must be addressed in light of sometimes complex natural and cultural conditions shaping their deposition, preservation, recovery and ultimate interpretation.

Table 7.1 lists archaeological sites in Rome, dating from the sixth century BC to the seventh century AD, with available faunal samples. The collection is relatively small, considering the long history of archaeological activity in the city. It should be appreciated, however, that animal bones have only been retrieved systematically from classical sites roughly since the 1980s, and even today they are not always collected or examined, with results published or otherwise disseminated. Temporally, the sites listed span from Rome's beginnings to its decline in Late Antiquity; however, fewer zooarchaeological data exist for earlier phases than for imperial or late antique times. Spatially, most bones derive from excavations in or near the Roman Forum, although some collections from areas further removed are noted. In general four categories exist: (1) rubbish from food processing and consumption; (2) disposal of animals, such as pets, pack animals and other working or entertainment beasts, most of which generally were not consumed by humans; (3) pests and associated vermin living in the city; (4) animal remains from ritual and sacrificial offerings. By far, the biggest zooarchaeological samples derive from food animals, although representatives from the latter three categories exist. Nevertheless, the distinction among these groups is not always explicit from the archaeological context. Moreover, animals

Table 7.1 *NISP frequencies for zooarchaeological samples from ancient sites in Rome*

Site	Dates (Cent.)	Type	NISP*	per cent NISP cattle	sheep/ goat
San Omobono (1962–4 seasons)	6–5/4 BC	Ritual	1588	16.0	46.3
San Omobono (1974–5 seasons)	6–5/4 BC	Ritual	2096	5.9	61.7
Niger Lapis	6–5 BC	Ritual	Na	cattle sacrifice	
Via Sacra	6–5/4 BC	misc. waste	93	52.7	17.2
Aqua Marcia	2 BC	misc. waste	5	60.0	20.0
Aqua Marcia	1 BC–AD 1	misc. waste	178	24.2	4.5
Forum Transitorium	Flavian	misc. waste	73	12.3	9.6
Caput Africae	AD 1	misc. waste	41	4.9	9.8
Quirinale	AD 1	misc. waste	1279	3.8	14.5
Aqua Marcia	AD 1–2	misc. waste	149	7.4	13.4
Aqua Marcia	AD 2–3	misc. waste	86		23.3
Caput Africae	AD 2–3	misc. waste	177	0.6	23.7
Crypta Balbi (Mithraeum)	AD 3–5	Ritual	429	3.7	11.4
Schola Praeconum	AD 5	misc. waste	1736	8.6	33.2
Meta Sudans (US 3641 and 3180)	AD 5–7	misc. waste/ games	2826	12.7	17.6
Crypta Balbi	AD 7	misc. waste	3923	6.1	29.5

* NISP (= Number of Identified Specimens) for all animal taxa (does not include shells). See MacKinnon 2004 for references to individual sites, except: Crypta Balbi (De Grossi Mazzorin 2004; De Grossi Mazzorin and Minniti 2001).

often fulfilled numerous roles in ancient Rome, roles that may intersect categories listed above.

FOOD ANIMALS

Figure 7.1 displays mean NISP[1] frequencies for the three major mammalian meat taxa, or animal groupings, for ancient Rome over

[1] NISP (=Number of Identified Specimens) is a count of the number of bones identified per taxon from a zooarchaeological assemblage. It is a fairly common quantifier in zooarchaeological research.

			per cent NISP							
			wild			other				
…uid	dog	cat	animals	rodent	chicken	avian	fish	reptile	amphibian	other
	0.8	0.9			0.1		0.1	1.1		shells (4)
	1.8					0.4	0.2	0.1	0.1	
						vulture				
	6.7	0.6			3.9	1.1				shells (7)
					1.4					shells (9)
	2.4				2.4	2.4				
		0.9			3.7	1.4				shells (179)
	1.3	1.3			2.7	1.3				shells (16)
					4.7	1.2	2.3			shells (17)
	0.6			1.1	4.0		1.7			
		0.7			24.0	4.2	0.9			
	1.4	0.1	0.1		7.6					shells (405)
.9	5.3	1.3	1.3		9.0	2.4	1.7	0.2		
	1.1	1.0	3.3	1.8	6.2	0.7	1.0	0.2		shells (376)

time. Statistics from individual sites are pooled and averaged according to broad temporal periods (i.e. Republic, imperial, Late Antiquity). Sacrificial assemblages are excluded. The data indicate a progressive increase in pig consumption throughout antiquity, presumably a reflection of the value of pork to the Roman diet. Although meat did not dominate ancient diets (see Chapter 15), pork, when available and affordable, was a favoured food for the Romans. As prolific breeders and providers of no other significant resources beyond their meat, pigs could be kept at lower production costs than other domesticates, like cattle and sheep. Consequently, pork dishes dominate meat recipes, such as those of Apicius. The increase in pork consumption in Rome might reflect shifting market demands to capitalize on this commodity, perhaps a sign of increased wealth and urbanization. The rise may also

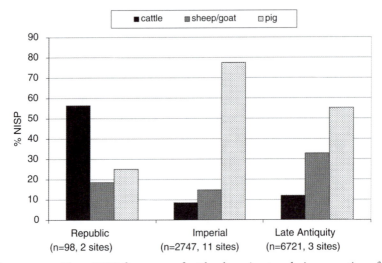

FIGURE 7.1 Mean NISP frequency of cattle, sheep/goat and pig across time, for sites in Rome.

have been fuelled by the *annona* schemes implemented by imperial and late antique emperors. Under these systems, free rations of pork were distributed to Roman citizens, about 2 kgs per person per month for Late Antiquity. Archaeological and ancient historical evidence indicates that farms in central and southern Italy carried the bulk of the burden in supplying Rome with pigs. Moreover, Rome appears able to sustain traditional dietary patterns of high pork consumption throughout the fourth and early fifth centuries AD, at a time when rural Italy was shifting towards more sheep and goat pastoralism. Such a pattern attests to the city's wealth and influence in terms of food supply networks and *annona* schemes.[2]

Cattle were important in antiquity, but principally as work animals, pulling ploughs, hauling wagons and other duties. Although veal was marketed in ancient Rome, generally as a luxury considering its high price relative to beef, cattle were chiefly consumed as older individuals, after serving as traction and/or brood stock. Higher NISP percentages for cattle during the Republic arguably indicate a reliance on these animals as plough beasts, at a time of agricultural growth. Their

---

[2] For further details about the *annona* schemes, and supplying Rome with pork, see Chapter 15, as well as Sirks 1991 and MacKinnon 2004.

decline afterwards, however, marks a concomitant shift to pig husbandry among many herders, as market demands changed, and accessible cattle pastures in Italy dwindled at the expense of other agricultural pursuits.

Sheep and goat NISP values for ancient Rome typically register their lowest figures in imperial contexts, coincident with pork increases. Economically, sheep factored more as wool producers, although, as with veal and beef, sufficient and consistent demands for lamb and mutton existed among Roman cities, with meat markets catering to suit. A trend, in Rome, towards increased sheep and goat percentages from imperial to late antique times appears, but the shift is not as noticeable in urban areas as among rural sites in Italy, which tend towards decentralized, small, pastoral operations at this time, as the empire experiences economic and social conflicts.[3]

Although domestic mammals contributed the bulk of Rome's meat, domestic fowl, including chickens, ducks, and geese, also factored. Zooarchaeological data confirm their presence, with rather small, but consistent, contributions of c. 2 per cent of total NISP values across time.[4] Wild mammals also figure infrequently among zooarchaeological samples from Rome, but certainly enough to confirm marketing of game, a luxury foodstuff. Wild birds, including thrushes and other songbirds, were available, some of which could derive from specialized aviaries set up in wealthier suburban or rural villas, although similar aviaries also may have existed in gardens of elite urban homes. Pigeons and doves were similarly maintained in aviaries, perhaps in cotes or pens on rooftops in urban areas (Juvenal 3.201–2; Plautus, *Miles Gloriosus* 162; Manilius, *Astronomica* 5.364–80). Dormice, another Roman culinary delicacy typically bred in suburban and rural locales during antiquity, also need not be restricted solely to these places. Specialized jars (improperly called *gliraria*, but now known as *vivaria in doliis*) used to fatten dormice were recovered from excavations just outside Rome, with further examples noted in Pompeii and other urban centres.[5] Finally, fish also factored in urban diets, but probably in relatively smaller numbers compared to mammals and birds, given available zooarchaeological data.[6] While Rome's fish derived chiefly from marine and river sources, decorative urban fishponds were not unknown among elite residences in the city.

---

[3] King 1999.   [4] MacKinnon 2004; De Grossi Mazzorin 2005.
[5] Colonnelli et al. 2000.   [6] MacKinnon 2004.

Pet animals

Modern concepts of 'pet' imply personal relationships of intimacy and mutual understanding between animals and humans. In contrast to food animals, pets are often permitted access to household rooms, are given names and are not consumed. While there are certainly cases of pet-keeping in classical antiquity, many of which seem to parallel contemporary notions of the idea, caution should be exercised in linking such relationships too closely with modern pet culture.[7] Moreover, the line between 'pet' and 'work animal' was certainly blurred in antiquity for some taxa. Sheep dogs, hunting dogs, guard dogs, even draught- and performing dogs are noted in ancient texts, iconography and faunal remains; many may have been named and cared for as pets as well. A similar situation applies to horses, which could have been considered 'pets' despite also serving more utilitarian roles as cavalry or riding mounts, racehorses, draught animals, brood stock or other 'work' responsibilities. Less common pet animals in ancient Rome included cats, birds, hares, weasels, fish, and even monkeys and similar exotics. Domesticated cats were rare in Rome until the end of the fifth century AD. Until then they were presumably imported from Egypt, where they were traditionally venerated as sacred animals.

Ample evidence for pet dogs in ancient Rome exists. Inscriptions and other ancient texts preserve anecdotal tales, epigrams, colourful descriptions, cherished memories and even funerary epitaphs about them. A famous example is the grave stele for Helena, the pet so loved it was deemed a 'foster child' by its owner (Fig. 7.2). This sculpted image is only one instance of many such representations of dogs from Roman iconography, which include images in all manner of media. Perhaps more importantly, pet dogs are often depicted accompanying images of the deceased on lids of sarcophagi or on funerary couches, perhaps a testament to canine faithfulness in life and the afterlife. Finally, zooarchaeological data from Rome and elsewhere attest to a vast range of dog breeds and sizes during antiquity; the Romans certainly bred and introduced new types. Toy breeds become more prevalent during imperial times, probably as a status symbol. At the same time, there is a dramatic diversification of dog varieties, ranging from 20 cm

---

[7] Gilhus 2006, 29 suggests the label 'personal animals' be used instead of 'pet' in reference to ancient human–animal relationships, to avoid confusions with modern concepts of pet-keeping.

FIGURE 7.2 Marble gravestone of Helena, AD 150–200. Inscription reads: 'To Helena, foster daughter, incomparable and praiseworthy soul'.

to over 70 cm at the withers, or shoulder height.[8] Metric data for dog bones from sites in Rome are limited, but available data indicate three general groups: (1) smaller breeds, less than 35/40 cm in height; (2) medium-sized breeds averaging between 50–60 cm; (3) larger varieties, above 60 cm. Medium-sized individuals predominate, which is typical across most ancient Roman sites, rural or urban. Dogs of all ages are recorded among faunal samples from Rome, attesting to local births of pups. Much as today, dogs of all varieties and ages were part of the urban fabric of ancient Rome: smaller toy breeds, such as the Maltese, were often selected as pets; larger breeds, like the Mastiff, performed well as guard dogs; while numerous types of mutts and other strays rummaged the streets.

[8] De Grossi Mazzorin and Tagliacozzo 1997.

SACRIFICIAL ANIMALS

Animal sacrifice was a common component in Roman pagan ritual. Specific rules dictated aspects such as which victims were sacrificed, which age categories, which colour, which parts of the carcass, among other characteristics, depending upon the occasion and deity commemorated.[9] Three general groups may be recognized. First, public festivals and ceremonies, as marked on the Roman calendar, typically required some type of animal sacrifice. Second, private offerings, such as those to various guardian and household spirits (e.g. *lares*) were another potential source of animal sacrifice. Third, augury (i.e. the reading and interpreting of signs) was practised as required. Auspices ranged from observations of behaviours of certain taxa, especially birds and chickens, to the reading of internal organs (i.e. divination) of sacrificed animals.

Domestic pigs, sheep, goats, cattle and chickens were the commonest species sacrificed in ancient Rome, in both public and private contexts. Generally, these taxa could be supplied through the same rural and suburban networks that provided Rome with regular, dietary meat, although in some cases sacrificial animals may have been specially bred, raised or kept (in rural, suburban or even urban locations) to ensure compliance with ritual specifications. Many Roman sacrifices also included a component of feasting, which, for some of Rome's poorest, may have been a chief source of dietary meat.

Animal sacrifice diminished throughout antiquity, as Christianity, which forbade the practice, grew in popularity. Still, some rituals involving animals continue into Late Antiquity. Excavations at the Crypta Balbi in Rome, for example, uncovered a mithraeum, dating to the third to fifth centuries AD, with evidence of sacrificed chickens.[10]

EXOTIC ANIMAL IMPORTS FOR THE AMPHITHEATRE GAMES

Alongside a supply of food, work, pet and sacrificial animals, Rome also required exotic animals for entertainment purposes, most notably for wild beast hunts, or *venationes*, in the amphitheatre and circus. Such

[9] Kadletz 1976 details these specifics for individual deities, as noted from the ancient sources.
[10] De Grossi Mazzorin 2004.

shows were probably introduced around the third century BC, but their earliest recorded reference in Rome is from 186 BC when Livy (39.5.7–10; 39.22.1–2) tells of an event with lions and leopards. Henceforth, the spectacles continue, culminating in the exhibition of hundreds, even thousands, of exotic animals in *venationes* throughout the imperial period.[11] Although the last beast shows noted in some detail were those sponsored by the emperor Probus in AD 281 (*Historia Augusta, Probus* 19), we can be assured by the comments of Symmachus (*Epistulae* 2.76; 9.117), about complications in acquiring and transporting African beasts, that these hunts continued into the late fourth century AD, and presumably later as well. The last recorded *venationes* in Rome were apparently in AD 523 (Cassiodorus, *Varia* 5.42), but there are few details for these.

Archaeological faunal evidence for exotic beasts in Rome is slim. Rumours of exotic animal bones retrieved from early excavations near the Colosseum cannot be verified in the absence of these bones, or of detailed reports discussing them. Only one site, that of the Meta Sudans, located about 50 m south-west of the Colosseum, provides unambiguous indication, in the presence of sixteen bear bones, two leopard bones, an ostrich fragment, and several red deer, roe deer, wild boar and fox remains from excavations of a fifth- to seventh-century AD fill of a drain.[12] In addition, many horse bones were also retrieved. It seems logical to relate these materials to amphitheatre and circus games, and if so, their location suggests that at least some exotic beasts were buried nearby. Still, these are hardly the extensive numbers or species diversity one would expect to find, even factoring in retrieval and preservation biases that can severely reduce a zooarchaeological assemblage. Available animal bone data, therefore, attest to much less grandiose versions of *venationes* in Rome than those illustrated through ancient texts or iconography.

PESTS

The numeric rise and spread of mice, rats and other commensal animals, such as house sparrows, is often associated with urbanization. As urbanization advances, through colonization and expansion, so do

---

[11] For detailed listings and further commentary on these, and other references to exotic animals in Roman *venationes*, see Jennison 1937 and MacKinnon 2006.

[12] De Grossi Mazzorin 1995.

commensals. There is evidence that during the last millennium BC, the Phoenicans and Greeks inadvertently brought the house mouse (*Mus musculus*) into the western Mediterranean, while the Romans themselves appear responsible for importing and dispersing the black rat (*Rattus rattus*), among other pests, throughout their empire.[13]

Mice and sparrows figure occasionally in Roman texts and iconography. Charting their existence and spread, zooarchaeologically, is complicated, given that bones from small taxa are not systematically recovered from archaeological sites, and that taphonomic forces can easily displace tiny bones across stratigraphic levels, rendering chronological placement tricky. Nevertheless, although sparrow bones are noted sporadically, mouse bones have been recovered from excavations throughout Italy, including Rome, among contexts across the entire Roman period, attesting to their early association with urban societies here, and their persistence over time. Still, house mice are not the only small 'pest' mammals recorded in Roman urban centres, including Rome. Wood mice, voles and shrews are also noted. Although they are not true commensal pests, the presence of these small mammals may relate to the existence of gardens and orchards within Roman urban settings, habitats conducive for them. At present, however, there are insufficient zooarchaeological, textual and iconographical data to quantify and assess the incidence and prevalence of mice, sparrows and similar pests in ancient Rome. No doubt, just as in many cities today, these taxa were an everyday nuisance to tolerate and control as necessary. Some assistance in this regard came from cats, whether domesticated or not, which, alongside the ferret, seem to have acted chiefly in destroying rodents during Roman antiquity.[14]

The situation involving the black rat in Rome and, further afield, across the empire is complicated. This species (*Rattus rattus*) is crucial in the spread of bubonic plague (microbes being transferred via fleas carried by the rats), so its movement can help illuminate patterns of disease transmission and plague epidemics during antiquity. Solid archaeological evidence for rats in Roman Italy, be this in the form of rat gnaw marks on other bones; owl or other predator pellets containing rat pieces; or actual rat remains preserved *in situ*, is still somewhat controversial. The presence of rat bones in fourth- to second-century BC levels in Corsica, and among second-century BC contexts from Pompeii and Minorca, suggests movement of this species into the western

---

[13] Cucchi and Vigne 2006.   [14] Engels 1999.

Mediterranean during republican times.[15] Still, only scattered and often isolated rat remains have been identified from other ancient sites on the Italian mainland, with more secure evidence chiefly for late Roman and medieval contexts, and, as yet, no rat bones noted among any Roman contexts from excavations in Rome itself. Ancient texts are also of little help in providing a timeline, given that classical Latin and Greek lacked distinguishing words for 'rat' and 'mouse', lumping both together as *mus* (Latin) and *mys* (Greek). Certainly, all the elements conducive for rat colonization and expansion existed in ancient Rome, even if the zooarchaeological evidence, as yet, cannot confirm their presence in the city during antiquity. First, Rome lies on a major shipping and transport route, conducive for the movement of rats, which might stow-away on carts, ships and other vessels. Normally, black rats have a limited range of active movement, and do not venture much beyond 200 m. Second, black rats prefer grain, which makes it all the more likely that they infiltrated Rome as part of the many food shipments directed to the capital. Finally, high population densities, apartment block (*insula*) housing and the potential for poor sanitation conditions within Rome, would have all contributed to the spread of rats in the city, once these animals had been initially transported there. Routine street cleaning and waste disposal, proper storage of foodstuffs, construction in brick, stone and concrete (as opposed to wood), and even the use of predators, such as cats, would help in controlling rats in the city of Rome, but once established, it would be difficult to eradicate black rat populations from the city. Clearly, rats, like mice and other vermin, were a regular component of urban life, even if their prevalence is not documented correspondingly in the archaeological, textual and iconographical evidence for the city.

CONSEQUENCES OF ANIMALS IN THE CITY

Pooling together the range of animals present in ancient Rome – food animals, pets, working animals, sacrificial animals, exotic show animals, pests – highlights the diversity of taxa and the array of conditions needed to acquire, maintain, market and control such beasts. Estimating numbers of animals is always problematic. There are no clear records of these from ancient sources, but rough estimates derived

---

[15] Statistics and data for the discussion of rats in the ancient Mediterranean context derive from McCormick 2003.

on the basis of dietary contributions and comparisons with other pre-industrial cities yield an absolute low estimate of approximately 60,000 pigs, 2,000 sheep and goats and 7,500 cattle, up to a high estimate of ten times these numbers.[16] A midpoint between these ends: 300,000 pigs, 10,000 sheep and goats, and 37,500 cattle might be a compromise for the annual domestic mammalian meat needs of imperial Rome, at its height. A total of c. 5,000–10,000 for horses, donkeys, mules and traction oxen seems reasonable; however, the bulk of these were probably stabled in the suburban areas of Rome and used in the city as needed, rather than being kept there permanently. However, essential mill animals and some special horses were an exception.[17] Pets might account for perhaps another 5,000–10,000.[18] Exotic show animals would vary with imperial and elite expenditures on games, but an average figure of 1,000 per year does not seem unreasonable. Sacrificial animals might account for another 20,000–50,000 per year, if one factors in smaller domestic offerings. Caligula (Suetonius, *Gaius* 14.1), it is claimed, sacrificed 160,000 animals, during a three-month celebratory period, perhaps an exaggerated figure, but still a guide to the aggregate importance of animals in ancient ritual. Although exact numbers are impossible to calculate, collectively, the number of animals present, or required, in ancient Rome potentially rivals the human population, and certainly far exceeds it if one includes all types of birds, game animals and fish, stray cats and dogs, and vermin like rats and mice in this mix.

Food animals probably presented the biggest logistical challenge for Rome. How and where were livestock, which supplied the city's meat, kept and raised? Practicalities limited any large-scale husbandry activities in Rome itself. Although animals may have pastured within the city in unpopulated sections during its foundation, or in abandoned

---

[16] For imperial times: using a range for meat consumption of 5–50 kg/person/year (there is great controversy here; see Kron 2005 and Jongman 2007); a population of Rome at 1,000,000; NISP statistics from Table 7.1, above, which convert to c. 60 per cent pork, 10 per cent mutton and 30 per cent beef when available meat weights are calculated (see MacKinnon 2004: 190–239). By comparison, late eighteenth- and early nineteenth-century Genoa (a city upwards of 100,000 people) recorded annual figures of c. 2,000 oxen, 6,000 cows, 60,000 sheep and 2,000 pigs (Balzaretti 2004, 108).

[17] The Genoa statistics are: c. 1,500 mules, c. 2,000 donkeys, and a few horses (Balzaretti 2004, 108).

[18] By comparison, it is estimated that Paris in the 1840s, a city of comparable population to ancient Rome, had 100,000 dogs (Robert 1888: 7), so one-tenth to one-twentieth this value for all pets dogs and otherwise does not seem an unreasonable estimate for Rome.

zones during Late Antiquity, urban space was certainly at a premium for human occupants between these periods. Domestic food animals, by necessity, were mainly raised on rural and suburban farms during antiquity.[19] At some point these animals, or at least their products, had to be imported to Rome for marketing or distribution.

Despite a presumed importance of markets in everyday urban life, much of our knowledge about livestock markets in antiquity remains obscure. Two are referenced for ancient Rome: the Forum Boarium and the Forum Suarium. The most famous of these is the Forum Boarium, or cattle market, located south of the Circus Maximus, next to the Tiber. It is the only livestock market in Italy to have left archaeological traces, even if defined by neighbouring roads, buildings and temples, leaving no actual forum structure.[20] Varro (*De lingua Latina* 5.146) and Livy (21.62.3) and an inscription found in the area (*CIL* 6.1035) attest selling cattle in this area. Presumably, its proximity to the river facilitated the transport of animals (if they were brought in this way), as well as shipments of hay and fodder necessary to feed the animals (if they were kept for short periods near the market before slaughter or sale).

Whatever activities occurred in the Forum Boarium, it appears that its function as a livestock market ended quite early, perhaps by the second century BC, and certainly before the Principate. Cicero (*Pro Scauro* 23) mentions the area as a place for legal business, while Livy (*Epitome* 16) and Tertullian (*De Spectaculis* 5.6.) say it was a spot for gladiatorial contests.

The Forum Suarium is first mentioned in Livy (10.23.2, 22.57.6, 23.10.8, 27.37.17, 29.37.1), then in two inscriptions of about AD 200 (*CIL* 6.3728), and in documents of a later date (*Not. Reg.* VII; *Pol. Silv.* 545; *Codex Theodosianus* 14.4.4.4; Philostratus, *Heroicus* 283). This market was situated in Regio VII of Rome, between the Via Flaminia and the Pincio, and the junction of the modern Via Due Macelli and Via di Propaganda.[21] Given the importance of pigs to Roman life, it is surprising that the Forum Suarium is relatively obscure. Perhaps this is due to its position, somewhat removed from the central core of the city. Pigs could have been herded to nearby holding pens or grounds before being sold here. Areas to butcher the pigs may have been located

---

[19] There is a large body of scholarship examining ancient Roman animal husbandry on suburban and rural farms. See MacKinnon 2004 and White 1970 for discussion and further references.

[20] Frayn 1993, 145.   [21] Frayn 1993, 148.

in the vicinity, but again there is no archaeological or ancient textual evidence to confirm this. Indeed, there is little evidence to confirm the location of butchery shops and slaughterhouses in Rome. Certainly, as exists today in Italy, neighbourhood shops selling fresh and preserved cuts of meat probably existed in residential areas of ancient Rome, but the more odious tasks of slaughter and initial carcass processing would have been conducted far away from residential sections. Two texts support this hypothesis. The first is an inscription denoting the import of meat to a butcher near Rome's Temple of Libitana, probably on the Esquiline, where there was a market (*CIL* 6.33870). The second comes from Plautus (*Pseudolus* 326–31), who mentions slaughtering animals 'outside the gate' (of Rome). Zooarchaeological evidence helps confirm some import of animal sections and body parts into the city, in the presence of a disproportionately higher number of bones from primary and secondary cuts of meat at sites within the city. Suburban and rural sites, by contrast, record more head and lower limb sections, presumably thanks to their role in supplying Rome with better cuts of meat.[22]

A suburban location was also desired for other activities involving animals, specifically tanning and hide-processing. Juvenal (14.200–5) and Martial (*Epigr.* 6.93) mention regulations to locate tanners in peripheral quarters on the Tiber, while an inscription (*CIL* 6.1117 and 1118) found in the zone of the Septimiana Gate mentions a corpus of tanners (*corpus coriariorum*) found in Trastevere. Considering the foul chemicals used in tanning hides, as well as the animal wastes generated, a location outside, downwind and downstream of urban, residential Rome is warranted.

Large-scale imports of animals and their products to Rome certainly required sufficient space, planning and organization. There is mention of fields, the Campus Boarius (*CIL* 6.9226 and 6.37806) and the Campus Pecuarius (*CIL* 6.9660, although, curiously, as yet, no Campus Suarius), either of which could temporarily maintain herds. Nevertheless, such a system does not mean that other domestic livestock were not maintained within the city on a more regular basis. Unfortunately, it is difficult to prove to what extent Rome's inhabitants kept and raised food animals on their urban premises. Key factors, including available stall space, and access to yards, pastures and other feeding grounds, are essential, as are considerations of noise, smell, hygiene and other practicalities. It would be unreasonable to keep larger mammals,

---

[22] MacKinnon 2004.

such as beef cattle, unless they served foremost as traction beasts in the city, as opposed to simply food animals. Medium- and small-sized animals (i.e. sheep, goats, pigs and fowl) seem more likely candidates to be raised inside the city, if space and society permitted. Certainly it would be unfeasible for most of Rome's inhabitants to maintain any livestock in the city itself, but wealthier individuals could easily raise a few fowl, and perhaps a sheep, goat or pig, in the rear confines of a *domus*, in much the same way that some households today maintain backyard animals. Some animals destined for ritual purposes, and under strict breeding regimens to maintain the necessary physical character- istics and temperament, may also have been raised in urban areas for convenient sacrifice.

Although most food animals were probably raised outside Rome, the situation is different for working animals, such as horses, donkeys, mules and oxen, which were needed within the city. Images of equids and oxen fulfilling various duties – transporting goods and riders, mili- tary and *cursus publicus* responsibilities, hauling carts and wagons, pulling ploughs, rotating mills and presses – abound in Roman visual culture.[23] Wheel ruts on Roman streets, alongside bone remains of equids and oxen from urban contexts, some with pathological conditions sugges- tive of work stress,[24] attest to the frequency of these animals in cities, including Rome. Work animals could be rented as required (*Histo- ria Augusta, Elagabalus* 16.1), for those without their own stock. At times, the cacophony of animal traffic had to be regulated (e.g. *Historia Augusta, Hadrian* 22.8; *Elag.* 4.4; Suetonius, *Gaius* 39.1). Nevertheless, despite these sources, very little archaeological evidence is available to determine where and how work animals were housed while in Rome. Presumably, many were kept in suburban farms, venturing into the city as required; however, some must have been housed inside Rome on a more regular basis. As yet, no securely attested archaeological traces of stables exist in Rome. Although the Roman agricultural writers out- line aspects of stable construction, recognizing these archaeologically is complicated, given their often nondescript nature, and potential to be used for multiple purposes, not just for animals. Stables have been identified in Pompeii (e.g. House of Chaste Lovers), but their dimen- sions and flooring generally are not specific enough to assign them, unambiguously, as rooms for oxen, horses or other livestock.

[23] E.g., Toynbee 1973; Hyland 1990; Johnstone 2004.
[24] E.g., De Grossi Mazzorin et al. 1998.

Some aspects of the mechanics of trade and importation of exotic animals can be reconstructed. In the case of supplying Rome, exotic animals were shipped overseas, typically unloaded at Ostia, and subsequently barged up the Tiber. The transfer was not always smooth. Pliny (*Historia Naturalis* 36.40) tells of a sculptor at the docks who was attacked by an escaped leopard. Once in Rome, some animals could be stored in subterranean rooms and pens at the Colosseum itself, but these seem principally designed to provide only temporary housing prior to the shows. *Vivaria*, or stockyards, furnished longer-term storage. There are some references to *vivaria* in the ancient texts and even mention of what may be interpreted as ancient zookeepers, or *custodes vivari* (*CIL* 6.130); however, only conflicting evidence for the whereabouts of these stockyards exists, and, as yet, no archaeological traces of them. Given their large spatial requirements, *vivaria* would only be practical in suburban areas of a city, and presumably beyond the city gates in the case of Rome. Ancient references to them, however, are scarce, and biased in favour of Late Antiquity, making it difficult to assess their applicability to earlier imperial and republican times. Nevertheless, one inscription (*CIL* 6.130) records a possible *vivarium* outside the *Porta Praenestina* in Rome, while Procopius (*De bello Gothico* 5.32.10–11; 5.33.14–17) mentions another *vivarium* (near the *Porta Labicana*, according to most authorities) where apparently lions and other untamed beasts were kept. The relationship between these two *vivaria* is unknown; it is possible that they refer to the same place. Nevertheless, few architectural or physical details are available that might help distinguish such an area archaeologically, and even then subsequent modification and development of the region has probably obliterated most structural clues.

Finally, the presence of such a range of food, work, pet and exotic animals in Rome prompts questions about hygiene, health, safety and waste management. All cities, including ancient Rome, generate waste, from both human and animal inhabitants. Several references attest to dung, filth and carcasses littering streets (*CIL* 1.2.839; Suetonius, *Vitellius* 12.2). Estimates record that a population of *c.* 1,000,000 in early imperial Rome would generate about 50,000 kgs of body wastes daily.[25] Factoring in animal dung and urine, butchery and food waste, dead carcasses and related garbage increases such amounts. While efforts were made by Rome's inhabitants to remove waste from the city, animals can also help in this regard by consuming organic refuse, even excrement.

---

[25] Scobie 1986, 413.

Pigs were commonly kept in medieval cities in this regard,[26] and it seems logical to extrapolate this practice back to antiquity, even if available data cannot confirm exactly where and on what scale this occurred. No definitive pigsties are noted in the archaeological record for Rome, although pigs and other animals could have been kept in any manner of nondescript stalls, rooms or yards among houses or other buildings in the city. They may also have roamed more freely. Zooarchaeological, ancient textual and iconographical evidence indicates the existence of at least two breeds of pigs in Roman Italy: a large, fat variety, and a smaller, leaner breed.[27] The larger variety is more prevalent in urban locales, and could have been maintained as a refuse feeder, before ultimately being consumed itself. The ancient texts provide some clues about urban pigs. Plautus (*Captivi* 4.1.807–8) complains that pigs kept by millers to feed off waste from milling and grinding create such a stench that no one can go to the mill. Horace (*Epist.* 2.2.72–5) mentions a muddy sow rushing down the street in a description of urban (presumably Rome's) hustle and bustle. Ausonius (*Epistolarum liber* 10.6.25–6) recounts a similar scene of a dirty sow roaming the streets of ancient Bordeaux. Dogs and other animals, whether kept in houses or straying through the city, could act in similar fashion, feeding on urban refuse. Suetonius (*Vespasian* 5.4) mentions a stray dog that brought a human hand into Vespasian's dining room.

Despite efforts at waste removal, no doubt Rome fostered numerous pathogens, which thrived in areas of poor sanitation.[28] Animals exacerbated disease transmission under these conditions, not only through contamination of living conditions and water supplies, but also through more direct routes, such as vectors for rabies, plague and malaria (if one considers mosquitos and fleas), and transmitters of zoonotic diseases (i.e. those passed from humans to animals), including bovine tuberculosis. Uncontrolled roaming of animals, such as dogs and pigs, coupled with close living conditions between humans and animals in crowded urban environments, would augment disease complications. No doubt Rome saw its share of health problems, as testified in numerous complaints about diseases found in the ancient sources, as well as diagnoses and cures for many of these as outlined in medical (e.g. Celsus' *De medicina*; Galen's volumes) and veterinary (e.g. Vegetius' *Mulomedicina*) texts.

---

[26] Keene 1982.   [27] MacKinnon 2001.
[28] See Chapter 3, for a more detailed discussion of disease and death in ancient Rome.

Further reading

For a general overview of animals in Roman life, especially as regards ancient textual and iconographical evidence, see Keller 1909–13, Jennison 1937, and Toynbee 1973. Focused studies of individual taxa, such as Merlen 1971 (dogs), Engels 1999 (cats), Hyland 1990 and Johnstone 2004 (horses), and MacKinnon 2001 (pigs) are also available. For amphitheatre animals, see MacKinnon 2006. White 1970 remains an essential source of data for ancient animal husbandry practices. MacKinnon 2007 provides an overview of the field of zooarchaeology within classical archaeology. Detailed analyses of zooarchaeological results for Roman sites in Italy specifically, e.g. MacKinnon 2004, and the Roman world generally, e.g. King 1999, are available. Many excavation reports also contain individual analyses of faunal material recovered, with organizations such as the International Council for Archaeozoology ICAZ and the Associazione Italiana di Archeozoologia sponsoring conferences and publication venues for research. Bodson 2000 reviews pet-keeping in ancient Rome, with further references to the philosophy and practice of this as discovered from ancient sources, including iconography. Kadletz 1976 collates data for animal sacrifice in Roman religion, sorting things by deity, festival and taxon. For information about meat consumption in Rome, and the mechanics of its marketing and distribution see Corbier 1989, Frayn 1993, Sirks 1991, Chioffi 1999 and MacKinnon 2004. Rubbish disposal in antiquity is discussed in Scobie 1986 and Dupré Raventós and Remolà 2000, with some mention of dogs, pigs and other animals as trash feeders.

PART II

THE URBAN FABRIC

8: THE URBAN TOPOGRAPHY
OF ROME

Elisha Ann Dumser

Rome's urban topography was a vital expression of the power and authority of the Roman state. In his *Ten Books on Architecture* (*c.* 25 BC), Vitruvius praises Augustus:

> you cared not only about the common life of all men, and the constitution of the state, but also about the provision of suitable public buildings, so that the state was not only made greater through you by its new provinces, but the majesty of the empire was also expressed through the eminent dignity of its public buildings.
>
> (*De arch.* 1. pr. 2)

Yet a complete understanding of Rome's urban topography remains elusive. For evidence, we rely on literary sources and archaeology, but texts tend to favour the elite, and the longstanding interest of archaeologists in major public monuments has led to unbalanced excavation efforts. The centre of the ancient city, especially the Forum and Palatine, has been subject to extensive scientific investigation, yet surrounding urban areas have seen less archaeological activity (Map 8.1). Even as attitudes and interests change, the fact that Rome remains a vibrant, living city will always, for the best of reasons, limit the areas in which archaeological investigation can be carried out. Combined, these factors skew our picture of the ancient city: the monumental city centre and major imperial projects are fairly well-known, whereas neighbourhoods on the periphery and 'minor' private structures are often extrapolated from limited archaeological and textual data. That said, our knowledge of the ancient city is vast, and this chapter can provide only a lightly sketched overview of Rome's changing topography from 200 BC to AD 350.

MAP 8.1 Plan of Rome in the early fourth century AD.

THE REPUBLICAN CITY

The centre of republican Rome, both physically and politically, was the Forum Romanum (Map 8.2). Situated in the valley between the Capitoline, Palatine and Velia, the Forum was an open, trapezoidal expanse loosely defined by the civic and religious buildings at its borders. Along the north and south sides ran the Basilica Fulvia and Basilica Sempronia, large enclosed structures founded in the early second century BC to house legal, commercial and financial transactions. Along the shorter east and west ends ranged religious buildings and venerable monuments, including the temples of Castor, Vesta, Saturn and Concordia, as well as the Regia and Atrium Vestae. The west end of the Forum was especially dedicated to political use during the Republic and was the site of the Rostra, Comitium and Curia. Scattered throughout the open plaza were numerous honorific statues and modest sacred sites and shrines, some of great antiquity.[1] In addition to its everyday political, legal and commercial uses, the Forum was a desirable locale for prominent funerals and the frequent site of gladiatorial games.

Given the political significance of the Forum Romanum, it comes as little surprise that the neighbouring hills became prime sites for elite housing in the Republic. Remains of several luxurious republican *domus* have been recovered just east of the Forum on the Velia, while literary and archaeological evidence indicates that the Palatine was a sought-after neighbourhood for politically ambitious aristocrats. Besides their close proximity to the forum, Palatine residents benefited from the hill's numinous aura, and among its many temples and shrines stood the Hut of Romulus, an iron-age dwelling associated with the revered city founder and preserved with exacting care through the ages (Dion. Hal., *Ant. Rom.* 1.79.11). The Aventine was especially associated with the plebs, and its religious foundations included cults with plebeian facets, such as Diana Aventina, Ceres and Flora. The urban poor lived in decrepit conditions. Infamous was the Subura, a slum known for its filth, damp, noise and violence located in the valley between the Viminal and Esquiline. 'Residential' neighbourhoods differed significantly from those in the west today: even the most elite regions in Rome were 'mixed-use' with residences, shops, warehouses, religious dedications and light industry all found within a single area.

---

[1] Chapter 11.

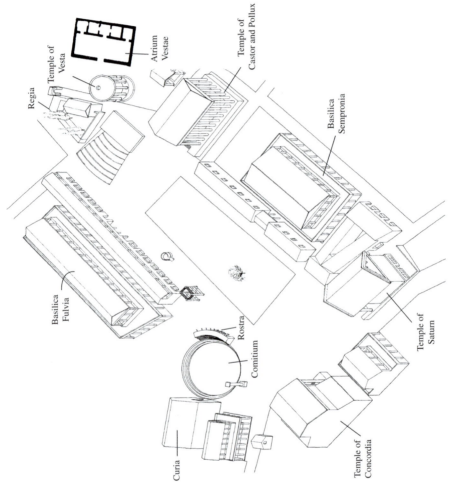

Regia

Temple of
Vesta

Atrium
Vestae

Temple of
Castor and Pollux

Basilica
Sempronia

Basilica
Fulvia

Rostra

Comitium

Curia

Temple of
Saturn

Temple of
Concordia

MAP 8.2 The Forum Romanum in the second century BC.

Religious observances were seamlessly interwoven with daily life in ancient Rome such that architecture to facilitate worship – sanctuaries, altars and shrines – could be found throughout the city. One of the most important sanctuaries was the Capitoline temple of Jupiter Optimus Maximus, Juno and Minerva. Originally dedicated in 509 BC, the Capitolium was rebuilt several times in the Republic and figured prominently in official rituals. There, new consuls offered sacrifice as they took office and triumphal parades concluded with dedications and a sacrifice to Jupiter. Major religious monuments like the Capitolium were usually situated around heavily trafficked public areas such as fora. At the neighbourhood level were smaller sanctuaries and compital altars, and residences often featured personal shrines to the domestic *lares* (household gods). Foreign cults like those of Isis or Bellona were frequently located outside the *pomerium*. Likewise tombs were located outside the city, most often in highly visible locations along major roads, because of prohibitions against intramural burial.[2]

Mercantile centres in the Republic were clustered along the Tiber. Between the Forum Romanum and the Tiber were the Forum Boarium and Forum Holitorium (the 'cattle market' and 'vegetable market', respectively). Substantially rebuilt in the early second century BC, these fora featured facilities for trade and commerce, open space for market days, a harbour (the Portus Tiberinus) and embankments along the river, as well as religious monuments including a number of altars and shrines dedicated to Hercules. Several bridges connected this busy hub with the Trans Tiberim (west bank of the Tiber): the Pons Sublicius was an ancient crossing built up on wooden pilings, while the Pons Aemilius was Rome's first stone bridge (by 179 BC, perhaps as early as 241 BC). By the mid-first century BC, the Pons Cestius and Pons Fabricius connected the Tiber Island to both banks as well. Further south along the Tiber below the Aventine was the Emporium, a district of warehouses and quays that served as Rome's most important depot for seaborne trade. Here stood the Porticus Aemilia, an immense warehouse (487 × 60 m) whose scale testifies to the frequency of trade in Rome by the mid-first century BC, while its form – fifty barrel-vaulted bays built of concrete – marks an important development in Roman architectural technology.[3]

---

[2] Chapter 12.
[3] The identification of this warehouse as the Porticus Aemilia is debated; for a summary, O. Harmanşah, 'Porticus Aemilia (Emporium)', in Haselberger et al. 2008, 201–2.

During the Republic, Rome had a central market, or *macellum*, directly north-east of the Forum Romanum.

As their building names suggest, the patrons of important civic structures like the Basilica Sempronia or Pons Fabricius were most often individuals of significant public standing (here, Ti. Sempronius Gracchus and L. Fabricius). Self-interest motivated their generosity, as public works bearing the family name advertised their munificence and helped sway public opinion in the donor's favour. Alongside public buildings, increasingly luxurious and impressive *domus* were erected as a patron's home became an important means to express personal power and influence his network of clients. Triumphant generals with political aspirations were soon expected to use manubial spoils to fund public buildings, often temples erected in fulfilment of a vow sworn on the eve of battle. By the late Republic, private patronage by Rome's political elite had reached monumental proportions as demonstrated by the extravagant theatre erected by Pompey the Great. Rome's first permanent stone theatre, the Theatrum Pompeii (55 BC) was located on the Campus Martius and boasted a temple dedicated to Venus Victrix atop a spacious *cavea* (*c.* 11,000 capacity) connected to a large *quadriporticus* filled with greenery and artwork.

In the late Republic splendid architectural works like the Theatre of Pompey existed largely in isolation, oases of grandeur amidst a decaying city that lacked adequate provisions for the regular maintenance of its infrastructure and public buildings. Prior to the reforms of Augustus, Rome's urban administration was largely the responsibility of censors and aediles, who let contracts for new building and maintenance work. Given their short terms of office (eighteen and twelve months, respectively), the accomplishments of such magistrates were limited. Moreover, practical maintenance, such as road repair and sewer work, brought little prestige and was often overlooked in favour of far more popular and politically profitable ventures, such as commissioning a new building or, for aediles, sponsoring lavish games. As Rome's population grew to nearly 1 million in the late Republic, the density of her residential areas made water an increasingly important commodity, yet only four aqueducts served the city's expanding needs (Aqua Appia, 312 BC; Anio Vetus, 272 BC; Aqua Marcia, 144 BC; Aqua Tepula, 125 BC). By the late first century BC, the ill-effects of Rome's deficient infrastructure and administration were openly apparent: the city had become dangerously derelict, and her crumbling infrastructure was unable to accommodate the load imposed by her tremendous growth.

More was at stake, however, than just safety and upkeep. Rome had come to govern an expanding empire, and the shortcomings of her urban image became a matter of concern for her leading citizens. Rival cities in the Hellenistic east boasted Hippodamian (grid) plans and gracious public amenities absent from Rome. A Macedonian embassy in 182 BC reportedly found Rome's urban appearance laughable since the city 'was not yet adorned in either its public or private spaces' (Livy, *History of Rome*, 40.5.7). Cicero described Rome's 'multi-storeyed houses piled one on top of the other, its narrow alleys and lack of decent streets' (*Leg. agr.* 2.35.96). Livy served as an apologist for its haphazard layout, writing that after the Gallic sack of 390 BC 'Romans, in their haste, were careless about making straight the streets... For this reason... the appearance of the city is like one where the ground has been appropriated by settlers rather than divided [following a plan]' (Livy, *History of Rome*, 5.55.5). Rome's appearance utterly failed to reflect the status and dignity of a world power, and as individuals such as Julius Caesar and Augustus gained unprecedented influence, they sought a remedy.

Julius Caesar took on the role of Rome's benefactor with vigour and determination in the mid-first century BC. Much like his contemporary Pompey, Caesar looked to public works as a means of self-aggrandizement and political advancement, yet his projects were unmatched in scale and ambition. He replaced the ageing Basilica Sempronia with the Basilica Iulia; paid for the restoration of the Basilica Paulli; began to rebuild the Curia; initiated construction of the Saepta, a voting hall in the Campus Martius renowned for its mile-long portico; added the first permanent seats to the Circus Maximus; and augmented Rome's civic space with the Forum Iulium. Focused on architectural works that would serve the needs of the people, Caesar's patronage sought to maximize his standing in the contentious political arena of late republican Rome.

With the Forum Iulium, Caesar introduced what would become a signature urban element in Rome: the imperial forum (Map 8.3). Adjacent to the Forum Romanum, Caesar's forum (dedicated in 44 BC, but completed under Augustus) rivalled its venerable predecessor in size and grandeur. At its centre was an open rectangular piazza enclosed by colonnaded porticos on three sides. Behind the porticos were *tabernae* (modest rooms) used primarily for government business. Axially positioned was a temple to Venus Genetrix; its dedication was a direct allusion to Caesar's familial ancestry (the *gens Iulia* traced its roots to Aeneas and thus ultimately to Venus) and a deliberate jibe at Pompey's temple

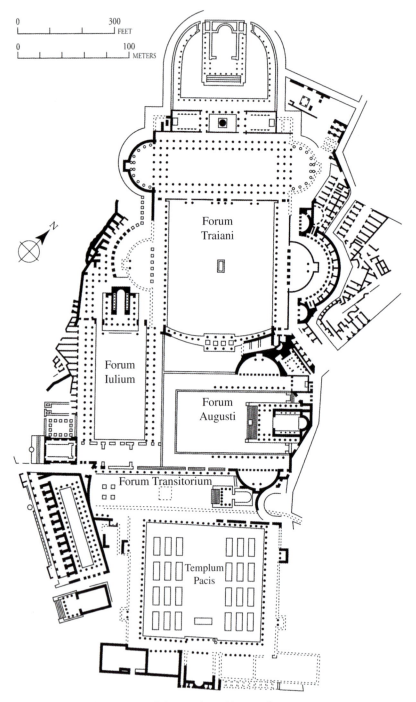

0 _____ 300
FEET

0 _____ 100
METERS

N

Forum
Traiani

Forum
Iulium

Forum
Augusti

Forum Transitorium

Templum
Pacis

MAP 8.3 Plan of the imperial fora in the mid-second century AD.

to Venus Victrix. Connected to the Forum's south-west corner was the newly rebuilt Curia. With the Forum Iulium Rome had at last gained an orderly civic space for government business: adorned with decorous colonnades and a gracious temple, Caesar's Forum emulated the Hippodamian fora of eastern Hellenistic cities in its regularity and beauty.

Yet the Forum Iulium, like Pompey's theatre in the Campus Martius, remained a grand monument of personal propaganda isolated within an urban landscape unequal to Rome's increasing prominence. By all reports, Caesar sensed this deficiency and sought to remedy Rome's failings. In addition to the numerous structures he had already realized, in 44 BC Caesar began construction of a permanent theatre on the west slope of the Capitoline (Dio Cass. 43.49) and planned a large temple of Mars and a public library for the Campus Martius (Suetonius *Caes.* 44). Caesar also hoped to straighten the course of the Tiber and thus augment the available land on the Campus (Cic. *Att.* 13.33a). Alongside these physical changes, Caesar named additional aediles to care for the city and drafted new laws to govern Rome's urban concerns (the *Lex Iulia municipalis*, adopted after his death). Left largely unrealized at the time of his murder on 15 March 44 BC, Caesar's plans 'to adorn and decorate the city' (Suetonius *Caes.* 44.1–2) represent an important step beyond the norms of republican patronage, because his interest extended beyond singular monuments to encompass the health of the city as a whole.

THE AUGUSTAN CITY

Despite Caesar's efforts to address Rome's lack of urban amenities and suitable infrastructure, in 44 BC the city was still deficient and Augustus earned praise for the actions he took to resolve the issue. Around 25 BC, Vitruvius commended Augustus for 'the provision of suitable public buildings, so that . . . the majesty of the empire was also expressed through the eminent dignity of its public buildings' and described the emperor's building programme as 'large scale' with 'edifices that will correspond to the grandeur of our history and be a memorial to future ages' (*De arch.* 1.pr.2–3). Writing a century later, Suetonius echoes Vitruvius when he offered one of the most famous descriptions of Augustan Rome's changing urban fortunes.

> [Rome], which was a city not adorned in accordance with
> the majesty of the empire and which was prone to flooding

and fires, was transformed to such an extent under him [Augustus] that he could justly claim to have found a city of bricks and left it a city of marble.

(*Aug.* 28.3)

By the end of his reign Augustus had brought about fundamental changes in Rome's physical topography and urban infrastructure, substantially improving the appearance and administration of the empire's capital. He commissioned a wealth of important new monuments,[4] and though his efforts could be seen throughout Rome's diverse neighbourhoods – for instance his restoration of eighty-two ageing temples in 28 BC would have touched upon all areas of the city (*Res Gestae* 20.4) – his patronage revolved around three primary regions, the Campus Martius, the fora and the Palatine.

The southern Campus Martius had been a locus for building in the late Republic, but under Augustus the entire campus was transformed through new building and restoration works. Augustus built the Theatre of Marcellus and a wooden stadium; restored the Via Flaminia, the Theatre of Pompey and two porticos, the Porticus Octavia and Porticus Octaviae; constructed his Mausoleum and its surrounding public gardens; and erected the Horologium, a giant sundial built in conjunction with the Ara Pacis Augustae, an altar erected by the senate to celebrate the peace Augustus brought the empire. Augustus' works in the Campus Martius were complemented by those of his staunch ally and supporter, Marcus Agrippa, who built the 'Stoa of Poseidon' to celebrate his naval victories at Naulochos and Actium; began construction of the Diribitorium and Porticus Vipsania; dedicated the Pantheon; and founded Rome's first large-scale public bath complex, the Thermae Agrippae. To meet the water demands of the *thermae* and the adjacent Stagnum Agrippae, Agrippa completed the Aqua Virgo in 19 BC, one of Rome's first new aqueducts in over 100 years.[5] This suite of monuments, known as the *monumenta Agrippae* (Tacitus, *Ann.* 15.39), had an axial orientation not seen elsewhere in Rome and lent the Campus Martius an air of Hellenic organization and grandeur. Under Augustus, the Campus Martius had become a 'spectacle that

---

[4] The exhaustive list of Augustan buildings runs three full pages in Haselberger 2007, 261–3.

[5] Two other new aqueducts, the Aqua Iulia and Aqua Alsietina, were opened under Augustus as he recognized the importance of meeting Rome's growing need for potable water.

one can hardly draw away from' for there are 'colonnades all around it in very great numbers, and sacred precincts, and three theatres, and an amphitheatre and very costly temples in close succession to one another, giving you the impression that they are trying . . . to declare the rest of the city a mere accessory' (Strabo 5.3.8). No longer characterized by a smattering of republican monuments, the Campus Martius had been vested by Augustus and Agrippa with an unusual, stirring beauty and amenities that rivalled the city itself.

The heart of the city was not lacking for Augustus' attention either, for there he studiously completed the monuments begun by Caesar and then launched a programme of additions that transformed the Forum Romanum into a celebration of the imperial family. Defining its perimeter were monuments erected or restored by Augustus or his immediate family members: the temples of Concordia Augusta and of Castor; the Curia; the Porticus of Gaius and Lucius in front of the Basilica Paulli; the temple and rostra of Deified Caesar (which initiated the regular practice of dedicating temples to deified rulers); the Basilica Iulia; and several honorific arches.

To this, Augustus added Rome's third forum, the Forum Augusti in 2 BC which was heavily indebted to Caesar's forum for its design (Fig. 8.3). It too centred on an enclosed rectangular piazza defined by colonnades and had an axial temple, here dedicated to Mars Ultor, 'Mars the Avenger', to acknowledge Augustus' defeat of those responsible for Caesar's death as well as allude to his recovery of the military standards lost to the Parthians. Complementing the refined architecture and lavish building materials was a sophisticated sculptural programme celebrating the lineage of Augustus and the *gens Iulia*. Like Rome's two other fora, the Forum Augusti existed primarily to serve jurisprudence and government business, especially matters relating to foreign policy. Just as Augustus transformed Rome's government from a republic to a principate, his architectural commissions ensured that major *loci* for civic transactions in Rome – the Forum Romanum, Forum Iulium and Forum Augusti – were 'Augustan' spaces that proclaimed the power of Rome's new emperor.

The third centre of Augustan patronage was the Palatine, where he erected an expansive residential complex at its south-west corner near the Hut of Romulus. Overlooking the Circus Maximus were *domus* for himself, his wife Livia and Agrippa. While elite *domus* routinely contained a mix of public and private spaces, Augustus' own residence was unique in its public components. It featured a prominent entrance graced by symbols of his office, a pair of Greek and Latin libraries, and a direct connection to the adjacent temple of Apollo Palatinus, dedicated by Augustus in 28 BC. Nearby, Augustus erected a public colonnade, the Portico of Apollo, and renovated the temples of Magna Mater, Victoria and Victoria Virgo. Over the course of his reign, the south-west Palatine became a spectacular assemblage of houses, temples, porticos, libraries and sacred sites worthy of a Hellenistic monarch.

Though largely invisible, Augustus' administrative reforms are just as important as his architectural patronage. In 7 BC, Augustus replaced the existing administrative system with a new organization based on fourteen regions, each subdivided into many *vicus* (neighbourhoods).[6] The Augustan system effectively extended the official definition of the city beyond the *pomerium* and Servian Wall to encompass previously unrecognized areas like the Campus Martius, Trans Tiberim and Emporium. In addition, Augustus introduced curatorial boards staffed with a bureaucracy of experts and funded by the state that were responsible for the upkeep of Rome's essential infrastructure, such as roads, water and sewer systems, public buildings and the Tiber embankments. Augustus also established Rome's first standing fire brigade, the *Cohortes Vigilum* (*c.* AD 6), a corps of 7,000 freedmen based in seven barracks throughout the city.

Just as significant as what Augustus built in Rome was his decision *not* to build a new circuit of defensive walls. By the time of Augustus, the Servian Wall had fallen into disrepair and had lost its functional capacity. Dionysius of Halicarnassus reports that 'the wall is hard to find because of the buildings surrounding it in many places' (4.13.5). Moreover, the city had expanded appreciably in the intervening centuries and now extended far beyond the line of the fourth-century BC wall. Augustus' decision not to commission a new defensive circuit, and the public's acceptance of this choice, is an appreciable measure of his success at instilling peace after decades of military violence, and in fostering the widespread belief that adopting an imperial system would maintain that peace indefinitely. The decision to forego a defensive wall made Rome a highly unusual city in the ancient world, an 'open city' defended by 'the belief that it is not walls that protect men, but men that protect walls' (Strabo 5.3.7).[7]

---

[6] Chapter 10.

[7] The concept of Augustan Rome as an 'open city' originates with Frézouls 1987, and has been taken up by Haselberger 2007 among others.

With the changes introduced by Augustus, Rome had become worthy of her status as an imperial capital. No longer a deficient city that left her residents shamefaced and visiting ambassadors in mocking laughter, Augustan Rome gleamed with new monuments and attractions: the Campus Martius rose up as a new city to rival the old in architectural majesty; three fora set a suitable stage for government business; new aqueducts fed her neighbourhoods with water; her streets were safer from fire and flood; public buildings no longer languished in disrepair but were maintained by dedicated curatorial boards; and, boldly confident in the peace inaugurated by Augustus, Rome stood as an 'open city'. In light of such profound changes, Suetonius' famous assertion that Augustus 'found a city of bricks and left it a city of marble' (*Aug.* 28.3) seems unjust in its understatement.

IMPERIAL ROME

Among the profound shifts the Principate brought to Rome was a new perception of who was responsible for the city and its monuments. In the Republic, commissions were sponsored by the politically ambitious and the burden of upkeep shared by the patrons of major buildings and magistrates with limited capabilities. Now emperors were expected to lavish the city with architectural benefactions as well as see to the proper maintenance of existing monuments and infrastructure. Emperors embraced this task with different levels of ardour. Some, like Augustus and Vespasian, demonstrated a keen awareness of the political and economic advantages of architectural patronage, while others such as Tiberius or the Antonine emperors, to judge from their lacklustre building records in Rome, regarded such munificence as an obligation to be cursorily addressed. Imperial patronage encompassed a range of building types. Some were religious or political in motivation, like temples or fora, while others were geared to please Rome's fickle populace, such as amphitheatres, porticos and other venues for entertainment and leisure pursuits. Large public bath complexes were an especial imperial benefaction, and after Agrippa set the fashion, new *thermae* were erected by Nero, Titus, Trajan, Commodus, Caracalla, Decius, Diocletian and Constantine. Emperors also funded less glamorous projects, such as new aqueducts and harbour works. Though imperial benefactions were clustered in the centre of the city and Campus Martius, by the early fourth century AD imperial monuments could be found throughout the city and accounted for at least a fifth of Rome's area.[8]

Following imperial patronage, the second leading cause of change in Rome's urban topography over the empire was growth. Over three centuries of imperial leadership, Rome became ever larger and denser. While many neighbourhoods retained their republican character – government in the fora, mercantile activities by the Tiber and state religion on the Capitoline – their supporting architectural infrastructure was often enhanced. As the empire grew, Rome required new facilities for an expanding bureaucracy and the many new residents attracted to the capital. Existing neighbourhoods increased in density and a number of new residential areas developed as the city expanded outward. Unchanged, however, was the mixed character of Rome's urban fabric, which blended housing, religious monuments, commercial structures and imperially commissioned public buildings.

During the empire, official business related to governance, legal matters, banking and commerce continued to be transacted in the Forum Romanum and imperial fora, which were augmented by three additional fora (Fig. 8.3). Vespasian built the Templum Pacis (AD 75), which differed notably from the fora erected by Caesar and Augustus. Though the Templum Pacis served – just as earlier fora had – as a venue for personal propaganda, specifically as a reminder of the peace Vespasian had restored to the empire, it did not serve government business. Instead, its porticos displayed art objects and spoils from Vespasian's military campaigns and its rectilinear piazza was filled with orderly rows of greenery and water works – in all, a pleasurable respite from the rigours of Rome's dense urban fabric. Built into one side of the *quadriporticus* was a temple dedicated to Pax (Peace), but its subdued appearance was utterly unlike the visually dominant temples of Venus Genetrix and Mars Ultor. A few decades later, Domitian began the Forum Transitorium (dedicated in AD 97 by his successor Nerva), which was essentially an aggrandized passage for the Argiletum, a major thoroughfare leading from the Quirinal to the Forum Romanum, with an axial temple dedicated to Domitian's patron goddess Minerva at one end. The largest and most luxurious of the imperial fora was the Forum of Trajan, which was designed by Apollodorus (*c.* AD 112) and considered one of Rome's most beautiful buildings for centuries to come (e.g. Amm. Marc. 16.10.15,

---

[8] Given the serious lacunae in our knowledge of the ancient city, the area covered by imperial commissions is best considered an educated estimate rather than a precise figure.

writing *c.* AD 390). Twice as large as the Forum of Augustus, the Forum of Trajan had the familiar open piazza framed by colonnaded porticos but instead of an axial temple it featured the spacious Basilica Ulpia, dual Greek and Latin libraries, and the Column of Trajan, a 128-foot honorific column carved with relief sculpture commemorating Trajan's military victories in Dacia. After Trajan's death in AD 117, his ashes were interred in the base of the column and an axial temple erected to Deified Trajan.[9] The imperial fora were unique to Rome. Other Roman cities might have a forum that emulated the Forum Romanum in its function and architectural components, but only Rome, as the capital of the empire and home of the emperor, had the need and the imperial patrons to support a magisterial complex of six fora. Rome was a world capital, and the emperors ensured it had the physical resources to support that role.

In the Principate, Rome's mercantile facilities such as ports, warehouses and docks continued to be clustered along the Tiber, and the Emporium remained the city's epicentre for trade. Improvements to the harbour at the mouth of the Tiber sponsored by Claudius and Trajan increased the ease of shipping. Though the republican *macellum* near the Forum Romanum was supplanted by the Templum Pacis, two other central markets were built: the Macellum Liviae (early first century AD) on the Esquiline, and Nero's Macellum Magnum on the Caelian (AD 59). Most Romans conducted their daily shopping locally, and at the neighbourhood level commerce was carried out primarily in small *tabernae* (shops or stalls) that lined the streets.

In Rome's residential areas, the elite continued to favour hilltops for their *domus* and proximity to the city centre remained a prized commodity. In the first century AD, the Caelian became popular with Rome's elite and the Aventine emerged as an increasingly fashionable locale. *Horti*, expansive villas with lush gardens, were located at the periphery of the city, and large areas of the Esquiline, Pincian and Trans Tiberim were given over to these exclusive estates. Those at the opposite end of the social spectrum lived in slums like the Subura or in dense housing on the slopes of the Esquiline, Oppian and Viminal. During the Principate, the Trans Tiberim region grew into a vital neighbourhood especially popular with foreign residents and Jews (most of the eleven known synagogues are located in this region). Throughout Rome *insulae*, large multi-storey apartment buildings, sprung up

---

[9] For the ongoing debate concerning the layout and components of the Forum of Trajan, especially the site of the temple to Divine Trajan, see Claridge 2007.

to house the swelling population.[10] Typically built as rental properties by wealthy landlords, *insulae* were especially prevalent in the valleys between hills and in lower-class neighbourhoods like the Trans
Tiberim. Though many *insulae* were certainly well-built, literary tradition holds them to be overcrowded, damp, rickety, structurally suspect
firetraps.

The Palatine remained home to the emperor, whose residence
grew over the centuries to encompass almost the entire hilltop. Eschew-
ing Augustus' *domus* on the south-west Palatine, Tiberius constructed a
new palace, the Domus Tiberiana (after AD 14), overlooking the Forum
Romanum. After AD 80, Domitian added the Domus Augustana to the
southern Palatine. Designed by Rabirius, Domitian's impressive new
residence had suites of monumental public halls, lavish private apartments and spacious gardens. Under the Severan emperors came the last
major expansion of the Domus Augustana, which included the Septi-
zodium (AD 203), a monumental three-storey fountain oriented towards
the Via Appia. The Palatine residence continued in use through the
fourth century with occasional restoration and additions, such as the
appealing bath suite erected by Maxentius (*c.* AD 306–12).

All Roman emperors were expected to bestow architectural largess
upon Rome, but some, distinguished by their extraordinary interest in
architecture, left an indelible mark on the city's urban topography.
Augustus was one such ruler and Nero was another. After a devastating
fire in AD 64 ravaged ten of Rome's fourteen regions, Nero instituted
new building codes intended to limit damage from the frequent fires that
continued to plague the city. He also seized a huge tract of land opened
by the blaze to the east of the Forum Romanum. There, his architects
Severus and Celer built the Domus Aurea, an imperial residence of
unprecedented size and magnificence. The main entry from the Forum
Romanum proceeded along a mile-long colonnade punctuated by the
Colossus of Nero, a 120-foot tall bronze portrait of the emperor (Suetonius *Nero* 31). Much of the usurped land was transformed into a
bucolic country landscape in the heart of the city, while the walls of the
domus itself 'were overlaid with gold and studded with precious stones
and mother of pearl' (Suetonius *Nero* 31). Such excess was despised by
Nero's contemporaries and the enormous size of the Domus Aurea was
an especial affront. Suetonius quotes verses that were written on the
city's walls or spread verbally, saying that: 'Rome has become a house;
citizens, emigrate to Veii! But watch out that the house does not extend

[10] Chapter 9.

146

that far too' (*Nero* 39). Martial's reaction is more succinct: 'one house took up the whole city of Rome' (*Liber de Spectaculis* 2.4).

Such excess could not be left uncorrected, and after assuming power in AD 69 Vespasian moved to rectify the situation. A number of art objects from the Domus Aurea were put on public display in the Templum Pacis, and in the midst of its expansive pastoral landscape he erected the Flavian Amphitheatre, Rome's first permanent venue for gladiatorial combats, animal hunts and the other events comprising *ludi* (games). Better known as the Colosseum (a name deriving from its proximity to Nero's Colossus), the amphitheatre was begun by Vespasian in AD 72 and completed by his son Titus in AD 80. Dedicated concurrently with the Colosseum in AD 80 were the Baths of Titus, a public bath complex erected atop one wing of Nero's Domus Aurea. With the Amphitheatre and Baths, Vespasian and Titus courted popular support: not only did they construct two well-received venues for public entertainment and leisure, but by reversing Nero's excesses and 'returning' a substantial part of the city to its residents, they cemented their reputation as populist emperors.

The reign of Hadrian represents a high point for imperial patronage in Rome, for his long, stable rule and deep personal interest in architecture combined to produce a building programme rivalled by few others. His actions included broad, city-wide initiatives such as restoring the *pomerium*, restructuring the brick industry and personally vetting those who wished to restore a compital shrine. Yet Hadrian is best known for the stunning new monuments he erected. Two religious dedications, the Pantheon and the Temple of Venus and Roma, exemplify the virtuosity that makes Hadrianic architecture so engaging. After Agrippa's Pantheon was damaged by fire in AD 110, Hadrian rebuilt it with significant structural changes. Drawing upon the Roman architects' mastery of arcuated forms, the Pantheon's spectacular concrete dome sheltered an unbroken interior space of stunning expanse.[11] In contrast, Hadrian's Temple of Venus and Roma, the largest temple in Rome, followed Greek precedents and featured a double peristyle of fifty-foot columns (no building in Rome had a larger order), a rectilinear design and walls of hewn stone (*opus quadratum*) built by Greek masons.

[11] Fundamental aspects of the Pantheon have been questioned in recent years. Using brickstamp evidence, Hetland 2007 suggests that Trajan rather than Hadrian began its construction. Davies et al. 1987 question whether the Pantheon's oft-lauded design represents the architect's original intention or results from a compromise occasioned by a lack of suitable building materials.

The architectural zenith achieved in Hadrianic Rome depended upon an ideal set of circumstances: Hadrian's long 21-year reign, the stability of the empire and its full coffers, and the emperor's avowed interest in architectural design (e.g. Dio Cass. 69.4.1–5).

In contrast, imperial patronage reached its nadir during the third century AD. Political, military and economic instability created a 65-year 'crisis' after the reign of Caracalla ended in AD 217. During this period, Rome saw over twenty different emperors, each dealing with urgent military challenges at the empire's borders, steep inflation crippling the economy and constant threats to his tenuous hold on imperial power. In such conditions, it is unsurprising that architectural patronage lagged in Rome. Though some significant commissions are known – for instance, the Temple of Sol Invictus Elagabalus (a Syrian sun god) on the Palatine by Elagabalus in AD 221 or the Aventine Baths of Decius *c.* AD 250 – major imperial building works are rare in the mid-third century AD. The largest public work of the age, the Aurelian Wall (*c.* AD 271), a 19 km defensive circuit, offers a vivid testament to the unstable conditions at Rome. In an age of civil strife and barbarian incursions, Rome could no longer afford to be the 'open city' of Augustus. Moreover, in such tense economic times, Rome could barely afford to build the wall itself, and up to one-sixth of its length comprises reused structures that lay in its path.

Only with the return of strong imperial leadership under the Tetrarchs did Rome witness a brief reversal in the steep decline of its fortunes. After a fire in AD 283 cut a destructive swath through the Forum Romanum and Forum Iulium, Diocletian responded with a programme of restoration and new construction. He repaired the damaged structures and restored functionality to the civic centre of Rome, overhauled the brick industry and together with his co-ruler Maximian embarked upon a steady twenty-year building campaign, which included a magnificent new bath complex on the Quirinal, the Thermae Diocletiani (*c.* AD 305/6). To celebrate their *vicennalia* (twenty-year anniversary of rule), Diocletian and Maximian redefined the physical space of the Forum Romanum with brilliant clarity and economy by installing a series of columnar monuments at its perimeter. Following in their footsteps was Maxentius, who built a series of astounding structures just east of the Forum Romanum: he rebuilt Hadrian's temple of Venus and Roma; erected the Basilica Nova, the largest cross-vaulted space in antiquity; and commissioned a dramatic domed rotunda and audience hall.

Maxentius' commissions proved to be the last major civic buildings erected in Rome. After Constantine vanquished Maxentius in AD 312, he displayed little interest in the city. Constantine seldom visited and built even less: a well-received restoration of the Circus Maximus and a bath complex dismissed as 'not much different from the others' (Aur. Vict. *De Caes.* 40.27) were the only non-religious structures he could call his own.[12] The Arch of Constantine and the rededication of Maxentius' buildings in Constantine's name were acts of the Roman senate and herald a change in patronage in Rome – in the face of imperial lack of interest in the fourth century AD, Rome's senators and high-ranking magistrates, especially the urban prefect, became her leading patrons. Though they were wealthy, their resources could never match those of an emperor, and so their building efforts were often on a reduced scale and, like those of their republican ancestors, reflective of the patron's personal interests.

On 11 May AD 330 Constantine sounded the death knell for Rome as a vital political centre with the dedication of his new imperial capital at Constantinople. Ironically, the path for Rome's salvation came from Constantine as well: his commissions of Christian churches signalled a new direction for Rome as a capital of Christendom. Under Constantine's guidance and patronage, Rome's first monumental Christian church, the Lateran Basilica, was erected on the Caelian as the *cathedra* for the bishop of Rome (*c.* AD 313–24). A few years later, Constantine sponsored a *martyria* church on the site of St Peter's tomb (now the Vatican; consecrated in AD 333). Built and endowed with imperial resources, the size and grandeur of Constantine's churches rivalled any imperial commission in the city. To those expecting traditional imperial architectural largess, Constantine's patronage must have been disorienting, for instead of focusing on the political needs of the capital or the entertainment of its residents, Constantine lavished resources on a religion that, while followed by many, was only decades removed from official imperial proscription. Yet over the coming centuries, as Christianity steadily supplanted traditional Roman beliefs, Constantine's vision of Rome as a Christian capital would prevail and carry the Eternal City through the next 1,600 years.

FURTHER READING

Stambaugh 1988 remains a useful introduction to Rome's changing topography and includes a chronological account of building works

---

[12] For a more traditional account of Constantine as a 'significant' architectural patron in the imperial tradition, see Johnson 2006.

by leading republican citizens and emperors, as well as thematic chapters on urban life. For specific structures, consult their entries in *LTUR*, Richardson 1992, or Haselberger et al. 2008. For an overview of Rome, Claridge 1998 and Coarelli 2007 are useful. On the republican and Augustan city, Favro 1996 is essential; complementary are Favro 1992 on the city's administration and the assessments of Augustan Rome found in Purcell 1996 and Haselberger 2007. For the Forum Romanum, consult Coarelli 1983 and Giuliani and Verduchi 1987. On the imperial fora, see Anderson 1984 and Packer 1997. For Flavian Rome, see Darwall-Smith 1996. Boatwright 1987 offers a comprehensive account of Hadrianic Rome. Curran 2000 has a useful overview of the third and fourth centuries. For Maxentius' patronage in Rome, see Dumser 2005 and Cullhed 1994, esp. 49–60. For Constantine's religious and civic patronage, see Johnson 2006 and Holloway 2004. Brandenburg 2005 details early church building in Rome.

9: HOUSING AND DOMESTIC ARCHITECTURE*

Glenn R. Storey

This chapter is devoted to the housing and domestic architecture of the city of Rome. That means that virtually any structure that was used as living space is relevant. Therefore, we will explore typical architectural configurations of the city of Rome that served as the domestic context for the urban inhabitant.

Discussion (both scholarly and popular) of Roman houses is dominated by attention to elite, aristocratic housing. When people think of a 'Roman house', they automatically think of the houses of Pompeii. Pompeian houses mostly pre-date incorporation into the Roman polity and so, in one sense, Pompeian houses are not Roman houses at all. Nevertheless, the houses of the elites showcased in the Vesuvian cities reasonably continue to be thought of as *the* quintessential houses of Rome because they entered the archaeological record as Roman houses.

Beyond the fancy houses of Pompeii, people may have heard that the Romans had apartment houses and that some of them were tall enough to count as 'skyscrapers', which is an attractive notion to moderns because that allows them to forge a connection to the ancient Romans. So, it is commonly known that the Romans had houses or apartments. The Romans themselves recognized these two basic kinds of houses, the elite aristocratic houses, which they called *domus* ('mansions' or 'town houses'), and apartments for the rest of the urban population, called *insulae* ('residential units'); this distinction almost, but not quite, covers the full variety of residences Romans occupied.[1]

---

* I would like to thank Paul Erdkamp for the invitation to contribute to this volume. I also thank Geoffrey Kron for valuable suggestions and insights. Any errors are my own. All photos in the figures are by the author.

[1] *Domus* in language and in archaeology is not a controversial term. However, the term *insulae* very much is. It seems to indicate an architectural/residential unit (Storey 2001, 2002). Priester 2002, 23–36; 238–77 and Storey 2004 review the various possible archaeological correlates for Roman domestic terms.

The aim of this chapter is to introduce briefly the variability of houses in Rome, not an easy task, given the basic scholarly dilemma, beautifully illustrated by Simon Ellis prefacing the second edition of his *Roman Housing*: 'Among peers who have commented on the publication, some have said that it talks too much about aristocratic housing, whereas others have said it does not say enough. It is thus appropriate that the text remains unchanged.'[2] This chapter, indebted to Ellis's tome, sympathizes. No matter; we can review and appreciate the breadth of contexts that Romans called 'house and home'. And, to appreciate the evidence and its variety properly, a close combining of documentary and archaeological evidence in the discussion is required.

Lastly, Rome, as a socially stratified hierarchical imperial society, does prove the archaeological truism that the character of housing reflects the social structure in place, meaning that the bigger the house, the higher the social status. The Egyptian word for their monarch, *per-ah-ah* (coming down to us as 'Pharaoh' through Greek), literally means 'Big House', an unmistakably clear marker that the person with the biggest house is king. So it was with Rome. The English 'palace' comes from the name of the hill in Rome, the Palatine, which Augustus established as the residence of the imperial family. That complex is certainly the largest residential structure in Rome. Because it is well documented elsewhere, we will say little of it here. We will instead concentrate on the three main categories of houses that were typical in Rome: shops, apartments and elite houses.[3]

DOCUMENTARY EVIDENCE: RESIDENTIAL TERMINOLOGY

Let us begin with a brief review of some terms. The words *house, home, abode, domicile, residence*, etc. all refer to the living space occupied by one or more persons. Of course, an important component of this definition is the human group of people who do the occupying. In most languages, including Latin and English, the words for this residential unit are ambiguous as to whether referring to the architectural structure for the residence, or the more abstract notion of the residential group as a unit. The *Oxford English Dictionary* (online) defines the word *house*:

[2] Ellis 2000, viii.
[3] A recent publication on the Palatine, with references, is Cecamore 2002. Ellis 2000, 80 concurs with this typology of shops, apartments and aristocratic houses.

'I.1 A building for human habitation; *esp.* a building that is the ordinary dwelling-place of a family . . . b. The portion of a building, consisting of one or more rooms, occupied by one tenant or family . . . '

Thus the term 'house' covers the basic notion of the architectural/ residential unit, the physical place that is occupied by a human group, whether one separate building, or only a portion of another. In the nineteenth-century censuses of the United Kingdom, this distinction caused the census-takers some grief in recognizing a unit that should be counted as a 'house'. Similar ambiguity confronted the Romans because many of the Latin passages from antiquity referring to residences and domestic architecture are unclear about the character of the configuration described. Moreover, the terms could be used in different ways in different periods and contexts. But for Romans it was basically the same: houses could be either a separate building standing alone, or a portion of one separable from other residences within the same building.[4]

The most common Roman terms for residence are *domus, domicilium, sedes, habitatio*. English derivates for some of these are easily recognized. Latin is also ambiguous whether the physical structure or the abstraction of the cohabiting group is meant. But what was the inhabiting unit? Despite recent questioning, the consensus remains that the Roman household was basically a nuclear family. Differences between 'households' (basically the kin of a family unit) and 'housefuls' (the kin of a family plus servants, tutors and lodgers) have been posited. The evidence still strongly suggests nuclear family habitation in most Roman houses, especially those of common Romans, who might also have a lodger or a slave or two. Roman household sizes probably consisted of around five persons, two adult spouses and children, or children and a slave.[5]

SHOP-HOUSES

As with any other big city, Rome had a population of transients. References to them are sparse but unmistakable: a rent dodger with his family and possessions appears in Martial *Epigrams* 12.32.1–25 as someone who will end up under the bridge or on the slopes of hills with other beggars or in a 'shuttered up archway' (cf. *Epigr.* 10.5.4–7). Aside

---

[4] Storey 2002, 431, and n. 87 for the UK census. For terms used differentially depending on period and context, Storey 2004, 79–81.

[5] The 'households' versus 'housefuls' distinction is emphasized by Wallace-Hadrill 1994. Cf. Chapter 6.

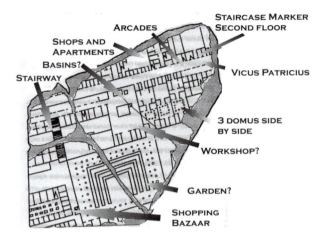

FIGURE 9.1 Fragment 11 of the Marble Plan of Rome, showing the Vicus Patricius running along the top with buildings on both sides fronted by shops.

from those minimalist 'houses', the smallest Roman residence with sufficient frequency to count as typical is the shop; in Latin, *taberna* (origin of English 'tavern'). A *taberna* was the most common house in Rome.

Possibly an Etruscan word, *taberna* originally meant a simple shelter such as a 'tent', 'shack' or 'hut'. Later, the term meant habitation in general, developing the specialized meaning of 'shop' ('hut for business', Isidorus of Seville, *Etymologiae* 15.2.43; cf. Horace, *Carmina* 1.4.13–14, where the houses of the poor are *tabernae*). The interchangeability of meanings was not unnatural, given that craftspeople manufactured and sold their wares in their shops, living in or above those shops. *Taberna* implies both a place of business and a residence (most Roman houses were both), best translated as 'shop-house' (Ulpian, *Digesta* 50.16.183 and 50.16.185). Shops were ubiquitous in Rome, Pompeii, Herculaneum and Ostia, where four basic types are recognized: (1) shop alone, (2) shop with backroom; (3) shop with mezzanine apartment; and (4) shop with both backroom and mezzanine apartment. These four types cover the vast majority of possibilities.

Figure 9.1 shows a typical configuration mapped on Fragment 11 of the Marble Plan of Rome. The Marble Plan of Rome, known as the *Forma Urbis Romae* (*FUR*), was made during the reign of Septimius Severus between AD 203 and 207. Given the dearth of excavated examples of common houses in Rome, the *FUR* is the best evidence we have for the ordinary, typical residential districts of imperial Rome, and its accuracy is attested chiefly by its resemblance to the actual cityscapes of Pompeii and Ostia, especially the latter. The four basic types of shops listed for Ostia hardly do justice to the sheer variety of shop combinations found on the *FUR*, where sixteen different configurations with almost 100 examples can be found. Shops were adjacent to private houses, in single rows, back-to-back, in every possible combination around courtyards, with and without colonnades, arcades and porticos, backing onto corridors and alleys, with and without backroom, with olive or wine presses with basins; there are even shops with their own pavements in front of them, and shops arranged as purely shopping bazaars. Finally, the shops around important public monuments such as the Circus Maximus or the Temple of Peace (where the *FUR* was displayed) attest to state interest in revenue from these properties.[6] Figure 9.2 shows still-standing examples.

APARTMENT HOUSES

The true poverty of ancient Rome is defined by life in the tiniest, most cramped upper-floor apartments in apartment houses. Two passages of Livy have been used to suggest that multiple-floor apartment buildings were known as early as the late third century BC. Livy (21.62.3, 218 BC) states that an ox had climbed to the third floor (*tertiam contignationem*) of a house, and he reports (36.37.2, 191 BC) that two bulls reached the top of a building (*in tegulas*). Both of these reports could be anachronistic, that is, Livy was transposing the character of buildings in his own time to the earlier situation. Another passage, dating to 200 BC, Plautus' *Amphitruo* (863–4) has Jupiter say: 'I live in an upstairs apartment [*cenaculo*] . . .' Varro (*De lingua Latina* 5.162) discussed residential apartments (*cenacula*) in upper floors in the first century BC; the term had evolved from being a second-floor dining room to mean any upper-floor apartment.

Given this evidence, the height of these apartment buildings has long been an issue. A quick search of internet sites devoted to

---

[6] Cf. Ellis 2000, 78 and 188. Girri 1954 assigned the four types to Ostia and others have applied it to Rome as well, e.g. Packer 1971, 6 and n. 7. Reynolds 1996 is a thorough analytic review of the *FUR* with references. Stanford University's Digital *Forma Urbis Romae* Project (Koller et al. 2006) is a major internet-based research project devoted to the *FUR*. The various shop configurations are illustrated in Reynolds 1996, 358–86, figures, with appropriate comparisons from Pompeii and Ostia.

discussions of Roman houses turns up statements that apartment houses had anywhere from three to twelve floors, with heights of eight, nine, ten and eleven being mentioned, without references. A popular view of buildings with dizzying heights is clearly entrenched. The scholarly view has generally allowed these numbers.[7]

We must, however, distinguish the typical from the exceptional. The staircase evidence of the *FUR* data seems to indicate the number of floors in a structure, strongly suggesting that the vast majority of structures had only two floors (an example is shown in Figure 9.1, upper right, marked). Although some tall residential buildings in Rome were indeed present, only 13 per cent of all buildings had five or more floors, with the Insula of Felicles (Tertullian, *Adversus Valentinianos* 7: 1–3) probably serving as the tallest for its time, topping out at eight floors. Thus, such buildings were not typical. Imperial legislation limiting the heights of buildings was directed at this small subset of tall buildings. Most buildings in Rome (and Ostia) were on the order of one, two or three floors. Four and five floor buildings were common enough but not dominant.[8]

One argument favouring such tall buildings is that there were many comparable later multiple-floor residential structures, largely built of wood and brick. Although evidence for European residential structures of multiple stories, from the sixteenth century on, seems strong, there is no logically compelling argument that, if later multi-floor structures were commonly five-plus floors, the ancient Roman structures must also have commonly been five-plus. But, because there are reports that Glasgow and Edinburgh had apartment houses from seven to thirteen floors, it seemed reasonable to investigate these possibilities further. Data from three sources were compiled with fifty examples of apartment houses from Europe 1844–1973 in drawings or photos: 70 per cent had one to four floors, 26 per cent had five and six; the 4 per cent that were above were recent (since 1950). The *FUR* data suggest 82.9 per cent one to three floors, 15.7 per cent four to six, and 1.4 per cent six to eight floors. These results suggest similar distributions, but

---

[7] Storey 2003 attempts to reconcile a sceptical view of the evidence for tall buildings in Rome with the frequent reports about them, using the important study of Pedroni 1992. The majority scholarly view is reflected by Claridge 1998, 56 stating that 'Insulas twelve storeys high are mentioned in Rome in C1 [first century] BC', but no reference is given.

[8] The evidence on tall buildings in Rome is analysed fully by Priester 2002. Although agreeing with the standard view he also states that we don't really know what was typical (Priester 2002, 141–2).

also that neither in Rome, nor elsewhere in Europe before 1950, were apartments typically higher than five floors.[9]

Another popular argument in favour of restoring many upper floors to Roman buildings is that the thickness of ground-floor walls could be used to extrapolate for the number of floors. That assumption can no longer be maintained. The reason is quite simple. Roman engineers had no way to test their concrete and so they generally built thicker matrices than was strictly necessary, using too much wood. Various scholars have suggested a rule of thumb for wall thickness and height of building. One recent version suggested that a 50 cm wall could support two floors, 60–65 cm three, 80 cm four, 90 cm five, and 1 m to support six floors. This idea was tested using 1,273 wall thickness measurements from 308 buildings in Rome, Pompeii, Herculaneum and Ostia, using two statistical procedures, linear regression and discriminant analysis. The result was that neither statistical procedure had much predictive value. This is best illustrated by the fact that there is barely half a centimetre's difference in Pompeii between one and two-floor structures; for Ostia, only a couple of centimetres' difference in ground floor wall thickness distinguishes two- from four-floor structures.

For Ostia, Meiggs believed that a 59 cm wall was sufficient to bear five floors but that 'provides no evidence for their existence, for the Romans notoriously often built more stoutly than was necessary'.[10] Ulrich demonstrated that Campanian builders probably used more wood in their joists than was strictly necessary, while Ostian builders used less wood, depending more on brick projections on which to support the floor, spanning smaller intervals. In both cases he suggested that the builders 'knew little enough about the engineering principles that could have resulted in a safe floor carried by a lesser number of structural timbers'.[11]

Nevertheless, Ostian buildings dating from the second century AD are built of concrete with brick facing. The use of concrete in

---

[9] Storey 2003, 12, and n. 39 discusses examples of documentary reports unconfirmed by contemporary prints of city skylines. For Glasgow, Smith 1974, 212 states that stone buildings were often seven and eight storeys with some reaching thirteen, but provides nothing other than documentary evidence for it. The *FUR* data are compiled in Storey 2003, 26, table 4.

[10] Meiggs 1973, 241.

[11] Ulrich 1996, 151. Stevens 2005, 113, 122 n. 9 credits F. Sear with rules of thumb which she rightly characterizes as 'a bit random and not substantiated by archaeological data'. Hermansen 1982, 51, n. 27 promulgates the rules given. Storey 2003, 13–16, 25–6 provides the details of the test study.

these upper floors would have drastically increased the weight. The increased load-bearing requirements placed on the structure overall would have been extremely stressful for the foundation and load-bearing walls. And, without reinforced concrete, the weights of the floors in the buildings were extremely limiting, making it likely that most of the concrete residential structures of Ostia were two, at most three, floors.

There has been some suggestion that reinforcing iron bars were used by the Romans in concrete. Although some very limited use of iron bars may be attested, it is clear that no such material is commonly found in the residential structures. Ulrich demonstrated that the joisting for the floors in upper stories was with wood. Carbonized wood is found in Herculaneum; in Pompeii and Ostia, wood impressions are common in the holes for joists. Iron bars oxidize and could have completely rusted away since Roman times. However, a tell-tale trace of iron oxide rust trails would be common in the walls of Roman structures, if reinforcing via iron bars had been common. There are some such traces scattered around the Vesuvian cities and Ostia, but they seem part of modern stabilizing efforts. Although Ulrich felt that Ostia's concrete upper floors were relatively strong, the totality of their weight in large blocks would have been substantial.[12]

A good example of the massiveness of these structures is the complex covering Region 3 Block 10 at Ostia, including the Caseggiato degli Aurighi (3.10.1), Baths of the Seven Sages (3.10.2), the Caseggiato della Serapide (3.10.3) and the apartment house of 3.10.4 (Fig. 9.3). This massive concrete complex raises the question as to how many upper floors could run the entire extent of the structure. Possibly there were only three floors, with a staircase in 3.10.3 going to the roof. We could test fragments of the remaining concrete mass and see if the materials analysis would give some idea as to its load-bearing capability. Such concrete tensile strength analysis is expensive and would need to be done in numerous places in the structure to give a reasonably definitive answer. Figure 9.3 shows the massive matrix of this structure and a large collapsed concrete mass (upper right) that could provide a sample for testing. It is a pity that the excavation of Ostia was deficient in modern archaeological technique, because proper mapping of the collapsed rubble around the structure would have given a good idea of the amount of material that had fallen from the structure, thus

---

[12] The suggestion of iron bars is from Kron (personal communication, 2009) and Oleson 2008, 269–73. Ulrich 1996, 140–1, 147 deals with the wood joist traces.

FIGURE 9.2 Two shop-fronts from the third century AD, partially walled up, opposite the Church of SS. Giovanni e Paolo on the Caelian Hill.

allowing a reasonably accurate reconstruction of the whole. Whenever the unexcavated portions of Ostia are excavated, the clearing of the apartment houses will allow mapping and measurement of the collapsed rubble. That would help answer the question.[13]

However many floors there were, the upper floor apartments may not have been pleasant living. Martial's *Epigrams* (2.53; 3.30.3–4; 8.14.5–6) refer to an apartment as a *cella*, possibly a one-room apartment. Today, such a unit would be called an 'efficiency', but that would do violence to the term because such Roman rooms were virtually without services, and the walk-up was taxing. In *Epigrams* 11.32 and 11.56.3–8, Martial described the minimum amenities for these garrets: a hearth, a bed infested with lice, a mat patched with absorbent reeds, a slave, a bolt, a key, a dog, a cup, and a water pot with a broken handle. Martial (*Epigr.* 1.86) demonstrates, with 'Novius is my neighbour, and we can shake hands from the windows', the relative lack of privacy in an apartment as opposed to a private house, a situation that was probably as true then as today. But here, in the suggested close-packing of the buildings, tenants could shake hands from adjoining rooms, or buildings – or perhaps even across the street. Passages from the jurists

---

[13] Packer 1971, 182, 185 judged the 3.10 complex to be 4 Serapide and 5 floors Aurighi.

FIGURE 9.3 Block 3.10 at Ostia. Upper left, the ruins of the *Aurighi* complex; upper right, massive concrete matrix; lower left, second-floor wall remains; lower right, thick concrete second-floor remnant.

suggest that a *cenaculum* had a number of rooms, some even sharing rooms between two floors, a situation known in Ostia, and probably true for Rome as well. The owner of the ground floor dwelling might or might not own the upstairs apartments, and it was also quite normal for upper apartments to have stairs opening directly onto the street (Ulpian, *Digesta* 43.17.3.7) and in the Ostian examples. These sources suggest a complex situation. Conjoined structures with different functions could sometimes be treated as separate units or as one unit, both physically and in legal terms.[14]

Martial (*Epigr.* 2.53) described a ceiling as so low that one had to stoop to enter it, and one archaeological example suffices to bear him out. These structures probably resembled tiered 'wedding cakes', as illustrated in Figure 9.4 which shows Gismondi's reconstruction of the Ara Coeli Insula, the only reasonably full ruin of a large multiple-storey

---

[14] Stevens 2005, cf. Reynolds 1996, 375, 377, figs. 3.24 and 3.26.

FIGURE 9.4 Roman apartment buildings. Left, the Ara Coeli Insula on the west slope of the Capitoline Hill, the modern ground level being at the third floor of the ancient. Upper right, Gismondi's reconstruction of the Ara Coeli Insula in the Museum of Roman Civilization, Rome. Lower right, floor plans and cross-section of that structure (north is to the left).

apartment still extant in Rome, abutting the Capitoline Hill. Each upper floor was slightly shorter and covered a smaller area. Martial's inhabitants clearly dwelt in these poorer, smaller fourth and fifth floor units. The situation was probably fluid, as it is today in modern cities. Cicero, *Epistulae ad Atticum* 16.32.2 and 14.9.1, as well as the jurists Paul, *Digesta* 19.2.56, Alfenus, *Dig.* 19.2.27, and Labeo, *Dig.* 19.2.60 all show the tug-of-war between tenants and landlords and imply that rent-dodging was common. Tenants with unstable sources of income probably inhabited various apartments, always keeping one step ahead of the *insularius* (apartment landlord or manager) at rent-collection time, 1 July of every year (Petronius, *Satyricon* 95.1.8; *CIL* 6.6299 and 9383; Pomponius, *Dig.* 7.8.16.1 and 50.16.166, preamble).

Apartment buildings in Ostia have been arranged into three basic types: (1) the buildings accommodating the shop unit; (2) buildings with ground floor apartments as the characteristic unit; and (3) buildings with large workshop rooms on the ground floor. All three of these types were frequently arranged around a courtyard (Fig. 9.5 shows how both *domus* and *insula* ideally could be incorporated into a courtyard), which is an architectural element that was greatly favoured in all types of Roman housing, as was the inclusion of some kind of reception room. Ellis discusses the importance of courtyards and reception rooms in the evolution of the Roman house, and how even middling and poor Romans aspired to both. So, courtyards are a common feature, whether for private enjoyment in *domus* or as shared space in the *insulae*. Eight examples of irregularly arranged houses with courtyards are found on the *FUR*. Ostia is typified by what is usually called the *cenaculum* or *medianum* type of apartment arrangement. The former designation indicates multiple rooms; the latter indicates a hallway fronting these rooms, which served as the reception room to the house. At Rome, this type of complex is rare, but known. In both cities, irregular configurations of flats/houses are reasonably common, which creates a blurred distinction between *insulae* and *domus*.[15]

ELITE HOUSES

We now turn to the most well-known examples of Roman houses – the houses of the elite aristocrats. The focus here will be on the urban house characteristic of the city of Rome, not on the well-known *villae* and *domus* of Pompeii and Herculaneum. The elite houses in the city, the *domus*, have a layout including courtyards and receptions rooms, patterned after the rural estate of the Romans, the *villa*. *Domus* can be thought of as urban *villae*. These houses are usually called 'atrium-peristyle' houses because they have both of these architectural features – basically forms of open courtyards – the first being an Italian feature, the latter an import from the Greek east. These were clearly the most ubiquitous form of elite housing in Rome.

Ellis traces the evolution of the atrium-peristyle house demonstrating how the atrium became less important than the peristyle as time passed in the imperial period. What does not change is the necessity of having some form of courtyard as an integral feature of the elite house

[15] Floor plans in Figure 9.4 are after Priester 2002, 47–114. The Ostian typology is Packers's (1971, 6–15). Ellis 2000, 73–85 concurs in general. Reynolds 1996, 375–7, figs. 3.24 and 3.26 shows the basic relevant apartment configurations for both Ostia and Rome although he calls the Roman version of the *medianum* apartment, a 'corridor flat'. Ellis on courtyards and reception rooms is 2000, 182–3 and irregular flats/houses 2000, 80–5. The eight examples are given by Reynolds 1996, 374, 378, figs. 3.23 and 3.27.

throughout the long trajectory of those houses. He also reiterates the necessity of a reception room, which basically evolved from the atrium to the dining room (*triclinium*) to courtyards that become audience halls in Late Antiquity (some with apses that were also becoming the defining feature of Christian churches), when elite houses became grander and more exclusive. These Roman houses, throughout their history, in their unifying elements of peristyle, *triclinium*, and elaborate and expensive decoration, are a form of 'blatant self-promotion' for elites.[16]

There is, however, a paradox about these kinds of houses in Rome. *Domus* in Rome are probably both much larger (the biggest houses of the wealthiest of the elites) and at the same time significantly smaller than their counterparts in the Vesuvian cities (that is, a large number of typical *domus* were comparatively small). There are few remains of *domus* in the city of Rome, despite much documentary reference to *domus*. Examples from which size could be determined in two separate sources (only about twenty) suggest a mean size in Rome of from 1,000 m² or as much as 2,700 m² depending on how they are grouped and averaged (whether the best archaeological examples of individual houses that are part of the Palatine complex are included), with the best measure of central tendency falling between 1,300 and 1,500 m². Thus, the typical size of *domus* is about twice that of houses in Pompeii and Herculaneum, where the largest houses averaged about 700 sq m. Naturally, one would expect *domus* in Rome to be bigger because that is where the greatest concentration of wealth in the empire was located. Figure 9.6 is the plan of an average *domus* of the High Empire; Figure 9.7 is a very modest medieval house type that might have originated in the ancient city.[17]

The paradox is that many *domus* in Rome are likely to have been smaller than their counterparts elsewhere. The reason is the topography. Both Ostia and Pompeii sat on rivers at the edge of the sea. Rome sits amidst numerous hills which define the urban landscape. Atrium-peristyle houses could not easily fit into the spaces and on the slopes, so were made smaller. The evidence for this is suggested by the *FUR*, which shows *domus* more unobtrusively than in the Vesuvian cities

---

[16] Evolution of the atrium-peristyle house, Ellis 2000, 182–3; quote 2000, 190. Works devoted to promotional use of house architecture: Wallace-Hadrill 1994; Hales 2003.

[17] Usable examples are from *LTUR* 2.391–426, figs. 7–67 and Haselberger et al. 2008, 104–17, and fold-out maps. Wallace-Hadrill 1994 used a sample of over 600 houses from Pompeii and Herculaneum arranged in Type 1 smallest to Type 4 largest, with 700 sq m being the mean for Type 4. Figure 9.6 is adapted from *LTUR* 2.410, fig. 37.

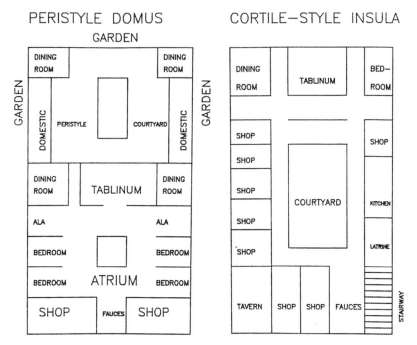

FIGURE 9.5 Idealized *domus* and *insula* plans centred on a courtyard.

(which were partly resorts). Certainly the overall number of *domus* in Rome outstrips the Campanian towns and Ostia. Evidence from the fourth-century *Regionaries* suggests there were 1,800 *domus* to 46,000 *insulae*, probably apartments although there is controversy whether units or structures are meant. It probably meant apartment houses, in the sense with which we began: an architectural/residential unit that is a home, but not the whole building of multiple residences. Twenty-five times the number of apartments to houses seems a reasonable ratio because if the 46,000 statistic were buildings with numerous apartments in them, the number of apartments would have so overwhelmed the number of *domus* that elite housing would have appeared negligible, which it certainly wasn't in the ancient city.[18]

---

[18] Reynolds shows only four examples of *domus* on the *FUR*, in contrast to many *tabernae* (Reynolds 1996, 145, 382, fig. 3.31). They appear smaller than the Bay of Naples comparanda. Storey 2002 reviews and analyses the *Regionaries* data, concluding that the term *insulae* there must refer to individual architectural/residential units, not separate structures.

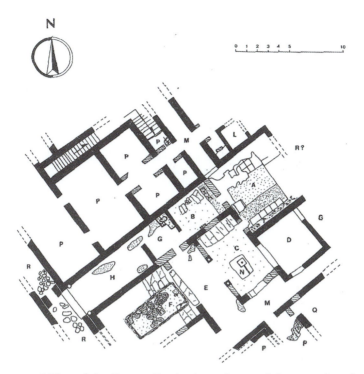

FIGURE 9.6 Plan of the Domus Gaudentius, a house of the second to fourth centuries AD on the Caelian Hill, of middling size for Rome, juxtaposed to shops and apartments.

THE CITYSCAPE OF HOUSES

We thus have reviewed the three main types of housing in the city of Rome: the shop-houses, the apartments and the elite houses. We have explored how all three types show several varieties in Rome. How were these houses distributed across the cityscape? Many documentary sources and the *FUR* show that the character of that cityscape could be quite varied, it being common for a mixture of domestic or commercial functional elements (*CIL* 4.138 from Pompeii mentions mezzanine apartments, luxury apartments and *domus*), or a private house (*domus*), shops (*tabernae*), workshops, to be conjoined in the same fabric – there was virtually no zoning. The kinds of structures reviewed here occurred in close proximity and were often built as one complex or were added onto an existing complex over time. Gardens (which were a favoured addition to many a Roman house, see Fig. 9.5, top left), the

FIGURE 9.7 A thirteenth-century house in Rome on the Campus Martius. Such a house might well have evolved from the shop and mezzanine apartment configuration or the small atrium-peristyle houses seen on the *FUR*.

houses, storerooms (an important adjunct to houses), shops and apartments were located in close proximity within the ancient city (e.g. Scaevola, *Dig.* 8.2.41, discusses testamentary arrangements for a complex with a *domus*, storeroom, garden and apartment). Rome was not an unbroken mass of dwellings, although clearly more thickly built-up than the countryside, hence the term *continentia tecta* ('contiguous' (or 'continuous') 'roofed-over structures') described in the jurists (Marcellus,

Dig. 50.16.87; Paul, *Dig.* 50.16.2; Macer, *Dig.* 50.16.154; Ulpian, *Dig.* 50.16.139).

Referring back to Figure 9.1, the *FUR* fragment is the best representative of the houses of Rome. It shows arcades, shops, apartment houses, a shopping bazaar, as marked. In the centre along the street are a row of similar structures, the centre example being possibly a school or workshop (it has basins, but a distinctly *domus*-like plan); to the right are three atrium-peristyle *domus* (though small and could have evolved into the medieval house of Fig. 9.7); the large rectangular feature at the bottom is a possible pleasure garden at the top of the long flight of stairs with a putative decorative hydraulic ornament. This figure shows the houses of Rome and is as good evidence as any of the 'warren of anonymous domestic and commercial architecture that filled the city'.[19]

FURTHER READING

The three leading sources for the question of Roman housing are McKay 1975 [1998], Barton 1996 and Ellis 2000; the latter is most up to date, but all three are eminently readable. Works on the Roman villa are numerous; the most recent summary is that of Smith 1997. Some differences in elite houses between central Italy and northern Italy and the provinces are set out by George 1997. Priester 2002 offers the best archaeological account of the scant information on the apartment houses of Rome, with references and especially good illustrations. The critical importance of archaeological artefact assemblages for the proper study of houses could not be fully addressed here, but is best illustrated by Allison's 2004 study on the household artefacts of Pompeii. Briefly, Ellis 2000 thinks that the architectural implications of room function are far more important than the artefact assemblage information. Allison's careful reconstructing of the poorly documented artefactual data of Pompeii suggests great multi-functionality of room use as opposed to the architecture. Clearly, architecture, decoration and artefacts – together – provide the evidence about room use we require. New Testament scholars have produced some good summaries on

---

[19] Figure 9.1 adapted from and discussed by Rodriguez-Almeida 1981, 86–92, fig. 21, p. 89, and pl. 10. Reynolds 1996, 386, fig. 3.35 suggests that the presence of the basins as marked indicates a workshop, possibly with an olive or wine press. The shape of the building certainly suggests a converted atrium-peristyle house, just like its neighbours. The quote is from Reynolds 1996, 304, caption to fig. 2.9.

lower-class housing in Rome, focused on St Paul's sojourn in Rome, and how houses came to be used as churches. Osiek and Balch 1997 is a good example of this context. How houses shaped Roman identity, especially of elites, is discussed by Wallace-Hadrill 1994 and Hales 2003. The Roman house at the end of the empire is explored by Ellis 1988, and there are several good articles on the housing of the later Roman empire in the *Late Antique Archaeology* series published by Brill (Leiden). Dyson 2009 provides extensive commentary on issues of residence in Rome.

10: REGIONS AND NEIGHBOURHOODS

J. Bert Lott

The urban community is neither an undifferentiated mass nor a haphazard collage of buildings and people.[1]

Modern cities are not undifferentiated wholes but rather are regularly subdivided into smaller, often overlapping, units by topography, by the built fabric of the city, by the inhabitants for social reasons, and by the civic government for administration. This web of sub-configurations is familiar to the inhabitants of modern cities. We would recognize that similar kinds of businesses sometimes cluster in the same location, that people often choose their residential location based on attributes such as class, ethnicity and religion, and that government creates school districts, police precincts, fire districts and historical zones. Where we can study it – particularly at Pompeii – the urban fabric of ancient Italian cities was not as heavily differentiated according to class, ethnicity, family or occupation as modern cities. Rome, however, was more differentiated than most because of its size, the more diverse population drawn (by choice and not) to the imperial capital and a traditional view of the city as a conglomeration of multiple settlements and people. Certain kinds of speciality businesses clustered together, e.g. booksellers around the Fora and goldsmiths on the Sacra Via, and businessmen joined together with their neighbours to form clubs to pursue common religious or mercantile interests. The homes of aspiring politicians clustered on the Palatine in the late Republic, and the hill became a virtual compound for the imperial family thereafter. In the second century BC an enclave of Africans gave their name to a neighbourhood, the Vicus Africus, and in the empire Sulpicii, freedmen of the Sulpicii Galbae and their descendants, are regularly found living on the south-west slope of the Aventine where they had spent their servitude working in the warehouses and granaries of the noble family.

[1] Timms 1971, 1.

Some zones of the imperial city, like the Campus Martius, were given over almost entirely to public works and public spaces, and certain areas, such as the unsafe and unsavoury Subura described by Juvenal (3.8–9), took on particular personalities that set them apart in reputation and, evidently, in geography as well.

In 7 BC, on the cusp between republic and empire, the first Roman emperor, Caesar Augustus, created a new comprehensive scheme for organizing the space of Rome, restructuring the city into fourteen regions and numerous neighbourhoods (*spatium urbis in regiones vicosque divisit*). These divisions were based at least to some degree on existing patterns that dated back to the third century BC and they persisted until the sixth century AD. The vast amount of information needed to execute such a change had been collected the year before, in 8 BC, as part of a *lustrum* and census of the city. The new divisions were important both to the administration of the city throughout the empire and to the creation of a way for successful freedmen, locked out of most avenues for social advancement, to participate in urban culture in a non-disruptive fashion.

Two ancient authors inform us of the changes. First the imperial biographer Suetonius includes them in a list of other improvements to the urban infrastructure accomplished by Augustus.

> He [Augustus] divided the area of the city into regions (*regiones*) and neighbourhoods (*vici*) and enacted that magistrates allotted annually should look after the former and that officers (*magistri*) chosen from the people of each neighbourhood should look after the latter.
>
> (*Augustus* 30.2)

Second, as part of his discussion of a fire that was intentionally set by property owners around the Forum, the historian Cassius Dio says:

> These men [the arsonists] gained nothing; but the neighbourhoods (*stenōpoi*) were then put in charge of officers whom we call *magistri vici* (*stenōparchoi*) chosen from the people. These men were allowed to use the *toga praetexta* and two lictors, but only in the areas under their administration and on certain days, and they were given control over the force of slaves that had previously been associated with the aediles to save buildings that caught fire. The aediles, however, together with the tribunes and

praetors, were still assigned by lot to have charge of the whole city, which was divided into fourteen regions. This is also the present arrangement.

(55.8.6)

Fire, flood and plague were recurring nightmares in ancient cities. However, even if fire (and fraud) provided the immediate impetus for Augustus' reorganization, the reforms were consistent with two important characteristics of the Principate.[2] First, Augustus began a trend towards regularization and professionalization in all areas of administration. In addition to the system of neighbourhoods and regions, Augustus created the *vigiles* who fought fires, the urban cohorts who policed the city, and boards of *curatores* who looked after the water supply, the food supply, the roads to and from the city, the maintenance of buildings and the control of floods. In particular, the urban prefect (*praefectus urbi*), who had served a largely symbolic role in the Republic as the consuls' deputy, came by the height of the empire to oversee in the emperor's name almost all aspects of the city's administration and government including the regions and neighbourhoods. Second, Augustus actively worked to align every level of society and every place in the city with him and his new dynasty, the Domus Augusta. The reorganization of the neighbourhoods in particular provided the means by which a formerly disruptive and uncontrolled element of the urban plebs was co-opted into the new order.

REGIONS

Romans from Augustus' day believed that their city had been divided into regions and neighbourhoods from time immemorial. The Greek immigrant Dionysius of Halicarnassus, who wrote during the reign of the first emperor, tells us that King Servius Tullius created the system in the regal period:

> After Tullius had surrounded the seven hills with one wall,
> he divided the city into four regions, which he named after
> the hills, calling the first the Palatine, the second the
> Suburan, the third the Colline, and the fourth the
> Esquiline region; and by this means he made the city
> contain four tribes, whereas it previously had consisted of

[2] See Chapter 23.

but three. . . . And over each region he appointed
commanders, like heads of tribes or villages, whom he
ordered to know what house each man lived in. After this
he commanded that there should be erected in every street
by the inhabitants of the neighbourhood chapels to heroes
whose statues stood in front of the houses, and he made a
law that sacrifices should be performed to them every year,
each family contributing a honey-cake.

(Dionysius of Halicarnassus 4.14.3)

Dionysius' account of the origins of Rome's regions and neighbourhoods is certainly anachronistic to some degree. Augustus took great
pains to locate antique precedents for what was, in fact, a complete
reimagining of the Roman city and state; and he was not above wholesale fabrication (e.g. Livy 4.20.7; Cassius Dio 51.24.4). The syncretism
of the four urban tribes, Collina, Palatina, Suburana and Esquiliae,
which were not regionally based in the historical period, with the supposed Servian regions is very problematic – not least because the four
regions so defined would not have covered the entire city space, which
would seem to be required if regions were to serve as the administrative
units of the city. The reality of a republican 'city of four regions' has
therefore been called in question.[3] But it is unlikely that Dionysius could
have posited the regal origins of such a system if there were no practices within current memory that could be interpreted as the vestiges
of the system. We should not therefore cavalierly dismiss the existence
of regions in republican Rome just because Dionysius' account of their
origin is suspect.

Indeed, there is good reason to believe that a quadripartite division
of the urban space for administrative purposes – though not necessarily
for the political purposes espoused by Dionysius – existed perhaps as
early as 367 BC when the total number of aediles, the magistrates who
had charge of maintaining the urban space, was increased to four. The
four republican aediles regulated the city's markets, produced a number
of important sacred entertainments and exercised a general supervision
of the city (*cura urbis*). The last included maintenance of public streets,
public spaces, and public order, the delivery of water to public fountains
and basins, and oversight of some aspects of the city's food supply. Indeed
the so-called *lex Iulia municipalis* requires the four aediles to decide which
part of the city (*pars urbis*) each will take charge of within five days of

---

[3] Fraschetti 1990, 190–200.

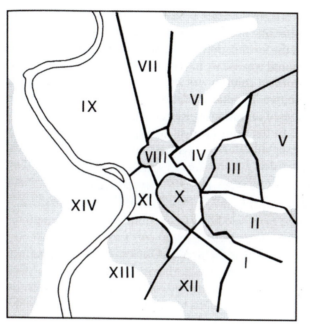

Key
I   Porta Capena
II   Caelimontium
III Isis et Serapis
IV   Templum Pacis
V   Esquiliae
VI   Alta Semita
VII Via Lata
VIII Forum Romanum
IX   Circus Flaminius
X   Palatium
XI   Circus Maximus
XII Piscina Publica
XIII Aventinus
XIV Transtiberim

MAP 10.1 The fourteen Augustan regions

entering office (*FIRA* 1.13 = ILS 6085).[4] It is unlikely that the aediles
redrew the boundaries for the four *partes* each year, so a *de facto* system
like the regionary system instituted by Augustus must have existed.

In 7 BC Augustus' fourteen new urban regions (*regiones*) superseded any earlier divisions, encompassing the entire city. They were
originally known simply by number. They were numbered counter-
clockwise around the city beginning in the south, with region XIV
added across the Tiber (Map 10.1). The regionary catalogues also list
names for each region derived from a place, building or street in the
region, but these names do not appear in earlier references to the regions
in literature or epigraphy.[5] They may either be a mistake (taking the first
item in each region's inventory as a name) or reflect unofficial usage.
Still, the regions are often identified in modern scholarship by these
names.

No boundary markers for the Augustan regions have been found
in the city but the regions must have had clear – and knowable –
borders in order to serve as administrative divisions. Our knowledge

---

[4] Nicolet 1987, 1–25.   [5] For monuments within the regions, see Chapter 8.

of the layout and extent of the new regions depends primarily on two catalogues of important monuments in the city listed region by region. These regionary catalogues date from the fourth century AD and probably derive from a Diocletian original. Obviously our knowledge of the regions depends on our knowledge of the location of the monuments noted in the regionary catalogues so the boundaries are better known for regions where the catalogues list monuments whose locations are more securely known. Inscriptions that note a region or that can be assigned to a particular region supplement our knowledge. For example, an altar erected by a certain *C. Clodius C. l. Euphemus negotiator penoris et vinorum de Velabro a IIII Scaris* must have stood right at the border between region VIII and region XI, which according to the regionary catalogues respectively contained the a*quam cernentem IIII scauros* and the Velabrum.

While it seems clear that the *recensus* of the city in 8 BC provided the data necessary for the redistricting in 7 BC, the rules used to draw up the regions are unclear. Except for the Tiber (only region XIV lay across the Tiber), the borders of the regions do not seem to follow the natural or fabricated topography of the city – they do not, for example, follow the Servian Wall or major thoroughfares. The urbanized area of the city and the fourteen regions extended well beyond the traditional boundary of the *pomerium*. The regions are not of equal size, at least as they existed in the fourth century (it is important to remember that 300 years separate Augustus' creation of the regions and the composition of the regionary catalogues). Were they intended to have roughly the same population or same surface area in linear feet of public streets? The cohorts of the *vigiles* were equally divided among them, suggesting the regions required equal amounts of fire services. The boundaries of the regions must have changed over this time as the city expanded so that no portion of the city fell outside a region. The regions may also have required rebalancing in light of major alterations of the city's layout such as the rebuilding after the great fire of AD 64.

Augustus placed each region under the administrative oversight of a senatorial magistrate, an aedile, tribune or praetor chosen annually by lot. In the Republic, the four aediles alone had shared the *cura urbis* dividing the city into four areas. However, in the late Republic the task of looking after the city's streets had become too much for the aediles, and other magistrates had stepped in to help with – or to perform – the aediles' duties on several occasions (Cassius Dio 41.36.3, 49.46.12, 53.2.2). Augustus, therefore, regularized what had been an *ad hoc* response, although street cleaning continued to be considered an aedilician task, as is shown by the famous story of Caligula covering the future emperor Vespasian in mud for failing to keep the streets clean as aedile (Suetonius, *Vespasian* 5.3; Cassius Dio 59.12.3). Not surprisingly, the regionary magistrates do not appear very often in the historians: not every aedile turned out like Vespasian. In addition to street cleaning, the regionary magistrates had charge in particular of regulating the imperial cult practised in the neighbourhoods: the worship of the Lares Augusti on the holiday of Compitalia. In this capacity they are found in epigraphy authorizing the repair of neighbourhood shrines (e.g. *CIL* 6.449–4532). We don't know what other kinds of construction required the approval of a regionary magistrate, but surely anything that encroached on the public streets would require their approval. The regionary magistrates performed other sacrifices appropriate to their region (e.g. they officiated at rites for Vulcan along the line that marked the extent of the great fire of AD 64). In addition to street maintenance and the neighbourhood's imperial cult, the regionary administration also managed fair commerce: the official weights and measures were supplied and certified region by region (*ILS* 8630–8634), a duty that the republican aediles had also fulfilled (Cicero, *Epistulae ad familiares* 8.6.5) and one that neighbourhood officers might duplicate in their own neighbourhoods (see below on Numerius Lucius Hermeros). Cases of commercial fraud were investigated in the regions before being judged by the urban prefect. Ulpian (*Digesta* 1.12.1) reports a case of bank fraud in the late third century perpetrated by a slave who defrauded residents of Region XII (Piscina Publica). In the fourth century the urban prefect Tarracius Bassus condemned a long list of business owners, listed by neighbourhood and by region, noting the name of the regionary *denuntiator* who had uncovered the evidence (*CIL* 6.31893–31901).

The systems of independent magistrates (who had other duties in addition to the *cura regionum*) did not allow for any centralized administration of the regions and also created a potential conflict between the individual regionary magistrates and the urban prefect, who had authority on the emperor's behalf over the entire city, including most judicial matters. Domitian was praised for not interfering with the magistrates when he was urban prefect, which implied of course that such interference was normal. Replacing the magistrates with supervisors (*curatores*) and subordinating the regions and neighbourhoods to the urban prefect solved the problem. When exactly the change took place is unknown, but the final testimony for a regionary magistrate is AD 109.

In AD 136 the fourteen regions raised a statue of Hadrian collectively. The inscribed base lists a low class *curator* and *denuntiator* (investigator) for each region before listing the neighbourhood officers by neighbourhood. The dedication may correspond to the change, but it is hard to believe that the *curatores* listed on the base, who were mostly freedmen, could be the men who replaced the regionary magistrates. We do know that by the reign of Septimius Severus the regions were overseen by consular supervisors, one of whom is known from region IIII (*consularis sacrae urbis regionis IIII* (*CIL* 14.2078)). The emperor himself evidently took over responsibility for managing the imperial cult practised in the neighbourhoods, separating the administrative activities managed through the regions from the religious activities.

The primacy of the new conception of the regionary city, as opposed, for example, to the earlier Rome 'of seven hills' (*septimontium*) is demonstrated by the regular description of Rome after 7 BC as 'of fourteen regions' (*urbs sacra regionum XIV*). Despite the regions' artificial origins and clear association with matters of city services, the lower class residents of the regions did act communally, primarily to honour the emperor. For example, the *plebs urbana quae habitat in regione urbis XIII* along with their neighbourhood officers collected bronze to make a statue of Augustus' adopted son Gaius Caesar (*CIL* 6.40323). In 136, the *magistri vicorum urbis regionum XIIII* appear together on the Capitoline Base (*CIL* 6.975). However, most collective activity was based not in the regions but in the neighbourhoods, whose supervision was always a central part of the *cura urbis*.

NEIGHBOURHOODS

After reporting Servius' creation of four regions, Dionysius turns to neighbourhoods:

> After this he (Servius) commanded the inhabitants of every neighbourhood to erect in the streets shrines to heroes whose statues stood in front of the houses, and he made a law that there should be annual sacrifices there and that each family should contribute a honey-cake. He also ordered that slaves should assist the officiants at the sacrifices performed on behalf of the neighbourhood, since the service of slaves was pleasing to the heroes. The Romans continued in my day to celebrate Compitalia – so named after *compita*, which is a word for street – in the

most solemn and sumptuous manner a few days after the
Saturnalia. And they still observe the ancient custom in
connection with those sacrifices, propitiating the heroes by
the ministry of their servants, and during these days
removing every badge of their servitude, in order that the
slaves, being softened by this instance of humanity, which
has something great and solemn about it, may make
themselves more agreeable to their masters and be less
sensible of the severity of their condition.

(Dionysius of Halicarnassus 4.14.2–4)

Again there is reason to doubt the regal origin of the neighbourhoods,
but there is no doubt that generally recognized neighbourhoods existed
at Rome in the Republic. There can be debate whether the neighbourhoods of the republican city were clearly demarcated spatially or
whether they had any official standing in civic governance or administration. In Livy, neighbourhoods are regularly the unit of the city used
by the aediles to accomplish particular tasks, such as the distribution of
food, within their allotted *pars* of the city (Livy 25.2.6–10, 30.26.5–6).
A special *census* of the urban population, probably for the purpose of
the food distribution, called a *recensus* was taken *vicatim* through the
city (Suetonius, *Caesar* 41). Neighbourhood leaders had some official
standing that allowed them to wear the clothing of officers of the state
on certain occasions within the confines of the neighbourhood (Livy
34.7.3–10, Cicero, *In Pisonem* 8). In the second century BC the foreign
king Philip II could even mistake the neighbourhood leaders for civic
magistrates (*ILS* 8763).

Whatever their involvement with the aediles in urban administration, the primary activity in the republican neighbourhoods was
the cult of the Lares Compitales or Viales, practised in the city by
neighbourhoods at crossroads shrines called *compita*, and the celebration
of the midwinter holiday of Compitalia. This cult was, as Dionysius
says, the purview of Rome's lower classes, the *infima plebs*, who came
together around Compitalia for games and entertainments organized by
neighbourhood leaders. The celebration of Compitalia created a social
cohesion among lower-class residents that, in the late Republic, was
exploited by politicians seeking power outside the traditional routes
of senatorial advancement. Men such as Clodius organized groups of
thugs *vicatim* and used them as an effective cudgel in civic politics.[6] To

---

[6] For rioting associated with the Compitalia, see Chapter 24.

prevent this, there were repeated attempts to forbid or curtail the cel-ebrations (*ludi*) in the neighbourhoods that accompanied Compitalia, though the holiday itself could not be done away with. It is within this context of disaffection and the attempted repression of neighbourhood activists in the final years of the Republic that the creation of Augus-tus' organized neighbourhood structure should be considered, not in the context of the distant historical precedent presented by Dionysius (though Augustus himself regularly relied on antique precedent as the public justification for his actions).

Neighbourhoods and *compita* did not disappear in the late Repub-lic and administrative activities such as the *recensus* continued to be performed *vicatim*. Nevertheless, the suppression of the compital cel-ebrations and the organizations that performed them had a negative effect on the neighbourhoods: infrastructure was allowed to decline and *compita* were even abandoned to private individuals. As part of a larger campaign to restore the capital after years of civil war, Augustus attempted to rebuild the neighbourhood shrines as well. In 10 BC he rescued a *compitum* on the Esquiline from private hands, restored its shrine and decorated it with a new statue of Mercurius (*CIL* 6.30974, 6.31572). Statues of other gods for other neighbourhoods followed in 9 and 8 BC (6.30771, 6.30772, Suetonius, *Aug.* 57, Cassius Dio 54.35.2). However, the potential for the neighbourhoods to provide an alternative power base for ambitious politicians or revolutionaries remained, as the career of one maverick aedile, Egnatius Rufus, shows (Velleius Pater-culus 2.91.3–2.92; Cassius Dio 53.24.4–6). As aedile Rufus organized a private fire brigade to gain the support of the urban plebs; when he was prevented from illegally standing for the consulship of 18 BC, civil disturbances followed that were so severe that Augustus was recalled from abroad and Rufus executed. When in 7 BC Augustus undertook a systematic reorganization of all the city's neighbourhoods he was not only restructuring the delivery of city services, he was transforming a disruptive element of urban society into a prop for the new regime. This is not necessarily surprising. John Mollenkopf points out that the co-optation of 'movements that challenge urban governments' is one of the central processes of urban politics over time.[7]

Defining neighbourhoods, spatially or socially, is a particularly difficult task. Spatially, neighbourhoods are diffuse entities focused on an identifiable centre or core but with outer limits that are fuzzy and subject to debate. Their shape depends neither wholly on natural social

[7] Mollenkopf 1992, 27.

cohesion nor wholly on administrative planning and enforcement. At Rome, the neighbourhoods centred on a *compitum*, literally a crossroads but in its urban form a street altar or shrine for the neighbourhoods' Lares. The state holiday for the neighbourhoods' protective spirits, Compitalia, derived its name from the *compitum* where each neighbourhood's Lares resided. The neighbourhoods that surrounded the *compita* were called *vici*. The republican scholar Terentius Varro says that, 'a *vicus* consists of houses' (*LL* 5.159) and 'the urban *vicus* derives from the word 'street' (*via*) because there are buildings on either side of the street' (*De lingua Latina* 5.145). In his *Etymologiae* (15.2.22), Isidorus, a seventh-century AD bishop of Seville, offers a definition of the urban neighbourhood, saying, 'urban dwellings themselves . . . make up a *vicus*. The inhabitants of a *vicus* are called *vicini*. Streets are the thin spaces in the middle of *vici*.' A *vicus* comprised a group of dwellings along either side of a street along with the inhabitants of the dwellings. (Since they aligned closely with streets, *vicus* is used often in ancient authors like the modern 'street', especially to give directions or describe a route through the city.) One of the most important topographical resources for ancient Rome is provided by the fragments of the Severan *Forma Urbis Romae*, a large marble map of the city installed on a wall in the temple of Peace in the early third century AD. At least four individual *vici* appear on the surviving fragments of the plan (Fig. 10.1). Since the map identifies few urban features and monuments by name, the inscriptions underscore the centrality of the neighbourhoods in the conceived form of the city. The names were inscribed down the course of a street and certain features might be taken for *compita* (Fig. 10.2). The extent of the Vicus Stablarius, however, was certainly equal to, or greater than, the area covered by its name on the marble plan. Thus the neighbourhood included a run of around 100 m of a street flanked by small houses, shops and apartment houses.

Since Augustus' reforms, however, assigned important administrative tasks to the neighbourhoods, the entire space of the city must have fallen within one or another neighbourhood after 7 BC. Many old neighbourhoods were retained but new ones must have been created in 7 and thereafter when the boundaries of the city were expanded or when the street plan of the city was adjusted. Pliny the Elder tells us that there were 265 neighbourhoods (*compita Larum*) in the city in his day, a figure that relates to the Flavian city after the great fire of AD 64 and the massive construction and destruction projects of Nero and Vespasian (*Historia Naturalis* 3.66–7). Virgil (*Aeneid* 8.116–17) offers the figure of 300 neighbourhood shrines in the city, and Ovid (*Fasti* 5.145–6)

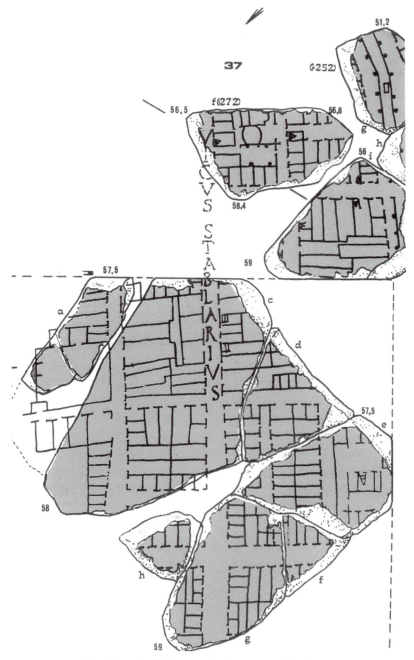

FIGURE 10.1 The Vicus Stablarius on the Severan marble plan.

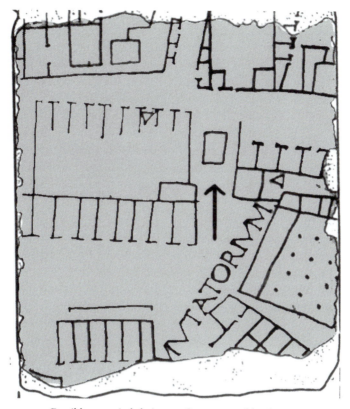

FIGURE 10.2 Possible compital shrine on Severan marble plan.

says 500. The regionary catalogues both list over 400 *vici* in the city. We know about 120 by name. Unlike the regions, neighbourhoods were linked to a small residential space in the city. New neighbourhoods must have been created when the urbanized space expanded or was readjusted (e.g. the Vicus Statuae Verris was created under the Flavians[8] and the Vicus Compiti Acili went out of existence in the late first century AD).

Socially, participation in the neighbourhoods of the imperial city continued to be primarily the purview of freedmen and other lower-class citizens as it had been in the Republic. Neighbourhoods can serve as a learning ground for new urban residents.[9] Both Suetonius and Cassius Dio report the creation of new neighbourhood officers (*magistri vici*) chosen from each neighbourhood's residents. We do not know

[8] Palmer 1978–80.   [9] Hollnsteiner-Racelis 1988.

how the *magistri* were selected, but since we know most of the attested *magistri vici* from their expensive gifts to their neighbourhoods, some wealth may have been a requirement. Most, but not all, neighbourhoods chose four *magistri* each year, and the names of hundreds of individual *magistri vici* are known from the empire. Sometimes a second college of *ministri vici*, slaves who served as attendants to the freed *magistri*, served some neighbourhoods. The *magistri* had the right to wear the special togas of civic magistrates and to be preceded by lictors, and the officers of several neighbourhoods proudly presented themselves wearing their togas and using lictors on altars they donated to their neighbourhoods (Fig. 10.3). The neighbourhoods reckoned a new era beginning usually, though not always, with 1 August 7 BC. Officers identify themselves according to this new era as the first, second and third board of officers (*magistri primi, magistri secundi, magistri terti*) well into the second century and beyond (e.g. the central shrine of the Vicus Iovis Fagutalis in AD 109 lists the *magistri anni CXXI* (*CIL* 6.452)).

The new neighbourhoods and their officers certainly played an important role in the city's administration. They were charged with helping to control fires, they were the basis for the *recensus* of the city's population, and they looked after the local distribution points for the city's water supply. Numerous neighbourhood dedications from around the city to the goddess who stopped fires, Stata Mater, attest that the neighbourhood officers took their new duty seriously, at least until Augustus transferred it to the newly created *vigiles* in AD 6. However, the celebration of Compitalia continued to be the primary focus of neighbourhood activity, but Augustus emphatically joined neighbourhood religion with the commemoration of the emperor and imperial dynasty. The Lares Compitales or Viales were renamed the Lares Augusti, in honour of the emperor. In some instances the worship of the Genius Caesarum, 'Virility of the Caesars', was added to the worship of the renamed Lares in order to signal the neighbourhood's attachment to the new dynasty as well. Augustus personally provided new cult statuettes of the Lares Augusti for each neighbourhood to use in its celebrations. One neighbourhood proudly recorded the emperor's visit and gift as the heading of its calendar and list of neighbourhood officers:

> Imperator Caesar Augustus, pontifex maximus, consul for the eleventh time, holding tribunician power for the seventeenth time, gave the Lares Augusti to the officers of the neighbourhood.
>
> (*Insc. Ital.* 13.1 279–89 no. 20, 13.2 90–8 no. 12)

FIGURE 10.3 Altar of the Vicus Aesculeti showing *magistri vici* sacrificing and with an inscription identifying the era of the neighbourhood.

The *magistri* from across the city came together annually to parade with their statuettes as part of the Ludi Augustales instituted after the first emperor's death. In the neighbourhoods new, more elaborate *aediculae* were erected to house the new Lares Augusti. Many neighbourhoods also installed new compital altars decorated with the statuettes and other symbols recalling the dynasty (laurels, *corona civica*) or even decorated with important contemporary scenes involving Augustus and the *domus Augusta* – the officers of the Vicus Sandaliarius installed an altar in 2 BC that commemorated the departure of Augustus' adopted son Gaius Caesar to take command over the eastern provinces on its front face (Fig. 10.4), depicted the two Lares Augusti on one side

FIGURE 10.4 Altar of the Vicus Sandaliarius (front), showing Augustus, Livia and Gaius Caesar.

(Fig. 10.5), and on the rear showed a collection of symbols associated with Augustus (Fig. 10.6).

ONE NEIGHBOURHOOD: THE VICUS COMPITI ACILI

In 1932 the construction of the Via dei Fori Imperiali near the intersection of the modern-day Via del Colosseo and the Via della Polveriera

FIGURE 10.5 Altar of the Vicus Sandaliarius (side), showing Lares Augusti.

unearthed the podium, steps and portions of the inscribed architrave of a small rectangular shrine and the fragments of an inscribed altar from the *aedicula* of the Vicus Compiti Acili. The *compitum* stood on the edge of the district called Carinae, above the head of the Sacra Via, at the intersection of two major streets, the continuator of the Sacra Via along the course of the present day Via della Polveriera (running south-west– north-east) and a street running north-west–south-east from the Vicus Cyprius past the Compitum Acili and across the Colosseum valley to the Porta Capena. The neighbourhood of the Compitum Acili was probably this street from the Vicus Cyprius across the saddle between the Velia and the Oppius to the Compitum Acili (approximately 150 m).

FIGURE 10.6 Altar of the Vicus Sandaliarius (rear), showing Augustan symbols.

The neighbourhood's crossroads and shrine therefore stood at the edge of the neighbourhood, where it met an important thoroughfare into the city.

The shrine stood not just near but in an actual crossroads (as *in situ* street pavement and drains surrounding it show) on a small rectangular podium (2.8 × 2.4 m) raised 1.4 m above street level (Fig. 10.7). An inscription carved into the architrave clarifies the context and meaning of the shrine.

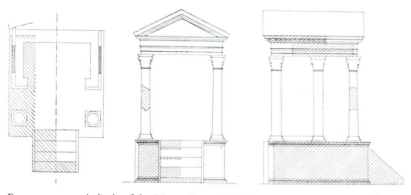

FIGURE 10.7 *Aedicula* of the Vicus Compiti Acili.

> When Imperator Caesar Augustus, pontifex maximus, with
> tribunician power for the eighteenth time, imperator for
> the fourteenth time, and L. Cornelius Sulla were consuls,
> the second board of officers for the Vicus Compiti Acili
> built and dedicated this shrine.

> (*AE* 1964, 74a)

Below this the names of the four freedmen who served as the *magistri
secundi* for the Vicus Compiti Acili appeared in smaller, but still prominent, letters. Three of the four names can still be read on the fragment of
the architrave: [M.] Licinius M. Sextiliae l(ibertus) Diogenes, L. Aelius
L. l(ibertus) Hilarus, and M. Tillius M. l(ibertus) Silo. A small piece
of the altar from the shrine was also found. The fragment bears part
of the altar's dedicatory inscription, 'the *magistri* of the Vicus Compiti
Acili for the year 10', followed by the remains of two names M(arcus)
An[t]onius [–]rionis l(ibertus) Felix and L(ucius) Venuleiu[s] Turanni
l(ibertus) Bucci[o] (*AE* 1964, 74b).

The Compitum Acili (named after an important republican family with property in the area) existed at Rome as early as 219 BC
when Rome's first Greek doctor settled in the neighbourhood. In
7 BC Augustus reorganized the Vicus Compiti Acili along with Rome's
other neighbourhoods. Two years later, in 5 BC, the second board of
magistri donated a new compital shrine for the neighbourhood; eight
years later, the tenth board of officers donated a new altar for the shrine.
The neighbourhood of the Compitum Acili did not survive the Julio-
Claudian dynasty. It stood on land that the emperor Nero cleared for
the Domus Aurea. Later the space was incorporated into the Flavian
structures surrounding the Colosseum.

One *MAGISTER*: Numerius Lucius Hermeros

The career of one *magister vici*, Numerius Lucius Hermeros, is particularly illustrative. Hermeros served as *magister* three times for a neighbourhood that ran through the Forum Boarium under S. Maria in Cosmedin. Even though he must have been wealthy, Hermeros had reached the apex of the opportunities for public service for a man of his station. Hermeros marked each of his three years in office with the donation of a valuable gift to the neighbourhood. In the first year of his *vicus*, Hermeros and two others dedicated a statue to Mercurius Augustus (*CIL* 6.283). In year 11 of the neighbourhood (AD 4/5) Hermeros (as *magister iterum*) and two new colleagues donated a set of gold and silver scale weights to the neighbourhood and built a shrine to Hercules to house them (*CIL* 6.282). Finally as *magister tertium* Hermeros donated a statue of Venus Augusta (*AE* 1980, 54). The gods Hermeros honoured, Mercurius Augustus, Hercules and Venus Augusta, were not just important in Augustan Rome in general but had specific resonance with the Forum Boarium where Hermeros' neighbourhood lay. The Forum Boarium was the centre of the worship of Hercules in Rome. The only known state temple of Mercury in Rome overlooked the Forum Boarium. Finally, the oldest temple of Venus at Rome, that of Venus Obsequens, stood nearby. Hermeros' choices also reflected the commercial nature of the district where his neighbourhood lay. Both Mercury and Hercules were closely associated with commerce. The gold and silver weights Hermeros provided as *magister iterum* were presumably for neighbourhood residents to use in their businesses. Indeed the fairness of weights was so important that only nine years later along with the *magistri* of the year 19 Hermeros and his colleagues revalidated the accuracy of their gift (*CIL* 6.282). Venus (Augusta) played a central role in Augustan religious ideology, but Hermeros' gift related to his activities as *magister vici* as well. The inscribed base is decorated on the front with a pair of doves drinking from a bowl and on the side with a dove feeding its nestlings. Doves are a token of Venus, and the drinking composition is not unique (cf. Pliny *Nat. Hist.* 36.184) and the motif of abundant sustenance is a common one in Augustan art. However taken together, drinking and feeding recall two primary duties of the *magistri vici*: to maintain a neighbourhood's fountains and the lists of those eligible for the grain distributions. In one statue Hermeros alluded to a local temple, imperial religion and his own activities as neighbourhood officer.

Mercurius and Venus together also evoked the two halves of Hermeros' *cognomen*, *Herm(es)* and *eros*. Hermeros' name changed slightly but significantly over his career. In his first term in office he is called N(umerius) Lucius N(umerii) l(ibertus) Hermeros. In his later terms he is named on his gifts as N(umerius) Lucius N(umerii) l(ibertus) Hermeros Aequitas. Evidently Hermeros acquired the second *cognomen* Aequitas (Fairness) sometime between 7 and 5 BC. The public set of precious metal scale weights that Hermeros donated and evidently agreed to maintain ensured fair commerce and Hermeros' neighbours responded by offering him the new name Mr Fairness, an honorific *cognomen* that recalled those given to victorious generals in the Republic and the emperor's own new name Augustus.

FURTHER READING

For the regions, any further investigation should begin with the basic articles in *LTUR* by A. Fraschetti (*storia*) and D. Palombi (*topografia*). For the discussion over the existence of republican regions and *vici*, Fraschetti 1990 is essential (but not necessarily correct), as is Wallace-Hadrill 2003. For the regions in later times, see Frézouls 1987. For the governance of the regions, see De Robertis 1935, Panciera 1970, Palmer 1974. For *vici* in the late Republic, see Laurence 1991. For a discussion of Augustus' reforms of the *vici*, see Lott 2004. For an earlier treatment of regions and neighbourhoods as part of Augustus' reforms of urban administration, see Favro 1996. For studies of individual neighbourhoods, the many articles published by R. E. A. Palmer and S. Panciera should be consulted. The best available text and commentary for the regionary catalogues is given by Valentini and Zucchetti 1940–53; see also Arce 1999. For the marble plan, see Carrettoni et al. 1960 and Rodriguez-Almeida 1981. For a general treatment of city services, see Robinson 1992. Wallace-Hadrill 2008 appeared too late for consideration here, but should be consulted.

11: MONUMENTAL ROME

R. Don Miller

Ancient Rome was a city of monuments. Even today, visitors
walking the streets of the city marvel at the grandeur and magnificence of the architectural remains, some of which have
stood intact for more than 2,000 years. From the bronze equestrian
statue of Marcus Aurelius that crowns the Capitoline Hill, to the imposing Colosseum dominating the cityscape, monuments assumed many
varied forms. Owing to constant rebuilding in the city over the past two
and a half millennia, countless monuments have been destroyed, particularly those of the republican period. Nevertheless, much can be discerned about the nature of these monuments from the literary sources,
in addition to the evidence supplied by numismatics, epigraphy and
archaeology. But how is a monument to be defined? The grammarian
Festus (*Epitome* 123L) suggests one definition, declaring that 'a monument is anything... which has been made for the memory of someone,
such as temples, porticos, literary works, and poems'. The poet Horace
(*Carmina* 3.30.1–5) even goes so far as to designate his own collection of
works 'a monument more lasting than bronze, and higher than the site
of the regal pyramids, one that no destructive storm, no furious north
wind can destroy, nor the countless succession of years or the passing
of seasons'. Thus, the most important characteristic of a monument
is that it served to perpetuate the memory of a particular person or
event.

PUBLIC MONUMENTS IN REPUBLICAN ROME

As in any society, the Roman elite were generally responsible for commissioning public monuments. Throughout the republican period the
governing class subscribed to a set of competitive social values, the
most important of which was the moral quality of *virtus*, perhaps best

defined as 'virtue' or 'manliness'.[1] *Virtus* consisted primarily in winning personal glory and prestige by performing great deeds on behalf of the Roman state, for which warfare provided the greatest opportunities. The prize that these men endeavoured to obtain was the high esteem of their fellow citizens, which manifested itself most clearly in the forms of *gloria et laus*, glory and praise, prerequisites for anyone seeking political office. In order to transform military success into political advantage, however, the ruling class needed a means of publicizing their achievements before the wider citizen body. Two spectacles in particular facilitated this transmission: the triumphal procession and funeral ceremonies for distinguished men. Yet these events were transient in nature. Funerals lasted for only a day, as did most triumphs. The ruling class needed to devise another method for prolonging public awareness of their military success beyond these immediate celebrations, hence the erection of commemorative monuments and public memorials in civic spaces.

One of the most common victory monuments in republican Rome was the votive temple. Frequent wars provided numerous opportunities for the construction of new temples. The usual practice was for a magistrate with *imperium* to vow a temple whilst on campaign, with work commencing upon his return to Rome following the successful conclusion of the war.[2] The construction of a temple offered clear political advantages to its builder. Since the vowing of a temple served the direct interests of the state, which would benefit from the introduction of a new deity to the Roman pantheon, a general who made such a vow created the public impression that he placed the interests of the state above his own. Moreover, the erection of a temple created a structure that would be closely linked with the commander, whose name and personal achievements were recorded for posterity in the dedicatory inscription above the doors to the sanctuary, thereby providing a means of perpetuating glory not just for himself, but also his family. From the middle of the second century BC onwards, there are an increasing number of references to temples by the names of their founders. The temple of Fortuna Huiusce Diei constructed by Q. Lutatius Catulus, for example, was referred to as the *aedes Catuli* (Varro, *Res Rusticae* 3.5.12). Likewise, the temple of Honos et Virtus built by C. Marius was

---

[1] Harris 1979, ch. 1 discusses the value system of the Roman elite.
[2] For more on the processes involved in the vowing and construction of a temple, see Orlin 1997.

known as the *monumentum Marianum* (Cicero, *Pro Plancio* 116; Valerius Maximus 1.7.5).

The primary reason for the association of certain temples with military commanders, however, derived from the frequent use of temples by these men as repositories for the public display of spoils and artworks seized from the enemy. M. Claudius Marcellus, for example, displayed a number of precious artworks from Syracuse in the temples of *Honos* and *Virtus* following his capture of the city in 211. According to the writer Livy, the adornments were so remarkable that foreigners from far and wide visited the temples simply in order to view them (Livy 25.40.3). As public life grew increasingly competitive in the second and first centuries, Roman commanders became even more ambitious with their building projects. Following his successful defeat of the Macedonians in 148, Q. Caecilius Metellus constructed a monumental four-sided porticus in the Circus Flaminius to enclose the twin temples to Jupiter Stator and Juno Regina (Velleius Paterculus 1.11.3). Not only were these the first marble temples in Rome, they also contained a number of statues by renowned Greek artists. The most impressive artistic treasure was the *turma Alexandri*, a bronze equestrian monument representing Alexander the Great and his companions who had fallen at the battle of the Granicus (Pliny, *Historia Naturalis* 34.64; Plutarch, *Alexander* 16.15–16). Metellus positioned this statuary group prominently before the twin temples, both in order to emphasize his success in Macedonia and to equate his achievements with those of the legendary general.

In the late Republic, temples began to focus attention solely on the individual achievements of the builder, rather than the deity in whose honour the sanctuary was constructed. This is most evident in the large-scale building programmes of Cn. Pompey and C. Iulius Caesar. Pompey utilized the immense booty amassed from his campaigns in the Greek east to create a triumphal monument of unprecedented splendour: a vast building complex consisting of a small shrine to Venus Victrix (the Conqueror), a multi-storied theatre, and a *quadroporticus* containing fountains and gardens decorated with captured artworks and war spoils. Faced with the challenge of surpassing his long-term political rival, Julius Caesar embarked upon an even more ambitious project: the construction of a new architectural monument bearing his name, the Forum Iulium. This was dominated by a temple to the goddess Venus Genetrix, the alleged divine mother of the *gens Iulii*. He embellished the forum with a number of priceless artworks and statues, the most magnificent of which were placed within the temple of Venus itself (Pliny, *Hist. Nat.* 9.116, 35.26, 35.156, 37.11). The entire complex was therefore designed to celebrate Caesar's supposed divine lineage, together with his unparalleled successes throughout Europe and the Mediterranean.

Another ubiquitous Roman monument was the commemorative statue.[3] It is uncertain when statues of this type were first erected in Rome. The Romans themselves understood the practice to have originated in the time of Romulus, who was credited with setting up the first public statue to commemorate his triumph over neighbouring tribes (Dionysius of Halicarnassus, *Antiquitates Romanae* 2.54.2; Plutarch, *Romulus* 16.8). The earliest known statues represented heroes of the early Republic. L. Iunius Brutus, the famous 'tyrannicide' who helped overthrow the last of the Etruscan kings, was epitomized in this fashion, as was Horatius Cocles, the warrior renowned for having allegedly defended Rome single-handedly against invading Etruscan forces (Cassius Dio 43.45.4; Livy 2.10.12).

This practice soon became widespread, with statues being set up for a range of reasons by a variety of social groups. The senate, for example, erected statues on a number of occasions in honour of diplomats who had perished whilst serving the state on public business. This custom afforded this body the opportunity publicly to acknowledge and celebrate what was arguably the most important of all public virtues: self-sacrifice on behalf of the *res publica*. Statues were also conferred on those who had performed some particularly noteworthy public service. Scipio Africanus was honoured in this fashion as a result of his extraordinary military success against Hannibal in the Second Punic War, as was Cato the Elder, in recognition of his continual and committed service to the state (Valerius Maximus 4.1.6, 8.15.2). By the late Republic, the senatorial awarding of statues had become largely sycophantic, designed to placate powerful political dynasts of the day; Sulla, Pompey and Caesar all received equestrian images on the rostra.

Commemorative statues were also granted on occasion by the Roman people, typically to those who championed their cause. One of the earliest such recipients was the Greek philosopher Hermodorus of Ephesus, whose statue was set up in the area of the Comitium in 451 in gratitude for his role in the composition of the first Ten Tables of Laws (Pliny, *Hist. Nat.* 34.21). The people chose to honour

---

[3] Lahusen 1983 provides the most in-depth examination of statuary in ancient Rome generally. For those without German, Stewart 2003 is also valuable.

L. Caecilius Metellus for a very different reason. As pontifex maximus in 241 Metellus risked his own life in order to rescue a number of sacred objects from the temple of Vesta after that structure caught fire. For this he received a portrait statue on the Capitol, accompanied by an inscription detailing the circumstances for which it was erected (Dionysius of Halicarnassus, *Ant. Rom.* 2.66.4). Statues were also bestowed for more trivial achievements. The curule aedile M. Seius, for example, had his statues set up on the Capitol and the Palatine merely for supplying the public with corn at a reduced price (Pliny, *Hist. Nat.* 18.16). Likewise, the praetor M. Marius Gratidianus was honoured with statues throughout the city simply for his introduction of a law to test and eliminate debased coinage (Cicero, *De Officiis* 3.80; Pliny, *Hist. Nat.* 33.132).

The majority of commemorative statues appear to have been set up on private initiative and celebrated either personal or ancestral achievements. The consul Sp. Carvilius, for instance, advertised his military success against the Samnites in 293 by dedicating on the Capitol two separate images fashioned from captured enemy spoils that had been melted down: a colossal figure of Jupiter together with a smaller self-portrait (Pliny, *Hist. Nat.* 34.43). His example was later imitated by the consul Q. Fabius Maximus, who erected his own equestrian image on the Capitol alongside a colossal bronze statue of Heracles that he had confiscated from Tarentum during the Second Punic War (Plutarch, *Fabius Maximus* 22.6). Both dedications simultaneously advertised individual achievements and religious fidelity. In several instances individuals also erected statues in celebration of their ancestors. M. Acilius Glabrio chose to emphasize his lineage by dedicating a gold equestrian statue of his father within the temple of Pietas as a memorial to the elder Glabrio's political career (Livy 40.34.5; Valerius Maximus 2.5.1). Perhaps the most elaborate display of ancestral imagery, however, was the series of gilded equestrian statues erected on the Capitol by Q. Caecilius Metellus Scipio representing earlier members of his adopted gens, the Cornelii Scipiones (Cicero, *Epistulae at Atticum* 6.1.17). Finally, portrait statues were presented to individuals by communities or collective groups in recognition of exceptional service performed on their behalf. The tribune C. Aelius was rewarded in this manner by the people of Thurii for assisting them in the defence of their city (Plin. *Hist. Nat.* 34.32). As pro-praetorian governor of Sicily, C. Verres received numerous public statues from the Sicilians, including a group of gilded equestrian images in the Campus Martius (Cicero, *In Verrem* 2.2.150, 2.2.167). Unlike the statues awarded to Aelius, however, these images were set up not out of reverence, but rather from fear and compulsion.

Considering the large number of statues that congested the public spaces of Rome, it is only natural that individuals soon began searching for ways in which to make their statuary stand out from the teeming crowds of images all around. This was achieved most effectively by placing statues atop columns and arches, a practice that had a long history at Rome. Indeed, columns of this type are amongst the earliest attested commemorative monuments in the city, first appearing at the beginning of the fifth century. The first known recipient was L. Minucius Esquilinus Augurinus, who received an honorific statue and column from the Roman populace for having reduced the price of corn during a time of famine (Pliny, *Hist. Nat.* 34.21). The majority of columns, however, were set up in celebration of military success. For example, C. Maenius was honoured in this fashion for his victory over the Latins in 338, as was C. Duilius in 260 for his defeat of the Carthaginians in a naval battle off the coast of Sicily (Pliny, *Hist. Nat.* 34.20; Quintilianus, *De Institutione oratoria* 1.7.12).

The commemorative arch, often considered one of the most characteristic Roman monument types, actually appeared relatively late in comparison with other forms of public commemoration, with the first known arches dating only to the second century.[4] The earliest were the three arches erected by the Roman commander L. Stertinius in 196: two were set up in the Forum Boarium, the other in the Circus Maximus (Livy 33.27.3–4). Nothing further is known about these arches except that they were surmounted by gilded statues of some sort. A few years later Scipio Africanus followed this example by erecting an arch on the Capitoline Hill, similarly adorning it with gilded statues (Livy 37.3.7). Once again, who or what was represented is unknown; the statues possibly depicted Roman deities or perhaps members of the *gens Cornelia*. The only republican arch for which there is any archaeological evidence is that erected by Q. Fabius Maximus Allobrogicus at the eastern end of the Forum Romanum, sometime after his victory over the Gallic tribes in 121 (Ps.-Asconius, *Comm. ad Cic. Verr.* 1.19). It was later restored in 56 by his homonymous grandson. The surviving dedicatory inscription records the *elogia* of the three members of the *gens Fabii* represented on the attic of the arch. Thus the arch appears to have been erected to venerate Fabius' ancestry rather than to publicize his military accomplishments.

---

[4] The starting point for any investigation into the commemorative arch in Rome is De Maria 1988. Kleiner 1985 examines arches erected during the Republic and under the Julio-Claudian emperors.

The same motivations that led to the construction of public monuments also influenced Roman commanders to commission historical paintings of their military achievements.[5] These types of paintings differed from other forms of public commemoration in that their impact on the viewer was more immediate; the spectator was able literally to 'see' the actual events that had transpired. The earliest examples of this medium are found in sepulchres and family tombs, the walls of which were frequently decorated with scenes depicting the accomplishments of those interred within, or else prominent ancestors. Pictorial representations were often utilized by Roman commanders to publicize successful campaigns against foreign adversaries. M. Valerius Maximus Messala, for instance, displayed a painting illustrating his defeat of the Carthaginians on the side of the Curia in 263 (Pliny, *Hist. Nat.* 35.22). Likewise L. Hostilius Mancinus exhibited in the Forum Romanum a painting representing his capture of Carthage during the Third Punic War (Pliny, *Hist. Nat.* 35.23). This practice was closely connected with the spectacle of the Roman triumph, as pictures portraying events from a successful campaign formed an integral part of the procession, at least from the late third century BC onwards. M. Claudius Marcellus included a representation of captured Syracuse in the *ovatio* he celebrated in 211, a clear allusion to his subjugation of the city (Livy 26.21.7). Scipio Africanus likewise incorporated pictures illustrating the key events of the battle of Zama in his triumph of 201 (Appian, *Bellum Punicum* 66).

PUBLIC MONUMENTS IN IMPERIAL ROME

The advent of Augustus effectively brought to an end the republican tradition of individuals erecting monuments on private initiative for personal glorification.[6] Deprived of their traditional arena for public display in Rome, the Roman elite were instead compelled to publicize their achievements in their native cities throughout Italy and beyond. Hereafter, public art and architecture within the city were regarded as the prerogative of the emperor, intimately bound to an ideological programme designed to promote the interests of both himself and his household. Despite this, members of the ruling class on occasion were permitted to restore and embellish at their own expense monuments erected by ancestors, as in the case of M. Aemilius Lepidus, who received permission from Tiberius to refurbish the Basilica

---

[5] See Holliday 1997.   [6] Eck 1984 explores this issue in detail.

Aemilia (Tacitus, *Annales* 3.72). Though the various forms of public commemoration that existed in the Republic continued to be employed under the empire, their meaning and function, along with the motivations for their erection, changed significantly.

Whilst arches in the republican period were erected exclusively on private initiative, under the empire the senate and people voted approval. At this time the arch was transformed into an instrument of political propaganda, conceived to celebrate the military achievements of the emperor and his family. Its effectiveness rested in its use as an imperial billboard of sorts: the dedicatory inscription on the attic informed viewers of the reason for its erection, whilst relief sculptures on the facade reinforced this message through their depiction of events associated with the victory. Statuary was an integral feature of these monuments, all of which were surmounted in antiquity by imperial imagery. As few arches have survived to the present day, representations of these monuments on coins are invaluable in reconstructing their visual appearance.

In general, imperial arches were erected to commemorate the conclusion of a successful military campaign. The first such recipient was Octavian himself, who was voted this honour by the senate following his defeat of Sextus Pompey at the battle of Naulochus in 36 BC (Cassius Dio 49.15.1). Indeed, during the course of his forty-year reign Augustus was accorded a number of arches within the city of Rome, the most prominent of which was arguably that set up at the eastern end of the Forum Romanum to celebrate his recovery of the lost Roman standards from the Parthians in 19 BC (Cassius Dio 54.8.3). Though succeeding emperors were also presented with arches, this appears to have occurred less frequently.

Arguably the best surviving example of this monument type is the triple-bayed arch of Septimius Severus positioned in the north-west corner of the Roman Forum.[7] As the inscription attests, the monument was dedicated in AD 203 to the emperor and his two sons, Geta and Caracalla, in commemoration of their victories in the Parthian Wars. The monument also fulfilled an important dynastic function in that it served to legitimize the political rule of the Severan line. The key events of the campaigns were represented on four large sculptured panels on the east and west facades of the arch, the inspiration for which was most likely a series of paintings depicting the war, previously commissioned by Severus for public display in Rome (Herodian 3.9.12). The arch

---

[7] For this monument, see Brilliant 1967.

originally supported a large statue group, which was later melted down, featuring the emperor in a triumphal chariot drawn by six horses, flanked by equestrian figures of his sons.

The practice of placing statues atop columns also continued under the empire, though all such monuments now commemorated the achievements of the emperor alone. The earliest extant example is the Column of Trajan.[8] This marble structure, almost 100 feet in height, was crowned with a colossal statue of the emperor in military attire (Aurelius Victor, *De Caesaribus* 31.11). The column was conceived to celebrate Trajan's victories in the Dacian Wars, thus its message was overtly ideological, emphasizing the *virtus* of the emperor and by extension the martial supremacy of the Roman state. The monument marked an important innovation in the development of relief sculpture in that the shaft of the column was decorated with a continuous spiral frieze depicting various events and scenes from the wars in Dacia, providing an important pictorial record of the campaign. Although not part of the original design, the base of the column also served as the final resting place for the ashes of the emperor and his wife (Cassius Dio 69.2.3; Eutropius 8.5). A column was similarly set up by the senate and people of Rome in honour of Marcus Aurelius, to commemorate his victories over the Marcomanni and the Sarmatians in a series of campaigns fought between AD 172 and 175 (Aurelius Victor, *Caes.* 16.14). It was closely modelled on that of Trajan, in terms of both height and the prominent spiral frieze on the shaft of the column, which portrayed notable episodes from the wars.

Although in the republican period new temples were constructed chiefly by victorious commanders, this practice effectively came to an end with the establishment of the Principate, after which only the emperor and members of his family erected temples at Rome. A major contrast can be seen in the tendency of emperors to rebuild or refurbish existing temples as opposed to constructing new sanctuaries. Augustus, for instance, boasted in his *Res Gestae* that in the year 28 BC alone he restored eighty-two temples (4.20). This practice is perhaps best exemplified in the Pantheon, the most well-preserved public temple in Rome.[9] Originally constructed in 27 BC by M. Agrippa, intimate associate of Augustus, the temple was later renovated in AD 125 by the emperor Hadrian, who, rather than claiming the credit for himself, chose to retain the original dedicatory inscription: *M(arcus) Agrippa*

[8] Lepper and Frere 1988; Packer 2001, 74–7.   [9] See MacDonald 1982, 94–121.

L(uci) f(ilius) co(n)s(ul) tertium fecit – 'Marcus Agrippa, son of Lucius, having been consul three times, made (this)'.

Furthermore, imperial rulers maintained the republican custom of financing temples with monies acquired from foreign campaigns, and continued the practice of dedicating war spoils within the confines of religious precincts. Temples were also dedicated on occasion to deities with whom the emperor claimed a close association. Augustus, for example, funded the construction of the temple of Mars Ultor – the centrepiece of his new forum – with booty seized during the course of the civil wars (*Res Gestae* 4.21).[10] The purpose of the temple was twofold: to remind viewers of the defeat of Caesar's assassins in 42 BC, and to recall his recovery of the Roman standards from the Parthians, subsequently deposited within the temple (Cassius Dio 54.8.1–3; *Res Gestae* 5.29). The emphasis on these victories was further enhanced by the various military functions ascribed to the temple and forum. Roman commanders returning from a successful war dedicated votive offerings within the temple, the senate met there to discuss declarations of war and the granting of triumphs, and governors departed for their elected provinces from the forum (Cassius Dio 55.10.2–3; Suetonius, *Augustus* 29.2).

The emperor Vespasian likewise promoted the cult of Pax (Peace) by constructing a large temple to the goddess as the focal point of his new forum, paid for from the spoils acquired during the Jewish War (Cassius Dio 65.15.1; Josephus, *Bellum Judaicum* 7.7.158–9). The entire complex was designed to commemorate his victories in that conflict, which culminated in the sack of Jerusalem and the destruction of its temple.[11] The dedication of a temple to Pax was particularly significant as it symbolized Vespasian's assertion that he had brought peace to the entire Roman world. To reinforce this notion he embellished the sanctuary with artistic treasures taken from the temple at Jerusalem, including gold vessels and the sacred menorah (Josephus, *Bell. Jud.* 7.7.161). In addition, the forum was decorated with a large number of artworks by famous Greek artists, many of which had been transferred from Nero's Domus Aurea following his assassination (Pliny, *Hist. Nat.* 34.84). The Jewish historian Josephus (*Bell. Jud.* 7.7.160) remarks that the temple housed objects that men had previously travelled the entire world to see.

---

[10] For an overview of the Augustan Forum as a whole, see Anderson 1984, 65–100, Favro 1996 and Galinsky 1996, 197–213.

[11] On the forum of Vespasian, see Anderson 1984, 101–18.

One of the most striking changes in religious practice under the empire, however, is the construction of new temples to deified emperors. This precedent was established by the young Octavian, who consecrated a temple to *divus Iulius* on the site in the Forum Romanum where Caesar's body had been cremated (Appian, *Bellum Civile* 1.4; Cassius Dio 47.18; *Res Gestae* 4.19). Though not all emperors were deified, almost all those that were received a temple, at least until the middle of the second century AD. The dedication of such a temple was a powerful propaganda tool that served to legitimize the political rule of the successor by strengthening his association with his predecessor.

As discussed earlier in this chapter, throughout the republican period the Roman elite both erected and received honorific statues in the public spaces of Rome, the most popular sites being the Forum Romanum and the Capitoline Hill. This changed in the empire as the awarding of public honours was now exclusively at the discretion of the emperor and the senate.[12] In fact, on at least two occasions statues were removed en masse in accordance with an imperial decree: Caligula destroyed a vast number of statues in the area of the Campus Martius, subsequently forbidding the erection of such images anywhere in the city without express imperial consent (Suetonius, *Gaius* 34); likewise, Claudius cleared statues congesting the thoroughfares of Rome, again forbidding the erection of images by private citizens without senatorial permission (Cassius Dio 60.25.2–3).

The purpose of these restrictive measures was to control competition within the city in order to ensure that the pre-eminence of the emperor remained unchallenged. As no private individual was permitted to celebrate a triumph after 19 BC, a substitute reward was created for commanders whose victories merited this honour, hence the custom of awarding a triumphal statue (*statua triumphalis*) was introduced. From the time of Augustus onwards, anyone deserving of triumphal honours was instead presented with a bronze portrait statue in the Forum Augusti (Cassius Dio 54.24.7–8, 55.10.3). The porticos flanking the complex also contained a series of images representing the *summi viri*, celebrated figures – both historical and mythical – from Rome's illustrious past, accompanied by inscriptions listing their most outstanding achievements (Ovid, *Fasti* 5.551–68; Suetonius, *Aug.* 31.5). The addition of triumphal statues for victorious commanders thus enhanced the overall programmatic message of the urban complex, specifically that ultimate glory was to be obtained by performing great deeds on behalf

---

[12] Lahusen 1983, 97–107.

of the *res publica*. Statues to men who had distinguished themselves in the arenas of war and public life – particularly consuls and praetorian prefects – were similarly erected in the Forum of Trajan (Cassius Dio 68.16.2; *Historia Augusta, Alexander Severus* 26.4; *Marcus* 22.7). Consequently, the awarding of a statue through imperial or senatorial decree became the only sanctioned form of public display by means of which members of the Roman elite could distinguish themselves.[13]

The majority of public portrait statues erected under the empire venerated either the emperor himself or members of his household. On occasion, such figures formed an integral component of imperial architectural complexes; the Forum of Augustus, for example, was dominated by an image of the emperor in a triumphal quadriga (*Res Gestae* 6.35). In addition, the equestrian portrait, rare until the late Republic, became a prominent method of celebrating the military prowess of the emperor, as exemplified by the bronze image of Marcus Aurelius on horseback still standing on the Capitoline Hill. This period also witnessed the emergence of a new, albeit rare, category of imperial statuary: the colossal image. The first such portrait statue was the *colossus Augusti* in the Augustan Forum, set up in honour of the emperor by one of his successors, possibly Tiberius or Claudius (Martial, *Liber Spectaculorum* 8.44). Likewise, a colossal nude image of the emperor Nero, fashioned of bronze and standing over 100 feet high, was erected in his private residence, the Domus Aurea (Suetonius, *Nero* 31.1). Later moved by Hadrian to a position immediately adjacent to the Flavian Amphitheatre, the immense statue ultimately imparted its name to that structure, known today as the Colosseum. Lastly, an immense seated statue of the emperor Constantine dominated the apse of his great Basilica in the Forum Romanum, large fragments of which still survive. If an emperor fell from grace, his images were sometimes torn down or destroyed by the disgruntled populace in an almost ritualistic fashion, a process commonly termed *damnatio memoriae*.[14]

Another monument type to evolve under the empire was the ancestral tomb. During the republican period a select number of prominent families – notably the Marcelli, the Metelli and the Scipios – erected large sepulchres along the Via Appia on the outskirts of Rome. This tradition was continued by Augustus, though on a far grander scale. He planned and constructed an enormous mausoleum to function as the final resting place for the Julio-Claudian *gens*. Sited in the

---

[13] As illustrated by Eck 1984.
[14] This topic is treated extensively by Stewart 2003, 267–99.

Campus Martius, the tomb was covered with an earthen mound and surmounted by a gilded statue of the *princeps* (Strabo 5.3.8; Suetonius, *Aug.* 100.4). In front of the tomb bronze tablets were set up on which were inscribed a list of Augustus' most important achievements, the *Res Gestae Divi Augusti* (*Res Gestae* 1.1; Suetonius, *Aug.* 101.4). Thus the tomb fulfilled a practical function whilst simultaneously serving to advertise the glory and power of the imperial family, as evidenced by its conspicuous location and considerable size. Hadrian similarly built a mausoleum not far from that of Augustus, surmounted by an image of himself in a four-horse chariot. Although the mausoleum was intended as a family tomb, the ashes of several Antonine and Severan emperors were ultimately deposited here as well.

Arguably the most impressive monument of the imperial era is the Colosseum, one of the largest and most enduring symbols of Rome.[15] This vast amphitheatre was constructed by Vespasian for the exhibition of gladiatorial contests and wild beast hunts; the inaugural events alone lasted for 100 days during which time more than 5,000 animals were killed (Cassius Dio 66.25. 1–4; Suetonius, *Titus* 7.3). Financed with his Jewish spoils, the structure stood on the former site of Nero's palatial residence, the Domus Aurea (Martial, *Spect.* 2.5–6; Suetonius, *Vespasian* 9.1). This in itself was a significant act as it was in keeping with Vespasian's policy of restoring to public use areas formerly appropriated by Nero for his private building schemes.

As discussed previously, Vespasian and Augustus both employed war booty for the construction of large imperial fora. A similarly ambitious enterprise, the Forum Traiani, was also undertaken by the emperor Trajan, though on a scale heretofore unimagined.[16] The completed project consisted of the forum proper, a large basilica (known as the Basilica Ulpia), two libraries (one Greek and one Latin) and Trajan's Column. Though the complex was planned first and foremost to provide additional space for civic business and the imperial law courts, it was also conceived to commemorate the emperor's achievements in the Dacian campaigns, the spoils from which paid for its construction (Aulus Gellius, *Noctes Atticae* 13.25.1). This was achieved not only by means of the monumental Column, but also through an expansive sculptural programme. Statues of captive Dacian soldiers lined the colonnades of the forum, whilst gilded horses and military trophies ornamented their roofs (Gellius, *loc. cit.*). In addition, the principal entrance to the forum took the form of a three-bayed arch supporting an image of Trajan in a

---

[15] See Coarelli 2001. [16] Anderson 1984, 141–77. Packer 2001.

six-horse chariot, a direct allusion to the triumph he celebrated for his victories. His martial supremacy was further reinforced by the strategic incorporation of his colossal equestrian portrait as the centrepiece of the open area in front of the Basilica Ulpia (Ammianus Marcellinus 16.10.15).

LATER ROMAN EMPIRE

The period between the assassination of Alexander Severus in AD 235 and the accession of Diocletian in 284 was an era of unprecedented crisis for the Roman empire. Political instability, brought about by widespread economic problems, the constant threat of foreign invasion, and the rapid succession of men vying for the Principate, meant there was little time, money or manpower available to spend on the construction of new public building projects.[17] Moreover, the tetrarchic reforms instituted under Diocletian diminished the prominence of Rome; the city was superseded by four new capitals in separate parts of the empire, each with its own ruler. Constantine's decision to transfer the seat of imperial government to Constantinople decisively ended Rome's pre-eminent position as the focal point for architectural patronage by Roman emperors. As a result, one of the last official public monuments to be erected in Rome was the arch which the Roman senate set up adjacent the Colosseum to commemorate the victory of the emperor Constantine over his rival Maxentius at the battle of the Milvian Bridge in AD 312. Though similar in form and function to previous imperial arches, this monument was unique in that it was decorated to a large extent with statues and sculptural reliefs appropriated from the monuments of earlier emperors – namely Trajan, Hadrian and Marcus Aurelius – with whom Constantine wished to be associated. Monumental Rome had finally reached its zenith.

CONCLUSION

Considering the vast range of commemorative monuments that existed in ancient Rome, it is ironic that so little physical evidence survives. In spite of this, much can be learned from the primary literary sources, which are often invaluable in reconstructing the nature and purpose of

---

[17] With the notable exception of the 12-mile-long defensive wall which the emperor Aurelian constructed around the city between AD 271 and 275.

such monuments, not to mention their external appearance. The testimony of ancient writers attests the importance of this visual medium, which played a central role in enabling the Roman elite to communicate their social values and to win everlasting fame. Yet in the end it seems that not everyone pursued glory through a commemorative monument. Plutarch relates that at the conclusion of Cato the Elder's censorship, the Roman people honoured him with a statue and inscription in the temple of Salus. Prior to this, Cato had mocked those who delighted in such honours, declaring that, although they did not know it, their pride rested purely on the work of sculptors and painters, whereas his own images, of the most exquisite workmanship, were borne in the hearts of his fellow citizens. And to those who expressed amazement that many insignificant men had statues whilst he had none, Cato replied: 'I would much rather have men ask why I have no statue, than to ask why I have one' (Plutarch, *Cato Maior* 19.4).

FURTHER READING

Readers looking for information on specific topics discussed in this chapter should first check the works listed in the notes. In addition, individual entries on many of the monuments can be found in Platner and Ashby 1926, Richardson Jr. 1992, and *LTUR*. Two excellent guides to the archaeological remains of the city are Claridge 2010 and Coarelli 2007. These should be supplemented with Nash 1961–2, who provides photographs of the most important monuments. A brief overview of Roman monuments generally can be found in Coarelli 1972, Stambaugh 1988 and Ramage and Ramage 2008. The topographical surveys by Patterson 1992 and 2010 are also valuable. For collections of primary source materials on the city and its monuments, see Dudley 1967 and Pollitt 1983. Eck 1984 examines the changes in aristocratic display between the late Republic and the early empire. The most in-depth studies on the architectural and propaganda programme of Augustus are Zanker 1988, Favro 1996 and Galinsky 1996. For a comprehensive study of the imperial fora, based on the available textual and archaeological evidence, see Anderson Jr. 1984. Moatti 1993 is useful for the history of the major monuments from the decline of Rome to the present day.

12: (SUB)URBAN SURROUNDINGS

Robert Witcher

Ancient Roman writers such as Dionysius of Halicarnassus (*Antiquitates Romanae* 4.13.4–5) observed the impossibility of locating the point at which Rome ceased and the countryside began. In contrast, modern guidebooks to the remains of the ancient city have less trouble, frequently delimiting their area of interest within the impressive and largely extant Aurelian Wall. However, this wall was not built until the late third century AD and has no relevance to the first millennium of Rome's history. By using it to define the ancient city generally, ten centuries of *sub*urban development are unintentionally re-designated as *intra*mural or urban. Such an impression is reinforced by scholarly works on the ancient city, which frequently neglect any consideration of the suburbs or hinterland as distinct spaces; paradoxically, this leaves the impression that Rome was the centre of an empire, but existed in splendid isolation from its immediate surroundings. This chapter aims to demonstrate the need for an integrated approach to city, suburbs and hinterland.

Ancient cities created physical and conceptual unity through the definition of boundaries – classifying those people, places and activities which were part of the city, and those which were not. This chapter draws on textual and archaeological evidence to explore how the boundaries between the city of Rome and its suburbs were defined. It goes on to consider the buildings and everyday activities that characterized the suburbs.

Particular emphasis is placed on the transformation of suburbs over time and space. Many formerly suburban areas were incorporated within the city as it expanded. However, the intention is not to chase the 'leading edge' of the suburbs as it moved out from the city, but to consider the broader zone which encompassed the historical evolution of Rome's suburbs. This will involve consideration of monuments and areas frequently (but mistakenly) regarded as 'urban'. For example, the

Ara Pacis has been incorporated into the fabric of the late antique, medieval and modern city, but was built within an explicitly *sub*urban context.

The study of Rome's suburbs has a long history which has developed in tandem with the expansion of the modern city; major bursts of urban development during the late nineteenth century and after the Second World War led to the rapid excavation of extensive areas within the ancient city's suburbs. Similarly, the renewed expansion of Rome over the past decade has instigated large-scale, well-funded excavations leading to new and unexpected discoveries. Simultaneously, the *Lexicon Topographicum Urbis Romae – Suburbium* (*LTURS*) has systematically catalogued a wealth of disparate and often unpublished information about key sites in a broad swathe of land *c.*5–10 km beyond the Aurelian Wall.

This renewed attention to Rome's suburbs coincides with a trend in recent scholarship towards the study of 'peripheral' phenomena – that is, socially marginal activities, often occurring in distinct liminal spaces, such as burial and rubbish dumping. Such studies have sought to shed new light on the ancient city by exploring the unremarkable activities through which societies mark out social norms.

Similarly, there has been a renaissance of interest in Rome's wider hinterland: new archaeological projects reveal ever more complex patterns and densities of towns, villas and farms which were closely integrated with the social and economic life of the metropolis. Again, this coincides with recent developments in the wider study of ancient economies and urban–rural relations, moving away from old debates, such as the 'consumer city', to more sophisticated interpretations informed by archaeological and comparative evidence.

With these new data and concepts to hand, this chapter will question two persistent preconceptions about Rome's suburbs. The first is the widespread and entirely negative perception of suburbs as characterized by a range of undesirable activities, such as burial, which were banished to the urban periphery. The second is a more sophisticated position which recognizes both positive (e.g. leisure, social freedoms, luxury) and negative (e.g. execution, burial, manufacturing and rubbish dumping) associations, but finds these contradictory. In short, the aim is to question the subordinate status of Rome's suburbs in our interpretations and to reinstate them as an integral and complex part of the study of the ancient city.

DEFINING THE SUBURBS

What is a suburb? Both ancient and modern definitions rely heavily on the concept of the city itself, i.e. they are defined as 'not urban'. Geographers of modern suburbs have developed elaborate typologies, but ultimately recognize the theoretical and practical difficulties of unambiguously distinguishing city from suburb in terms of any simple measure of physical form (e.g. building or population density) or type of activities (e.g. manufacturing, commerce, housing). Roman concepts and definitions were equally problematic.

Suburbium is a rather rare noun used almost exclusively to describe the area around Rome rather than urban hinterlands in general; much more common is the adjectival form *suburbana* used in conjunction with features such as villa estates. In this specific sense, 'suburban' meant not only physical proximity to the city, but alluded to an elite lifestyle. These villas were integral to the practice and display of aristocratic values such as *amoenitas*. Other terms such as *continentia aedificia* (built-up area) and *extra-urbem* (beyond the walls) were rather less ideologically loaded expressions pertaining to periurban spaces.[1] Each of these terms referred to subtly different aspects of suburban life, but all share a common difficulty regarding precise geographical definition. How then were city and suburbs defined on the ground?

The most obvious method of bounding a city is to build walls. Urban enceintes resolve ambiguities by categorizing those people and activities included and those excluded from the city. Three successive walls encircled Rome, each subject to realignment and rebuilding. Roman authors relate that the 'Romulean Wall' was first constructed during the eighth century BC around the Palatine Hill;[2] later kings expanded this circuit to include other hills (*LTUR* 3.315–17). The 'Servian' or Republican Wall, possibly established in the late sixth century BC and rebuilt during the early fourth century BC, comprised a 10 m high defensive circuit of large *tufo* blocks, extending *c.*11 km and enclosing *c.*426 hectares (*LTUR* 3.319–24). Finally, the Aurelian Wall, commenced in AD 271, comprised a 6 m high (later raised to 12 m) brick-faced concrete wall with towers and heavily defended gateways,

---

[1] Champlin 1982; Goodman 2007, 6.
[2] Excavations beneath the Palatine have revealed a sequence of walls starting in the eighth century BC. This has generated much debate about its possible relation to Romulus' wall; the issue remains open, not least because of the wall's rather undefensive character and location at the foot of the hill.

MAP 12.1 Republican and Aurelian Walls, plus key monuments.

extending *c.* 19 km and enclosing *c.* 1350 hectares (*LTUR* 3.290–314). Chronologically, therefore, it is possible to discern a sequence of ever-larger circuits of ever-greater defensive strength. However, for five centuries, during the late Republic and early empire, buildings extended far beyond the Republican Wall – Rome was effectively an 'open city'.

Walls fix stable urban limits; but as cities grow, such restrictive physical boundaries are overwhelmed and either demolished or absorbed into the urban fabric (e.g. *LTUR* 3.321; Livy 1.44). For example, stretches of the Republican Wall were left deep inside the imperial city, where they remained culturally meaningful in terms of urban rituals[3] and stood testament to the impossibility of containing Rome.

However, physical walls are only one means of defining the (sub)urban. The ritually defined *pomerium* was perhaps of even greater

---

[3] Wiseman 1998, 19–21.

TI CLAVDIVS
DRVSI F CAISAR
AVGGERMANICVS
PONT MAX TRIB POT

VIIII IMP XVI COS IIII

CENSOR   P P

AUCTIS POPULI ROMANI

FINIBVS   POMERIVM

AMPLIAꟼITTERMINAꟼITQ

FIGURE 12.1 Drawing of Claudian pomerial cippus based on *CIL* 6.40852, pt. 8, fasc. 2 (1996).

importance (*LTUR* 3.96–105). The *pomerium* dates back to the archaic city when a ploughed furrow was used to mark out the boundary of the city (Plutarch, *Romulus* 11.1–4; Varro, *De lingua Latina* 5.143); this line may or may not have coincided with the earliest urban wall (*LTUR* 3.315–17). During the regal period, the area enclosed by the *pomerium* was enlarged several times; the circuit then remained largely unchanged during the republican period, broadly coinciding with the Republican Wall. There was renewed interest in extending the *pomerium* during the early imperial period, when Claudius made an explicit connection between the territorial expansion of the empire and the physical expansion of the city (Tacitus, *Annales* 12.23–4). By erecting inscribed *cippi* (e.g. *CIL* 6.1231a = 31537d) which physically defined the course of the *pomerium* (perhaps for the first time, as no republican equivalents are known), Claudius promulgated this imperial connection, though

Boatwright suggests he 'created' this tradition in line with his anti-quarian and political interests. Vespasian and Titus subsequently further extended the *pomerium* within the same tradition (*CIL* 6.31538a–c).[4]

The *pomerium* defined the city by establishing a series of binary oppositions: *urbs* versus *ager*, Roman versus foreign, life versus death, military versus civilian. Laws and traditions accumulated around this symbolic line: for example, the Twelve Tables forbade burial within the *pomerium* (Cicero, *De legibus* 2.23 debates significance) and generals surrendered their *imperium* on crossing the *pomerium* and entering the city.[5] As a result there was a concentration of funerary and military activity (e.g. *Castra Praetoria*) beyond the *pomerium*. However, the sanctity of this boundary may have been exaggerated. For example, it is often claimed that potentially dangerous foreign cults such as Juno Regina and Isis were kept beyond the *pomerium*. Yet there are multiple exceptions to such a rule (e.g. Venus Erycina on the Capitoline) and there is no clear textual or epigraphic evidence for any universal legal requirement. Rather, concerns around individual deities have been generalized (e.g. Cassius Dio 40.47.3–4 on the demolition of intra-pomerial temples to Isis and Serapis in 52 BC). Orlin argues that the concentration of foreign cults on the Aventine, uniquely beyond the *pomerium* but within the Republican Wall, was not an act of exclusion but of integration. It was a transitional space which allowed foreign gods to make the physical and ideological transition to Rome.[6]

As well as walls and religious circuits, other types of boundary encircled and defined the city. For example, goods entering Rome were taxed at a series of customs stations forming an economic cordon beyond both the Republican Wall and the *pomerium*.[7] Such multiple and mobile boundaries mean that no single line definitively divided city from suburb/hinterland. Further, all of these boundaries were con-ceptually and physically permeable. For example, administratively, the legal power of the tribunes extended *passus mille* (one mile) beyond the walls (compare Livy 3.20.6–7 and Cassius Dio 51.19.6; this probably referred generally to the *continentia aedificia*).[8] In a broader conceptual sense, 'Rome' was never restricted to the physical city itself. Sanctuaries vital to Roman religious identity had long existed at nearby towns such as Lavinium. Finally, in a more mundane sense, people moved back and forth across these boundaries on a daily basis. Perhaps it was precisely

[4] Boatwright 1986. [5] Drogula 2007 for revisionist interpretation.
[6] Orlin 2002. [7] Palmer 1980. [8] Goodman 2007, 15.

because of such permeability that boundary definition and maintenance held importance.

It is often suggested that boundaries such as the *pomerium* shaped the suburban character through its reception of polluting and undesirable activities (such as burial, execution and rubbish dumping) excluded from the urban core. However, such an approach is inadequate for two reasons. First, it defines the suburbs in purely negative terms – activities were pushed out to the periphery. However, suburban areas could provide positive attractions. For example, artisans such as potters found land, access to resources and transport links.[9] As places of transit, suburbs provided opportunities for competitive display: roads provided highly visible locations for funerary monuments, whilst gates and arches choreographed movement. In the northern Campus Martius, Augustus found a new space, unencumbered by associations with other leaders, which could be ideologically manipulated for dynastic purposes. Other activities and buildings are likely to have been constructed in suburban areas for more pragmatic reasons; for example, the concentration of theatres and stadia in the Campus Martius probably reflects a simple lack of space with the urban core.

Second, the idea that the suburbs were defined by urban exclusion is inadequate, because the distinction between city and suburb was, in reality, blurred. As the city grew, suburban areas were drawn into the urban core. Such incorporation could comprehensively transform the character of an area. For example, the extensive republican cemeteries on the Esquiline were gradually tidied and regulated and, eventually, levelled and landscaped as part of the *horti* of Maecenas;[10] connotations of death, pollution and poverty were replaced with notions of leisure and refinement (Horace, *Satires* 1.8). In other areas, traces of former suburban identity persisted. For example, Claudius' extension of the *pomerium* left the Tomb of Bibulus well within the city. Such traces of 'suburban' activities may have been conceptually problematic, but their frequency must have normalized the situation; tombs and anomalous architectural forms were part of the *bricolage* of the city's fabric.

There was also the difficulty of actually perceiving the urban boundary and therefore potential ambiguity in the experience of these

---

[9] Evidence for pottery production at Rome is rather limited; however, activity appears to have focused on the clay deposits of the Janiculum on the west bank of the Tiber (Peña 1999, 31–3).

[10] Bodel 1994, 50–3.

spaces. For example, the pre-Claudian arches of the Marcia–Tempula–Julia aqueducts crossing over the Via Praenestina may have *appeared* to those arriving at Rome as the point of transition from *suburbium* to *urbs*, the edge of the city. But passing beneath the aqueducts and continuing along the road, travellers would have encountered tombs on either side of the approach to the actual city gate (Porta Esquilina) and the *pomerium*.[11] The exclusion of burial from the city may have been a legal requirement, but the realities of an expanding city and multiple urban boundaries may have blurred the *experience* of this legality. Similarly, there was no sharp division of *continentia aedificia* and green open space. Rather, gardens and groves penetrated the city, whilst urban-style building spilled into the countryside.

This blurred reality between city and suburb also helps to explain some of the perceived paradoxes of the suburban landscape. Both the immediate suburbs and the wider *suburbium* have been characterized as places of extraction and production (e.g. stone, *pozzolana*, fruit, vegetables, pottery, brick) but also as places of consumption (e.g. elaborate villas). The suburbs were slums and shanty towns, but also dotted with villas set within spacious gardens (e.g. *horti* of Maecenas, *LTUR* 3.70–4). They were cramped and dirty, but also green and open (in relation to Campus Martius, *LTUR* 1.220–4). Suburbs were beyond the city, but strictly regulated.[12] They were teeming with life, but places of the dead. In part, such seemingly discordant juxtapositions result from generalization of fragmentary topographical information, in part they also reflect the reality of extreme economic and social pressures on the leading edge of an expanding imperial metropolis. Whilst the rich and powerful dominated the urban core, the suburbs were the place to view the social structure of Rome in action – the achievement of high status (villas, *horti*, mausoleums), the aspiration to higher status (especially the funerary monuments of freedmen) and the utter lack of any status (squatters' huts, *putuculi* or public burial pits).

An excellent example of the apparently contradictory nature of suburban phenomena is the *hortus*. Traditionally, *horti* have been interpreted as large parks and gardens established by the elite during the late Republic and early empire. They were intended for leisurely retreat and the display of culture and status through the conspicuous consumption of expensive land and elaborate architecture and sculpture. However,

[11] Coates-Stephens 2004, 34.
[12] Note the management of cemetery areas on the Esquiline, Bodel 1994, 50–3. On production in the suburban area, see Chapter 18.

this interpretation bears the strong influence of the Renaissance imagination. Purcell stresses the parallel economic significance of *horti* as speculative investments – property to be bought and sold as land prices rose.[13] In other words, *horti* were both a 'green belt' *and* the basis for the city's further expansion.

Rather than pollution and waste exported over the urban boundary, the suburbs were integral to the well-being of Rome. Conceptually, the suburbs were perceived and represented as a fundamental component of the city. The marble *Forma Urbis* displayed in the Temple of Peace (*LTUR* 4.67–70) mapped not only the monumental urban core but also represented extensive suburban tracts, though few relevant fragments survive. In a more immediate sense, the suburbs were also vital to the survival of the city as the primary location for the importation and processing of food. Extensive warehouses were built in the suburbs to store imported grain, oil and wine (*LTUR* 4.67–70; 5.285). Large-scale mill complexes (*pistrinae*) at the Porta Maggiore and on the Janiculum (*LTUR* 3.270–2), powered by water from adjacent aqueducts, attest the industrial scale necessary to support the urban population.[14] But the location of these activities in the suburbs was not determined by simple expedience (e.g. cheaper land). The monumentality of aqueducts and warehouses indicates they were more than just functional buildings; production and supply were integral to Rome's expression of power. Nowhere was this more obvious than in suburban areas where boats, mule trains, ox carts and herds of animals congregated in the shadow of monumental aqueducts. Monte Testaccio (*LTUR* 5.28–30), the largest of several artificial hills of discarded amphorae, was as much a highly visible monument to Rome's power to command and consume surplus as it was to the need to manage rubbish dumping in an area of rising land prices.[15]

Beyond the inner suburbs lay the wider *suburbium*. Again, it is impossible to delimit its extent or to identify activities unique to this area. The villas of Roman aristocrats were densely clustered along consular roads and around suburban towns such as Tibur and Tusculum, particularly in the hills to the south and east of Rome.[16] This architectural form was hardly unique to the *suburbium*, but their numbers and close integration into the social, political and economic fabric of the city, as revealed for example through Pliny the Younger's letters (e.g. *Epistulae* 9.36), was distinctive. In particular, emperors confiscated

---

[13] Purcell 2007.   [14] Coates-Stephens 2004, 22–9.
[15] For rubbish dumping, see Dupré Raventós and Remolà 2000.   [16] Marzano 2007.

or constructed elaborate architectural complexes to which they could physically withdraw from the city to hunt, recuperate, receive guests or play the role of a traditional aristocratic landowner. As well as the singular complex of Hadrian at Tivoli, there was a host of others including the villas of Nero at Subiaco, Trajan at Arcinazzo, and that associated with Marcus Aurelius at Villa Magna.

The countryside was also densely occupied with small farms intensively producing food and luxuries for the urban market. The scale of production is amply attested by archaeological evidence for cisterns (to irrigate gardens and orchards), vine trenches, pits for olive trees, oil presses and wine cellars. But it is important to stress that these suburban settlements were not just producers for the urban market; the dense distributions of mass-produced pottery, imported marble and stamped bricks mapped by archaeologists is testament to a 'metropolitan' style of consumption on even the smallest farms.[17] Such closely integrated economic and social networks make it even harder to discern clear differences between urban, suburban and rural.

As well as dispersed 'rural' settlement, there were also many ancient Latin, Sabine and Etruscan cities such as Tusculum, Cures and Veii located in the *suburbium*. These maintained distinct civic identities, but as Rome increasingly monopolized the social and economic functions of these old cities, imperial patronage became an important means of support. Paradoxically, as Rome's immediate suburbs were gradually redefined as urban, these erstwhile independent cities were slowly redefined as *sub*urban, forming part of an 'extended metropolis'.[18]

Just as delimiting the start of the suburbs is an impossible task, so attempts to define the farthest boundary of the *suburbium* are equally spurious. Inevitably, the density of farms and villas declined with distance from the city, but there is no clear line beyond which the social and economic influence of Rome dissipated. Even if such a line did exist, it would have to have been mobile, shifting ever further from the city as economic pressures inflated the price of goods, and the construction of roads and bridges drew ever more distant areas into the immediate influence of the city.

In sum, Rome's suburbs cannot be defined in simple terms such as location, material form, or specific social and economic activities. Even incontrovertible 'truths', such as burial outside the *pomerium*, emerge as rather less straightforward in reality. In practice, the suburbs are best

[17] Witcher 2005. [18] Witcher 2005.

characterized by a distinctive *mobility* and *diversity*: that is, mobility of people and goods, but also mobility of the suburbs themselves, as well as a diversity of buildings, activities and ideologies.

A JOURNEY THROUGH THE SUBURBS

If Rome's suburbs defy definition, how else can we 'know' them? Guidebooks and topographical dictionaries often structure visitor itineraries along Rome's consular roads.[19] However, such accounts are composites of many periods, describing a city which no individual could ever have experienced. One approach is to investigate 'lived' spatial encounters at specific chronological moments. Favro (1996) presents two accounts reconstructing the experiences of pedestrians moving through Rome's streets – from the Forum Romanum along the Via Flaminia to the Milvian Bridge in 52 BC (*ibid.*: 24–41) and from the Milvian Bridge back to the Forum in AD 14 (*ibid.*: 252–80).[20]

Favro's journeys permit her to consider the profound impact of Augustus' urban programme on the everyday experience of the city. The following section presents a similar journey, with the specific aim of dissolving the stark conventional distinction between urban and rural, and instead exploring a single extended suburban space which encompasses monuments, such as the Ara Pacis, and practices, such as pottery production, which are rarely considered together. To complement Favro's two journeys (52 BC and AD 14), we move forward in time again. Likewise, our journey will also follow the line of the Via Flaminia, but will omit the Forum Romanum, Rome's urban heart, instead starting at the Porta Fontinalis in the Republican Wall. It will then continue via the Milvian Bridge some 20 Roman miles (*c.* 30 km) deep into the countryside of Etruria.

In contrast to Favro, we will not accompany fictional individuals with their own extensive personal memories of Rome's urban landscape and appreciation of its cultural history. Rather, we will use our own eyes, ears and noses. In more of a hurry, especially on the first stretch, and less well-versed in how to read the monuments encountered, we will be less contemplative of the broader cultural resonance of what we see and hear. Details of topography and debate can be found in the

---

[19] E.g. Messineo 1991.
[20] For other briefer examples, see Patterson 2000, 97–101; Purcell 1987b, 187–9.

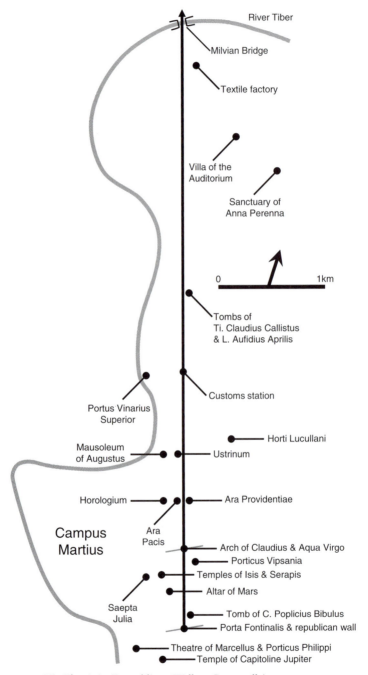

River Tiber

Milvian Bridge

Textile factory

Villa of the
Auditorium

Sanctuary of
Anna Perenna

0   1km

Tombs of
Ti. Claudius Callistus
& L. Aufidius Aprilis

Customs station

Portus Vinarius
Superior

Horti Lucullani

Mausoleum
of Augustus

Ustrinum

Horologium

Ara Providentiae

Campus
Martius

Ara
Pacis

Arch of Claudius & Aqua Virgo

Porticus Vipsania

Temples of Isis & Serapis

Altar of Mars

Saepta
Julia

Tomb of C. Poplicius Bibulus

Porta Fontinalis & republican wall

Theatre of Marcellus & Porticus Philippi

Temple of Capitoline Jupiter

MAP 12.2 Via Flaminia (Republican Wall to Centocelle).

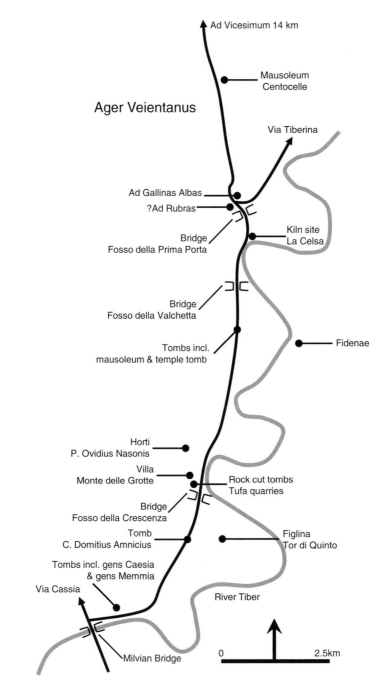

Ad Vicesimum 14 km

Mausoleum
Centocelle

Ager Veientanus

Via Tiberina

Ad Gallinas Albas

?Ad Rubras

Bridge
Fosso della Prima Porta

Kiln site
La Celsa

Bridge
Fosso della Valchetta

Tombs incl.
mausoleum & temple tomb

Fidenae

Horti
P. Ovidius Nasonis

Villa
Monte delle Grotte

Rock cut tombs
Tufa quarries

Bridge
Fosso della Crescenza

Tomb
C. Domitius Amnicius

Figlina
Tor di Quinto

Tombs incl. gens Caesia
& gens Memmia

Via Cassia

River Tiber

0   2.5km

Milvian Bridge

Map 12.2 (*cont.*)

relevant *LTUR(S)* entries. The more ephemeral structures and activities seen, heard and smelt are inevitably imaginary, but draw on textual, epigraphic and comparative evidence. Particular emphasis is placed on archaeological information, especially as we move further from Rome and textual evidence becomes disproportionately rarer. The results of recent archaeological discoveries in the suburbs of the modern city are also incorporated.

It is AD 79. Setting off from the Forum, we pass through the old Republican Wall via the Porta Fontinalis (*LTUR* 3.319–24, 328–9) and skirt the base of the Capitoline Hill. High above is the new Temple of Capitoline Jupiter recently rebuilt by Vespasian following its destruction during the Civil War (*LTUR* 1.226–33; Tacitus, *Hist.* 3.71); to our left is the curving facade of the Theatre of Marcellus (*LTUR* 5.31–5) and the Porticus Philippi (*LTUR* 4.146–8). The road turns north and runs straight into the distance (*LTUR* 5.135–7; 5.139–41). We pass a number of imposing republican tombs including that of C. Poplicius Bibulus (*LTUR* 4.295; generally Juvenal 1.170). The inscriptions on these buildings narrate the lives of the rich and influential individuals and families of the city.

As we walk north, we keep the Campus Martius to our left (*LTUR* 1.220–4); as the name suggests, we pass monuments associated with the military such as the Altar of Mars (*LTUR* 1.223–6). Many date back to when citizens gathered here for the census, to vote or to complete their military obligations. Further along is the Saepta Julia, an enormous colonnaded space; originally a voting precinct, it is now used for shows and gymnastic contests (*LTUR* 4.228–9; Suetonius, *Augustus* 43; *Nero* 12). Like so many grand buildings hereabouts, the Saepta is full of sculptures and artworks, many from the eastern kingdoms. We also pass the Temples of Isis and Serapis (*LTUR* 3.107–10), a splendid complex of buildings, porticos and exedra decorated with Egyptian obelisks and sphinxes. Beyond, towards the Tiber, lie theatres, baths, porticos and temples, as well as grand old houses and open spaces.

To our right is the Porticus Vipsania, a large colonnaded space which houses a map of the world (*LTUR* 4.151–3; Pliny the Elder, *Historia Naturalis* 3.16–17). We continue towards a triumphal arch; the inscription announces that it was built by Claudius to commemorate his conquest of Britain (*LTUR* 1.85–6; *CIL* 6.920; Cassius Dio 60.22). Until recently, the arch also marked the line of the *pomerium*. The inscription states that Claudius was entitled to move this ritual urban boundary following his successful foreign wars, which had extended the territory subject to Rome (*CIL* 6.40852). However, just four years ago Vespasian and Titus extended the *pomerium* still further north; the old pomerial *cippi* were buried and new ones set up by the roadside ahead.[21] Claudius' arch also carries the Aqua Virgo over the road; an inscription on an arcade further to our right recalls that the emperor rebuilt the aqueduct and restored the water supply to the Campus Martius (*LTUR* 1.72–3; Frontinus, *De aquaeductu* 1.10; *CIL* 6.1252).

Beyond the arch, the landscape opens out; looking back, the Aqua Virgo appears like a wall enclosing the city (see *LTUR* 1.223); beneath its arcades are the 'lean-tos' of squatters.[22] To our left is a spacious complex of monuments erected by Augustus to commemorate his family and the city's imperial destiny. Next to the road is the *Ara Pacis* (*LTUR* 4.70–4; 5.285–6), an altar within a precinct of richly carved marble celebrating Rome's past, present and future. It is matched on the opposite side of the road by Tiberius' *Ara Providentiae* (*LTUR* 4.165–6). Behind the *Ara Pacis* is the *horologium* (sundial, *LTUR* 3.35-7), a towering Egyptian obelisk covered with illegible hieroglyphs, which casts a shadow across a huge marble and bronze pavement. It is an impressive sight, but from the position of the sun in the sky, the monument's timekeeping seems to have become inaccurate (Pliny, *Hist. Nat.* 36.73)!

Just beyond, we pass the imperial funerary complex. Here, emperors and members of the imperial family are cremated within a large travertine enclosure (*ustrinum*, *LTUR* 5.97) and their ashes interred in the huge mausoleum by the river (*LTUR* 3.234–9). The latter is adorned with tall trees, Egyptian obelisks and long inscriptions detailing Augustus' achievements (*res gestae*).

On the hillslopes to our right are *horti* – amongst the trees and open areas, we glimpse the buildings and terraces of the Horti Lucullani, the most beautiful in Rome (*LTUR* 3.67–70; Plutarch, *Lucullus* 39.3). Many of these properties were owned by famous men of the Republic such as Lucullus whose names they preserve. Most now belong to the emperor, though those closest to the road have been sold for development. Indeed, labourers are building large brick-faced concrete *insulae* on the Campus Agrippae to our right (1.217).[23]

[21] *CIL* 6.31538a records Vespasian's northern pomerial expansion, but its original location is unknown.
[22] Scobie 1986, 402.
[23] Archaeological evidence for domestic architecture at Rome is comparatively poor and dominated by large, second-century AD *insulae*. There is limited evidence

Soon the Pincian Hill comes down towards the Tiber.[24] We pass a customs station for the collection of tolls on goods imported into the city; officials count carts of amphorae and flocks of animals on their way to market.[25] Down to our left are the docks and warehouses of the Portus Vinarius Superior (*LTUR* 4.156), where wine and other goods brought downriver from Umbria and Sabina are unloaded.

We pass a succession of funerary monuments – extravagant and humble, in old styles and new, commemorating young and old, individuals and families, rich and poor. There are inscriptions in Latin, Greek and unfamiliar languages proclaiming names, birthplaces, occupations, ages and the relatives left behind. On our right, we pass a couple of grand cylindrical mausolea of travertine, one perhaps a century old, and a complex of ornate funerary altars commemorating Ti. Claudius Callistus and the recently deceased L. Aufidius Aprilis and his freedmen (*LTURS* 1.167–9; 2.111). On the higher ground beyond are wealthy villas and *horti*. All along our route, boundary stones announce the owners of *praedia* (estates) bordering the road; here, between the Via Flaminia and the Tiber, is an estate belonging to Calpurnia (*LTURS* 2.54–5; *CIL* 6.29782).

Further along, on the high wooded hill to our right is the sanctuary of Anna Perenna (*LTURS* 1.59–63). On the Ides of March, people walk from the city to celebrate New Year and the coming spring (Ovid, *Fasti* 3.523–696). They drink much wine with the hope of living long lives (understandable after passing all those tombs!); they sing, dance and make magical offerings of coins, lamps, curse tablets and tiny figurines into a sacred pool. It is a far cry from the formal processions and sacrifices conducted on the Capitoline.

We catch up with some carts carrying night-soil out of the city to the market gardens.[26] Many of these plots are small patches of land worked by urban folk, but some are larger estates. We pass a grand but old-fashioned villa on our right; with its *tufo* block construction it is more like a public building than a private house. Despite the risk

---

for smaller-scale domestic architecture of earlier periods and especially the more ephemeral structures to be expected in the suburbs.

[24] Later, this was the site of the Porta Flaminia in the Aurelian Wall which enclosed the first *c*.2 km of the Via Flaminia – and the monuments along it – within the city limits. This newly urban stretch was renamed Via Lata (*LTUR* 5.139).

[25] Palmer 1980, 221–3 for the *ansarium* and *foricularium* as taxes on oil/wine and animals respectively. See Peña 1999, 39 n. 27 for alternative interpretation.

[26] Scobie 1986, 414.

of flooding, the villa sits on the plain surrounded by verdant gardens exploiting the rich soil and abundant water.[27]

As we continue, the road is lined with funerary monuments jostling for prime position. On our left is a large necropolis; the tombs are closely packed with dozens of inscriptions marking plots and commemorating the deceased, both individuals and families (modern Via Calderini). Beyond, the graves of the less well-off are marked by upturned amphorae.[28] Nearby, funerary pyres of the recently deceased burn and the bereaved mourn. On anniversaries and festivals such as *Parentalia*, relatives will return to make offerings and to share a meal. Some larger tomb plots are used as vegetable gardens (*cepotaphion* tombs), whilst some of the grander old tombs provide shelter for the destitute and privacy for prostitutes and their clients. Though places of the dead, these cemeteries are busy with the living.[29]

Next we pass a textile factory, an old building alongside the road. The smell of the urine and dyes used to treat the newly woven woollen cloth hangs in the air. We walk up the ramp onto the Milvian Bridge (*LTURS* 4.76–7) to cross the Tiber, passing beneath an arch erected by Augustus to commemorate his restoration of the Via Flaminia as far as Ariminum (see *CIL* 11.365). Below, are warehouses with boats and rafts unloading cargoes of bricks and timber from upriver. On the far bank is a road junction, surrounded by funerary monuments (e.g. to the *gens Caesia* and *gens Memmia*, *LTURS* 2.27–9). Here, the Via Cassia strikes north, whilst the Flaminia turns east along the Tiber. Many of the funerary monuments hereabouts commemorate military men – soldiers of the Praetorian Guard, the urban cohorts and the recently disbanded *Germani corporis custodes* (the private Batavian guard of the Julio-Claudian emperors; *LTURS* 2.254). On the higher ground above are more *horti* and villas (e.g. *Horti* of P. Ovidius Nasonis, *LTURS* 4.151–2). The succession of funerary monuments displays a bewildering mix of shapes, sizes and materials; here, on our left are some *columbaria*

---

[27] The Villa of the Auditorium, Carandini 2006b. The earliest structures date to *c.*550–500 BC with six subsequent phases of rebuilding/extension extending into the early third century AD; the substantial *tufo* block construction of the third-century BC phase remained the core of the villa until its abandonment. Flood deposits separated phases of occupation. Generally, this area had been assumed to be thinly occupied, apart from tombs, because of the flood risk. However, discoveries such as this villa indicate an intensively used landscape (Ricci 2002, 90).

[28] Amphorae burials are not attested at this particular location, but are documented at the better-preserved necropolis at Isola Sacra, north of Ostia (Graham 2006, 92–4).

[29] Graham 2006, 36–9; Scobie 1986, 402–3.

and mausolea and, on our right, a striking complex with an elaborate funerary altar and portraits of C. Domitius Amnicius (Tor di Quinto).

Out on the floodplain is a *figlina* or brickyard (Tor di Quinto). Artisans prepare clay, mould bricks and lay them out to dry. Thick smoke billows from the large kilns. By the river, workers load bricks onto rafts for transportation downstream.

We cross a stone bridge (across the Fosso della Crescenza) and red cliffs now rise up to our left. They are pock-marked with ancient rock-cut tombs and quarries used to supply stone blocks for the monuments of Rome. The fashion for brick-faced concrete has led to a recent decline in quarrying and the rise of *figlinae* instead. High above we glimpse another grand old villa (Monte delle Grotte); up there it must be fresher with splendid views back to the city. Below, the funerary monuments continue: mausoleums of marble, a highly ornate terracotta tomb in the form of a little temple, and so on.

On the opposite bank of the Tiber we see the small town of Fidenae. Five centuries ago, Rome fought the city of Veii for control of this river port. Today it is a sleepy place. Although the countryside around is full of farms, the owners sell their produce directly at Rome and few people now need to pay a visit to the old town.

Passing a continuous facade of funerary monuments, we cross a stone bridge (across the Fosso della Valchetta). Immediately beyond is a large manufacturing complex producing pottery (La Celsa). Men load kilns with delicate cups and plates for sale at market; a pile of misfired pots is dumped by the side of the road in the shadow of a towering mausoleum (*LTURS* 4.148–9).

We cross another stone bridge (across the Fosso della Prima Porta) and arrive at the small settlement of Ad Rubras.[30] Here, we pause for a rest and some food. Inns and a few houses jostle alongside yet more mausolea and rock-cut tombs. To our right, the Via Tiberina strikes off towards the sanctuary town of Lucus Feroniae; the *compitium* (crossroads) is marked by a fountain.[31]

On the cliffs above us – and projecting out on enormous buttressed terraces – is a grand villa known as *ad Gallinas Albas*. Augustus' wife

---

[30] The precise location of this settlement is unclear; the Peutinger Table locates it at the ninth mile of the Via Flaminia, i.e. near modern Prima Porta. However, some scholars have argued for a position further back along the road near Grottarossa (see Messineo 1991, 83).

[31] Messineo 1991.

Livia had inherited the estate from her first husband; it then became imperial property (*LTURS* 3.17–24). The story goes that an eagle dropped a white hen bearing a laurel twig into Livia's lap. She planted the twig at this villa and a grove grew from it; the emperors used these laurels for their crowns (Cassius Dio 48.52.3–4; Pliny, *Hist. Nat.* 15.137). Ominously, the trees suddenly died on the eve of the recent Civil War (Cassius Dio 63.29.3; Suetonius, *Galba* 1).

The Flaminia now climbs onto higher ground with extensive views across the *ager Veientanus*. The countryside is thickly settled. There are large, wealthy villas to which the senators and knights come to escape the noise and heat of the city. Most are working estates surrounded by fields and orchards. Many have large cisterns, prominently located on high ground, to provide water for baths and to irrigate gardens of vegetables and flowers for market. Some estates are connected to the Via Flaminia by private paved *diverticula*, down which mule trains laden with goods make their way to Rome. Dispersed around the villas are many small farms.

Gradually the funerary monuments become intermittent, but no less grand (e.g. Centocelle). Most are the tombs of wealthy villa owners commemorated on the roadside-edge of their estates. Even though the villas regularly change hands, the inscriptions on these monuments form lasting reminders of past owners. There are also large cemeteries for the everyday folk and slaves who live and work in the surrounding countryside. The workers in the fields are prematurely old; indeed, the further from Rome we travel, the fewer old people we see.[32] The city may be hot and dangerous but these rural folk have hard lives – no wonder so many migrate to Rome given half a chance!

As the sun sets to our left, we arrive at Ad Vicesimum (Madonna della Guardia), a road station 20 miles from Rome. The Via Flaminia is a former military road designed to move troops to distant places, hence it does not pass through any of the ancient towns in this area. However, a number of small roadside settlements have developed along the consular roads providing food and accommodation for travellers and services for surrounding farms. Hopefully, we can find a bed for the night.

---

[32] Skeletal evidence indicates that suburban populations had more pathological and chronic conditions and died significantly younger than urban populations, e.g. Cucina et al. 2006.

CONCLUSIONS

By engaging with the suburbs as a 'lived' space, our journey emphasizes that no clear line divided city from suburb from hinterland. Legal, religious and administrative boundaries ringed the city, but these were mobile, overlapping and permeable. Instead, the suburbs were defined *in practice*: agriculture, extraction, manufacturing, burial, entertainment, soldiering and the worship of foreign cults. Individually, none of these was exclusively 'suburban', but they found particular concentration in these areas. Some were excluded from the city; others were drawn to the opportunities on offer. It was the juxtapositions between rich and poor, production and consumption, leisure and death, military and civilian, enforced exile and voluntary escape which defined a distinctive suburban space. Indeed, Goodman argues that the urban periphery both created *and* resolved the tension between elite ideologies of the ancient city (walls, *pomerium*) and socio-economic realities (land prices, social competition).[33] But if the suburbs were a product of the city, they were also a microcosm of the wider world: triumphal arches, obelisks, works of Hellenistic art, and funerary monuments commemorating people from three continents. These evoked not so much the *city* as the empire beyond.

Further, by locating our journey at one specific moment in time, it is clear that the suburbs were always changing in terms of form, use and ownership; the memories of earlier people and landscapes were all around. Economic pressures, social opportunities, political expedience and serendipitous events – such as the great fire of AD 80 which would destroy much of the Campus Martius just traversed (Cassius Dio 66.24; Suetonius, *Titus* 8) – created the circumstances through which suburban areas were drawn into the urban core. Material traces of former suburbs created anomalies in the urban fabric which walls, laws and customs tried but failed to resolve. It is precisely such tensions and ambiguities around *sub*urbanity which inform us about what really mattered in ancient Rome.

FURTHER READING

Goodman 2007 provides a wide-ranging treatment of suburbs in the Roman west, including Rome; Patterson 2000 discusses Rome specifically. For burial, Graham 2006; for *horti*, Cima and La Rocca 1998;

[33] Goodman 2007, 233–4.

for rubbish dumping, Dupré Raventós and Remolà 2000; for villas, Marzano 2007. Definitions: *suburbium* etc., Champlin 1982; *pomerium*, *LTUR* 4.96–105.

The *LTURS* volumes catalogue (named) monuments in the immediate suburbs. Perhaps the most important of recent suburban excavations is the Villa of the Auditorium (Carandini 2006b). Morley 1996 draws on texts and archaeology to consider the relationship between Rome and its wider hinterland; also see Witcher 2005, 2006. Messineo 1991 provides a comprehensive and richly illustrated guide to the Via Flaminia.

PART III

❦

LOGISTICAL CHALLENGES

13: THE TIBER AND RIVER TRANSPORT

Steven L. Tuck

Romulus was admirably successful in achieving all the benefits that could belong to maritime cities, without incurring the dangers to which they are exposed. He built Rome on the bank of an inexhaustible river, whose equal current discharges itself into the sea by a vast embouchure, so that our city can receive all it wants from the sea, and discharge its superabundant commodities by the same channel. It finds, in the same river, a communication by which it receives from the sea all the productions necessary to the conveniences and elegancies of life, and possesses an inland territory beside, which furnishes it with an exuberant supply of provisions.

(Cicero, *De re publica* 2)

For a while the Syrian Orontes has been emptying itself into the Tiber.

(Juvenal 3.62)

ROMAN ATTITUDES TOWARDS THE TIBER

As this small sampling of quotes makes clear, the history, traditions and attitude of the Romans towards the Tiber mark a very complex and developing relationship. The reality of Rome's growth and interaction with the Tiber is arguably the most important geographical fact in the rise of the city. Romans were aware of its key role as a transportation conduit, fearful of it as a route for foreign influence, keenly aware of its place as a sacred boundary, but also frequently used it as a path to remove trash, wastewater or pollution from the city. Any examination of the Tiber and its relationship to the city of ancient Rome needs to take all of these relationships into account. Furthermore, while the preponderance of evidence is weighted towards the practical aspects of the Tiber including its key role in food supply, the symbolic aspects were always prominent in the minds of the Romans and need to be addressed to establish the Romans' attitude towards their crucial connection to the larger Mediterranean world. One of the most powerful examples of this attitude is the role of Tiber as the symbolic father of Rome, guiding Aeneas in a dream to the future site of Rome (Virgil, *Aeneid* 8.26–65).

At 409 km, the Tiber is the third longest river in Italy after the Po and the Adige and remarkable for its navigability, which made the eventual size of Rome possible while the river's major floods in contrast limited the expansion of the city into the flood plain near the river for many centuries. Ships in antiquity could sail up and down stream along at least 70 km of the lower stream to and from the Tyrrhenian Sea. This fact, coupled with the high cost of overland transport, especially of bulk commodities, meant that the Tiber fulfilled the key role of providing transport of Rome's important bulk commodities including food, notably grain, olive oil and wine, as well as stone, timber and the raw materials of Roman urban life. We would do well to remember the uniqueness of Rome's scale. At over 1 million inhabitants in the early empire, it was the largest city by far in the ancient Mediterranean world and the largest city in history until surpassed by nineteenth-century London. Its size and dense urban population were made possible by exploiting the benefits of the Tiber as Cicero eloquently stated in *De re publica*. It provided all of the positive aspects of a coastal community with the protections of an inland foundation, ensuring that Rome developed with adequate resources yet free from the dangers of attack and direct foreign influence found so lamentable by later authors such as Juvenal. Nevertheless, the Tiber also had a down side and the disadvantages of the river need to be assessed as well, because they were formative to the development of Rome.

The unpredictable and ultimately uncontrollable nature of the Tiber is arguably the source of much of the ritual that defined the river as a sacred boundary that needed propitiation. The role of the priests (*pontifices*) in that propitiation is thought to be the source for their titles, deriving from the word *pons*, the bridge that first crossed the boundary of the Tiber for the propitiation of which violation of the sacred they were responsible. The Janus figure herms that decorate the ends of the surviving republican Pons Fabricius demonstrate the potency of the river and the dangers in bridging it (see Figures 13.1, 13.2). The dedicatory inscription of the bridge, inscribed on the arches that bridge the left channel so that they can only be read easily by one sailing up or down the river, demonstrates the primacy of the river-borne perspective

FIGURE 13.1 Pons Fabricius.

to the bridge's patron (see Figure 13.3). Perhaps the most intriguing and powerful symbol of this religious engagement with the Tiber is the *Sacra Argeorum*, a ritual described by Plutarch and Dionysius of Halicarnassus involving the Tiber, human sacrifice and ritual disposal. In the ritual, which Plutarch refers to as Rome's great rite of purification, the priests and Vestal Virgins process to the Tiber carrying effigies of men, bound hand and foot, and then throw them into the Tiber from the Pons Sublicius, the oldest and most symbolically charged of the bridges over the river. The description in Dionysus is more complete, but can be excerpted to reveal the relevant elements:

> to appease the anger of the god by making effigies
> resembling the men they had been wont to bind hand and
> foot and throw into the stream of the Tiber, and dressing
> these in the same manner, to throw them into the river
> instead of the men . . . This the Romans continued to do
> every year even down to my day a little after the vernal
> equinox, in the month of May, on what they call the Ides
> (the day they mean to be the middle of the month); on this
> day, after offering the preliminary sacrifices according to
> the laws, the *pontifices*, as the most important of the priests
> are called, and with them the virgins who guard the

FIGURE 13.2 Janus figure herms on Pons Fabricius.

perpetual fire, the praetors, and such of the other citizens as
may lawfully be present at the rites, throw from the sacred
bridge into the stream of the Tiber thirty effigies made in
the likeness of men, which they call *Argei*.
  (Dionysius of Halicarnassus, *Roman Antiquities*, 38.2)

The meaning of the ritual is and always has been debated; it might
represent a ritual purification of the city with the effigies representing

FIGURE 13.3 Inscription on Pons Fabricius.

hostile forces expelled from the community by its religious authorities. Or it could represent a ritual human sacrifice operating prophylactically to placate the spirits that might threaten Rome in the following year. Note that Dionysius seems to believe that the ritual preserves the form of an earlier one in which actual men were thrown into the river. If this were the case, the latter interpretation could be the accurate one, although the reference in some sources to the men being over sixty years of age also implies a ceremony allowing for the disposal of non-contributing members of society. In either case the role of the Tiber is identical. With its constant flow, it represents the ideal location for the deposit of threatening or divisive material that in some way harms the city or whose destruction ensures the security of the city. The dumping of the Tarquins' grain into the Tiber after their expulsion is an example of this pattern (Livy 2.5). In much the same way the Vestals used the river and the Pons Sublicius during the Vestalia for their annual procession and deposit of the dust and ashes from the sanctuary of Vesta. The Tiber is more than just a convenient dump here; it is a sacred location itself that allows for the secure disposal of other sacred material.

It is this attitude towards the sacred which may inform the use of the Tiber for the bodies of Rome's enemies whether foreign or domestic. The disposal of bodies was subject to tight legal control in ancient Rome with extramural burial prescribed at least since the

fifth century BC. As we see in the accounts of the deaths of Tiberius
Gracchus, referred to as *paranomos hubristheis* (Plutarch, *Tiberius Gracchus*
19), and Gaius Gracchus and their followers, after they were killed
their bodies were thrown into the Tiber. This might have been simply
a matter of treating them as waste, but is more likely symbolically
associating them with parricides and other threats to the state whose
bodies were also thrown into the river in a ritual cleansing of the city.
The power of this form of removal of threats to the state is seen in the
imperial period with the disposal of the bodies, and even the statues,
of disgraced political figures such as Sejanus and calls for the same
treatment of the corpse of Tiberius himself upon his death (Suetonius,
Tiberius 75).

This attitude may also inform the actions of Sulla during his
famous triumphal banquet; the brief description in Plutarch's *Life of
Sulla* is worth quoting in full: 'Sulla feasted the people sumptuously, and
his provision for them was so much beyond what was needed that great
quantities of meats were daily cast into the Tiber' (Plutarch, *Sulla* 35). By
throwing the daily remains of meals into the Tiber he was accomplishing
two tasks. First, he is making a statement of beneficence and abundance
by disposing of rather than distributing the meals' leftovers. Second, by
removing the material from the city into a religiously charged feature,
arguably the largest and most prominent of the religiously charged
features of the city of Rome, he is associating his triumphal celebration
with older rituals in the city. Nero seems to have copied this behaviour
when he ordered a massive amount of grain to be disposed of in the
river (Tacitus, *Annales* 15.18). Of course, sometimes, the Tiber is a
dump. As the primary conduit for wastewater from the city, the Tiber
was the terminal location for Rome's extensive sewer system.

Roman sewers made the development of urban space in the low
areas of the city – the Forum Romanum, Circus Maximus and others –
possible. These sewers combined sanitary and storm drainage in a single
system that shed Rome's excess water and waste into the Tiber. Much
of that came from the Cloaca Maxima and its tributaries, an extensive
series of pipes, tunnels and open channels 1,600 m in length that served
to drain the former swamps in the city, remove the downstream water
from the collective aqueducts and the accumulated wastewater from a
large portion of the million inhabitants and animals that eventually were
to inhabit Rome. This system was joined by other sewers that drained
the valley of the Circus Maximus and the Campus Martius separately.
The outfall for all of this made its way to the Tiber. Owing to the lack
of backflow prevention it also served, however, as a conduit for waters

from the Tiber to pass up into the low areas of the city during the river's frequent floods.

FLOODING OF THE TIBER

To anyone familiar with the modern city of Rome either from photos or from personal autopsy, the notion of the dire threat of flooding in antiquity might seem curious. In fact, the modern city is isolated from the Tiber in a way that would be unrecognizable to an ancient Roman. The current embankment walls that create such a prominent barrier between the city and the river are a modern phenomenon from the period of 1876–1910 in the wake of the devastating 1870 flood. The modern city also rests on metres of fill, meaning that the same areas in antiquity were sometimes 5 to 10 m lower than comparable areas today. To understand the notion of flooding in ancient Rome it is first necessary to think away these walls and later fill and to note that ancient Rome was intimately linked to the river by a series of ports, docks and facilities supporting the transport of bulk commodities. The role of floods in the history and development of this was of primary significance. The story of the city's origin itself was based on the limits of a flood as the basket containing Romulus and Remus was deposited by the Tiber's flood waters in a spot on the slopes of the Palatine Hill. Rome may have been built on seven hills, but it was founded and kept fed and supplied because of the river and its floodplain. And that floodplain is necessary for a river that has the largest drainage basin in Italy.

All of the major transport facilities as well as many of the city's most symbolically important spaces and buildings were frequently and severely inundated by the waters of the Tiber in the thirty-four major floods known from literary and epigraphic sources from 414 BC to AD 411. It should be stressed that this number represents major floods and probably only a small percentage of the flooding events of antiquity when the annual rising of the waters of the Tiber would have covered areas adjacent to the river banks. The extent of flooding is revealed by analysis of the most detailed of the literary accounts, which name key buildings submerged in the floodwaters. Certainly the grain warehouses and harbour facilities of the Emporium area on the south edge of the city were affected as attested in the descriptions especially of the flood of AD 69. In addition and more damagingly those public buildings in low areas including the Forum Boarium, the Circus Maximus and the

theatres near the river are naturally repeatedly affected. The Forum
Romanum and the buildings within it including the Temple of Vesta
on the east side of the Forum are also mentioned as being underwater
during flooding, suggesting that perhaps 2–4 m of water covered the low
areas of the city. Perhaps most surprising is the extent of flooding. In one
instance Cicero describes a flood that passed up the valley of the Circus
Maximus and along the Via Appia, which modern analysis pinpoints for
more than 2.5 km from the Tiber's banks. Along with these buildings
and areas, the Campus Martius seems particularly prone. Accounts of
ancient floods reveal that the Campus was considered separately from
the other low areas of the city and also that it frequently flooded,
presumably from the north moving south, including areas of the Via
Flaminia/Via Lata down to the Theatres of Pompey and Balbus. While
the frequency of flooding is difficult to gauge, recent calculations have
concluded that major floods occurred every twenty years on average
and minor floods occurred every four to five years.

The results of flooding could be immediate in the damage and
destruction of buildings as well as the loss of life and personal property
that would result from rapidly moving waters sweeping through urban
areas. In some accounts, entire *insulae* collapsed from flooding and
people, animals and possessions were swept away by the waters of the
Tiber (Cicero, *Epistulae ad Quintum Fratrem* 3.7.1; Tacitus, *Historiae*
1.86; Cassius Dio 37.58.3; Symmachus, *Epistulae* 6.37; Orosius 4.11.6;
Augustine, *De civitate Dei* 3.18). Longer-term effects included weakened
structures, disease, injured Romans and food shortages. If the *horrea* near
the Tiber were flooded, spoiling the grain, and additional shipments
unable to sail up a rain-swollen river, the food supply for Rome would
be almost immediately imperilled.

To gain an appreciation of the effects of flooding, we might note
that of all the political, entertainment and commercial buildings of
Augustus, only those on the Capitoline and Palatine Hills lay outside
the zones that were inundated by major floods which occurred during
his Principate in 22, 13, and 5 BC and AD 5. The duration of floods is less
certain, but literary accounts record several floods that lasted from three
to seven days with the added details that boats were used to navigate the
flooded city during these periods (Cassius Dio 53.20.1, 57.14.7; Zonaras
11.3; Ammianus Marcellinus 29.6.17–18); the flood of AD 5 resulting
in the city being navigable by boat for seven days (Cassius Dio 53.33.5,
55.22.3). These were almost certainly the river boats generally used for
conveying goods and travellers up and down the river and to and from
the cargo ships to the docks. These will be the next topic addressed.

RIVER TRANSPORT, PORTS AND FACILITIES

The Tiber is the final corridor and its banks the terminus for all of the bulk goods that made their way to Rome including building materials such as imported stone and timber, living cargo, notably slaves and animals for the games including elephants, and food, especially the major commodities of wine, olives and olive oil, and grain. Since the tremendous ships of the grain fleet could not navigate the Tiber, their role in transporting the half a million tons of grain that came into Rome annually was taken by scores of smaller ships and boats of a variety of sizes and styles all fulfilling a myriad of functions along the river including transport of commodities, passengers, ferrying across the river, guiding ships into dock, transferring cargo and other tasks. Our knowledge of these is generally not direct. Although we are fortunate to have several extant boats, notably for our discussion those found in the harbour at Pisa, most of our information on the riverboats comes from written and artistic sources. It is also worth noting that the ships that transported this critical commodity were privately owned. Although the Roman state beginning in the late Republic offered a number of enticements to encourage participation in the grain trade such as tax incentives, subsidies and grants of citizenship, private owners rather than a state-owned merchant fleet took the considerable risks involved here.

During the middle and late Republic, literary accounts suggest that seagoing vessels would regularly sail up the Tiber without stopping at Ostia to transfer cargo to smaller vessels. For example, the description of the arrival of Magna Mater at Rome implies a long-range Mediterranean vessel in use on that occasion (Livy 29.10). Certainly the largest vessel ever attested sailing up the Tiber was that which carried Aemilius Paulus to Rome after his victory over the Macedonians in 167 BC. Livy (45.35.3) describes it as King Perseus of Macedon's personal ship, an enormous naval vessel powered by either eight or sixteen banks of oarsmen.

This was before the explosion of bridge-building in the late Republic and early Principate, which probably restricted the channel and subsequently led to the movement to river boats rather than seagoing vessels making the trip up the Tiber. Nevertheless, the ship, probably a large barge, that Caligula used to transport the obelisk for the Vatican Circus was extraordinarily large as well. The excavations of the ship's remains at Portus indicate that it was probably almost 100 m in length and displaced over 7,000 tons. Its passage up the Tiber to

FIGURE 13.4 Frieze of Tiber sarcophagus.

deliver the obelisk is something of a mystery as it must have required towing by oxen for much if not all of the distance. The largest of the river vessels was a form of merchant galley probably approximately 16 m in length compared to the 55 m in length of attested seagoing vessels of the grain fleet. Many reliefs including those from Trajan's Column as well as private tomb images illustrate heavy oar-driven vessels carrying cargo up the rivers of the empire (see Figure 13.4).

The use of these large vessels with their wide rowing profiles explains the necessity of continually working to keep a wide Tiber channel clear, a task Augustus himself oversaw along the river. A number of these cargo vessels were designed to transport bulk commodities from Ostia or Portus to Rome and back, sometimes with outbound cargo, but probably most often empty as the accounts of the clean-up from the fire of AD 64 make clear when these boats were used to remove debris from the city (Tacitus, *Ann.* 15). Clearly they were the major high-capacity vessels supplying Rome from the Tiber.

Given their size, however, many were not rowed upriver but instead towed by the *caudicariae*, the specialized tow boats which seem to have been developed specifically for this task along the Tiber. These vessels were equipped with a small sail, but their major power was towing either by men or oxen along the towpaths that framed the Tiber. The *naves caudicariae* were used to haul the larger cargo ships up the confines of the narrow river in a three-day journey from Ostia to the docks on the south side of Rome. Martial (*Epigr.* 4.64.22) records a reference to the rhythm of the chant as the *helciarii* trudged up the towpaths. Many reliefs from Ostia show these craft in use and emphasize their association with larger cargo vessels and critical role in guiding or powering them into position. It seems clear that they were indispensible in moving cargo ships up river and into docking along the banks of the Tiber. The creation of this unique form of ship as well as the employment of so many men as crews and rowers is a small element of the evidence for the complexity and reach of the trade up the Tiber. A variety of other small craft plied the Tiber as well as the large cargo vessels. We have attested the terms of *lintres, stlattae, cumbae, scaphae, lembi, lenunculi* and *lusoriae*. Among these are the critical tugboats and barges on which the entire system relies. The *linter* is a class of small boats with oars and sail used along rivers including the Tiber, as Propertius (1.14.3–4) testifies. The *stlatta* was another form of river boat of undetermined occupation while the *scapha*, a light service boat, seems to have been designed for unloading cargo and ferrying it to warehouses or to the docks from the larger vessels. The *lembus* and *lenunculus* were also used to transfer cargo and to fulfil the key duty of warping ships to the dock, both necessary at the multiple docking facilities along the Tiber at Rome. The *lenunculus* should be categorized as a type of barge, the mainstay of the cargo service. One of these flat-bottomed transfer vessels just over 15 m in length was excavated from the mud in the harbour at Portus and represents our best evidence for these critical small craft, which were essential to cargo ships that put up at anchorage rather than at a berth along the dock. Some of these craft as well must have been operated by the officials who oversaw the docking facilities and used to communicate with arriving ships to assign berths and tug or tow boats for manoeuvring the large vessels. While the overwhelming majority of these vessels were working boats, the *lusoria* was specifically a pleasure boat, perhaps of the houseboat type. Propertius' testimony of them on the Tiber demonstrates the use of the river by the Roman elite for pleasure sailing, perhaps in the vicinity of Rome itself. We should also consider the use of the river by fishing vessels, either fishing in the river or returning from the sea, whose names do not survive in the literary or epigraphic record.

This discussion of vessel types and their roles along the Tiber should not neglect the personnel that made all this work possible. Epigraphic evidence makes it clear that slave labour was, at best, a small percentage of the workforce. Instead, guilds of specialized workers fulfilled each of the key tasks involved in river trade and traffic resulting in wage labour for thousands of Rome's inhabitants. The *lenunculi* for example were rowed and crewed by guild members, the *lenuncularii*, organized into five guilds of further specialization known from a number of inscriptions. Similarly the *caudicariae* were manned by *cau-dicarii*, who were themselves divided into two guilds based on which stage of the river they transported goods on. In addition to the transport guilds, those actually moving the cargo by hand are represented includ-ing the *saccarii*, the sack men who carried sacks of grain; the *phalangarii*, amphora carriers; *saburrarii*, carriers of sand used for ballast; *urinatores*, divers who recovered goods lost overboard during unloading. In addi-tion, specialized labour was necessary on the docks and around the warehouses, including *geruli*, the longshoremen or dock workers; *hor-rearii*, the warehouse workers; *custodiarii*, warehouse guards; and *mensores frumentarii*, who measured the grain presumably upon offloading and storage in the *horrea*. All of this work was also supported by the efforts of the *fabri*, who constructed the equipment and buildings around the dock facilities, and the *fabri navales*, who built the ships. The overall picture we get is of a very crowded river with constant traffic. Perhaps hundreds of vessels, of which one hundred at any one time might be from the grain fleet (Tacitus, *Ann.* 15.18.2), moved up and down stream every day. Moreover, there was intermittent travel across the current and in and out of the docking facilities along the banks of the Tiber, which as the liminal space between Tiber and city deserve some extended consideration.

The docking facilities that made the transfer of bulk commodities into Rome were not a simple arrangement. They served the purposes of flood control, docking ships, allowing for loading and unloading, use of cranes, etc. These represented a vast set of buildings and works of which the tremendous Emporium district on the south side of Rome is probably the best-understood, but certainly not the only example and probably later than the Portus Tiberinus north of the Pons Aemilius and south of the theatres in the southern Campus Martius. The docks prob-ably developed early to supply Rome. Since Ostia was not founded until the second half of the fourth century, all Rome's long-distance trade probably travelled directly up the Tiber until then and docked at the city at facilities for which the evidence no longer exists owing to later overbuilding. After the development of Ostia, larger and larger vessels were gradually stopped at Ostia and then Portus with smaller ships and boats supplying the city. These changes led to alterations in the dock facilities at Rome, but never allowed for their elimination. Port facili-ties began development at Rome in the middle and late Republic until they eventually filled much of the left bank of the Tiber with stone and concrete embankments. These were constructed in a sporadic manner over the centuries with no overall strategy or plan, leading to a variety of designs, building materials and locations for docks along the Tiber. Their major purpose was to allow for the docking of ships coming up river, but secondarily they included buildings for storage of commodities as well as perhaps ship sheds for dry-docking ships for repair and maintenance. Ship construction is another matter and probably took place elsewhere than at Rome. The architecture for *horrea*, dry docks and ship sheds is very ambiguous in design, leading to uncertainty about the use of particular facilities. The general development of docks and their support systems is clear from the literary and epigraphic record.

The earliest large-scale construction projects we know of along the Tiber at Rome occurred in the early second century BC. At this period, the facilities at Ostia were restricted to sets of river docks as at Rome and the large merchant ships offloaded in open water, a risky procedure for ship, crew and cargo (Strabo 231–2), so the need for docks at Rome was very great. According to Livy (35.10.12) M. Aemilius Lepidus and L. Aemilius Paulus constructed a number of works including a portico and quay along the Tiber in 193 BC. Livy further records (40.51) that the quays were upgraded in 179 BC by the censors M. Aemilius Lepidus and M. Fulvius Nobilior. The next censors of 174 BC, Q. Fulvius Flaccus and A. Postumius Albinus, extended the quays and repaired the *horrea*, again according to Livy (41.27). The forms of the facilities are not precisely known, but sections of the embankments excavated in the preparation of the 1876–1910 embankments revealed paired steps leading from the Tiber up along low walls making the embankment each culminating in a walkway. Ships moored using projecting mooring rings carved from large stone blocks. The entire works were constructed of cut tufa and travertine and the form indicates that ships docked broadside to the embankment and were unloaded fore and aft, perhaps simultaneously. The locations of all these works are not securely identified, but from the descriptions and extant remains can probably be located at the areas near the Forum Boarium, alongside the Aventine near the Pons Sublicius and downstream at the Emporium area, which seems to be the primary focus of development during this period.

Later periods saw massive extensions and renovations of these facilities, providing tangible evidence of Rome's increased need for harbour facilities for the imported commodities necessary for the growing city. The largest next datable phase is that under Augustus, when there is evidence for storage rooms constructed dockside in *opus reticulatum* as an innovative feature (see Figure 13.5).

FIGURE 13.5 Tiber port overview.

His works also extended to what were probably the first constructed docks in the northern Campus Martius, adjacent to his Mausoleum. The success of this set of docks is proved by the use of the pavement around the Mausoleum under Hadrian to lay out the stone elements for the Pantheon, which seem to have been offloaded here and the final carving completed on the paved area near the river before they were carted half a Roman mile south to the Pantheon. The next datable phase of construction, which occurred under Trajan, is evidenced by the remains found along the bank of the Tiber near Monte Testaccio, with projecting travertine mooring rings each flanked by a pair of ramps leading down into the Tiber. These are comparable to those in the inner, Trajanic basin at Portus, which measure 15 m apart (height 1.10, width 0.75, depth 2.0, diameter of holes 0.45). Above them is a structure, all constructed of brick-faced concrete including a high embankment wall and quay along which are multiple levels of barrel-vaulted storage rooms similar to those found quayside at other imperial harbours, such as Caesarea Maritima and Lepcis Magna. The project is actually probably only a component of the harbour work that created the new basin, Portus Traiani Felicis, at the mouth of the Tiber. Eventually the port and warehouse facilities stretch along the left bank of the Tiber from the area of the Pons Sublicius south past the Emporium region, across much of the Campus Martius and finally along the right bank in the area of Trans Tiberim. Although the eventual image is of a solid line of port facilities, these were never planned in concert and instead seem to have grown almost organically in response to Rome's needs for imported goods, notably food.

Apparently always separate from the docks and facilities for commerce were the *navalia*, the ship sheds of the Roman war fleet. These were more developed than simple docks as the fleet required dry-dock facilities between deployments to preserve the ships and allow for maintenance, so should be understood as roofed sheds set behind docking areas that allowed ships to be drawn up out of the waters of the Tiber. These were built initially on the left bank of the Tiber adjacent to the Campus Martius and according to references in Livy were in place at least from 338 BC (Livy 8.14.12) with references to later rebuilding or extensions in 179 BC (Livy 40.51.6) and 167 BC (Livy 45.35.3). The structures were in use for their original purpose at least to the end of the Republic, and if the account of Procopius can be accepted they continued to survive into the sixth century, although their use had undoubtedly changed as the Roman war fleet was no longer stationed at the capital itself after the end of the first century BC. Their role throughout the period of their use seems to have been at least partially symbolic as they represented Rome's naval power in a tremendous building complex along the banks of otherwise undeveloped space until the time of Augustus. Some references also suggest a museum purpose as the *navalia* were used to display captured ships and the 'ship of Aeneas' (Plutarch, *Cato Minor* 39; Velleius Paterculus 2.45; Procopius, *De bello Gothico* 4.22).

In addition to extraordinary constructions, the docks, embankments and quays along with the bridges required continual as well as periodic maintenance. These along with the river itself needed officials who could oversee the clearing of the channel, the supervision of the banks and the removal of debris from along the river. Under the Republic, these works, like the constructions in the second century BC noted above, seem to have been undertaken by the censors. The censors of 55 BC, P. Servilius Vatia Isauricus and M. Valerius Messalla Niger, are referred to as *curatores riparum* on a series of cippi erected along the banks of the Tiber. The extent of their work is unclear, but at least part of it seems to have been designed to delimit the boundaries between public and private land. Under Augustus, as with so much else, this administrative structure changed with the establishment of a new office, the *curator alvei Tiberis*, responsible for the channel of the Tiber. This official may have been the one actually in charge of the clearing of debris from the channel and the removal of the protruding structures (Suetonius, *Augustus* 30). This arrangement was not to last, however. Following the massive flood of AD 15, described by both Tacitus and Cassius Dio, Tiberius created a board of five senators chosen by lot to regulate the flow of the Tiber (Cassius Dio 57.14.7–8). These *curatores riparum et alvei Tiberis* seem, judging by their title, to have had expanded authority over the censors as their mandate includes both the channel and the banks of the Tiber, effectively combining the republican censorial authority with the office created by Augustus. An additional two-man commission whose charge was to reduce the flow of the river presented their plan to the senate where it was rejected (Tacitus, *Ann.* 1.76. 79). Under Vespasian this board was replaced with a single official of consular status who was named the *curator riparum et alvei Tiberis*. His authority expanded under Trajan so much that an assistant of equestrian rank was stationed in an office at Ostia. The most important duties of these officials were the maintenance of the river banks and the facilities along them and ensuring that the navigation channel of the Tiber stayed clear. The former could involve architectural maintenance, shoring up of the banks or other duties as is attested in an inscription from AD 300 (*CIL* 6.1242). The latter was mainly accomplished through clearing navigation obstacles or dredging the channel of silt and debris. Naturally, these duties were not undertaken by the officials personally but were probably hired out to various guilds and so the work operated as part of the public jobs programmes for which imperial construction projects are noted. The major uncertainty in this organization was the responsibility for the bridges. It is unclear under the Principate if the bridges that were periodically damaged or destroyed by flooding were repaired or replaced by the *curatores* or by the Pontifex Maximus, from Augustus on the office held by the emperors.

The Tiber and its relationship to the Roman people is complex. It represents a sacred boundary, a repository, a drain and a dump. However, it also operated as the Romans' lifeline. In some ways its nature both threatened the city of Rome from floods and foreign culture, yet its navigability made the city's existence and growth possible. The Tiber itself became the basis for an extensive trade organization requiring the employment of thousands of Romans and the construction of large-scale facilities along its banks, including docks, warehouses, embankments, ship sheds and emporia, all serving as tangible evidence of the critical role of the Tiber for the city of Rome.

FURTHER READING

Jones 2005 assesses the complex relationship with the Tiber in Roman literature and culture. Most authors focus on the more practical with Aldrete 2007 providing a superb work on Tiber floods. On the administration of the Tiber and the government response to navigational needs see Meiggs 1973, and Aldrete 2007 notably tracks the development of new offices to ensure the food supply and infrastructure of navigation. Analysis of the ships that sailed the Tiber can be found in Gardiner 1995 and Casson 1971 and 1994. The evidence for docks, *navalia* and harbour works are discussed in Gardiner 1995, Hohlfelder 2008 and Aldrete 1999. The general architectural development of the Tiber area and its integration with the growing city of Rome is addressed by Favro 1996 and Haselberger 2008, 2007.

14: TRAFFIC AND LAND TRANSPORTATION IN AND NEAR ROME

Ray Laurence

There are many ways to measure population increase and its impact on the infrastructure of cities, but perhaps the most graphic example is seen in photographs and films of roads congested with stationary vehicles. These images are all too familiar to inhabitants of the modern *metropolis*, whether they live in Lagos, Los Angeles, London or Rome. Population growth was a feature of life in ancient Rome with regular increases of population postulated right through to at least the end of the first century AD (see Chapter 2). An aspect of living in Rome was a sense in which the streets of one's youth were increasingly congested by one's old age. The history of the *metropolis* in the modern world has been one that is entwined with the development of new technologies of transport that were not available in ancient Rome. In the nineteenth century, railways spread the *metropolis* over a larger geographical area. The following century saw a new emphasis on a planned *metropolis* that linked population growth to the development of transport infrastructure. However, the rates of population growth in the metropoles of Latin America, Asia and Africa in the late twentieth and early twenty-first centuries outpaced any attempt to develop the transport infrastructure. As a result, although we can identify limited planning in cities such as Lagos and a level of congestion that most westerners find astonishing, congestion of itself does not cause a city to cease to function. A traffic jam can be an inconvenience to those wishing to move from A to B, but it is an opportunity for traders wishing to sell goods and services to these stationary travellers.[1]

Perhaps, in looking at traffic and transport in Rome, we should put our concepts of speed of travel familiar to us from the modern western *metropolis* to one side and make a comparison with other cities in the

[1] Koolhaas et al. 2000; for the role of peddlers in the distribution of goods see Loane 1938, 149–50.

MAP 14.1 Rome showing Aurelian Wall (with gates) and roads radiating into the centre of the city.

ancient world. Rome was bigger than any other city, in both population size and urban area, Rome had far more people and far more streets than any other city (Pliny, *Naturalis Historia* 3.66; see Chapter 10). Owing to the size of its urban area, a feature of life in Rome was a need to travel over larger distances within the city (Martial, *Epigr.* 2.5, 5.22). This factor caused the experience of urban life to be fundamentally different from that found in other cities. However, the journey was not just longer in distance, it was temporally increased by the number of inhabitants moving around the city. The combination of longer distances of urban travel with increasing congestion in the streets produced a literary *topos* of a Rome whose streets were at a standstill as its inhabitants (in the case of the authors concerned, who were migrants to Rome, accidents in the streets seem to happen to visitors from overseas, e.g. Suetonius, *De illustribus grammaticis* 2) battled to reach their destinations. This was a different type of urban environment with a unique soundscape – what Horace and Pliny described as a roar or din (Horace, *Epistulae* 1.17.7–8, 2.2.79; *Carmina* 3.29.12; Pliny the Younger, *Epistulae* 1.9.7, 3.5.14).[2]

[2] Ramage 1984, 69–70.

TRAFFIC FLOW AND THE LAYOUT
OF THE CITY

The Forum (later fora) located on low-lying ground between the Capitoline, Palatine, Quirinal, Viminal, Cispian and Oppian Hills establishes a central point within the city. It was to the Forum that Horace imagined 200 wagons (*plaustra*) and three major funerals with trumpets converging (*Satires* 1.6.42–4; compare Seneca, *Consolatio ad Marciam* 11.2). Rome was a radiant city, whose urban expansion, whether across the Tiber or across the Esquiline, followed the major roads that converged on the Forum.[3] This was later confirmed in 20 BC with the establishment of the Golden Milestone between the imperial rostra and the Curia within the Forum Romanum (Cassius Dio 54.8.4; Pliny, *Nat. Hist.* 3.66; Plutarch, *Galba* 24.4; *Digesta* 50.16.154).[4] The imperial fora, unlike the Forum Romanum, were closed spaces into which the movement of traffic, both pedestrian and vehicular, could be controlled.[5] The pattern of traffic arteries radiating from, or converging on, the Forum Romanum was partly created by the physical geography of Rome's famous hills. However, there is another factor: the defensive circuit of walls known as the Servian Walls had in the past created a linear barrier to urban expansion. These walls were restored right down to the first century AD (Livy 22.8.6–7, 26.55.8; Appian, *Bellum Civile* 1.66); and the walls remained a topographical feature of the city during the imperial period (Cassius Dio 57.14.7, 62.20.1; Herodian 2.14.2, 1.12.8). The twenty-two republican gates through the walls formed the major traffic arteries into the old part of the city, even when the walls ceased to serve any defensive function (Suetonius, *Gaius* 27; Juvenal 5.153–5; Quintilian, *De institutione oratoria* 12.10.74).[6] Through the Republican Walls one entered what many writers regarded as a city of formless crooked streets (Cicero, *De lege agraria* 2.96; Livy 5.55.2–5; Diodorus Siculus 14.116.8–9; Plutarch, *Camillus* 32). Beyond the Republican Walls lay another set of thirty-seven gates to the city, those of the customs contractors, which later would coincide with points in front of the Aurelian Walls.[7] Gates naturally funnel traffic and become associated with concentrations of traffic trying to cross a boundary.[8] The other barrier to land transport

---

[3] Laurence 2008 for discussion of urban extension.
[4] Newsome 2009 for discussion of the centrality of the Forum Romanum.
[5] La Rocca 2001, 210–11.   [6] *LTUR* 3.324–34; Wiseman 1998.
[7] Palmer 1980 for discussion.
[8] Van Tilburg 2007, 85–94, 105–7 for discussion of gates and congestion in Rome.

was the Tiber: a number of bridges were added to that of the Pons Sublicius, the Pons Aemilius completed in 142 BC, the Pons Cestius and
Pons Fabricius in 62 BC, the Pons Agrippae from the Augustan age, a
Pons Neronianus from the first century AD, and finally the Pons Aelius
of AD 134.[9] The location of all these bridges provided initially connections between the Forum and what would become Trans Tiberim
(Regio XIV) and later under the emperors between the new monumental zone of the Campus Martius and monuments across the Tiber
(e.g. Hadrian's Mausoleum). There would also have been numerous
ferries crossing the Tiber at other points, but bridge-building would
seem to have been undertaken, certainly in the Republic, with a view
to the facilitation of traffic crossing the Tiber leading to or from the
Forum Romanum. When discussing transport, we need to remember
that the Tiber was itself an important transport artery bringing goods
and people to Rome from central Italy and ferrying food and other
resources from Ostia and Portus to the capital in the imperial period,
but it also in flood disrupted the flow of land transport. Finally, it needs
to be noted that traffic did not just go into the centre of Rome. People
lived their lives within the urban area of the city and beyond it in the
suburbium: an area of densely settled countryside that was intimately
connected with the city itself.[10] It was the roads leading from Rome
that facilitated the possibility of spending time in the Forum and then
to retire from the city to a villa located in the suburbs (Pliny, *Epist.*
2.17), and took goods from the markets in Rome to the villas of the
suburbium (Martial, *Epigr.* 7.31, 10.94).[11]

TRAFFIC CONGESTION AND THE ROMAN STREET

Today, visitors to Trajan's Markets can see the Via Biberatica – a wide
street with pavements (*crepidines*), almost 8 m in width, and lined with
shops (Figure 14.1). There is a very modern feel to this street with
a division between vehicles in the streets, driven across a surface of
durable basalt paving stones, and pedestrians passing at the sides on
the pavements (as they do today in nearby Via del Corso). We need
to appreciate that the surface of the Via Biberatica was a culmination

[9] *LTUR* 4.105–13 for sources and discussion.
[10] Witcher 2005; Goodman 2007, 7–38; Champlin 1982. Note also evidence for depots
outside Rome's customs barrier within the *suburbium* (Palmer 1980, 232).
[11] Purcell 1987a, 1987b.

FIGURE 14.1 Via Biberatica.

of a long evolution of experimentation to create a road surface. Livy (59 BC–AD 17) carefully recorded in his *History of Rome* (*Ab urbe condita*) the development of paved surfaces on the roads leading from the city and on the streets within the city. The Via Appia may have been laid out from Rome to Capua in 312 BC, but this was not a paved road (Livy 9.29.6). Improvements were made later. In 295 BC, a mile long path was paved in squared blocks from the Porta Capena in the Republican Walls to the Temple of Mars, and in 292 BC a 12-mile section of the road was paved in hard stone (*silex*) from this temple to Bovillae (Livy 10.23, 10.47). The stone (*silex*) used is usually interpreted as a leucitic basalt and it is this stone that replaces the surface of the section of the Via Appia from the Porta Capena to the Temple of Mars in 189 BC (Livy 38.28). The streets within the city were only paved with this hard stone in 174 BC and it is at this point that the roads outside the city are given a gravel rather than a clay surface (Livy 41.27.5).[12] The sources for the paving stones, including those of the Via Biberatica, can be located in the middle Tiber Valley and in the Alban Hills from where these high-density and durable rocks were transported to Rome (see Chapter 16).[13]

[12] Laurence 1999, 58–77.   [13] Laurence 2004; Black et al. 2009.

Although very durable, basalt paving stones can become quite slippery, especially if wet, and the narrow sloping streets of the eastern half of the city were the place of accidents for the unwary and especially for visitors, unaccustomed to moving through the city of Rome (Tacitus, *Historiae* 3.82, 2.88; Martial, *Epigr.* 5.22, 8.75). Many of Rome's monuments were located at the summits of hills and it is these locations that the poets Martial (*Epigr.* 5.22) and Juvenal (3.254–9) regarded as the destinations for both mule trains and wagons transporting marble or large timber spans for the restoration of the city's temples and monuments under the Flavian emperors. These streets leading up to the summits of the hills of Rome, for example the Clivus Suburbanus, were particularly susceptible to runaway wagons. There is a legal discussion involving a mule-drawn wagon on the Clivus Capitolinus slipping back and bumping into another wagon that careered down the hill killing a slave boy (*Dig.* 9.2.52.2). Martial includes in quite a number of his epigrams a representation of the surfaces of the streets of the city. The road surface is frequently described by Martial as muddy (*Epigr.* 3.36, 7.61, 10.10, 12.26). It is in this part of the street that a patron was carried in his litter with his clients following on foot negotiating the mud and dung lying on the road surface itself. Unless the street was obstructed by building work or shop displays or simply busy, other pedestrians used the pavements on each side of the road and managed if possible to keep their feet dry. However, Martial notes that the pavement and steps of the Clivus Suburbanus were dirty and never dry (*Epigr.* 5.22).

The maintenance of the streets as transport routes within the city and up to a mile from the city fell under the jurisdiction of the aediles.[14] The future emperor Vespasian singularly failed in his duty as aedile to keep the streets clean, providing an opportunity for the emperor Caligula to humiliate him by having the Praetorian Guard load down the fold of Vespasian's toga with mud/dung (Suetonius, *Vespasian* 5). Our understanding of the duties of the aedile in this area benefits from the survival of the bronze statute of 45 BC known today as the Tabula Heracleensis. This statute makes it clear that it was the responsibility of the four aediles to ensure that the owners of property fronting onto the streets of the city fulfilled their legal obligations to maintain the pavements and the road surface that adjoined

---

[14] Robinson 1992, 59–82. Van Tilburg 2007, 34, and 36 suggests that their jurisdiction extended to 10 miles from Rome on the basis of the unique circumstances arising in 209 BC following the report of a series of prodigies during the Hannibalic War (Livy 27.37.9). His argument is interesting but unconvincing.

their property. In practice, it may have been possible for an aedile to let a contract for the maintenance of the entire street and to ensure that the costs were borne by the property owners (the *possessores*). The aediles with four other magistrates (the *quattuorviri*) were responsible for the cleaning of the streets within the city and were aided outside the city by another two magistrates (the *duumviri*). What this involved was not so much street sweeping, but the removal of the build-up of mud, dung and other materials from on top of the paving stones (Ulpian, *Dig.* 48.11). An aedile would also remove any obstructions from the street, for example the delivery of some couches could have been left at the curbside and would have been legitimately removed by an aedile doing his duty and acting within the law (*Dig.* 18.6.13–14). There was careful provision to prevent the encroachment of private property over the pavement or into the thoroughfare of a street (Papinian *Dig.* 48.10), as well as to forbid the digging of holes in the street. The law also dealt with the prohibition of activities that would prevent access through a street: the disposal of animal skins or dead animals; the throwing of dung and fighting; and a prohibition of the putting out of goods in the street with the exceptions of wheelwrights and fullers drying clothes.[15] However, encroachment into the streets by barbers, bars, cooks, butchers, wine merchants can be identified within Martial's famous *Epigram* (7.61) that eulogizes Domitian's decision to ensure the streets of Rome were no longer encroached on. Encroachment reduced the streets (*viae*) of Rome into muddy tracks (*semitae*). The restoration moved not just the goods back into the shops lining the roads, but also shifted the pedestrians out of the mud of the street and back onto the dry pavement. The latter was an ideal, but the will to maintain it and to restrict the sale of goods to within the bounds of private space seems unlikely to have been achieved. The reality may have been closer to Seneca's (*De Ira* 3.35.3–5) muddy paths filled with dirty people and enclosed with the misaligned and cracked facades of the *insulae* (properties) that lined the streets. In any case, for Seneca (*De clementia* 1.6.1), the widest streets could easily have become filled with people flowing like a torrent, but the flow was impeded frequently by the activities of the city causing an individual to be held back, to slip and to be splashed as he made his way across the city (Seneca, *De ira* 3.6.4).

[15] For Tabula Heracleensis, see Crawford 1996, 355–91. See Robinson 1992, 59–82 for discussion of this text and other legal evidence. For street fights observed by the elite as they travelled the city, see Suetonius, *Aug.* 45.

The ban on vehicles in the centre of Rome

Congestion in Rome's narrow streets would seem to have become a recognized problem by the middle of the first century BC. A law was passed by Julius Caesar, extending the ban on women travelling in the city in carriages, as part of the Lex Oppia (Livy 34.1.3) to all wheeled traffic from sunrise until the tenth hour of the twelve Roman hours of daylight.[16] Carts that had entered the city at night could leave the city over this period of time, as could vehicles removing refuse. What this law created was a window of opportunity for those delivering goods within the customs boundary of Rome: the last two hours of daylight and then through the night itself. As we have seen above, the law did not ban all traffic: for example, there were exemptions for building materials for work on the temples of the gods, and any other construction or restoration for which a public contract had been let. The scale of this traffic and its dangers under the Flavian emperors is revealed in the works of Martial and Juvenal discussed above. Certain persons, unspecified, were exempt from the law. However, this law created a massive influx of traffic into the city over the course of the last two hours of daylight – a time perhaps, when the elite at least were in their homes or dining at the houses of others.[17] This was the time for deliveries to be made of goods brought to the city from outside Rome. With only two hours of daylight remaining, all the goods brought to Rome in wagons had to make their way to their destinations either before nightfall or with the aid of lamps after dark. For the inhabitants of the city, there was a sudden change from crowded streets of foot passengers to streets crowded with vehicles on a scale not seen during the rest of the day. What this law did was to restrict entry into Rome and thus alleviate congestion caused by the delivery of goods to the city and use of wheeled transport within the city for a substantial part of the day, rather than addressing causes of congestion.

Once the goods had reached their initial destination in Rome, there was a need to distribute them for delivery/sale to the population of the city. It has been calculated that 150,000 tonnes of wheat, 75 million litres of wine and some 30 million litres of olive oil would

---

[16] Tabula Heracleensis 56–61; Crawford 1996, 365 for text and 374 for translation; Robinson 1992, 73–6.

[17] For the temporal arrangement of life in the city, see Laurence 2007, 154–66.

have been required by the population each year.[18] These quantities appear particularly large, but to understand how transport might have functioned we need to define how much transport the distribution of these goods may have required. There were choices to be made in transporting goods: humans can carry them, equids could carry them or they might be placed in a wagon drawn by oxen or equids. To illustrate the scale of transportation, we will take the wheat required by the population, and consider how much of it may have been moved each day. With 410 tonnes of wheat being consumed each day within the city, it had to be moved to numerous locations across the city. However, just to shift 410 tonnes of wheat from A to B would have involved 10,250 loads for transport by porters, 4,315 loads for transport by pack donkeys, and 3,416 loads for pack mules. If wagons were used to transport the 410 tonnes of wheat, between 833 and 6,200 loads would be produced according to the size of the vehicle used.[19] All these calculations do is to translate a quantity of goods required by the population into load sizes according to the transport opportunities available in Rome. It may have taken more loads to distribute goods on the backs of donkeys, mules and humans than on carts; yet there were advantages to doing so. Not least the condition of the streets themselves, that as we have seen were crowded and even impassable to vehicles, and an additional reason was a ban on vehicles in Rome for the first nine hours of the day. More important, maybe, was the need to distribute goods to a whole variety of shops and other locations across the city. This factor may have made it preferable to have a larger number of people, donkeys and mules moving across the city with smaller loads, than a large cart delivering to a large number of locations. The labour power of the Roman plebs to perform the basic offloading, carrying and delivery of goods across the city should not be underestimated. However, the need to move goods put an additional pressure on the transport infrastructure of the city – the streets were crowded with people, donkeys and mules moving goods from place to place.

The elite's solution to the experience of crowded streets in the city, alongside a prohibition of wheeled transport, was for them to be carried in litters or sedan chairs, above the heads of the crowds below. Unlike their clients, such as Martial (*Epigr.* 3.36), following in their wake, the elite did not have contact with either the crowds or the mud

---

[18] Morley 2007, 577. See also Chapter 15.
[19] Figures from Raepsaet 2008, 588–9, 600. Compare Van Tilburg 2007, 75 for a similar calculation. On costs of transport generally, see Laurence 1999, 95–108.

under-foot (compare Juvenal 3.329–45; Martial, *Epigr.* 2.81, 4.51, 6.77 on status associated with litter-borne passengers). Carried on high at a speed of about 2.5 kph, the elite could look down on dirty streets filled with crowds of citizens clad in dirty clothes, a panorama of the environment of the *plebs sordida* that was such a contrast to their own marble-encrusted homes (Tacitus, *Hist.*1.4, 3.74; Seneca, *De ira* 3.35.3– 5; Calpurnius Siculus, *Eclogues* 7.26, 42, 46; Pliny, *Epist.* 7.17.9).[20] The literature of Juvenal and Martial provides a different view – exposing the elite to the view of their clients struggling through the mud-strewn streets in dirt-stained togas (e.g. Martial, *Epigr.* 1.104; Juvenal 3.149). The elite's view of this crowd was easily blanked out with the curtains of the litter closed (Cicero, *Philippicae* 2.106; Suetonius, *Nero* 9, 28). The litter bearers in the city were slaves, whose memorials are found in the tombs of wealthy families and alongside the messengers or runners associated with these households. These slaves were prominent not just within the household, but also on the street carrying their master.[21] Movement for their master was essential, but it was equally essential for the owner of these slaves to arrive at his destination in pristine condition – the purchase of a litter and slave litter bearers provided a solution that kept the elite out of contact with the dirt they saw in the streets of Rome. In short, the conditions faced in the crowded streets caused travel by litter or sedan chair to expand, by the end of the first century BC, with the result that attempts were made to restrict the use of litters to persons of a high status and/or of suffi- cient age (Suetonius, *Caesar* 43; Ovid, *Ars Amatoria* 1.488; Horace, *Sat.* 1.2.98).

TRAFFIC FLOW

We hear little about the actual timing of the flow of traffic within Rome; it is a subject only alluded to by authors.[22] We know that clients travelled to the morning *salutatio* from dawn through to the second hour

[20] Yavetz 1965 discusses the use of terminology for the plebs found in literature written by the elite. The terminology used for the plebs needs to be read within the more recent framework of the Roman Gaze – see papers in Fredrick 2002, especially those by Corbeill and Barton.

[21] Joshel 1992, 74–5, 88–91; Treggiari 1975b, 57. Note that within the imperial house- hold by the time of Claudius or Nero there was a *Corpus Lecticariorum* – a form of *collegium* or guild of litter bearers.

[22] For discussion, see Laurence 2007, 154–66.

of daylight, and might follow their patron in their litter or sedan chair until the tenth hour of daylight (Martial, *Epigr.* 2.5, 3.36, 4.8, 10.70; Horace, *Epist.* 2.1.104). From their houses, the senators travelled with a procession down to the forum (Q. Cicero, *Commentariolum Petitionis* 34, 36), where courts would begin their sessions and public business would continue through the day until the tenth hour of daylight. For those transacting business in Rome who came from out of town, it may have been advantageous to do so in the morning to allow them to travel from Rome in the afternoon. It is significant that the meetings in Rome of the Sulpicii bankers from Puteoli on the Bay of Naples tended to take place in the morning rather than in the afternoon.[23] All of these activities were concentrated around the Forum Romanum and the imperial fora and pedestrian traffic in the morning would gravitate towards this location. There appears to have been a break at midday (Plutarch, *Quaestiones Romanae* 84), which was followed for the elite at least by the eighth hour of daylight with the commencement of bathing (Martial, *Epigr.* 10.48.3; Vitruvius, *De architectura* 10.1; Suetonius, *Domitian* 16.2). Because the baths, certainly by the time of the empire, were distributed across the city, there would have been a movement of pedestrian traffic to these destinations in the afternoon. From the baths, the elite went home to dinner or were guests at dinner at another person's house – usually nine hours after sunrise (Martial, *Epigr.* 4.8). What is outlined so far is the pattern of elite male traffic, but what about activities that produced general traffic within the city? Shops tended to open according to the patterns of traffic around them – for example shops around the baths became busy when the bathers were arriving before or departing after their baths (Seneca, *Epistulae* 56). Generally, in Rome, the shops opened from the second hour through to the eleventh hour after sunrise (Pliny, *Nat. Hist.* 7.182; Petronius, *Satyricon* 12; Martial, *Epigr.* 9.59; Horace, *Sat.* 1.6.113), but the bakeries were open from dawn or even earlier (Martial, *Epigr.* 12.57). We should add to this pattern the sale by auction of goods both within the forum and the Saepta, and at other locations across the city.[24] In terms of traffic, the impact of auctions would have been most clearly visualized by the procession of slaves arriving in Rome to be taken for sale at the places of auction.[25] The bars

---

[23] Laurence 2007, 154, table 9.1.
[24] DeLaine 2005 explores this subject further, see also Loane 1938, 151–3; and Rauh 1989.
[25] Fentress 2005 on locations of the auction of slaves; Bodel 2005 for the process; Scheidel 2005 for numbers of slaves imported and sold in Italy.

or *popinae* opened from the third hour of daylight and could stay open late into the night (Cicero, *In Pisonem* 13; Juvenal 8.158; Ammianus Marcellinus 14.6.25). As can be seen the information is scarce; there is no sense of deliveries taking place, the activities of women of any status, and little information about the movement of children – although we do know that teaching took place from early in the morning. However, within the pattern that can be discerned we see traffic: beginning at dawn or even earlier; intensifying as activities commence in the forum and other central places; followed by further movement at midday away from the centre of the city on completion of some activities. Towards the middle of the afternoon traffic became focused on the baths and finally with a return home or to dinner at another person's home as evening approached.

Festivals and other religious events would have created very different patterns of traffic (see Chapters 25–27). For a start, many of these events were associated with processions that utilized wheeled transport and special provision was made for the Vestal Virgins, *Rex Sacrorum* and the *Flamines* within the document known as the Tabula Heracleensis and also for triumphing generals. By the end of the first century BC, the games and entertainments associated with these religious celebrations had gone up to a higher level. Julius Caesar staged plays in every *vicus* of the city. Rome would become within the next generation the city that needed three theatres rather than just one (Seneca, *De clementia* 1.6.1). The scale of entertainments promised by Julius Caesar drew crowds to Rome, who camped in the streets (*viae*) and in the alleyways (*vici*) of the city. The traffic problems and crowds in the city resulted in the crushing to death of quite a number of people, including two senators (Suetonius, *Caesar* 39). Much has been said with respect to the location of the Colosseum (dedicated AD 80) with respect to Nero's Golden House, but perhaps we need to see the Colosseum's position with respect to the street network of Rome – it lies at a central point where roads converge allowing the crowd of 50,000 or more to arrive from dawn, disperse for a break at midday and reconvene for an afternoon of further spectacles before returning home at the end of the day (Suetonius, *Claudius* 34; Cassius Dio 37.46.4; Tertullian, *Apologeticus pro Christianis* 15.5). The Circus Maximus, also, lies at a central point in the street network and perhaps it is no coincidence that the theatres of Pompey, Balbus and Marcellus were all located close to one another, so that only part of the city was affected by the crowds converging on the theatres to watch plays beginning at the second or seventh hours of the day (Horace, *Epist.* 2.1.189).

So far we have discussed the flow of pedestrians, but what about vehicles? As we have seen, these could not enter the city prior to the tenth hour of daylight. This presented the supply of the city of Rome with a logistical problem that could only be overcome by a response to the situation at an organizational level. If at the tenth hour the vehicles crossed the customs post and went into the city, did they return before dark? This seems doubtful, because a mule would travel at roughly 3–4 kph and its crew would have needed time to unload their goods prior to leaving the city. The Tabula Heracleensis does make provision for empty carts to leave the city after sunrise on the following day, so we might assume that the drivers stayed overnight in Rome prior to leaving the next day. So what we are looking at, in terms of land transportation to Rome, is a round trip with a stay overnight in the city. The question remains: how far did goods come from? If the carts crossed the customs boundary at the tenth hour, we could anticipate goods travelling in the region of 30–40 km to the customs boundary within that time span – perhaps less if heavily laden.[26] Presumably, what was taken into Rome by wagons was of a size that was larger than a normal load for a pack animal, in the case of a mule 150–180 kg. The yoking together of oxen could allow for considerable loads of 8–10 tonnes to be carried particularly for the building industry in Rome (Vitruvius, *De archit.*10.3.7–8), but it was slow at speeds of 1.6 to 3.2 kph with a total range each day of about 9–18 km.[27] There should be one important addition made to this model of supply: the presence of depots outside Rome's customs boundary to which goods were transported and stored prior to distribution within Rome.[28] However, even a short journey from a depot into the city need not have been completed by nightfall – certainly activities in the streets continued into the night perhaps preventing sleep for Rome's residents (Pliny, *Nat. Hist.* 26.111; Juvenal 3.232).

FROM THE CITY AND BACK AGAIN

Pliny the Younger pointed out in a letter (*Epist.* 2.17) that his villa at Laurentum on the coast to the south of Ostia was easily accessible from the city. This did not mean that he commuted in the modern sense on a daily basis, but instead could spend time on business in Rome and

---

[26] Raepsaet 2008 for full discussion of the distances and loads.
[27] DeLaine 1997, 128–9; Raepsaet 2008, 591–2; Lancaster 2005, 12–18 for sources of local building materials.
[28] Palmer 1980 for discussion of wine depots.

spend the later part of the day at his villa away from the city.[29] The journey of 17 Roman miles (*c.* 27 km) could be undertaken rapidly on horseback or more slowly in a carriage – since the roads leading to the villa from the major roads (the Via Laurentina and the Via Ostiensis) were not of the highest standard. There is an important point here: when considering communications, it was advantageous to own a villa close to the major roads leading to Rome, since these roads were designed for wheeled transport (Columella, *De re rustica* 1.1.19; Pliny, *Epist.* 1.24). As Pliny describes the journey to his villa, we see unfolding a quite different view from that found in the streets of Rome: a landscape of production, rustic beauty, mountains, the sea and the villas of the rich.[30] The elite travelled out of Rome to villas in this zone stretching out some 20–25 Roman miles along the major roads (e.g. Tacitus, *Ann.* 15.60.19; Suetonius, *Nero* 48; *Domitian* 17; Pliny, *Nat. Hist.* 14.50). The plebs living in Rome also saw this landscape, for beyond the *pomerium* (Rome's sacred boundary) lay the cemeteries to the dead – family burial plots were to be visited and particularly at the festivals of the dead in February (of course the poorest may have been buried in mass-graves with no memorial). However, travel from the city to the *suburbium* and back again was a key feature of elite culture at Rome. It is a life-style characterized by mobility between two locations that the elite did not call home, one of which was often located further away and associated with their place of birth.[31] The suburban villa, perhaps unlike a traditional rural home, had the features found in the city: a bath-suite, good water, a library or two, a *porticus* and dining rooms – it was a location like the urban house, set up for entertainment of visitors and the enjoyment of literary and intellectual pursuits. However, the view seen as you travelled through the landscape was rather different from that found within the city itself – variation of view and of landscape was a key feature of elite culture by the middle of the first century AD (see e.g. Seneca, *De tranquillitate animi* 2.13).

Within the city itself, travel was a feature of urban life. Owing to Rome's size, especially if we include the *suburbium*, journeys were longer than in other cities – after all it takes all of fifteen minutes

---

[29] Goodman 2007, 23.

[30] Purcell 1987b, 187–90 recreates a visual journey from the centre of Rome out onto the Via Tiburtina and into the *suburbium*. See Purcell 1995a for discussion of the view of production; see Champlin 1982 and Purcell 1987a, 1987b on the landscape of Rome's *suburbium*.

[31] Champlin 1982, 103–5. See Adams 2008 for survey of villas.

to traverse Pompeii. For those living in Rome, the urban journey presented them with not just obstacles in their way and what we might describe as congestion, but also a view of the city of Rome as a quite different urban phenomenon. This latter was characterized by crowds, dirt and congestion and was not seen in other cities on this scale nor over the same duration of journey times. Perhaps, it is this kinetic aspect of the city of Rome that produces the rhythm and disjuncture found in the genre of Roman satire.[32] There may be another imperative at work, too; the rebuilding of Rome under the Flavians in the wake of the fires of AD 64 and AD 80 was on a new scale and flooded the streets of the city with carts delivering goods to rebuild the city and develop its monuments.[33] The movement between the *suburbium* and the city was characteristic of urban living for the elite. Those resident on the outskirts of the city created another image of the metropolis: the *suburbium* by comparison to the city was a place of tranquillity, providing views of nature or the adaptation of nature that presented the sharpest of contrasts with Rome, which was associated with duties, *negotium* and movement about the city. As we have seen, travel in the city was a means to producing social distinctions between the man in the sedan chair and his clients following behind walking in the mud or dust of the streets. This was a distinction made even clearer in the Severan City, when Severus Alexander permitted the senators to use carriages with silver decoration, in an attempt to enhance the dignity of Rome (*Historia Augusta, Severus Alexander* 43). Perhaps this reform of the earlier ban on traffic simply enhanced and identified the status of the senators, replacing their litter with a carriage. The impact of the law on traffic flow would have been irrelevant to the lawmakers; what was important was that the elite were recognized as they moved across the city – and just perhaps, someone might have got out of their way.

FURTHER READING

There are few books that deal directly with this topic. Laurence 1999 discusses transport in Italy outside the city of Rome. Van Tilburg 2007 approaches the subject of traffic congestion, but in places does seem to be reading modern situations of congestion in the ancient evidence – yet this book is full of information. Palmer 1980 remains central for

---

[32] Larmour 2007; Miller 2007.
[33] Newbold 1974 discusses some of the consequences; see also Darwall-Smith 1996.

the understanding of customs duties at the edge of the city of Rome. Champlin 1982, Purcell 1987a and 1987b, Witcher 2005, and Goodman 2007 discuss the nature of land-use and the need to see the periphery of Rome as part of the urban experience of the city. DeLaine 1997 discusses the whole issue of transport for the building industry at Rome. For the text and a translation of the Tabula Heracleensis, see Crawford 1996. On the nitty-gritty of harnessing, size of loads and other matters Raepsaet 2008 provides nearly all the relevant details. Morley 2007 discusses distribution of goods in the city, but Loane 1938 is still worth referring to on this subject.

15: THE FOOD SUPPLY OF
THE CAPITAL

Paul Erdkamp

Apopular modern view sees the population of the Roman capital as unemployed, degenerate and dependent on imperial largess. Few phrases from the ancient literature are so often quoted as 'bread and games', Juvenal's brief expression of the corruption and corruptibility of the urban masses (10.81). In his view the Roman populace had sold to the emperors the rights and liberties they had had during the Republic. While the political dimension of Rome's food supply is beyond doubt, one may wonder whether the grain dole is adequately explained as a bribe. The feeding of Rome, a city of nearly a million inhabitants, tested the logistical, economic and organizational abilities of the Roman world to their limits. This is reflected in every aspect of the city's food supply: the urban diet and its shortcomings, the weaknesses of the urban food supply, the grain dole, and the state's involvement in the acquisition and distribution of food.

THE URBAN DIET

The diet of all people in the Roman world consisted largely of cereals: durum wheat for the better-off people and the inhabitants of cities, emmer wheat, barley or millet for the less fortunate. However, the diet of the rural dwellers, the majority of whom were involved in farming and could gather food from the wild, was more varied than that of the urban populace. The predominance of cereals in urban consumption was partly due to logistical considerations. High transport costs favoured foodstuffs with a high nutritional value and limited bulk. Moreover, grain is less perishable than many other foodstuffs, which means that it can be transported and stored with relatively little loss. On the other hand, it was owing to the city's status as political centre that in imperial times even the common people in Rome ate durum wheat instead of emmer, barley or millet. In contrast to the 'lesser' cereals, durum wheat was suitable for baking into leavened bread. Hence, if the populace is said to have been corrupted by the 'bread and circuses' offered to them by the emperors, it does not mean merely that they could fill their bellies daily, but that they could fill them with wheaten bread, a luxury for most subjects of imperial Rome.

An estimation of the amount of grain eaten on average by individuals in Rome depends on many unknown variables. While we can make reasonable assumptions about the size and stature of ancient Romans, it is more difficult to estimate their energy requirements, since we have little idea of how much physical labour the 'average' person living in Rome had to undertake. Even more importantly, while we can say that their diet was dominated by wheat, we cannot establish with any precision the role of other items in meeting their nutritional requirements, and we cannot express the nutritional status of people in Rome in figures. What we can say is that on average the annual consumption of wheat must have been in the range of 200 kg for an adult. Estimates in the range of 250 kg would either exclude the consumption of other foodstuffs or imply an implausibly high intake of calories, while much lower estimates would either have the people starve or underrate the dominance of cereals in the urban diet. A total consumption in the city of Rome of more than 150,000 tonnes of grain must be understood as a very rough estimate, since it is hampered by our inadequate understanding of the age structure, sex ratio and size of the city's population.

The main items of food, besides grain, were legumes, olive oil, wine and meat.[1] We may be sure that these were normal items of the diet of the common people in Rome, but it must remain unclear how regular and in what quantities they were eaten. Much of the evidence on diet in the ancient world does not pertain to the population of large cities. The rations of slaves or soldiers are not relevant as far as the population of big cities is concerned. However, a number of considerations point to a diet dominated by grain and bread. To begin with, the number of instances where authors refer to the supply of grain is vastly greater than similar references to legumes, olive oil, wine or meat. The sources, ranging from Livy's first decade on early Rome to Pliny's eulogy of the emperor Trajan, show an almost exclusive interest in the harvest, supply and price of grain. Second, Gaius Gracchus in 123 BC started the regular distribution to the urban populace of cheap grain, and for centuries grain remained the only item that was

---

[1] On the consumption of legumes, Corbier 1999. On meat, Corbier 1989, MacKinnon 2004.

distributed in such a way. It was only from Severan times onwards that olive oil was regularly distributed, while meat and wine were added even later. Third, from the first century BC onwards, people in Rome were aroused to violent demonstrations by the high price of grain, but similar occurrences due to the high price of wine are rare and only mentioned for the fourth century AD. In short, everything indicates that the urban populace fulfilled their nutritional needs largely by the consumption of cereals.[2]

An overview of the diet of the people living in Rome would not be complete if we were to pay attention only to basic foodstuffs and ignore the luxurious and exotic items that were eaten in Rome too – albeit not by everyone. For example, pepper was imported from southern India by way of Egypt, a trade route that flourished from Hellenistic times until the Portuguese arrival in the Indian Ocean more than 1,500 years later. In AD 92, Domitian ordered *horrea piperataria* to be built. It is amazing that pepper has become so very popular, Pliny the Elder (*Historia Naturalis* 12.29) writes, in view of the fact that bitterness is its main characteristic. Its popularity is reflected in the recipes of Apicius, nearly all of which include pepper. Peppers have even been found in military camps along the borders. Pliny the Elder shows a knowledge of various tropical fruits, such as bananas, but supply lines were too long to allow the importation of such perishable goods. The point to be made is that, despite the general emphasis on basic staple foods in ancient sources and modern literature, the well-to-do in Rome did not regard it as depraved to eat fish, fish sauce, mussels, fowl, eggs, mushrooms, figs and dates, melons, pears and apricots.[3]

THE DOLE

In 123 BC the Roman popular assembly accepted Gaius Gracchus' proposal for a grain law, according to which male citizens of Rome were given the right to buy a monthly ration of grain at a fixed and low price (6 1/3 *asses*). Gaius Gracchus introduced the grain dole as part of a series of measures taken to curry favour with the voters in Rome, but we should not see it solely as a bribe. Rome had grown tremendously in the previous century, and the food supply of such a large city, gradually

---

[2] Cf. Jongman 2007, 603–4, who, however, does not distinguish between urban and rural consumers.
[3] On luxurious and exotic foods, see e.g. Dalby 2002.

outgrowing the productive capacity of its direct hinterland, became increasingly vulnerable. A measure that would create some degree of stability in the grain market was not out of place. Moreover, and this might seem paradoxical, Gracchus may have intended to de-politicize the handing out of grain. The past decades had seen the increasing tendency of magistrates to employ public grain on their own initiative for distribution among the Roman populace, but such ad hoc measures by individual magistrates did not solve the capital's problems, while adding to those of the tax-paying provinces.[4]

The sources demonstrate that the grain dole remained a political issue until the end of the Republic, but the fact that we do not even know for sure what amount was stipulated by Gracchus' grain law may serve as an indication of the fragmentary and inadequate nature of our evidence.[5] The *lex Terentia Cassia* from 73 BC specified the monthly distribution of five *modii*, and it is likely that this was the amount from the start. Five *modii* (about 33 kg) is more than sufficient for an adult male. Such an amount might have fed two adult people, the more so if one of them was a woman. Recipients of the grain dole were male citizens from either 11 or 14 years old. In view of the much higher average age of first marriage for men, many recipients did not have a family to support.

At first the beneficiaries seem to have included all male citizens of sufficient age living in Rome. There is no mention of any further restrictions. However, with regard to the *lex Terentia Cassia* of 73 BC, Cicero (2 *In Verrem* 3.72) stated that 33,000 *medimnoi* would be sufficient for the monthly distribution of grain to the plebs, which implies about 40,000 beneficiaries. The total number of male citizens from age 11 or 14 onwards living in Rome must have been much higher. Cato the Younger is said to have widened the group of recipients in 62 BC to include 'the poor and landless plebs' (Plutarch, *Cato Minor* 26.1), which confirms that some sort of restriction was imposed previously. In 58 BC Clodius abolished the price, making the rations a free gift. In the 40s, the number of recipients appears to have risen to 320,000, inducing Julius Caesar to bring it down to 150,000. He did this in part by conducting a census district for district, employing the services of the *domini insularum*, i.e. the heads of the apartment blocks that housed many of the urban poor. Augustus, following Caesar's example, conducted a similar census and established the number of recipients at

---

[4] Erdkamp 2000. See also Garnsey and Rathbone 1985.
[5] In particular, Rickman 1980a, ch. 7.

about 200,000.[6] We do not have similar numbers for imperial times; we can only speculate that the number of recipients did not change significantly.

The *frumentationes* remained a privilege in later times. The recipients were entered on a list that was regularly revised.[7] In the first century AD, the members of the Praetorian Guard, the urban cohorts and the *vigiles* were added to the list. Trajan included 5,000 children, a gesture that was repeated by some of his followers. The epitaphs of several young children tell us that they had been entitled to receive public grain, which shows that being on the list provided a certain status.

Handing out grain to several hundred thousand people each month required a complex organization, spreading the actual distribution over various places and/or days per month. An inscription from the first century AD tells us that a certain individual received grain at entrance 42 on day 14 at the Porticus Minucia. Apparently there was now one distribution centre, which handed out grain to recipients allocated to specific days and entrances. The importance of the Porticus Minucia is reflected in the title of certain officials attached to the city's grain supply: *procurator Augusti ad Minuciam* and *praefectus Miniciae*. Furthermore, a *curator aquarum et Miniciae* is first attested for the reign of Septimius Severus.[8]

In the third century the handing out of grain was replaced by that of bread, which caused a major revision of the system, which, in turn, explains the curator's responsibility for both the aqueducts and the food supply. The emperor Aurelian is said to have handed out bread to the urban populace (*Historia Augusta, Aurelian* 35.1), which has often been interpreted as an innovation. However, there is good reason to date this change earlier. The distribution of bread implied a different organization, because grain could be stored for some time and thus handed out monthly, while bread required a more or less daily distribution. Moreover, the state had to take responsibility for the milling of the grain. This ties very well with the discovery of a large-scale watermill in Rome that was powered by the *aqua Traiana* and that was constructed at some time during the third century. Its construction gave the aqueduct an entirely new purpose, and therefore the watermill must have been built on imperial orders. In view of the emergence of the *curator aquarum et Miniciae* under Septimius Severus, it is most likely that this development dates to his reign.[9]

---

[6] Rickman 1980a, 175–82.   [7] Rickman 1980a, 188–91.
[8] Rickman 1980a, 192–7.   [9] Bell III 1994.

Septimius Severus changed the dole in another momentous way by adding a daily allowance of olive oil to that of bread. Already his predecessors in the second century AD occasionally distributed olive oil, but it was left to Severus to make this a regular gift (*Hist. Aug., Septimius Severus* 18.3). Alexander Severus is said to have restored the regular handing out of oil after it had been abolished under his predecessor (*Hist. Aug., Alexander Severus* 22.1). Finally, the emperor Aurelian is credited with adding the distribution of wine and pork to those of bread and olive oil (*Hist. Aug., Aurelian* 35.2 and 48.1).

VULNERABILITY

The grain dole did not feed the city of Rome. Not everyone was entitled to it, and until the reign of Septimius Severus the dole was limited to grain. The price of food was still a major concern for the capital's populace: accustomed to buy their food day by day, Tacitus (*Historiae* 4.38) writes, the common people have no interest in public affairs save the grain supply. They looked to the emperor to safeguard their interests: when Nero intended to leave the city, the Roman populace feared supply problems in his absence (Tacitus, *Annales* 15.36.4).

Several elements combined to make food prices such a pressing concern for the urban masses. First, their buying power was so low that most of their income was spent on food. Early modern figures on the consumption pattern indicate that the cost of daily sustenance used up about half or three-quarters of the income of the common people in European cities. Second, the income of many wage-earners was unstable and may have been threatened by seasonal fluctuations in employment, which were caused, for instance, by the decrease during wintertime of shipping and cargo handling or by a temporary slump in building activity. Third, when the price of grain rose, urban consumers had little recourse to alternative foodstuffs. It is clear that, if the daily sustenance consumed half of the income of an average household, the consequences of a prolonged doubling of prices were grave. Even if outright starvation was limited to beggars and vagabonds, the most fortunate among the common people had to eat into their reserves, while the less fortunate were forced to accept more frugal living conditions than they were accustomed to. Hence, price stability – or, at least, a limitation of price volatility – was something to be desired.

Famine did not occur in Rome as long as its authorities ruled overseas possessions. Not until the fifth and sixth centuries, when the empire had long been lost and Italy turned into a battle zone, did the Black Horse of the Apocalypse make its appearance in Rome. However, individuals in Rome may nevertheless have died of hunger and malnourishment. The story of the beggar shooing away the dogs that are awaiting his death in order to feed on his body illustrates that abject poverty was not absent from Rome, despite the empire's power and Rome's status as its capital. Lack of work or the inability to work, lack of food and increasing vulnerability to disease must have gone hand in hand for many among the destitute. Disease and disability surely made it impossible for some to acquire enough food to make it through the days. Starvation, in other words, was a cause of death, albeit operating in tandem with other causes.

The dominance of cereals in the urban diet must also have caused some degree of malnourishment among those who ate little else. Malnourishment is indeed indicated by ancient skeletal evidence, although it is not always possible to distinguish between the effects of a one-sided diet and those of diseases that hampered the body's intake of necessary nutrients and minerals. Being unaware of the condition, medical writers could not recognize its symptoms, as seems to be the case in the following passage, in which the second-century doctor Soranus (*Gynaikeia* 2.43-4) warns about the dangers of having babies starting to walk too early: 'If moreover it [the infant] is too prone to stand up, and desirous of walking, the legs may become distorted in the region of the thighs. This is observed to happen particularly in Rome.' Soranus continues by rejecting various causes that have been proposed, blaming instead insufficient care by Roman mothers. As Peter Garnsey has pointed out, the passage probably points to the occurrence of rickets in Rome, a condition that is caused by vitamin D deficiency, which, in turn, may be related to the predominance of cereals in the diet.[10]

Most people in Rome did not have to fear actual starvation, but that did not prevent many inhabitants of Rome making their disapproval clear when the price of grain rose. Food riots in Rome were directly related to the dole, first of grain, later wine and pork. From the first century BC onwards, the sources mention grain riots aimed at those people whom the rioters thought were responsible for the situation, which meant throwing stones at the consuls in the late Republic, at Octavian and Mark Antony in the time of the second triumvirate, throwing pieces of bread at Claudius during his reign, and demanding

---

[10] Garnsey 1999, 47–8.

the death of Cleander, an imperial favourite, from the emperor Commodus. In the fourth century the people responded to the high price of wine with violent protests, burning down the house of a leading magistrate. In one case we are told of demonstrations in Rome because of the high price of beef and pork (*Hist. Aug., Alex. Sev.* 22.7). Although the protests are dated to the reign of Alexander Severus, the passage may actually reflect the situation in Late Antiquity, when it was written. Just as in the case of wine, the regular distribution of pork altered the expectations of the Roman populace. The state had made itself responsible for an adequate food supply, and thus the people addressed the state's representatives when reality did not meet expectations. Moreover, riots were not caused by hunger – genuinely starving people do not protest – but by the rioters' perception of the violation of their rights. In the face of the possibility of a food riot by a violent mob, it was often opportune to live up to one's creed and to make sure that market supply was plentiful and the price 'just'. As the first-century BC historian Dionysius of Halicarnassus (*Antiquitates Romanae* 7.20) quite anachronistically wrote about fifth-century BC Rome: 'The consuls . . . took great care to supply the city plentifully with both grain and other provisions, believing that the harmony of the masses depended on their well-being in this respect.'[11]

SUPPLY AND TRANSPORTATION

Consumers in Rome ate foodstuffs from all over the Roman empire and even beyond. Pepper and other spices were imported from India and South East Asia. However, it is clear that most of the staple foods that the urban populace consumed either came from the direct hinterland of the city or from regions that offered relatively easy access to the capital. Logistical considerations determined that most of the meat eaten in Rome came from the Italian peninsula, including Cisalpine Gaul. However, Rome had become so gigantic that the food requirements of its nearly 1 million inhabitants exceeded the productive capacity of Italy. One should not forget that Rome's hinterland counted numerous smaller towns and cities whose inhabitants had to be fed as well.

In fact, Rome was only able to grow so very large because the Roman state had sufficient power and organizational ability to ensure an adequate supply of at least basic foodstuffs. Already at the end of

---

[11] In more detail, Erdkamp 2002.

the third century BC occasional shipments of grain from Sicily and Sardinia appear in the sources. Although these islands continued to play an important role in the capital's grain supply, they were soon surpassed by Africa. Under Augustus Egypt became Rome's largest supplier of grain, which it remained until the founding of Constantinople. Pliny the Younger observed that 'it was generally believed that Rome could only be fed and maintained with Egyptian aid' (*Panegyricus* 31). Seneca tells us that the arrival of the grain ships from Egypt in Puteoli was a cause for celebration (*Epistulae* 77). Africa was the second largest supplier of grain, and it also played an important role in the supply of olive oil. Most of the olive oil, however, came from southern Spain, as the Monte Testaccio – a hill near Rome consisting of millions of sherds of discarded amphorae used to transport olive oil – demonstrates.

However, the produce of Italy should not be dismissed as insignificant. Many among the rich or just well-to-do families living in Rome owned land in Italy. For example, Pliny the Younger, by no means an extremely rich senator, owned property in Tuscany and Cisalpine Gaul, while Maecenas supported the poet Horace by giving him a farm in Sabinum. The urban households of the rich and well-to-do, which varied from a few relatives and slaves to palatial workforces consisting of hundreds of slaves, undoubtedly ate grain, olive oil, vegetables, legumes, meat, cheese, honey and fruit from the produce of their estates.

All of the food consumed in Rome had to be transported some distance over land, if only from the river docks to the depots and from the depots to the consumers. Mosaics showing the unloading of ships demonstrate that the grain and olive oil were carried sack by sack and amphora by amphora, which is supported by the fact that the storage rooms of *horrea* were only accessible on foot. The movement of food offered employment for thousands of free and servile labourers. However, the food supply of Rome was only manageable if the largest part of the staple food was transported most of the way by river and sea. Rome was exceptional as a Mediterranean metropolis in the sense that it was not located downriver from fertile lands that were able to fulfil its needs, as Alexandria, Carthage and Antioch were. The upstream transportation of goods on the Tiber from the harbour at Ostia to Rome was undertaken by barges that were towed by teams consisting of either men or oxen.[12]

---

[12] See Procopius, *De bello Gothico* 5.26.9–11 for a description of ox-drawn tow-boats in the sixth century AD. In general, see Chapter 13.

Ships of all sizes were involved in the provisioning of the Roman capital, but the ships bringing grain and olive oil from Egypt, Africa and Spain tended to be larger than average. The emperor Claudius offered privileges to owners of ships of at least 10,000 *modii* (approx. 70 tonnes) burden, while later rulings specified either one ship of 50,000 *modii* or five ships of 10,000 *modii*. Since these rulings were intended to stimulate the involvement of as many ships as possible, 70 tonnes was below average. Small freighters offered advantages to shipowners and merchants who bought and sold a variety of goods at various markets: small ships could enter shallow harbours, and it was less difficult and costly to fill the hold of small ships with goods that one hoped to sell profitably. In contrast, the volume and constancy necessary for the provisioning of Rome stimulated the use of sizeable freighters.

The Apostle Paul was brought as a prisoner to Rome on such a grain ship, and his experiences, described in detail in *Acts of the Apostles* (27–28), graphically illustrate the physical difficulties of shipping grain from Egypt. Overseas voyages were regarded as too dangerous from mid-November to mid-March. While trying to find a safe harbour for the coming winter, Paul's ship was blown off course and wrecked on a small island. The ship's cargo was lost. Paul's guards finally brought him to another Alexandrian grain ship wintering in a nearby harbour. Owing to the distance and the winter break in long-distance shipping, freighters on the Alexandria–Italy route managed no more than one return trip each year. The largest single flow of food towards Rome – the grain supply from Egypt – was a time-consuming and risky affair, requiring the continuous service of hundreds of ships. Ships from Africa and Spain managed several return trips and hence the transportation of olive oil and grain from these provinces was less time-consuming and risky. Even so, feeding 1 million people was a huge logistical challenge that required every effort of the Roman state.

The question of how the authorities managed the transportation of the city's staple foods is closely related to the question of how they acquired the necessary grain, olive oil and other goods. Opinion on this matter diverges.[13] Scholars like G. Rickman assume that the authorities bought almost all the grain they shipped to Rome on the open market. He argued that the authorities required the service of a large number of merchants to supply the urban market with adequate amounts of

---

[13] For a more detailed analysis, see e.g. Herz 1988, Sirks 1991, Höbenreich 1997, and Erdkamp 2005.

grain.[14] One may point to people like M. Caerellius Iazymis, who is called a *codicarius, item mercator frumentarius* (boat-owner and grain trader) on an inscription from Ostia. However, while we cannot deny the involvement of trade, in my view the emphasis should lie with the state, not with trade: most of the grain supplied to Rome was state-owned, and hence the authorities needed the services of shipowners who transported grain rather than that of grain merchants who supplied it. It is difficult to say when this system arose, but this is the picture emerging in the sources from the first and second century AD.

Clear evidence first pertains to the reign of Claudius. Apart from building a new harbour at Ostia, he offered favourable conditions and privileges to the businessmen (*negotiatores*) who built ships 'of a capacity of not less than 10,000 modii of grain, and if that ship, or any other in its place, carries grain to Rome for six years'.[15] Most importantly, the authorities undertook to compensate the businessmen for any losses they incurred while serving the city's grain supply. The text does not clearly specify who owned the grain that was to be transported on the ships involved. However, Claudius was evidently interested in the services of shipowners, not traders who did not own ships. Moreover, we know that many shipowners had contracts for transportation with the *annona*, the department in charge of the grain supply of Rome. Claudius limited his privileges to those shipowners who held contracts with the *annona* for at least six years. Similar rulings, dating to the reigns of Hadrian and Marcus Aurelius, offer similar conditions to shipowners who serve the *annona*.[16] In short, the authorities responsible for the grain supply of Rome were eager to stimulate the cooperation of many shipowners, but there is no evidence for a similar policy towards merchants dealing in grain. Many businessmen may have been involved in both lines of business, but that does not alter the main point: the authorities, not having any freighters themselves, solicited the services of shipowners who would transport grain to Rome.

The authorities did not need the services of merchants supplying grain, because under normal circumstances they had recourse to sufficient grain for the state's overall needs. Rome's main source of grain consisted of the taxes-in-kind that were levied in almost all provinces. Already in the Republic, Rome had introduced levies of a fixed percentage of the harvest (a tenth in Sicily and Sardinia, a twentieth in Spain) and the sources make clear that taxes-in-kind were normal in

---

[14] Rickman 1980a, 72.   [15] Gaius, *Institutiones* 1.32c. Also Suetonius, *Claudius* 18.2.
[16] Callistratus, *Digesta* 50.6.65.5, 6; Scaevola, *Dig.* 50.5.3.

subsequent provinces. Most importantly, farmers in Egypt paid taxes in grain and other crops. In Egypt taxes were fixed at a certain amount per unit of land, not a percentage of the harvest, which is undoubtedly related to the relative reliability of harvests in Egypt. Moreover, the emperors held vast imperial domains throughout the provinces, in particular in Africa and Egypt, which offered rents in kind. Even on a conservative estimate Egypt offered sufficient tax grain (some 25–30 million *modii* each year) to fulfil a significant part of the capital's need.[17]

The sources also offer evidence of contractors who transported olive oil to Rome on behalf of the authorities, and again we may ask whether the olive oil supply of Rome reflects commercial channels that are supported by the authorities or state-dominated extraction that relied on businessmen for its distribution. One inscription, set up by *scapharii* (shippers of boats) in Spain in honour of Sex. Iulius Possessor, tells us that the latter, as *adiutor* of the *annona* in charge of the oil from Africa and Spain during the reign of Marcus Aurelius (AD 161–80), was responsible for the inspection of the oil, the organization of its transport and the payment of the transport charges to the shippers. The last two tasks mentioned demonstrate that the oil was already state-owned when it was transported to Rome, but the origin of the oil remains unclear. Another inscription mentions the same Possessor as *adiutor* of the *annona* connected to the depots (*horrea*) at Ostia and Portus, i.e. Rome's main harbours. The state's concern with transportation is shown by the fact that in another function Possessor was responsible for the navigability of the Guadalquivir, the most important transportation channel in Spain's main oil-producing region.

Other evidence consists of the stamps and writings (so-called *tituli picti*) on the amphorae in which the oil was transported. The stamps usually mention the name(s) of the owner(s) of the pottery which made the amphora, while the *tituli picti* contain the names of the trader or transporter, the names of the producers of the oil, and information pertaining to the amphora's weight and content. Many of the names on the amphorae also occur in inscriptions mentioning *navicularii* (shippers), *mercatores* (traders), *negotiatores* (businessmen) and *diffusores* (exact meaning unclear) involved in the 'oil business'. The evidence demonstrates the heavy involvement in the oil supply of Rome of people who are known to be involved in the oil trade outside of Rome. It must remain unclear, however, whether the people who traded in oil were either involved in selling oil to the state or were just

---

[17] Erdkamp 2005, 219–37.

using their ships and expertise to transport state-owned oil on the state's behalf.

It may be significant that under Septimius Severus the phrasing of the *tituli picti* changed: the names of private traders/transporters are replaced by the formula 'of our imperial lords...', followed by the name of the emperor. After AD 217 the imperial names disappear in favour of a phrase referring to the imperial treasury of one of the two Spanish provinces. These changes have been interpreted in various ways, but are usually taken to indicate a more direct involvement of the state in the production and distribution of oil.[18]

It seems clear that to a large extent the provisioning of the capital consisted of the distribution of state-owned grain and olive oil, but the involvement of trade channels cannot be ruled out, the more so regarding olive oil, which at least in the late Republic and Principate was seen as less essential. The supply of wine and other foodstuffs seems to have depended largely on the initiative of traders who were attracted by the numbers and aggregate buying power of Rome's consumers.

STORAGE AND DISTRIBUTION

The state was also much involved in the distribution of foodstuffs, if only by taking care of the necessary infrastructure such as wharves, warehouses and market buildings. During the Republic the scale on which foodstuffs were supplied to the city increased tremendously, and at some time this must have led to the building of warehouses. In the early second century BC port facilities were built along the Tiber, and warehouses surely were part of this development. Gaius Gracchus is said to have built *horrea* as part of the grain dole that he introduced. Various warehouses are mentioned for Rome, such as the Horrea Galbae, the Horrea Lolliana and the Horrea Agrippiana. Some of the early warehouses seem to have been built by private owners, such as the Sulpicii Galbae, but already during the first century AD most of the *horrea* became state-owned, in the sense of having become imperial property. Colossal warehouses were not only part of imperial Rome, but also of Ostia and Portus, where many overseas imports were stored before being moved to Rome. Because the *horrea* were crucial for the capital's food supply, they were built on a massive scale (thick walls, multiple stories), using the most modern techniques (ventilation, raised

---

[18] Recently, Broekaert 2008.

floors). Cost was obviously no issue, and much care was given to the avoidance of spoilage or theft. Storage facilities containing *dolia* (large vessels for liquids) suggest the storage of olive oil and wine on a massive scale. The *horrea piperataria*, i.e. the 'pepper warehouse', indicates the need for large-scale storage for this luxury item. It was probably not only used for pepper, but also for other spices coming from beyond the boundaries of the empire.

Storage space in the *horrea* was rented out in various types and sizes. Inscriptions mentioning the staff working there also reveal the presence of people involved in selling goods from the *horrea*. Although most of the goods mentioned are non-edible, it is likely that the *horrea* were part of the commercial distribution of many foodstuffs consumed in Rome. Unfortunately, the sources remain silent as to the exact nature of the channels through which staple foods such as grain and olive oil left the warehouses.[19]

At some time during the Republic a situation must have emerged in which most households in Rome relied on the service of professional bakers for their bread. Most houses in Rome must have lacked ovens, as was the case in Pompeii. 'Rise', Martial (*Epigr.* 14.223) writes, 'the baker is already selling the boys their breakfast'. The Latin term *pistor* does not distinguish between the milling of grain and the baking of bread, which reflects the fact that the *pistores* in Rome performed both services. In view of the vulnerability of flour to spoilage, it was safest to mill the grain just before it was baked. Moreover, in contrast to later times, when milling was often powered by wind or water, Roman bakers usually employed animal labour to turn the mills. Hence, there was no point in separating the milling from the baking process. It is only in the early third century AD that we see the construction of a large-scale water-powered milling facility along the Tiber in Rome, which reflects not only the scale of consumption in Rome, but also the concern invested by the city's authorities in ensuring a steady supply of bread.[20]

Various sources throughout the Mediterranean world indicate that the cost of bread was changed by varying its weight, not its price. The same is undoubtedly true of Rome: the emperor Aurelian is said to have used taxes from Egypt to increase the weight of the loaves of bread in the capital (*Hist. Aug., Aurel.* 47.1). The weighing of bread is depicted on the famous tomb of the wealthy baker M. Vergilius Eurysaces: large baskets filled with loaves of bread are being weighed, undoubtedly

---

[19] Rickman 1971, 173–6. [20] Bell 1994.

to ensure their prescribed weight. Eurysaces was a contractor (*pistor redemptor*) in the urban bread supply, but it is unclear what that term exactly means. Rome numbered approximately 250 bakeries in the fourth century. Trajan organized these bakers into a *collegium*, which may have made it easier for the state to employ the bakers on behalf of the *annona* and regulate their activities. The second-century jurist Gaius (*Institutiones* 1.34) informs us that Trajan offered privileges to owners of *pistrina* who processed at least 100 *modii* per day and who exercised their trade in Rome for at least three years. Apparently, the authorities closely monitored the bakeries that supplied the populace with bread. They continued to do so up to the end of the western empire (and beyond), but by then they had lost their grip on the Mediterranean's main grain-producing provinces.

Shops were omnipresent in Rome, and many of them must have sold food items. Cicero (*In Pisonem* 67) derided one of his political opponents by stating that his bread and wine were bought at the vendor, implying that a real gentleman employed his own baker and served wine from his cellar. Nevertheless, even wealthy consumers included in their cuisine goods they bought from specialized traders, and we should not underestimate the aggregate demand from the well-to-do citizens. Columella (*De re rustica* 3.2.1) advised his readers that the cultivation of 'table grapes' was only profitable near cities where one could sell them to merchants supplying urban markets. These merchants must have catered for the needs of those middle groups who could afford them, but could (or would) not obtain grapes from their own farms. Obviously there were sellers of vegetables, fish and meat. The common people bought their pork from the butcher, Varro (*Res Rusticae* 2.4.8, 10) says, adding that pork was imported from as far as Gaul. Cicero (*De officiis* 1.152), expressing contempt for small-scale merchants, specifies fish-sellers, butchers, cooks and poulterers. An inscription from Rome (*CIL* 6.96830) mentions a freedwoman who sold grain and legumes (*negotiatrix frumentaria et legumenaria*). Alexander Severus (*Hist. Aug., Alex. Sev.* 33) is said to have formed *corpora* of wine-dealers and vegetable-sellers. Pompeii offers evidence for garlic vendors, reflecting a degree of specialization that must have existed in Rome too (*CIL* 4.3485. Cf. 4.202).

FURTHER READING

Garnsey 1988 investigates the vulnerability of the ancient food supply to disruption and the various strategies employed to ward off hunger.

Erdkamp 2005 concentrates on aspects of the production, trade and distribution of grain. Rickman 1980a deals with the various aspects of the grain supply of the city of Rome. Tengström 1974 offers a study of the grain supply in late imperial Rome. A shorter introduction, offering an attempt at quantification, can be found in Aldrete and Mattingly 1999. Invaluable on diet in Rome are Garnsey 1991 and 1999. More generally, see Foxhall and Forbes 1982. Recent systematic analyses of bone data, in particular of trace elements in skeletons, add to our understanding of the diet in the ancient world. However, one should be wary of broad generalizations on the basis of small samples. General introductions are to be found in Kron 2005 and MacKinnon 2007 (see also Chapter 3). There are numerous detailed studies of the distribution of olive oil and wine in Antiquity. More general on olive oil are Mattingly 1996, Peña 1998, and Broekaert 2008. On wine, see Purcell 1985.

16: COUNTING BRICKS AND STACKING WOOD

Providing the physical fabric

Shawn Graham

Imagine the whole history of the city of Rome played out as a time-lapsed film. One would see it emerge, amoeba-like, from the landscape. Over time, the rhythms and flows of the city pulse with life, growing ever bigger. Towards the latter stages of the film, the city grows hard, and buildings are transformed to concrete and brick and marble. Enormous monuments emerge. The humans scuttle about. The pulse, the flow, the energy, the vitality of the city is constant, constantly renewing its exoskeleton: its built fabric.

This is the city of Rome. Viewed on this time scale, the city is clearly a living thing. I could have described it in terms of a giant machine, which would have focused the subsequent discussion in terms of interchangeable parts, closed-loop systems, and the people of Rome would be only so much background noise to the systems in which they are embedded. The metaphors we use to describe the city condition our thinking about it. By saying that 'the city is alive', I want to focus the attention on how the city is an emergent feature of the way its citizens interact. The city is a complex system.

CITIES AS NETWORKS

Cities are more than simple conglomerations of people. If cities were merely complicated (as a machine is complicated), then it would be true to say that a city is simply a very big village. A city is a place where, over the course of a single day, an individual might move into and out of many different worlds, depending on with whom (and where) they interact. The client meeting a patron in the Forum lives, for a time, in the world of high politics, but returns to a very different world when dealing with the bailiff of his fullery. Another way of thinking about these worlds is to consider them as different kinds of networks. The same individual can play different roles in different networks of social or economic ties.

What makes each city unique in its own way is the way these networks play across space, and how they become intensified in specific locations. Cities represent the intensification in a particular geographical location of multiple intersecting and overlapping networks. When we played the movie of Rome's history, what we observed was the intensification, collision and evolution of complex networks in one single place.[1]

We have to consider what flows through these networks. Some of those things will be intangible, like the exercise of power or social obligation, but they will leave traces for us to recover. In this chapter, I want to explore and examine some of these networks and the energy flows in them (that is, the goods that made up the city's fabric – the brick, timber, concrete, marble and the fuel) as they precipitate to form the exoskeleton of Rome. We always need to remember though that networks do not exist independently of the people within them. It is not enough that mere interconnections exist. Individuals matter and individuals must make something of these interconnections for the networks to work.[2]

Let us consider the question of scale first. How much energy was flowing through these networks? Take the network at the heart of Rome, coalesced around the figure of the emperor. In one particular case, the emperor Caracalla wishes to construct the most magnificent baths. This idea in his head is communicated to his underlings, and within a few short years, his Baths are constructed. In the resultant mobilization of men and resources, the networks called into being, repurposed or otherwise employed extend to the furthest reaches of the empire. The networks that formed around the emperor are not, however, the only ones that existed in Rome. Other, less formal and more ad hoc, existed as well. In this chapter, I will consider both.

THE BACKGROUND HUM: PERSPECTIVES

How do networks organize and structure an entity such as Rome? Some of these networks that provided material for Rome seem to have

[1] Graham 2009. On cities as networks, see Massey et al. 1999, and more generally, the work of the Centre for Advanced Spatial Analysis at University College London, casa.ucl.ac.uk.

[2] For example, see Laurence's 2001 discussion of the Antonine Itineraries and the transformation of Britain into a Roman province. For Laurence, the Itineraries are evidence of the purposeful reconfiguration of existing networks, over which people, goods and capital flowed, into a distinctly Roman pattern.

been self-organizing – like the Tiber valley brick industry. Others (like the marble trade) required a certain amount of top-down organization. Yet it is extremely difficult to disentangle each kind one from the other. The building industry of Rome is one area of ancient activity where these different networks leave traces for us to find.

In recent years, Janet DeLaine has pioneered the study of ancient buildings in terms of the raw energy involved in constructing them, by reverse engineering from the standing ruins to quantities of manpower and materials. In this she works from manpower constants developed over the nineteenth century in the context of railroad construction. She turned her method to the Baths of Caracalla to study the economic impact of this singular imperial building project.[3] Painstakingly measuring every wall, every elevation, DeLaine worked out that the average minimum workforce over the four main years of construction employed:

- 7,200 men directly on the production of materials and in construction
- 1,800 men and pairs of oxen for transport around Rome itself

These numbers rose to 10,400 and 3,200 respectively during the peak periods, to a high of 13,100 during the year 213 when the project was at its highest. For the centre block of the Baths, the quantities of materials used were:

72,000 m³ of pozzolana	12,300 m³ of quicklime
118,400 m³ of tufa	9,400 m³ of pumice
2,794,000 *bessales*	480,000 sesquipedales
815,000 bipedales	54,000 tubuli
7,200 m³ of rubbled brick in wall core	3,200 m³ of timber

DeLaine's work offers us the most detailed investigation of the social and economic impact of the Roman construction industry to date. By the logic of critical path analysis (i.e. before event Y can happen, event X absolutely must take place; before event X, W; and so on) she also worked out the scheduling of provisioning of all these men and

[3] On the Tiber valley brick industry, see S. Graham 2006; on top-down organization of the marble trade, see Fant 1993. On the Baths of Caracalla, see DeLaine 1997. Figures regarding manpower and materials for the Baths are all from DeLaine 1997.

material. What she was doing was mapping out the numerous flows of energy and material arriving at a single point in space and time.[4]

Picture the scene on a Roman road outside the city, all those men, all those wagons. How many wagons? A Roman road is only so wide, and the amount of material an ox-drawn cart may pull, only so much. DeLaine worked out nose-to-tail the implications of all that traffic. Clearly, for this enormous project to work, for it to be feasible, there is a patent implication of organization somehow.

It was formally organized, yet at the same time it was not. An enormous imperial building project created a deformation in the natural economic gravity of Rome, creating incentives for the smart operator to respond to. At the same time, without pre-existing structures – dynamic networks – in place, it would not have been possible (or would have been considerably more difficult) for the project to take place.

An imperial building project is a discordant note against the normal background hum of Rome. It is a distortion for us now, because it survives (and so attracts our attention), and it was a distortion then, because it warped the natural economic networks of the city. To set such imperial projects in perspective, I want to consider the creation of Rome's *entire* non-public building stock. In a later work DeLaine explores the economic implications, in terms of manpower and materials, for building different kinds of walls, all the same size.[5] DeLaine's figures and method provide us a means to estimate roughly the energy inputs for all of Rome. This exercise is fraught of course with numerous caveats and so on, and so must be considered more in keeping with being a thought-experiment.

ASSUMPTIONS AND CAVEATS

In order to simplify the calculations, let us assume that all of Rome's private building stock was made from brick-faced concrete. Brick-faced concrete was the major construction style from the mid-first century AD until the Middle Ages, and so accounts for the majority of the period covered in this volume (in reality Rome of course was an admixture of all kinds of buildings stock – timber-framed, *opus incertum*, *opus reticulatum*, brick-faced concrete, and so on). Note that we are also leaving out all public buildings, all temples, all precincts, and so on,

---

[4] Cf. Davies 2005, 140 on mapping economic flows in the ancient economy.
[5] DeLaine 2000a.

as well as not accounting for staircases, embankments or other kinds of urban furniture. What we are aiming to do is to make an estimate that we know to be an *underestimate*, so as to not overstate our case. By underestimating, we should end up with figures on the right order of magnitude. In another sense, though, we are over-emphasizing the importance of brick and concrete and under-emphasizing the role of timber. Much of Rome's housing and other building stock would have been more akin to timber-framed, wattle-and-daub construction prior to the first century AD; indeed, well into the imperial era many upper floors and interior partition walls would also have been timber framed. I do attempt to account somewhat for timber requirements, though this is the area where our knowledge is most uncertain.

The next problem is one of coming up with an estimate of how many buildings stood in Rome, on average, over the period with which we are concerned, and how big they were, on average. Ostia plays an important role here. I follow the work of Storey, who uses the evidence of Ostia and the Regionary Catalogues for Rome to test various hypotheses concerning the meaning of the term *insulae*. He decides that *insulae* most likely refers to 'enclosed unitary units within the fabric of a single city street block . . . basically, but not necessarily exclusively, apartments within a structure'. For the purposes of his analysis, he calls these 'architectural/residential units'. He then looks at the average number of these ARUs per building per hectare, comparing them with the ratio of *insulae* to *domus* recorded in the Regionary Catalogues; calculating from the Regionary Catalogues for Rome using the Ostian figure of 6.84 units per hectare, gives a resultant 9.9 buildings per hectare.[6]

In part two of his study, Storey then uses a geographic information system to work out how many such 'architectural/residential units' might fit into one of Rome's Augustan regions. He estimates that there

---

[6] The problem of upper floors is discussed somewhat in Adam 1994 and more fully in Chapter 9. On the subject of the density of housing stock in Rome more generally, see Chapters 2 and 9. In the estimation of the number of buildings used for housing – whatever their type – I follow Storey's 2001 and 2002 articles. I follow his figures here because of his methodology for determining the meaning of *insulae*, and for determining what could literally fit in the space used in Rome. Note that his conclusion on the average areal size of a residential unit coincides with Morley's argument based on the *Forma Urbis Romae*. All calculations that follow, obviously, depend on these initial assumptions. However, even if this argument of Storey's was found to be wrong in some regard, it is simply a matter of plugging a new number into DeLaine's method to arrive at new figures.

were approximately ten to fifteen buildings per hectare which could be considered 'apartment buildings' of the style we know from Ostia. The size of the city at its height was on the order of 1,400–1,800 hectares. Assuming 1,400 hectares for the size of Rome, with 10 buildings per hectare, we end up with 14,000 buildings.

Storey estimates from a comparison of evidence from Ostia, Pompeii and Herculaneum that a typical four-story building (that is, it had four floors: ground, first, second and third) had roughly 156 m² of space on each floor (a compromise that would be 'typical for an apartment building, a small domus, or a large shop and workshop'). Assuming that such buildings are square, it would have sides 12.49 m long. It would stand about 12 m tall. DeLaine's 'typical' section of wall is also based on examples at Ostia, and she uses the figure of 0.59 m. Assume that each floor would be roughly 0.59 m thick as well. That leaves us with a building containing about 620 m³ of material. It then becomes a matter of applying DeLaine's algorithms to work out the amount of men and materials for such a city.

The caveats to this exercise are numerous and obvious. There is no accounting for bricks used in arches, for instance, and there were of course many other kinds of buildings and structures in Rome (not to mention the aqueducts stretching into the hinterland). It is important to remember that we are not trying to produce *the* correct figure here; rather, we want to illustrate the *magnitude* of Rome's appetite for resources and energy. In this way, we can describe the shape, texture and relative size of some of these different flows, and delineate something of the shape of the networks that carried them. We can extract and highlight the self-organizing versus the top-down dynamics at play, and contrast the distortions of the imperial programmes with the general background hum.

COUNTING BRICKS[7]

A square building with an area of 156 m² has sides roughly 12.49 m long. The exterior, at four stories of 3 m each, is 12 m high.

---

[7] Following DeLaine 2000a, 254–7. It is also possible to move the resultant figures around, using DeLaine's approach, to arrive at estimates of the actual manpower involved in making these materials, though that is outside of the scope of this chapter.

Assume that the wall is 0.59 m thick. Laid out flat ('unfolding' the four walls into one plane), that building can be considered like a wall that is 50 m long, 12 m high, 0.59 m thick.

Assuming 14,000 such buildings, arranged as a wall, we have a structure that measures 700,000 m long, 12 m high, 0.59 m thick.

Volume of facing bricks, on such a wall: 700,000 × 12 × 2 (inside and outside facing): 17,000,000 m^2 of facing; the facing is 0.14 m deep, thus: 2,400,000 m^3.

There are 72 facing bricks per square metre of wall, thus: 17,000,000 × 72 = 1,200,000,000 bricks or 600,000,000 *bessales*.

The volume of those bricks: 0.00066 × 1,200,000,000 = 800,000 m^3.

The volume of the core equals the volume of the wall less the volume of the facing. 700,000 × 12 × 0.59 = 5,000,000 m^3, 5,000,000 − 2,400,000 = 2,600,000 m^3.

DeLaine estimates that, given an average size of a piece of rubble used as aggregate in a typical Roman wall, that there are about 1,820 pieces per m^3. In which case we are looking at 4,700,000,000 broken up pieces of tufa and other stone aggregate, with a volume of about 1,600,000 m^3.

The volume of mortar in that wall equals the volume of the wall, less the volume of the facing, less the volume of the aggregate, or roughly 2,600,000 m^3.

The mortar is an admixture of lime and pozzolana. Allowing for a ratio of 1:3 lime to pozzolana, and also allowing for a 25 per cent loss of volume on mixing, we get:

Pozzolana: 2,400,000 m^3
Slaked lime: 800,000 m^3
Quicklime: 300,00 m^3.

Producing the quicklime requires, roughly, 2.75 tonnes of fuel/m^3, so 900,000 tonnes.

Firing the bricks takes roughly 0.45 tonnes of fuel/1000 *bessales*, so 300,000 tonnes.

This model of the city envisions a vast, uniformly tall city, which is a gross oversimplification. The vast majority of buildings, on the order of 80 per cent, would have only one to three stories, while the remainder would rise from four to eight floors, so varying from 6 to 20 m. Of the 14,000 estimated buildings in Rome, let us assume nearly 12,000 would average two floors (3 stories: ground, first, second), with another 2,000 with five floors, and 140 with seven floors.[8]

An underestimate of the amount of materials in the building fabric of a Rome covering 1,400 hectares, with a density of 10 buildings per hectare, with heights varying from two to seven floors gives us:

	Two floors	Five floors	Seven floors	Total
Pozzolana	1,500,000 m³	600,000 m³	50,000 m³	2,150,000 m³
slaked lime	500,000 m³	200,000 m³	20,000 m³	720,000 m³
bessales bricks	400,000,000	150,000,000	10,000,000	560,000,000
caementa for core (rubble aggregate)	1,000,000 m³	400,000 m³	30,000 m³	1,430,000 m³
fuel for materials production (coppiced wood)	700,000 tonnes	300,000 tonnes	20,000 tonnes	1,020,000 tonnes

At first blush, these numbers seem staggering. The Caesarian edict limiting daylight travel on the roads of Rome, which includes carts and wagons related to construction (*Lex Julia Municipalis*, line 56), seems to make an awful lot of sense. How much of a nightmare was it to move this material around?

DeLaine considered the question for the Baths of Caracalla, and I shall use her numbers here (assuming, given the scale we are discussing, that the practical differences of using different sources for materials do not make much difference):

	Distance from quarry or port to site Roman miles	Trips/unit m³ or 1,000 bricks	Time/trip loading/ unloading hrs	Maximum round trips/ 12 hr day
pozzolana	2.3	4	3.31	3
Lime	1.2	3.9	1.84	6

(*cont.*)

[8] The percentages used are Storey's from Chapter 9, rounded to 83 per cent (1–3 stories: I calculate for 2 stories), 16 per cent (4–6 stories, 5 stories) and 1 per cent (6–8 stories, so 7 stories).

(*cont.*)

	Distance from quarry or port to site Roman miles	Trips/unit m³ or 1,000 bricks	Time/trip loading/ unloading hrs	Maximum round trips/ 12 hr day
bessales	1.2	7.5	1.77	6
Tufa	1.2	4.25	1.82	6

These are trips using an ox cart to move the material. If we use these constants, we get roughly:

	Number of trips necessary	Number of hours	Number of 12 hr days
pozzolana	9,000,000	30,000,000	9,000,000
Lime	3,000,000	5,000,000	900,000
bessales	4,000,000	7,000,000	1,000,000
Tufa	6,000,000	11,000,000	2,000,000

... or 13,000,000 days of work for a single ox cart. However, if we imagine that all of this building stock was erected over about 350 years (first to fourth centuries AD), and we further imagine that the construction season lasted 220 days each year, that gives us 77,000 days of work. How many oxen would be necessary to do this much work? Divide the amount of work done (remembering that each trip uses a *pair* of oxen), by the available amount of days, and we get about 350 pairs of oxen.

However, it is unreasonable to imagine that construction happened, every day, for every one of those years. The record shows that construction was much more punctuated. Construction would peak in the years after major fires, earthquakes or other such events. Buildings fell down from time to time. The Great Fire of AD 64 left only four regions untouched, three were utterly destroyed and seven were heavily damaged, according to Tacitus (*Annales* 15.40.2); Cassius Dio suggests two thirds of the city were devastated (62.18.2). Other similar conflagrations happened in 80 and 238, for instance. While Tacitus and Dio might be exaggerating for effect, it has been estimated that at least a quarter and perhaps a third of the housing of Rome was destroyed in the fire of 64.[9] This estimate allows us to scale our estimate of materials and transport requirements into a snapshot of time following the fire, from 64 through to the end of Vespasian's reign, or fifteen years:

Materials required to rebuild 1/4 of Rome (assuming the same ratio of building sizes as in the previous estimate):

pozzolana	537,500 m³
slaked lime	180,000 m³
bessales bricks	140,000,000
caementa for core (rubble aggregate)	357,500 m³
fuel for materials production (coppiced wood)	255,000 tonnes

There are 3,300 working days – assuming no interruptions – during that fifteen-year period. A single ox cart would take over 3 million days to move this amount of material; about 2,000 teams of oxen could shift this material working flat out over the fifteen years. This was the context of the Flavian building projects, a workforce already in production making all of the materials necessary for the fabric of Rome. The Flavian projects would have increased demand for materials and transportation. DeLaine estimated for the Baths of Caracalla – an extremely intense project – that within Rome 1,800 to 3,200 pairs of oxen were used, and somewhere between 4,000 and 5,000 pairs of oxen were in use for the building industry (including monuments and other public works) as a whole.[10] (Figure 16.1 gives a sense of the difficulties of using oxen in the narrow streets of Rome.) Our estimate here then is on the right order of magnitude. The amount of activity would have tapered off over time, as the city recovered from the disaster, only to wax again with the next one, or with the next major building project.

The background noise of the Roman building industry brought an enormous amount of material into the city of Rome, but contrary to what we might have imagined, it was not an unmanageable amount. At least that is, until an imperial project began, at which point the amount of activity could triple or more!

[9] Newbold 1974.
[10] As an aside, DeLaine estimated that, assuming an ox cart is 4.5 m long, and leaving 2 m between carts, a maximum of 250 carts could be on each Roman mile of road at any one time (DeLaine 1997, 190). Our 1,200 ox carts could be packed tight into 5 miles of Roman road. See also Chapter 14 on congestion within the city and the times when deliveries could be made.

FIGURE 16.1 Teams of oxen struggle to drag Mussolini's obelisk through the crowded streets of Rome in 1929.

STACKING WOOD: AN OUTLINE OF THE TIMBER INDUSTRY

The flows of energy and materials required to build a Rome of concrete and brick are only a portion of the total flows of non-perishable goods.

Securing good timber supplies was a state concern from as early as 192 BC, when the city set aside port facilities to handle the import of timber for construction (Livy 35.41.10).[11] Wood was required for cooking and for heating as well. The timber industry was thus not just an industry connected with constructing Rome, but with sustaining Rome. One estimate suggests that a total population of 50 million around the Mediterranean would require 75,000 tonnes of wood every day; a Rome of 1 million of those people might be assumed to use one-fiftieth of that wood, or 1,500 tonnes every day. The major heating fuel source was not logs of wood but rather charcoal. It takes roughly 10 kg of wood to produce 1 kg of charcoal. When burnt, charcoal provides 1.67 times more energy than wood. Charcoal's advantage lies in its lightness and portability, and its ability to give off a higher temperature. Burning charcoal for heating or for cooking gives off less smoke and particulate matter than burning a comparable amount of wood, but one could imagine that a cold day during the Roman winter would have been a hazy unpleasant mess. Vitruvius (*De architectura* 2.9.5–17) lists the different species of wood in common use in his day, and Columella (*De re rustica* 12.2.13) discusses wagon loads of squared timber, which suggests that some wood was produced on estates for the wider market.[12]

It is something of a myth to suggest that the timber industry of antiquity led to wholesale deforestation. Horden and Purcell's work on 'microregions' and interconnected ecologies – networks – argues that modern ideas about deforestation neglect the fact that a forest, or a woodland, provided more resources than simple building timber or charcoal:

> Woodlands offer food directly, by routes ranging from
> apiculture to hunting. Its different forms can be used as a
> primary resource for timber, brushwood, charcoal and
> so on. It can be managed in many ways, from charcoal-
> burning to 'modern'-type silviculture. But it can
> also be used indirectly, again being improved or managed
> in many different ways, as a reserve of wild food or as a
> pasture for several different types of domesticated animal,

[11] Casson 1965, 31–2; see also Chapter 13, and Graham 2005.
[12] On the demand for wood around the Mediterranean, see Le Houerou 1981. On charcoal, see Horden and Purcell, 2000, 334–5; on timber for construction see DeLaine 1997, 93.

especially pig and goat. These indirect uses increase the potential of the forest without inevitably destroying it.[13]

Once again, the difference between the background hum of Rome and the top-down directives of the imperial house contrast. Provisions were made to set aside tracts of land in the Tiber Valley to provide fuel for the imperial baths, while others were left to provide from the production of their own estates or via purchase. We can advance the hypothesis that the production of charcoal or other forest products (pitch, resin, cork, dyes, wagon axles and so on) could have been self-organized in the same way as the brick industry was. Brick was not the only material stamped in the Roman world. Evidence exists for stamping on bitumen, on a squared timber from AD 63 on the Thames, on timbers in the circus of Arles, and of course on marbles. Given that stamps and brandings are known on ancient timbers from elsewhere in the Roman world, we can imagine bricks being shipped down-river on rafts of squared timbers that were themselves destined for sale: uncut as rafters, or sawed into formworks, or shuttering for concrete foundations.[14]

The role of the timber industry in provisioning Rome has been neglected by scholars up to now. If the assumptions regarding the other building materials used in Rome come with cartloads of caveats, any figures regarding timber use would be doubly-loaded, for timber was not just a building material used in the eventual finished building, but also as a tool, as a form for concrete foundations, as scaffolding to be reused elsewhere,[15] as rafts to bring other materials down the Tiber, as formworks for arches, as a source of charcoal, as a fuel for slaking lime or baking clay. But, given our assumptions about the private building stock of Rome above, we could perhaps make a tentative estimate of the amount of timber used in the roofing of Rome. If a roof tile measures on average 50 cm wide, and one side of the roof is about 12 m long (or over 40 Roman feet), then we are looking at 24 beams per building;

---

[13] Quotation is from Horden and Purcell 2002, 332–3. On microregions, see Horden and Purcell 2000, 328–41; on deforestation see Hughes and Thirgood 1982.

[14] On set-aside land in the Tiber Valley used as a source for fuel for the baths, see Horden and Purcell 2002, 184; Hemphill 1987. Bitumen: Agostini and Pellegrini 1996, 57–8. Squared timber from the Thames: Brigham et al. 1996, 36. Timbers from the circus of Arles: M. Fuegere, pers. comm. 2000. Marbles: Fant 1993, 145–70.

[15] DeLaine's study of the patterning of put-log holes in the fabric of the Baths of Caracalla enabled her to conclude that 85,000 put-logs for scaffolding were needed (DeLaine 1997, 126).

with 14,000 buildings, that is roughly 300,000 roof beams alone – roof beams that would have to be replaced over time, whether because of rot, weather damage, or fire. Clearly, this is a rough-and-ready calculation, and a gross underestimate, but the point is not to determine exact numbers, but to obtain a measure of scale. Imagine the river and road traffic implied by 300,000 40-foot beams, and Juvenal's fear of being crushed by a fir-log (amongst other things) seems entirely justified:

> . . . up comes a huge fir-log swaying on a wagon, and then
> a second dray carrying a whole pine-tree; they tower aloft
> and threaten the people. For if that axle with its load of
> Ligurian marble breaks down, and pours an overturned
> mountain on to the crowd, what is left of their bodies?
>
> (Juvenal 3.254–8)

The timber industry – and forest products more generally – are an important lacuna in our knowledge and understanding and would reward further study.

COMPLEXITY AND PROVISIONING ROME

In the aftermath of the fire of 64, Nero offered various incentives to encourage quick rebuilding. He also famously set up new building codes and widened streets. Widening the streets had the effect of dispossessing many landowners of their properties; the fire itself had deprived many more of their wealth. Funds for rebuilding were tight, and some of Nero's measures to raise funds from property owners had the effect of transferring that pressure to the tenants themselves, driving up rents in an already tight housing market. The sudden demand for building materials would have led to a spike in their price, leading to development of clay resources, felling of timbers and so on in the hinterland of Rome.[16] Organizing this extraction and transportation of materials from the hinterland to the building sites of Rome depended on intensifying existing networks, or creating them from new.

The picture I have been developing is of a low background noise of some complexity, punctuated by bursts of extreme activity. It is these bursts of activity that I wish to explore now, using the evidence of brick and, more precisely, the networks of personal connections implied in

---

[16] On the social and economic aftermath of the Great Fire, see Newbold 1974.

the stamps on the brick, as an indicator material for the other principal materials (excluding marble).

Network shape is important, because it affects how materials move over it – some networks require many steps between participants for material (or information) to get from one side to another, while others allow for extremely fast penetration. Particular network shapes result from different formation dynamics: some spontaneously self-organize, while others require top-down intervention. The brick industry in particular bears many characteristics of what is called a 'small-world' network, or one in which a handful of participants are exponentially well-connected to the rest of the network; these also tend to be self-organizing. These individuals act as short-cuts, allowing information to move through and penetrate deeper than otherwise would be the case.

This is important because it implies two things. One, that the brick industry was largely self-regulated: no governmental control needs to be suggested to account for what we can see of the industry, archaeologically. The patterning of interconnections between named individuals in the stamps is sufficient. Two, that 'shocks' to the network – such as the periodic surges of imperial building projects, or the demand for building materials in the wake of major fires – could have chaotic results. In a small-world network, an external shock can have counter-intuitive results. A large event might not wreck the system, but a simple nudge at just the right time could bring the whole edifice crashing down. This implies that the supply of building materials would sometimes be able to rise majestically to meet demand, but at other times fail abysmally. Small-world networks also cast into stark relief the difference between the global effects of the network itself and the local effects for individuals within that network.[17]

This means that a description, such as this chapter, of events at the global or macro scale (the background hum) describe a completely different world from that of the micro scale, because they exist at different levels of complexity. This is the problem of trying to understand levels of complexity. One point of view regards levels in terms of control, as a hierarchy. The classic example here would be the structure of an army, with privates, corporals, sergeants, up to the generals. Another approach regards levels as containers: a day is made up of hours, which are made up of minutes, which are made up of seconds. The difference

[17] On networks and network shape in the brick industry, see S. Graham 2006, ch. 6; Graham and Ruffini 2007. On small worlds, see Watts 1999 and Barabàsi 2002.

between the two levels is clear, for thirty privates do not make one corporal. Finally, there is another way of viewing levels, as 'emergent'. In this view, levels are defined by the pattern of interactions between actors – a traffic jam emerges from the interactions of its constituent, ever-changing component automobiles.[18]

It is in this sense that I view the provision of building materials to Rome, and the building industry of Rome more generally. The brick industry has been seen as the classic industry demonstrating the finger of the state operating in the economy (a view going back to H. Bloch in a 1959 publication), since over time the names of private landowners become replaced by the imperial family. This I think is to confuse the problem of levels: what happens in terms of production, and how production is organized, might be at a different level of complexity from the global ownership of land. In which case, it is the pattern of landowning which emerges from the patterns of production, and not the other way around. The urban fabric of the city was brought together by a process operating at a different level of complexity than that recorded in the individual stamped bricks.

This is particularly in evidence when we consider the problem of the year 123. This consular dated year when Paetinus and Apronianus were consuls appears so frequently in brick stamps that Bloch was led to suggest that there must have been an order from on high in that year for all stamps to be marked with the date; this is the foundation for arguing that the industry, the provisioning of building materials, was organized by the state. In point of fact, when we examine the number of examples of stamped bricks known today carrying particular years – when we examine the relative rate of dated stamps – we find that there is a fairly regular saw-tooth patterning with peaks at the years AD 110, 115, 120, 123, 127, 130, 135, 138, 142, 145, 148, 154, 159 and 164. On average, the length of time between peaks is four years, although the most common period (the mode) is five years.

This pattern is reminiscent of the patterns of land tenancy in the Roman world. Ethnographic and anthropological studies of modern peasant–landlord relationships in the Third World have demonstrated that tenant farming is a method which actually increases productivity at the expense of the peasant's independence. By leasing out undersized plots, the landlord forces the tenant to overproduce to pay the land rent

[18] U. Wilensky, 1998, 'NetLogo Wolf Sheep Predation Model', Center for Connected Learning and Computer-Based Modeling, Northwestern University, Evanston, IL, <www.ccl.northwestern.edu/netlogo/models/WolfSheepPredation>, 4.

and also to feed himself and his family from the same allotment. By using short-term contracts (which in practice are rarely ever cancelled) the landlord uses the continual threat of eviction to intimidate the tenant. Economies of scale can thus be achieved using many small-scale land units, a significant difference from modern economies. The contracts used in land tenancy were most likely the same ones used to organize brick production, as has been deduced by the appearance of certain elements in the text of brick stamps.

The staggering pattern around the five-year mark in the stamping rates of bricks carrying consular dates is strongly reminiscent of that land-tenancy situation, where landlords try to exercise control over their tenants by creating instability over the terms of their leases. The saw-tooth patterning also suggests a turnover of *officinatores*. Comparison with the history of other extractive industries suggests that the brick industry would have suffered repeated cycles of oversupply and price collapse. When the price was rising, more land was exploited for brick, but when the price collapsed, the shock meant that the *officinator* was driven out of business or could no longer afford the land rent. The decline in absolute numbers of examples and types of stamped brick carrying dates over time from the high in AD 123 to when consular dates cease to be used is evocative of other industries in other times and places where shocks and shakeouts tended to consolidate the industry in the hands of the few. Consolidation emerges from the patterning of landholding in the immediate environs of Rome, whence come the bricks.

The year 123 itself, however, does not appear to be fundamentally different from other years in terms of number of examples of stamped brick per type, meaning that there is no need to posit some form of government intervention that year concerning stamping rates or the organization of production. It might, however, represent a real increase in the amount of land exploited for brick production: a boom in land rents. It would be a situation analogous to the 'rush' which happens in the early days in extractive industries (as in timber or gold) when everyone is trying to open up as much land as possible. Demand for brick in the year prior to AD 123 must have been enormous (or at least, the *expectation* of a sudden increase in demand was) to foster such a run on the land; this run could have been precipitated by the announcement of future plans for public/private building programmes (an example may be the evidence for Rutilius Lupus storing brick in anticipation of the emperor's return after AD 117 and the resumption of building activities). This complex network behind the brick industry was not therefore immune from shocks.[19]

CONCLUDING THOUGHTS

In conclusion, when we study the provisioning of materials to Rome, whether brick, rubble, timber or marble, we need to be aware of the scale of use, and the likely kind of networks in which the people involved were embedded, and over which the materials themselves flowed.

The Baths of Caracalla alone used 6,330 m³ of marble weighing over 17,000 tonnes, requiring over 9,000 ox-cart days just to move the marble from the Emporium to the site. Marble was exotic. It was expensive. It required enormous amounts of manpower to extract it, move it, and build with it. Consequently, it carried associations of wealth, power and prestige, and it attracted the direct attention of the imperial bureaucracy. Brick did not, during the normal course of events (the background noise in Rome), attract the same attention. Six hundred million *bessales* bricks appear to be an enormous number, but set that against 200 years of production, and we have an annual production of 3 million – or one to two kiln loads per day per productive year.[20] But keep in mind some lacunae in the estimation of production: no *tubuli*, no roof tiles, no *sesquipedales*, no *bipedales*, no *dolia*, no ceramic sarcophagi. The background hum of production had to be much higher than one kiln load per day per year. Because the production of the brickyards was always in demand, one way or another, there was a concomitant ability to weather the peaks in demand – the imperial building projects – without compromising supply. That is not to say that

---

[19] Bloch's argument for government control: Bloch 1959, 237. On the stamping pattern in stamped bricks, see S. Graham 2006, 85–7. Tenancy and the organization of the exploitation of land are discussed in Foxhall 1990, 100–2: threat of eviction, and the use of under-sized plots; contracts in brick stamps, see *LTUR*, cf. De Neeve 1984. The history of other extractive industries: Graham 2005, 106–24, Darvill and McWhirr 1984, 241. Shakeout and consolidation: Graham 2005, S. Graham 2006, 73–91. Stockpiling of brick by Rutilius Lupus: Bloch 1959, 236.

[20] DeLaine 1997, 118 remarks that at peak efficiency, a brick kiln could probably have managed nine firings per season, but for a kiln with one worker only two firings would be possible; within the scenario outlined in this chapter and assuming one worker per kiln, a brick industry comprised of 110-220 kilns would certainly be reasonable, given the numbers of unique stamps known in the industry.

those peaks were met successfully by every participant in the market, just that the market, as an emergent level of complexity from the individual participants, was able to continue. It accomplished this even whilst shaking out the smaller participants, over time, leading to the concentration of productive units in fewer and fewer hands.

With regard to marble, the uniformity of the stamps points to government control, administration and marketing: the hallmarks of a top-down directed network. The diversity of brick stamps, coupled with the near ubiquity of certain types, points to a bottom-up, emergent and dynamic network. What is particularly interesting about this bottom-up network is the way it could scale up to meet the needs of the unpredictable building booms of Rome. On the other hand, we always must remember that these networks were composed of individuals. The secondary markets in sarcophagi that 'borrowed' from the official state networks for provisioning marble, and the aftermarket in luxury marbles once the state had met its needs, illustrate some of the ways in which individuals made the most of their connections: as always seems to be the case, it's not what you know, it's who you know.

FURTHER READING

DeLaine's *Baths of Caracalla* (1997) is the foundation for understanding the economic, social and physical impact on Rome of the construction industry. For construction more generally, see Adam 1994. For the broader impact on the wider Mediterranean basin, and especially for the idea of interconnected micro-regions, see Horden and Purcell 2000. For other materials supplied to Rome, see Papi 2007. On the ancient timber industry, the standard is still Meiggs 1982. For the brick industry as a complex system, see S. Graham 2006; for the use of stamps more generally on a wide variety of materials, see Harris 1993. On complexity and network dynamics, see Barabàsi 2002.

17: WATER SUPPLY, DRAINAGE AND WATERMILLS

Christer Bruun

The aqueducts and the sewers of ancient Rome would deserve to be included among the wonders of the ancient world. Unfortunately, by the time the water supply was fully developed in the early third century AD, the canonical list of the 'seven wonders' had long since been drawn up by Hellenistic intellectuals, who had no idea that Rome would one day be supplied by eleven aqueducts. Nor did they anticipate that Strabo (5.3.8) would admiringly write about artificial rivers flowing through the city and emptying into the Tiber, that according to Pliny nothing in the world was more wondrous than the *abundantia aquarum* of Rome (*Historia Naturalis* 36.123), or that Dionysius of Halicarnassus would rank the aqueducts and the sewers among the most important achievements of Roman culture (*Antiquitates Romanae* 3.67.5).

THE HISTORY OF THE AQUEDUCTS

The beginning was modest. In 312 BC the censor Appius Claudius Caecus, one of the leading men of his time and involved in a number of important reforms, began work on the Via Appia as well as on Rome's first aqueduct, which was named after him. The Aqua Appia was only 16 km long and ran under ground for its whole stretch, which is why its course has not yet been identified. At the time, Rome was engaged in a difficult war with the Samnites, and the Via Appia which led south to Campania was strategically important. The importance of the Aqua Appia is less clear. It terminated near the commercial river harbour and the Forum Boarium, below the Palatine (Frontinus, *De aquaeductu* 5.5), and one can only conclude that Rome's social and economic development had made its introduction necessary. It came from the same direction as the Via Appia, and there were possibly synergy effects between these two major projects. As far as we know, there was no model for an urban aqueduct on this scale in Italy. Influence from the Greek world is one possible source of technological inspiration, while hydraulic expertise could definitely be found among Rome's neighbours the Etruscans, who excelled in drainage work and tunnelling. Legend has it that the famous Cloaca Maxima, which drained the Forum valley, goes back to a period when Rome was under the sway of rulers of Etruscan origin. Undoubtedly drainage work took place in the archaic period; part of the surviving Cloaca dates to the early Republic.

Three other aqueducts were built during the republican period, normally with censors or praetors in charge: *Anio* (*vetus*) in 272–269 BC, Aqua Marcia in 144–140 BC and Aqua Tepula in 126–125 BC. At that time Rome had already entered the late republican phase, which may explain why no further aqueducts were built for almost a century. That period of social and political conflicts, until Augustus took control in Rome, was not conducive to a long-range costly project such as the construction of an aqueduct, although the first century BC was a period of growing population and increasing demand for urban amenities.

Under the direction of Augustus' loyal follower M. Vipsanius Agrippa major investments in the water supply were made. In 33 (or 40) BC the Aqua Julia was introduced, in 19 BC the Aqua Virgo and in 2 BC the Aqua Alsietina. Half a century later in AD 52 the two largest aqueducts (by volume), the Anio Novus and the Aqua Claudia, were inaugurated by the emperor Claudius, after their construction had been begun under Gaius. In 109 Trajan inaugurated the Aqua Traiana, financed with the booty from the conquest of Dacia, while Caracalla, during his sole reign (211–17), added new sources to the Marcia and built a new branch from it to his Baths. Severus Alexander (222–35) is normally credited with a final aqueduct, called Aqua Alexandri(a)na, but there is some debate about whether the arches which can still be seen in Rome may not belong to Caracalla's expansion of the Marcia.

Indeed the physical remains of the eleven (or ten) aqueducts have always constituted a point of departure for the study of Rome's water supply. Ashby's classic investigation of the course of the aqueducts in the countryside is still valuable, but there is much recent work and new discoveries are continuously made. There is also a useful guide by Aicher on what can actually still be seen, while the Parco degli Acquedotti in the eastern outskirts of Rome allows visitors, for the price of a subway ticket, to walk among the majestic arches which inspired generations of landscape painters from the Romantic period onwards. Within the city, water was conveyed both on arches and in underground conduits. The identification of these remains is relevant also for the study of urbanism and social history, besides engineering.

SEWERS AND WASTE DISPOSAL

The sewer network, on the contrary, has been poorly mapped out, although we can assume that drainage received attention on a par with the water supply. The narrative sources are mostly silent; repairs on the already existing network were carried out by the censors in 184 BC, and new ones were built where needed (Livy 39.44.6, cf. Dionysius of Halicarnassus, *Ant. Rom.* 3.67.5). Under Agrippa, repairs on the Cloaca Maxima took place. At that time, the 'veritable rivers that flowed through the city and the sewers' impressed the geographer Strabo (5.3.8). Inscriptions do not help much; no more than a handful of craftsmen or entrepreneurs concerned with the *cloacae* are known.

The best we can do when creating a picture of the treatment of waste water in Rome is to use comparative material from towns like Pompeii and Ostia. Waste products and filth were disposed of in many ways, and Rome's residents had unequal access to the various amenities. There were public latrines (the one in the Largo di Torre Argentina is still visible), which surely were flushed by aqueduct water, as was the latrine in many a rich *domus*; possibly they existed in some high-rise buildings as well (shared by the residents). Affluent houses benefiting from a private conduit normally let their surplus water flow out into the gutter, where it might perform a cleaning or flushing function before ending up in one of the covered underground sewers. The overflow from public fountains served a similar purpose, as did the rainwater run-off from every kind of building. There were strict rules in Roman law prohibiting owners of real estate from flooding neighbouring properties. Then again, the most primitive form of waste disposal was to use cess pits, and this probably occurred in Rome as well; there were workers (*stercorarii*) who could be used to empty them at intervals.

THREE KINDS OF SOURCES FOR MODERN SCHOLARSHIP

The archaeological remains of the aqueducts, the distribution network (including, for instance, fountains and cisterns), and the latrines and the sewers represent one of the three types of sources that scholars studying Rome's water supply need to use. Inscriptions provide another essential source of information. There are not many monumental texts in Rome that concern the aqueducts, some of the most important being the three inscriptions on the *Porta Maggiore* arch (which carried the Anio Novus and the Claudia), recording the construction by Claudius and repairs by first Vespasian and then Titus (*CIL* 6.1256–8 = *ILS* 218). Relatively common are the standardized markers, *cippi*, that were set up along the course of the aqueducts outside the city to indicate the distance and the protected zone along an aqueduct. Most frequent are inscriptions on lead pipes (*fistulae*), which number some 800 in Rome alone and are still often neglected by scholars, although they contain crucial information on, for instance, administration, distribution and manufacture. In classical literary texts there are a few minor instances that pertain to Rome's water supply, mostly passages that shower praise on the aqueducts. Important beyond comparison is Sex. Iulius Frontinus' *De aquaeductu urbis Romae*, 'On Rome's water supply', written around the year AD 100 by the then *curator aquarum*, the city's 'Water Commissioner'. In fifty-three pages (in the recent Cambridge edition) Frontinus presents information on, among other topics, the history, the topography, the volume of water and its distribution, and the administration of Rome's aqueducts. Of great general historical interest are the *senatus consulta* (all from 11 BC) and the *lex Quinctia* (from 9 BC), which created the *cura aquarum* proper and which he quotes verbatim. The work provides a unique survey of one sector of Roman urban administration, but its use as a historical source is less straightforward than is sometimes assumed, because Frontinus' motives for writing coloured his treatment and selection of material. Besides the reason Frontinus gives for composing his work, 'for my own instruction' (*aq.* 2.3), one can at least discern the wish to compliment the ruler, promote his own activities and immortalize Roman civilization. It is crucial for our understanding of Rome's water supply, and of Frontinus' *De aquaeductu*, to consider all the various sources together; in particular the *fistula* inscriptions shed important light on Frontinus' treatise.

THE *CURA AQUARUM* OF ROME – A MODEL CASE OF ROMAN GOVERNMENT

Owing to the many and varied sources relating to it no administrative branch in the Roman world is as well known as Rome's water supply during the empire. Every so often a discussion of Roman imperial administration uses the *cura aquarum* of Rome as an example. For the republican period, though, little information is available, besides the fact that aediles and censors seem to have been given the task of supervising the building of new aqueducts, and praetors had jurisdiction in conflicts involving water (*CIL* 10.4842.65 = *ILS* 5743; 10.8236; Frontinus, *aq.* 129.5). It is not known who the officials in charge of overseeing the day-by-day working of the aqueducts were.

There was development when Agrippa began the programme of building new aqueducts. He exercised control over the water supply both while holding various elected offices (consul, aedile) and by virtue of his investments in this sector, with steady support of the Princeps, as *operum suorum et munerum velut perpetuus curator*, as Frontinus puts it (*aq.* 98.1, 'as if in charge of his own achievements for life'). A major change took place after Agrippa died in 12 BC. In the following year the senate enacted a number of decrees (*senatus consulta*) that established a proper *cura aquarum* with a high-ranking *curator aquarum* at its head. In 9 BC the people passed a law, the *lex Quinctia*, which further defined the *cura aquarum*. Frontinus cites the *senatus consulta* and the *lex Quinctia* verbatim, often with a brief summary in his own words or a comment (*aq.* 100–1, 104–11, 125–9). One of the considerable problems when studying Rome's water supply is to identify which of the clauses were still valid by Frontinus' time, and why he does not make a greater effort to outline how matters were handled when he wrote, since it is obvious that some changes had occurred.

The creation of the *cura aquarum* was typical of the Augustan period. To let an ally of the Princeps such as Agrippa, while for most of the time holding no elected office, handle an important part of the government of the capital could not but antagonize the senatorial order. The post of *curator aquarum*, which Suetonius (*Augustus* 37) lumps together with the other *nova officia* that Augustus devised (*excogitavit*), was a way of integrating the senators by conferring an important task on a distinguished member of that order. The *senatus consulta* of 11 BC make it clear that the *cura aquarum* was founded on the emperor's initiative (*aq.* 99), although formally the decisions were made by the senate in 11 BC and in 9 BC by the assembly. The *curator* was always nominated by the emperor.

No corresponding *curator* for the *cloacae* is known before the early second century, when to the title of the official in charge of the Tiber and its bank, the *curator alvei et riparum Tiberis*, was added 'et *cloacarum urbis*'. How the upkeep of the sewers was organized during the first century is unknown, and we have very few details, except for the names of a few curators, after that.

Frontinus says that the *curatores aquarum* were leading senators (*aq.* 1) and the list of sixteen predecessors he gives confirms this (*aq.* 102). The curatorship was a ceremonial one in many ways; no technical expertise was required of the curator, and it seems that curators were not always present in Rome; hydraulic and other relevant knowledge was to be found primarily or even exclusively on the lower levels of the organization. Among the experts that were part of the workforce Frontinus mentions *architecti* (engineers), *silicarii* (pavers), *tectores* (plasterers) and common *aquarii* (*aq.* 100.1, 117.1). In Agrippa's times, a force of 240 slaves and freedmen had been employed for aqueduct work. In his testament, they were bequeathed to Augustus, who donated them to the Roman state with the intention that they continue to serve the water supply. The emperor Claudius increased that number by 460 men from among the imperial slaves and freedmen (*aq.* 116.4). (Of these, only about a dozen appear in funerary inscriptions over a period of some 200 years, which is an indication of how poorly the population of Rome is present in the epigraphic record.) Frontinus also reports that from Claudius onwards imperial procurators were seconded to the aqueducts (*aq.* 105.2).

DEBATES ABOUT THE *CURA AQUARUM*

In current scholarship there are two main debates relative to the aqueduct administration. One concerns the role of the over fifty procurators (more than in any other Roman administrative sector) that have some connection with the water supply of Rome. A handful of *procuratores aquarum* appear in inscriptions on stone, but a vast majority of procurators (all without any epithet such as '*aquarum*') are known from inscriptions (stamps) on Roman lead pipes, where they appear in the *sub cura* formula, which indicates that they performed some official task. Their number is so large that they cannot all be the *procurator aquarum* as it used to be thought, and the most likely situation is that they supervised various public works involving also the installation of a water conduit.

Another puzzling feature is that after the tenure of Frontinus no *curator aquarum* has been securely identified during a period of some ninety years. The office may have been left vacant during the second century, although it seems odd that the emperor should have abstained from bestowing that honorific office on loyal senators. Then, in *c.* AD 190, senators of consular rank with the title *curator aquarum et*

Minuciae (also spelled *Miniciae*) begin to turn up in funerary and honorary inscriptions that cite senatorial careers (their *cursus honorum*); some fifteen such officials are known down to the reign of Constantine the Great.[1]

WATER, GRAIN DISTRIBUTION AND GRAIN-MILLING

The free grain distribution to the Roman population took place in the Porticus Minucia in the Campus Martius, and the assumption is that from *c.* 190 (or possibly earlier) the water supply and the grain distribution were joined under a *curator aquarum et Minuciae*. Why that reform was carried out is debated. One explanation sets out from the hypothesis that the headquarters of the *cura aquarum* was located in the Porticus Minucia where the grain distribution took place.

Another theory focuses on the fact that water power was used for milling grain in Rome (see also Chapter 15). It would seem to make sense to have the same organization direct both the aqueducts and the production of flour that was used to bake the bread which supplanted the distribution of free grain. Yet there are chronological problems with this theory, as the watermill on the Gianicolo that used the water of the Aqua Traiana is dated to after AD 200, thus it postdates the first *curatores aquarum et Minuciae*.

There is archaeological evidence for watermills also in the Baths of Caracalla, and late-antique millstones were recently identified on the Palatine. At an even later date, when the aqueducts had been cut off during the Visigothic siege in 537, floating watermills were placed in the Tiber (Procopius, *De bello Gothico* 5.19.19–25).

---

[1] The possibility that no *curator aquarum* was nominated after Frontinus is puzzling. Statistical arguments have shown that the absence of secure evidence for a *curator aquarum* during the second century AD is significant and does not seem to depend purely on chance. Perhaps imperial financial procurators were in charge instead? One may compare the various inscriptions that name as many as fifteen of the less distinguished *curatores alvei et riparum Tiberis et cloacarum urbis* during the same period (up to *c.* AD 190). There was apparently a new development from the early 190s onward, when a senator of consular rank is known from a *sub cura* inscription on a lead pipe and as *curator aquarum et ad fraudes Minuciae* (a very odd title, worth more discussion) in an inscription on stone; see comprehensively Bruun 2006.

PUBLIC WORKS, CONTRACTORS,
PLUMBARII AND FINANCES

Although thanks to the inscribed *fistulae* we possess the names of senators and equestrians who were in charge of projects that involved the instalment of water conduits, we have no details about the organization of such works, and above all we lack information on how the building of new aqueducts was organized. It is generally thought that the *curator aquarum* was not in charge of new projects. The emperor financed them, and those procurators who oversaw the imperial finances would have been responsible for aqueducts as well as for other building projects. The *curator aquarum* was in charge of the upkeep of the existing aqueducts, however, and this was a central task of his. Frontinus writes that the *curator* had to guarantee the flow of water 'day and night' (*aq.* 103.4), and he also remarks on the constant need to repair the existing structures. Wear and tear and damages inflicted by inclement weather, for instance freezing temperatures in the winter, required vigilance. Frontinus recommended that repairs be carried out in the spring or in the fall (*aq.* 122.3). Interestingly enough, he warns against too readily believing those who urge that repairs are required, clearly in order to avoid fattening the purse of dishonest contractors who were keen to engage in unnecessary projects (*aq.* 119). Although the workforce of the *cura aquarum* was able to handle some repairs, the Roman practice during the imperial period would have been to offer larger tasks to private contractors (*redemptores*), as had been done during the Republic and Agrippa likely did too. Only one such contractor can be securely identified, a certain Paquedius Festus who was responsible for an aqueduct tunnel under Mons Aeflanus near modern Tivoli (Tibur) and who calls himself *redemptor operum Caesaris et publicorum* (*CIL* 14.3530).

The manufacturing and installation of lead pipes was handled by other specialists, the *plumbarii* (or owners of *officinae plumbariae*). Some 300 are known from Rome, all from the imperial period, which makes this profession one of the numerically best represented in our sources. The *cura aquarum* surely had men in their ranks who were capable of lead working, but none have been securely identified. No very clear pattern emerges when studying the *plumbarii* who manufactured the pipes that were installed under supervision of imperial officials. Sometimes we are dealing with imperial freedmen or with men who carry imperial names (Iulius, Flavius, Aurelius). The latter could be imperial freedmen too, or they may have had some relation to such individuals (through descendants or freed slaves). Most of the *plumbarii* will have been working for the 'free market' (i.e. private employers) and no relation to the *cura aquarum* needs to be assumed.

We have little information on the finances of the *cura aquarum*. The building of the Aqua Marcia in the 140s BC is said to have cost 180 million *sestertii* (*aq.* 7.4), which gives an average cost of 2 million per km in those early days. That price agrees with the report that the Anio Novus and the Claudia cost 350 million *sestertii* c. AD 50 (Pliny, *Hist. Nat.* 36.122). The only other sum mentioned in the context of the *cura aquarum* is Frontinus' reference to the sum of 250,000 *sestertii* that during the reign of Domitian was the annual total received as a tax from the owners of private water grants (*aq.* 118.3). Considering what the costs for the aqueducts and the *familia aquaria* must have been, that sum seems rather negligible.

TECHNICAL ASPECTS OF ROME'S WATER SUPPLY

The total length of Rome's aqueducts is over 500 km. The longest was the Aqua Marcia with 91 km, which makes it one of the longest ever built by the Romans. The lengths of all the nine aqueducts existing by the time Frontinus wrote are given in his work, as well as a breakdown of what portion of each aqueduct ran underground and what portion on arches. Carrying the aqueduct on arches was much less common, but the general notion that the aqueducts were elevated in this way derives in part from the fact that arches were used when approaching Rome over the Campagna, in order to preserve the height, as well as in several places inside the city (the Arcus Neroniani, the branch crossing the Caelian Hill to the Palatine, is conspicuous). Roman engineers relied on gravity to convey water to Rome, which means that extensive surveying was needed before an aqueduct could be built. The slope of the aqueducts of Rome varies from a mere 0.2 m per km (Aqua Virgo) to an average of around 3 m per km. Mechanical water-lifting devices were not used, except perhaps in private contexts, but pressure conduits represented one way of conquering valleys; aqueduct bridges, of which there are many in the countryside, represented the other. Pressure conduits, called (inverted) siphons by classicists, are not known in the countryside around Rome, though, but they were used in the capital in several instances in order to supply the hills without having to build cumbersome bridges. Water was conducted from a cistern in a closed pipe by making use of the physical law of communicating vessels to another cistern at its destination, where water gushed forth at almost the same level from which it had departed. There is recent work on siphons in Rome and more is needed. Meanwhile, one often sees references to what purports to be the longest siphon built in Rome, leading from the cistern next to the Baths of Diocletian to the Capitol. In reality there is no plausible evidence for it. Siphons were normally built of lead, and some water mains in Rome may have been of lead too, but otherwise the Roman engineers built in masonry. Crucial was the waterproof mortar that they used to line the interior of the aqueducts (the *specus*) with. The *specus* varies in size from aqueduct to aqueduct, but it was normally large enough to enable a man to enter, in order to carry out cleaning and repair work. The construction technique changed over the centuries as the practice of Roman builders developed. Blocks of tufa which were preferred during the Republic were replaced by concrete with a brick facing from the later first century AD. The rusticated white travertin facing preferred by Claudius can be seen on some arches of the Aqua Virgo in central Rome.

MEASURING THE VOLUME OF WATER

One of the most often discussed topics relating to Rome's water supply is the amount of water available for the Romans. There is a considerable debate here, although no one will dispute that the inhabitants of Rome, in a general sense, were well provided with water. The figure of 1 million m^3 per day is often given as the total capacity of Rome's aqueducts, or 1,000 litres per day per person, estimating the population at 1 million. Such a per capita amount is enormous, and still today exceeds the consumption in the best-provided (or most wasteful) cities. Yet a critical look at the data at our disposal forces us to revise and qualify the above figure considerably. Scholars have traditionally set out from delivery figures given by Frontinus. He gives the volume of water delivered by each aqueduct in *quinariae*. The problem is to convert the Roman *quinaria* into a modern measure for water delivery such as litre per second or cubic metre per day. That operation can in fact not be carried out with any kind of precision, because in order to reach an accurate value, one needs to consider the velocity of flowing water. This the Romans could not do, and the task was in fact not mastered until the mid-nineteenth century. Various ways in which the Romans might nevertheless have devised their *quinaria* measure so that it can be converted straight into a modern measure (and yield the above figure) have been suggested, but some scholars neglect parts of the whole picture, and other ideas, though ingenious, lack confirmation in ancient sources. The soundest way to approach the question of the delivery of the aqueducts seems to me to be the investigation of the ancient *specus* carried out by some scholars, who have from the residue left on the walls by the calcium-rich water concluded up to what level the aqueduct was filled in antiquity. Then by measuring the slope of the aqueduct and the roughness of the wall – both factors that influence the velocity of the water – they have calculated the maximum amount of water the aqueduct could deliver. In addition, when the maximum figure is compared to Frontinus' *quinaria* number for that particular aqueduct, a range for the *quinaria* can be found. These calculations have shown that the estimate for the water delivered daily to Rome must be revised downwards by a fair amount. Instead of 1 million m^3 per day, a figure in the range of 520,000–635,000 m^3 (before the *Traiana*) seems more reasonable, which is still a very large amount indeed.

THE UNEQUAL DISTRIBUTION OF WATER

The other question to discuss in this context is distribution, which will affect the living conditions of the average Roman. In this respect, the Roman system differs decisively from current practice. The hierarchical nature of Roman society was reflected also in the access individuals had to water. Frontinus dedicates large sections of his treatise to the water distribution in Rome, and he also gives overall figures for the destination of the water: 17 per cent was distributed *(sub) nomine Caesaris* (to the emperor or to particular destinations which the emperor has singled out, such as imperial baths or the barracks of the Praetorian Guard); 44 per cent went to the public, *usibus publicis*, while over 38 per cent was destined for private individuals (*privatis*) (*aq.* 78.3). The percentages are calculated from the measures in *quinaria* given by Frontinus. Even though we now know that these measures cannot be exact, they should roughly respect the actual proportions, and, above all, they show the proportions that the *cura aquarum* (and the emperor) found acceptable.

The water that was delivered to the public supplied fountains and local water basins, and commoners were also able to fetch water from the monumental terminal fountains of the aqueducts, one of which, near the central railway station, today is known as the Trofei di Mario; the Fontana di Trevi and the Acqua Paola fountain on the Gianicolo represent similar structures from the early modern period. It was the duty of the *cura aquarum* to see to it that these fountains and water basins were continuously supplied. According to Frontinus (*aq.* 78.3), there were over 750 installations that provided Rome's population with water: *castra, opera publica, munera*, and especially the smaller *lacus*. He proudly reports as a novelty that each *lacus* was supplied by water from two aqueducts so that even if one was temporarily shut down for service or because of malfunction, the residents would not suffer too much (*aq.* 87.5). Archaeologists have not been able to verify Frontinus' description, and quite possibly part of what we are told in the sources is exaggerated. So, for instance, is it claimed in an official document, the so-called Fasti Ostienses, that when Trajan introduced the new Aqua Traiana in AD 109 it provided water to every city region. Yet the Aqua Traiana approaches Rome on the right side of the Tiber, where only one of Rome's fourteen regions is situated, and although there are clear indications that water from the Traiana crossed the river, it is difficult to believe that it could have supplied all of the city on the left side.

THE PRIVILEGED FEW: HOLDERS OF IMPERIAL WATER GRANTS

In his treatise, Frontinus devotes much more space to private water grants than to water for *usus publicus*. That is understandable, because these grants were an imperial privilege reserved for the elite, to which Frontinus belonged and for whom he mainly wrote. He informs his readers that during the Republic private conduits had been extremely rare and were only given out to the most deserving citizens by general acclaim (*aq.* 94.1). The new aqueducts he introduced allowed Agrippa to be much more generous, and during his administration of the water supply a register of private water right holders was established. Frontinus seems to have consulted and benefited from Agrippa's *commentarii* (lit. 'notes') concerning the *cura aquarum* (*aq.* 99.3). After Agrippa the right to bestow a private water grant was taken over by the emperor and was still an imperial privilege when Frontinus wrote (*aq.* 99.3). He makes it clear that it was a much-sought-after privilege to receive the right to instal a private conduit. The size of the conduit was determined in the imperial grant, as was the cistern (*castellum*) from where it was to draw water (*aq.* 103, 105–6). Each private conduit had to be connected to the cistern through a *calix*, a short bronze 'ajutage' (*aq.* 36.3–4). Yet no *calix* has ever been found in Rome, and the system may never have been fully implemented. Grants were given for life, to individuals or to associates. They could not be inherited or sold, Frontinus writes, although in this regard he is less than clear and mixes quotes from official regulations with contradictory comments. This conundrum cannot be resolved without considering the full range of sources, primarily the *fistula* inscriptions.

Frontinus does not mention the name of any holder of an imperial water concession; instead the inscriptions on lead pipes contain hundreds of names. Normally, names in the nominative are accompanied by the verb *fecit* and indicate the manufacturer of the conduit, while names in the genitive indicate possession of the water conduit and hence of the imperial grant, although a few seem to refer to the owner of the *officina* who manufactured them, or to an official under whose *cura* the conduit was installed. It used to be thought that a law laid down that owners apply their names on the conduits, but a careful reading of Frontinus disproves this notion. It is likely for practical reasons that many but not all lead conduits in Rome carry inscriptions with irregular frequency. (A conduit was made up of individual *fistulae*, up to *c.* 3 m in length; some, all or none of these *fistulae* may carry an inscription.)

The names of the putative water right owners in Rome have been collected (they total some 300) and, where possible, identified. Among the identified owners the social elite dominates, and it seems that the families of former consuls are particularly well represented, at the expense even of ordinary senators (including family members). There are also a few powerful equestrians and some imperial freedmen. From this material it appears that even average senators could not be assured of a water concession, although only 600 senators belonged to the senate at any one time, while the emperors did not abstain from singling out a few trusted equestrians and *Augusti liberti* with this privilege. Women represent some 20 per cent of the total. In light of all this, it is all the more surprising to find a fair amount of names among the concession owners that cannot be identified and in many cases seem to belong to commoners. Some of them may in fact be owners of an *officina plumbaria*, while in other cases we may be dealing with owners of industrial establishments (fulleries, baths), which were granted water due to their socially valuable services (*aq.* 94.4). More work is needed here.

WATER CONSUMPTION AS A CULTURAL PHENOMENON — LIKE 'BREAD AND GAMES'

The pattern among the holders of an imperial water grant, and the details about improprieties and theft among the *aquarii* that Frontinus relates (*aq.* 112–13, 114.1) lead to a surprising conclusion: water was a scarce commodity in imperial Rome. The emperor and the imperial administration struggled continuously to satisfy the needs of the inhabitants. This sounds paradoxical in the light of the immense amounts of water conveyed to Rome. Water consumption is, however, more of a cultural than a demographic phenomenon (this is why the attempts to calculate the population of Rome based on the capacity of the aqueducts are methodologically unsound [see also Chapter 2]). The demand for water is elastic and once it became fashionable among the wealthy elite to have a *domus* provided with garden, fountains and a bath there was no way the *cura aquarum* could satisfy every request. The emperor had to negotiate continuously between the demands from various groups, and the percentages cited above show the outcome of this balancing act (before the introduction of the Aqua Traiana). A small elite of private concession owners (probably no more than a few thousand at any one time) were allotted almost the same amount of water as the general public, around 1 million people. In addition, much of the water delivered at the public fountains and water posts for common consumption was never put to use because water flowed continuously day and night, as Frontinus says (*aq.* 103.2, 104.2). The question whether some saving mechanisms employing cisterns were in use during the dark hours is, however, worth a serious study; the technology existed. All considered, however, the average Roman could probably consume a decent amount of water on a daily basis, perhaps around 60–80 litres per person. In addition, there were the public baths.

Small public baths existed in Rome already during the republican period, but the first large so-called imperial bath was built by Agrippa, and eventually Rome was to have three such structures, built by Trajan, Caracalla and Diocletian respectively, all enormous in size. The Baths of Caracalla, covering an area of over 320 x 330 m, is thought to have been able to accommodate 10,000 visitors per day. Although the imperial baths consumed large quantities of water, they represented a form of luxury that the commoners of Rome could enjoy for free and that the emperor was expected to provide. Plenty of water in the baths and at the fountains had a symbolic function, signifying well-being and abundance. In fact 'water' should be added to Juvenal's famous saying that the emperors bolstered their rule by providing the people with 'bread and spectacles' (*panem et circenses*, Juvenal 10.81). Major aqueduct enterprises often resulted in new imperial baths, and the main purpose of the Aqua Alsietina seems to have been to supply Augustus' Naumachia, a venue for mock sea-battles.

WATER AND HEALTH ISSUES

For personal hygiene, numerous smaller commercial baths were also available. Indeed the water of Rome potentially fulfilled a major function in safeguarding public health in Rome. The practice of letting fountains overflow continuously on the one hand wasted important resources, but on the other hand the overflow was used to flush the sewers and to clean the streets, thereby performing a very important task indeed. A population of 1 million people produced some 50,000 kg of solid bodily waste per day. The Romans were aware of the salubrious effect of their water, and Frontinus remarks that the air in Rome after some recent improvements of the water supply was much purer (*aq.* 88.1, 3). Yet most scholars doubt that these measures would have been enough to improve public health in Rome to the degree that the city could avoid the common fate of cities in pre-industrial societies: that mortality exceeded births (cf. Chapter 3). There are 'optimists', though, who wonder whether Rome's unique water supply might not have created an exception.

The water supply of Rome has also been blamed for much evil, indeed for the downfall of the empire, inasmuch as the lead conduits have been thought by some to have caused lead poisoning among the population. This theory was first advanced in the nineteenth century and is still frequently cited, although it has been refuted many times. First, only part of the distribution net consisted of lead pipes. Second, it was mostly the aristocracy who used lead conduits, but lead was known to give water a less pleasant taste, and there were other sources for drinking water. Above all, in Rome almost all aqueduct water contains a high level of calcium, which forms a protective layer inside conduits; thus very little lead would ever dissolve. The fact that an unhealthy concentration of lead in bones from the Roman period is occasionally found is a different matter; there were many other reasons for this (for instance cooking ware, wine sweetened with lead sugar, atmospheric pollution from lead processing).

FURTHER READING

For modern accounts of the aqueducts, also focusing on the physical remains, see Ashby 1935; Treggiari 1986; Aicher 1995 (especially useful for the visitor to Rome). On the Aqua Alexandrina, see Coates-Stephens 2003, 81–113. On the *cippi*, Mari 1991, and *passim* in *CIL* 6.1243–60, 31558–71, 37030–6 for those published earlier.

On the sewers, still valuable is Narducci 1889, who was an eyewitness to many public works in Rome in the late nineteenth century. See Reimers 1989 on the literary sources, and Bauer 1993 in particular on the Cloaca Maxima. For all aspects of waste removal, see Panciera 2000, with Chini 1995 on a new public latrine.

For any topographical feature with a name (such as Aqua Claudia, *statio aquarum*, Thermae Traiani, etc.), the corresponding entry in the *LTUR* should always be consulted. Many inscribed *fistulae* from Rome are found in *CIL* 15.7235–7734, but later scattered discoveries have added a similar number. In general on this material, see Bruun 1991, and the Introduction to my edition of the *fistula* stamps in the Vatican Museum (in preparation). For the text of Frontinus, with extensive commentary, see Rodgers 2004; new translations in Evans 1994 and Rodgers 2005. There is also the new Italian edition with commentary by Del Chicca 2004. For the latest on the nature of Frontinus' work, see Rodgers 2004, 12–14; Saastamoinen 2003; and Bruun 2007.

On the *cura aquarum* and Roman administration, see Bruun 1991, 140–271; Eck 1995–8, vol. 1, 161–78; Bruun 2006. For the *familia aquaria*, see Bruun 1991, 190–4.

Wikander 1979 was the first synthesis on grain-milling using water power in Rome. Recent discoveries are discussed in Wilson 2000 and 2003. For the building of Rome's aqueducts and engineering, see Van Deman 1934; Ashby 1935; and Hodge 1992 (later reprinted). On entrepreneurs, see Bruun 2003a, on the *plumbarii*, see Bruun 1991, 304–68, and several later works, such as Bruun 2003b and 2010. On the volume of water and the impossibility of accurately defining the *quinaria* measure used by Frontinus, see Bruun 2004. In general on distribution in Rome, see Evans 1994; Wilson 2007. The private owners are presented in Eck 1995-8, vol. 2; in *LTUR* 2, under *domus*, and are discussed in Bruun 1991, 63–9, Bruun 1997, and Bruun 2003b.

On large imperial baths in Rome, DeLaine 1997 is the best single study. Fagan 1999 has much material pertaining to Rome; see also *LTUR* 1 and 5, under *balneum*, *thermae*. On the topic of whether the Romans wasted their hydraulic resources, and on health issues: Bruun 2000, Scobie 1986, and Chapter 3 in this volume.

PART IV

WORKING FOR A LIVING

18: INDUSTRIES AND SERVICES[*]

Wim Broekaert and Arjan Zuiderhoek

T he city of Rome was an unusual place. Capital of the only world empire in European history, it was a huge city of marble in a largely agrarian society, attracting people, goods and ideas from all corners of its vast imperial hinterland. With over 1 million inhabitants around the time of Augustus, it was the largest city in European history until the rise of London *c.* 1800, and of a size similar to the capitals of Song China and Tokugawa Japan.[1] How were all these people housed, clothed and fed? The food supply system of the city of Rome is already dealt with elsewhere in this volume, so here we concentrate on economic activity in and immediately around Rome itself. We shall mostly focus on imperial Rome, though we do occasionally cite material from the late Republic. What kind of occupational structure characterized such a pre-industrial, imperial super-city? How did those million or more people gain a living, and how and where did they acquire what they needed or desired?

In what follows, we shall explore some of the main categories of economic activity in and immediately around imperial Rome, i.e. (sub)urban agriculture, manufacture, construction, services, commerce and finance.[2] First, however, something needs to be said about one of the most striking features of the imperial capital's internal economy: the highly specialized nature of professional activity within it.

SPECIALIZATION

The degree of occupational specialization has been a major feature of models of urbanization ever since the archaeologist V. Gordon Childe

---

[*] We would like to thank Koen Verboven for his help with some aspects of this chapter.
[1] Scheidel 2007, 79.
[2] We shall not deal systematically with associations of craftsmen and traders (*collegia*), for which see Chapter 20.

famously included the presence of 'full-time specialist craftsmen, transport workers, merchants, officials and priests' among his ten criteria for distinguishing pre-modern cities from villages.[3] Whereas in small rural societies almost anyone was able to make and grow almost anything, the densely populated environment of cities rendered a high degree of self-sufficiency impractical and encouraged the creation of myriad economic niches in which often high levels of skill were required. This feature can be traced in any of the major pre- (and post-) industrial cities and capitals.

It is, however, a curious characteristic of Roman society that even comparatively small towns often show a remarkable degree of occupational specialization. Thus we are aware of some 85 different trades in Pompeii, whereas for late antique Korykos in Asia Minor, some 110 (!) different professions are on record.[4] By way of comparison, 101 different jobs are on record for thirteenth-century Paris and over 99 for Florence in 1427.[5] The high level of urbanization (higher than in much of medieval and early modern Europe), especially in the empire's core areas (Italy, North Africa, western Asia Minor), might well account for this phenomenon.[6] Nowhere was this truer than in the imperial city of Rome itself with its 1 million-plus inhabitants, where we know of some 200 different trades, though more could no doubt be found in the city's extensive epigraphic records. This high degree of specialization can be explained by the capital's specific market conditions. The continuous massive demand for both ordinary commodities and luxury goods stimulated the development of a safe and stable market in the capital. The everyday needs of ordinary citizens and the more demanding spending patterns of the elite created a market in which an extremely large variety of products could be sold. Therefore, it was economically viable for artisans to focus on the production of very specific merchandise, while merchants were able to specialize in just a few commodities. Hence, nowhere in the Mediterranean world would a customer find such a concentration and diversity of specialized goods.[7]

---

[3] In his classic paper on 'The urban revolution', Childe 1950, 11.
[4] Though it should be noted that sometimes individuals are recorded as having carried out several professions. For the data see Hopkins 1978b, 72ff.; Jongman 1991, 185–6.
[5] Treggiari 1980, 56.
[6] See Jongman 2000 for this argument in the context of a discussion of the textile industry in Roman Italy.
[7] See Treggiari 1980, 56; Von Petrikovits 1981; Wissemann 1984. Some examples of very specialized crafts and services: *CIL* 6.8173: *faber intestinarius* (specialist in finish

There was, however, also a darker side to the exceptional level of occupational specialization at Rome. The city had grown to its enormous Augustan size largely due to massive migration from mid-republican times onwards. The excess labour generated by continuing migration created a large pool of unskilled workers ready to tap for construction-minded emperors (see below). Yet in between such bouts of public building, and given the absence of organized social security (the grain dole, or *cura annona*, only reached part of the population – resident Roman citizens – and hardly sufficed to support a family), many of the poorest created informal employment for themselves as a survival strategy.[8] As in many third-world cities today 'the fantastic fragmentation of services and retail sales' at Rome therefore at least partly reflects a dysfunctional labour market, with many poor seeking refuge in informal street trading, selling low quantities of goods for low prices, mostly to equally poor customers.[9]

Ultimately, it was the spending power of the urban-based landowning elites and the demand exercised by the mass of ordinary people gathered around them to service their needs that turned Roman cities into complex, pluriform urban economies, with the city of Rome as the prime example. Thus, the occupational diversity serves as an important guide to the deeper economic structures of the imperial capital.

(SUB)URBAN AGRICULTURE

The reader might be surprised to find a section with the above title in a chapter on Rome's urban economy, but the fact is that in most

carpentry and interior woodwork); 8756–7: *corinthiarius* (worker in Corinthian brass); 9812: *pistor similaginarius* (baker using the finest wheat flour); 9104: *abietarius* (dealer in fir); 9141: *alipilus* (a slave who plucked the hair from the armpits of the bathers); 9143: *anatiarius* (dealer in ducks); 9210–11: *brattearius* (dealer in thin plates of metal and gold-leaves); 9214: *aurivestrix* (woman making and selling gold-decorated luxury clothing); 9402: *faber oculariarius* (specialist in inserting artificial eyes in statues); 9443: *glutinarius* (glue-boiler); 9456: *harundinarius* (dealer in limed twigs); 9476: *iatralipta* (ointment-doctor); 9611–13: *mulomedicus* (mule-doctor); 9793: *pictor quadrigularius* (painter of little four-horse teams); 9810: *pistor magnarius pepsianus* (dealer in bread that promotes digestion); 9819: *plutearius* (maker of balustrades); 9935: *tibiarius* (flute-maker); 9943–9: *topiarius* (ornamental gardener); 9981: *vestiplicus* (clothes-folder or ironer).

[8] Holleran 2011 develops this argument in considerable detail.

[9] Hopkins 1978b, 107, n. 19 for the quote; Holleran 2011 discusses comparative evidence as well.

pre-industrial cities the separation between urban and rural production was not as clear-cut as is often supposed. Transport, especially over land, was slow and expensive, thus it made eminent sense to produce the most perishable commodities (e.g. fruit, certain vegetables, dairy products) in close vicinity to their main centre of consumption. Consequently, we commonly find a zone of intensive horticulture and dairy farming in the suburban areas and immediate hinterland of (larger) pre-industrial towns.[10] The Roman *suburbium* of the late Republic and early empire, roughly defined as the area within 30 km of Rome (with a little extension up the Tiber valley) and bounded by the Monti Sabatini, Sabini and Tiburtini, the Alban Hills and the sea, fits this pattern perfectly.[11] We have, for instance, evidence for the growing, within this region, of pears at Crustumerium (Pliny the Elder, *Historia Naturalis* 15.53; Columella, *De re rustica* 5.10.18), mulberries, apples and figs at Tibur (Pliny, *Nat. Hist.* 15.97; Horace, *Satires* 2.4.70–1; Columella, *Res rust.* 5.10.11), turnips at Rome (Pliny, *Nat. Hist.* 19.77), leeks at Ostia and Aricia (Pliny, *Nat. Hist.* 19.110; Martial, *Epigr.* 13.19; Columella, *Res rust.* 10.139), cabbages also at Aricia (Pliny, *Nat. Hist.* 19.140), onions at Tusculum (Pliny, *Nat. Hist.* 19.105), the keeping of boars at Tusculum and Laurentum (Varro, *Res rusticae* 3.3.8; Martial, *Epigr.* 9.48, 10.45), and production of milk also at Laurentum (Pliny the Younger, *Epistulae* 2.17).[12] These are but a few examples, and more could be found, but they suffice to convey the general impression.

Their proximity to the urban market, in which such goods would always fetch high prices, ensured suburban farmers of a steady return supply of manure, tools, labour, but above all grain for consumption from the city, allowing them to specialize in high-value cash crops.[13] As mentioned earlier, the sheer size of Rome's urban market encouraged some highly specialized forms of production. Martial remarks on the roses grown at Rome in his day, stating that formerly these had to be imported from Egypt (*Epigr.* 6.80; also Varro, *Res rust.* 1.16.3: violets and roses). Other sources point to the production of almonds (Pliny, *Nat. Hist.* 15.90), to beekeeping (Varro, *Res rust.* 3.16.10–11), to aviaries

---

[10] This observation is based on Von Thünen's famous model of 'The Isolated State', applied to Rome by Morley 1996.

[11] See Morley 1996, map 2.

[12] Morley 1996, 83–90, 107. Note that the fact that a certain product is attested as having been produced at a certain locality does not necessarily imply that that locality *specialized* in the production of the commodity in question.

[13] Morley 1996, 86.

for the provision of exotic birds (Varro, *Res rust.* 3.3.7, 3.5.1–17), and especially to the so-called *pastio villatica*, that is, for instance, the raising and fattening of thrushes, pigeons, peacocks, and the keeping of fishponds and snail enclosures, all to enliven elite dinner parties in the city (e.g. Pliny, *Nat. Hist.* 9.168, 10.45).[14]

Much (but certainly not all) of this market-oriented specialized agriculture, from cultivating fruit trees to fattening peacocks, will have taken place on the suburban villas of Rome's elite.[15] However, agricultural activities in Rome were neither limited to the *suburbium*, nor exclusive to the upper classes. Like their counterparts in other premodern cities, many less well-off inhabitants of Rome kept their kitchen gardens, which Pliny the Elder describes as the poor man's *ager*, providing the owner with (part of) his or her daily sustenance (*Nat. Hist.* 19.51–2). At Pompeii, it appears that many smaller gardens were planted with fruit and nut trees and vines, while below the trees, cabbages, onions and herbs were cultivated.[16] The situation at Rome is unlikely to have been different.[17]

CRAFTSMEN, ARTISANS AND WORKSHOPS

The task of just feeding, clothing and housing Rome's 1 million-plus inhabitants demanded huge efforts, not only from the surrounding imperial hinterland, which supplied much of the raw material (foodstuffs, wool, stone, wood, metals), but also, and especially, from the great numbers of craftsmen and workers who turned the raw materials into finished products. Consequently, Rome was a hub of constant, relentless and frenetic activity. 'There is no place in this city', the poet Martial complained, 'where a poor man can either think or rest: one's life is denied by the clamour of schoolmasters in the morning, corn-grinders at night and the hammers of bronze-smiths day and night' (*Epigr.* 12.57.3–6). His colleague Juvenal likewise despaired over the constant rattling of carts through Rome's narrow streets, providing

[14] On *pastio villatica* and its profitability in the vicinity of Rome see Rinkewitz 1984, 13–20.

[15] Morley 1996, 86–90. See Cato, *De agricultura* 7.1, 8.2; Varro, *Res rust.* 1.16.3.

[16] Jashemski 2008. The shape of the roots can still be studied because casts were made of them by filling up the spaces they left in the earth, in a manner similar to the way plaster casts were made by filling up the cavities left by decayed human corpses.

[17] See Horden and Purcell 2000, 110–12 for ancient and medieval comparative evidence.

the city with countless loads of wood (fir and pine) and Ligurian marble and numerous other products (3.232–60).

Most urban artisanal production and distribution was small-scale, even in as large a city as Rome. Yet its combined economic impact was far from negligible. Roads bustled with business activities. Many streets were lined with shops and workshops, which were a very visible and familiar part of the urban commercial life. The numerous inscriptions of Roman artisans working in the famous Via Sacra testify to this thriving business life.[18] Most of the commodities manufactured and sold in these shops were probably destined for local use and consumption.

The workshop indeed was the typical Roman production unit, larger 'factory-style' enterprises being few and far between, and often state-sponsored (such as the *officinae* 'between the temples of Flora and Quirinus' mentioned by Vitruvius (*De architectura* 7.9.4), which processed cinnabar ore or *minium*, the product of state-contracted mining operations in Spain, to produce 'Pompeian red' paint). Workshops producing the same type of goods would often cluster in specific neighbourhoods (*vici*), as in many medieval and early modern European cities. Thus in Rome we find, for instance, the *vicus materiarius* (neighbourhood of the carpenters; *CIL* 6.975), the *vicus lorarius* (harness-makers; 9796), the *vicus . . . ionum ferrariarum* (iron workers; 9185), the *vicus turarius* (perfumers; Horace, *Epistulae* 1.20.1; Porphyrio, *ad loc.*), the *scalae anulariae* (stairs of the ring-makers; Suetonius, *Augustus* 72), and so forth.[19]

Roman shops were easily recognizable by their wide entrances. Part of the merchandise was displayed at the store fronts on counters (Pliny, *Nat. Hist.*10.121), where customers could handle the goods (Horace, *Sat.* 1.4.71–4). A wider selection could be found inside (Martial, *Epigr.* 9.59). Most of the shops were part of large houses and had upper levels and back rooms that were used as storage room and dwellings. The modern separation of living and working space clearly did not apply to Roman business life.[20] Signs, frescoes and small texts often indicated the identity and specialization of the artisan. On the front of a Pompeian house, the walls on either side of the doorway are

---

[18] Inscriptions mention goldsmiths (*CIL* 6.9207), engravers (9221), garland-dealers (9283), metal-casters (9418–19), jewellers (9434–5), pearl-dealers (9546–9), wholesale traders (9662), dealers in paint and unguents (9795), flute-makers (9935) and honey-dealers (*AE* 1971, 42).

[19] Frank 1940, 223, n. 15 lists the evidence.

[20] DeLaine 2005 for shops in Ostia; MacMahon 2005a for Britain; Pirson 2008 for Pompeii.

decorated with frescoes representing Venus and Mercury as protective gods and several work activities, such as wool-combing and felt-making. The owner too is depicted and below is written 'Verecundus'. This man is probably to be identified with M. Vecilius Verecundus, who in a Pompeian graffito is called 'a textile-dealer'.[21] The woman portrayed selling clothing in a room with several shelves and textiles was most likely his wife. The image the frescoes convey of simultaneously producing and selling no doubt revealed the most recurrent combination of business activities in Roman shops.[22] Moreover, Verecundus' wife selling the workshop's produce highlights another common feature of these small shops: production was consigned to slaves, who worked together with and/or under the supervision of their master, while he and his wife were responsible for commercializing the goods.

From a consideration of the basic structure of workshops we now turn to the goods produced and sold there, and the people who made them. We only have space to discuss some paradigmatic examples and we have therefore opted for food and textiles. Food processing and textile production both rank high among pre-industrial urban economic activities, as both were vital to the survival of the urban populace. Since grain was the staple food of ancient Rome, we turn to bakers first.

Bread could easily be baked at home, in a small earthen crock or oven. However, as this process demanded a continuously burning fire, it was quite unsafe, as well as relatively expensive in terms of fuel, for each family to bake their own bread, especially in a fire-prone urban environment such as Rome. Hence, baking was mostly entrusted to the *pistores* or bakers. They were probably organized in at least two *collegia* (*AE* 1994, 197 and *CIL* 6.1002: *corpus pistorum*; 22: *corpus pistorum siliginiariorum*). Another part of the *pistores'* responsibility was processing the grain destined for the emperor's corn distributions.

So far, no bakeries have been discovered in Rome (they may have been situated close to the large *horrea* where the grain was stored), but we can safely assume that bakers' workshops were comparable to the ones found in Ostia. Today, eight bakeries have been identified there, yet on the basis of a calculation of the production rate of the millstones found scattered throughout the town, Bakker assumes there must have been at least twenty.[23] Given that during Ostia's heyday the population amounted to some 40,000 inhabitants, theoretically one bakery would fulfil the needs of 2,000 people. If we can justifiably apply this ratio to

[21] *CIL* 4.3130 (*M(arcus) Vecilius/Verecund/us vestiar(ius)*).
[22] Clarke 2003, 105–12.   [23] Bakker 2001.

Rome, the capital would have numbered at least 500 bakeries. Given the minimum production of bakeries attached to the *annona* of 100 *modii* (875 kg) of grain according to a ruling of Trajan (Gaius, *Institutiones* 1.34), 500 bakeries may very well be a reasonable guesstimate for a population of over 1 million people.[24]

Next, we turn to textile manufacture, which in pre-industrial societies came second only to the production and distribution of food.[25] Producing plain clothes was quite a laborious process: spinning, washing, carding and weaving required significant effort (for literary descriptions, see Catullus 64.311–19 and Ovid, *Metamorphoses* 6.53–128). Additionally, clothes could be dyed. Since this process involved the use of urine and soda (Pliny, *Nat. Hist.* 28.174; 35.196 and 198), fulling was entrusted to specialist *fullones*.[26] We can safely assume that, in the city of Rome as elsewhere in the empire, some unknown part of an individual family's needs were covered by spinning and weaving in the household (for spinning and weaving on urban and rural *villae* see Virgil, *Georgica* 4.347; Martial, *Epigr.* 9.65.11; Columella, *Res rust.* 12.3.6 and *Digesta* 33.7.16.2 where the *mulieres lanificae* are considered to belong to the *instrumentum* of an estate for inheritance purposes). Both freeborn and slave women engaged in textile production, which doubtless was a crucial part of the female household economy (Livy 1.57.9; Tibullus 1.3.83ff.; 1.6.77).

Obviously, not every family was able to produce all the clothing its members needed and many will have had to buy clothes (Dio Chrysostom, *Orationes* 7.105). Since evidence for the manufacture of textiles from raw material for sale in the urban market is extremely scanty at Rome (only three inscriptions mention weavers: *CIL* 6.6361–2 and 9290)[27], it seems likely that plain cloth was brought to the capital from Italy and the provinces and subsequently processed in shops.[28] Several authors mention the import of the famous black wool from Spain (Martial, *Epigr.* 12.65; Strabo 3.2.6) or linen from Egypt (Cicero, *Pro Rabirio Postumo* 40). These linen and woollen fabrics were then manufactured into clothing by the numerous *lanarii* (*CIL* 6.9489–94), *sagarii* (6.9864–72) and *vestiarii* (6.9961–78 and 28629–35) active in the city. It seems likely, however, that Rome also imported some finished clothing. This at least is suggested by the presence of a textile merchant from Gaul (6.9962: *vestiarius Narbonensis*) in the capital. Furthermore, a few cities

---

[24] See also Chapter 15.   [25] Horden and Purcell 2000, 359–61; Jongman 2000, 188–9.
[26] Bradley 2002; Flohr 2003.   [27] See Jongman 1991, 163–5 for a Pompeian parallel.
[28] Jongman 1991, 157.

in the Roman empire, such as Patavium, Tarsus and Laodicea, were renowned for their high-quality textiles (Strabo 5.1.7; Dio Chrysostom, *Orat.* 34.21–3). Those luxury clothes could no doubt be found on the Roman market too.

Merchants-producers, who most likely ran their own workshop, also specialized in niche markets of the textile industry, such as slippers (*CIL* 6.9284 and 9404; Martial, *Epigr.* 2.17.3), women's shoes (6.9897), boots (6.9225), fur clothing (6.9431), feather-embroidered clothes (6.7411 and 9813) or silk (6.9678 and 9890). More luxurious, gold-embroidered clothes could be bought from an *aurivestrix* (6.9214).

CONSTRUCTION

Construction was probably the largest sector of production in imperial Rome, and one of the most visible. Its remains still surround the modern visitor to the city. Public construction, in Rome, was truly an imperial affair, and the city profited from publicly sponsored building programmes the likes of which were not seen again until the early modern era or later. No expense was spared, in terms of funds, manpower or materials, in providing the imperial capital with its aqueducts, bath houses, temples, fora, palaces and monuments, many of which counted among the largest or most splendid of their kind.

A good illustration of the extent of imperial outlay on public building and its impact on the city's economy is provided by the Baths of Caracalla, the largest of their kind when completed in AD 217. Their total cost of construction has been estimated as the equivalent of 120,000–140,000 tons of wheat, enough to feed 500,000 people for a year, i.e. about half the capital's entire population.[29] During the main period of construction, between AD 212–16, some 16,000 people in and around Rome are likely to have been engaged in work connected to the Baths.[30] If we factor in other public construction projects taking place in Rome and its surroundings during Caracalla's reign (among others, the baths at Castra Albana, the Porticus Severi, and repairs to buildings on the Palatine, the Horti Sallustiani, the Pantheon, the

---

[29] DeLaine 1997, 219; Jongman 2001, 1079–81.

[30] DeLaine 1997, 193, 196: that is, the 13,100 men required in the peak year 213 (referred to by Graham in Chapter 16) but with 1,600 decorators required at a later stage of the building process, 500 skilled quarry workers producing *selce* required at the early stages and extra ox-cart drivers needed in 212 added.

Praetorian Camp and the Tiber wharves and banks), the total number of individuals active in the building trade or professions connected to it rises to between 20,000–30,000, or about 15–24 per cent of all adult males in and around the city.[31] Given that episodic large-scale public building projects were a structural feature of early and high imperial Rome (think, for instance, of Nero's Golden House, the Colosseum, Domitian's Domus Augustana, Trajan's Baths and Market, and so forth), it seems justified to project the Severan situation back in time, and argue that this level of employment in the building trades is in the right order of magnitude for first- and second-century AD Rome as well. This, in turn, suggests the continuous presence in the capital of a large and flexible workforce, both skilled and unskilled, that could be mobilized quickly and effectively (the Baths of Caracalla were built in just six years). Who were these people, what did their work consist of, and how were they organized?

During the Republic, public building work was farmed out by the censors to private contractors (*redemptores*) who functioned as, and were in fact organized as, the *publicani* who farmed Rome's taxes in her provinces. Upon winning a contract, they subcontracted the work to professional builders, who either had their own staff of specialist (slave) craftsmen and/or sublet the work still further.[32] Under the Principate, public building, both construction and repair, increasingly came to be controlled by the imperial bureaucracy. From Augustus onwards, maintenance of the roads, the water system (aqueducts) and public buildings and shrines was the responsibility of permanent boards, each under a curator (the *curatores viarum*, *aquarum* and *operum publicorum* respectively). Eventually, and possibly by Domitian, a permanent office for public construction was established, the *opera Caesaris*. To each of these boards or offices, a permanent corps of public skilled or semi-skilled slave workmen and an office staff of freedman or freeborn administrators were attached.[33] Thus, the *curator aquarum* had under his command a corps of 700 public slaves, among whom could be found various classes of workmen: *vilici* (overseers), *castellarii* (reservoir keepers), *circitores* (inspectors), *silicarii* (pavers), *tectores* (plasterers) and others (*alii opifices*). These were deployed at the water reservoirs and fountains in the various regions of the city. The office staff or *apparitores* (attendants) consisted of *architecti*, *scribae* (secretaries), *librarii* (clerks), *accensi*

---

[31] DeLaine 1997, 197–201. DeLaine 2000b, 132, 135–6 estimates 20,000 on average for Rome, but suggests higher estimates are plausible.

[32] Anderson 1997, 79–88, 95–107.   [33] Anderson 1997, 88–95.

(assistants) and *praecones* (heralds) (Frontinus, *De aquaeductu* 98.3–99.1, 100, 117, 119).[34]

It is clear, however, that despite their permanent workforce the imperial boards and offices could by no means avoid contracting out part or even most of their work (see e.g. Frontinus, *Aq.* 119: it is up to the *curator aquarum* to decide what part of the work is to be carried out by public contractors and what by his own workforce; see also *Aq.* 124). This was either because the amount of work exceeded the capabilities of the curator's own workforce or because the work required specialist skills not found among the curator's staff, or both. The *curatores* could then turn to numerous specialized contractors (*redemptores*), each of whom would usually take on some (small) part of the building work planned.[35] These were men such as L. Paquedius Festus, who was a *redemptor operum Caesar(is) et puplicorum* (sic) and worked on the Claudian aqueduct (*CIL* 14.3530) or Ti. Claudius Celadus, who was a *redemptor intestinarius*, arranging for the carpentry needed to complete a building (*AE* 1925, 87). Contractors such as these are likely to have employed their own small *familia* of skilled workers, but would probably often have sublet part of the work again to skilled builders and their teams, the sort of men that could be found, for instance, in the *collegium fabrorum tignuariorum*, the association of builders.[36] It has been plausibly suggested that the membership of this *collegium*, about 1,300 men strong, consisted of master builders (freedman or freeborn), each of whom headed a small team or 'firm' of eight to ten skilled (slave) craftsmen or even fewer, and would hire extra day labourers as and when the job required (though of course *redemptores* and *curatores* could hire temporary unskilled labour as well).[37] Other *collegia* associated with the building trade at Rome, such as the *marmorarii* (marble workers), the *fabri ferrarii* (blacksmiths), the *mensores aedificiorum* (building surveyors) and the *pavimentarii* (pavement layers), may have been organized along similar lines.[38] Both written evidence (Vitruvius, *Archit.*

---

[34] Brunt 1980, 84–6; Anderson 1997, 92–5.

[35] See e.g. *Dig.* 50.10.2.1, where it is stated that the *curator operum publicorum* transacts business with the *redemptores* on behalf of the state, implying that this was a normal course of affairs.

[36] Anderson 1997, 88–95, 108–18. Some *redemptores* might themselves have been members of *collegia*, as was Ti. Claudius Onesimus, *redemptor operum Caesaris* and *magister quinquennalis* of the *collegium fabrorum tignuariorum*, see *CIL* 6.9034.

[37] DeLaine 1997, 199–200, 202–5; DeLaine 2000b, 121, 132; see also Brunt 1980, 84–8.

[38] It should be noted that not all (master) craftsmen need to have been members of *collegia*. Some no doubt operated autonomously.

7.1.3, 7.3.10; Statius, *Silvae* 4.3.40–58) and archaeological research on individual buildings would suggest that construction workers generally worked in small groups or gangs, often termed *decuria* (though this need not imply that all gangs consisted of just ten men), an observation that reinforces the picture just sketched of organization and deployment of construction workers via *collegia*.[39]

The rationale behind all this contracting and subcontracting, and the small size of permanent (slave) workforces kept by the various leading actors at different levels of the construction 'hierarchy' was of course that public building projects, though often large-scale, were episodic in nature. It made little economic sense for *curatores*, contractors or builders to keep on a very large, permanent workforce that could only be employed to its full extent occasionally, especially not one consisting of slaves, who needed to be housed, fed and clothed on a permanent basis. Moreover, contractors or master builders could never predict in advance how much labour they were going to need for the next project in which they became involved. Better then to have a flexible system that would quickly enable one to hire the necessary manpower and expertise when and where this was needed. It is this line of argument that has also led scholars to the conclusion that the bulk of unskilled labour on major building projects was in fact provided by the mass of poor free inhabitants of Rome (occasionally supplemented by convicts), who were hired as temporary wage-labourers on building sites. Keeping on permanent large slave gangs for the purpose would simply have been too expensive, and would have kept the plebs out of work (the *locus classicus* here is Suetonius, *Vespasian* 18).[40]

Private building continued unabated, occasioned by both the insatiable demand for ever more luxurious living spaces among Rome's elite and the sheer necessity of providing cheap housing for the urban masses, often in *insulae* (blocks of flats) let by elite owners at great profit. Here, contracting flourished as well, and much the same system of subletting probably operated (see Cicero, *Epistulae ad Atticum* 12.18.1, 12.36.2 on contracting for private projects, 12.32.2 and 15.26.4 on *insulae* Cicero owned; see also Venuleius *Digesta* 45.1.137.3 on the construction of *insulae*).[41]

---

[39] DeLaine 1997, 172–3, 204; Lancaster 1998 on the construction of Trajan's markets.
[40] Brunt 1980; Anderson 1997, 117–18, 119–27; DeLaine 1997, 201. However, Erdkamp 2008, 429–30, argues for the employment of seasonal migrants from the countryside rather than the urban poor. See also Chapter 19.
[41] Anderson 1997, 75–9, 95–112; DeLaine 2000b, 123–8.

SERVICES

In dealing with the mass of service-providers in the capital, we need to distinguish between those operating on the free market and those associated with large households. As the living standards of wealthy Romans required flocks of servants, many service activities were in fact carried out by their *familiae* of slaves and freedmen (Juvenal 1.64–8; Martial, *Epigr.* 3.82). Joshel claims that in Rome nearly 75 per cent of the slaves with an occupational title can be linked to a wealthy household. The famous *columbarium* of the Statilii lists nearly 120 slaves working in the household as teachers, architects, surveyors, doctors, midwives, barbers, hairdressers, masseurs, oilers, readers, entertainers, bath attendants, child nurses, bodyguards, room and table servants, cooks, provisioners, caretakers, gardeners, social organizers, animal tenders, runners and bearers, financial agents, administrators, secretaries and copyists (*CIL* 6.6243–6381).[42]

The same occupational diversity is visible in the inscriptions of service-providers working outside the household. It is obviously impossible here to cover in its entirety the wide range of economic activities that can be qualified as services, but we shall mention some of the most important sectors.

We can start with Juvenal's famous attack on Greek influences on Roman *mores*, where he provides a quick list of Greek trades, many of which can easily be considered as services:

> Grammarian, orator, geometrician, painter, masseur,
> soothsayer, rope-dancer,
> doctor or magician: a hungry Greek claims to be a
> professional in every science.
> Let him go to hell!
>
> (3.76–8)

Education (Plutarch, *Cato Maior* 22.5; Virgil, *Aeneid* 6.847–53; Horace, *Epist.* 2.1.156–60), theatre and entertainment, and body care and medicine (Pliny, *Nat. Hist.* 29.6.12–21; Cicero, *De officiis* 1.42.151) were indeed all important sectors of the urban service economy. In the leisure sector, special mention should be made of the Roman libraries and bath houses. Although officially belonging to the emperor's private property, the use of libraries was perceived as a public service. The

---

[42] Joshel 1992, 74–5.

personnel, mainly slaves and freedmen belonging to the *familia Caesaris*, were responsible for arranging volumes, acquiring new books, making and checking copies, and assisting readers.[43] However, the most famous public service, offered by successive emperors from Nero to Constantine, was the provision of thermal baths (*thermae*).[44] Apparently conceived as wellness centres, baths also included gardens, libraries, sports halls, rooms for body care and various shops offering food and drinks. Roman literature offers a few descriptions of the variety of service-providers and paints a vivid picture of swarming stokers, water pourers, anointers, masseurs, trainers, doctors, hawkers and cloakroom attendants (Juvenal 6.419–23; Seneca, *Epistulae* 56.1–2; for an inscription of a cloak attendant in the Baths of Caracalla, see *CIL* 6.9232).

We next turn to the various establishments providing the capital's inhabitants with food, drink and lodgings, that is, the pubs and bars. A small Roman pub usually consisted of three guest facilities, that is, an L-shaped stone or sometimes wooden counter, often stuccoed and decorated with paintings and marble, a small eating area, and a latrine. Behind the counter, food and drinks were stored on shelves and in additional niches. Wine was served straight from the *amphorae*, stacked horizontally in large racks. Dry foodstuffs like vegetables, grain, beans, nuts and dried fruit were conserved in large *dolia* (storage vats), which were built into the counter. The proprietor and his assistants used a stove and other cooking facilities to serve hot meals like soup, porridge and meat (Suetonius, *Tiberius* 34; *Nero* 16; Cassius Dio 60.6.7 and 62.14.2). Larger and more luxurious taverns were equipped with dining rooms, gardens, bedrooms and a separate kitchen (*CIL* 4.807 advertises the presence of a *triclinium* in a Pompeian bar).

In Roman literature, inns had a bad reputation: as the upper classes usually relied on family and friends to find lodgings, inns were said to attract poor and even untrustworthy tenants (Juvenal 8.171; Petronius, *Satyricon* 95–8; Ammianus Marcellinus 14.6.25 for poor people in the capital spending the night drinking in pubs). Consequently, there was no need for luxurious accommodation or quality food and drinks.[45]

The actual number of pubs and hotels spread throughout the city is difficult to gauge. However, by making use of the Pompeian excavations, a rough estimate is possible. A recent count of Pompeian

[43] Houston 2002.　[44] Heinz 1983; Nielsen 1990; DeLaine 1997.
[45] MacMahon 2005b; DeFelice 2008. On prostitution in bars and brothels, see Chapter 21.

inns and taverns lists ninety-four *tabernae* offering food and drinks, and fifty-one businesses serving overnight guests.[46] Assuming a comparable distribution in the 40 per cent of the city that has not yet been excavated, Pompeii should have numbered approximately 156 *tabernae* and 83 houses offering lodgings for a population of some 15,000 people. If the same population–businesses ratio did apply to Rome, the capital might have counted at least 10,000 *tabernae* and 5,500 hotels. To contemporary city dwellers, a number of one *taberna* for every 100 citizens may sound astonishingly high, but this compares rather well to sixteenth- and seventeenth-century figures for English cities, which often had one alehouse per 12–20 households or 90–110 inhabitants.[47]

Finally, we take a look at the providers of 'dirty' services, that is, the collectors of garbage and refuse. Services connected to the hygiene of a capital the size of imperial Rome were evidently of great importance, because the population produced about 40 to 50 tons of body waste each day.[48] As Roman law forbade throwing excrement and corpses out into the street (*Dig.* 43.10.1.5, but see Juvenal 1.131), waste management was a vital service. A clear distinction between the public and private sector needs to be made. Rome provided basic public facilities such as latrines (*foricae*) and a sewer system, the upkeep of which clearly was an imperial duty. Yet, keeping the capital clean was also partly a private business. Private sewers and latrines were obviously to be cleansed by the owner's slaves (Petronius, *Sat.* 27.3–5 and 47.5; Martial, *Epigr.* 3.82; *Dig.* 43.23.1–2). Human excrement was gathered by *stercorarii* (*Dig.* 33.7.12.10). A graffito from Herculaneum mentions 11 asses as the price for emptying a cesspit (*CIL* 4.10606). The manure was then sold to farmers and used as fertilizer in urban and suburban agriculture (Columella, *Res rust.* 10.84). Urine, necessary for dying textiles, was collected by fullers, who placed small vessels in the street (Martial, *Epigr.* 6.93.1).

COMMERCE

The Italian hinterland and the provinces provided Rome with most of the products it needed, either as raw materials or as finished commodities. This constant stream of goods turned Rome into a hub of

---

[46] DeFelice 2008, 483, n. 1. [47] Clark 1983, 39–63. [48] Scobie 1986, 413.

commercial activity. Countless merchants ensured the supply of consumer goods: more than 25 per cent of all Roman inscriptions mentioning a *negotiator* were found in the capital and by adding the Ostian
documents, this figure increases to 35 per cent. Inscriptions set up by
mercatores display a similar pattern: 25 per cent are from Rome, while
Ostia adds another 30 per cent.[49]

The sale of goods took place on various markets, which often
specialized in particular foodstuffs. There were a number of open-air
markets, such as the *forum boarium* (cattle market: Ovid, *Fasti* 6.477–8;
Livy 10.23.3; 21.62.3; 22.57.6; 24.10.7), *holitorium* (vegetable market:
Varro, *De lingua Latina* 5.146), *piscarium* (fish market: Livy 26.27.2;
Varro, *Ling. Lat.* 5.146–7; Plautus, *Curculio* 474), *suarium* (pork market:
CIL 6.3728 and 9631) and *vinarium* (wine market: *CIL* 6.9181–9182).
Distribution was also facilitated by the construction of market halls and
arcades, such as the *basilica Iulia* (Cassius Dio 56.27; Suetonius, *Aug.*
29; Pliny, *Epist.* 6.33; Suetonius, *Gaius* 37) and the *macellum magnum*,
built by Nero (*CIL* 6.1648 and 9183; Cassius Dio 62.18). Furthermore,
merchandise was sold in warehouses and storage rooms which functioned as markets, such as the *horrea Galbana* (*CIL* 6.9801, 33886 and
33906), *horrea Agrippiana* (*CIL* 6.9972 and 10026) and *horrea Nervae* (*CIL*
6.33747).

Second, goods were sold at auctions (*ad hastam*). Auctions were
used for the sale of slaves, real estate, bulk commodities and small samples
of luxury items. Depending on what exactly was being sold and the
possibilities for display of the goods, auctions could be held in various
settings. A simple street corner would suffice for small sales (Horace,
Epist. 1.7.63–6; Juvenal 7.9–11), while bulk commodities were usually
offered up for sale on the forum, at markets or in auction halls (Cicero,
De lege agraria 1.7; Quintilian, *De institutione oratoria* 25).[50]

Lastly, no doubt temporary stalls were set up daily, providing
passers-by with a variety of goods and services. Ambulant hawkers
usually sold snacks and refreshments in public places (*Dig.* 14.3.5. 9)
or offered their goods door-to-door (*Dig.* 14.3.5.4). Seneca was much
bothered by the constant shouting of 'the cake-seller with his various
cries, the sausage-man, the confectioner, and all the food-sellers hawking their wares' at the public baths (*Epist.* 56). Another lively picture of
Roman hawkers is given by Martial, who claims that a certain Caecilius
is no better than

---

[49] Verboven 2004 and Broekaert 2010.   [50] García Morcillo 2005.

such a thing as strolls around in the quarters beyond the
Tiber, and barters pale-coloured sulphur matches for pieces
of glass; such a one as offers boiled peas and beans to the
idle crowd; a master and keeper of snakes; or a common
slave of the salt-meat-sellers; or a hoarse-voiced cook
carrying around smoking sausages in steaming shops.

(*Epigr.* 1.41)

However, Rome was not only a major consumer city, but also
functioned as an export and transit centre. Merchants supplying the
Roman market evidently tried to find a decent return cargo and ensured
both the export of Roman and Italian merchandise, and the re-export
of surplus imports. The transport activities of shippers working for the
governmental grain supply system (*annona*) were crucial here. Since
the trip to the capital was more or less subsidized by the government,
and since shippers had to return for the next cargo of Baetican oil or
African grain anyway, they might as well take a load of goods for sale
back with them. If necessary, shippers even traded in bricks and tiles,
which were easy to pile up and increased the ship's stability. Although
provincial demand for building materials would never be sufficiently
high to justify specialization, shipping bricks and tiles from the capital
as an (additional) retour cargo was a quick and easy solution to fill the
hold. Profits would be modest, but not negligible. Thus, major concentrations of bricks produced in the workshops around Rome are found in
the Spanish, Gallic and African provinces, especially in large provincial
ports such as Carthage and Tarraco.[51] The same 'spontaneous redistribu-
tion' mechanism explains why large quantities of western commodities
destined for Rome were re-exported to *annona*-provinces.[52]

FINANCE

Rome was the single largest financial centre in the western Mediterranean. Over half the inscriptions of Roman money-changers, bankers
and money-lenders were found in the capital.[53] The various banking services were necessary to support the city's thriving business life.
Indeed, Cicero was well aware of the bankers' crucial role in the Roman

[51] Tomber 1987; Rico 1995.
[52] This might account for the concentration of Spanish olive oil amphorae found in
the Alexandrian harbour. See Lyding Will 1983.
[53] Andreau 1999, 35.

economy, as he claims that they were enjoying favours from 'all orders' (*Off.* 3.8). In Rome, professional bankers worked in little shops or at trestle tables. Many were situated in the immediate vicinity of the forum, close to the capital's commercial centre.[54] Others set up their business wherever clients required their services. We can trace bankers operating on the markets (*macella*) or the *fora* where specific merchandise was sold, like the Forum Vinarium or the Forum Boarium.[55] No doubt they were lending and collecting money and offering credit to merchants and buyers. Bankers, however, were not only dealing with professional businessmen. They also engaged in assaying coins, money exchange and the reception of deposits. We are rather well informed about the actual functioning of Roman banking. Evidence on interest rates on loans is quite abundant: rates fluctuated between 4 and 12 per cent per year. Since bankers were supposed to make a living, we can safely assume that interests on loans were mostly higher than those on deposits. Each client had a separate deposit account (*ratio*), on which all operations were recorded. However, bankers did not keep up-to-date records nor did they send their clients information on the accounts. One had to pay a visit to the banker, who would then calculate the balances. Overdraft was possible, until one of the parties – the banker or his client – decided to close the account.[56]

CONCLUSION

> The occupations and trades in the city, if all are considered, are many and of all kinds, and some of them are very profitable . . . But it is not easy to name them all separately on account of their multitude, and equally because that would be out of place here.
>
> (Dio Chrysostom, *Orat.* 7.109–10)

Like many of his contemporaries, and like modern historians, the Greek orator was struck by the wide range of professions that could be found in the cities of the Roman empire. Yet their sheer variety meant that Dio could not find space to discuss all of them in his oration, and we have

---

[54] Andreau 1987.
[55] *CIL* 6.9183 (*argentarius macelli magni*); 9181 (*argentarius de foro vinario*); 1035 (*argentarii et negotiantes boarii huius loci qui invehent*).
[56] Andreau 1999, 36–45 and 90–9.

found ourselves in similar straits in this chapter. The examples we have given, however, attest to the remarkable occupational diversity that once existed in the imperial capital. In this respect, Rome was in principle no different from other pre-industrial capitals. What was different, at Rome, was the scale. If Rome was indeed the ultimate consumer city, it required a complex urban economy consisting of myriad different activities to sustain that unprecedented level of consumption.

FURTHER READING

Joshel 1992 is the essential survey of occupations at Rome, mainly based on epigraphic sources. See also Treggiari 1980. For occupational specialization see Petrikovits 1981, Wissemann 1984. On suburban agriculture see Morley 1996, ch. 4. See MacMahon and Price 2005 on crafts, trades and services, and the structures of the workplace. On the building industry see Anderson 1997, DeLaine 2000b. For finance and banking, see Andreau 1999.

19: LABOUR AND EMPLOYMENT[1]

Cameron Hawkins

At its height, ancient Rome was a centre of consumption with few rivals in the ancient world. Not only was the city home to an enormous population by pre-industrial standards, it was also a forum for conspicuous consumption on the part of an increasingly wealthy imperial elite. These processes combined to ensure that the city created an immense and concentrated demand for goods and services of all types, and by extension an enormous demand for labour. The funerary epigraphy of the city's inhabitants offers some sense of the scale of that demand for labour, for it reveals a degree of occupational specialization that would have been impossible to sustain in its absence, particularly in those sectors of the market that catered to the needs of the wealthy.[2]

The demand for labour in Rome was met by a diverse working population that was split along lines of both gender (male and female) and legal status (freeborn, freed and slave). My goal in this chapter is to determine how and why workers in these several categories came to be distributed across various sectors of the economy. I hope to show that while this distribution was affected by expectations about working roles arising from distinctions in gender and status, those expectations were not determinative in and of themselves. Rather, they shaped the options available to urban producers who devised labour management strategies in response to a pervasive problem: the impact of seasonality on the urban market.

GENDER, LEGAL STATUS AND WORK

Our literary sources trace the rough outlines of gender expectations that shaped the working roles of both men and women. Because of

---

[1] This chapter draws heavily on my dissertation, Hawkins 2006.
[2] Joshel 1992, 176–82 catalogues the known occupations in the inscriptions.

beliefs concerning women's temperament, character and sexual honour, women were expected to perform tasks that were not only situated
within a domestic context, but were also in many cases directed toward
household consumption. These tasks included rearing children, processing foodstuffs, producing textiles and managing the household stores.
Men, on the other hand, were thought better suited to tasks that placed
the individual in contact with the wider physical, social and economic
environment. These included agriculture, commerce and production
for the market.[3]

In practice, these gender expectations constrained the working
roles of women more so than those of men. They did so in the first
instance by limiting the access of freeborn women to formal training in
marketable skills. The surviving apprenticeship documents from Roman
Egypt show that freeborn women rarely learned technical skills in a
formal context. Of the forty documents that we possess, roughly a
quarter record the apprenticeships of both male and female slaves, while
fully three quarters record the apprenticeships of freeborn boys; only
one may refer to the apprenticeship of a freeborn girl. In all probability,
this reflects a pattern that was not unique to Egypt but was instead
typical of the Roman world as a whole.[4]

The occupational inscriptions from Rome reinforce this conclusion. In the inscriptions, not only do women bear occupational titles
less frequently than do men, they are also attested in fewer occupations:
whereas Susan Treggiari catalogued some 225 occupations for men, she
found only 35 for women, many of which involved either service and
distribution or the manufacture of a narrow range of consumer goods
(mostly textiles). Moreover, the women named in these inscriptions
were not wholly, nor even predominantly, freeborn: many were slaves
or freedwomen who had presumably acquired their skills at the instiga-
tion of their owners.[5] The distribution of female occupations therefore
shows that even if slave women had more access to formal training than
did freeborn women, the range of trades in which they acquired skills
was nevertheless still narrowly constrained by social expectations about
gender.

Economic realities meant that these expectations were often bent:
in spite of the fact that agriculture was conceptualized as a quintessentially male activity, women indisputably engaged in agricultural work
at certain times of the year. That said, when social expectations did

---

[3] Columella, *Res rust.* 12.pr.1–10.   [4] Saller 2003, 194–5.   [5] Treggiari 1979.

bend in response to economic pressure, women's participation in the economy was still channelled in ways that reflected their poor access to formal training. Those who directed their labour towards the market often held jobs that drew on skills they had acquired in the household or that could be practised at home, like spinning. Others chose occupations in which they could train on the job, such as street-trading, or assisted their husbands by minding sales counters or by performing other ancillary tasks in the family business.[6]

While gender expectations thus clearly did play some role in structuring the distribution of labour in the Roman economy, the same cannot necessarily be said about perceived distinctions between slave and free workers. Opinions concerning the ideological impact of slavery on conceptions of work are mixed: it is not clear whether the freeborn population came to perceive certain occupations as servile and unfit for free men or not. Nor can actual patterns of employment be readily reconstructed, since our sources focus on slaves and former slaves to the virtual exclusion of the freeborn. It is therefore almost impossible to give precise answers to most questions about the distribution of slave and free labour in the urban economy.[7]

What we can say with certainty is that both slaves and the free worked in a large number of overlapping positions. This was a result of the ease with which Roman slaveholders could accommodate slavery to the full spectrum of jobs that were available to the free. Roman law gave slaveholders considerable latitude to deal with their slaves in whatever way they pleased, and thus made it possible for them to enforce or solicit compliance from their slaves in numerous different contexts. When slaves held jobs amenable to direct supervision, slaveholders could employ both the threat and the reality of punishment to keep them in line; when slaves held positions that required personal initiative and diligence, slaveholders could just as easily rely on the promise of rewards, including manumission.[8]

Although the nature of our evidence means that we cannot directly assess the relative importance of free or slave labour in many sectors of the economy, there is a general consensus that slaves were

[6] Women and agriculture: Scheidel 1996. Women and non-agricultural employment: Apuleius, *Metamorphoses* 9.5 and Saller 2003, 193–7.
[7] On the ideology of slaveholding and perceptions of work, see Bradley 1994, 65 and Scheidel 2002, 182. Joshel 1992, 46–9 and 124–8 discusses the challenges of reconstructing the distribution of free and slave labour.
[8] Scheidel 2008, esp. 107–15.

predominant in the domestic service sector. The occupational inscriptions may support this view in spite of the obvious interpretative difficulties. In the inscriptions of freeborn and freed workers with occupational titles, we find mention of only a very small subset of the numerous jobs that were associated with domestic service. Since attestations of occupation in this group are otherwise relatively common – at least among freed slaves if not among the freeborn – it seems tempting to conclude that domestic service really was mostly the province of slaves.[9]

To the extent that this was true, however, it was not the exclusive product of expectations concerning the proper roles of free and slave labour. Instead, economic considerations were equally important. The domestic service sector of the economy was primarily a forum for competitive display, and it had emerged as such no later than the beginning of the second century BC. The timing of this development was crucial, for it took place in a period when free labour was scarce because of heavy political and military commitments on the part of freeborn Roman citizens. Because transaction costs in the labour market were correspondingly high, free labour was therefore difficult to recruit and retain. Slaves, however, were readily accessible, and as members of the Roman elite competed with one another by expanding their household retinues, they turned to slave labour in order to fill this particular niche. Gradually, this trend may have been reinforced by the growing importance of social domination in Roman conceptions of status, particularly domination over slaves. The domestic service sector, already oriented towards conspicuous display, provided a natural stage on which the elite could display such domination for the benefit of their peers.[10]

SEASONALITY AND THE DEMAND FOR LABOUR

If slavery affected the distribution of labour in Rome's economy, then it clearly did not do so exclusively because attitudes concerning slaves and the free produced social expectations about the kind of work appropriate to each category. Instead, economic considerations clearly influenced preferences for slave labour in the one sector in which they

---

[9] Bradley 1994, 65; Joshel 1992, 98–100.
[10] Scheidel 2008 (slavery and transaction costs); Joshel 1992, 149–51 and Bradley 1994, esp. 66 (domestic slavery, domination, and conspicuous display).

did predominate, domestic service. If we hope to elucidate further the patterns of employment in the Roman economy, it therefore seems best to examine the economic context in which other employers – namely, the producers of the various goods and services in demand in Rome – lived and worked, and the impact this context had on their labour-management strategies.

If conditions in other pre-industrial economies are any indication, then that context was characterized above all by seasonal fluctuations in the urban demand for goods and services. In early modern Europe, seasonal changes in the weather had a profound impact on trades that were practised out-of-doors or that depended upon the shipping season: winter weather routinely decreased the need for labour on construction sites and along the docks in many cities. Seasonal changes in consumption patterns, on the other hand, could affect entire sectors of the urban economy simultaneously. In early modern London, the first half of the year was known as the Season – in these months the royal court was in residence, parliament was in session, and wealthy visitors from all over the country flocked to the capital and spent their money in its shops. Summer reversed the pattern: parliament adjourned, the court moved to its summer residence, and the demand for goods and services in London diminished noticeably.[11]

Comparable phenomena shaped economic life in ancient Rome. Seasonal changes in the weather, for instance, had a demonstrable impact on jobs in transportation and building. In the transport sector, the weather dictated the navigability of both the Mediterranean and the Tiber and therefore generated seasonal fluctuations in the demand for a host of services: not only those of porters who unloaded ships at the nearby ports of Portus and Ostia, but also those of bargemen, animal handlers and porters who moved goods from seaside warehouses to those in the capital. Demand for these services peaked during the height of the shipping season between May and September, when it furnished work for several thousands. The weather also clearly affected the demand for services in the building industries: in the first century AD, Frontinus noted that because Roman mortar and concrete did not set well in hot weather or when subjected to frost, construction on the aqueducts was best performed between 1 April and 1 November, with a hiatus during the hottest part of the summer (Frontinus, *De aquaeductu* 2.123). Since mortar and concrete had been in widespread use in many building trades since the second century BC, construction

[11] Schwarz 1992, 103–23.

work in general was presumably seasonal for much of the core period of Roman history.[12]

Seasonal changes in consumption patterns likewise affected the demand for goods and services in most sectors of the urban economy. Many urban residents found that their ability to consume goods and services changed dramatically over the course of the year not only because grain consumed a large portion of their budgets, but also because grain prices fluctuated. They tended to be at their lowest immediately after the harvest when supplies were most plentiful, and as stores were depleted during the year they increased to a seasonal peak just before the next harvest. In a typical year, they could increase twofold towards the end of the cycle.[13] The ability of average urban residents to consume other goods or services was therefore strongest in late summer and autumn and weakest by the spring, with predictable consequences for those who catered chiefly to the needs of these customers.

The largest fluctuations in the consumption of goods and services in Rome were arguably caused by seasonal changes in the size and composition of the population that was present in the city at any given time. These changes affected most socio-economic strata in the city and, by extension, both low-end and high-end markets for products and services. For those who catered to the basic needs of the urban population or to low-end markets, seasonal migration caused fluctuations in the number of potential customers in the city for two reasons. First, rural inhabitants came to the city seeking work during the winter and spring (possibly in the tens of thousands – see below), and while in town they would have made regular purchases of foodstuffs and incidental purchases of other low-end goods and services. Second, when these individuals returned to the countryside before the peak of the agricultural season, they were arguably joined by numerous residents of the city who left town to seek temporary employment as farm hands at the most critical times of the agricultural year: in June and July (the cereal harvest), in August and September (when olive trees were tended) and in October and November (the vintage and the sowing of the coming year's crop).[14]

[12] Aldrete and Mattingly 1999, 192–204 (the shipping season and labour demand); Anderson 1997, 145–51 (concrete); Brunt 1980, 93 (seasonality and construction).
[13] Erdkamp 2005, 147–55.
[14] Shaw 1996b identifies a seasonal pattern in the dates on which Christian women married in late antique Rome, and suggests that this pattern was dictated in part by the annual cycle of agricultural labour. If so, it may suggest that inhabitants of the city sought harvest work in the countryside with some regularity.

CAMERON HAWKINS

Urban producers who catered to a wealthy clientele likewise contended with a population of potential customers that fluctuated in size and composition during the course of the year. Wealthy Italians and residents of the provinces made occasional trips to Rome, whether to strike up relationships with members of the Roman elite, to tour the public monuments, or as members of embassies to the emperor. The courts also attracted wealthy litigants who came to settle disputes in the capital, for although magistrates in the *municipia* and *coloniae* of Italy did enjoy some independent jurisdiction, it was limited by municipal charters that transferred many criminal cases to Rome, along with civil suits in which large sums were at stake. At the same time, wealthy residents of Rome had reasons to leave the city periodically: during the early imperial period, as men of Italian and provincial origin increasingly penetrated both the senate and the panels of jurymen, Rome became home to men who had ties to cities or estates in Italy or in the provinces and who therefore had reasons to split their time between Rome and their other domiciles.[15]

Two factors ensured that there was a seasonal pattern not only in the movements of wealthy visitors and residents, but also by extension in their ability to consume goods and services in the capital. The first, of course, was the agricultural calendar: the correspondence of Pliny the Younger demonstrates that the intensity of activity on medium-sized farms and agricultural estates during critical times of the agricultural season often demanded the personal attention of landowners, even those of senatorial rank (Pliny the Younger, *Epistulae* 8.2, 10.8.5). The second was Rome's climate, which was notoriously unhealthy during the late summer and early autumn. At this time of year pathogens – including typhoid, tuberculosis and falciparian malaria – caused a seasonal peak in morbidity and mortality. Contemporary observers were fully aware of the seasonal character of this phenomenon and preferred to avoid Rome during the summer for precisely that reason.[16]

Seasonal fluctuations in the Roman population were so pervasive that they gained recognition on an institutional level. According to Suetonius, Augustus established official recesses for both the senate and the courts: the former occurred in September and October, the latter in

---

[15] On municipal jurisdiction see Jones 1960, 75–7 and Brunt 1988, 225–6; on the composition of the senate, see Talbert 1984, 29–38; on the composition of the judicial *album*, see Brunt 1988, 231–6.

[16] See Chapter 3 above and Scheidel 2003, 163–9 for seasonal morbidity and avoidance strategies.

342

November and December (Suetonius, *Augustus* 32.3, 35.3). The recess of the senate clearly took place at the height of both the agricultural and malarial seasons. The recess of the courts was delayed until later, perhaps because Augustus wished to balance the desire to offer a recess against the need to ensure that legal business was actually wrapped up with minimal interruption before new juries were empanelled at the beginning of the year. But in spite of this delay in the official period of recess for the courts, Pliny the Younger indicates that in practice legal business fell off earlier in the year: July, he claims, was a relatively quiet month in the courts (Pliny, *Epist.* 8.21.2). Moreover, by the time of Marcus Aurelius, if not earlier, litigants could not compel adversaries to appear in court during the harvest or vintage, both of which occurred well before the official judicial recess; this stipulation gave institutional recognition to what was undoubtedly a long-established preference among landowners to be present on their estates at critical times in the agricultural year (*Digesta* 2.12.1, 2.12.3).

Seasonality clearly had a pervasive impact on the size and composition of the population resident in the capital at any given time, and hence on the overall demand for goods and services in the city. But what impact did it have on the demand for labour? In the service sector, the answer was mixed. In large and wealthy households where members of the elite maintained servants for reasons of conspicuous display, seasonality was arguably unlikely to have had much of an impact. But for employers and workers who sold their services on the market, the situation was much different. Many of these people – distributors, construction workers, hairdressers, doctors and so forth – provided services that were consumed more or less instantaneously, and for that reason it was difficult for them to substitute their labour over time. Seasonal fluctuations in the demand for their services inevitably entailed seasonal fluctuations in the demand for their labour.

Nor were manufacturers immune to the effects of seasonality. In theory, they could have distributed their labour evenly over the year by stockpiling goods during periods of low consumer demand for sale later in the season. In practice, however, two considerations militated against this strategy and generated seasonal fluctuations in the demand for their labour too. First, many manufacturers – particularly those who catered to a wealthy clientele – worked on a bespoke basis, producing goods to order for clients with individualized tastes. For instance, Apuleius, impressed by sample pieces on display in a carpenter's workshop in North Africa, commissioned from this artisan a devotional statue and other small items that were to be made to his specifications

(Apul. *Apologia* 61). The Roman jurists regularly assumed that artisans working in other high-end products like gold jewellery followed this same business model (e.g. *Dig.* 19.2.2.1, 19.2.13.5). Though some bespoke manufacturers were able to stockpile partially finished goods during the off season – for example, rough portrait busts to which they would later add specific features – they nevertheless could not entirely eliminate the seasonal character of production.

The second objection to stockpiling goods arose because this strategy was inherently risky, based as it was upon the hope that an investment in raw materials and labour could be recouped in the future without incurring a loss. While there certainly must have been well-capitalized producers who were willing to bear these risks, well-stocked retail shops were the exception rather than the rule in Rome. Instead, most Roman manufacture was in the hands of artisans who ran small, highly specialized workshops that did not require large reserves of capital. Most likely they had no such reserves at their disposal in any case, and were not in a position to amass large stockpiles of goods. Thus, labour requirements were seasonal for many manufacturers regardless of whether or not they produced mostly for a bespoke market.[17]

Comparative evidence suggests that these fluctuations in the demand for labour were likely to translate directly into fluctuations in employment. In early modern Europe, producers who regularly employed labour adapted to comparable fluctuations by tailoring both their output and their labour consumption to prevailing levels of consumer demand. In most cases they did so by maintaining only a small workforce of permanent employees all year round, hiring additional workers on short-term contracts when consumer demand increased. In this way they were able to expand their output during peak periods of demand, while ensuring that they were not saddled with the costs of underemployed labour during slumps.[18]

Our sources from the ancient world rarely comment on issues pertaining to urban labour markets, but there are indications that Roman producers may have followed comparable strategies. In the first place, we do find evidence that producers in ancient Rome – like their early modern counterparts – hired workers on short-term contracts. Columella assumed that urban slaveholders routinely encouraged their slaves to seek paid work, provided that those slaves remitted some of their

[17] On the risks of stockpiling, see Stedman Jones 1971, 33; Holleran 2012 discusses the structure of the Roman retail trade.
[18] Sonenscher 1989, 130–73, Schwarz 1992, 117–23.

earnings as a regular tribute. The fact that this tribute was computed on a daily basis suggests that employers hired and paid such slaves by the day (Columella, *De re rustica* 1.pr.12). Likewise, Apuleius imagined that a free skilled worker could find short-term or even daily employment in the workshop of another artisan (*Metamorphoses* 9.5–7). Finally, the jurists imply that employers in the building trades were often reliant on short-term help that they hired by the job (e.g. *Dig.* 45.1.137.3). It is tempting to conclude that these sources reflect the efforts of Roman producers to supplement small permanent workforces with additional hired help in periods of peak demand.[19]

It was also possible for Roman producers to adapt their workforces to prevailing levels of demand in a way that their early modern counterparts could not, namely by exploiting features of the Roman slave system. Roman law not only permitted Roman slaveholders to free their slaves, it also permitted them to demand labour services from some of these freed slaves as compensation for manumission.[20] These labour services – the so-called *operae libertorum* – were measured in units of a day, and the number of *operae* that any given slave might owe in exchange for his or her freedom was typically specified as part of the process of manumission. There is no way to determine how many *operae* a slave would typically promise in exchange for manumission, but Ulpian suggests that one thousand days of work may not have been an exceptional price to pay for one's freedom (*Dig.* 38.1.15).

For urban producers seeking to tailor their workforces to prevailing levels of demand, manumission in exchange for *operae* offered several advantages. Freed slaves were not only expected to discharge their *operae* at the convenience of their patrons, but were also expected to do so by practising any specific technical skills they had acquired as slaves. Since patrons were only required to support their freed slaves financially when the latter were destitute, urban producers who manumitted slaves in exchange for *operae* were therefore simultaneously able to minimize operating costs (by reducing the number of dependants whom they needed to maintain from their household stores) while retaining control over skilled workers whom they could call upon as and when necessary.

---

[19] See Beare 1978 on Columella and Martin 1989, 43–72 and 115–16 for hiring practices in the building trades.

[20] Waldstein 1986 offers a comprehensive discussion of freedmen and *operae*. For the concepts discussed in this and the next paragraph, see especially 130, 223–38 and 283–7.

Our sources suggest that urban producers employed this strategy with some regularity in order to tailor their output to prevailing levels of demand. In their funerary epigraphy, for instance, many artisans chose to depict themselves as the proprietors of businesses that were staffed by freed slaves.[21] Julian, the jurist of the second century AD, offers evidence of a more direct nature in his analysis of the rule stipulating that patrons were expected to use the *operae* of their freedmen personally rather than to rent them out. He argues that there are legitimate exceptions to this rule, reasoning that 'doctors often produce as freedmen slaves who are skilled in this same craft [of medicine], whose *operae* they cannot otherwise continually use except by hiring them out. And the same things can be said in the case of other craftsmen' (*Dig.* 38.1.25.pr. 2). Implicit here is not only an assumption that doctors and other urban producers owned skilled slaves, some of whom they regularly manumitted in exchange for *operae*, but also an assumption that such producers had only intermittent demand for the labour of their own freedmen. The seasonal fluctuations in consumer demand that were characteristic of the Roman economy offer the best explanation for all of these observations: when read in this context, the funerary epigraphy and Julian's comments suggest that doctors and artisans controlled the *operae* of freed slaves and called them in as necessary in order to increase production during periods of elevated demand.

LABOUR MARKETS AND THE DISTRIBUTION OF LABOUR

If seasonality did exert a strong influence on the labour management strategies of Roman producers – namely, by encouraging them to maintain only small permanent workforces and to expand these as necessary in response to temporary surges in consumer demand – then it seems reasonable to suppose that it may also have had a hand in the way in which various categories of labour were distributed in the urban economy. In this final section, I suggest that employers made decisions about whether to employ hired help or freedmen in periods of elevated demand on the basis of the ways in which seasonal pressures interacted with transaction costs in different segments of the labour market.

The transaction-cost approach begins with the observation that recruiting workers is never a straightforward process, but instead entails

[21] Joshel 1992, 128–45.

real costs, all of which are amplified when employers work on a bespoke basis and need to adapt quickly in response to changing consumer demand. More specifically, employers must expend time and effort on locating workers with appropriate skills, on negotiating contracts and on enforcing the terms of those agreements. In societies in which hired labour exists alongside alternative sources of labour, employers often weigh the transaction costs associated with different labour regimes against one another and make recruitment decisions partly on the basis of that assessment, all in the hope of recruiting and retaining workers with minimal cost and effort.[22]

When urban producers in ancient Rome sought to hire short-term help on the labour market, the severity of the transaction costs they encountered depended largely on the ratio between employers and employees in any segment of the market. Generally speaking, when workers are abundant relative to employers, then the market is thick: workers are easy to locate, they have little leverage when negotiating contracts and transaction costs are correspondingly low. In Rome, unskilled and semi-skilled labour must have been relatively abundant, though some workers undoubtedly sought agricultural employment at certain points of the year (see above). This thick market was buttressed by a constant stream of permanent migrants to Rome, many of whom arrived from the countryside with only limited training in non-agricultural work and consequently sought casual employment or joined the ranks of street-traders and hawkers.[23] Gender also played a role in swelling this segment of the market: as we have seen, because freeborn women lacked access to formal training, when they engaged in market production they tended to do so by working in unskilled or semi-skilled occupations. As a consequence, many may have spent their time working in short-term jobs for a succession of employers in low-skill trades.

Furthermore, during periods of low labour demand in the agricultural sector, seasonal migration had the potential to expand dramatically the supply of unskilled labour in the capital. This was so because of structural challenges inherent in peasant cultivation, the most pressing of which was the need to balance the productive inputs of labour and capital. While liquidity constraints have historically made it difficult

[22] Hanes 1996 formulates this basic approach in the context of British and antebellum America; Scheidel 2008 applies it to the ancient Mediterranean.
[23] See Scheidel 2008 on changing labour market conditions in the early Principate, and Holleran 2011 on migration, hawking and street vending.

for peasant cultivators to acquire additional parcels of farmland, their households tend to fluctuate in size and composition throughout their lifecycle. This produces a surplus of household labour relative to productive capital and thus underemployment for many of its members, particularly after the harvest. In a number of historical contexts, peasant cultivators have therefore sought to complement work on the farm with paid employment in order to increase the labour productivity of their households and to reduce the risks of exclusive dependence on agriculture. When local opportunities for employment were wanting, this necessitated seasonal migration.

Known examples of seasonal migration in pre-industrial contexts show that it can happen on a massive scale: more than 100,000 people a year sought seasonal work in Italy during the nineteenth century, gravitating towards the agricultural region of central Italy, toward cities in the north, or towards Rome. We can only guess at the scale of seasonal migration in Roman Italy, but there is no doubt that it took place. Peasant farms that could supply migrant workers continued to exist alongside agricultural estates in parts of Italy, and on occasion our sources even mention migrant workers explicitly. During the first century AD, for instance, agricultural workers crossed into Sabinum every year from Umbria to help with the harvest (Suetonius, *Vespasian* 1.4). Evidence from an admittedly late source is no less interesting: the fifth-century author Constantius of Lyons wrote that Germanus of Auxerre, while travelling from Gaul to Italy, encountered a party of workmen (possibly builders) who were returning to their homes after a spell of paid work in Gaul (Constantius, *Vita S. Germani* 31). The timing of their journey, which took place before the feasts of Saints Gervasius and Protasius on 19 June, suggests that they were peasants returning to their farms in time for the harvest after seeking paid work elsewhere during the spring. Rome itself, with its enormous aggregate demand for goods and services, was an obvious destination for migrant workers of this sort.[24]

While the supply of unskilled and semi-skilled labour available for hire in Rome was therefore relatively abundant, particularly in periods of low labour demand in the agricultural sector, the same was not true of the supply of skilled labour. In part, this was so because

---

[24] For discussions of seasonal migration and its relationship to peasant cultivation in the early modern world, see Lucassen 1987 (esp. 95–9, 116–19 and 235–60); on comparable phenomena in the ancient world, with discussion of the relevant sources, see Erdkamp 2005, 55–87 and Erdkamp 2008, 424–33.

trades in the capital had reached a high enough level of specialization by the late Republic to demand skills that were not widely available in the countryside. Consequently, immigration from Italy, whether seasonal or otherwise, did not necessarily enhance the supply of skilled labour in the city. Moreover, within Rome itself, access to training was not unlimited: most trades were taught through apprenticeship, and a young man's access to training therefore depended on his ability to find an instructor who was willing not only to take on additional full-time labour, but also to invest in the training of a potential future competitor.[25] Finally, because of the low level of capitalization in most trades and the high aggregate demand for goods and services in Rome, opportunities existed for those with training to establish businesses or clienteles of their own and become potential employers in their own right rather than employees of another.

If the above analysis of the Roman labour market is correct, then employers faced a very different transaction cost regime when hiring unskilled or semi-skilled labour than they did when hiring skilled workers. The thickness of the market in unskilled and semi-skilled labour meant that employers in search of workers of this calibre faced relatively low transaction costs for much of the year. On this view, employers who could get by with unskilled or semi-skilled help may have been content to meet their demand for workers by relying on the labour market. Many employers in the building trades who worked for the state or for private clients fell into this category: though they needed a certain amount of skilled help, they also demanded a considerable amount of menial labour, which the unskilled segment of the Roman population and seasonal migrants were both capable of supplying. Likewise, in trades demanding skills that were widely distributed and in which quality was less important than price – basic textile manufacture and the like – employers may have been able to meet many of their seasonal demands for labour by hiring semi-skilled resident or migrant workers. Employers in this category may have recruited even the members of their smaller permanent workforces on the open market, particularly when the political and military commitments of the free citizenry fell off during the Augustan period and this segment of the labour market became even more fluid.[26]

---

[25] For an economic analysis of the incentives and risks associated with apprenticeship, see Smits and Stromback 2001.

[26] Brunt 1980 discusses skilled and unskilled labour in the building trades; for changes in urban labour markets see Scheidel 2008.

Where skilled labour was necessary, however, the comparative thinness of the market meant that employers faced comparatively high transaction costs when they sought to hire help in periods of elevated consumer demand. In these circumstances those who controlled the *operae* of freedmen were potentially able to secure the labour they needed with considerably less effort than those who relied on the labour market. Because freedmen were expected to discharge their *operae* at the convenience of their patrons, employers who controlled the labour of former slaves had access to skilled help at very short notice and did not need to waste time and resources searching for workers and negotiating contracts. There were admittedly some risks inherent in this strategy: like other urban residents, some freedmen may have temporarily left the city to find employment on agricultural estates during the harvest or the vintage, while others must have found it tempting to renege on their obligations in periods of high demand when their labour was at a premium. In practice, however, the first of these dangers was mitigated by the fact that the demand for urban products and services – and thus urban employers' demand for labour – was likely to drop off during precisely those periods of the year in which freedmen might seek agricultural employment. More importantly, patrons could circumvent the second danger by using incentives to solicit the compliance of their freedmen, thereby minimizing their costs of enforcement: the funerary epigraphy suggests that urban producers transmitted property to their freedmen in their wills with some regularity (e.g. *CIL* 6.37824), and the possibility of receiving an inheritance may have been enough to persuade many freed slaves to remain in the good graces of their patron. Given the time-sensitive nature of much of their work, urban producers who controlled the labour of freedmen therefore enjoyed real advantages over those who relied exclusively on the market to secure skilled help in periods of elevated demand; for that reason, most employers of skilled labour probably preferred to adapt their workforces to the pressures of seasonality by relying on slavery and manumission in exchange for *operae* rather than by relying on hired help.

Gender and legal status were therefore neither the exclusive nor even necessarily the primary determining factors in the ways in which the working population of Rome was distributed across various sectors of the urban economy. Instead, that distribution was the product of an elaborate interplay between multiple factors. On the one hand, the seasonality of economic life in the capital strongly influenced the basic labour-management strategies of urban producers. On the other hand, the precise ways in which urban producers pursued these strategies were shaped in turn both by the impact of gender and legal status on the character of urban labour markets and by the degree to which they facilitated alternative arrangements. Ultimately, for the people who lived and worked in ancient Rome, divisions of gender and status may have been less noticeable in day-to-day life than another division engendered by the dominant patterns of employment: the division between those who practised one occupation for most of the year and those who did not.

FURTHER READING

Treggiari 1979 is fundamental reading for those interested in work and gender, but it is now dated and should be read in conjunction with Saller 2003. Bradley 1994 provides an overview of Roman slavery and includes a chapter on slave labour, and Scheidel 2008 complements it with an important analysis of causal factors underlying the widespread adoption of slavery in the Roman economy. Brunt 1980, Aldrete and Mattingly 1999, and Erdkamp 2008 all address seasonality and its consequences. On freedmen and *operae*, the standard work is Waldstein 1986. Finally, see Schwarz 1992 for a comparative analysis of seasonality and labour markets in another pre-modern context.

20: PROFESSIONAL
ASSOCIATIONS

Jinyu Liu

C alled *collegium*, *corpus*, *sodalitas*, *koinon*, *synodos*, *synergion*, *hetaira* and so on, an association would be an organization of some durability with formal structural features such as collegial magistrates, member lists, common treasury and patrons. Closely associated with the urban development under the *Pax Romana*, the associations played a dynamic role in structuring the social and economic world of the sub-elite in the cities in the imperial period. Their significance in social integration, as well as in building status and social credibility among the artisans and tradesmen, has been increasingly brought to the fore. Much of the ongoing research is not specific to the city of Rome, but the *c.* 700 inscriptions from Rome alone and the overwhelming number (*c.* 500) and varieties of associations found at imperial Rome certainly make it a central area of study. Before the imperial period, however, the evidence for the existence and activities of associations is much more scarce and confusing; as a result, their earlier history at Rome is shrouded in uncertainty.

ASSOCIATIONS IN REPUBLICAN ROME

In principle, according to a clause of the Twelve Tables preserved in Justinian's *Digest*, members (*sodales*) of an association had the right to enter into any agreement (*pactio*) as they wished as long as they did not violate public law (*Digesta* 47.22.4 Gaius). According to the jurist Gaius, this clause may have derived from Solon's legislation. However, neither the citation from the Twelve Tables nor the Solonian provision can be independently verified. To be sure, voluntary association was hardly an unfamiliar concept among the Romans or the Italians especially after the mid-Republic, as shown by the various Roman or Italian associations in Delos and Rhodes. In the city of Rome itself, however, the extant literary and epigraphic sources only give us a fleeting glimpse of a few associations, such as the *collegium mercatorum* connected with the temple of Mercury (Livy 2.27; *CIL* 10.3773 = 1.2672, 112–111 BC) and the *collegium Capitolinorum* for the games in honour of Jupiter Optimus Maximus (Livy 5.50.4 and 52.11). Both *collegia* were instituted by the public authorities. The existence of an association of flute players (*tibicines*) as early as 312 BC is plausible but not certain (Livy 9. 30.5–10; Valerius Maximus 2.5.4). An association of playwrights and actors (*scribae, histriones*) may have already been formed by 200 BC (Festus, *Epitome* 446. L), perhaps influenced by the organizations of the Dionysiac artists that were common in the Hellenistic world. We also hear of a *collegium* of poets in the 90s BC (Valerius Maximus 3. 7. 11). Judging by their orthography, a handful of inscriptions referring to associations may be datable to the first century BC or AD (e.g. *ILS* 7282, *AE* 1927, 167, *CIL* 1.2984b). The uncertainties involved in dating these inscriptions would mean that it is not always clear whether these associations date from the republican period or early Principate.

The literary sources regarding the origins of professional associations all come from the imperial period, and seem to reflect heavily reconstructed or reworked narratives. Pliny the Elder (*Historia Naturalis* 34.1; 35.159) knew of a ranked list of *collegia* whose origins can be traced back to the reign of Numa, the alleged second king of Rome. The *collegium aerarium fabrum* (bronze-workers), for instance, ranked third, and the *collegium figulorum* (pottery-makers), seventh. Plutarch (*Numa* 17.2) also ascribed to Numa the creation of craft associations of musicians, goldsmiths, builders/carpenters, dyers, leather-workers, curriers, bronze smiths and potters, and an additional group that included all the remaining trades. In Florus (1.6.3), however, it was the sixth king, Servius Tullius, who distributed artisans into associations based on the census. Although details vary, all of these accounts hinged on the supposed antiquity of certain occupationally defined groups. This alleged antiquity, however, cannot be taken at face value. As Gabba (1984) has aptly argued, the attribution of the creation of specific associations to a king may have been an invention in the late Republic and/or early empire in response to the hostility towards associations and intensified restrictions imposed on them.

In the chaotic last years of the Republic, associations incurred more official attention than ever before. Entangled in the political struggles, they became and were seen as many things, especially ready-made structures for electoral support, factitious conflicts, mass mobilization and street violence.[1] Politicians coveted their support, but were also eager to deprive their opponents of any potential support from the associations, as shown in Cicero's oscillating attitudes towards *collegia* (Q. Cicero, *Commentariolum Petitionis* 30; M. Cicero, *Pro Sestio* 34 and 55). Asconius' (d. AD 76) commentaries on Cicero's speeches are our main sources for the restrictive legislation levelled at associations in the late Republic. According to Asconius (7C), a senatorial decree (*senatus consultum*) dating to 64 BC abolished 'those *collegia* that seemed to have been established in conflict with the public interest'. Publius Clodius Pulcher, the popular tribune, reportedly not only restored these *collegia*, but also established numerous new ones by virtue of the *lex Clodia de collegiis* passed in 58 BC (Cicero, *In Pisonem* 4.9; Asconius 8C; Cassius Dio 38.13.2). In Cicero's hostile and derogatory language, the associations created under Clodius were described as being made up of destitute (*egentes*), half-starved dregs, prisoners and slaves (Cicero, *De Domo sua* 45, 54; *Pro Sestio* 34; *Pro Flacco* 18). The turbulent economic, social and political character of the late Republic led to the connection between associations and sources of unrest. It is this very connection, both real and perceived, that put the Roman associations in a sensitive position with respect to the state.

LEGAL STATUS UNDER THE EMPIRE

Both Caesar and Augustus took steps to clean up the associations, using 'antiquity', according to Suetonius, as the criterion to separate legitimate *collegia* from the unlawful ones (Suetonius, *Caesar* 42.3; *Augustus* 32.1). It is presumably against this background that lists of 'ancient associations' (*collegia antiqua*) became composed and circulated. Associations were abolished 'with the exception of a few established ones which the public interest (*utilitas civitatis*) wished for, such as those of the *fabri* and *fictores*' (Asconius 75C). In these words, Asconius seems to be speaking of the eventual effect of these restrictive measures. Interestingly, Asconius gives us a different criterion of differentiation, namely, *utilitas civitatis*. Asconius is commenting on Cicero's remark that 'as for the Cornelii, there are so many that an association (*collegium*) of them has been formed'. *Utilitas civitatis* here means public good or interest in a general sense as opposed to factional goals. It does not necessarily imply

---

[1] See also Chapter 24 on riots.

that the association had to assume specific duties assigned by the state or the city.

Certain types of professional associations were most likely organized or reorganized under the impulsion, if not necessarily compulsion, of the authorities in the early empire. Such might have been the case with several associations of musicians (*symphoniacii*), flute-players (*tibicines*) and lyre-players (*fidicines*), who were all specified as those 'who perform for public religious ceremonies' (*qui sacris publicis praestu sunt* – CIL 6.2191–2193, 240, 1054, 3696). The association of the *symphoniacii* was permitted by the senate to assemble; it was also sanctioned by an unspecified Julian law promulgated by the authority of Augustus (*lex Iulia ex autoritate Augusti*) for the purpose of games (*ludorum causa*; CIL 6.4416=2193=ILS 4966). It is often assumed that the Julian law in question was a special law governing *collegia*. Yet it may be more appropriate to situate this particular law within the context of the Augustan 'restoration' of religion, as musicians were indispensable elements in games (*ludi*) and state religious ceremonies.

In reconstructing the legal situation of *collegia* in the imperial period, we are faced with serious chronological gaps in our sources, as the legal citations concerning *collegia* mostly date to the late second and third centuries AD. But the concept of the right to assemble (*ius coeundi*) seemed to have become better defined in the imperial period. The formal recognition of a *collegium* took the form of an imperial or senatorial grant of the right to assemble, which was also the prerequisite to other legal rights at least from the second century on. The procedure of acquiring and granting *ius coeundi*, however, was by no means clear. The law contrasted legal associations with illegal ones, but not all the *collegia illicita* were considered subversive gangs: the penalty for *collegia illicita* was often just dissolution, and the members could divide up their common funds (Marcian *Dig.* 47. 22.3; Tacitus, *Annales* 14.17). Nevertheless, the jurist Ulpian emphasized that anyone who should usurp a *collegium illicitum* would be severely penalized (*Dig.* 47.22.2). To understand the associative phenomenon at its full complexity, then, it is important to emphasize the double-edged effect of official regulations. On the one hand, they could be used by the rulers as tools of control; on the other hand, the law would provide privileges and protection to the accepted *collegia*, and thus be instrumental in their development. The development of the associations that were connected with Rome's food supply, for example, accelerated under Trajan, who actively promoted the use of the collegial structure for public purposes. A *pistor* (miller/baker), for example, could only obtain special privileges through *collegium* membership (Aurelius Victor, *De Caesaribus* 13.5; *Fragmenta Vaticana* 233). The *collegium pistorum* of Rome also possessed the right to *corpus habere* from the very beginning, that is, the legal capacity to hold common property, to be represented by an agent (*actor* or *syndicus*), and to sue and be sued as a collective entity rather than a number of individuals (*Dig.* Gaius 3.4.1.pr.2). Such a right was only extended to the other types of authorized associations in the course of the second century AD, many of which were perhaps established on private initiative.

What complicated the picture was that organizations of the lower orders that were called *collegia* could vary widely in nature. There were the so-called *collegia domestica* composed of household staffs of the wealthy families. In the imperial household in particular, staffs with specialized duties ranging from the chamberlains (*cubicularii*), masons (*structores*), doormen (*ostiarii*), cooks (*coci*), litter-bearers (*lecticarii*), bath attendants (*unctores*), tent-makers/carers of the awnings (*tabernacularii*), to food tasters and waiters (*praegustatores*) were organized into *collegia* (e.g. *CIL* 6.9310, 8750, 8961, 6218, 8872, 8582, 9093, 9004, 37765; *AE* 2004, 210). The emperor's personal bodyguards (*corporis custodes*), who were mostly recruited from the German tribes subject to Rome, formed a *collegium Germanorum* under the Julio-Claudians (*CIL* 6.8802–09; Suetonius, *Galba* 72). It is more appropriate to consider it as a subdivision of the *familia Caesaris* than an association of soldiers. In terms of the household *collegia*'s formations and activities, the *paterfamilias* would have been the primary source of approval or disapproval. On the other end of the spectrum, *collegium* as an organizational pattern was widely applied in organizing the *apparitores*, or 'civil servants' including *scribae* (secretaries), *viatores* (messengers), *praecones* (heralds) and *lictores* (fasces bearers) who served the magistrates of various ranks.[2] The public character of the *collegia apparitorum* as part of the working mechanism of the *respublica* separated them from the other types of sub-elite groups. Although the *apparitores* were salaried and often recruited from freedmen, it was not business or trade but their attendance on the magistrates that articulated their social identity. In this category we should also count organizations like the *collegium victimariorum* (sacrificial assistants) who were specified as 'those who serve the priests, magistrates and the senate' (*CIL* 6.971=31217 = *ILS* 4963; AD 129).

It is not always clear whether the word *collegia* or *corpora* in the legal excerpts included the *collegia apparitorum*, or if it only referred to what modern scholars would consider as private and voluntary associations

---

[2] Waltzing 1895–1900, 1.54–5, 3.2–16; Purcell 1983.

linked with a particular occupation, cult, neighbourhood, or all three. Whatever the case, the proliferation of all kinds of *collegia* in imperial Rome suggests that the official regulations may in fact have had a positive impact on the development of associations. The law provided a broad infrastructure for the gradation and differentiation of the associations; as such, it formed one type of articulation for the character of the Roman associations. The legal infrastructure apart, the larger socioeconomic environment of the capital city, which was characterized by urban transformation, population expansion and influx of immigrants in the early empire, provided a wide range of social stimuli for the formation of associations.[3]

PARTICIPATION IN THE EPIGRAPHIC CULTURE

Many associations and their members were active participants in the epigraphic culture in imperial Rome. Inscriptions, therefore, form the bulk of our sources, which mainly consist of epitaphs, dedications, member lists (*alba*) and records of benefactions. Many of the inscribed texts were terse, highly formulaic and geared towards an advertising end: sociability, conviviality, legal privileges and interactions with benefactors were among the favourite subjects in the epigraphic media. As such, we are much better informed about the associations' aspiration to respectability and their formal sides than we are about the less 'dignified' and more mundane aspects of the collegial life. How were the members recruited? Did the associations intervene when the members conflicted with each other in professional areas? Did the associations facilitate information flow with respect to job opportunities, price fluctuations, technological innovations or the reputation of individual artisans? Did members of a professional association stand a better chance in obtaining public contracts? Could members borrow money from the associations, some of which were quite well endowed? If a professional association shouldered specific public service(s), how was the service carried out in practice? These are the sorts of questions about which the epigraphic sources tended to be either silent or elusive. Take the *collegium fabrum tignariorum* (builders and carpenters), for example. It may have been founded in the republican period, experienced a reorganization

---

[3] Patterson 2006.

in 7 BC, and continued to prosper throughout the imperial period.[4] We know quite well that it boasted at least 1,300 members in the third century AD, erected inscriptions in prominent places such as the forum and perhaps owned a club hall in the Palatine area or at the foot of the Capitoline Hill. Tiberius Claudius Onesimus, a chief magistrate of the said *collegium* in the eighteenth *lustrum*, was a contractor on public works (*CIL* 6.9034). We may reasonably conjecture that his fellow members might have had an easier time obtaining sub-contracts. The inscriptional evidence, however, neither contradicts nor confirms the speculation. In western cities other than Rome, the smiths, carpenters and builders often joined a single association called the *collegium fabrum*. We learn from Pliny's letters that the *collegium fabrum* could function as a fire-brigade. Yet there is no sign that the *collegium fabrum tignariorum* or any other related associations at Rome had any fire-fighting functions until the fourth century AD (Symmachus, *Relationes* 14.3).

We are deprived of information concerning those associations which failed to leave any traces in epigraphy either because they or their members could not afford inscriptions or because the epigraphic references did not survive. This necessarily means that our knowledge of the associations is confined to the wealthier ones which could take full advantage of the epigraphic media. Despite all the limitations of the epigraphic sources, they do reveal a world of the associations widely varied in terms of their history, size, judicial status, visibility in the city and the socio-economic standings of their members.

COMPOSITION, ORGANIZATION AND FUNCTION

What percentage of Rome's population belonged to an association? It is difficult to reach a solid estimation, especially since the sizes of the associations were often unknown to us. The official minimum group size was three. But the limit on the higher end was seldom spelled out in our sources. The larger associations were often divided into different units called *centuriae* or *decuriae*. The largest association known at Rome, that is, the *collegium fabrum tignariorum*, was at one point divided into sixty *decuriae*, each comprising at least twenty-two members. An epitaph of uncertain date (*CIL* 6.10147) seems to show that there were at least sixteen *decuriae* in the *collegium scabillariorum*. But many other

---

[4] Pearse 1974, 1976–7.

associations were probably much smaller. The *collegium Aesculapii et Hygiae*, for example, would admit no more than sixty members. It is also impossible to assess how many of the collegial members were new immigrants. What is clear is that *collegia* that clearly identified themselves on the basis of geographical origin or ethnicity were not a common occurrence in the epigraphic record. The current state of our source does not allow us to be assertive on the issue of whether associations had the effect of blocking out the new immigrants or rather served as support structures.

Judging from the inscribed member lists that have survived, none of the associations were dominated by a small number of families. Father and son were indeed found among the members, yet we can hardly speak of hereditary membership. The collegial members were mainly a mixture of freedmen and freeborn. The proportion of freedmen members, however, is not easy to determine. We do not have a sample of the member list of every association. Even on the lists we do have, status indicators were not always included, and we have to resort to the less reliable criteria such as the onomastics. Among the *collegium fabrum tignariorum*, 46 per cent bore non-Latin *cognomina*, which were often but not always securely associated with servile origin.[5] Nor did Latin *cognomina* necessarily indicate freeborn status. Among the magistrates of professional associations at Rome, only about 14 per cent can be securely identified as freedmen, while the status of the majority (79 per cent) was uncertain.[6] Although associations provided freedmen with a social space to construct personal prestige, they by no means exclusively or predominantly catered to freedmen. It should also be noted that the freed population was by no means a homogeneous group, but had a wide spectrum of socio-economic levels. Imperial freedmen, for example, were frequently involved not only in associations that were attached to the imperial household but also in those that did not seem to be connected with the imperial household. [Ti. Cla]udius Aug. [Ac]ratus, for example, seemed to have been a member of the sixth *decuria* of the *conlegium scabillariorum* (percussion musicians associated with pantomimes?) (*CIL* 6.33194 = *ILS* 7297).

It is reasonable to assume that entrance fees or monthly contributions were common features among the associations. Yet, as far as the city of Rome is concerned, we have little information as to how much membership might have cost. None of the extant by-laws of the associations from Rome specified admission fees or monthly dues.

---

[5] Pearse 1974, 129.   [6] Royden 1988, 229.

The majority of the association members known to us beyond a simple name were collegiate magistrates who seemed to have been men of some substance. This is, however, largely due to the biased nature of the epigraphic evidence. Within the same *collegium*, there may have been a wide spectrum of financial and social status among the members. Indeed, *Dig.* 50. 6.6.12 made a contrast between 'those who increase their wealth and are able to bear compulsory public obligations of the cities' (*qui augeant facultates et munera civitatium sustinere possunt*) and the poorer members.

Compared with the municipal cities, Rome boasted many more associations whose titles suggested highly specialized trades. Apart from the *collegium fabrum tignariorum*, several other building-related associations, including those of the *pavimentarii* (pavement-layers), *marmorarii* (marble masons), *sectores serrarii* (stone sawyers), and *subrutores* (demolition men), were also active. As far as the smiths are concerned, there were the associations of the ring-makers (*anularii*), goldsmiths (*aurifices*), bronze workers (*aerarii*), and ironsmiths (*fabri ferrarii*) (*CIL* 6.1892, 9144, 9202, 36771). We even learn of an association of shoe and sandal manufacturers (*collegium fabrum soliarium baxiarium*), which was divided into three *centuriae* and had a *schola* by the Theatre of Pompey perhaps as early as the first century AD.[7]

Shared occupation was supposedly the defining characteristic of the *collegia* whose titles mentioned professions. The *collegium* of the *fabri tignarii* of Rome, for example, proudly advertised their work tools on their altar (*CIL* 6.30982 = *AE* 1975, 13). The association of the fishermen and divers (*piscatores, urinatores*) on the Tiber depicted men rowing boats in a river on a statue base (*CIL* 6.1872 = *ILS* 7266). The jurists indeed spoke of associations whose members were recruited on the basis of their trade (*artificium*) as a distinct category of corporations (*Dig.* Callistratus 50.6.6.12). The link to a particular occupation, however, did not mean that all the practitioners of a trade had to become members of the corresponding association, or that each and every professional association admitted artisans and/or tradesmen of its titular trade only. In general, it seems that whether or not to accept outsiders was up to individual associations. At one end of the spectrum, some *collegia* took strict measures to prevent 'outsiders' from gaining entry. An excellent example is the *collegium* of the *negotiatores eborarii aut citriarii* (merchants of ivory and citrus wood products) under Hadrian (*CIL* 6.33885 = *ILS* 7214), in which membership was strictly limited to these merchants.

---

[7] *CIL* 6.9404 = *ILS* 7249; Bollmann 1998, A 16.

But other associations apparently maintained a fair degree of openness regarding recruitment, and were not closed to persons who were not in the same trade. As the membership in certain professional associations carried legal privileges such as exemption from guardianship, admission of outsiders who were attracted to such privileges seemed rather common after the latter half of the second century AD. Roman administrators and jurists were apparently aware of such a phenomenon. The principle governing the granting of such privileges rested with the ability of the members to show that they were *artifices dumtaxat* who were actively engaged in the relevant trade (*Dig.* 50.6.6.12).

The openness of the membership profile only illustrates one aspect of the complexities in the composition of the professional *collegia*. It must also be noted that, more often than not, we can only surmise an association's functions or its membership base from its title, which was not always a reliable index to either. A *collegium Silvani Aureliani* was in fact an association of gladiators (*CIL* 6.631 = *ILS* 5084; AD 177). There seemed to be more than one association of the *sagarii* (garment-dealers) at Rome. One was called *collegium Herculis Salutaris c(o)h(ortis) primae sagariorum*, which apparently took Hercules, the patron deity of the first cohort of the Praetorian Guards, as their own patron deity (*CIL* 6.339 = *ILS* 7315). The *sagarii* by the Theatre of Marcellus styled themselves as *cultores domus Aug(ustae)*, and made a dedication to Trajan (*CIL* 6.956). The make-up of the *corpus pausariorum et argentariorum* is puzzling. The *pausarii* had formal roles in the worship of Isis. Indeed, the *corpus* had an unmistakable connection with the cult of Isis and Osiris, for whom it built a temple (*mansio*) (*CIL* 6.30745 = *ILS* 4353). But how the *argentarii* (money changers) fit in is not at all clear. Similar examples abound, which makes drawing a clear-cut distinction between professional and cultic associations elusive.

Scholars have repeatedly noted that the associations were formed *ad exemplum reipublicae*. The terminologies for magistrates – *quinquennales, duoviri, curatores* – were all borrowed from the municipalities. The use of apparitorial titles such as *lictor, viator* and *scriba* was also quite common. They might have been either submagistrates or simply honorific titles. The common members were often called *plebs* or *populus*; the decisions of the associations were referred to as *decreta ordinis*. Many associations had their own temples, *schola* or other types of meeting places. The *negotiatores frumentarii*, for example, were authorized by Vespasian to build a temple in the designated place (*CIL* 6.814). The *aenatores Romani* (musicians who played bronze wind instruments) seemed to have a temple of their own, which was located near the north-eastern slope of the Palatine Hill, and was repaired by Claudius in AD 51–4. The temple housed statues that the *aenatores* put up to the emperors and imperial members in the Julio-Claudian dynasty.[8] An association may have its own birthday and dating systems. Apart from the *collegium fabrum tignariorum*, several other associations dated their eras by *lustrum* (five-year cycle). The *collegium aromatariorum* (pharmacists or spice dealers?), for example, counted at least twenty-eight *lustra* (*CIL* 6.384). As for the sociological significance of the associations' resemblance to a miniature city, however, scholarly interpretations vary. Many emphasize the associations' conformity to the dominant elite value systems and principles. A quite different view that goes beneath the superficial resemblance between the associations and the cities holds that the associations in fact amounted to a 'symbolic order' of the non-aristocrats. This 'symbolic order' was an alternative to the civic order in which their positions were defined by inferiority and exclusion.[9] This understanding seems particularly to suit the city of Rome, where the associations were seldom part of public banquets or ceremonies. In the municipal cities, the decurions, the *Augustales* and the associations were sometimes mentioned together as recipients of prorated distributions. This mode of integration was simply not feasible at Rome. Some scholars thought the associations were incorporated into the imperial processions as in the case of Pertinax's funeral (Cassius Dio 75. 4) and Gallienus' entrance into Rome (*Historia Augusta, Gallienus* 8.6). Yet, judging by the context, the organizations of the *apparitores* were meant in the former case, and it is far from clear that the word *collegia* referred to all kinds of associations in the latter.

PATRONAGE OF ASSOCIATIONS

In contrast to many western cities where the *collegia* of various types were often mentioned together in the epigraphic records as sharing patrons and benefactions, rarely do we find associations at Rome mentioned together as joint recipients of benefactions. The title of collegial patron did not seem to confer enough prestige to attract high-ranking personages at Rome, which was not the case at Ostia. Senatorial or equestrian patrons of associations were far from common at Rome before the fourth century AD. Magistrates of associations seemed to have been the main sources of material benefits. Imperial freedmen and slaves also

[8] *CIL* 6.40334, 40307; Bollmann 1998, 260–1.   [9] Verboven 2007.

featured frequently as benefactors/donors to associations, regardless of whether they were officially affiliated with these associations or not. The gifts ranged from statues of deities or reigning emperors, altars, building decorations, buildings, cash distributions and banquets to burial slots. In the first century AD, for example, L. Sextilius Seleucus, a *decurio* of the *collegium centonariorum*, gave the association a monument with a marble base and two bronze candlesticks, each in the shape of Cupid holding a candle. In addition, he also established a foundation of 5,000 *denarii*, the annual interest of which – 600 *denarii* – was to be used perhaps for celebrations on the birthday of the deified Augustus (*CIL* 6.9254 = *ILS* 7244). Some of the gifts from the magistrates may have been compulsory, others may have been a show of generosity. Through such generosity, collegiate magistrates may have been able to advance to the rank of patron, as the 'cursus' of Flavius Annius Ann(a)eius Lemonia Fortunatus seemed to indicate. Having held all the honours of different grades in the association of fishermen and divers and thrice served as the chief magistrate (*quinquennalis*), he was granted the title of *quinquennalis* for life, and was eventually honoured as the patron. On the occasion of his being offered the title of patron, he gave 12,000 sesterces to the association. The annual income from the fund was to be distributed to the members on his birthday. In addition, he, along with a fellow member, donated a silver statue weighing three pounds. On the occasion of its dedication, the patrons and members received different amounts of cash distributions according to rank (*CIL* 6.29700).

Collegial banquets were much more than simple merrymaking; rather, they constituted special occasions invested in the elements of formality. The organization of banquets, the dining places, as well as the manner of dining, were carefully regulated by the *collegium* by-laws. Notably, distributions and food and wine portions were hierarchically structured; furthermore, the convivial occasions were by no means randomly chosen but revolved around the associations' benefactors or patrons as well as the reigning emperors.[10] The by-laws of the merchants of ivory and citrus wood products, for example, contained detailed regulations in these regards. The tetrastyle building where the *negotiatores eborarii aut citriarii* were to dine was very likely the gift of a certain Iulius Aelianus. Among the four dining occasions stipulated in the by-laws, two were in honour of the emperor Hadrian, and two others were to be held on the birthday of Iulius Aelianus and that of his son respectively (*CIL* 6.33885 = *ILS* 7214). Conceivably, the change of benefactors

---

[10] Liu 2008.

and the emperors would affect the calendar and the rhythm of collegial activities as well as the organization of an association. The emphasis on the emperor(s) deserves particular attention. In fact, the Roman associations were actively involved in emperor worship. They were often found to make dedications to the living emperors or imperial family members, the guardian spirit (*numen*) or the well-being (*salus*) of the imperial household (*CIL* 6.240, 1117–18, 30745, 31220a, *AE* 1912, 38). Statues of living emperor(s) were among the gifts that the associations tended to receive. Marcus Ulpius Aeglus, an imperial freedman and procurator of the Mausoleum of Divus Augustus, for example, donated a brass bust of Trajan to the *collegium faenariorum* (hay salesmen, *CIL* 6.8686 = *ILS* 1577). An honorific inscription put up by the *corpus piscatorum et urinatorum totius alv. Tiber.* (fishermen and divers of the Tiber) to Tiberius Claudius Severus, a *decurialis lictor*, their patron and three times *quinquennalis*, provided an illuminating summary of the range of benefits that an association might receive through the intervention of a patron (*CIL* 6.1872 = *ILS* 7266; AD 206). He was honoured for three deeds. First, together with his son, he put up the statues of the emperor Caracalla and his mother, perhaps in the association's meeting place. Second, he donated 10,000 sesterces to the *corpus*, from the yearly interest on which all the members were to receive distributions on his anniversary. Last but most importantly (*praesertim*), he helped the *corpus* acquire a special navigation right (*navigatio scapharum*). This inscription vividly illustrated the multi-faceted nature of the Roman associations: from emperor worship to material benefits, from conferring honour on a benefactor to negotiating licences or privileges. In addition, Tiberius Claudius Severus served as a link between the association and high-ranking personages such as his son, who was not specified as a member or patron but as being of equestrian status. The navigation right was likely to have been obtained from a high-ranking magistrate, to whom Severus might have access in his capacity as a high-ranking *apparitor*.

FUNERARY CLUBS?

The earlier opinion that there existed a distinct legal category of 'burial associations' (*collegia funeraticia*), which were authorized en masse, has been discarded.[11] The current scholarly opinion holds that all associations may have had a funerary dimension. As far as the city of Rome

---

[11] Ausbüttel 1982.

is concerned, however, it is not easy to gauge how significant the associations were in providing burials for the members. Statistically, only a small minority of all the commemorated individuals at Rome can be identified as members of an association. They were also not necessarily buried in the collegial tomb, or commemorated by their own association or individual fellow members. A *decurio* of the *collegium fabrum tignuariorum*, who died at nineteen, for example, was buried in the tomb built by his father (*CIL* 6.9407 = 30601.1). It is by no means rare to find members, especially magistrates, of an association buried in the family tomb that they built for themselves, their wives, their freed(wo)men and their descendants (e.g. *CIL* 6.9408, 9677). A small number of epitaphs seemed to have been erected by a *collegium* for its members. The members of the *collegium marmorariorum* (marble masons), for example, set up an epitaph for Quintus Marcius Iovinus (*CIL* 6.9550). But whether the marble masons owned a tomb of their own is not clear. Nor do we know whether the burial was funded by a special *funeraticium* that came out of the membership dues. In the early imperial period, a *columbarium* measuring 384 ft² *(CIL* 6.7860) on the Via Salaria accommodated at least six members of the *collegium centonariorum*. Judging by the onomastics, they all seemed to have been related to the original owners of the tombs. But not all of those interred inside the *columbarium* were affiliated with the *collegium*. There was also another tomb at Rome inside which, among others, two *centonarii* were buried, both of them freedmen of one Marcus Octavius. Both tombs appear to have been family tombs. The members were buried inside as part of the *familiae*.

Indeed, not all the associations or the subunits within associations had their own communal tombs. Those associations or subunits that did have their own burial sites or slots may have either commissioned them with the communal funds or obtained them as a result of the benefactions from members or external benefactors. Perhaps in the first century BC, the synod of Greek singers had a tomb built out of its common money (*AE* 1927, 167; *LTUR* 4. 298). In the late first century BC or early first century AD, the *duovir* of the *collegium anulariorum* gave the *collegium* a tomb measuring 625 ft² that he had built with his own money (*CIL* 6.9144 = *ILS* 7284). M. Licinius Mena, a freedman and twice curator of the *synhodus Magna Psaltum* (singers and/or musicians), restored the collective tomb of the *collegium* on Via Labicana (*CIL* 6.33968 = *ILS* 5246). The *collegium scabillariorum* seemed to own a communal tomb near Porta Maggiore, which was under the supervision of the association's curators (*CIL* 6.33193). The tomb(s) of an association or its subunits did not have to be an independent/separate cemetery but could be acquired within a larger *columbarium*. For example, by the will of L. Mamilius Felix, who was most likely a member of the tenth unit (*decuria*) of the *collegium fabrum tignuariorum*, thirty-two burial niches (*ollae*) were to be reserved for twenty-two specific members of the *decuria* and ten future members (*CIL* 6.9405 = *ILS* 7238). These niches evidently belonged to a larger communal tomb owned by L. Cincius Martialis, who specified himself as a *quinquevir*, perhaps of the *collegium*. The association of the *symphoniacii* had burial slots in the Vigna Codini *columbarium*, part of which was also occupied by the *socii coronariorum* (wreath makers?) (*CIL* 6.4414–15). Within the imperial household, the *collegia* of the staffs also had funerary characters. For example, Ulpia Cynegis donated a tomb to the *collegium Aesculapi et Hygiae structorum Caes(aris) n(ostri)* (the association of (the worshippers of) Aesculapius and Hygia (who are also) masons (working for) the emperor) but reserved twelve urns and two sarcophagi for herself and her freedmen (*AE* 1937, 161). P. Aelius Pyramus, one of Hadrian's freedmen and head doorman in the imperial palace, stipulated that when his family line ended, the chief doormen and the members of the *collegium ostiariorum Caesaris nostri* may claim the right to the tomb that he and his wife built for their son, themselves, their freedmen and their offspring (*AE* 2004, 210). A head chef also left similar instructions to the *collegium cocorum* (*CIL* 6.8750 = *ILS* 29899).

Given the many different ways by which a collegial member obtained burials and commemorations, and the varied socio-economic background of the members, the significance of the associations' involvement in providing funerary assistance may have had quite different meanings to different members. It may have relieved a financial burden for some, offered affirmation of group solidarity for others, or fulfilled the role of a relative for still others – especially those without direct relatives. As to the more affluent members, they were more concerned with engaging the association in the continued performance of commemorative rites. C. Turius C. f. Lollianus, for example, donated funds to the *corpus mensorum machinariorum* to perform sacrifice on designated days (*CIL* 6.9626 = *ILS* 7267). Interestingly, the development of the associations' funerary dimensions seemed to have coincided with the decline of the phenomenon of *socii monumenti*, which was particularly popular in the first century BC–first century AD. The partners (*socii*) were a definite number of persons, who shared a burial lot and whose names were usually listed on the tomb markers. The interaction of the *socii* did not necessarily go beyond sharing a tomb, which distinguished them from a *collegium*. But the boundaries were not always easy to draw.

DEVELOPMENTS IN THE FOURTH CENTURY

If the inscriptions from the first three centuries provided a relatively well-rounded picture of the various aspects of the associations, our understanding of their activities after the third century becomes limited to their services to the city of Rome or the state. Notably, over the course of the third century, the *utilitas publica* of several *collegia* was transformed into *munus*. The *munus navicularium*, for example, was introduced in the early third century AD, then further evolved into a *munus patrimonii*, that is, an obligation resting on the member's landed property, at the end of the third century.[12] The term *navicularii* no longer represented an occupational title but a service, as in the case of the bakers/millers (*pistores*), importers of pork and of meat from sheep and cattle (*suarii*, *pecuarii* and *boarii*) and so on. The performance of one *munus* granted exemption from other *munera*; but *ad hoc* impositions of services or levies on the collegial members could occur. Several very elaborate honorific inscriptions for patrons date to after the reign of Diocletian. The urban prefects, who were now in charge of *collegia*, were featured prominently among the collegial patrons, which represented a visible change from the first three centuries. The *collegium fabrum tignuariorum* made a dedication to L. Aelius Helvius Dionysius, who had been curator of public works and became urban prefect in AD 301 (*CIL* 6.1673 = *ILS* 1211). The *corpus magnariorum* (the association of wholesale dealers) put up a bronze statue for their patron, Attius Insteius Tertullus, urban prefect in AD 307–8, referring to his benefaction (*munificentia*) towards the *corpus* (*CIL* 6.1696). The *corpus coriariorum* (leather-workers or tanners?) erected a statue to their 'worthy patron', urban prefect in AD 334/5 and later consul, for through his efforts their quarter (*insula*) was restored to its former state in accordance with laws of the previous emperors Severus and Caracalla (*CIL* 6.1682–3 = *ILS* 1220–1). Slightly outside our period, examples from Symmachus' family illustrate the role of the urban prefects as intermediaries between the emperors and the *collegia* (*CIL* 6.1739–42; *Codex Theodosianus* 14.2.1; Symmachus, *Relat.* 14.3). Since this period, however, inscriptions gradually tapered off. As a result, accounts from the perspective of the associations, however subjective, became overshadowed by the rhetoric of the authorities.

---

[12] Sirks 1991.

F u r t h e r   r e a d i n g

For collection of the epigraphic material, see Waltzing 3.167–324 nos. 612–1378. Newer inscriptions about the associations of Rome have not been systematically sorted out, but can be collected from *AE*. Catalogue and examination of the archaeological data related to *collegia* can be found in Bollmann 1998. For particular types of associations, see Pearse 1974 on the *fabri tignarii* and Sirks 1991 and Broekaert 2010 on the *navicularii* (shippers). Royden 1988 provides a prosopographic study of the collegial magistrates. For general discussions of the significance of associations in Roman social history, see in particular Ausbüttel 1982, Joshel 1992, Van Nijf 1997, Bollmann 1998, Patterson 2006, Tran 2006, Verboven 2007. Perry 2006 discusses what influenced the modern historiography on *collegia*. For a global analysis of how professional associations may have functioned as private-order, reputation-based enforcement mechanisms that institutionalized trust-networks, see Hawkins 2006, especially 78–138.

21: SEX AND THE CITY

Thomas A. J. McGinn

MAPPING MORALITY

The widespread and easy availability of sex, above all sex for sale, in the urban setting is perhaps one of the better-known clichés in Roman literature. Horace in his *Epistles* teases the bailiff of his country estate for pining over the attractions of Rome, among which figure prominently the brothel, the (greasy) bar/cookhouse, the tavern and the prostitute with her flute.[1] Columella puts bars (*popinae*) and brothels (*lupanaria*) on a list of urban pleasures, opining that a slave who indulges in such things is unreliable.[2] Tacitus in his *Histories* cites prostitutes and their haunts as customary and common features of city life that contrast pointedly with the bloodshed that accompanied the street-fighting between Vitellian and Flavian forces in December 69: here you have battles and wounds, there you have baths and bars; you find blood and piles of corpses juxtaposed with prostitutes and those like them.[3] Other sources indicate that sex was also accessible outside the city. Varro observes that lodgings were commonly installed on rural estates along roads in order to serve the needs of travellers, and we know that prostitutes offered their services in at least some of these places.[4]

Still other evidence suggests that sex was not universally available within cities. For example, in an oft-cited passage Seneca provides an idealized moral distinction between good places and bad, which turns on an association of the latter with prostitution:

> Why do you unite things that are unlike, or, rather,
> completely different? Virtue is something lofty, exalted and
> king-like, undefeated and untiring. Pleasure is low, slavish,

---

[1] Horace, *Epist.* 1.14.18–26. [2] Columella, *De re rustica* 1.8.2.
[3] Tacitus, *Historiae* 3.83.2.
[4] Varro, *Res rusticae* 1.2.23; Suetonius, *Claudius* 38.2 (the scene is possibly urban); *CIL* 9.2689 (= *ILS* 7478), a joke but still apt for our purposes.

weak, perishable, whose hangout and home are brothels
and bars. You will find virtue in the temple, in the Forum,
in the senate-house, standing in front of the city walls,
covered with dust, sunburned, with calloused hands.
Pleasure you'll find more often hiding out, lurking in the
shadows, around the baths, the sweating-rooms, the places
afraid of the aedile. It is delicate, languid, soaked in
unmixed wine and perfume, either pale or painted with
cosmetics and laid out like a corpse.

(Seneca, *De vita beata* 7.3)

Seneca links *Virtus* with temple, Forum and senate-house, an association that in reality seems to have been far from watertight, in that it is
not difficult to cite evidence that ties the presence of prostitutes to all
three of these venues, or at least their near vicinity.[5] Perhaps for this
reason, in the end he relocates *Virtus* to the edge or outside of the city
entirely, evidently transformed into an idealized soldier or agricultural
worker. The latter alternative stamps Seneca's discourse as a variant
of the city:bad/country:good theme so popular in Roman moralistic
writing.[6] The passage from Horace described above falls within the
same tradition, which suggests that the information it conveys should
be treated with care. The same is true for Columella, who may in fact
depend on Horace, at least in part. For Tacitus, unlike Seneca (perhaps),
there are no good places in the city. He juxtaposes the peacetime pleasures of a corrupt metropolis with the savagery of civil war in a manner
that suggests the two phenomena are in fact related, manifestations of
a society whose moral calculus has gone horribly awry. We may safely
conclude that all four of these authors write in a moralizing vein, not
as urban topographers, either in a prescriptive or a descriptive sense.

Such evidence encourages, or should encourage, some hesitation
on our part over the precise status of prostitution as a feature of Roman
urban life. It was evidently practised outside as well as inside the confines
of the city, where it seems to have been widespread, though its exact
extent was liable to exaggeration. Not too many years ago I published a

[5] On prostitution near temples, see Plautus, *Poenulus* 265–70; Dio Chrysostom 7.133–
4; Juvenal 6.489 (Isis as a *lena*), 9.24. On prostitution in the Forum, particularly in
front of the senate-house, see Seneca, *De beneficiis* 6.32.1 (Augustus' Julia depicted
comporting herself as a prostitute); McGinn 2004, 92, 247–8.
[6] See, for example, Wallace-Hadrill 1991, 244–9. The essays collected by Rosen and
Sluiter 2006 have much to say about values, but surprisingly little on sex.

book on the economy of prostitution in the Roman world, in which I argued, among other things, that prostitution was in fact a fairly diffuse phenomenon in the Roman city, though far from a universal one, and that, while the numbers and locations of brothels and other venues where sex was sold remain uncertain for the vast majority of cases, there is no reason to think that these were restricted in any significant way, in other words, that the Roman government pursued a policy of moral zoning that reduced their numbers and restricted their locations.[7] I am grateful that the reception of this argument by scholars has been, almost from the start, overwhelmingly favourable. A number of them have questioned or explicitly rejected the thesis of moral zoning.[8] I hope that I do not seem ungrateful if I express the concern that acceptance of this point in some cases threatens to paint over what were shades of grey with black and white.

To make the point as simply and plainly as possible, a list of 'possible brothels' is not the same as a list of proven brothels. The uncertainty over the numbers and locations of brothels in the Roman city cuts both ways. While making it impossible, in my view, to sustain a thesis of moral zoning, it does not render such an argument absurd, and poses serious challenges to drawing further conclusions based on the relevant evidence, both archaeological and literary in nature. What I propose to do in what follows is briefly to review this evidence with an eye to its limitations as much as its potential for illuminating our understanding.

SITES FOR PROSTITUTION

Not only the literary tradition but also the epigraphic and archaeological record suggests that prostitution was indeed widespread. It was associated with taverns which often had rooms for sex in back

[7] McGinn 2004 (an elaboration of an argument made in McGinn 2002).
[8] See, for example, Ellis 2004 (makes a similar argument for Pompeian bars – profitability, not moral zoning, determined their location – and further issues a useful caution on using Latin tags for identifying the archaeological remains of venues for the 'hospitality industry'); Varone 2005 (pushes the epigraphical evidence too hard in reconstructing the details of prostitution in Pompeii); DeFelice 2007 (over-criticizes the theory of moral zoning and evinces hyperscepticism over the number of brothels, misunderstanding the relationship between literary and archaeological evidence): Guzzo and Scarano Ussani 2009 (in the context of a counterproductive quibble over the meaning of 'brothel'). See also Laurence 2007, 82–101, for a half-hearted defence of the moral zoning thesis, attempting to discard the term, but not the thing itself.

and/or upstairs,[9] lower-class residences or lodgings (which we might describe as inns), places of public entertainment such as circuses, theatres and amphitheatres (in whose arcades prostitutes evidently solicited customers even on days without performances), and of course baths (where food, drink and sex were all often for sale). Much of this evidence is tendentious or otherwise unreliable, and scarcely signifies that, for example, every tavern or every bath offered prostitution. Its cumulative weight nevertheless is probative of a strong link between such places and the practice of venal sex overall.[10]

The same can be said of the evidence for the occasions on which prostitutes plied their trade. These included markets, fairs, festivals, circuit courts, public shows of every kind, dinner parties, indeed, any event where potential clients might gather. It is clear that some prostitutes were mobile, and travelled in order to be present at these opportunities, though in this case mobility should not be confused with freedom.

Another way in which the sources convey the widespread nature of prostitution concerns prostitutes more directly than brothels and other venues for the sale of sex. The elite Roman male, to whom we owe the vast bulk of our evidence, did much to exaggerate the presence of prostitutes in the Roman city. This was because he was liable to identify almost any lower-class woman as a prostitute, especially if she worked in a trade that exposed her to indiscriminate contact with males outside her family. Such contact would have been routine in any imaginable part of the Roman service economy, such as selling vegetables in the marketplace or serving wine in a bar. So Martial's insinuations about the behaviour of the Suburan *tonstrix* reflect, in my view, this simple bias, instead of presenting evidence that permits us to conclude that hairdressers typically worked as prostitutes.[11] A similar point holds for Plautus' *alicariae* ('mill-girls'), whose identification as prostitutes owes as much to modern ideas of whore-taxonomy as ancient attempts to make sense of the text, which is far from clear.[12] This does not mean of

---

[9] The better-known examples include, aside from the evidence of Horace, Columella and other authors cited above, Catullus' *salax taberna* ('sexually provocative tavern'): 37.1.

[10] For more evidence of prostitution in such places and for what immediately follows in the text, see McGinn 2004, ch. 2.

[11] Martial, *Epigr.* 2.17; cf. Plautus, *Truculentus* 405–6.

[12] Plautus, *Poenulus* 266. Festus 7L takes a sexual joke (*alicariae* = 'women who deal in grain' becomes 'women who grind' or 'are ground') and turns it into a job description: see Adams 1983, 335–7.

course that no mill-girl or hairdresser ever doubled as a prostitute. The evidence does allow us to draw the conclusion that the vast majority of prostitutes were of low status, meaning slaves, ex-slaves, or living in conditions close to slavery.

We have no way to be absolutely certain, then, whether the Pompeian (h)alicaria Glyco, as a prostitute, is a part-timer or this term simply functions as slang for 'prostitute'.[13] The sad truth is that the elite male misogyny of our literary texts almost certainly blurs to the point of unrecognition a flourishing part-time and casual economy of prostitution. This leaves us ill-equipped at times even to interpret a simple epigraph in a satisfactory manner.

To put the problem another way, there is a parallel danger of hyperscepticism over the extent of prostitution in the Roman world. Its widespread nature is suggested (though not, I must emphasize, proven) by a wealth of comparative evidence that shows lower-class women in a variety of trades who do supplement their incomes by resorting to prostitution.[14] In other words, it is quite possible to read the bias of the sources as a kind of backhanded acknowledgement of the existence of part-time and/or cyclical prostitution in the Roman world. What is more, not all prostitutes remained in a brothel, but went out to solicit customers or simply worked in the streets independently of a brothel. Thus the presence of prostitutes in the Forum and other public spaces is securely attested, whatever exaggerations may safely be ascribed to class and gender bias.

The breadth and variety of this evidence is suggestive. Any attempt at quantification is clearly out of the question, but it is clear that prostitution must be regarded as a major service industry in the Roman world. Although, as we have seen, brothels did exist in rural areas, prostitution was overwhelmingly an urban phenomenon, regarded as one of the distinct pleasures of life in the town. In cities, prostitution seems to have been fairly pervasive, at least in lower-class contexts, a fact supported by evidence that not only the prostitutes themselves but the clients of the establishments surveyed here were themselves typically of low status.[15] Even so, considerations of commercial advantage, rather

[13] *CIL* 4.3999, 4001.   [14] McGinn 2004, ch. 2.

[15] One aspect of this evidence lies in the generally low prices charged for sex. These typically range from 1 *as* to 16 *asses* (= 1 denarius), with 2 *asses*, the price of a loaf of bread, the most common. Prices attested for Pompeii fall mostly towards the lower end of the scale, while the evidence for Rome suggests they tended there to be on the higher side.

than Christianizing concerns with public morality or the aesthetics of the public sphere, determined the widespread presence of venal sex in Roman urban contexts. We do well all the same to remind ourselves, as often as necessary, that while prostitution was widespread, it was not universal.

MATERIAL EVIDENCE

To steer a safe course between the Scylla of underestimating and the Charybdis of overestimating the presence of venal sex in the Roman city remains a challenge when we come to a more direct and detailed examination of the archaeological evidence. The bulk of this (by far) derives from Pompeii, but Rome itself presents possible brothels as well.[16] I define 'brothel' as a location open to the public where sex is the principal business or, at any rate, is a major component of the business of the place, and where two or more prostitutes can work simultaneously. The identification of brothels, certainly in Pompeii, has depended on the application of three criteria adapted from those origi-nally set forth by Andrew Wallace-Hadrill. First, there is the criterion of design, including, above all, the presence of masonry beds and/or the size of rooms and their relationship to each other, such as a series of small rooms lying off a common corridor. The second feature is erotic art, meaning scenes of explicit lovemaking typically displayed in the form of wall painting. Next are explicit graffiti, naming, for example, prostitutes, specific sexual acts and the prices charged.

The application of these criteria is fraught with difficulties. Not one of them is essential to the operation of a brothel, ancient or mod-ern. In fact, not one of these criteria has so far been employed to identify brothels in any other culture known to me, with the (very) partial exception of ancient Greece.[17] Each by itself can be attributed to contexts that are actually or potentially distinguishable from the practice of prostitution. Such a layout of rooms (and even, at times perhaps, masonry beds) is consistent with the operation of an inn or lodging-house. Wall paintings with such content are found in pri-vate homes. There is a possibility that at least some of these graffiti

---

[16] For evidence of brothels and the practice of prostitution from other cities, see McGinn 2004, ch. 8.

[17] Some of the essays in a recently published collection address this issue regarding venues for prostitution in ancient Greece, with criticism of Wallace-Hadrill's criteria: Glazebrook and Henry 2011.

might be intended as insults or jokes, so that they should not be used to identify a brothel. Rarely do all three appear together and rarely can they be said to be really probative (or even nearly so) in terms of their kind, quality or sheer amount. Most tellingly, perhaps, the criteria are best suited to identify the famous Purpose-Built Brothel (or *Lupanar*) in Pompeii (which is scarcely in need of identification as such), making their use in other contexts a somewhat circular exercise in reasoning.

Nevertheless, this evidence is all that we have and all that, for the foreseeable future, we are likely to have for the purpose of identifying brothels in Rome, Pompeii and elsewhere in the Roman world. Used with due caution, it can help us identify possible brothels. The challenge of identifying brothels in the material record may be compared to that of tracking the presence of slaves, a familiar problem in archaeology. The coincidence is perhaps not entirely casual, given the low status of most Roman prostitutes.[18]

Scholars have identified as many as three possible brothels at Rome. More than sixty years ago, Giuseppe Lugli argued that a building excavated in the early years of the twentieth century was to be regarded not as an aristocratic *domus*, as had been thought, but precisely as a brothel.[19] The building is located at the intersection of the so-called Clivus Palatinus and a street identified as the Sacra Via, just west of the Arch of Titus, and dates from the early to mid-first century BC (*c.* 80–*c.* 50) to AD 64 (the time of the Neronian fire), to omit possible remodelling(s). There were (at least) two levels, a ground floor, which has been reconstructed with some of the features of an upper-class town house, including an atrium, partial peristyle and tablinum, and an underground level, which had a bath complex and as many as sixty-two small rooms that in most cases seem to have featured a bed (part masonry and part wood) and a drain. Lugli argues that the dimensions of these

---

[18] One can reasonably point to the presence of loom weights as a possible criterion for identifying brothels. Not given for Roman brothels, they were found in large numbers in the famous Athenian Bau Z3, 153 examples, according to the excavators: Knigge 2005, 71. This establishment has been identified as a possible tavern brothel. The loom weights do not guarantee the identification as a brothel, but precisely in the context of a tavern suggest as much. One reason concerns the presumed status of the prostitutes as slaves or similar. Weaving will have occupied their time when they were not selling drink or sex. See the essays by Glazebrook and McGinn in Glazebrook and Henry 2011.

[19] Lugli 1947.

small rooms, or 'cellae' were such as to argue for the building being used as a brothel.[20]

In the context of this discussion Lugli identifies a second brothel in a building even closer to, if not actually in, the Forum adjacent to the so-called temple of Romulus and close in date to the first. A third example Lugli sees in a structure uncovered in 1901 in the Forum Boarium, next to (and partially underneath) the so-called Arch of Janus, again close in date.

At Pompeii, I have located forty-one possible examples, of which I believe about half are more likely than the rest. This does not mean that there were forty-one brothels at Pompeii, or even that there were twenty-six or twenty-three brothels. The evidence can, for the most part, only suggest possibilities, and not dictate certainties. Such uncertainty is useful to the extent that it underlines the unlikelihood that a policy on moral zoning existed. In other words, the fact that we cannot for certain rule out the possibility that any of the forty-one were brothels makes it difficult for us to assume that brothels were zoned in or out of certain parts of the city.

A similar point holds regarding cribs. A crib was a small, crude building or room which was used by a prostitute who did not work in a brothel and which is often clustered with other cribs in an alley or along a roadway. They are frequently known by the modern term *cellae meretriciae*. Cribs were an important non-brothel venue for prostitution. Their identification, however, depends on the same three criteria that hold for brothels, and we experience similar difficulties in applying these criteria. While no cribs have emerged in the very thin material evidence for the practice of prostitution in Rome, I have been able to identify thirteen possible cribs in Pompeii. Of these, eleven open directly off the street, while the other two are found at the back of a bar, constituting two distinct subtypes.

It is possible to identify with some degree of confidence three categories or types of brothels. One of these is purpose-built, meaning that the structure was designed and constructed precisely as a brothel. Only one of these is known from Pompeii and, in fact, from the entire Roman world. This is the famous *Lupanar*, newly renovated at the time of writing and possibly the single most popular tourist attraction in

---

[20] More recently, Tomei 1995 has argued that the building is a *caupona-lupanar*, a view rejected by the building's excavators, who view it as an aristocratic *domus*. See Carandini and Papi 2005.

the contemporary archaeological site of Pompeii. It contains five small rooms on the ground floor, each with a masonry bed that must have supported some sort of mattress and/or cushions in antiquity. On the upper walls of the passageway that connects the rooms is a series of erotic paintings. Five more rooms are upstairs, accessible by a separate entrance stairway and a balcony. Of these rooms, only two are securely identifiable as '*cellae*' on the order of the five downstairs, while a third possibly qualifies as one, despite its greater size. To be sure, no masonry beds, erotic paintings or erotic graffiti are recorded for this level. The other two rooms are better regarded as banquet halls that differ in size, but that, especially in the case of the larger one, mimic an elite atmospheric.[21]

There are more than 100 graffiti, many of them erotic, in and around the building. It is worth emphasizing that this Purpose-Built Brothel is unique for another reason. It stands as our most certain example of a brothel, not only in Pompeii, but, once again, in the entire Roman world. This makes it very difficult to generalize from, though some have found the temptation to do so irresistible.

A second type is that of the tavern/bar/cookhouse (typically – if tenuously – identified by the Latin terms *taberna/caupona/popina*), often outfitted with rooms for sex in the back and/or upstairs. The terminology (sometimes, though this is not without difficulties) supports a distinction between places that offered lodging in addition to food and drink, namely lower-class lodgings or inns, and those that operated as a combination of bar and fast-food restaurant, namely taverns. There is some support for this distinction in the archaeological record, though the terminology, it cannot be sufficiently emphasized, cannot take us very far in this direction. This record also yields examples of taverns with what were probably lodgings, so that we should recognize two subcategories, the tavern with and without lodgings. The line can thus be a thin one between this type and the third category, precisely that of lower-class lodgings or inns, in that food and drink were often available here as well. But the same is also true of the first type, represented by the Purpose-Built Brothel, suggesting that while brothels show some

---

[21] Personal observation, March 2009. This configuration of space need not depress estimates of the total numbers of prostitutes who worked in the brothel. The banquet halls may have allowed more to work simultaneously, and/or some might have been brought in from elsewhere for special occasions. One wonders all the same whether at times the upstairs functioned as a lodging and entertainment centre where venal sex was just one of the attractions, and less exclusively as a 'brothel'. And, appearances to the contrary, did the same hold for the downstairs as well?

typological differences, these cannot be pressed too hard. Brothels are notoriously difficult to identify as brothels, so that it comes as no surprise that problems in the excavation and/or preservation of some sites will present challenges in the assignment of a possible brothel to one category or the other. Again, the existence of these categories hardly signifies that all taverns or all lower-class lodging houses were venues for prostitution. The presence of one or more of the three criteria described above typically indicates possible brothels, and no more.

NUMBERS OF BROTHELS AND PROSTITUTES

The numbers of possible brothels and cribs generated by this survey raise a perfectly reasonable question.[22] How many brothels could a city the size of Rome or Pompeii sustain? The answer is strictly impossible to know. For one thing, we do not know how many people lived in ancient Rome, above all, in the fourth century, the era of the Regionary Catalogues, which tell us more or less precisely that there were forty-five or forty-six brothels in the capital at that time. The current consensus among scholars is, to say the least, cautious about assuming a sharp decline in the city's population as early as the fourth century, meaning that as many as a million people might have lived in Rome then. Such a figure makes that of forty-five or forty-six appear relatively small. Perhaps these are all large, purpose-built brothels, or were simply large enough to qualify as tourist attractions, even if not purpose-built. Perhaps the number was pitched low so as to avoid creating the wrong kind of impression about the capital. If so, however, it is difficult to see why they are mentioned at all. Another possible explanation is that these were brothels that had come into the ownership of the state by the usual means of acquisition, meaning purchase, gift, bequest and so forth. Not all of these explanations are mutually exclusive.

A similar point holds for the population of Pompeii, and its relation to the number of presumed brothels. The usual guess is about 10,000, but this remains merely a guess. Even if it were a certainty, it would be pointless simply to attempt to extrapolate numbers of brothels from this or any other population figure. The clients of Pompeian brothels, like the prostitutes themselves, all but certainly hailed not only from the town itself but from the surrounding territory, other towns in the area,

---

[22] On what follows, see McGinn 2004, ch. 6.

and, ultimately, from the entire Mediterranean world. The population of Pompeii and its surrounding area has been rated as high as 36,000. Much of the rural population must have consisted of unmarried male agricultural workers. These men, unless they were slaves in chains, were prime candidates as clients of Pompeian prostitutes. The important point is that the number of brothels is likely to have been influenced as much or more by the number of visitors to the town than by the number of persons who lived there. Neither number can be known to us.

Perhaps it is more interesting to inquire after the number of prostitutes sustained by these cities. With Rome it is impossible to know where to begin. With Pompeii, again, it seems fruitless to reason downward by relying on overall population estimates. That leaves estimating upwards, based on the number and size of brothels, an uncertain undertaking, as we have already seen. Nevertheless, it can be a valuable heuristic exercise. If we accept a number of brothels that is just under half of those I list as possible, namely twenty, and postulate an average of four prostitutes in each brothel, this gives a base of eighty brothel prostitutes. Most *possible* Pompeian brothels were small, like Pompeian hotels. A wealth of comparative evidence also supports the idea of relatively modest-sized brothels. The Purpose-Built Brothel, on the other hand, was larger, featuring perhaps a dozen or more prostitutes. If we add to this figure for brothel prostitutes a dozen women working in cribs and another dozen 'independent' streetwalkers (some of whom may have worked near the theatres, amphitheatre and baths) we arrive at just over 100 prostitutes for Pompeii. This estimate does not attempt to account for part-time or seasonal prostitutes, and so is intended to be conservative in nature. The total would represent just over 1 per cent of the population, if this was indeed 10,000, though this number remains uncertain, as we have already seen.

Whether this total of 'just over 100' is itself too large or too small is strictly impossible to say. The former seems unlikely, however. Prostitution, like other aspects of human sexuality, though it is found in a broad number of cultures, configures itself differently in different societies. Information drawn from a wide variety of contexts in past time shows that the numbers of prostitutes as a proportion of a given population can show significant differences from one to the other. It is left for us to decide whether ancient Rome resembled those cultures with higher percentages of prostitution or those with lower. If we examine the factors that played a role, for example, in the phenomenon of high proportions of female prostitutes in Europe and the United States from the mid- to late nineteenth and early twentieth centuries, we find some that were foreign to the Roman experience, such as industrialization, rapid urbanization and mass migration. Others, however, were not unknown and may have been worse for Rome, including poor opportunities for female employment and dim prospects of marriage for many lower-status males. The phenomenon of slavery may help explain elevated levels both of supply (slave prostitutes) and demand (slave customers) for Roman society. A better comparison for Rome may lie with the ratios of prostitutes from cities in southern France and Germany in the medieval and early modern periods. This too would support a relatively high level at Pompeii.

If it seems safe to conclude in any case that brothels were widely diffused in Pompeii (meaning they were not confined to specific zones) and that the numbers of prostitutes were relatively high (compared both with some other cultures and with what the moral zoning thesis seems to suggest), the next problem to confront is whether it is safe to generalize from conditions there to those prevailing in other Roman towns, including Rome itself. Did Pompeii, for example, enjoy such close links to a number of other areas that it possessed the status of a 'gateway settlement'?[23] The question is a vital one for us, since if Pompeii was a gateway settlement, the number of prostitutes working there would conceivably have been well above any number we might postulate as typical (it is impossible to speak of 'average') for a Roman city of its size and situation.

In fact, the problem of the typicality of Pompeii is a traditional one in the scholarship on a number of different levels. We must perforce remain focused on a very specific aspect of a much more general issue. Just how exceptional was Pompeii with respect to prostitution?[24]

First, the sheer bulk of evidence for erotic life in general that has been recovered from Pompeii, especially when contrasted with the leaner yield from Herculaneum, prompts the suggestion that the situation there was unusual, more conducive to the experience of *amor* than elsewhere in the Roman world. This seems unlikely, however. Pompeii was no Baiae, if it is indeed correct to assume that Baiae actually lived up to its reputation. Pompeii was known as a port city, a good place to purchase an oil press, not as a hotbed for *la dolce vita*. For

---

[23] On the concept of gateway settlement, see Horden and Purcell 2000, 133, 399.
[24] What follows is of necessity summary. For more detail see McGinn 2004, ch. 6.

this reason, it seems reasonably safe to generalize from the evidence of Pompeii in erotic matters, including venal sex.

The second set of conditions discouraging generalization is more intractable. It has been argued that in the period following the devastating earthquake of 62 the need for housing at Pompeii was acute, because many residences were damaged and because a massive rebuilding campaign attracted a large transient population of workers from the countryside, most of whom would have been male. Aside from hotels, these workers patronized other service outlets, including bars and brothels. Pompeians were not, it would seem, slow to exploit their urban properties and so transformed many residences into hotels, taverns, etc. in order to accommodate this increased need.

While the 'earthquake hypothesis' may well explain, in part, the evident diffusion of brothels in Pompeii, proof for this argument is not adequate at this point. Closer examination of these establishments at Pompeii may shed light on the extent to which the earthquake and its aftermath encouraged, indirectly, the practice of prostitution. At present, we may cautiously conclude that it had some impact, however limited. One correlate of this conclusion is that a gender imbalance existed, with more men, perhaps many more, than women. At the same time, prostitutes perhaps formed a higher percentage of the female population than one expects to find in other Roman cities that did not experience Pompeii's difficulties in this period. Even so, the Pompeian evidence suggests that brothels were a widespread feature of Roman urban life. To this extent, it does seem safe to generalize from the material remains of Pompeii. Most importantly, we can conclude that the precise numbers and locations of brothels in Roman cities were a function of economics and not of morality or a public policy directed at relegating prostitution to the backstreets of Rome, Pompeii, or elsewhere.

ATTITUDES AND ATMOSPHERICS

It is hardly the case, of course, that Roman aristocrats regarded brothels favourably.[25] The evidence they have left behind is unequivocal in denouncing such places as filthy and poorly lit. This testimony bears the mark of an elite sensibility so that it must be discounted

[25] See, for example, Seneca the Elder, *Contr.* 1.2.21; Petronius, *Satyricon* 7; Ulpian, *Dig.* 4.8.21.11; Paul, *Dig.* 47.10.26. For more evidence on what follows see McGinn 2004, ch. 3.

to some degree. The same holds for another horror of the brothel registered by the ancient sources, the close proximity of persons from varying social levels. Upper-class Roman males, it is worth pointing out, might as easily find other sexual opportunities, such as in marriage or with their household slaves. The brothel, like prostitution itself, was supposed to reinforce the social hierarchy, but could, through implicating upper-class visitors in its 'evils', threaten to overturn it. Some Romans thought it dishonourable even to set foot in these places, and many of those who did found it expedient to cover their heads in order to conceal their identity. Brothels were regarded as extremely inauspicious.

What really distinguished brothels as 'bad' was the combination of class mixing and atmosphere of criminality that pervaded them, first and foremost in the elite imaginary, but not only there. In this respect, a wealth of comparative evidence backs up what we have from antiquity. Brothels in various cultures, including the Roman, have been characterized by beatings, rape, murder, robbery, theft and the destruction of property. The combination of such factors as the consumption of alcohol, the close contact among persons of different social classes and the presence in particular of young men prone to impulsive behaviour, might generate explosive results. A great deal of noise was produced by drunken, often obscene, singing and violent, often bloody, confrontations. Another common phenomenon was gambling, which, despite its being for the most part illegal, was rife throughout taverns and brothels. A basic premise of the brothel was to celebrate various forms of transgression, not just the sexual.

It is certainly clear that the Romans associated an atmosphere of disorder and criminality with the operation of such enterprises. It is impossible precisely to determine to what extent this evidence reflects upper-class prejudice or social reality. The casual nature of some of the references suggests, however, that the evidence should not be viewed simply as a reflection of elite bias.[26] We have seen that both prostitutes and clients tended to be of low status. One might rather easily conclude, as others have done, from the expressions we have of this hostility, and the reality we can glimpse behind them, that Romans were inclined to locate brothels in out-of-the-way places.

[26] See, for example, Plautus, *Mercator* 408–9, *Persa* 568–9; Propertius 2.5.21–6, 2.19.5–6, and other evidence cited in McGinn 2004, ch. 3.

Policy and moral geography

The problems of the brothel, however, did not loom so large as to prompt such a direction in official approaches to brothels. A measure of social control was afforded by the collection of a tax imposed on prostitutes and pimps and collected by civilian authorities in some places and in others by the military. The aediles in Rome and, we may reasonably suppose, their equivalents in other cities were entrusted with the oversight of brothels, but this meant above all the preservation of public order, without resort to an elaborate system of regulation or repression. A more convincing conclusion than a thesis of moral zoning is that the social pathologies associated by the Romans most intimately with the brothel were thought to have been contained there, for the most part. Thus it was possible to maintain the correct physical distance from venues for venal sex simply by avoiding them. There was neither an ideological nor a legal basis for the topographical isolation of prostitution. The idea that brothels themselves should be zoned in or out of certain areas appears to be a Christianizing (and post-Christian) phenomenon.

Social distance was also a concern. Members of the Roman elite, with only a very few possible exceptions, did not want to risk identification as a pimp. The social prejudice against pimps was very strong, and was manifested in a series of legal disabilities levied upon them. For example, they were excluded from holding municipal office and from sitting on town councils by the late republican regulations recorded on the Tabula Heracleensis.[27] Pimps also figured on a list of types of persons restricted in their capacity to make procedural requests relevant to private lawsuits before the urban praetor. They were among a very small group of types forbidden to marry freeborn persons by the Augustan marriage law. Together with prostitutes, gladiators, trainers, beast-fighters and actors, they formed a category that stood at the core of disgrace, a category that was both legal and social in its implications.

Sensitivity over this subject was sharpened by the fact that many upper-class Romans made considerable sums from the business of prostitution. The jurist Ulpian indicates as much in a famous excerpt from

---

[27] For greater detail on what follows, see McGinn 1998, chs. 2–4, 9. For more on upper-class investment in brothels, see McGinn 2004, ch. 2.

his commentary on the urban praetor's edict.[28] Ulpian almost casu-
ally suggests that the sale of sex was diffuse, and that the line between
honourable and dishonourable was impossible to draw in a topographical sense. Many *domus* in Pompeii were surrounded by businesses that
appear to have been owned by the proprietor of the house. No evidence exists of any concern that the presence of brothels might lower
property values, a familiar refrain from modern contexts. If anything
the reverse was true. A brothel might add value to an *insula* containing
an aristocratic *domus*, at least for some.

These factors helped, I argue, to make it all the more imperative
to draw a bright line between honour and dishonour in a more purely
social sense. One way to evade identification as a pimp was to resort to
middlemen, persons of low status who could operate a brothel and pass
on a healthy share of the profits to the upper-class owner. It is unclear
just how many intermediaries, that is, how much social insulation,
were required, but the bar does not seem to have been set all that
high, and probably depended in the end on the status of the owner. In
this way, members of the elite might enjoy the benefits of this cash-
rich business while avoiding the social obloquy and legal disabilities
directed at pimps. Moral zoning, or any kind of zoning, meaning the
topographical restriction of venues for prostitution into or away from
certain places, was hardly needed to make such a system function.

These observations suggest another point to make about the numbers of brothels and their location in the urban context. Brothels and
related businesses tended to cluster together, constituting, in Pompeii,
an 'Eros Centre' surrounding the Purpose-Built Brothel in *Regio* 7 and
mini-versions thereof, in *Regio* 1 stretching from the *Porta Stabiana* to
the *Insula del Menandro*, and in *Regio* 7 at *Insula* 13. These were districts
that catered to a variety of needs and desires associated with the sale of
sex.

CONCLUSIONS

Considerations of profit appear to have dictated the numbers and locations of brothels in Rome, in Pompeii and in other Roman cities, so
that we would expect any patterns that emerge to exemplify the results
of a loose and informal practice of commercial clustering that fostered
a mix of residential and retail establishments, including brothels, rather

[28] Ulpian (15 *ad edictum*), *Dig.* 5.3.27.1.

than of a top-down, officially imposed 'moral geography'. The Romans did not shrink from eroticizing – actually or at least potentially – the atmospherics of their cities. The sum of the weird marginality imposed on Roman prostitutes was to stand as outcasts openly for all to see in the urban centre.[29] Prostitution, or at any rate the idea of it, was never far to seek in this context.

This does not mean of course that venal sex was universal at Rome or in any other Roman urban centre. The decision to instal and operate a brothel was always a matter for the individual property owner. By the same token, no one, including the authorities, was in a position to prevent such exploitation. The moral geography of Rome, Pompeii and other cities was no more than the sum of these individual choices.

What more can we say about the sheer frequency of prostitution? Much remains to be done, especially with the archaeological record. Caution is all the more obligatory, however. The vast uncertainties, surveyed above, that are generated by the kind and quantity of our evidence should give us pause in assuming just how much sex was for sale in the ancient Roman city.

FURTHER READING

In this present essay I avoid citing bibliography that appears in my book apart from a very few exceptions. The reader is directed to McGinn 2004 for fuller citation of primary and secondary sources for some of the points made here. McGinn 1998 is a study of the legal rules affecting the practice of female prostitution at Rome during the central part of Rome's history, a period extending from c. 200 BC to AD 250. It examines the formation and precise content of the legal norms developed for prostitution and for those engaged in its profession, with close attention paid to their social context. McGinn 2004 is a study of the evidence for the business of prostitution in the Roman world. The main focus is on the economics of venal sex, meaning precisely the manner in which it was sold, a subject that extends to the ownership, operation, staffing and location of brothels, as well as to various aspects of non-brothel prostitution.

---

[29] On the marginalization of prostitutes, see McGinn 2011.

PART V

RULERS AND THE RULED

22: CIVIC RITUALS AND POLITICAL SPACES IN REPUBLICAN AND IMPERIAL ROME

Adam Ziolkowski

T he *Shorter Oxford Dictionary* defines *civic* as 'Of or proper to a citizen or citizens', 'of, or pertaining to citizenship' and 'civil (opposed to military, ecclesiastical, etc)'. The last definition would have made little sense to the Romans in whose notion of the civic life politics and public cult, mainly performed by officers of state, not priests, made an inseparable whole. Since, however, public religious activities are treated elsewhere in this volume,[1] I shall include only those which formed an integral part of the civic ritual in our restricted sense.

In spite of its Italian and Mediterranean empire, Rome of the last two centuries BC was still a city-state of the *polis* kind, in which ideally the whole of the communal life took place in the open, under the gaze of all, and especially in which matters of common interest were the object of public discussion and decision-making by, again ideally, all members of the community. Public activities involved two paramount institutions: the politically organized citizenry and the magistrates (on the senate, see below). Citizens participated in two distinct political organizations: the people (*populus*) with its magistrates and the plebs (the same citizenry except for some few patricians) with its tribunes, both sovereign in that decisions by both were binding for the whole community (see Map 22.1).

The people and their leaders met publicly in two zones, intra- and extra-urban: the civic and economic centre in the valley of the Forum Romanum/Comitium between the Capitol, the Palatine and the Velia, and the plain of the Campus Martius in the bend of the Tiber north-west of the city, originally reserved for military training. This dichotomy was linked with the twofold nature of the *populus*, which exercised its power both as an organization of 'civilians' and as a body

---

[1] Chapter 26.

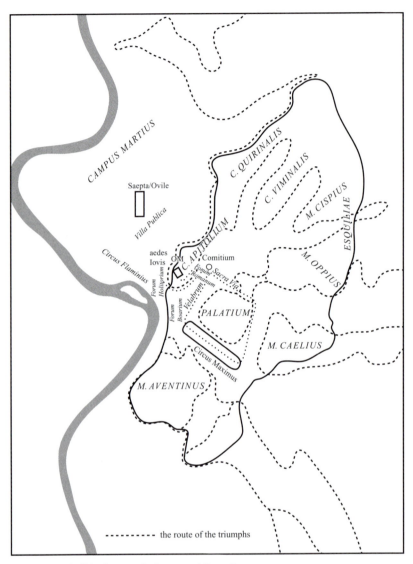

MAP 22.1 Political spaces in late republican Rome.

of quasi-warriors. Since activities of a military nature were forbidden within the ritual boundary of the city (*pomerium*), the people as citizens-in-arms met exclusively in the Campus Martius, leaving the zone of the Forum for activities of a strictly civilian or urban nature. The latter were not as circumscribed, though: their outer limit ran 1 mile beyond the *pomerium*, including, among others, the whole of the Campus Martius as well. This limit held for the plebs, inherently 'civilian', and so for the power of the tribunes too.

ACTORS AND RULES OF CIVIC RITUAL UNDER THE REPUBLIC

The fundamental rule of the civic life was that the chosen leaders of the community, magistrates and tribunes, were its only active element; the people, the fount of power and law, were completely passive. As an institution, they existed latently; they came into being at the summons of the magistrate. Any mass meeting, any political assembly, had to be convened by a competent officer, who then strictly supervised it, having the power to dismiss it when things were getting out of control. There were two sets of circumstances which made the people's purposeful coming together legitimate: a voting assembly of the people (*comitia*) and the plebs (*concilium plebis*), and a mass-meeting of citizens summoned by a magistrate or a tribune to present to them some political or judicial matter (*contio*) without putting it to a vote. Without proper guidance, a gathering was but a crowd (*multitudo*), undesirable and potentially dangerous. Livy expressed this fundamental rule in a speech to the people, put into the mouth of one of the consuls of 186 BC, authors of the bloody repression of the cult of Bacchus:

> Your ancestors did not want to gather fortuitously and
> without good cause but only when either, after the military
> standard had been set up on the citadel, the army was led
> forth for the purpose of holding a voting assembly, or
> when the tribunes decreed a gathering of the plebs, or else
> when one of the magistrates called out a public meeting;
> they were of the opinion that wherever a crowd is, there
> should be present a lawful leader of the crowd.
>
> (39.15.11)

The people exercised their sovereign prerogative of decision-making according to a political arithmetic different from the Greek (and our) principle of one voter, one vote. In an assembly they voted within units corresponding to subgroups into which the citizen body was divided, with the majority in the unit counting as the unit's vote. The subgroupings were two, centuriate and tribal, one originally based on the citizens' contribution to the military potential of the community, later translated into property qualifications, the other on domicile or property holding. In the former the citizen body was divided into 193 centuries, split between five classes according to wealth, in the times under discussion including one century of propertyless *proletarii*. In the latter each citizen was a member of one of the thirty-five territorially based *tribus*.

The centuriate assemblies (*comitia centuriata*) were gatherings of citizens in their capacity as warriors: though unarmed and in the toga, the civilian uniform of Roman citizens, they were officially referred to as the *exercitus* (fighting force), and their main functions were the election of the highest magistrates, consuls and praetors vested with *imperium*, the regal right to command and declare war. As such, they were held outside the *pomerium*, in the central Campus Martius. The tribal assemblies (*comitia tributa*) were innately civilian and their natural place was the Comitium, an appendix to the Forum Romanum reserved for political meetings. The first group to start to assemble by tribes were the plebeians; the *populus* and its magistrates followed their example for electing lower office-holders and legislating.

Depending on the purpose for which it had been summoned, an assembly could be electoral, legislative, but also judicial. In Rome, as in every classical city-state, jurisdiction was an integral part of politics. Penal trials were institutionally and procedurally an affair of the community: they were judged by assemblies (only the *comitia centuriata* could pass sentences on capital charges), by judges appointed by magistrates (praetors and aediles), or by special courts which legally had to be established by a duly passed law (*lex*, hence the official name of the procedure: *iudicium publicum*). In private lawsuits the magistrates also played a prominent part. The Roman private trial consisted of two stages, the first of which took place before the praetor, who decided which legal action would be brought to solve the case and appointed a judge, or judges, to decide the issue. Only this second stage – the real trial – was private both as regards the status of the person(s) of the judge(s) and the fact that it could take place anywhere, including a private house; the former involved some of the highest magistrates and took place in some of the most exalted public places of the city.

The lifeblood of the political life of the Republic were *contiones*. By custom and since 98 BC by law, the proposed bill or judgment had to be posted up to 'three market-days' (*trinum nundinum*, twenty-four days) before the vote; during the interval the proposer informed the people of the measure he was going to put before the assembly and conducted a public discussion of its merits at several *contiones*, the last of which immediately preceded the vote. But the *contiones* were more than an indispensable element of the voting procedure: they were the forum in which any matter of public interest could be presented and debated, thus countering to a certain extent the muteness of the people in political matters. Admittedly, during a *contio*, apart from the officer who had convened it, only those whom he asked to address the meeting spoke, and only on the matters raised by him; but if he allowed only his own supporters to speak, his adversaries among the magistrates and tribunes summoned their own *contiones* to attack his measure. It paid better to ask one's opponents to present their views as well.

Of the main performers in the civic ritual only the magistrates vested with *imperium*, consuls and praetors, and the tribunes of the plebs had the right *cum populo/plebe agere* (to deal with the *populus* or the *plebs*), in other words – to convene the people to assemblies. External symbols of magistracy were few and austere: a purple-bordered *toga praetexta*, an elevated platform (*tribunal*) on which they transacted public functions, seated in the chair of office (*sella curulis*). The tribunes of the plebs, despite their power being in some respects superior to that of the consuls, were strictly speaking civilians; as such they bore no symbols of their rank and their equivalent of the *sella curulis* was a common bench (*subsellium*) strategically placed in the Comitium to make them available to give help (*auxilium*) to any citizen threatened by an arbitrary measure of a magistrate. Consuls and praetors also had at their disposal lictors, attendants with bundles of rods (*fasces*) on their shoulders. The lictors – two for a praetor, twenty-four for the consul 'holding the *fasces*' (whereas each praetor present in the city had a separate sphere of activity, and hence his own pair of lictors, the consuls, as long as they remained in Rome, alternated monthly the power and all the twenty-four lictors assigned to them) – were not a surrogate police force, e.g. they never used their rods to disperse a crowd. They surrounded the magistrate as visible symbols of his supreme power; and they ceremoniously unfastened their rods at his order only to flog a culprit he had indicated, usually a person opposing his will (such, at least, was the theory; in practice, within the city, Roman citizens had long since been protected from arbitrary action of the magistrate). The symbolic role of the *fasces* and those who carried them manifested itself most spectacularly when the magistrate walked – on foot, as any other citizen – through the city. The lictors went in a single file before him and all save the Vestals were obliged to give way to them. Thus, when they were in an important urban thoroughfare, very narrow (the republican Sacra Via measured twenty feet in width, plus sidewalks) and crowded, a line of *fasces* appeared above people's heads, passers-by rushed sideways, pressed upon each other and against the walls of buildings, making an opening for the magistrate and his retinue. And vice versa: breaking up the *fasces* was the most ostentatious gesture of defiance to the magistrate and his authority.

The ancient city-state was the community of gods and men; hence civic ritual perforce included cultic elements. In Rome every politically significant act, every public address started with the office-holder's prayer (*precatio*) that the action he had in mind may prove to be advantageous to the Roman people. But the *Wunderwaffe* of the cultic apparatus of the Republic was the technique of public auspices through which the magistrate learned Jupiter's attitude to the action he was going to undertake.

The first purpose of the civic ritual *sensu largo* was to maintain the gods' goodwill towards the Republic (*pax deorum*). The crucial factor in producing this was the maintenance of communication between the divine and human element of the community through correct handling of divine signs (*signa*). The *signa* were divided into two main categories: *prodigia*, unsolicited signs sent by the gods to inform the community about the state of the *pax deorum*, and *auspicia* through which Jupiter expressed his opinion on public actions about to be undertaken or already begun. More important were the regular *auspicia impetrativa* (solicited), an almost exclusive domain of the magistrates. Before convening an assembly, starting a trial, departing to a province, engaging in battle, etc., the magistrate performed an *auspicium*, i.e. asked Jupiter whether he approved of the action being conducted that day; if the god said 'no', it was the magistrate's duty to postpone the action and try another day. *Auspicium oblativum* occurred when an unfavourable unsolicited *signum* was reported to the magistrate after his own propitious *auspicium impetrativum*, when the action for which he had taken the auspices was already in progress; it signified Jupiter's having withdrawn his approval for the action and led (or was supposed to lead) to its abandonment.

The prodigies kept the Romans informed about the gods' attitude towards the Republic, enabling them, when portents signalled that something had gone wrong, to take steps to appease the gods' wrath. But the auspices went one better: if carefully observed by the magistrates, everything in the Republic proceeded in accordance with the gods' will. The best illustration of the Romans' conviction that no politics worthy of the name were possible without auspices is their adoption by the tribunes of the plebs. In theory, the *auspicia populi Romani* were an exclusive preserve of the magistrates, like the *toga praetexta* and the *sella curulis*. But when the political prerogatives of the tribunes caught up with those of the magistrates *cum imperio*, the urge to adopt the auspices became irresistible on the part of the tribunes and, we can safely add, their plebeian constituency in general. By the end of the Republic we see the tribunes still contented with a simple toga and the lowly *subsellium*, but at the same time using (and being subject to) a whole range of auspical techniques.

Finally, a word about the senate, readily treated by ancient and modern writers as the ruling body of the Republic. Without wishing to get entangled in the hotly debated question of the nature and extent of its power, it suffices to note that officially and effectively it had no independent standing, being an advisory body of magistrates *cum imperio* and (possibly since the late third century BC) tribunes. Individually, the senators were members of the *populus* and, except for a handful of patricians, the plebs; as senators, they met at the summons of a magistrate or tribune in the place he had indicated to discuss matters he wanted to carry through himself or put to vote in an assembly; their recommendations (*senatusconsulta*) were addressed solely to him. This, together with the total lack of contact with the people and the closed and un-public, often outright confidential, character of its sessions (the senate met indoors, in the Curia, its old meeting-place in the Comitium, and in temples), the senate's ties to magistrates and tribunes rather than populace made its sessions a category apart among political activities, to which the notion of civic ritual (an open-air affair by its very nature) hardly applies.

The extent to which civic rituals were the essence of the community is expressed in the notion of *iustitium*, a cessation of all public business in the event of great calamity or other cause of grief. The ancients emphasized that whereas the Parthian Great King's mourning consisted in abstaining from feasting and hunting, the Romans did it by desisting from courts (Suetonius, *Caligula* 5).

PUBLIC SPACES

An indispensable feature of a public space was an elevated platform which served the presiding office-holder as his *tribunal*. If he was a magistrate, the platform had to be a *templum*, a place inaugurated (i.e. given the religious status of a *res sancta*) by the augurs, priestly experts on auspices; but the tribunes quickly started to run plebeian *contiones* and assemblies from *templa* as well. Apart from the *tribunal*, for *contiones* and sessions of public courts an open space to accommodate the audience sufficed; but places in which assemblies were held had to be arranged in a way that would account for the peculiarities of the Roman voting procedures, starting with the unique system of indirect voting. In order that the citizen body would be broken into a number of groupings at the moment of the vote, the subgroups of voters had to be physically isolated from one another. Another peculiarity was the technique of casting and counting the votes one by one, in stark contrast to the primitive Greek showing of hands and judging the results by eye. Queues of voters had to be channelled in a way that would prevent disorder and abuse.

All this was relatively easy to achieve in the extensive and largely empty Campus Martius. The voting space of the *comitia centuriata* was a huge rectangle (*c.* 310 x 120 m) enclosed by a fence of wooden boards, divided internally by wooden screens into a number of alleys which allowed simultaneous voting of a number of centuries – hence its name: Ovile ('sheepfold') or Saepta ('enclosures') – between, broadly speaking, today's Corso Vittorio Emanuele to the south, the Via del Seminario to the north, Via dei Cestari/Via della Minerva to the west and Via del Gesù to the east (see Figure 22.1). Since the reform of the *comitia* there were thirty-five or thirty-six alleys, one for each unit of *iuniores* and *seniores* of each class plus – possibly – one more for the *centuria inermis* voting with the particular class (like the *fabri* with the first or the *proletarii* with the fifth). The width of the alleys (*c.* 2.5 m) made it possible for several men to stand abreast; but since they voted one by one, they had to approach the spots where the votes were being taken in file. For this purpose the alleys ended in *pontes* (literally 'bridges'), wooden gangways slightly elevated above the ground. As long as the voting was oral, members of a unit walked up the *pons* to the *rogatores* ('those who ask'), officials who asked the voters the names of their candidates or their answer to the question put by the magistrate, and recorded the returns on tablets; with the introduction between 139 and 107 BC of the written ballot the voters indicated their choices on small tablets covered with wax, which were handed to them when they were entering the *pons*, and placed them in baskets or urns at its far end. Behind the *pontes* stood the *tribunal* (called *templum* to emphasize its being inaugurated, but also *pons*, which implies a wooden structure) from which the presiding magistrate (and, in electoral assemblies, the candidates) watched the progress of voting. Undoubtedly, with the written ballot a structure was set up close to the *templum* to sort and count votes (*diribitorium*, from *diribere*, 'to sort'), though our republican sources do not mention it. The Ovile was used only for voting; the

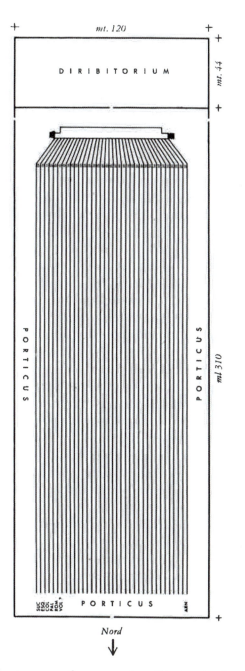

FIGURE 22.1 Saepta, proposed reconstruction of the interior for voting. Drawing by Lucos Cozza.

preliminary *contio* had to be held outside yet close by, possibly in the other civic area *par excellence* of the Campus Martius, the Villa Publica south and east of it. The Villa Publica was also used for gatherings of the *populus* for the purpose of taking the census, essentially a quinquennial review of the citizen body by the censors, who assigned citizens to appropriate centuries and tribes. The conclusion of the census was the ceremony of *lustrum*, the purification of the citizen body assembled in centuries by the Ara Martis (Altar of Mars) which stood either within the Villa Publica or next to it.

Within the *pomerium* voting assemblies were held in the Comitium and (plebeian assemblies only) in the *area Capitolina* in front of the temple of Jupiter Optimus Maximus on the Capitol. The *tribunal* of the Comitium, the Rostra (from ships' beaks (*rostra*) which adorned the structure), was situated between the latter and the Forum Romanum; in the *area Capitolina* the tribunes used as the *tribunal* the podium of the temple of Jupiter. Both areas were minute compared to the Ovile – the Comitium was a circle of *c.* 1600 m², the *area Capitolina* an irregular piazza of *c.* 3000 m² – which must have created considerable difficulties in any decently attended assembly. One way of coping with them was to call the tribes to vote one by one to a single precinct leading to one or several *pontes*, with the whole area divided by means of easily dismantled ropes; but since even this was not enough for electoral assemblies which attracted the greatest attendance, they were transferred to the Ovile, where all the tribes could vote simultaneously, which greatly simplified and sped up the proceedings. The electoral *comitia tributa*, presided over by the magistrates, probably moved there soon after the reform of centuries. The tribunes may have been more reluctant; the electoral *concilium plebis* in 133 BC, which led to the murder of Tiberius Gracchus, was still convened in the *area Capitolina* and, before being broken off, clearly took place with tribes voting in succession. But in that year there would have been many special reasons to hold the tribunician elections in the holiest place of Rome; and nine years later we find Tiberius' younger brother elected tribune in the Ovile.

The other solution was to move the assemblies to the Forum Romanum, much bigger than the Comitium (5000 m² or more), though always crowded with people engaged in non-political activities. It seems that it was used for *contiones* since the building of the Rostra (which probably faced the Forum, not the Comitium); in the first half of the second century BC an effective second *tribunal* was created on the opposite side of the Forum. But it was only in 145 BC that the tribune C. Licinius Crassus first held a *concilium plebis* in the central piazza of the Forum. Others quickly followed suit; in the first century BC it was the normal place of legislative assemblies, magisterial and tribunician.

Contiones could be convened anywhere, though their usual site was the civic centre of the Forum Romanum/Comitium/*area Capitolina*. Another public space often chosen for that purpose was the Circus Flaminius, once the southernmost part of the Campus Martius, created in 221/220 BC by the censor Gaius Flaminius. An empty area outside the *pomerium* (but within 1 mile of it and so accessible both for the tribunes and for the holders of military *imperium* who could not cross the *pomerium*, located very near the Porta Carmentalis through which triumphal processions entered the city, bordered by temples whose podia made excellent inaugurated *tribunalia*) was ideal to hold *contiones* in which generals in command, usually those waiting for a triumph, sometimes for a long time, could participate. In an emergency a *contio* could be held in the nearest inaugurated place commanding a large open area.

The original seat of jurisdiction was the Comitium, the site of the *tribunal* of the praetor, since 242 BC of the *praetor urbanus*, administering lawsuits between citizens. The *tribunal* of the *praetor peregrinus*, who took over lawsuits involving foreigners (*peregrini*), was surely located in the Forum, where trials by judicial assemblies or *ad hoc* judges or juries were commonly held with the exception of high treason cases judged by the *comitia centuriata*. Trials for crimes and serious public offences were gradually taken over by standing jury courts presided by praetors (*quaestiones perpetuae*), Forum-located as well. The first, for extortions, was established in 149 BC; two others were created before the end of the century. In 80 BC Sulla brought their number up to six, presided over by all the six praetors other than the *urbanus* and *peregrinus*, who were overloaded with private lawsuits. His reform and the subsequent rebuilding of the civic centre were probably the occasion when the urban praetors moved their *tribunal* to the Forum as well.

CIVIC ACTIVITIES IN THEIR URBAN SETTING DURING THE LATE REPUBLIC

Throughout the Republic, the civic life of the community was centred on the Forum Romanum/Comitium and the Capitol; it shifted to the Campus Martius only once a year, at the time of the elections. Until

Sulla the elections started a few weeks before the beginning of the magistrates' year (15 March till 154 BC, 1 January afterwards; the tribunes assumed office on 10 December), since 80 BC in July (i.e. in the hottest period of the year, but when the day is the longest). Before sunrise of the appointed day the consul (in the elections of lower office-holders the *praetor urbanus*) performed the auspices; in the morning the people were summoned by a herald to the Campus Martius (for the *comitia centuriata* by a trumpeter and the raising of a military standard at the outpost on the Ianiculum on the opposite side of the Tiber), where the president, after a prayer, solemnly asked the people to vote. In the *comitia centuriata* it started with the selection by lot of a *centuria praerogativa* ('first asked') of *iuniores* of the first class, which entered the Ovile and voted ahead of the others; after the announcement (*renuntiatio*) of its vote other centuries of *iuniores* went in and voted simultaneously, then those of *seniores*, then the equestrian centuries. Once their results had been announced, it was the turn of the second class; after the announcement of its vote, of the third; etc. The president announced the names of successful candidates as they reached the majority (ninety-seven centuries or eighteen tribes); when all the posts were filled, the assembly was dissolved. This meant that, had the upper classes been unanimous in their voting, the lower would not have had a chance to exercise their right to ballot; but this eventuality, according to theoreticians of the late Republic prevailing in the good old days, was but wishful thinking on their part. In practically all the consular elections about which we have some detailed knowledge, the struggle went on to the last centuries, or to sunset, when the voting had to stop. In the tribal electoral assemblies all tribes voted at the same time, with the lot deciding the order of announcing results.

With the elections over, the centre of gravity of the civic life returned to the Forum (see Map 22.2). At the beginning of the year consuls and praetors had to have their regal *imperium* formally conferred upon them by the *lex curiata*, a law passed in the Comitium by the assembly of thirty *curiae*, the oldest subdivisions of the Roman community, allegedly created by Romulus: a venerable fossil, with thirty lictors representing the *curiae*, always voting in the affirmative. Afterwards it was the customary whirlpool of *contiones*, sessions of courts, oath-taking by officials, letting out state contracts, etc., usually taking place simultaneously in various parts of the piazza, competing among themselves and with other activities for which the Forum served as the stage (shows, banquets, religious celebrations, funeral orations, triumphal processions, etc.) to attract the attention of the crowd. The most important, though

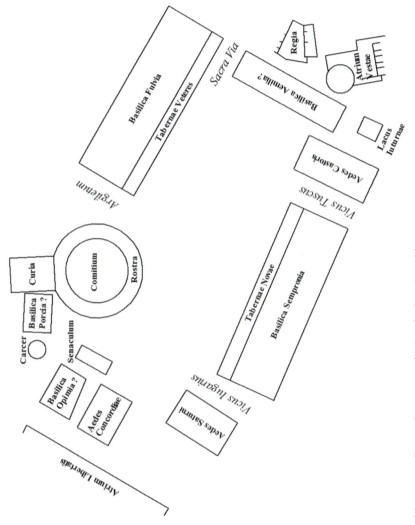

MAP 22.2 Forum Romanum during the late Republic.

not always the best attended (it seems that in this respect nothing could beat a good gladiatorial show), were legislative assemblies. They were also preceded by the president's *auspicia* and started with a *contio* in which after the prayer the draft of the proposed measure was read. The signal for the assembly *sensu stricto* was the bringing in of the urn for the lot to select the order in which the tribes went to vote. While the lots were being drawn, the crowd broke into tribal units. The tribes went into the voting area one by one, with the results announced once the counting of its vote was done. Unlike the electoral assemblies, the voting went on to the end, also after the majority had been reached.

Whereas nothing but a wholesale desertion of the audience could stop a *contio*, assemblies were subject to a number of procedures which could hinder their progress or annul their results. During the last century of the Republic a legislative assembly could be stopped by a personally delivered veto of a tribune of the plebs; but until the tribunate of Tiberius Gracchus in 133 BC there plainly existed safeguards which prevented its misuse. Tiberius himself found a way to nullify the obstinate veto of his colleague Marcus Octavius by putting forward a motion to deprive him of the tribunate, and even without this extreme measure, in later generations only those intercessions succeeded against stones and fists of determined voters which were backed by an adequate physical force. The state religion was more difficult to counter. Every assembly could be stopped by an *auspicium oblativum* endorsed by an augur present at the meeting; and in the last generations of the Republic we witness an auspicial technique of pure political obstruction: *de caelo servare* ('to watch the sky'), taking of auspices by a magistrate or a tribune the day for which another office-holder had convened an assembly. An unfavourable sign announced by the former to the latter automatically vitiated the procedure (hence the name of the technique: *obnuntiatio*, 'announcement against'); and if the president disregarded it, the results of the assembly could be annulled as carried through *contra auspicia*. Caesar, inventive and resolute, during his first consulate in 59 BC coped with this difficulty by surrounding the Forum, to which he had summoned the assembly to vote his furiously contested first land distribution bill, with squads which prevented the other consul and three tribunes from reaching the tribunal and delivering the *obnuntiatio*; and without the actual announcement, the signs they had seen (or pretended to have seen) had no value whatsoever. Others quickly learned the lesson: during the last decade of the 'free' republic political struggle lapsed time and again into fighting for physical control of both assembly-sites;

those who managed to occupy the Forum or the Ovile (preferably the night before the assembly) and hold it against their competitors, prevailed.

Probably the most spectacular public ritual, and certainly the most passionately sought-after honour, half-religious and half-military in nature, was the triumph – the procession of a victorious general and his soldiers, with leading prisoners and choice spoils on display, through the City to the Capitoline Temple, to thank Jupiter for victory – the only occasion in peacetime when armed men were permitted to cross the *pomerium*. The route of the procession – from the Porta Carmentalis to the Velabrum (a valley between the Capitol and the Palatine) and the Forum Boarium (Cattle Market), thence along the foot of the Palatine to the Sacra Via which brought it to the Capitol – marked with triumphal arches and temples built by generals from war-booty (*ex manubiis*), led through three chief areas of religious ceremonies: the Circus Maximus, the Forum Romanum and the Capitol itself. The triumphator, *ornatus Iovis* (attired as Jupiter) – seated in a *quadriga*, wearing a wreath and an embroidered toga, his face painted red and a sceptre in his hand – was plainly recreating to some extent the role of the god; this is why behind him stood a servant repeating: 'remember that you are mortal'. The soldiers who followed the chariot made similar apotropaic gestures: their ribald jokes and songs about the general were originally meant to allay the gods' displeasure at such an exaltation of a mortal.

Mention should also be made of a highly ritualized civic activity, in theory by private individuals, but in fact engaging even the highest magistrates, which went on all the time, in all sorts of public space – not only in the aforementioned 'political areas', but with equal intensity in streets, circuses and theatres: electioneering. In Cicero's day candidates for public office donned a snow-white *toga candida*, during or soon after the elections for the following year. Canvassing consisted essentially in the candidate's going around the city, surrounded by a suite (the bigger and more eminent the better, preferably including the consuls) of *deductores* (those who accompanied him on his way to the Forum) and *assectatores* (those who were always at his side), gripping the hands (*prensatio*) of passers-by and soliciting for their support. Dozens of groups of candidates with their suites forcing their way through the crowd down the Via Sacra, moving around the tribunals of the Forum, mixing with throngs of spectacle-goers, were one of the most characteristic features of the city's landscape all the year round.

ADAM ZIOLKOWSKI

CAESAR AND AUGUSTUS: THE TIME OF CHANGE

Judging by the phraseology of contending parties, the two decades of civil wars which sealed the doom of the free republic (49–30 BC) were one great struggle for liberty. In fact, the two generations from the elder Caesar's second dictatorship in 48 BC to the younger's death in AD 14 can be considered an interlude when various authoritarian arrangements (the fundamental aspect of which was the discretionary and secret character of decision-making) were being tried along with strict observance of traditional civic rituals. Of course, with the loss of freedom of speech, and especially with the effective emasculating of the tribunes of the plebs, *contiones* and *iudicia publica* became pale shadows of their republican selves, and the legislative assemblies – a mere formality. The electoral assemblies fared slightly better, at least under Augustus, who in 27 BC made relative freedom of election of magistrates an essential feature of his regime.

It was during that interlude that the place of electoral assemblies in the Campus Martius acquired a monumental aspect – almost as an illustration of that Parkinson's Law which states that perfection of design is attained only by institutions in decay. First to intend a remake of the wooden precinct of the old Ovile in marble was Caesar while still in Gaul. His plans were executed by Lepidus and completed by Agrippa, who in 26 BC dedicated the huge Saepta Iulia, flanked by two sumptuous porticos glittering with exotic marbles and works of art. The Diribitorium (see above), which closed the complex from the south, was completed fourteen years later, after Agrippa's death, most probably because of difficulties with finding the 100-feet-long tree-trunks which made up its roof, one of the architectonic wonders of the city. The other traditional area of civic rituals, the Forum and the Comitium, underwent a complete transformation. The latter practically vanished with the building of the Forum Iulium and the new senate-house, the Curia Iulia; the republican Rostra were abolished and their site became an open area in front of the Curia. The Forum, reduced in size by splendid new structures encroaching on it from all sides – the great new Rostra from the west, the temple of deified Caesar (Divus Iulius) and the second Rostra from the east, the huge basilicas from the south (Basilica Iulia) and north (Basilica Paulli) – and paved sumptuously with slabs of travertine, which covered underground shafts and galleries used for theatrical and gladiatorial shows, lost its last economic functions and ceased being a setting for spectacles. It remained the civic centre as the site of *contiones* and legislative assemblies, much less frequently summoned than before; but a good part of its judicial functions were transferred to the new 'imperial' fora: the Forum Iulium and the neighbouring Forum Augustum, or hidden in the basilicas (see below).

Deprived of so many functions, the Forum acquired a new one: that of the scenery of the public actions of the monarch. By virtue of his personal powers Augustus was empowered to convene *contiones* and assemblies; but the public activity which probably took up most of his time was dispensing justice. In Rome, it was a novelty: republican magistrates presided over jury courts or appointed judges, but themselves neither heard cases nor delivered verdicts. Since, however, in the ancients' conception, dispensing justice was the quintessential activity of a ruler, petitioners flocked already to the elder Caesar for judgment regardless of his official position. Augustus, too, so meticulous about the legal basis of his privileges and powers, administered justice without bothering about formalities.

The result of all these changes was the change of everyday life in the Forum: once vibrant with conflicting oratory of speakers and shouts and jeers of the crowd, it became tame and passive, or, in the phraseology of the new regime, more dignified (it remained, though, the centre of popular disturbances). With the gagging of the Forum-based traditional channels of dialogue between the populace and its leaders (now rather the ruled and their ruler) this vital role was progressively taken over by places of spectacle.

CIVIC CEREMONIAL UNDER THE EMPIRE

The Augustan formula for Rome – autocracy in a republican garb – in general lines outlived him by over two centuries. Yet already during his long reign the double process began whereby the apparatus inherited from the Republic shrank dramatically in scope and importance, supplanted, though not completely, by specifically imperial institutions and procedures which quickly acquired a ceremonial of their own. This process went hand in hand with the development of the city, which can be summarized as an effective marginalization of the traditional civic spaces of the Forum and the Ovile/Saepta, and a steady expansion of the imperial complexes north-east of the Forum, on the Palatine and in the Campus Martius.

Let us start with the republican heritage. The moment Augustus died, his successor Tiberius dealt a crushing blow to the traditional prerogatives of the citizens in general and the civic rituals in particular, by transferring the elections of magistrates and tribunes to the senate. In theory, the principle of popular choice stayed on; in practice the people's role was reduced to approving, *en bloc* and certainly by acclamation, the list of office-holders for a given year elected in the Curia. In this form the electoral assembly 'survived' to the early third century, and probably much longer. The Saepta Iulia remained an important mark on the map of Rome, but chiefly as a place of gladiatorial and acrobatic shows. Symptomatically, when the Diribitorium, now entirely useless in its primary role though occasionally used for theatrical performances, burned down in AD 80, no one bothered to replace its marvellous roof; it was left unroofed and the only trunk saved from the fire was displayed as a curiosity in the Saepta. A side-effect of depriving the people of its most important prerogative was the disappearance of public electioneering. In reality, canvassing for posts went on as before, but unobtrusively, in the antechambers of power and houses of influential power brokers.

The legislative assemblies soldiered on in their traditional form, yet ever less frequently. Augustus, who on the one hand made it a rule to present all his new regulations to the senate and promulgate them as *senatusconsulta*, on the other was very particular about having the more important among them validated as *leges*, with full ritual. His successors bothered less and less about such ratifications, in practice giving the *senatusconsulta* the force of laws. The legislative assemblies became not only a formality, but a dispensable one at that, except the *comitia tribuniciae potestatis*, which confirmed the *senatusconsultum* granting a new emperor his prerogatives. Apart from these so-called *leges de imperio*, the last known *lex* was the agrarian law of the emperor Nerva from AD 97 or 98.

Writers of the late first and second century AD still referred to the Forum as the centre of traditional judicial activities, but this was just a metaphor. In their days, only one public, i.e. open to general observation, activity of this kind was located there, more precisely in the Basilica Iulia: the centumviral courts, the longest-lived vestige of old procedures, presided over by a praetor and quoted as one of the last refuges of forensic oratory. Soon after Augustus' death almost all the criminal cases involving senators and more eminent members of the equestrian order vanished from public sight behind the doors of the Curia, taken over by the senate with the consuls as presidents, leading to the disappearance of the public courts for embezzlement, extortions and *lèse-majesté*. Other criminal courts gradually disappeared as well, supplanted by jurisdiction by new officials created under the empire, especially the prefect of the city (*praefectus urbi*). It is only logical to situate their courts in the imperial fora, in the post-Augustan Templum Pacis and Forum Traiani rather than in the already crowded Forum Iulium and the Forum Augustum. Apparently, the *tribunal* of the *praetor urbanus* moved out of the Forum as well: the only explicit post-republican report we have situates it in the Forum Augustum.

The Forum Romanum was left to the emperor in his most republican persona: as a super-magistrate of sorts treating with the *populus*. The legislative assemblies have already been mentioned; as for *contiones*, our sources make it clear that addressing the people from the Rostra was a regular activity of an emperor, on a par with speeches in the senate. The lasting role of the Forum as the political centre is underscored in the last attempt of the members of Piso's conspiracy against Nero in AD 65 to turn the scales even after the disclosure of the plot by asking Piso to go to the Rostra and call the citizens – the news of important events invariably brought great crowds to the piazza – to fight the tyrant (Tacitus, *Annales* 15.59.1). Another kind of imperial activities with the Forum as the setting – celebrating major moments of a reign – also had a republican tradition behind it. Carrying the dead to the Forum before burial and delivering from the Rostra speeches in their praise had been an old privilege of Roman nobles, now monopolized by emperors and their families, with the celebrations of Augustus' funeral as the precedent.

Jurisdiction, an emperor's most time-consuming public activity, though long administered principally in the Forum, was not bound to one place (like the traditional courts) and could be exercised anywhere. A remark by Cassius Dio shows that by the reign of Hadrian the Forum had acquired competitors: 'he ... adjudicated with the help of leading men, now in the Palace [or 'on the Palatine'], now in the Forum or the Pantheon, and in many other places, on a *tribunal* to make his acts public' (Cassius Dio 69.7.1). Most significant is the mention of the official imperial residence on the Palatine, already in its relatively modest Augustan phase referred to by the name of the hill (*palatium*). The notion of the residence of the ruler as a public place was slow to emerge. Augustus' house acquired the official status of a *publicum* in several stages between 36 BC and AD 3 on exclusively religious grounds, and the only public (if not strictly civic) actions that took place therein during his reign were frequent sessions of the senate in the 'domestic' temple of Apollo Actius. The complex of imperial palaces, which under Domitianus embraced the whole Palatine, was formally made accessible to the Roman people (only in part, no doubt) by Nerva under the name of *aedes publicae* (public complex). We do not know where exactly in the palace Hadrian held court; but we hear that Septimius Severus used for this purpose a hall called Auditorium.

The private and public character of imperial residences resulted in the once strictly private custom of *salutatio* – a formal morning call paid by a client on his patron – becoming a quasi-public ritual, with the vestibule and the open space before the main entrance to the Palace (Area Palatina) serving as a waiting-area for crowds wishing to greet the ruler (or present him with a petition). Another old custom that became a great official celebration, which engaged most of the state officials and attracted enormous crowds of spectators, was an emperor's entry into the city after a long absence (*adventus*), often little different from a triumph.

Civic and civic-like rituals, and public places in which they were celebrated (those mentioned above and frequent extraordinary acts, like periodical burning by the emperors of record of debts to the state in the Forum Traiani, the most magnificent piece of architecture and urban design in Rome before the building of the present Saint Peter's), were just a part of the year-round ceremonial of the community of the master people, from the first citizen to the last, with the whole of the Campus Martius and the city's centre as its scenery. Other rites – religious ceremonies and especially shows: equestrian, gladiatorial, theatrical – were as good or better a setting for regular contacts between the emperor and the *plebs urbana*, the representative of the ever growing millions of Roman citizens. In view of the centrality of this relationship the mid-third century AD, when the emperors moved permanently from Rome to the empire's embattled frontiers, marked the end of an era. When 100 years later Ammianus Marcellinus, Jerome, Augustine and others give us a view of the Rome of their day, the picture is not that of the capital of the world, but of a sanctuary to two idle and pretentious classes collectively known as *senatus populusque Romanus*. In this sanctuary many old civic rituals certainly survived – e.g. the continuance of the early imperial system of office-holders suggests continuing twofold elections by the senate and the people well into Late Antiquity – but only as interesting relics.

FURTHER READING

On Roman political institutions Mommsen 1887–8 remains irreplace-able; so does, on assemblies, Taylor 1966. The standard reference book on the city's topography is now *LTUR*; for discussion of the topography and functions of Rome's public spaces in historical context, see monographs by Coarelli 1983, 1985, 1989 and 1997. An analysis of the working of the court of the urban praetor is in Frier 1985. The many aspects of public auspices are treated in Linderski 1986. On the working of the Republic in general and the role of the Forum as the central stage of Roman politics, see Millar 1984, 1986, 1989 and 1998. Civic rituals and public space as aspects of the urban reality are examined by Purcell 1994 and 1996. On the emperor's position in the public life of Rome, see Millar 1977.

23: POLICING AND SECURITY

Benjamin Kelly

In a city like Rome, whatever level of security of person and property existed must have been achieved through a variety of mechanisms, many of them invisible and unconscious. In a multitude of sophisticated ways, psychological inhibitions to the formation of criminal designs would have been created and reinforced. Various methods of surveillance and supervision are likely to have restrained those who still formed such intentions. Earlier chapters of this volume have discussed these subtle ways in which social control and public order would have been maintained: relevant here are institutions such as the family, slavery, patronage, *collegia*, as well as the authorities' attempts to guarantee basic needs such as food and water. But in most societies, such mechanisms of control are never entirely successful. Casual references suggest that Rome was no different, even though nothing precise can be said about levels or patterns of 'crime' (either in the sense of acts regarded as punishable by the law or of acts seen as serious wrongs by society at large).[1] In Rome, awareness of crime led to conscious attempts to restrain criminality, and to apprehend and punish those who committed crimes. This chapter discusses the question of how the state, community and individual tried to cope with threats to person and property at this conscious level.

THE IDEA OF PUBLIC ORDER

Earlier generations of scholars often approached this question with the assumption that all civilized societies need professional, specialist police forces, and sometimes manipulated the evidence to try to find one in

---

[1] E.g. Martial, *Liber spectaculorum* 9(7); Pliny, *Epistulae* 3.14.6–8; Pliny, *Historia Naturalis* 19.59; Suetonius, *Aug.* 43, Tacitus, *Ann.* 4.22, 13.44, 14.42. On crime in Rome generally, see Robinson 1992, 204–6; Ménard 2001. On legal and lay definitions of 'crime', see Harries 2007, 1–11.

Rome.[2] There has quite rightly been a reaction against this approach, with scholars stressing that such police forces were exceptionally rare before the nineteenth century. It is a far from universal expectation that the state should provide agents to carry out 'policing' – that is, to do such things as patrolling the city to deter offenders and catch them red-handed, hunting down criminals after the fact, and assisting the courts with the detention, prosecution and punishment of offenders.[3] It is conceivable that the manpower resources at the disposal of the authorities in Rome were intended simply to deal with political threats. However, in literary accounts of riots during the Principate there are signs of an underlying assumption that state agents should repress riots in Rome and elsewhere, whether political in origin or not. From the period of the Principate, there is evidence of the idea that the imperial authorities did or should take steps to ensure public order throughout the empire.[4] This is seen, for instance, in Epictetus' statement that 'Caesar appears to provide us with great peace, there are no longer any wars, or battles, or large-scale banditry, or piracy, but at every hour it is possible to travel the roads, or sail from the rising to the setting sun' (Arrianus, *Epicteti Dissertationes* 3.13.9–10). There is no reason to think that the imperial authorities were expected to keep order in the empire at large, but not in Rome itself. Indeed, Augustus acted on this expectation by posting guards around the city during public spectacles to prevent muggers from taking advantage of the deserted streets to prey on the few people not attending the spectacle (Suetonius, *Augustus* 43). Two centuries later, the jurist Ulpian stressed the urban prefect's duties in relation to public order in the city, writing that 'it seems the peace of the populace and good order of the games are responsibilities that fall to the urban prefect; and he should even have soldiers on policing duties (*milites stationarii*) dispersed around to guard the peace of the populace and to report back to him what is being done and where' (*Digesta* 1.12.1.12).

The expectations lying behind these statements are also reflected in discussions in the ancient sources about what various types of official should or did do in relation to petty criminality. Such statements are good evidence for mentalities, even if not for what really happened.

[2] E.g., Hirschfeld 1913, 576–91; Echols 1958; Freis 1967, 41, 44.

[3] Nippel 1984, 20; 1988, 7–9; 1995, 2–3, 113–18; Sablayrolles 2001, 130.

[4] Riots: Kelly 2007, 156–60. Order throughout the empire: Brélaz 2005, 26–39. For examples of the authorities acting on these expectations: Appian, *Bell. Civ.* 5.132; Suetonius, *Aug.* 32; *Tib.* 37.

The sources assume that, during the Republic and early Principate, the aediles, amongst their many other duties, had the task of supervising markets and baths, as well as having coercive powers which included the exaction of fines. There was also a board of three minor magistrates, the *tresviri capitales*, many of whose duties could be called police duties. They oversaw the prison and the executions carried out there (*Dig.* 1.2.2.30). Plautus also assumes that they rounded up escaped slaves during their nightly patrols. The ancient sources take it for granted that the *tresviri* exercised some form of criminal jurisdiction, or at least the power to carry out preliminary inquiries. One text also states that the *tresviri* had the task of investigating crimes, although just what this investigative activity was meant to involve is quite unclear.[5]

The early years of the Principate saw the establishment of urban and praetorian cohorts, as well as the *vigiles*, a paramilitary force that conducted night patrols and extinguished fires. The prefects in charge of these three new forces were vested with criminal jurisdictions at various stages. The jurist Paulus states that the *praefectus vigilum* ('prefect of the *vigiles*') can hand out minor corporal punishments to those negligent in relation to fires, and that he has criminal jurisdiction over 'arsonists, burglars, thieves, robbers, and those who harbour them', provided they are not serious or notorious offenders, in which case the praetorian prefect has jurisdiction (*Dig.* 1.15.3.1). An imperial rescript imposed on the *praefectus vigilum* a positive duty to seek out escaped slaves and return them to their owners (*Dig.* 1.15.4; cf. Paulus, *Sententiae* 1.6a.6). Various inscriptions also suggest that the ranks of the *vigiles* (and also of the urban cohorts) included officials with tasks connected with the arrest, interrogation and incarceration of suspects.[6] The jurisdictional competence of the *praefectus vigilum* and the penal infrastructure evidently put at the disposal of the *cohortes vigilum* seem to be best explained by the assumption that the *vigiles* were expected to apprehend various types of criminals during their nocturnal patrols.

Something similar can be said of the urban cohorts. The juristic sources assign the urban prefect a wide-ranging jurisdiction over matters including theft, the fraudulent administration of trusts, forged wills, sharp practice in markets, dishonesty on the part of bankers

---

5   Aediles: Plautus, *Rud.* 372–3; Seneca, *De vita beata* 7.3, *Epist.* 86.10; Tacitus, *Ann.* 13.28; Varro ap. A. Gellius, *Noct. Att.* 13.13.4; cf. Martial, *Epigr.* 5.84. *Tresviri capitales*: Cascione 1999, esp. 85–117, 157–60 (on jurisdiction); Lintott 1999, 102 (on rounding up escaped slaves); Varro, *De lingua Latina* 5.81 (on investigative functions).
6   Robinson 1992, 191–4; Sablayrolles 1996, 225–6, 232.

and money changers, unlawful *collegia*, adultery, offences by freedmen against masters and cruelty to slaves.[7] By the early-third century, Ulpian was able to write that the urban prefect had jurisdiction of 'absolutely all crimes' (*Dig.* 1.12.1). In a discussion of Augustus' establishment of the urban prefecture as a permanent office, Tacitus claims that the emperor was motivated by a desire to have an official 'to keep the slaves in order, and that part of the citizens that would be reckless and turbulent unless it feared force' (Tacitus, *Annales* 6.11). The urban prefect can hardly have been expected to do all of these things in person: it must have been assumed that he would use the impressive manpower resources at his disposal to assist him. The wide-ranging statement of Ulpian quoted above certainly takes it for granted that the prefect would use his troops for surveillance and the repression of general criminality.

'POLICING' AND THE STATE

The idea that state agents should have a role in repressing minor criminality was certainly present, especially during the Principate, at least in the minds of some members of the governing elite. This raises two questions: to what extent did these ideas result in effective action; and what reaction did the state's attempts at policing provoke amongst ordinary people in Rome? These questions are to a certain extent interrelated: effective policing relies to a large extent on community cooperation; and the efficiency and honesty of a police force will in turn shape the community's perception of it. Answering these questions is made difficult by the fact that the sources contain virtually no cases showing state agents policing mundane criminality. There are some reports of soldiers keeping order at public spectacles and repressing riots, and a few Christian martyr-acts depict the urban prefect and his cohorts persecuting Christians.[8] But there are no reports of actual cases in which they dealt with more mundane crimes like burglary, theft or assault. Some progress can be made, however, by considering the structural features of the 'policing' institutions of the city.

The first relevant fact is that, during the Republic, and also during the early fourth century, sheer lack of manpower must have hindered

---

[7] Freis 1967, 45; Mantovani 1988; Robinson 1992, 190–1.
[8] Spectacles: Cassius Dio 61.8.3; Tacitus, *Ann.* 13.24–5. Riots: Cassius Dio 73.13.4, 74.13.4; Herodian 1.12.6–9; [Seneca] *Oct.* 780–855; *Historia Augusta, Didius Iulianus* 4.6; Tacitus, *Ann.* 12.43, 14.45, 14.61. Christians: Freis 1967, 23–8 for references.

the state's attempts at policing. During the Republic, the lack of a standing army and the taboo on exercising military command within the *pomerium* meant that any 'policing' was left up to civilian officials (Aulus Gellius 15.27.5). In the late Republic, there were only four aediles and three *tresviri capitales* at any one time. Both the aediles and the *tresviri capitales* were probably accompanied by a few burly attendants (Plautus, *Amphitruo* 153–62; Varro ap. Aulus Gellius, *Noctes Atticae* 13.13.4), but a few dozen men cannot have had much of an impact on regulating mundane criminality in the late republican city, with its population pushing into the hundreds of thousands. The establishment in the early Principate of the *vigiles* and the praetorian and urban cohorts represented an impressive increase in the manpower resources potentially at the disposal of the state for policing duties. Precision is difficult, but the numbers of men in these cohorts probably fluctuated between around 10,000 in the first century to something over 20,000 in the early third. There are signs, however, of a significant reduction in military manpower in Rome under Diocletian. The praetorians were then completely disbanded soon after the battle of the Mulvian Bridge in AD 312, and the urban cohorts and *vigiles* also disappeared in the course of the fourth century.[9] We hear that when Flavius Leontius, urban prefect in AD 355–6, quelled a riot, he used his attendants (*apparitores*) to do so, presumably lacking the military manpower that his predecessors had once enjoyed (Ammianus Marcellinus 15.7.2).

Second, none of these military or paramilitary bodies was in any sense a specialist police force. During the Republic, the *tresviri capitales* had another major claim on their time and energy: the organization of fire prevention measures (*Dig.* 1.15.1). In the Principate, the *vigiles* took over this task, and the demands of detecting and fighting fires must have dramatically reduced the manpower available for their policing duties. For their part, the praetorians were involved in ensuring the security of the person of the emperor, even when he was outside the city. Members of the praetorian cohorts were at times deployed outside the city on other tasks as well. In Rome, they were also involved in the collection of various taxes introduced by Caligula on litigation, foodstuffs and trades such as prostitution. As for the urban cohorts, we know that in the

---

[9] Inhibitions to military policing during the Republic: Nippel 1984, 20; Sablayrolles 2001, 129–30. The size of the military and paramilitary forces during the Principate: Freis 1967, 36–42; Panciera 1993, 262; Coulston 2000, 81. Disappearance of these forces in the fourth century: Durry 1938, 393–4; Freis 1967, 19–22; Sablayrolles 1996, 59–65.

fourth century at least they had some role in the collection of customs duties at the gates of the city.[10]

Then there is the question of how we should imagine the city population's interactions with these institutions. One relevant factor here is surely the absence of serious mechanisms of accountability. Suggestive is the situation in Rome in the second half of the sixteenth century. In that period, there was a police force organized along military lines, provided by the papal state. There were attempts to regulate police conduct, but these were largely nugatory, to the point that the city population loathed the police force, thanks to its heavy-handed, violent and extortionate behaviour. The hostility of the population then served to undermine effective policing further.[11] In ancient Rome, there are no signs of any police accountability mechanisms at all. Victims of improper conduct by soldiers in Rome would have had little chance of obtaining redress through the courts. Juvenal complains that grievances against soldiers were heard in the military camp, with soldiers acting as judge and jury, and it is plausible that court cases involving soldiers really were heard in the camp by military judges. True, the praetorian and urban cohorts were under military discipline, but the disciplinary standards of the Roman army were hardly known for ensuring that soldiers treated civilians with integrity. We hear, for instance, that after the great fire of AD 64, soldiers of the praetorian and urban cohorts and the *vigiles* took to looting the city rather than safeguarding law and order. In second-century Carthage, the soldiers posted there on policing duties seem to have run extortion rackets, demanding money from pickpockets, bath-thieves, gamesters, and Christians in return for protection from prosecution or other forms of harassment.[12] One suspects that, in the absence of safeguards, similar problems would have been encountered in Rome.

The sources certainly contain signs of friction and alienation between civilians and the various military and paramilitary bodies

---

[10] Manpower limitations of the *vigiles*: Rainbird 1986, 151; Nippel 1995, 96–7. External deployment of praetorians: Durry 1938, 274–80; Passerini 1939, 191–6. Praetorians and tax collection: Suetonius *Cal.* 40; McGinn 1998, 256–64. Urban cohorts and customs duties: *Codex Theodosianus* 4.13.3 = *Codex Iustinianus* 4.61.5; Freis 1967, 46.

[11] Blastenbrei 2006.

[12] Cases heard in military camps: Juvenal 16.7–34; Campbell 1984, 251–2, 431. Looting in AD 64: Cassius Dio 62.17.1, cf. Tacitus, *Ann.* 15.38. Extortion by soldiers in Carthage: Tertullian, *De fuga in persecutione* 13; McGinn 1998, 260–1.

stationed in the city.[13] On various occasions during the third century, crowds are said to have attacked the praetorians, and vice versa.[14]
Epictetus also stated that soldiers in Rome would act as *agents provoca-
teurs*, tempting people to make disloyal statements about the emperor
and then arresting them (Arrianus, *Epict. diss.* 4.13.5), a practice that
cannot have inspired civilian confidence in the city's military forces.
Studies of the epigraphic evidence have suggested a certain social distance between civilians and urban soldiers and *vigiles*. For soldiers stationed in Rome, rates of family formation were low, no doubt in
part thanks to the ban on the marriage of soldiers in the period from
Augustus to Septimius Severus. When urban soldiers did marry or
take concubines, these tended to be of fairly low social origin. And
there is scant sign of other forms of social contact: for instance, there
is a striking absence of dedications set up by soldiers and civilians in
cooperation.[15]

COMMUNITY 'SELF-POLICING'?

Thus, factors such as a lack of manpower and proper specialization,
as well as a distant or downright hostile relationship with the city
community, are likely to have seriously retarded the effectiveness of
'policing' institutions in the city. The total lack of known cases of
state agents carrying out acts of policing in relation to petty crimes
is consistent with this conclusion. The question then arises of just
how social control and personal security were achieved. One suggestion that has been urged very strongly is that the community essentially policed itself. There is evidence for a range of rituals dating back
into Rome's earliest history according to which individuals and groups
expressed disapproval using methods which ranged from defamatory
songs through to fully fledged lynchings. Some scholars, impressed
by the apparent similarity between these rituals and collective rituals
of disapproval in more recent European societies such as *charivari* and

---

[13] *Pace* Sablayrolles 1997, there is no evidence that the *vigiles* were regarded as figures
of sympathy who were part of the conviviality of Roman street life. Neither their
portrayal as inept buffoons nor their nickname proves anything (Petronius, *Sat.*
78; Tertullian, *Apologeticus pro Christianis* 39). Buffoons need not be likeable, nor
nicknames affectionate.
[14] Cassius Dio 80.2.3; Herodian 2.4.1, 7.11.6–12.7; *Hist. Aug., Maximini* 20.6.
[15] Panciera 1993; Sablayrolles 1996, 396–406.

Katzenmusik, have seen these as examples of the city community polic-ing itself.[16]

The Law of the Twelve Tables (mid-fifth century BC) apparently threatened capital punishment 'if anyone should chant (*occentavisset*) or write a song which brings infamy or ill repute (*flagitium*) to another'. The verb *occentare* has been taken to be part of the language of pop-ular justice, referring to rabble-rousing chanting before a wrongdoer's house. In reality, the word is so archaic that its meaning is impossible to recover with clarity. The resonances of *flagitium* are clearer: there is an etymological connection between *flagitium* ('ill repute'), and *flagrare* ('to burn') and *flagellare* ('to flog'), suggesting that originally this ritual included the flogging of the target or the burning of his or her house. Closely related too was *flagitatio*, the practice of demanding property with shouts. This could be done before a house or in some other pub-lic place, like the forum. Two other practices are also usually grouped under the rubric of 'popular justice'. One is *squalor*, the act of going around in public with shabby clothing and dishevelled hair as a way of casting odium on someone who had committed a supposed wrong. The second was the practice of people who were in the process of being robbed or attacked calling on the assistance of neighbours and passers-by. In this connection, the sources usually mention the formula *implorare Quiritum fidem* ('to call upon the good faith of the citizens') or similar. The sources for the Principate mention a variant on this, depicting people calling on the good faith (*fides*) of the emperor, either in person, or in the form of his image or statue.[17]

These rituals of popular justice are most vividly attested in Plautus. In the *Mostellaria*, the money-lender Misargyrides, who has lent money to the prodigal Athenian youth Philolaches, approaches the youth's slave in public. The money lender engages in *flagitatio*, demanding the payment of interest owed (Plautus, *Mostellaria* 603–5). Another relevant scene occurs in the *Rudens*, when two freeborn women, who had been captured by pirates and sold to a pimp, seek refuge in a temple. The pimp tries to drag them out, but a slave friendly to the women calls on the *fides* of the people of Cyrene, and various men in the vicinity duly come to their aid (Plautus, *Rudens* 615–26). But the problem with Plautus,

---

[16] Veyne 1983, esp. 12–25; Nippel 1995, 39–46; Krause 2004, 61–2; Ménard 2004, 10, 71, 118.
[17] *Occentare*: XII Tab. 8.1; Usener 1913, 359–60; Rives 2002, 283–4. *Flagitatio*: Usener 1913, 360–73; Lintott 1999, 9–10. *Squalor*: Lintott 1999, 16–21. *Fidem implorare*: Lintott 1999, 11–16.

as ever, lies in knowing just how his fictional world, influenced by its Greek models, correlated with the actual realities of the city of Rome in his day. It is clear enough from the existence of a technical Latin vocabulary of *flagitatio*, and also from the mention of these phenomena in the Twelve Tables, that these were ancient Roman practices. Yet it is far from clear that the representation of these institutions in Plautus reflects what was happening on the streets of Rome in 200 BC. And even if Plautus is describing what happened in the Rome of his day, these scenes cannot be assumed to represent routine practices in the cosmopolis of AD 200.

Indeed, when we look at the so-called rituals of popular justice in the cold light of history, the case for community self-policing starts to look weak. Even if we take at face value all the reports of concrete cases of this sort of behaviour in the city of Rome, there are still not very many. Moreover, most of these are essentially political protests. There are very few non-political cases, only one of which could be called a 'popular justice' response to a homicide (Seneca, *De clementia* 1.15.1), and none of which is a reaction to a mundane crime such as a theft or assault.[18] Nor can cases of political protest carried out according to traditions of 'popular justice' be taken as evidence of contemporary communal responses to mundane criminality. Such political protests could well have been self-consciously archaizing, with acts of verbal protest and political violence being implicitly legitimated by traditions about methods of plebeian agitation and self-help in the early Republic.

But perhaps it is too much to demand concrete cases. Scholars who have argued for the role of 'popular justice' in day-to-day social regulation have also pointed to the various passages, mostly in works of poetry or fiction, containing generalized references to supposed popular justice practices, or fictitious situations involving these rituals. In Catullus 42, the poet calls upon his poems to encircle a certain woman and demand back the tablets on which they are written, which she has supposedly stolen – in other words, to engage in *flagitatio*. To take

---

[18] Political protests: Appian, *Bell. Civ.* 1.32–3, 1.54; Ammianus Marcellinus 27.3.8; Asconius 93 C; Cicero, *De domo sua* 14, *Epistulae ad familiares* 1.5b.1, *De lege agraria* 2.13, *Epistulae ad Quintum Fratrem* 2.3.2, 2.11.1; Cassius Dio 50.10.2, 55.27.1–3, frag. 95.3; Diodorus Siculus 36.16; Florus 2.4; Livy, *Periochae* 74; Plutarch, *Pompey* 48; Suetonius, *Caesar* 80, 85, *Aug.* 55, *Gaius* 27, *Nero* 39, 45, *Domitian* 14; Tacitus, *Ann.* 1.72, 4.28–9, 6.39, 14.42–5, 15.49; Valerius Maximus 9.7.4. Non-political cases: Cato ap. A. Gellius, *Noct. Att.* 17.6.1; A. Gellius, *Noct. Att.* 4.5; Pliny, *Hist. Nat.* 10.121–3; Seneca, *Clem.* 1.15.1; Statius, *Silvae* 1.2.26–30; Tacitus, *Ann.* 3.36; Valerius Maximus 7.8.5.

another example, in the *Satyricon* Encolpius claims that when set upon and forced to perform unspeakable acts by Quartilla and her two lusty maids, he attempted *invocare Quiritum fidem* ('to appeal to the good faith of the citizens'). But these could be taken as light-hearted allusions to quaint practices that endured in cultural memory, even though they did not often occur in the streets of Rome in the time of Catullus or Petronius. It is also true that several classical jurists hold that 'popular justice' practices, including *flagitatio* and *squalor*, could give rise to an action for personal insult (*iniuria*).[19] Yet it is dangerous to assume a situation was common simply on the basis that it was discussed by the jurists.

Even if we can convince ourselves on the basis of these various types of evidence that the customs of 'popular justice' were still widespread in the late Republic and Principate, it does not follow that they contributed much to public order and social regulation. For one thing, both the 'real' and the imaginary cases were not really instances in which a clear collective consciousness was outraged. Rather, they were attempts to negotiate ethical problems whose solution was unclear and contested. Take, for instance, the case reported by Seneca, in which a member of the equestrian order flogged his own son to death. Members of the *populus* (including both fathers and sons) waylaid him in the forum and stabbed him with styluses. Augustus barely managed to rescue him by appearing in person (Seneca, *Clem.* 1.15.1). There was, however, a belief that fathers had the legal right to kill their own children. This belief was possibly a myth sustained by the rhetorical strategies of authoritarian fathers trying to resist threats to their authority from other family members. But if it was a myth, it was one in which many Romans believed.[20] The outraged crowd in the forum was thus not enforcing a clearly defined norm, but rather taking a stance on a morally and legally murky issue. The crowd's sense of right and wrong was not indicative of the collective morality of the community at large, but merely of the moral feeling of the members of that particular crowd. So we should not see rituals such as *flagitatio*, *squalor* and lynching as tools for the enforcement of defined norms, but rather as tactics designed to enforce a particular view in a disputed case. The same applies *a fortiori* in political cases.

There is also a class dynamic visible in various concrete cases such as the near lynching of the member of the equestrian order by members of the *populus*, and also in Tacitus' report that in AD 21 various low-status people (including slaves and freedmen) had been shielding

---

[19] *Dig.* 47.10.15.2–10, 27; Gaius, *Institutiones* 3.220.   [20] Shaw 2001, 56–77.

themselves behind portraits of the emperor to cast odium on people of reputation.[21] These tactics were also used to try to redress other power imbalances, and negotiate a variety of social tensions, including those between male and female, young and old, and patron and client. For example, we hear of a second-century BC case in which a woman lent money to her husband. When the marriage soured, she instructed a slave to follow the man around demanding the money back (Cato Maior ap. A. Gellius, *Noctes Atticae* 17.6.1). We can perhaps read this case as one in which *flagitatio* was used as a tactic in a marital dispute, and was prompted by the woman's realization of the difficulties that she would face suing her own husband. These were not, therefore, occasions on which the whole community would spontaneously rally together to stigmatize and punish a deviant. Rather, they were used by a section of society, often to pursue sectional interests, or by individuals to pursue individual interests.

Nor did these rituals necessarily function as methods of orderly dispute resolution: indeed, they were sometimes themselves potentially a threat to public order. An inscription from Cnidos shows Augustus reproaching that city for failing to check a man who had been coming by night before a house and engaging in a sort of *flagitatio*: the emperor says that this behaviour had threatened the safety of the whole community (Sherk *RDGE* no. 67). In the emperor's mind, therefore, there was a close connection between nocturnal protests before someone's house and large-scale disorders. A legal compilation dating to around AD 300 also assumes that the singing of defamatory songs was a threat to public order (*disciplina publica*) (Paulus, *Sent.* 5.4.15). And one suspects that this fear was well founded: the goal of rituals such as *flagitatio* was to gather bystanders and inflame their disapproval. It probably was not a large step from that to a genuinely riotous situation. Particularly during the strife of the late Republic, these ancient traditions were in fact appropriated by organizers of mobs to legitimate political violence.[22]

The rituals of collective disapproval, should, therefore, be seen as something more complex and dangerous than the mechanism by which a community policed itself in the absence of an effective state police force. In fact, they might have threatened public order more often than they maintained it. The attested cases look more like tactics in disputes that revealed structural tensions in society. Cases of straightforward

---

[21] Tacitus, *Ann.* 3.36. See too [Quintilian] *Declamationes minores* 364; Seneca the Elder, *Contr.* 10.1; Tacitus, *Ann.* 4.28–9.
[22] Lintott 1999, 6–21.

crimes like thefts, assaults and murders being treated in this way are rare to non-existent. Community 'self-policing' is unlikely to have been much of a factor in controlling mundane criminality.

SELF-DEFENCE

One is left with the problem of how people managed to achieve basic security of person and property in a city without an effective police force, and in which the rituals of collective action were as likely to threaten public order as to preserve it. The answer might be that order simply was not kept – that levels of crime and violence were far higher than would be considered acceptable in most modern cities. Alternatively, it could be that the more subtle mechanisms of social control mentioned above were relatively successful at limiting crime, rendering explicit attempts by state and community to combat crime largely otiose. We simply lack the statistical evidence needed to choose between these scenarios. But casual references certainly suggest a belief that the city was not crime-free, and for protection against such crime as did exist, what must have really mattered were not the state's efforts at 'policing', or the community's willingness to 'police' itself, but individuals' capacities to protect themselves. In this regard, classical Rome would have been no different from most pre-modern European cities. In sixteenth-century Rome, for instance, the rich travelled the streets with armed retainers and people of all classes went around 'armed to their teeth' with weapons including sticks, daggers, swords and wheellock pistols.[23] They felt the need to be so armed in spite of the fact that for most people the carrying of weapons was illegal – so great was their fear of the lawless streets.

In classical Rome, lawyers and legislators recognized the grim reality that citizens had to defend themselves. Roman law permitted the use of lethal force not only to protect one's person from attack, but also to protect one's household from thieves (both daytime and nocturnal).[24] This need for self-protection is illuminated by the elder Pliny's statement that members of the plebs living in apartments had been forced to give up their window box gardens and block up their windows as a result of a terrible outbreak of violent burglary (*Hist. Nat.*

---

[23] Individual's role in self-protection in classical Rome: Nippel 1995, 97; Sablayrolles 2001, 130; Krause 2004, 46–7. Sixteenth-century Rome: Blastenbrei 2006, 86.

[24] *XII Tab.* 8.12–13; *Collatio* 7.2.1, 7.3.2–3; *Dig.* 9.2.5 pr., 48.8.9; Macrobius, *Saturnalia* 1.4.19.

19.59). Even if the belief in a crime wave was merely a moral panic, the popular response is still interesting. The people did not clamour for more police or form vigilante squads: they boarded up their windows and hoped for the best.

The need to take private measures for one's own security is attested in a mass of incidental detail in the sources. Consider first the aristocratic urban house. It is true that in the aristocratic house public and private space were conflated, since clients and others were permitted entry to some rooms (Vitruvius, *De architectura* 6.5.1–2). Yet it was entry very much on the owner's terms. Literary descriptions assume that houses presented strong, closed doors to the street. A passage in Ovid suggests that windows facing the street tended to be high and inaccessible (*Ars Amatoria* 2.244–6), and the remains of houses in Ostia and Pompeii tend to confirm this. The doors of the great house might be opened for the morning *salutatio*, but several casual comments suggest that, at least during the Principate, doormen would control entrance even during this ritual (Martialis, *Epigr.* 5.22; Seneca, *De constantia sapientis* 14.1–2). And texts from both the Republic and the Principate suggest that at other times of the day and night doors were shut, and doormen firmly in control of who came in. Seneca assumes that doormen would be armed with large sticks to help repel unwanted visitors (*Const.* 14.2).

When the proprietor of an aristocratic house (or his or her family) moved around the city, it would sometimes be in the presence of a retinue. We hear of the great politicians of the late Republic moving around with retinues of supporters and clients (e.g. Sempronius Asellio ap. Aulus Gellius, *Noct. Att.* 2.13.4). Even when political violence was not at issue, there are signs that the rich sometimes moved around with attendants. In his third satire, Juvenal imagines that a nocturnal bully looking for a brawl will avoid the man who passes by in a scarlet cloak with a long column of attendants carrying torches and lamps (3.282–5; cf. Propertius 2.29a). The literary and epigraphic records also attest the use of litter bearers (*lecticarii*), who by definition were strong men likely to deter any street crime against their charges. Suggestive here is the epitaph of a certain Iucundus, a *lecticarius* for a member of the aristocratic house of the Statilii Tauri, which boasts that 'as long as he lived, he was a man and defended himself and others' (*CIL* 6.6308). In fourth-century Rome, these practices continued: Ammianus complains both about those who pass through the streets of the city 'without fear of danger', accompanied by huge retinues of slaves, and about women who travel the city in closed litters (Ammianus Marcellinus 14.6.16–17, 28.4.8). The children of the great households would also be accompanied by *paidagogoi* as they walked the streets. These attendants had multiple functions, but one was to keep their charges safe (e.g. Appian, *Bellum Civile* 4.30).

It would be a mistake, of course, to assume that every time a high-status person trod the streets, he or she was accompanied by a bevy of bodyguards. But the evidence does suggest that people with the necessary resources could employ a range of techniques to keep themselves safe. Wealth and social status, in other words, would have been the only true guarantors of security. The poor could give up their window-box gardens and block their windows, but one needed to be a slave owner or have access to other types of dependants to be truly safe on the streets, especially at night. Finally, when attempts at self-defence failed and one became a crime victim, self-help was relevant in another sense. From the late Republic onward there were various standing criminal courts available in which crimes against person and property could be tried. In the absence of public prosecutors, it fell to private individuals to bring prosecutions. Social position and wealth were again very relevant here, since they afforded access to legal advice and representation, the manpower physically to bring a criminal into court,[25] not to mention a chance of being taken seriously by judges and jurymen who would be members of the elite. In this second sense, therefore, social status was relevant to self-help against criminals.

CONCLUSIONS

Although some members of the Roman elite believed that the state should have a role in ensuring security of person and property, it is unlikely that the soldiers and officials entrusted with this task were terribly successful. Nor is there much evidence of genuine 'self-policing' by the urban community, especially during the Principate. Rather it would have been for individuals to keep themselves and their property safe as best they could. This conclusion is, of course, a matter of emphasis. It would be rash to claim that the *vigiles* never managed to round up a thief in the streets at night, or that angry neighbours never lynched a murderer. Rather, what I suggest is that individuals' security was probably more the result of their own efforts than those of the state or the community. And I particularly think that we should abandon the cosy communitarian notion that rituals like *flagitatio* ensured the

---

[25] Krause 2004, 64.

enforcement of some collective consensus. When it came to security, as with so many basic necessities of life, the city of Rome must have been a profoundly differentiated and unequal society.

FURTHER READING

Any further reading should begin with Nippel 1984; 1995. These works collect the relevant ancient evidence, and offer an analysis that takes the study of Roman policing to a new level of sophistication. Also fundamental for the Republic is Lintott 1999, 89-106, which analyses policing institutions and provides an assessment of their role that is perhaps somewhat less understated than that offered by Nippel 1984 and 1995. Lintott also discusses the archaic traditions of 'popular justice' and their role in legitimating the political violence of the late Republic (1999, 6–21). Fuhrmann 2012 offers a thorough discussion of policing institutions during the Principate, not only those in Rome but also those in Italy and the provinces. Harries 2007 discusses the structure of the criminal courts of the late Republic and Principate, and the construction of 'crime' in lay and legal discourses.

24: Riots

Gregory S. Aldrete

The inhabitants of ancient Rome seem to have been a riotous lot. For the 575-year period from 200 BC to AD 375, there were at least 154 episodes of unruly collective behaviour in the city of Rome that could be considered riots (an overall frequency of 1 riot every 3.7 years). Even in the often sketchy accounts offered by the primary sources, the overwhelming majority of these incidents (72 per cent) involved physical violence, and many (25 per cent) were serious enough that one or more people were reported as having been killed.[1] The worst of these could result in pitched battles in the streets, hundreds of deaths, widespread looting, acts of arson and even the lynching of leading magistrates of the state. These alarming bare facts have often led to stereotypes in which Rome and ancient cities in general are characterized as lawless and violent places, and their inhabitants, especially the poor, are portrayed as disorderly, fickle and brutish louts perpetually looking for an excuse to explode into an uncontrolled frenzy of urban violence. The reality of riots in ancient Rome, however, is considerably more complex. Many outbreaks, including some of the most destructive, were organized, instigated and exploited not by the indigent, but rather by Rome's political and social elites. Furthermore, acts of violent urban collective behaviour often occurred within the constraints of a tacit but nevertheless well-recognized set of informal societal norms. For the purposes of this chapter, a riot will be defined as a type of urban collective action utilizing violence or the threat of violence in order to obtain a goal, express a grievance, or make known an opinion.

Any discussion of riots or public order in ancient Rome must begin with a reminder that the city did not possess anything resembling

---

[1] These percentages are almost certainly too low given that the primary sources often do not give any details whatsoever of the riot, but merely state that one took place. Space limitations preclude offering the ever-growing list of Roman riots and accompanying citations here, but I hope to include the full list in a future publication on this topic.

a modern police force, whose purpose is to maintain public order, protect the populace, and deter, apprehend and punish criminals.[2] During the Republic, urban concerns (including keeping general order in the city) were the responsibility of the *aediles* and other minor officials; however, they lacked effective means of enforcement. Complicating matters during this era was the prohibition on military forces within the boundaries of the city; thus the most obvious recourse for quelling riots, calling in the troops, was unavailable. The situation changed somewhat during the empire, when a number of military units, including the praetorian cohorts, the urban cohorts and the *vigiles*, were established at Rome. None of these groups, however, was explicitly tasked with quelling rioting. Nevertheless, by the beginning of the second century AD, there were some 15,000–20,000 members of various military or paramilitary groups permanently stationed in the city of Rome who, at least in theory, might be used to suppress riots.

FREQUENCY AND HISTORICAL OVERVIEW

While one can calculate an overall frequency of roughly one riot every four years for the period of 200 BC to AD 375, this is a misleading statistic since the actual distribution of riots was extremely sporadic. Some of this effect is probably due simply to the relative richness or scarcity of the sources; in well-documented periods, we are more likely to hear of every riot that occurred, whereas for eras with sketchy sources, riots may have gone unrecorded. Nevertheless, while we know of some intermittent riots scattered throughout the third and second centuries BC, the pace of rioting does seem to have increased substantially during the turbulent period of the late Republic. From 133 BC to 70 BC, there were some eighteen riots; then rioting reached a dramatic peak in the 60s and 50s BC. Indeed, nearly half the known examples (73 out of 154) date to this brief but particularly unstable time during the city's history. Large-scale urban violence became endemic in this era largely because factions, and especially individual politicians, organized armed gangs composed of their slaves, freedmen and clients as well as hired thugs, and employed them to intimidate their enemies and to disrupt speeches, trials and public meetings. Skirmishes among these groups frequently resulted in riots, as did their attempts to interrupt

---

[2] On policing Rome and keeping public order, see Nippel 1995, and Chapter 23.

or influence the outcome of public proceedings. The sort of violence incited by these figures was far greater than could be suppressed by the existing system and traditional methods such as senatorial appeals. The riots of this period are somewhat atypical in that, unlike the usual model of urban rioting in which riots are sparked by the poor or the politically or socially disenfranchised, the instigators of most of the riots of the late Republic were men from the very highest social, political and economic strata of society.

The early Roman empire was also a comparatively riot-prone era, with thirty-five riots dating to between 31 BC and AD 96 (a still impressive rate of one every 3.6 years). From these figures, it is clear that the mere presence of new military detachments in Rome, such as the Praetorian Guard, was not sufficient to deter riots. As power shifted from senate to emperor, both the nature and the setting of riots likewise shifted. In the late Republic, most riots had been instigated or manipulated by elites for their own purposes, and the space in which these most commonly occurred was the Roman Forum. In the early empire, the typical riot became a request from or protest by the urban plebs directed towards the emperor, and the most common setting became an urban ritual or public entertainment. During the late Republic, a well-established tradition of the urban plebs making known their feelings about prominent figures or government policies in the theatre or at public entertainments had already existed, and this trend intensified under the empire, with the circus becoming a familiar setting for such demonstrations. At these specific places and times, a tacit agreement and expectation arose that the emperors would tolerate a range of behaviour and criticism that would not normally be allowed. While the majority of these interactions between ruler and ruled were relatively non-violent, they did on occasion become more acrimonious, and theatre or circus demonstrations were a frequent flashpoint for riots in this period.

Accounts of riots virtually disappear from the primary sources for the second century AD, whether due to the increased military presence, the relative economic prosperity or the benign rule of the Antonine emperors. With the political instability of the third century AD, however, riots in the city again turn up in the sources with some regularity, a trend that continues into the fourth century AD (twelve riots over 175 years, a rate of one every fourteen years). By this point, the emperors appear to have grown less tolerant of protests, and in riots of the later empire, the emperors were particularly quick to summon the military and crush them. Accordingly, the accounts of riots during this era include a number of pitched battles in the streets between soldiers and civilians and high casualty figures.

Overall, then, was Rome a particularly riotous city? Even if one discounts the glut of riots during the 50s and 60s BC as an aberration, Rome still averaged an impressive one riot every 6.6 years for the rest of the period between 200 BC and AD 375 (81 riots over the remaining 555 years). How does the frequency of riots at Rome compare to that of other cities of the time? Riots were by no means unique to Rome, and examples exist from other cities in Italy and throughout the Roman empire. Rioting in other cities was often provoked by economic concerns, but it could be initiated by a wide range of causes. The famous riot of AD 59 in Pompeii, for example, which began in the amphitheatre during a gladiatorial contest and resulted in many deaths, seems to have stemmed from nothing more than intra-city enmity between partisans of Pompeii and those of the rival town of Nuceria. The sheer size of Rome makes it difficult to compare with other cities, but one such possible point of comparison is with the great metropolis of Alexandria. In the primary sources, Alexandria was routinely denigrated as being a particularly unruly city, and this characterization has often been echoed by modern scholars. However, an actual analysis of known Alexandrian riots between 30 BC and AD 215 reveals only sixteen incidents, yielding an average frequency of just one riot every fifteen years – far less than the rate of riots at Rome in almost every period.[3] While this impression is, as always, subject to the vagaries of the surviving sources, it does seem fairly safe to say that Rome was indeed an especially riot-prone city, and that this characteristic is likely linked both to its unusual size and to its peculiar status as the political capital of an empire and the home (at least for most of this period) of those who ruled over it.

CAUSES OF RIOTS

Historically, some of the most common provocations for riots are famine, taxation and resentment over real or imagined injustices, and ancient Rome experienced riots that had their roots in all of these causes. Food shortages in particular were a recurrent source of tension in the city.[4] Rome's unprecedented size of around 1 million inhabitants by

---

[3] Barry 1993.

[4] On food riots see Garnsey 1988 and Erdkamp 2002. On the food supply system for Rome generally and associated problems, see Chapters 13–17 in this book.

the early empire posed an enormous logistical problem that was solved only through the importation of food on a massive scale. Maintaining a sufficient food supply for Rome was viewed as one of the central concerns of the state, and failure to do so quickly aroused the wrath of the city's inhabitants. Since it seems that this responsibility included not only taking steps to ensure that enough food reached Rome but also guaranteeing that the price was affordable, ancient Rome could be seen as having a 'moral economy' analogous with that proposed by E. P. Thompson and others for early modern England.[5] The dangers of neglecting the provisioning of the city were readily acknowledged by ancient authors. Seneca, for example, offers a frightening image of the volatile atmosphere that would develop in the city if Rome's rulers did not ensure an adequate food supply: 'a hungry people neither listens to reason, nor is appeased by justice, nor is bent by any entreaty' (*De brevitate vitae* 18.5). He asserts that such a situation can only lead to 'the city's destruction and famine, and the general revolution that follows famine' and warns that 'those in charge of the grain market will be faced with stones, sword and fire' (*Brev. Vit.* 18.5–6). Not surprisingly, given the scale of the system, the vagaries of ancient agriculture and the difficulties with transport, there were many times when the system broke down, resulting in shortages. On at least nineteen occasions, famine, or the fear of famine, was so severe that riots broke out at Rome (BC: 75, 67 (twice), 57 (twice), 41, 40, 38, 22; AD: 6, 7, 19, 32, 51, 68, 189, 356, 359, 364). It did not require actual starvation to provoke a food riot; shortages or simply a threat to the food supply could incite a violent response. Surely the angry crowd that famously pelted Claudius with bread crusts in the Roman Forum in AD 51 cannot actually have been suffering from starvation or they would not have chosen such missiles, however stale they might have been (Suetonius, *Claudius* 18.2).

Another frequent provocation for urban riots is economic concerns, especially resentment over debt laws, the imposition of a new tax, or simply anger over an existing one that is perceived as being too high or somehow unjust. For example, a series of debt riots occurred in 48 BC (Cassius Dio 42.29–32), a new tax on freedmen sparked violent protests not just in Rome but all over Italy in 31 BC (Cassius Dio 50.10.3–4), and circus crowds petitioned Caligula for relief from excessive taxation (Josephus, *Antiquitates Judaicae* 19.24–6).

---

[5] The 'moral economy' concept has spawned substantial debate beginning with the publication of Thompson 1971. For bibliography on this debate and with specific reference to its applicability for ancient Rome, see Erdkamp 2002.

By far the most frequent cause of riots during the Republic was politics, with disputes over elections and laws proving especially volatile sparks to urban violence. Unruly behaviour among candidates and their partisans was already disrupting elections as early as 185 BC (Livy 39.32.10–13), and these sorts of disturbances quickly grew in frequency and violence during the last century of the Republic. By the 70s BC, nearly every election was accompanied with riots and fighting among rival political gangs, as exemplified by the ongoing feud between Clodius and Milo and their respective patrons and supporters during the 50s BC. This intense spate of urban violence culminated in the death of Clodius during one scuffle, and the subsequent trial of Milo. Over the course of these events, there were multiple riots, open warfare in the streets among organized armed gangs of several hundred per side, burning and looting of houses, and many deaths. Relative order was restored only by Pompey bringing in his soldiers and effectively establishing military rule.

During the early empire, political concerns continued to be a source of urban unrest. During the reign of Augustus alone, violence over the election of magistrates broke out in 21 BC, 19 BC, and AD 7 (Cassius Dio 54.6.2; 54.10.1; 55.34.2). Even after the people lost their formal vote, they continued to express political opinions through protests and riots in favour of or against political appointments. Unpopular praetorian prefects were frequent targets of this sort of demonstration. Public invective was aimed at Sejanus (Cassius Dio 58.11.3–4), Tigellinus (Plutarch, *Galba* 17.4), and Cleander (Cassius Dio 72.13.1–6; Herodian 1.12–13), and in each case, the emperor ultimately ordered the prefect's execution. Through riots for or against potential candidates, the urban plebs of Rome often became involved in disputes over the imperial succession, especially at moments when the succession was unclear or during periods of actual civil war. This happened in AD 41 following the death of Caligula (Cassius Dio 58.11.1–5, 12.1), in AD 68 and 69 after the death of Nero (Suetonius, *Nero* 45; Cassius Dio 64.19–20; Tacitus, *Historiae* 1.81, 3.70–5, 3.80–4.1), and in AD 193 (Cassius Dio 74.13.3–5; Herodian 2.7.2–3; *Historia Augusta, Didius Julianus* 4.2–5), 196 (Cassius Dio 75.4.2–5), 238 (Herodian 7.7.3; *Historia Augusta, Gordianus* 13.6) and 308 (Herodian 7.10.5–9, 7.11.6–12.7) during various civil wars over the succession.

The plebs also felt entitled to give violent expression to their opinions about more personal decisions made by the emperors, as when Nero's declaration that he would divorce Octavia so that he could marry

Poppaea caused mobs to storm the Capitol and destroy statues of Poppaea (Tacitus, *Annales* 14.59–62). Rarer were apparently spontaneous demonstrations of the Roman people sparked by what they perceived as some kind of injustice. An interesting example of this type happened in AD 61 when the city prefect was murdered by one of his slaves and, as prescribed by ancient tradition, all the rest of his many slaves were also sentenced to death (Tacitus, *Ann.* 14.42–5). Supposedly the people were so moved by the planned execution of such a large number of innocents that they spontaneously gathered outside the senate-house and called for the pardon of the doomed slaves. When the sentence of execution was confirmed, the mob threatened the senate with torches and stones. Their efforts were fruitless, however, as Nero enforced the order, using overwhelming military force to restrain the crowd.

CHARACTERISTIC BEHAVIOUR AND SYMBOLIC ACTIONS

Urban rioters of all historical eras tend to engage in a fairly standard set of behaviours: they stage marches (often from one space of symbolic significance to another); they chant slogans (both advocating their cause and denigrating their opponents); they perform petty acts of vandalism (for example, smashing windows, doors, street signs, etc.); they loot stores and houses of valuable objects (or, in food riots, of basic staples); they make threats through symbolic actions (described in more detail below); they skirmish with rival gangs or mobs (or sometimes are content with mutual displays of intimidation); they threaten hated individuals with violence (and, occasionally, actually lynch them); they set fires (a more serious action that often provokes a response from the authorities); and finally, they attack or are attacked by representatives of the government (such as police, soldiers or militia). These behaviours are all familiar enough to require little further elaboration. The one type of behaviour that deserves special discussion, however, is symbolic actions, since many of these are specific to the Roman context.

The Romans' penchant for festooning their public spaces with a dense forest of commemorative statuary offered a fertile environment for symbolic actions. These statues often became the focal point for urban unrest, and a number of riots culminated in the pulling down of or attack upon the statue of a hated public figure. Thus, in 55 BC, statues of Pompey were stoned by an angry crowd (Plutarch, *Cato Minor* 43.1–5); in 40 BC, statues of Mark Antony and Octavian were

smashed during food riots (Cassius Dio 48.31.5); in AD 20, statues of
Piso were destroyed by a mob blaming him for the death of Germanicus
(Tacitus, *Ann.* 3.14); in AD 31, a mob calling for the arrest of Sejanus
attacked his statues (Cassius Dio 58.11.3–4); in AD 62, statues of Poppaea
were smashed (Tacitus, *Ann.* 14.59–61); and after the deaths of the
unpopular emperors Caligula in AD 41 (Cassius Dio 58.11.1–5, 12.1),
Domitian in AD 96 (Suetonius, *Domitian* 23.1) and Maximinius Thrax
in AD 238 (Herodian 7.7.3; *Historia Augusta, Gordian* 13.6), their statues
were pulled down by mobs (or in the case of Domitian, by senators).
Crowds might also express their hatred for an individual by attacking his
house, a symbol closely associated with his identity. This was a popular
type of behaviour during the late Republic, when Cicero, his brother
Quintus, Milo, Lepidus and the assassins of Julius Caesar all had their
houses burnt or damaged by vengeful mobs. A similar displacement of
hostility felt for a group being directed against its 'home' can be seen in
the burning or threatened burning of the senate-house, as happened in
44 BC and 56 BC. This type of behaviour did not end with the Republic –
as late as AD 364 and 365, enraged crowds are attested as having burnt
down the houses of the city prefects (Ammianus Marcellinus 27.3.4,
8–9).

In all of these instances of crowds destroying statues, houses and
fasces, the crowd is directing its hostility against an inanimate object as
a way of threatening or warning an individual. Oddly enough, these
then are really examples of rioters showing restraint, since they are
deliberately substituting a lesser act of violence (attacking or destroying
an object) for a greater one (attacking or killing a person). The implied
threat, however, is clear – act as the crowd wishes, or the next attack
may be directed against the person himself.

Another symbolic mob action was to break the *fasces* held by the
lictors of a particular magistrate as a way of indicating displeasure with
him or suggesting that his authority or acts were illegitimate. In 67 BC
at a public meeting concerning the *Lex Cornelia*, the consul Piso was
stoned and had his *fasces* broken by a mob (Cassius Dio 36.39.3); in 59
BC at an assembly, the consul Bibulus had his *fasces* broken and suffered
the further indignity of having a bucket of excrement dumped over his
head (Cassius Dio 38.6.3; Plutarch, *Cat. Min.* 32.2); and the next year,
Pompey's lictors had their *fasces* broken by some of Clodius' followers
(Cassius Dio 38.30.2).

There are a number of additional instances of symbolic actions by
Roman rioters. One interesting example involves a crowd protesting
against a legal process perceived as being corrupt. In 58 BC, at the

trial of Vatinius, rioters disrupted the proceedings and destroyed the voting urns and the seats of the judges (Cicero, *In Vatinium* 33–4, *Pro Sestio* 135). Selecting the urns and seats for destruction was plainly a symbolic statement that the rioters felt the legal process to be unfair. Another action with an unmistakable symbolic message was performed by the members of the crowd during the food riot of AD 51 who pelted Claudius with stale bread crusts. One of the standard behaviours of crowds was to engage in the stoning of public figures, and the crowd on this occasion appears to have substituted a less violent (but very appropriate) alternative missile as a warning to the emperor that he was expected to ensure an adequate supply of grain for the city.

LEADERSHIP AND ORGANIZATION

While it is relatively easy to assemble a list of riots in ancient Rome and perhaps even to speak of different categories of riots and types of riotous behaviours, it is much more difficult to analyse issues of leadership, organization and participation. Did these riots have leaders, and if so, how did they mobilize their supporters or instigate the riot? Who took part in such events, and what were their motivations? As usual, one of the greatest problems is the nature of and biases in the available sources, which are uniformly written from an elite perspective. Such sources tend to indulge in unhelpful stereotypes of the inhabitants of Rome, especially the poor, as being gullible, fickle, and congenitally prone to irrational violence. Here it becomes necessary to distinguish between spontaneous riots and those that have been planned. Some riots are truly spontaneous and arise unexpectedly from a random incident, but many, if not most, of ancient Rome's riots were set in motion or planned by a group or individual. We will look first at this latter type of riot and the means by which one could intentionally provoke a riot and even guide its course.

Fortunately, with some of Rome's riots, it is quite easy to identify the core leaders and participants. This is especially the case for many of the political riots of the late Republic. For these, we have contemporary sources that identify leaders, followers and motivation. One example is a food riot of 57 BC initiated by Clodius in which he attempted to scapegoat Cicero for the high grain prices (Cicero, *Epistulae ad Atticum* 4.1.6–7, *De domo sua* 6–7, 10–16, *Epist. ad familiares* 5.17.2; Cassius Dio 39.9.2–3). Clodius instructed the members of his gang to spread out through the city at night, mobilize the urban plebs, stir up their resentment over high food prices and direct it against Cicero. In the morning, Clodius led the angry crowd, spearheaded by an armed group of his own followers and slaves, to the Capitol, and threatened the senate. Clodius' lieutenants instigated stone throwing, and then the crowd, again prompted by Clodius' gang, began chanting anti-Cicero slogans. Even though some aspects of this event may have been spontaneous, and while it eventually involved large numbers of ordinary citizens, Clodius and his followers can nevertheless be seen at every step provoking and controlling events. Clodius' men agitate and mobilize the plebs during the night, they act as the leaders of the march and, by virtue of their arms, lend it menace, they instigate the stoning of the senate, and they act as claque-leaders to encourage and direct the hostile chants of the crowd. The identity of some of the actual participants is even hinted at in one source that specifically refers to one of Clodius' lieutenants, a certain Sergius, as 'an agitator of shopkeepers' (Cicero, *Dom.*13).

Rome's *collegia*, or professional organizations, also offered fertile ground for organizing riots and recruiting participants, and this potential probably accounts for the authorities' periodic attempts to ban or restrict these organizations. Violence prompted by the tribune Manilius' proposal in 67 BC to distribute the votes of freedmen over all the tribes was an example of a riot in which the *collegia* were probably used to mobilize the populace (Asconius 45, 65C; Cassius Dio 36.42.1–36.43.2; Livy, *Periochae* 100). The riot broke out at the festival of the Compitalia, which was itself staged by *collegia*, and the audience at the festival was heavily composed of freedmen, slaves and *collegia* members who had the most to benefit from the proposed legislation. Before the festival began, Manilius had probably coordinated with some of the *collegia* to initiate the riot, and once it had begun, the natural audience of the festival would have been receptive to its aims.

PARTICIPATION

By calling upon their slaves, freedmen, clients, household servants and guards, prominent politicians could readily summon a decent-sized group of followers who could act as the core group to instigate or respond to a riot. This natural nucleus of rioters was often supplemented by hired professionals. To provide a tough contingent of fighters if things turned really violent, thugs trained in the use of weapons were often hired. Typically, these were drawn from the ranks of current and former gladiators as well as ex-soldiers. Even in incidents such as those described above where there was a primary group of participants, however, the organizers were still counting on large numbers of additional people joining in.

This raises one of the trickiest and most debated issues among historians and sociologists who study riots: Why do ordinarily law-abiding bystanders going about their daily lives abruptly and voluntarily transform themselves into violent rioters on the spur of the moment? The apparent ease with which this routinely happens has led to much speculation (often from an elitist perspective and with a pejorative tone) about the 'madness of crowds', 'the contagion of the mob', 'the herd instinct' and 'the group mind'. While the classism and racism that influenced some of these studies have been discredited, whether due to biology or culture, there is nevertheless a strong allure to being one of the group. Furthermore, as a member of a group, one attains an undeniable power and anonymity that facilitate otherwise atypical behaviour. These impulses can be readily exploited by those who hope to instigate a protest or riot, and there is ample evidence of such attempts to manipulate crowds in ancient Rome.

A first precondition necessary for a riot is that the cause or provocation must be one that a sufficient number of random bystanders will agree or sympathize with to such an extent that they themselves will join the rioters. This precondition has important ramifications for those hoping to spark a riot. The riot must occur in a public space where large numbers of people will be present, and furthermore where a sizeable percentage of those same people are likely to be sympathetic to the grievance or cause of the rioters. This at least partially explains why so many riots began in the Roman Forum and at gatherings such as festivals, theatrical performances and public entertainments. By choosing the specific location and the situation, initiators of riots could also hope to maximize the chances that certain groups who might be in accord with their aims would be present. Such was clearly the case in the example of the Compitalia cited above, in which Manilius chose a venue where he could count on a large audience of like-minded spectators.

Therefore, if one is planning a riot, one must begin by mobilizing as large a contingent of one's friends and supporters as possible in order to provide a core group of rioters. Then, one must select a physical space and a time for the riot that will offer the best chance that large numbers of sympathetic bystanders will be present who might be induced to join the riot. If the cause were one that had widespread support, then the ranks of the rioters would naturally swell, but even in cases where the bystanders were neutral, they might still participate in order to be part of the group action. The readiness of spectators to join in when those around them are applauding or chanting is familiar to anyone who has attended modern sporting events such as soccer or football games. This desire to be a part of collective action is nicely illustrated by an ancient example: a partisan of Piso was easily able to prompt a crowd in Carthage to join him in passionately chanting pro-Pisonian slogans even when, as Tacitus notes, they had no real knowledge of the political situation or, presumably, any actual allegiance to Piso (Tacitus, *Hist.* 4.49).

While the instigator of the demonstration in this example was merely an enthusiastic amateur, ancient Rome possessed actual professionals who could be hired to stir up the emotions of a crowd and direct it towards desired verbal or non-verbal collective actions. Such men, who were known as claque leaders, seem to have evolved in the theatre, where an actor or theatre owner could hire them to blend into the crowd and initiate applause for a performance. The goal of such men was to prompt as enthusiastic a crowd response as possible, but yet to make it appear a completely spontaneous reaction. Thus, the best claquers were those whose manipulation of the crowd went unnoticed. Given the importance during the late Republic accorded to the reception that prominent politicians received from the audience when they appeared at public venues, the techniques of the theatrical claque leader were soon copied by politicians, who organized their own claques to manipulate audience reactions. In the food riot of 57 BC mentioned above, Clodius' men are explicitly described as acting as claque leaders initiating chants against Cicero, both stirring up and directing the emotions of the crowd for the desired effect. Instances of claque manipulation of crowds at riots abound in the primary sources, and include examples where the claquers were not followers of a politician but rather were simply hired opportunists. At games after the assassination of Julius Caesar, a group 'hired for that purpose' shouted for Brutus and Cassius to be recalled (Appian, *Bellum civile* 3.24). The profession of claque leader continued into the empire, and their activities are described in some detail by Pliny the Younger, who labels them *laudiceni*, literally 'those who applaud for their dinners' (*Epistulae* 2.14.4–8). Pliny reports how these men brazenly hang around the law courts and sell their services to one orator after another. For a fee, 'seats can be filled, a huge crowd assembled, and endless cheering raised'.

Such claque leaders are certainly not unique to ancient Rome. One of the more celebrated later instances of claque leaders occurred in France during the early 1800s, when such men were employed at various theatrical and musical venues, including the Paris Opera, in order to whip up acclaim for the performers or, in some instances, to provoke opprobrium. So confident were these men of their ability to spark the desired crowd reaction that they routinely presented their employers with a price list of options ranging from inciting 'ordinary applause' for the modest sum of 5 francs to guaranteeing 'unlimited curtain calls' for a fee of 50 francs. On the negative side, they could offer that the performers would be deluged with 'sneers, laughter and other indications of disapproval'. One group of claquers formally organized and sold their services under the name L'Assurance des Succès Dramatiques.[6]

Professional claquers would have provided those who were planning a riot with a convenient source of individuals skilled in manipulating crowds and provoking their behaviour. The ready adaptability of the techniques of claque leader to initiating riots is illustrated by the Antioch riots of AD 387, in which the instigators of the riot are identified as professional theatre claquers (Libanius, *Orationes* 19.28, 20.3, 46.17; John Chrysostom, *De Stat.* 2.3, 3.1, 5.3, 6.1, 17.2). Further illustrating the applicability of theatrical claquing to inciting riots is Tacitus' account of a man named Percennius, who early in his life during the reign of Augustus made a living as a theatrical claquer, and eventually ended up as a disaffected Roman legionary in Pannonia (*Ann.* 1.16). After the death of the emperor, it is Percennius who is credited with having stirred up the soldiers to mutiny by employing precisely the same techniques that he had honed in the theatre. Tacitus describes him as being able to play systematically upon the soldiers' resentment, finally bringing them to 'a frenzied pitch of rebellion' by virtue of 'his experience gained in stage rivalries which had taught him the art of inflaming an audience'.

While it is possible to discern the intent and organization behind many riots, particularly those of the late Republic, there are others that seem to be truly spontaneous outbreaks stemming from popular feeling. While these riots may not have been planned, they do almost always originate in a specific precipitating incident. Such moments, sometimes termed 'flashpoints', typically occur when long-standing resentments are finally brought to a boil by a trigger event, often trivial in nature, resulting in a riot.[7] The famous riot which broke out during Mark Antony's funeral oration for Caesar, which culminated

---

[6] Cohen 1998, 136.   [7] Waddington et al. 1989.

in the impromptu cremation of Caesar's body in the Forum and the destruction of the Curia, may have been of this type. The crowd was already simmering with anger against Caesar's assassins, so that Antony's provocative oratory coupled with inflammatory visual displays, such as a gory wax effigy emphasizing Caesar's wounds, acted as the 'flashpoint' which sparked the riot.

CONCLUSION: THE COMPLEXITY AND UTILITY OF RIOTS

One of the main problems that makes riots such a slippery phenomenon to study is the seeming contradiction that while almost every riot, whether planned or spontaneous, originates from a specific impetus, much of the behaviour during a riot, and many of the participants themselves, may not actually be motivated by the instigating cause. There is no doubt that some riots are precipitated by very large numbers of people sharing a common purpose, and thus issues of motivation, leadership and participation can be analysed in a fairly straightforward manner. Collective behaviour is a complex phenomenon, however, and in reality many – perhaps most – riots are more amorphous in how they develop and play out. Consider a hypothetical example in which a riot might be initiated by a distinct group of several dozen individuals with a specific political grievance whose predetermined goal is to march to the house of a political opponent and throw stones at it. In the general street confusion that ensues, however, a number of opportunistic individuals might join the crowd, break into nearby shops and loot them for personal economic gain. Another bystander might take advantage of the situation to exact personal revenge by beating up or even killing a neighbour with whom he had a feud. Still others, caught up in the atmosphere of chaos, might begin to set fires, eventually burning down an entire neighbourhood. When soldiers show up and attempt to disperse the crowd, all of these groups, together with other hitherto uninvolved bystanders who harbour a general resentment against authority, join together to fight with the soldiers, resulting in yet more injuries, deaths and destruction of property. Thus, what was intended as a minor political protest grows into a large-scale riot involving hundreds or even thousands of individuals, widespread acts of looting, vandalism, violence and arson, and numerous injuries and deaths – yet none of these effects were the intended result of the small group that began the riot.

Further problematizing any analysis of such an event is how the available sources would describe it. The ultimate participants were motivated variously by politics, greed, personal revenge, anarchic joy in destruction and anti-authoritarianism. An author writing long after it occurred, however, would not know of the various groups and motivations that contributed to and escalated the riot; he would only know perhaps how it started and the final results, and thus would be likely to blame everything that happened on the politically motivated initial group. The author might well also lump all the rioters together and thus ascribe to the initial group a far larger membership than it in reality had, and similarly would attribute much greater support for their political cause than in fact existed. While written narratives of riots (both ancient and modern) tend to stress uniform behaviour by and intent of the rioters, in reality, most riots were probably of a similarly mixed nature and motivation as in this hypothetical example, and any attempted analysis of a riot needs to be mindful of this complexity.

Riots were a surprisingly common feature of life in ancient Rome. Their prevalence has often been diagnosed as symptomatic of a fatal breakdown in government and a dangerous inability to maintain public order. This interpretation may well be true for some specific periods, such as the late Republic, but the frequency of riots even in times of relative stability and peace suggests that riots served an additional societal function. It is also notable that, despite periodic incidents of real violence, both Rome's populace and its leaders often displayed considerable restraint during riots. Within limits, riots appear to have served a useful function in ancient Rome as a tacitly allowed informal institution for popular expression, and thus constituted a form of communication that was acknowledged by both ruler and ruled.

FURTHER READING

The riots of the late Republic have received by far the most scholarly attention due to a combination of extensive sources for this era, the political significance of the associated events, and the involvement of prominent figures. On these riots, see Lintott 1999, Vanderbroeck 1987, Nippel 1995 and Mouritsen 2001. Riots at Rome during the early empire are discussed by Africa 1971, Jory 1984, Nippel 1995, and Yavetz 1987 and 1988. For riots of the second to the fourth centuries AD, see Browning 1952 and Ménard 2004. Kelly 2007 and Vanderbroeck 1987 offer excellent discussions of the sources in reference to riots, and the problems with bias. On the special nature of emperor–plebs interactions, see Yavetz 1987 and 1988, Griffin 1991, Aldrete 1999 and Sumi 2005. The literature on crowds, mobs and what is now termed 'collective behaviour' is vast, but some basic surveys of the development of thought on these issues, with additional bibliography, can be found in McClelland 1989, Waddington et al. 1989, Marx and McAdam 1994 and Miller 2000.

25: 'ROMANS, PLAY ON!'

City of the Games

Nicholas Purcell

THE GAME, THE AUDIENCE AND THE EVER-RETURNING YEAR

In the modern imagination, the ancient city of Rome is tied inextricably to Games: consider the emblematic Colosseum, whose impressive ruin has come, alongside the dome of St Peter's, to stand for the city. Complementary images of history, art and touristic value for our generation, arena and dome were opposites in earlier popular history too. Christian Rome had an antitype in the imagined city of the heathen games at which the martyrs suffered; and the violence and cruelty of the arena remains one of the most powerful popular associations of ancient Rome. Though the Circus Maximus is less easily imagined from its site and remains, its chariot races still vividly evoke an ancient Rome of surprisingly extended holidays. The place and the monument, in both cases, symbolize the world of spectacles.

Both amphitheatre and circus also stand for the spacious indulgence of awe-inspiring numbers of – inevitably – ordinary Romans, less blamed in our day than by earlier generations but no more understood. Our reception includes an indignant sense of waste in reckless expenditure, much of it public, on a worthless audience, of intrinsically depraved tastes, and still further spoiled – morally and politically – by the whimsical or self-interested blandishments of the powerful. So the pleasure, excitement and disorder of the audiences thus also loom large in the reputation of the Games, and oppression, subversion, dissidence, misrule, carnival and role-reversal reinforce the appeal of the subject for a less deferential age. Few aspects of Roman history do more to locate it in contemporary ethical and political narratives, and it is duly prominent in scholarly and popular writing about Rome: though there is a substantial dissonance between the disapproval built in to representations of the Roman Games and the general political and moral values of twenty-first-century first-world 'western' societies.

All these modern perceptions are prominent in ancient texts too – an essential element in how Romans presented and reflected on their city and its society. Those who devised and paid for the Games already used the awe-inspiring statistics and logistics in a rhetoric of excess, like the superabundant and conspicuous indulgence of a huge population of the privileged. Their visual prominence in what remains of the city's ancient landscape is no coincidence. Documentary evidence leaves us in no doubt about the passions and thrills which the Games gave their intended audiences. For ancient writers, all too familiar with archaic Greek theories of aristocracy, the fervid, abandoned atmosphere of the spectacles reflected and promoted ordinary people's corrupt and dangerous nature – especially in big crowds – so the ethical critique of the Games became a commonplace of Latin philosophical writing. Simultaneously, envious outsider observers of Rome made the Games an emblem of all that was disgusting in the special status of the imperial capital. Finally, the opposition between Christianity and the Games, Church and Arena, became a vital strand in Christian self-modelling from at least the generation of Tertullian. Christian antipathy shows how the Games were far more than a contingent, frequently deplorable, form of behaviour – a mode of being, a vehicle of identity, from which provincial Romans felt excluded, and from which Christians sought to exclude themselves.

It follows from this that the people who watched, who played, deserve the fullest attention from the historian of Roman Games. This is one of the very few areas of ancient history in which anything of the behaviours and priorities of such large groups of men and women can even hazily be discerned. Romans' participation in the Games is a large part of what we can today observe them actually doing, and it deserves better than criticism or condescension.

We begin, then, not among the scores of thousands of spectators in the Circus, nor in the monumentally capacious and detached Colosseum, but making a trip with the poet of the *Fasti* up the Tiber from the city to the water-meadows where modern Rome's concert-hall now stands. It is 15 March, and Ovid describes the 'happy festival of Anna Perenna':

The plebs comes out in couples: scattering amid the
greenery, they find a place to settle down and drink, some
managing in the open air, but a few putting up
awnings . . . Warmed by sun and wine they make their
prayer to live as many years as they down glasses, and drink

by numbers . . . There they sing the songs they've learned at
the theatres, and putting the wine-bowl aside, join in
clumsy dance . . . They are unsteady on their feet as they
head for home, and are a spectacle for passers-by – when
they rejoin the throng people say how lucky they are.

(Ovid, *Fasti* 3.523–42)

Dedications to the Nymphs from the apple-tree grove of the nymph
Anna, who was also the ever-returning year, pinpoint its site and confirm Ovid's picture, adding vivid detail about the playfully competitive
atmosphere, and how it fits a wider culture of the Games.[1]

These texts eloquently reflect the sensibilities of the slaves and
ex-slaves who were so prominent in Rome's enormous populace. The
pleasant warmth of spring counterpoints the precarious lifespan of a
dangerous environment and the transience of the time of the turning
year; the suburban location is a deliberate antithesis to the archetypal
City 2 miles to the south. Wine conduces to pleasure, but also to a
mirthful informality, and the slave–patron relations which pattern society are evoked in a new way, and against the holiday mood of relaxed
self-determination. This is one of a set of Roman festivals of careful
role-alteration, in which the subaltern are allowed the limelight for a
single day. Here the reversals are less dramatic than at the Saturnalia,
but still serve to orient participants and observers around the social
order. Sharing the festival means community solidarity; competition
and partisanship express individuality, and in this case – strikingly –
the individuality of the plebeian *couple*. In all its literary artifice, Ovid's
poem evokes a festival which itself embodied the values of sophisticated
dramatic culture. The newly discovered dedications by ex-slaves answer
to the literariness of the learned poet, as they seek to fix the moment
for ever in the metre of the comic 'songs they've learned at the theatres'. Writing on stone verse in the popular metre of the comic stage
is important, but so is the wish to represent and be represented at all.
The audiences of the Roman theatre here extend the life of the theatre,
becoming performers themselves. Through the cult of Anna, indeed –
and it is vital to remember that this was a religious occasion – we can
see the permeability of Roman society to the messages and practice of
the spectacles, and the power of the medium to express and shape experiences far beyond the Games proper. (The crowds returning to town
'are the entertainment of the people'.) At the heart lies the auspicious

[1] Piranomonte 2002.

greeting to the returning festival-goers: they were lucky. Games were religion with a winner: and that was always good news ('people say how lucky they are'). Between inscription and poem, a popular culture emerges, highly conscious of physical locality, in which time, good fortune and commemoration are celebrated through participatory festivals where performance problematizes and recreates social status and social bonds. For the populace at large, the watched and participant audience, all Roman Games functioned similarly, between life-time, city-time, memory, competition, performance, status and group.

A LANGUAGE OF THE LUDIC

Rome's public spectacles are traditionally, and reasonably, distinguished by their settings, circuses, theatres and amphitheatres. The state's religious festivals, *Ludi*, are, quite correctly, differentiated from the private *munera*, which included most of the spectacles of the arena. Competitive, agonistic shows may be contrasted with expository or epideictic ones, and games classified according to the status of the participants.[2] But we should not over-classify. All three principal strands in the history of the Games share in the 'ludic', the information, values and behaviours common to all play in public in the city of Rome, from the greatest festivals to tavern-gambling. Games offered an adaptable language of public life, a medium in its own right, drawing on a (naturally) ever deeper and richer anecdotal memory, through which deliberate statements could be made in a language which was perceived and believed to be deeply traditional and essentially Roman, even while its speakers, its grammar, and its functions changed. This medium is a much more rewarding subject of inquiry than the rather tired categories of 'sport' or 'entertainment'.

The spectacles were rich in messages and symbols. The thought-world of and around the Games was part of the treat and the pleasure. Richly textured meaning was among the signs of an urbane existence in which the non–elite could participate too. Their participation involved direct communication between players, audience and organizers, a dialectic in which the literal importance of the message is attested by allusions in the evidence to the media of communication between those responsible and the audiences: and it matters that these are sometimes dependent on some at least of the spectators being literate. The

---

[2] Potter 2006, 388.

audience, then, must come first. The Games were the People's, and they are the subject's foundation and core.

The People had a history, and their perceptions and discourses changed. The evidence for the ludic is abundant, but uneven. Historians have been tempted to treat the stories of different kinds of Games separately, and in pursuit of each to lump together different moments in the history of Games at Rome, when in fact different phases, even chronologically quite close, reflect importantly different parts of a complicated and changing history.[3] Nor is it helpful to sketch a single developmental story leading breathlessly towards the high imperial system. That said, the People's perceptions as expressed in the ludic were very closely linked with their position in a world which they came to dominate.

Public contests were common to most ancient Mediterranean cultural traditions, and they had a profound role in shaping many identities. The contribution they made to the system of identities that we call Roman drew on a far wider world than the city of Rome (starting, as we shall see, with a rich and ancient Italian background). But the centrality of Games to the fabric of life at Rome, within the city, and to the historical memory of all-conquering Rome, also had a far-reaching effect across the Roman world. Perceptions of space and time came to distinguish Rome from all other cities in the ancient Mediterranean. The Games are among the most important elements in that distinctiveness.

So this chapter's title comes from another medium apparently remote from the roar of the crowd in circus and amphitheatre, but which is actually a microcosm of the ludic universe. On a marble slab for the play of a two-person gambling board-game in Late Antiquity, the places were marked out with the letters of the inscription 'the Parthian is bound, worsted the Briton – Romans, play on!'[4]

THE ROMAN GAMES

The first and greatest Roman festival also concerned imperial destiny. The Ludi Romani, *the* Roman Games, in honour of the three Gods of the Capitoline Hill, Rome's city-protectors, Jupiter, Juno and Minerva, and above all Jupiter Optimus Maximus, always retained a conceptual

---

[3] Beard 2007 identifies and avoids the problem.   [4] Purcell 1995b, 25.

primacy among the Games.[5] Every aspect of Capitoline religion was intimately linked to Roman identity, and its annual festival, which bore the name of the community itself, and at first marked the end of the civic year, may be as old as the Temple of Jupiter, for which archaeology has confirmed a late sixth-century BC date.

Tradition linked the new cult of the Capitol to a wider transformation of the cityscape, recounting how the last kings reclaimed two wet valley-bottoms as the sites of civic authority, the Forum Romanum, and religious festivals with competitive Games, the Circus Maximus. In the nascent *poleis* of contemporary Greece, new types of citizen-space emerged, of sometimes more cultic, sometimes more institutional flavour, to accommodate processions, dances, performances or regulated physical competition. At Athens, the archaic Panathenaic procession linked the new *agora* to the sanctuary of city-protecting Athena on the Acropolis above. So too at Rome, the Capitolium was tied to the public meeting-places beneath by processions, and above all, in the Ludi Romani, the circus procession (*pompa circensis*), in which transportable statues of the deities were moved on lavish floats through the city to honorific places prepared for them as spectators of the Games in the Circus. Procession and Games were observances in which everyone, elite and citizenry, men and women and gods, could participate.

The place of the Ludi in the city of Rome cannot, then, be understood apart from Roman religion – the religion of the people at large. Few religious acts involved more members of the community than the *pompa*. The glad participation of large numbers of the people was essential, and the focus, for both procession and Games, was the divine images.[6] The religiosity of the Roman community was proudly displayed, because this was how the state obtained the most necessary gifts of the gods: present prosperity, harmonious government, a good future, and, specifically, the military successes which guaranteed them all. The Ludi were therefore intrinsic to the continuous and essential process of discerning and influencing the will of the gods. The uncertainty of the result was a major part of the point: special games were held on campaign, and in times of crisis. If the displays looked anxiously towards the future, they reassured through their continuity with a past in which, the rites proclaimed, the community had always succeeded in persuading the gods to maintain their favour. Forum, Circus and Capitol always retained an important linkage in the duties

---

[5] Unchallenged until 220, Scullard 1981, 40; in general 183–7. Bernstein 1997.
[6] Potter 2006.

and privileges of the community and its leaders. Priest and city-official resembled each other: business and pleasure did so too, since both had to take their place in a system which was concerned above all with maintaining the successes brought by the favour of the deities. So the processions of the Capitoline gods involved the Circus too; spectacles for public celebration might take place in the Forum; political life and competitive games alike took place both in more secular spaces and in divine sanctuaries. To the end of Antiquity, the crowd at the festival was still in some sense the *populus Romanus* assembled, an image of the Roman state.

The long valley of the Circus Maximus was well suited to equestrian competitions. Chariot races were the first and original Games.[7] Horse- and chariot-racing were prominent in the Greek and Etruscan milieux in which early Roman society shared, and the Romans later believed that their first Ludi – named for their city and identity – were an occasion when outsiders could come to participate in the celebration of the gods who supported the Roman state: the better to express community solidarities, all ancient spectacles, indeed, were about outsiders.

ELOQUENT CONTROVERSIES

In the middle Republic, new military and diplomatic horizons encouraged new festivals and spectacles. Conquering Italy, resisting Pyrrhus and fighting Carthage brought interactions with Greek and Italian communities which transformed Rome. The Romans believed that *ludi scaenici*, theatre competitions, had been brought from Etruria in 364 (and the enthusiasm of the west for the Greek stage in this period makes this a plausible enough general date).[8] In the aftermath of the First Punic War, Livius Andronicus' stage performance at the Ludi Romani in 240 BC was a turning-point in Roman cultural history. Another new spectacle in the same period was gladiatorial combat, attested at aristocratic funerals from 264.[9]

Challenge and failure worked alongside the spoils of success. The crisis, uncertainty and anxiety of wars with the Gauls and Hannibal

---

[7] Taylor 1937, 285 for the normal pattern of the republican *ludi* with clear logical and chronological priority of the *circenses*; Humphrey 1986, 10–18.
[8] Livy, 7.2.1–6; Festus 436. Early history and varied character, Wiseman 2008, 132–7.
[9] Livy: Gruen 1990, 80–4; Taylor 1937; gladiatorial Games, Welch 2007, 18–26.

changed Roman religion profoundly, and Games changed too. New festivals, often for outsider deities, performed once in an emergency, were subsequently made permanent. The Ludi Apollinares, about which we are quite well informed, are typical. Vowed in 212, they were made annual in 208; they had an important place for *ludi scaenici*.[10] Games for Ceres, who protected Rome's provision in grain, and the Ludi Megalenses, for the Anatolian Mother whose invitation to Rome helped win the Hannibalic War, followed over the next years.[11] The creative half-century from 220 to 173 crystallized the distinctive games-rich religious calendar. The link with the desperate religiosity of survival politics helps explain why regulating the Games that the Romans had enthusiastically introduced proved so problematic politically and morally over the next 150 years.

Domestic politics reinforced the consequences of defeat and victory. There were close ties for a magistrate between leading the procession of the Ludi, and being borne in the triumphal chariot.[12] And from the first, charioteers brought the aristocrats who sponsored them great glory.[13] The People, though, wanted more than a passive share in the Games. The narrative of the gradual empowerment of the Roman people included claims about how the Ludi Romani were expanded, and by the Hannibalic period the festival of the high establishment had acquired a popular pendant, the Ludi Plebeii, mirroring the ancient Games but a couple of months later: this willingness to iterate and to duplicate became a feature of Roman Games culture.[14] The highest military and political elite steadily escalated their public munificence and with it the lavishness of the games they gave from booty or to commemorate political success.[15] Competition between private displays such as the first *munera* and the community's celebrations can plausibly be deduced.[16] No doubt deliberately, elite flamboyance was counterpointed with involvement in funding by the state itself. The primary possessor of the wealth on show at the Games was thus to be

---

[10] Scullard 1981, 159–60; Gruen 1990, 127.

[11] Gruen 1992, 186, wrongly dated to 201; Scullard 1981, 101–3. Interventions in the Circus in early second century, Humphrey 1986, 69–71.

[12] Livy 5.41.2 compares the dress of the *triumphantes* with that of the *pompam ducentes*.

[13] Thus Rawson 1981 (1991, 390–4).

[14] The *Ludi plebeii* are first mentioned in 216, Livy 23.30.17: see Scullard 1981, 196–7. Their role as counterpoint to the Ludi Romani: Coarelli 1997, 78–100.

[15] Rawson 1981 (1991, 398) observes the increasing importance of manubial games in the record of the second century. Cf. Flower 2004.

[16] Thus Potter 2006, 389.

the Roman community, whose resources were made specially visible in the notorious practice of *instauratio*, the repetition of games when a ritual mistake was made – frequent in the early second century BC, this was still a daunting cost in the reign of Claudius. The sums were carefully noted, and frequently debated: Rome's first historian noted that 5,000 minae of silver had been spent every year on the Ludi Romani (Fabius Pictor fr. 16 Peter; cf. Livy 40.44.12). The system of the four *factiones* in the Circus, responsible for meeting the expenses of the chariots, charioteers and horses, and named for the colours which the *aurigae* wore in the races, is a likely by-product of the subordination of the expenditure on the Games to the public sphere (though the rich could still join in as contractors; Livy 24.18.10). The multiplication of permanent festivals changed Roman citizens' year. They came to live the Games, since the festivals patterned the civic and personal calendar. The amount of time devoted to them (alongside cost) became another potent way of quantifying and displaying the ludic.

As a religious act, above all, the *ludi* were a central concern of the *res publica*. Participation was part of the duty to public life which elite (for all their sneers at the Ludi) and populace shared. The Games were linked to the People's victories at war, and behind the Greek allusions of the festivals lurked the basic citizen-training of the *gymnasion*.[17] Much in the language of the ludic (including the role of the Campus Martius) derived from military training. The analogy between gladiators and soldiers was regularly drawn but not easily delineated. So assembling the People for the Games, with all their Greek or Italic elements, was directly political. Even if the first *munera*, gladiatorial games and wild-beast hunts, were private, they were held in the Forum itself.[18] The audiences of Plautus and Terence, then, were not passive recipients of the ludic. Their participation in every level of spectacle culture can be seen in their enthusiastic celebration of the local festivals of the urban crossroads. Part of the patterns of city-existence across the Italic and Roman diaspora, these observances are fascinatingly displayed in the paintings and altars of the Lares Compitales at Delos, for instance.[19] Poised between the religion of house and street or neighbourhood,

---

[17] Wallace-Hadrill 2008 has an important section on this theme.
[18] Vitruvius, *De architectura* 5.1.1 for the tradition: it has been argued that the stands constructed in the Forum shaped the architecture of the elliptical spectacle buildings which we call amphitheatres, Welch 2007, with Wiseman 2008, 158–62.
[19] Hasenöhr 2003.

they display the religiosity of the urban matrix, and its celebration of local rivalries and of the economy of the city. It is natural that such games should be so contentious in the popular politics of the end of the Republic, and an important ingredient in the urban settlement of Augustus. Cicero (*Pro Sestio* 50) listed voting-assemblies, meetings addressed by magistrates, and gatherings for the Games as parallel occasions for the expression of the popular will (and could allege that it was the most reliable).

But the elite could not leave the Games alone (even as competitors), and this added further to their contentiousness. The sheer complexity and technical virtuosity of organizing spectacles advertised skill, power and wealth. Aemilius Paullus, the final conqueror of Macedon, famously said that the organization of games and the logistics of war required similar and related skills (Polybius 30.14; cf. Livy 45.32.11). The organizer gained hugely from being part of his spectacle.[20] As providers of games, Roman magistrates, pursuing popular influence, drew on and elaborated patterns of benefaction long familiar in the Greek world, and which included banquets and other luxurious perks.

Alongside their cost, every aspect of the Games therefore came to be regulated – and hotly debated. The clothing of the audience in general, of particular status groups within it, and of the presiding official, was carefully prescribed. Strong feeling about whether the audience should be seated famously led to the demolition of the first permanent theatre-building in 155 BC.[21] The demeanour of the spectators had powerful implications, and theatrical laws prescribed seats of honour and the distribution of places according to a strictly hierarchical vision of society.[22] In control and licence, the Games performed social order, mirrored it through role-reversal, and buttressed it through framing and limiting the unpredictable and the play of chance.[23]

The urgency of the debates about the management of the Ludi reflects the intimacy of the link between the Games and senses of what it was to be Roman. Roman religious spectacle had been highly receptive to the splendour of processions elsewhere in the Mediterranean world, just as the *ludi scaenici* had been heavily indebted to Greek drama; but the reception of both created something culturally distinctive. By the middle of the second century BC, it was Rome's

[20] Wiseman 2008, 153–75, esp. 157.
[21] Wallace-Hadrill 2008, 160–9, with earlier bibliography. [22] Rawson 1987.
[23] Potter 2006, 385, cf. 408 on 'radical changes of fortune' and the appeal of spectacle.

practice that was imitated. Antiochus IV of Syria set up a Roman-style procession in his capital, in which he aimed at a remarkable inclusiveness of religious representation – so giving us a glimpse of what was thought to be so efficacious about the way in which conquering Rome worshipped (Polybius 30.25.13).[24] That was what the world saw in the Ludi.

GAMES OF THE CAESARS' VICTORIES

By 146 BC, the Roman people, in addition to its political and social self-consciousness, could claim to have conquered the world: it was 'dominus gentium populus'.[25] The Games came to be a central part of a well understood system by which the rewards or perks, the *commoda*, enjoyed by the conquering Romans, advertised this success. Thus, the rebellious peoples of the Italian interior just before the Social War sought to kill a comic actor on stage at Asculum just because he was such a celebrity among the Roman People.[26] In the Games, Rome's power was made explicit.

The power of the people was, as in the preceding period, the opportunity of its leaders and the mirror of their ambition. The stakes were rising. The development of popular politics brought a steady escalation of the cost and allure of magistrates' Games, culminating in the unsurpassable extravagances of aedilician Games of the 60s and 50s BC. The age when the political importance of the Ludi is eloquently presented by Cicero was that in which aspiring statesmen regularly became 'ensnared by the People's and senate's redoubled applause, echoing down the wedged seats' (Virgil, *Georgica* 2.508–10). The greatest leaders of the late Republic had to transcend the attainments of lesser competitors in this field too: so Sulla, Pompey and Caesar, completing the adaptation of the games to the celebration of political personality, ushered in the spectacle-culture of the imperial period. Games had always marked the victories of the Roman people; now, with the Victory Games of Sulla and Caesar, they offered a medium by which the victories of their most successful leaders could be added to the historical catalogue of popular achievement. Augustus' Ludi Saeculares of 17 BC developed the capacity

---

[24] Cf. Günther 1989. [25] The phrase is Caligula's: Suetonius, *Gaius* 35, 3.

[26] Diodorus Siculus 37.12, with Rawson 1985, 469–71. On the theory of the *commoda*, see Purcell 1994, 687. The funeral of the charioteer Felix also shows the development of the celebrity culture: Rawson 1981 (1991, 397).

of the Games to evoke distant past and glorious future to a new level of complexity.[27]

Just as the satisfaction of the people, the reckless outpouring of wealth and the self-display of the magistrate reached back into the middle Republic, so did the continuing ties between the Games and the gods. These made it possible for the dynasts to use the divine associations of the festivals as a vehicle for their most ambitious bids for status. To this repertoire of representation and rite, from the time of Julius Caesar, the honours of the emperors and their families were progressively added. The triumph provided ancient precedent for using Capitoline celebrations for personal glory, and it was easy to extend triumphal honorifics to the Ludi Romani and other Games, including the symbolic chair or statue of the honorand in the *pompa* and at the spectacle, and new festivals for significant birthdays, or extra events where the birthday fell in a pre-existing festival. The new festivals of the end of the Republic imitated the traditional ritual sequence, beginning with a divine *pompa*.

The clearest sign of change in the culture of the spectacle was massive investment in their settings. The architectural lavishness which had paradoxically become characteristic of temporary buildings for Games was made permanent.[28] Building types used elsewhere in Italy for spectacles were redeployed at Rome on impressive scales. Pompey's Theatre, dedicated after his Triumph of 55 BC, an architectural and engineering tour de force, ended the long debate on the desirability of seating at plays. Caesar's embellishment of the Circus Maximus transformed the ancient seat of the Ludi Romani into an unparalleled urban space. Amid a flood of projects and investments, large and small, two further theatres and the first permanent amphitheatre at Rome were added by Augustus and his supporters, completing the monumentalization of the Ludi and adapting the spectacle culture of the Roman past to the needs of the new regime.[29] Augustus is attributed with carefully nuanced and suggestive reasons for assiduous participation in the Games: the honour of those who gave them, the comely and ordered behaviour (*eukosmia*) of the mass of the population and the necessity of being seen to share in the religious festival – essential principles from the long history of the Ludi (Cassius Dio 57.11.5). But the new political order

---

[27] Schnegg-Köhler 2002; Potter 2006, 386, cf. 401–3.

[28] A point memorably made by Wallace-Hadrill 2008 (see n. 21 above).

[29] Pompey: Sear 2004. Caesar, Humphrey 1986, 73–6; Welch 2007. Theatres of Marcellus and Balbus, dedicated 13 BC, Sear 2004.

was as faithfully reflected in the ludic medium as the old. A major change has been discerned, from the politics of the public meeting in the Republic to those of the spectacles under the empire: so the first stone amphitheatre seems to stand for the imperial victory over the senatorial popular politic.[30] Augustus' personal munificence certainly changed the place of *munera* in the Roman system.[31] But the reality is more complex.

The three types of spectacle now became more special-ized. Circus-races, stage displays and fights between people and between people and animals developed more clearly separate tra-jectories. The Campus Martius, long linked with military training, popular assemblies, some of the early Ludi and the triumph, and with a complex cultic topography, became the part of the city most prominently associated with the Ludi after the valley of the Circus Maximus, as well as Rome's 'suburb more beautiful than the city', and the monument of the *domus Augusta* (Strabo 5.3.8). Spectacle-topography helped convert Rome into a display piece of Hellenistic royal urbanism. At the same time, the conformation of the civic year, and the record of Roman history, to Augustus' achievements required the founding or revival of festivals and a creative development of the language of Games.[32]

The members of the *domus Augusta* joined in as spectators, patrons and fans: and the emperors took up the fascinating dialogic rela-tionship between leaders and audience which had started in the late Republic, and which endured to sixth-century Constantinople.[33] The full participation of the imperial household in all types of specta-cle became essential, but the Circus remained the principal focus. The Games united the people in rivalry, and made it visible, now more than any other public activity. Their collective behaviour made them part of the show. It could be orchestrated, no doubt; but the Circus was also the location for *spontaneous* demonstrations (Cassius Dio 59.28.11). The licence shown for free speech (including siding with the other faction from the emperor – there were now only two, Blues and Greens) and direct political criticism was part of the imperial consensus.

But the elite could not be omitted from the ludic system, and the Games continued to play a vital part in magistrates' careers. This clearly remained one of the principal honours of magistrates in the

---

[30] Hopkins and Beard 2005, 40–1.   [31] Thus Wiedemann 1992, 41.
[32] Feeney 2007, 138–211.   [33] Yavetz 1988; Cameron 1976; Wiedemann 1992.

imperial system: the praetor was the main impresario of games after
22 BC.

A new epigraphy (*ILS* 9349) of the Games does credit to all
involved:

> In the consulship of Drusus Caesar and C. Norbanus
> Flaccus, Menander, the slave of C. Cominius Macer and C.
> Cornelius Crispus, driver in the pairs, won the prize at the
> Ludi Martiales which the consuls gave, with the horses
> Basilisk and Countryman, and at the games of the Victory
> of Caesar which the praetors P. Cornelius Scipio and Q.
> Pompeius Macer gave with the horses Hister and Corax.

As at Anna's festival, the whole community is involved; everyone, in a
sense, won prizes: and everyone was cemented more permanently into
the architecture of the new monarchy.

GAMES FOR THE CITY AND THE WORLD

Omens and portents in the Colosseum, in the early third century,
foretold disaster worldwide – filled with visitors from the whole
empire, it stood for all Rome's world (Cassius Dio 79.26.1). Roman
identity was still eloquently expressed in the ludic, sign, above all,
of an extraordinarily *urban* culture, distinct from the unsophisticated countryside (a distinction that was already visible in the rites
of Anna Perenna).

The architecture was the most obvious urban dimension, but the
city was people too: the 'cast of thousands', whose skills made the *ludi*
possible – actors, stuntmen, athletes, charioteers, gladiators. Their status
varied from servile and marginal in the case of gladiators, who might
even be condemned criminals, through the more ordinary *infames*, the
actors, to charioteers (not *infamis*, though unacceptable for the elite).
Audiences had the strongest sense of performers as individuals, and the
elite loved to mix with them too: an entourage of unsuitable company
of this kind was a sign of the (over-)cultivated life from Sulla to Lucius
Verus (Plutarch, *Sulla* 2.2; Suetonius, *Vitellius*, 12; *Historia Augusta*,
Verus passim). Hardly less important than the players, the artisans whose
technical virtuosity made possible the marvels of the spectacles, and
their unique expressions in the cityscape, advertised and ornamented
the milieu of *technitai* and *ergasteria* which was intrinsic to Rome's urban

identity.[34] The diverse origin of the personnel of the *ludi* matters too: the Roman community managed its cultural relations with alien systems through the control of the skills of outsiders.

Festivals further continued to shape Rome's residents' distinctive experience of time. Roman excitement about the festival calendar (yet another rhetoric of ludic excess) has enthused modern observers: the proportion of the year devoted to festival has become a Celebrated Fact. In AD 354 – the record – a Calendar gives 175 *festivi* and 65 *circenses*.[35] Special occasions were extra: the extreme is the total of 123 days for Trajan's Dacian triumph (Cassius Dio 68.15).[36]

The spectacles retained a sufficient link with cult to be a plausible source of indignation and warning to Christian writers. The cosmic symbolism of the Circus, as recorded in late texts, suggests registers of supernatural speculation accessible to wider audiences than the literate.[37] In the Circus, people lived their past and their city's: but they also laid down markers for the future and expected to find signs of what would happen next to them and to the *res publica*. The Ludi Romani at first marked the end of the civil year, and it is striking that the 'last horse-race before the Saturnalia', by that date the *ludi plebeii*, was still at the end of the second century AD seen as an especially ominous occasion.[38]

Roman games drew on the ever more elaborate spectacle-cultures of the rest of the empire, while maintaining Roman distinctiveness and primacy, and after Rome's conquest of the world other ludic traditions were shaped in turn by their dialogue with this defining aspect of the victorious community. Rome's ludic culture was reciprocally patterned by this imitative homage. Characteristic of the Roman community as a whole, the Games were necessarily replicated wherever the *populus Romanus* was on display – in the *coloniae* or the bases of the army: Roman commanders retained the impresario virtuosity of Aemilius Paullus.[39] In addition, benefaction disseminated the characteristic advantages of the capital – circuses, thermae, amphitheatres – across the more ambitious communities of the empire.

---

[34] Purcell 1994 for this milieu in the urban society of Rome.
[35] Edwards 1993, 110. Augustan calendars give 66 days; a reform of Marcus Aurelius limits festivities to 135 days.
[36] Hopkins and Beard 2005, 51 emphasize that the days were not continuous.
[37] Nelis-Clément and Roddaz 2008.
[38] Cassius Dio 74.4.3 (192); 76.4.2–6, the outbreak of Civil War (195).
[39] See, for instance, Cassius Dio 56.25.3, *hippodromia* for Augustus' birthday, celebrated in the field.

Meanwhile, from the age of Pompey and Caesar, the content of the *munera* spoke eloquently of what it was to wield overwhelming power across the globe. Thus the 400 bears and 400 Libyan beasts slain at the games for the belated dedication of the Temple of Augustus, in AD 37, evoked the northern and southern extremities of Rome's reach (Cassius Dio 59.7). The games of the amphitheatre explicitly evoked victory over all enemies, natural or human, civilized or barbaric, but the ideology of Victory permeated other spectacles too.

Most importantly, the surprisingly free exchanges between emperor and people at the Ludi were a central element in the web of communication which expressed and instantiated the position of the emperor in the body politic and in the empire. They concerned every aspect of the running of the Roman world, including the high politics in which senators or imperial confidants were involved. In AD 193 a revealing public denunciation took place at the games, in which we are specifically told that the senators and the populace played integrated roles (Cassius Dio 74.2). Dio makes it sound as if the populace was consciously expressing its restored freedom of speech. The crowds had been trained in rhythmic shouts in honour of Commodus, which they now subverted by making ridiculous changes. Displaying political consciousness still more strikingly, they greeted individually senators who were known to have been particularly suspected by Commodus: 'Go for it! Go for it! You're saved! You've won!'

SIXTY EXTRAORDINARY YEARS

The Principate of Nero introduced a change of pace, and the two generations from his Juvenalian games to the death of Trajan represent an acme in the history of the ludic. Emperors never invested more in the Games at Rome than over this period, which saw the consolidation of their function in an imperial monarchy based on a semblance of popular consensus, and a successful blending of Greek and Roman historical traditions. Nero's absolutist experiments were reinforced by the need for self-definition of the Flavian monarchy and its adoptive successor-system. Nero had favoured a hybrid Hellenism in introducing gymnasium-culture to Rome more explicitly than ever before, in the Thermae Neronianae, and established a populist and innovative enthusiasm for Ludi which his successors were bound to continue.[40]

---

[40] Champlin 2003, 53–83.

Two initiatives, above all, wove a new pattern of Roman and Greek spectacle in the Flavian age: the Amphitheatrum Flavium (Colosseum), monument of Vespasian's conquests in the east, with its technical Greek label and Roman imperial gentile name attached – and the Agon Capitolinus, the elaboration of a new festival in honour of the Capitoline cult to mark Domitian's rededication of the Temple of Jupiter, situating Roman Games in the *periodos* and conjoining the Greek concept of competition to the most Roman of imperial terms.[41] More than ever, the new emperors faced the necessity of outdoing all conceivable rivals. Both plans must be understood through the rhetoric of scale and expense, easier for us to see through the massive wreck of the amphitheatre, though, as the Piazza Navona, the Agon or Hippodrome which was built to house the new oecumenic festival is as familiar a part of Rome's landscape today.[42] Both entailed an extensive supporting infrastructure, and both transformed Rome's topography, reworking Nero's Golden House as a public space in the one case, and further developing the Campus Martius suburb in the other. And both also reoriented Rome's position in the networks of spectacle, which spanned Greek and Latin-speaking worlds alike.

Trajan's final monumental rebuilding of the Circus Maximus, which cemented the dominance of chariot-racing as the most popular and most important of the Games, completed the repertoire of architecture in the capital for the Antonine age and its sequel (though the gymnasium culture continued to develop in parallel with the *commoda* of the plebs in the Games through the mighty complexes of the great Thermae, which were added steadily to the city-scape for two more centuries).[43] It is easy to exaggerate the impact of gladiatorial *munera*, despite their huge cost.[44] The diversions of the plebs in Antonine Rome remained multiple and intricate. The philosophical doctor Galen feared that athletics, because of their high repute in public life in the Antonine empire, could beguile the young away from intellectual excellence, whereas they were unlikely to be tempted by 'acrobatics or tightrope-walking or whirling in a circle without feeling giddy' (Galen, *Protrepticus* 9 [K1.20–1]). Athletics certainly had a prominent place in the Rome of his day.

[41] Hopkins and Beard 2005; Lancaster 2007. Amphitheatre-literature of this moment: Coleman 2006. For the Agon, Caldelli 1993.
[42] Cassius Dio 59.7.3 for the rhetoric of excess.   [43] Humphrey 1986, 102–6.
[44] Hopkins and Beard 2005, 93 for the relative rarity of the grandest games.

Alongside Hellenism, however, in these interventions, the *Roman-ness* of the Games was restated in a manner which reached back to the grandeur of the first Capitoline temple six centuries before – through the aspiration to control. The symbiosis of the spectacle-culture of Rome with empire-wide power was equally and interdependently visible in the second century in what the emperors prescribed for Rome, how that related to what the subjects of Rome aspired to, and in the integrated regulation of the Games of the city and the world by imperial authority. The Colosseum and Marcus' careful control of provincial expenditure on gladiators – the Capitoline Agon and the fine-tuning of the whole *periodos* across the world by imperial fiat – these were expressions of a single system of domination, in the ancient, but ever-changing, languages of the Games.[45]

FURTHER READING

Scholarship on this subject is arranged around the three principal venues of theatre, circus and amphitheatre, and inclined to follow classifications suggested by analogies with modern sport. But Manuwald 2011 is a good recent introduction on the theatre; for the circus, see Humphrey 1986 and Nelis-Clément and Roddaz 2008. There is a huge bibliography on *munera*: see for instance Welch 2007, Wiedemann 1992. The small book by Hopkins and Beard 2005 on the Colosseum is very stimulating, but see the excellent review of Lancaster 2007.

Of more general settings, the general culture of the *Ludi* at Rome is not well served in English. Bernstein 1997 is the basic modern work, but Scullard 1981 is still useful. For the place of games in the Roman world at large, Clavel-Lévêque 1984 is still a classic. On the theme of spectacle more generally conceived, Potter 2006 makes a number of extremely useful points clearly, but is very compressed, and too concerned with the *munera*. See also the varied papers in Bergmann and Kondoleon 1999. For the social and political aspects of the games at Rome, see Flower 2004 on the Republic; Hekster 2005 on the empire; Cameron 1976 and Yavetz 1988 are still valuable.

[45] Hadrian's regulation of the *periodos*: *AE*, 2006, 1403a–c.

PART VI

∽

BEYOND THIS WORLD

26: The urban sacred landscape

Andreas Bendlin

Placing religion in the urban landscape

It is well known that Rome's first *princeps*, Augustus, claimed to have turned a 'city of bricks' into a 'city of marble' (Suetonius, *Augustus* 28.3). One of his ambitious early building projects, the Palatine temple of Apollo, dedicated in 28 BC, was constructed from white Italian marble: its capitals, entablature and doorframe displayed a sophisticated colour scheme of mainly yellow, ochre and gold. Study of Apollo's sanctuary makes us better understand the contemporary claim, however tendentious, that Augustus had indeed golden temples (*aurea templa*) constructed for 'gods made of clay' (Propertius 4.1.5), and that an unsophisticated religious architecture of tuff and travertine limestone had been replaced by a new sacred splendour (Ovid, *Ars Amatoria* 3.113).[1] However, Varro's 'Divine Antiquities', dedicated to the *pontifex maximus*, Caius Julius Caesar, in presumably 46 BC, remind us that the Roman sacred landscape does not make itself fully understood only through the study of its sacred buildings, no matter how splendid they appear in the imperial urban landscape. Varro not only discusses the temples, shrines and altars of Rome but also covers sacred groves and possibly even private tombs outside the city walls. His account includes the deities, 'holidays' (*feriae*) and games (*ludi*) of Rome. Varro also explicates festivals and rituals: those performed by or on behalf of the *populus Romanus* in its entirety, those of Rome's urban and suburban subdivisions – the *curiae*, *pagus*, hills and neighbourhoods (*vici*) – and last but not least the ritual celebrations of clans (*gentes*) and families.

Indeed, one immediate impression a visitor to Rome during the imperial period must have had was of a city abuzz with ritual activity of every description, and of a boundless number of diverse deities

---

[1] Cf. Zink and Piening 2009.

populating every corner of the urban landscape. When the time-travellers in Keith Hopkins's fictional travelogue, *A World Full of Gods*, 'visit' Roman Pompeii, they see a town replete with gods and goddesses everywhere, not only in the temples, shrines and small chapels but also at crossroad altars and in cult niches along the streets, in the living quarters and in shops. They see gods being carried along in procession, painted on the walls, depicted on reliefs and altars, or gazing command-ingly from their statue bases in the crowded open spaces.[2] The modern reader – whose religious background, either by faith or socialization, may lie in one of the major monotheistic traditions, or who regards the conceptual and spatial separation of secular and sacred realms as a natural given (a view that must disregard the historical contingency of any such separation) – will find it hard to fathom, let alone reconstruct, the very sensation of witnessing the local polytheistic system of Rome at work.

The Roman jurists developed, and Rome's political authorities employed, a system of distinctions to define the conceptual boundaries of religion in the urban landscape, of which the distinction between the two domains of *sacrum* ('sacred') and *publicum* ('civic' rather than 'public') is the most prominent. According to Aelius Gallus, who wrote during the late Republic, the *sacrum* encompassed whatever the civic community consecrated to a deity. The ritual of consecration was autho-rized and carried out by the civic authorities and rendered the deity the owner of what now became a *res sacra* ('sacred thing'), which included the deity's temple, the altar, the sacred images and any money or object the deity might receive (Festus 424 Lindsay). But as we shall see below, ancient distinctions between the *publicum*, the *sacrum* and the realm of private or individual religious activity – the latter remaining ill-defined throughout the republican and imperial periods – can tell us only so much about the diversity of religious life in Rome.

Few ancient cities could compete in size and grandeur with Rome the cosmopolis, the centre of a vast trans-Mediterranean empire, where during the Augustan period a hypothetically estimated 750,000–1,000,000 people of varied demographics were living.[3] The demo-graphic implications of the size and heterogeneity of the late repub-lican and imperial city for an understanding of its religious life are momentous. Since the mid-Republic, Rome was rapidly outgrowing the city contained by the republican city wall and the four republi-can regions credited by tradition to the king Servius Tullius, as large numbers of migrants continued to arrive in the prospering capital of an ever-expanding empire. The 'pull' of Rome intensified the urban sprawl, which blurred the republican distinction between urban and suburban zones. Augustus' administrative reorganization of the city into fourteen regions, which included both previously urban and suburban regions, implicitly acknowledged this ambiguity.

The 'pull' of the city also transformed its sacred landscape and arguably calls into question the very definition of what religion in Rome meant. Some have suggested that we view the urban sacred landscape not simply as a geographical space but also as a cultural matrix of Roman *lieux de mémoire* (to borrow the memorable phrase by the French cultural historian Pierre Nora), 'places of memory' of past events and actions of historical significance that shaped the social and religious identity of Rome's population. But as we shall see below, there was no unequivocal relation between the religious belief systems of Rome's inhabitants and the 'ideoscape' (to borrow a term by the social anthropologist Arjun Appadurai) of Roman religion, that is the idealized master narrative of religious ideas, images and representations entertained by the city's socio-political elite. Specifically 'Roman' *lieux de mémoire* do exist but they fragment easily in the urban sprawl; the socio-political, economic, cultural or religious frames of memory that the classicist chooses to apply condition their modern reconstruction. Whose *lieux de mémoire* are we trying to recover?

The definition of the urban sacred landscape is further complicated by the fact that it always included the *suburbium*, even though yet another marker of spatial separation between the city and the extra-urban space was applied: Rome's sacred boundary, the *pomerium*, usually explained as *post-moerium* ('beyond the wall'), was an inaugurated strip of land.[4] According to tradition it was originally drawn by Romulus (Tacitus, *Annales* 12.24). In the historical period consecrated boundary stones marked its course. Livy insists that this strip should really be understood as existing on both sides of the wall, and that neither the strip inside nor that outside the wall should be cultivated or covered with buildings – the latter condition apparently ignored in Livy's own time due to the contingencies of the city's continuous expansion (1.44).

The *pomerium* defined the inner line of the *ager effatus*, a space demarcated by the augurs in which auspices were taken by observing the flight or sound of birds, and whose outer perimeter, about 6 Roman miles from the city, was symbolized by more boundary stones. This outer perimeter marked the original termination of the *ager*

---

[4] Cf. Catalano 1978, 479–91; Rüpke 1990, 29–57; Andreussi 1999.

Romanus, the combined zones of the city inside the *pomerium* and of the *ager effatus* outside, as defined by the augural lore (Varro, *De lingua* 5.33). One would mount the Auguraculum on the Arx or on the Quirinal to observe the signs in an aerial corridor (*templum*) along visual axes that cut across the city and the *ager effatus* (Livy 1.18.6–10). The fourth-century Regionaries still list yet another augural spot, Romulus' Auguratorium on the Palatine, no doubt a *lieu de mémoire* of cultural rather than ritual significance. The augural system thus created a very specific 'Roman sacred landscape'; under the Republic, sacred and secular buildings could not obstruct the visual axes of the aerial *templum*.[5] The Terminalia and the Ambarvalia, two Roman festivals which took place on the outer perimeter of the *ager Romanus*, provided yet another ritualization of Roman spatial boundaries.

Since the auspices were taken in an aerial corridor coextensive with the geographical range of the original *ager Romanus*, the *pomerium*'s function as an augural spatial marker between *urbs* and *ager effatus* must have been of comparatively minor importance. Its main role was in the separation of the spheres of *domi* ('at home' in the city) and *militiae* (literally, 'in a zone of warfare'). Neither the army nor anyone openly carrying arms was allowed inside the *pomerium* (an ideological construct historical reality could not be expected to reflect accurately), and the centuriate assembly, which was by Roman tradition the assembly of the militarized citizen body and sometimes called *exercitus* ('army'), convened in the city's military parade and exercise ground, the Campus Martius ('Field of Mars'), outside the *pomerium*. In theory the *pomerium* was coextensive with the city walls and its consecrated boundary stones had to be moved forward whenever the walls were. In practice the late republican *pomerium*, despite its extension under Sulla, did not include the Aventine and appears to have played no role in the Augustan reorganization of the city regions. Claudius' decision to move the *pomerium* because he had added territory to Rome's empire brought the Aventine and a small part of the Field of Mars within the sacred perimeter of the city. And Vespasian, with explicit reference to Claudius' action (*CIL* 6.930), further extended the sacred boundary by once again moving the consecrated boundary stones. Yet no contemporary observer would have failed to notice that there no longer existed any ritual relation between the city's administrative boundaries and its *pomerium*.

Vitruvius must have Rome's sacred landscape in the 30s BC firmly in his mind when he suggests that one situate the triad of Jupiter, Juno

---

[5] Cancik 2008, 62–80.

and Minerva on the city's highest hill-top and place Mars' sanctuary in an extra-urban location (*De architectura* 1.7.1). The Capitoline triad of Jupiter Optimus Maximus ('Best and Greatest'), Juno and Minerva on the Capitoline Hill was a living symbol of the republican, and to a lesser extent the imperial, *res publica*, and its religious significance was inextricably entangled in Rome's political rituals (never mind that the Capitolium was not the highest among Rome's seven hills). Consuls and praetors sacrificed to Jupiter Optimus Maximus and made vows when entering office, and foreign kings as well as allied communities of the second and first centuries BC left dedications to the god. At his temple the *triumphator* concluded his triumphal procession. Republican treaties and the Sibylline Books, the Greek oracular texts of the Romans, which the priestly college of (*quin*)*decimviri sacris faciundis* controlled and interpreted, were deposited inside the temple (the latter until Augustus, a *quindecimvir* himself, had them transferred to 'his' Palatine temple of Apollo).

According to Vitruvius Mars was placed in an extra-urban location to protect the city walls from an outside enemy and to prevent armed conflict among the citizens. The god's republican cult sites could indeed be found outside the *pomerium*: one sanctuary was situated between the first and second milestones of the Via Appia, another in the Circus Flaminius in the southern Campus Martius. There existed also an altar of Mars in the open area of the Villa Publica in the Campus Martius, the site of the Roman census and the army's *lustratio* before a military campaign. Caesar's plan to erect a monumental temple of Mars that would dwarf all others in the suburban Campus Martius, while extravagant in other respects, still continued to reflect the ritual distinction of the two spheres of *domi* and *militiae*.

It fell to Augustus to break away from this religious convention. A shrine of Mars Ultor (the Avenger) was planned for the Capitoline Hill, but the temple of the deity was eventually to become the centrepiece of the new Forum of Augustus; either location was clearly inside the *pomerium*. To soften Augustus' religious innovation, the iconography of Mars Ultor appears to have emphasized the peaceful aspects of the warlike god, and he was paired with Venus.[6] The Augustan relocation and reinterpretation of the god could be understood by contemporaries as fulfilment of the *princeps*'s claim to bring peace to Rome, which is also the message of the altar of Pax Augusta ('Augustan Peace') dedicated in the Campus Martius in 9 BC.

[6] Zanker 1988, 195–201.

It is sometimes suggested that the *pomerium* also served as a sep-arator of Roman and foreign gods, with only the former permitted to receive public cult inside the city's sacred perimeter. Unequivocal ancient support for this view does not exist, however, and what little there is appears rather late. Furthermore, the question of which cri-terion defines the qualities of being Roman or foreign in the urban sacred space is exceedingly difficult to answer. Vitruvius, in the above-mentioned passage, regards the city walls as a crucial divider, rather than the *pomerium*, and suggests the placement of Ceres, Venus and Volcanus as well as Mars in extramural sanctuaries so that the population may be safeguarded. His reasoning is informed by a tendency to assign one specific function to a deity: Volcanus stands for fire, Venus represents sexual appetite, and the worship of Ceres requires a place of quiet and awe. But no 'pomerial rule' can be deduced from Vitruvius' stipulations and related texts. Indeed, had such a rule existed, the placement of the Ara Maxima ('Greatest Altar') of the 'Greek' Hercules in the Forum Boarium just inside Romulus' *pomerium* would have been highly prob-lematic: at this altar the god received worship according to 'Greek ritual custom' (*Graeco ritu*) – Greek ritual custom, it should noted, as imagined by the Romans.

We would fail to understand the urban sacred landscape, if we reified ancient or modern ethnic stereotyping and tried to deduce a normative system where 'Roman', 'Greek', 'eastern' or 'foreign' deities could easily be identified. For instance, the temple of Apollo Medicus ('the Physician'), a cult import of allegedly 433/1 BC, stood between the Forum Holitorium and the Circus Flaminius. The sanctuary of Aesculapius on the Tiber Island, just across the Tiber from Apollo's, was imported in 293/1. Both temple dedications were the senate's response to an epidemic, and both gods were representative of the Greek tradition of healing cults. Aesculapius was allegedly imported in the form of a sacred snake directly from Epidaurus, a major centre of the Asclepius cult in the Greek world. The respective locations of these two sanctuaries outside the republican city wall reflect the Greek custom of placing healing cults in extra-urban sanctuaries. But the adoption of these Greek gods and the patterns underlying their Greek cults should be seen as an adaptation of the Roman sacred landscape to the wider Mediterranean world, reflective of a more general 'interconnectedness' to that world, rather than as a divisive marker of the 'foreignness' of the gods involved.

Often the placement of sacred buildings must have been dic-tated by the availability of suitable space and a sense of administrative expediency, a parameter that Vitruvius barely hints at when he suggests that temples of 'the other gods' be erected in a location suited to the sacrifices they receive. Sometimes, the location of pre-existing sanctuaries may have prevented the construction of yet another temple to the same deity in the same area. On the other hand, such concentration may have made duplication particularly attractive, as was the case with Mars or Hercules, to whom several shrines were dedicated near the Circus Maximus. In such cases, new temple building projects would deliberately enter into competition with an already existing sacred landscape dedicated to these gods. Throughout Rome's republican and imperial history, political considerations and competition among the elite played a more significant role in the placement of publicly sanctioned temples than religious scruple or sacred restrictions, even though the latter could always be invoked to oppose the plans of an opponent if it suited the political situation, flexible and endlessly open to interpretation as it was.[7] The evolving Roman sacred landscape is the result of constant development, with each generation renegotiating previous traditions, rules and boundaries and rewriting the sacred landscape's spatial matrix.

LOCATING THE GODS IN THE URBAN LANDSCAPE

In the Roman imagination, the number of the deities who inhabited Rome was vast and even exceeded the actual size of the human population (cf. Pliny, *Historia Naturalis* 2.16). There were not only the many gods of the traditional pantheon; all male freeborn Romans also had their own guardian deity, their *genius*, and all female Romans also had their own Juno. The cult of the *genii locorum* ('of places') abounded in the imperial sacred landscape, as there was no place, no neighbourhood and no commercial quarter without its own protective *genius*.[8] Then there were the Lares *familiares*, pairs of divine protectors of the household. Shrines of the Lares *compitales* at the crossroads (*compita*) were centres of cult in the city's neighbourhoods, and a wide variety of Lares, with variable epithets, were thought responsible for the protection of alleys and waysides (*semitales*) and fields (*rurales*) and of those travelling

---

[7] For a critical discussion of the 'pomerial rule', see Ziolkowski 1992, 266–79; Orlin 2002. For a case study of the link between mid-republican temple placement and political competition, see Muccigrosso 2006.

[8] Cf. Bodel 2008.

on roads (*viales*) or by sea (*permarini*). The reorganization of Rome's regions and neighbourhoods by Augustus, the latter numbering 265 under Vespasian and more than 300 in the Regionaries, was accompanied by a radical transformation of the *vici*'s compital cult. Freedmen and freeborn *vicomagistri* (and, in subordinate roles, slave *ministri*) were charged with the worship of a divine triad of two Lares *Augusti*; later compital cult could include the genius of the Augustus as well.[9]

There also was a clear correlation between the number and diversity of the city's human inhabitants and the number and heterogeneity of its deities and cults. By the imperial period the city could be viewed as an epitome of cultural and religious plurality, and as a just reflection of the plurality of the *oikoumenē* she ruled, to paraphrase Athenaeus, a Greek author of the turn of the third century AD then living in Rome (1.20b–c). The perception of the capital as the home of all the gods contained by Rome's *imperium* and the image of all those gods as migrants to Rome recur with topical regularity in pagan and Christian literature since the Augustan period.

Neither new citizens nor migrants without Roman citizenship were willing or even expected to abandon their gods and forgo their own religious traditions. They brought the gods of their respective fatherlands (*patrii di*) and mother-cities, who required accommodation in Rome. Roman traders and soldiers brought deities they had encountered in distant lands. Densely populated Trastevere on the west bank of the Tiber, a 'suburban' area under the Republic with a *pagus*-style administration and an incremental religious infrastructure of cults and festivals all of its own, became one hub of immigrant religion: Jewish presence is documented since the first century BC and imperial evidence can be found for the so-called eastern cults of Astarte, Palmyrene Baal, Hadad or Jupiter Heliopolitanus, and for the cult of the Christians. But immigrant religion was spread out over other parts of the city as well, such as on the Aventine, in the Campus Martius, or along the Via Appia outside the Porta Capena.[10]

To be sure, the accommodation of new gods and cults characterizes local polytheistic systems throughout the ancient world, the limits imposed upon such diversification of a community's local religion notwithstanding. However, the 'liberty to adopt gods' as exercised by the political community (*libertas adoptandorum deorum*: Tertullian,

---

[9] Cf. Wallace-Hadrill 2008, 259–312; Chapter 10.
[10] Cf. Noy 2000a; Lampe 2003, 19–66; Chioffi 2008.

Ad nationes 2.8) seems to have been carried farther in Rome than elsewhere. Tertullian's political metaphor highlights a defining feature of Roman civic ideology: Roman citizenship was characterized, at least in principle, by its comparative openness, as foreigners as well as freed slaves could be adopted into Rome's citizen body; Roman foundation myths envisage Rome to have been a settlement of migrants and emphasize the degree of upward social mobility available to newcomers to the city. The Asylum, an enclosed sacred grove of trees situated in the hollow between Capitolium and Arx and a religious *lieu de mémoire* that was allegedly established as a sanctuary by Romulus to attract refugees of all backgrounds to settle in Rome, perpetuated this very ideology. The Asylum was located just north of a temple of the god Ve(d)iovis, which according to one tradition had been founded by the Sabine Titus Tatius, a foreigner who settled in the city to share power with Romulus.

A related logic operated in the case of the gods: both the republican and the imperial *res publicae* were dedicating sanctuaries to a host of divine newcomers as Rome and her empire continued to expand. Since the beginnings of the city, a correlation can be charted between the expansion of Roman contacts and influences – first across Italy and then throughout the Mediterranean and beyond – and the respective origins of the deities who found their home in Rome. But the political elite expected to impose its own rules on the process of adopting gods: in AD 220, the emperor Varius Avitus scandalized the Roman establishment by installing the Emesene sun god Elagabalus, whose priest in Emesa he had been since his youth, as the supreme deity of the Roman pantheon. Soon the emperor preferred to be addressed by the name of the deity, but the residency of the sun god in a splendid new temple on the Palatine did not outlast Avitus' short reign and the deity was quickly returned to Emesa following his assassination.

Elagabalus' example shows that only a fraction of Rome's gods obtained permanent civic recognition and public worship. But to all gods the ever-expanding urban landscape provided infrastructure, notwithstanding the hostility of Rome's socio-political elites and parts of its native population towards the immigrant traditions of Carthage, Egypt, Gaul, Germany, Judaea or Syria.[11] Despite the denunciation of these immigrant cults as *superstitiones* ('superstitions') by a Roman political elite intent on closely controlling the urban sacred landscape – with the term *superstitio* increasingly denoting the religious behaviour of the

---

[11] Cf. Isaac 2004; Gordon 2008.

469

ethnographic Other since the late Republic – the means at the elite's disposal and its willingness to control religion in the city were often limited, and there was no such thing as a canon of Roman deities an inhabitant would be obliged to worship.

The crucial proviso in the adoption of new gods is that Rome's socio-political elite always drew a line between those cults accorded public worship by sanction of the elite – only they would fall within the domain of *sacrum* discussed above – and all those deities not sanctioned by the *populus Romanus* or the authority of the senate. In fact, the republican and early imperial historiographic and antiquarian tradition credits Rome's mythical 'kings' with the introduction of many gods and the establishment of the most pertinent rituals and religious offices, suggesting a primordial void, as it were, that was filled by successive generations of rulers. This literary trope, which amounts to a retrospective reification of religious authority, no doubt mirrors the sentiments of Rome's ruling elites. With this trope they create an idealized religious 'ideoscape' that can be retrojected to, and hence justified by, the distant past. Any development in the recent past needs the authorization of the elite, who make adherence to the 'ancestral custom' (*mos maiorum*), that infinitely flexible criterion of Roman elite self-reflection since the second century BC, the yardstick by which acceptance by the political public is decided (Cicero, *De legibus* 19.3, 23, 26).

We can trace the nexus between socio-political power and the evolution of the urban sacred landscape back to the early sixth century BC, when a permanent, rather than transitory, sacred landscape first becomes visible.[12] The data imply a link between urbanization and the control of public space by a socio-political elite, in particular in the Forum and on the Capitoline Hill, two early focal points of political and religious life. Moreover, these data point towards an early interdependence between the socio-political and religious realms, as the construction of a religious infrastructure, administered and financed by the elite, generated the framework for elite-controlled communal cult in an increasingly monumentalized sacred landscape. Rome's first extant monumentalized archaic temple, the sanctuary of Sant'Omobono in the Forum Boarium, can be dated to before 550 BC. The comparatively huge Capitoline temple of Jupiter Optimus Maximus, Juno and Minerva dates to the late sixth century and the temple of Castor in the Forum to the early fifth century. The sanctuaries of Diana on the Aventine and Saturn in the Forum certainly belong to the same period.

---

[12] Cf. Cornell 1995, esp. 92–113; Chapter 1.

Subsequent expansion of the city's sacred landscape by Rome's socio-political elite can be seen as a correlate of the conflicts, imperial aspirations, successes and military setbacks afflicting the *res publica*.[13] The juridical tradition categorizes as 'foreign cults' (*peregrina sacra*, Festus 268 Lindsay) deities imported in times of war and during internal crises, but the systematization of these cults as 'foreign' does not reflect social and religious practice. Festus' list includes the 'Greek' Ceres, whose Aventine temple also housed Liber Pater and Libera. At least one Augustan Greek observer regarded this triad as a Roman transfer of Greek Demeter, Dionysus and Kore (Dionysius of Halicarnassus, *Antiquitates Romanae* 6.17.2). Their Aventine temple was by tradition founded in the early years of the fifth century BC; in the republican period, it served as the headquarters of the plebeian aediles and included an asylum. The Aventine sanctuary's focus on plebeian political ideology may explain the hesitation of the Augustan regime to restore it immediately after a fire in 31 BC; the sanctuary's eventual rededication did not materialize until the reign of Tiberius (Tacitus, *Ann.* 2.49). Aventine Ceres symbolized a partisan yet still Roman focus of identification, which belies the cult's categorization as foreign.

In 396 BC Juno of Etruscan Veii accepted, or so the story goes, a Roman vow offering the goddess a temple in Rome and abandoned the people of her native city for the Aventine, where she received cult as Juno Regina ('the Queen'). The combination of the ritual of *evocatio* of the main deity of a hostile city and the related if conceptually distinct subsequent offering of a place of worship in Rome (either element could exist independently of the other) is difficult to locate with certainty in the historical record but may have occurred more frequently.[14] The fourth and third centuries BC witnessed several cult imports. This was one way by which the senate responded to prodigies or domestic crises (as in the cases of Apollo Medicus and Aesculapius). Following the Roman military disaster at Lake Trasimene, Venus from Mount Eryx on the western, Punic side of Sicily, moved into a temple on the Capitolium in 217, thus providing Punic support in the fight against Hannibal of Carthage. On the brink of victory over the Carthaginian forces, the Romans transferred the Mater Magna of Mount Ida ('the Great Mother', the Greek Cybele) to Rome in 204; her temple on the Palatine, dedicated in 191, among other things expressed the Roman elite's strong eastern ties.

---

[13] On republican temple foundation, cf. Ziolkowski 1992, Aberson 1994, Orlin 1997.
[14] Gustafsson 2000.

Underneath the original platform of the Palatine temple of Mater Magna excavations have unearthed a number of statuettes of Attis, the companion of the goddess in her cult in the Greek east, datable to the second century BC.[15] The literary sources suggest that the republican authorities attempted to marginalize un-Roman elements of Cybele's eastern cult by excluding Romans from holding the goddess' priesthood (Dionysius of Halicarnassus, *Ant. Rom.* 2.19). By implicit contrast, these small and inexpensive terracotta figurines of Attis suggest that there were devotees of his at Rome shortly after the official introduction of the cult of Mater Magna, and hence long before the early imperial period when the official cult of Attis is documented in the Roman calendar. It is impossible to say whether the dedicators of these terracottas belonged among the Roman population or whether they were migrating devotees of the cult who became attracted to Rome by the new Palatine sanctuary. Religious migration of that kind was common, as is suggested by the later, literary case of Lucius, the fervent devotee of Isis who settled in 'sacrosanct' Rome to be in constant attendance of the deity in her sanctuary in the Campus Martius (Apuleius, *Metamorphoses* 11.26).

Upon closer examination the 'foreign cults' of Aesculapius, Ceres, Mater Magna and Isis challenge the strict conceptual boundaries drawn by the Roman literary sources. Nevertheless, these sources reflect a sense of unease on the part of Rome's socio-political elite. It is significant that from roughly the second quarter of the second century BC the number of civic cult imports and new temple dedications declined, at the same time as the city expanded demographically and an increasing number of migrants imported their gods. Even the aedilician practice of funding new temples from the proceeds of fines, which is documented five times between 304 and 195 BC, came to an abrupt halt. This retrograde process can be related to another recent development: the city's socio-political elite now emphasized the differences between Romans and foreigners and increasingly policed the boundaries of its citizen body. When new deities entered the official Roman pantheon, more often than not it was in fulfilment of the vows of victorious commanders. For instance, in 101 BC Caius Marius financed the double temple of Honos and Virtus on the Velia from war booty. His choice of divine addressees took as its inspiration a double temple to the same deities that the conqueror of Syracuse, Marcus Claudius Marcellus, had restored and extended. By choosing 'Honour' and 'Manly

---

[15] Cf. Beard et al. 1998, vol. 1, 97–8; Pensabene and D'Alessio 2006, 36–7.

Virtue', the *homo novus* ('new man') Marius also made a political claim: the two deities in question belonged among a number of abstractions receiving worship at Rome that embodied the competitive value system of individual excellence, which the socio-political elite of the Republic had internalized.[16] A line can be traced from the temple dedications of mid- and late republican *nobiles* such as Marcellus and Marius, Pompey and Caesar to the Augustan and later imperial endeavours to transform the urban sacred landscape into focal points of individual and dynastic, rather than 'republican', self-representation.

Augustus' control of temple building and repair illuminates the ideological changes that took place in the imperial sacred landscape. Throughout the late Republic, individual members of the socio-political elite could be expected to repair shrines using their own funds. Such practice continued into the early stages of the impe-rial age (Tacitus, *Annales* 3.72). But with the rise of autocracy, the restoration and construction of sacred buildings, just as of public buildings in the city overall, increasingly became the prerogative of the *princeps*.[17] When referring to his restoration of eighty-two temples, Augustus' use of republican constitutional formality (*'ex auctoritate sen-atus'*) misrepresented the facts of early imperial *realpolitik*; in fact, given the sheer size of Augustus' transformation of the urban landscape, he could even afford to restore the Capitolium and the theatre of Pompey with its temple of Venus Victrix ('the Victress') in the Campus Martius without advertising his authorship (*Res Gestae* 19–20).

Moreover, the transformation of the urban sacred landscape by successive imperial autocrats was ideologically loaded, and they were not above manipulating the *lieux de mémoire* of the republican past. This applies in particular to the first *princeps's* attempts to reconfigure the republican social memory through construction of new temples and other sacred buildings for the purposes and aims of his imperial *res pub-lica*. The construction of a temple of Divus Julius ('the god Julius', i.e. Julius Caesar) at the east side of the Forum, with a speakers' platform that showcased the prows of enemy ships captured at Actium, transformed the area into a venue of dynastic self-representation; buildings of the imperial cult would from now on occupy strategic locations through-out the urban landscape. But it did not go unnoticed, for instance, that Augustus merely restored and rededicated the temple of Jupiter Feretrius on the Capitoline Hill, which was by tradition the oldest

---

[16] Cf. Clark 2007.   [17] Eck 1984.

temple of Rome and had been dedicated by Romulus, the first founder of the city, as Livy (4.20.7) points out.

POPULATING THE SACRED LANDSCAPE

Throughout the year the inhabitants of Rome would be able to witness, and sometimes actively participate in, civic religious celebrations of various kinds. In addition to having a large number of religious holidays and festivals,[18] the Romans dedicated an ever-increasing quantity of holidays to civic games (*ludi publici*), often on the occasion of a temple foundation or the anniversary thereof. The games attracted large crowds not only from Rome but also from the city's immediate hinterland, from Italy and, increasingly, from an even wider, trans-Mediterranean area. Processions (*pompae*) from a temple to the Circus formed an integral part of these games, which provided viewers with an opportunity to experience at close distance the cult statues of the gods (e.g. Ovid, *Ars Amat.* 3.2.43–58). The processional routes were carefully orchestrated and comprised many landmarks of political, cultural and religious significance, which could be manipulated to suit the prevailing ideological needs: in the imperial period the *pompa circensis* included focal points of the so-called imperial cult. Military victories were celebrated with games as well, and Sulla's *ludi Victoriae* ('of Victory') in 81 BC, and likewise Caesar's in 45, established a pattern of military victory celebrations that the *principes* of the imperial age perfected. *Supplicationes* were civic rituals of supplication to the gods in times of crisis but also served as civic thanksgivings to commemorate escape from danger, military victory, and more generally success (Livy 41.21.11). In their gratulatory function, these supplications increasingly focused on the achievements of a powerful individual or the emperor, and the days of public celebration increased commensurately: for instance, the senate decreed fifty-five *supplicationes* on account of the affairs successfully conducted under Augustus' auspices, amounting to 890 days altogether or an average of sixteen days of celebration for each thanksgiving (*Res Gestae* 4.1).

Under the Republic the aediles oversaw the organization of the *ludi publici* and the maintenance or restoration of civic temples, shrines and altars, the regular supervision of the physical state of sacred buildings, of temple wardens and temple property, while Augustus

---

[18] See Chapter 27.

created the office of 'curators of sacred buildings and public works and places'. The sacred realm, however, did not always rely on civic or imperial money. When work on the temple of Aesculapius on the Tiber island was carried out in the first century BC, the aediles assigned the task to a private contractor, who in turn would be paid from the donations and fees the sanctuary was receiving from ordinary worshippers (*CIL* I².800: *de stipe Aesculapi*). The monetary value of such fees and donations could be substantial, as is shown by anecdotal evidence: in the Capitoline temple Augustus deposited a donation of 16,000 pounds of gold, as well as pearls and other precious stones valued at 50,000,000 sesterces (Suetonius, *Aug.* 30).

This donation may have been an inadvertent result of Augustus' construction of the temple of Jupiter Tonans ('the Thunderer') in the immediate vicinity of the Capitoline triad. Following the dedication of this new temple, Jupiter Optimus Maximus complained to Augustus in a dream that competition with his new neighbour decreased his own revenues: people were flocking to the other sanctuary, which was rendered even more fashionable by imperial patronage. Although Augustus restored the traditional priorities of religious propriety by according Jupiter Optimus Maximus his due (Suetonius, *Aug.* 91.2), this episode suggests that we envisage the urban sacred landscape as a space shaped by allegiance to traditional religious choices on the one hand and attraction to fashionable new religious 'brands' on the other. Temples, deities and cults (traditional and recent, permanent and migratory) were providers of religion to a heterogeneous and fragmented urban landscape: every day humans of all ages, genders, ranks, ethnicities and persuasions frequented the sacred buildings and places of the various divine addressees *of their choice*, where they left a small fee or cash donation,[19] made vows and dedications, or sacrificed and prayed in pursuit or fulfilment of some concern. There existed a religious market characterized by competition among these providers, demand from the population and a desire to explore a variety of religious options.[20]

The city's temples and shrines constituted respectable micro-economic systems in their own right. Their porticos and open plazas served as spaces of market activity. Some sanctuaries, such as the temples of Castor, Mars Ultor and Ops, offered the opportunity to deposit money and valuable objects, apparently in the form of sealed deposits on which no interest would accrue. Sanctuaries charged individuals

---

[19] In general, see the contributions in Scheid 2009.   [20] Bendlin 2006.

for the use of their infrastructure (Tertullian, *Ad Nat.* 1.10.24), which included the services of the temple's personnel and which covered the commodities of daily cult practice, from the supply of sacrificial animals to the provision of warm water (*CIL* 6.820), and from the use of the sanctuary's congregational spaces and kitchen facilities to the purchase of devotional souvenirs.[21] A comparatively unregulated religious market, rather than civic control or a consistent policy on the part of the city's elites, sustained religious life in the urban sacred landscape.

It is not hard to link the provision of religious services by temples and cults to the needs and demands of their urban and suburban consumer base. Concerns for health, sustenance, procreation and material security are reflected in the literary evidence, in the epigraphic record of Roman sanctuaries, and in the contents of votive deposits like those of Aesculapius and (presumably) Minerva Medica on the Esquiline, the latter datable from the fourth to first centuries BC. Furthermore there existed a wide range of independent providers of religious services: lower-class *vates* ('seers'), *harioli* ('diviners'), street augurs, *sortilegi* ('fortune-tellers by means of lot') and *haruspices* populated the Circus (e.g. Cicero, *De divinatione* 1.131–2). *Isiaci coniectores*, dream interpreters associated with the cult of Isis, can be found in Rome since the late Republic. Divination on the subject of death – of the emperor, no less – by astrologers and *haruspices* was regarded *lèse-majesté*, and the practitioners of the art were repeatedly banned from Rome (e.g. Cassius Dio 56.23; Suetonius, *Tiberius* 63.1). The 'witches' and sorcerers of Latin literature are a reflection of the female and male drug-sellers of Roman antiquity; notwithstanding their portrayal by the socio-political elites as criminal, foreign, lower class or otherwise marginal (e.g. Livy 8.18.2–11; Paulus, *Sententiae* 5.23.14–19), these people were often quite ordinary providers of medical and religious services. They were an integral part of Roman religion as well.

The urban sacred landscape emerges from this chapter as a differentiated geographical and cultural configuration. Yet even though the existence of its many religious micro-ecologies may eschew simple classifications, they are not so fundamentally fragmented as to prevent meaningful historical analysis. Quite on the contrary, it has been the aim of this chapter to show how the Roman sacred landscape as a geographical and historical configuration was continuously being constituted and

---

[21] In general, see Stambaugh 1978, 568–91; Egelhaaf-Gaiser 2000, 227–476.

reconstituted, created and recreated, constructed and reconstructed by the inhabitants of Rome.

FURTHER READING

Beard et al. 1998, Scheid 2003, and Rüpke 2007a and 2007b provide good introductory accounts of religion in the city of Rome. Bibliographical surveys are published at regular intervals in the journal *Archiv für Religionsgeschichte*. Balty et al. 2004–12 presents archaeological, epigraphic and literary evidence pertaining to a wide range of rituals and ritual contexts such as cult places, dedications, prayer, procession, sacrifice, etc. For a reconstruction of Rome's sacred topography, the entries in *LTUR* and in Haselberger et al. 2008 are fundamental. Roman temple architecture, largely ignored in this chapter, is discussed in Stamper 2005 and Schollmeyer 2008. The Augustan transformation of the urban sacred landscape has been covered extensively; see Zanker 1988, Haselberger 2007. Other pertinent literature is mentioned in the notes to this chapter. A truly comprehensive monographic account of the complexity and variability of religious life in the city of Rome remains to be written.

27: STRUCTURING TIME

Festivals, Holidays and the Calendar

Michele Renee Salzman

... one important aspect of the ritual calendar at Rome (and of the exegesis that went with it) was its capacity to project Rome and Roman history, and to adapt the image projected. The calendar was one way (and a changing way) for representing 'Roman time'. It was not, of course, the only way.

Beard (1987)

The Romans created time machines that we still inhabit, and they were working creatively on time from the beginning of our historical understanding of their culture.

Feeney (2007)

Writers of the Augustan age and later attributed the earliest Roman calendar to the city's founder, Romulus, or to its second king, Numa, the creator of Roman religion.[1] Although not historical, the attribution of the calendar to two of Rome's venerated foundational figures reveals the importance of calibrating time and projecting it onto a calendar. In historical times, these tasks fell to the priests and magistrates of the city; since the same aristocrats held both positions, it was clearly they who determined the temporal priorities of the city. So, while the agricultural cycle provides one strand in the city's annual calendar, it was the civic/political and religious cycle of the growing city that was central to Rome's elites. Indeed, elite concern to link Rome's civic/political and religious institutions (which the Romans conceptualized through the figure of their founding kings) remained at the heart of how Romans structured their temporal patterns in the early Republic and continuing into Late Antiquity. New developments in the political life of the city thus engendered not just new civic

---

[1] Plutarch, *Numa* 18–19; Macrobius, *Saturnalia* 1.16.2-6; Livy 1.19.6–20.7. For Romulus, see Ovid, *Fasti* 1.27.

temporal patterns, but religious ones as well. Similarly, changes in Roman religious life affected the civic/political temporal patterns of the city and its inhabitants.

It is this essential link between the political and religious life of the city projected by Roman calendars that I will focus on in this chapter. My aim is not merely descriptive. The political and religious changes that altered Roman calendars also provide insight into how the Romans perceived, conceptualized and remembered key elements of their history and identity, as Mary Beard rightly noted in the epigraph cited above. This chapter considers four periods in Rome– the pre-Julian middle and late republic; the age of Julius Caesar; the Augustan and early Julio-Claudian Period; and the post-Constantinian fourth century. These periods present important changes that can be documented by the public calendar of Rome. Despite these changes, the link between the religious and the political institutions that lie at the heart of the city's structuring of time lasted well into the fourth century AD and beyond, even after the adoption of Christianity by a series of emperors beginning with Constantine. In fact, Roman ways of structuring time as projected by their calendar have enduring relevance; as Denis Feeney observed, their time machine – the Julian calendar – is still in use today, albeit with some improvements in the mechanics of time measurement.

THE PRE-JULIAN CALENDAR OF THE REPUBLIC

Our sources say that the priests of the city's cults originally announced at the beginning of each month the holidays to be celebrated in the coming days, thus providing an oral 'calendar' of holidays and rituals throughout the year. The most likely historical beginning of a written calendar for Rome is linked to the 450 BC publication of the Twelve Tables by the Decemvirate; many scholars believe that this first set of laws also contained a calendar of holidays on which legal actions could not proceed. J. Rüpke has argued that this calendar, like the laws, was the result of plebeian pressures for access to this information. A century and a half later we hear of a calendar in a public space, and this again in response to continuing plebeian demands for greater access to information. According to the Augustan historian Livy (9.46.5), the curule aedile Flavius in 304 BC posted in the Roman forum a calendar of the year designating the legal days for conducting business inscribed on white tablets. This calendar probably also listed the dates for the meetings of the assemblies (*comitia*) alongside the holidays. From this point on, priests and magistrates were responsible not only for determining the days of the year for holidays in the annual ritual cycle, but for publicizing these days on calendars.

A century later, we hear of another innovation in calendrical practice; in 189 BC the consul M. Fulvius Nobilior compiled the first attested commentary on a Roman calendar. To the names of the holidays he added such information as the aetiologies of the names of the months. He deposited this calendar in the temple of Hercules and the Muses, which he had recently built in Rome. Probably, Fulvius' commentary was painted or inscribed on the wall of this temple for decoration and for informational purposes, like the only surviving pre-Julian calendar, the Fasti Antiates Maiores (see Fig. 27.1).[2] Fulvius' commentary likely inspired the remarkable annotated marble wall calendar of the Augustan age that has come to light in modern Palestrina, ancient Praeneste.[3]

It is due to the popularity of the habit of inscribing calendars on stone or painting them on walls for public display in Rome and in other towns in Italy during the early Julio-Claudian period that we know as much about the Roman calendar as we do. Of the forty-eight extant calendars from the Italian peninsula from Roman times published by A. Degrassi in his magisterial study, forty-four date to the reign of the Julio-Claudians, with the bulk clustering around the rule of Augustus and Tiberius.[4]

STRUCTURING TIME IN THE PRE-JULIAN REPUBLIC

From the extant calendars and the exegetical literature devoted to them, we can see how the Romans structured their year in the republican period. The Romans divided the year into twelve months according to the courses of the moon. Because the moon does not complete the thirty days in each month needed to fit with the cycle of the sun, eleven days are missing compared to the full solar year. Hence the priests who were in charge of managing the calendar added intercalary days to keep their lunar calendar in line with the solar year. Every other year they had to add 22 or 23 days (an intercalary month) after the holiday of

---

[2] Degrassi 1963, 156–66. [3] Michels 1967, 6. [4] Degrassi 1963, xxiiiff.

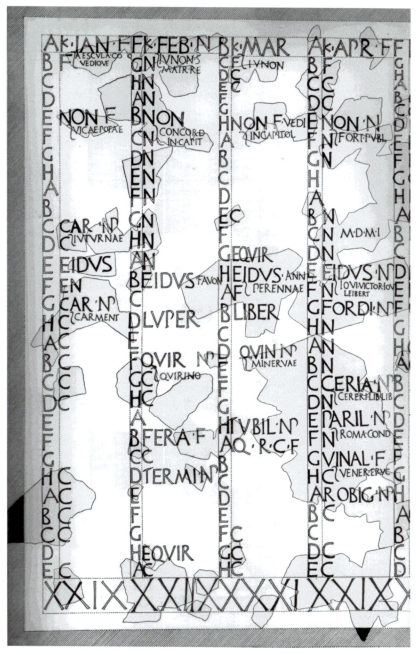

FIGURE 27.1 Pre-Caesarian calendar, Fasti Antiates.

the Terminalia (23 February) to make the 355-day lunar year match the 365¼-day solar year.

It was the priests as well who, on the Kalends (the first of each month) sacrificed to Juno and invoked Janus, the god of beginnings, to help give 'birth' to each new month. A minor priest who performed this sacrifice on the Capitol Hill would announce on what day the Nones (either the fifth or seventh, depending on the month) would occur. On the Nones, a priest (*rex sacrorum*) published an edict announcing all the regular fixed festivals up until the next Kalends. This ritual continued until the end of the Republic, in conjunction with inscribed, public calendars. The magistrates, however, announced the movable feasts (e.g. the urban praetor announced the Compitalia); other lesser priests or magistrates, or even specific groups, announced the lesser religious holidays. In these basic time-keeping tasks we see the shared responsibility of magistrates and priests that reinforced the link between the civic/political and religious spheres.

Since the priests announced the Kalends of each month, they also announced the New Year. In the earliest times of the Republic (ancient authors attribute this to Numa) the year began on 1 March. Some scholars have attributed this spring date for the New Year to the agrarian origins of the calendar and the community that used it; even in the late empire, religious and popular celebrations in March retained in communal memory the earlier opening of the year in March.[5] But by 153 BC, when the consuls began to enter office on the Kalends of January in accord with Roman law, the priests began the religious year on 1 January as well. This alignment of New Year rituals again indicates the close ties between the political/civic and religious temporal life of Rome. This link is apparent as well if we consider how the Romans designated their years.

Unlike our modern numbering of years from a set point (i.e. the year zero or the birth of Christ), Romans designated their years by the names of the two consuls. Hence, Consular Lists (Fasti Consulares) – in Latin the word *fasti* is used for both calendars and such lists – generally accompanied the annual lists of Rome's holidays in inscriptions painted on temple walls and in books. These Consular Lists enabled the inhabitant of Rome to locate a moment in time in the past. However, only after 153 BC was the consular year coterminous with the beginning of the new civil or new religious ritual year. Dating by consular year was the standard way to date a year, and continued

[5] Michels 1967, 99.

until the emperor Justinian in AD 537 introduced dating by regnal year instead.[6] This dating indicates the close ties between the calendar and the state.

It was also important for the inhabitants of republican Rome to know when farmers would come to sell their produce to city dwellers. By the middle Republic, every eighth day was a market day or *nundinae* (the numbers were calculated inconclusively). This was marked on the calendars with a recurring cycle of the letters A to H, beginning on 1 January and continuing through the year. Constructing an eight-day civic calendar week was highly unusual in the Mediterranean world; as Rüpke observed, the Romans took no account of the months in aligning their continuous civic weekly cycle on a solar, not lunar year.[7] Because the eight-day week was important to Rome's elite, on the market day, the wife of one of the high priests (the *flamen Dialis*) sacrificed a ram to Jupiter (Macrobius, *Saturnalia* 1.16.30). Fearful of the possibilities for political unrest caused by an influx of farmers, the Roman elite determined by the third century BC that regular public assemblies could not be held on market days, although the law courts remained open.

Along with this civic eight-day week, the Romans in the late Republic encountered the seven-day solar week of Hellenistic astrologers; from the early and middle years of Augustus' rule we have two calendars that included the seven-day week (marked by the letters A–G) along with the older (i.e. pre-Caesarian republican) eight-day market week.[8] In the second half of the first century AD, the planetary names of the seven days of the week (e.g. Saturn, Sun, Moon, Mars, Mercury, Jupiter and Venus) became increasingly familiar as well. Yet, the seven-day week with its day of rest did not become the basis for the Roman structuring of time (as it did eventually for the Jews in the early Principate).

The holidays and festivals of the pre-Julian calendar

Reconstructing the cycle of holidays and festivals in the pre-Julian republican calendar has been greatly aided by the survival of the one

---

[6] Bickermann 1980, 69.   [7] Rüpke 2007b, 198–9.

[8] For the seven-day weeks in calendars from the age of Augustus, see the *Fasti Sabini*, nos. 5 and 37, ed. Degrassi 1963.

pre-Julian calendar extant from the Republic. The Fasti Antiates Maiores is dated to 84/55 BC and comes not from Rome, but from Antium, a Roman *colonia*; we can see that it followed closely the official calendar of Rome as befitted its status as a colony, even if it did not exactly duplicate all of the holidays of the city. The Fasti Antiates' fragmentary information can be supplemented by extant literary and epigraphic evidence. Indeed, the brightly coloured letters on it – N, F, NP, C, EN – are explained by later writers. Of particular help is the testimony of the fifth-century writer Macrobius (*Saturnalia* 1.16.2-3), whose exegesis of the calendar depended on the Augustan scholar Varro (*De lingua Latina* 6.1-26):

> Numa divided each month into days, which he
> distinguished by calling some festival days (*festi*), some
> working days (*profesti*), and some half-and-half days
> (*intercisi*). The festival days were consecrated to the gods,
> the working days were left to men for them to regulate
> their affairs both public and private, and the half-and-half
> days were common to both the gods and men. The festival
> days included sacrifices, banquets, public games and
> holidays; the working days comprised propitious days,
> *comitiae* days, and days suitable for the passing of a
> judgment; as for half-and-half days, each individual divides
> them up for himself. . . on those days, religion authorizes
> the exercise of justice at certain hours and not at others.

In the pre-Julian calendar of the Republic, there were some 235 days for human affairs labelled *fasti* and marked with an F on calendars. Of these, some 192 were designated as days when it was possible for the public assemblies to meet; these were designated by a C in the calendar.

There were 109 named days to honour the gods, designated as N or *nefasti* in the calendar. Of these named holidays, some 61 were considered as public holidays (*feriae publicae*), which is likely the significance of the inscribed NP on these days in the calendar. On public holidays – *feriae, dies festi, dies feriales, or dies feriati* – rituals to honour the gods were performed and legal and political activities could not be carried out as the law courts were closed and the assemblies did not meet.[9] The day, in essence, belonged to the god or goddess so honoured. On the

---

[9] Michels 1967, 69–73; cf. Cicero, *De legibus* 2.19, 29, 55.

half-and-half days (marked EN and generally identified as *endotercisus*, an archaic form of *intercisus*), the morning and evening were for the gods while the periods in between were for men to conduct their business in law court or assemblies. If the priests of the state cults performed the proper rituals associated with a Roman holiday, there was no obligation for the populace at large to perform any specific act of worship. No popular participation was required.

Nonetheless, the people of Rome benefited from the holidays celebrated in the city and recorded by Roman calendars. The rituals performed on these days were intended to win the good will of the gods and hence ensure the continuity and survival of the city as a whole. The inhabitants of the city could be spectators for these rites and were the beneficiaries of the most typical ritual action, the animal sacrifice. After the priests of the cult performed the appropriate animal killing on behalf of the people in the front of the temple of the divinity honoured and had scrutinized the internal organs for signs of divine favour, the meat was distributed for public consumption. And because Roman holidays were intended to honour the gods for the benefit of the people, these rites and the animals sacrificed were funded by the state.[10]

In addition, the inhabitants of Rome could watch the Games held in conjunction with public holidays. The Games, or *ludi* in Latin, were not strictly speaking holidays. Law courts were not necessarily closed during the public games nor was there an official cessation of work; this meant that parts of Rome could and did continue to function and do business on these days. Still, the public games – theatrical events, circus races or gladiatorial combats – that were celebrated in conjunction with religious holidays were a great attraction and diversion for many in the city. And since the public games, too, were meant to honour the gods and were for the good of the people, they were funded by public monies and administered by state magistrates with priests present to perform whatever religious rituals were required.

Macrobius further divided the holidays in the Roman calendar into four distinct types – fixed, movable, extraordinary and market days (*Sat.*1.16.5–6). Only the fixed holidays (i.e. held on set days in appointed months) were noted in the civic calendar. Macrobius cites examples of fixed holidays that go back to what the Romans considered the earliest times; the Agonalia (9 January, 17 March, 21 May, 11 December) whose significance was uncertain in antiquity and remains uncertain today; the Carmentalia (11 and 15 January)

---

[10] Festus 248L and Macrobius, *Saturnalia* 1.16.4–8.

concerning the correct formulae for prayer; and the Lupercalia (15 February), a ritual running of young men through Rome to ensure fertility and/or to celebrate the end of the agricultural year. Macrobius considered these as ancient holidays, although their ritual meanings had certainly changed over the centuries.

Macrobius' second category of holiday, the movable holiday, included the days 'proclaimed annually by the magistrates or priest to be held on specific days which may or may not be set days'. Macrobius again cites some examples that scholars associate with the early Republic, including the Latin Holiday (*Feriae Latinae*); the Seed-Sowing Holiday (*Feriae Sementivae*); the Country-District Holiday (*Paganalia*); and the Neighbourhood-Shrines Holiday (*Compitalia*). Some, like the Compitalia, were later fixed; in this case, the Compitalia became linked with the Genius Augusti and the imperial cult so that in the Calendar of 354 it was celebrated with public games from 3 to 5 January. Similarly, the Roman Games (*Ludi Romani*) of 13 September and the Plebeian Games (*Ludi Plebeii*) of 13 November, which date to the early Republic, were later fixed in the calendar of Rome; both games were central to the promulgation of Roman identity as they honoured the city's patron deities, the Capitoline triad of Jupiter, Juno and Minerva.

The third category, 'extraordinary' days, are, as Macrobius notes (*Sat.* 1.16.6), set by the consuls or praetors for specific reasons, such as, for example, to give thanks to the gods; to expiate a wrong; to consult the auspices; to pronounce vows; etc. These, naturally, would occur when the situation demanded, and so were not included in the public calendar of the city, whose primary function was to fix and make public the system of days for civic and religious action. Fourth, Macrobius considers market days as festivals because on these days 'villagers and country folk . . . attend to their private affairs and market their wares'.

Varro observed, in his *De lingua Latina* 6.12, that the Romans divided the year in accord with 'the division made by nature' (*naturale discrimen*) and with 'the names of the days as given by the city' (*civilia vocabula dierum*). Varro thought that the civic named days 'were instituted first for the sake of gods and then for the sake of men' (*prius qui deorum causa, tum qui hominum sunt instituti*).[11] Following Varro's categorization, John Scheid has divided the Roman republican year into two great cycles, one tied to the agrarian year, and one to the civic/religious year.

---

[11] Scheid 2003, 48–54.

The outline of the agricultural cycle of the year is articulated by the calendar of the city of Rome and retained long after the city had become dependent upon commerce for its survival. The agrarian holidays focus on grain and grape production and storage. If we think of this cycle beginning in the spring, we commence with the Cerealia (19 April), devoted to the goddess Ceres, protector of the growth of grains and of the fields. Concern for the opening of the jars of new wine explains the next spring holiday, the Vinalia (23 April). Sacrifice is made to personified 'Rust' (or Blight) to protect the standing wheat at the Robigalia (25 April). The harvest again requires a round of holidays to placate the gods. So, to ensure the grape harvest, a second wine festival, the Vinalia (19 August), was celebrated, followed by the *Consualia* (21 August), a holiday to ensure divine aid in storing the grapes. The *Opiconsiva* (25 August) similarly was devoted to storing cereal products. The opening of the stored foods also necessitated placating the gods, and this appears to be the object of the *Meditrinalia* (11 October), when the new wine was sampled, and the *Consualia* (15 December), when the stored grain was tasted.

Tied to the agricultural cycle are the holiday times associated with the military year; early Romans were both farmers and soldiers. The *Quinquatrus* (19 March) and the *Tubilustrium* (23 March and 23 May) have been linked to the lustration of arms and trumpets at the beginning of the campaigning season, while the sacrifice of a horse at the '*October Horse*' (15 October) and the *Armilustrium* (19 October) have been tied to the end of the military season as the Roman farmer/soldier retired for the winter.[12]

The civic/religious cycle of holidays marked N in Roman calendars focus on ensuring the well-being and continued prosperity of the city. So, the *Vestalia* (9 June) is devoted to Vesta, the goddess whose flame symbolizes the hearth and very life of Rome. The *Liberalia* (17 March) commemorates when young citizens adopted the adult dress of the toga. Several other festivals are also closely linked to the civic well-being, even if they are only vaguely understood. These include the *Poplifugia* (5 July); the *Quirinalia* (17 February); the *Regifugium* (24 February); and the days described as: '*Quando rex comitiavit fas*' (literally, 'when the king held the *comitia*, the day is *fastus*', 24 March and 24 May). The concern to appease the spirits of the dead lies at the centre

---

[12] Rüpke 1995, 214–25, has suggested that these holidays were not tied to the military, but to the temporal divisions of the month. This conjecture, though possible for the Republic, remains at odds with Roman exegesis on these days in the empire.

of several civic holidays, including the *Larentalia* (23 December), the *Feralia* (21 February), and the *Lemuria* (9, 11, and 13 May). The *Saturnalia* (17 December) celebrates the end of the year, and the *Terminalia* (23 February) commemorates boundaries and endings in general.

In addition to these holidays the republican calendar included six great public games or *ludi*. These games, whether in the form of theatrical shows (*ludi scaenici*) or circus games (*ludi circenses*) were, in principle, intended to conclude the sacrifices that were performed as part of the public holidays. So, for example, the sacrifices and public banquets in honour of Jupiter on 13 September and 13 November were the heart of the holiday, *Epulum Iovis*. By the late Republic the sacrifice was preceded by nine days of theatrical games and followed by four days of chariot racing in the Circus Maximus, designated as the Roman and Plebeian Games accordingly. The magistrates who presided at the games were dressed as triumphing generals, a detail that supported the views of the Romans that the games originated in votive offerings by victorious generals to honour Rome's patron deity, Jupiter Optimus Maximus. Indeed, triumphing generals continued to celebrate victory games in Rome throughout the Republic, although only two are recorded as annual events in Rome's calendar: the games to honour Sulla from 26 October to 1 November and those to Caesar from 20 to 30 July. The Roman reluctance to commemorate humans in the civic calendar began to change with Caesar and would accelerate under Augustus and his family. However, the popularity of the public games in conjunction with the holidays to honour Rome's gods met the needs of urban dwellers, and, as we shall see, the days devoted to games expanded to such a degree that the emperors of later centuries periodically reduced the times allotted to such events in Rome.

RESTRUCTURING ROMAN TIME: JULIUS
CAESAR'S REFORM OF THE CALENDAR

As early as the third century BC, neglect and manipulation of the Roman civic calendar year (based as it was on the priestly determinations of the new moon and the intercalary days) left the Roman calendar at variance with the solar year. The political and military disruptions of the late first century BC only exacerbated this situation; Suetonius (*Julius Caesar* 40.1) tells us that the College of Priests inserted days or months as it suited them. In 44 BC, the New Year (1 January) would have fallen on what was actually 14 October, 45 BC according to the sun. Surprising to a modern eye, Varro in his *De lingua Latina* (cited above), which was written before Caesar's reform of the calendar, was not concerned by this; indeed, Varro did not connect the civic with the agricultural/natural cycle of holidays, nor does it seem an issue for other republican authors.[13] But this disjuncture between the natural and civic cycle did raise the concern of Julius Caesar who, as *pontifex maximus* and new ruler of Rome, had the authority and the power in 46 BC to realign how Romans structured time.

After the lavish victory celebrations and public games to honour Caesar's fourfold triumph in 46 BC, Suetonius tells us that Caesar's first domestic reform was to reorganize the calendar (*Jul.* 40.1): 'He linked the year to the course of the sun by lengthening it to 365 days, abolishing the short extra month and adding an entire day every fourth year.' Following one last correction in 8 BC, the Caesarian calendar thus functioned like a modern calendar, except that an intercalated day was added every fourth year after 24 February, not after 28 February. This act virtually revolutionized the accuracy of the Roman calendar. Now, it was 'for the first time feasible in the Mediterranean world to have the civil and natural years in harmony under the same standard of representation'.[14] This reform brought an accuracy to Rome that could not but impress contemporaries. As Denis Feeney astutely observed, Varro's *De re rustica*, written in 37 BC just after Caesar's reform, does something that would have not been possible just ten years before when he linked seasonal phenomena with Roman calendrical dates.[15]

Greater accuracy and reliability were probably part of Caesar's motivation, although Suetonius does not say so. It was, however, within the realm of Caesar's authority as *pontifex maximus* (the priest in charge of the priestly colleges and hence of the calendar) to undertake this reform. Suetonius associates Caesar's calendar reform with his efforts to revive and improve the political institutions of Rome; after the calendar reform, Suetonius goes on to describe Caesar's reorganization of the senate and his establishing of new guidelines for debtors. In addition, as Feeney suggests, calendar reform fits nicely with Caesar's personal views about the desired relationship between nature and the calendar; in his grammatical work *On Analogy*, Caesar proposed a harmony between nature and grammar and between nature and the calendar.[16] But these motivations pale compared to the glory that accrued to the

---

[13] Feeney 2007, 198–200.   [14] Feeney 2007, 196.   [15] Feeney 2007, 200.
[16] Feeney 2007, 197.

one who, through his regularization of the times, controlled the cosmos. Thus, while Caesar relied on the Greek astronomer Sosigenes (who had accompanied Caesar to Alexandria) for the technology to oversee the calendrical reform (Pliny, *Historia Naturalis* 18.211), it was Caesar's name that now replaced the 'fifth month' of the old calendar year (i.e. beginning in March). Every user of the calendar of Rome – which spread to Italy and the western empire – would be familiar with and reiterate his name, along with the commemorations and games in his honour.

With Caesar the calendar itself became a new means to honour the ruling elite. Imperial calendars record the addition of public holidays on the anniversaries of Caesar's victories at Munda (17 March), Alexandria (27 March), Thapsus (6 April), Ilerda and Zela (2 August), and Pharsalus (9 August). His adopted son, Augustus, added the commemoration of Caesar's birthday on 12 July.[17] This was the first time that a festival to a human being was incorporated into the public calendar of Rome, an extraordinary accomplishment by the man who undertook the task of completing Caesar's reordering of time and, along the way, established a new political and religious Roman identity that was projected through the Roman calendar.

ON AUGUSTAN TIME: THE JULIO-CLAUDIAN PRINCIPATE AND THE ROMAN CALENDAR

After Caesar's assassination on the Ides of March 44 BC, even his calendar fell in need of repair. (Some scholars have pointed to the machinations of Caesar's successor as *pontifex maximus*, Lepidus.) In 8 BC, Augustus corrected and celebrated Caesar's reformation of the calendar; he then accepted the renaming of the month of August in his honour, an act too that symbolically joined him to his father, whose month (July) came directly before his.[18] This reformation was timed to coincide closely with the dedication of a monumental Sundial, the Horologium, in the Campus Martius in Rome a year earlier. Like Caesar's calendar, the Augustan Horologium was made possible with the help of Egyptian science: the gnomon of this massive sundial was an Egyptian obelisk that Augustus, as *pontifex maximus*, had brought to Rome and dedicated to

---

[17] Fraschetti 1990, 15–16.   [18] Bennett 2003.

the Sun.[19] Like Caesar, Augustus sought to improve upon how Romans kept time.

Under Augustus, the political transformation of the Republic into the Principate (essentially a monarchy) transformed how the inhabitants of the city spent their time; these changes were also reflected in public calendars in Rome and Italy. Whereas in the Republic holidays were devoted to honouring the gods or were tied to the agricultural cycle, the calendar under Augustus became increasingly cluttered with holidays and games commemorating the new *princeps* and his family. These reflected and helped implement a vast shift in Roman civic and religious identity. How great a change this was can be grasped perhaps by the fact that for centuries before Caesar, no human being had been recorded in a public Roman calendar as the recipient of a holiday. With Caesar and increasingly often with his adopted son, Augustus, that changed. Now, the birthdays, death days, apotheoses, accessions to priesthoods, comings of age, dedications of temples, and victories in battle of the *princeps* or the *princeps'* family were included and commemorated in the public calendar of Rome. In 19 BC, the first Roman festival named after a historical human being, and the first new festival incorporated in the calendar as named holiday, the Augustalia of 12 October, was made an annual event.[20] This remained in the calendar down to the middle of the fourth century. (This focus on the *princeps* and his family also explains why no triumphs other than those of Augustus and his family were celebrated in Rome after that of Cornelius Balbus in 19 BC.)

An additional temporal indicator of the Augustan transformation can be seen in the Consular List that was used to indicate the year. The Consular List that probably accompanied the calendar erected by Augustus in the area of his father's temple at the east end of the Roman Forum broke with Roman chronographic tradition in significant ways. In addition to a list of the consuls of the years from the beginning of the Republic, Augustus' Consular List, the *Fasti Capitolini*, included the years from the time of the foundation of the city (calculated as occurring in 753 BC) next to the traditional Consular Lists. With this, Augustus challenged the temporal as well as political authority of consular dating; now the consuls and the Republic were merely one stage in the history of the city.[21]

Given the Augustan transformation of the Roman structuring of time, both annually in terms of Consular Lists and daily in terms of the

---

[19] Buchner 1982, 10.   [20] Michels 1967, 141; Taylor and Holland 1952, 140.
[21] Feeney 2007, 172–82.

calendar, it is not surprising that Augustus put up so many calendars in public spaces; indeed, most of our extant wall calendars from Rome and Italy, as noted above, date from the age of Augustus and peter off with the emperor Claudius (AD 41–54).

A CALENDAR FOR THE EMPIRE: THE *CODEX-CALENDAR OF 354* AND THE CITY OF ROME

After the Julio-Claudian period, our knowledge of how Romans structured the public calendar of Rome depends almost entirely on chance references or exegetical discussions. Not until the third and mid-fourth centuries do we have access to another calendar from Rome. A large public building excavated under S. Maria Maggiore that came to light in 1966 preserved a frescoed wall calendar.[22] This discovery made clear that the habit of inscribing calendars on walls continued in the city, although this calendar's fragmentary text added little new to our knowledge of how inhabitants used their time in the post-Augustan city. It is only in the middle of the fourth century that we have a rich and full source of information for the civic calendar of Rome; preserved in a book that survives only in Renaissance copies of a lost Carolingian original, the *Codex-Calendar of 354* presents a full year, a wealth of information for how Romans spent their time in the fourth-century city.[23]

The most striking change in the urban calendar of the fourth century as compared to the Julio-Claudian period is the sheer increase in the number of days devoted to holidays and public games (*ludi*). In the fourth century, there were 177 days for holidays or public games and circuses, including ten days set for gladiatorial shows. This contrasts with the first-century AD calendars, in which there were an estimated 53 days for public games. Of course, it would be wrong to think that the fourth-century city came to a standstill for 177 days of the year. Participation in the rituals and/or watching the games still remained optional. As long as priests and magistrates performed the proper rites and the gods were satisfied, the inhabitant of Rome would benefit. Nor did a spectator have to spend the entire day at the games. He could

---

[22] Salzman 1981, 215–27. However, there are differing arguments about the dating of this frescoed wall cycle from a public building in Rome.

[23] Salzman 1990, 250–68 for the manuscript tradition of the Codex-Calendar of 354.

do business at a law court in the morning – for these remained open on days designated for public games (*ludi*) – and drop by to watch the remainder of the games in the afternoon.

Nonetheless, the vast increase in days devoted to public games and the addition of games to Roman holidays that in the first century AD had not been so celebrated attests to their tremendous popularity and importance in defining the public, civic and religious meaning of a holiday for a Roman citizen. It was important that the emperor be present as much as possible in the minds of the spectators who enjoyed the games as part of their civic rights. No wonder, then, that 98 of the 177 public games noted in the calendar of 354 were connected to the emperor and/or his family (excluding the ten days devoted to gladiatorial combats). Of these, the reigning emperor and his family were predominant. Of the nine imperial victories taking up some fifty days of the year, all but one can be securely identified with the reigning Constantinian dynasty. Moreover, these Constantinian victories are uniquely and elaborately celebrated, with five days of *ludi* preceding one day of *circenses* on which twenty-four races are noted. In keeping with this presentist focus, only the anniversaries of the reigning dynasty – its birthdays, accessions to Caesar, accessions to Augustus – are regularly recorded with a second day of votive games (*ludi votivi*), a temporal extension that distinguishes the dates of the ruling emperor and his family from those of earlier deified emperors.

The fourth-century calendar of Rome, like earlier calendars, publicized the set religious holidays celebrated in the city. The remaining sixty-nine days of public games in the fourth-century calendar were in honour of the pagan gods of the Graeco-Roman pantheon. These holidays reveal how essentially conservative the Romans were in their deities and in the times devoted to them. Indeed, thirty-seven of the sixty-nine days of public games in the fourth-century calendar were the same public holidays found in calendars from the late Republic. (Only the victory games to Sulla and to Caesar were omitted; the victories of previous dynasties were not generally allowed to remain on Roman calendars.) Another sign of Roman conservatism is the fact that some twenty-four festivals and ceremonies without games and circuses that were noted in calendars of the mid-first century AD were preserved (albeit with some name changes) in the mid-fourth-century calendar of Rome. Moreover, less than half – some thirty-one days of the sixty-nine days – of the games devoted to festivals in honour of the gods were new, that is, post mid-first-century AD.

The deep tie between the civic/political and the religious that lay at the heart of the Roman calendar of the Republic can also be seen as central to the calendar of the fourth century, judging from the most popular religious cults (based on frequency and type of celebration); here too, the political influence of the emperor is clear. The support of the tetrarchic rulers for Jupiter, Hercules, Mars and Sol (the Sun god) helps explain the predominance of these four deities in the city's calendar. Indeed, in the case of Sol, the late third-century emperor Aurelian's special attention to this deity and his establishment of a new college of priests of Sol staffed by Roman aristocrats, along with a massive new temple in the city, were also key factors.[24] Even the two most popularly attested cults 'new' to the calendar after the Augustan Principate – Attis (worshipped with the Magna Mater) and Isis (including her consorts, Sarapis and Osiris, and her child, Harpocrates) – can be linked to imperial support; the emperor Claudius was the first of several emperors to expand the worship of Attis and the Magna Mater (or Cybele) with a public holiday; the Flavians began the official recognition of Isis and her consorts.[25] Both cults, we know, were also popular among Rome's senatorial elite.

We wish we knew more about the actual celebrations that took place during Roman holidays. Indeed, while interpretation of the rituals changed to reflect contemporary understanding, how the actual rituals themselves changed – if at all – is not often known. So, for example, at the Vestalia on 9 June, Ovid (*Fasti* 6.249–309) describes how the Vestals made the 'holy' cakes to be offered to the goddess on this day, which opened a period of time for cleansing the inner rooms of the temple; the dirt was ritually removed and the period of purification concluded, on 15 June, with the closing of the temple; this last is mentioned in the calendar of 354 as 'Vesta is Closed' (*Vesta clauditur*). It seems likely that the rituals of purification and cleansing continued into the fourth century, but we do not have specific evidence of this nor of the contemporary interpretation of this particular ritual. Of course, this holiday did not raise the more problematic issue of animal sacrifice which, since Constantine's reign, was openly challenged by Christians. Despite later laws restricting animal sacrifice, there is little to indicate that animal sacrifices as part of the celebration of most Roman holidays had ceased to be performed by pagan priests in public in Rome in 354.[26] That would be challenged in the coming decades.

---

[24] Halsberghe 1972, 122–6, 144; Salzman 1990, 149–53.
[25] Salzman 1990, 164–76.   [26] Salzman 1990, 205–9.

The inclusion of pagan holidays and festivals noted in the Codex-Calendar of 354 may be surprising to a modern reader given its date, some four decades after Constantine had embraced Christianity in the city of Rome. Yet the centrality to Roman identity of the public games and traditional holidays helps explain the willingness of Christian emperors to underwrite the games and the public cults that were linked to them. Moreover, the inhabitants of Rome remained predominantly pagan; the elites of Rome were among the most resistant to religious change in the western Roman empire.[27]

Yet Christian times and rituals needed to be known by the Christian recipient of the Codex-Calendar of 354; hence a virtual calendar for Christian usage was appended in the form of two lists of dates to commemorate the Depositions of Martyrs and of Bishops recognized by the bishops in Rome. This separate but equal status for Christian holidays indicates that Christian rituals had not yet been integrated into the civic/political or religious life of the city. But the inclusion of two separate lists of Depositions would have seemed useful to a Christian in Rome. Indeed, utility also explains why the Codex-Calendar of 354 included a Consular List; now its owner could determine the year as well as the holiday in the year.

These appended lists of the Depositions of Bishops and Martyrs demonstrate that inhabitants of Rome simultaneously lived in different temporal structures, the civic/traditionally pagan as well as the Christian. We see this same willingness to live under different temporal spheres when we consider how the Codex-Calendar of 354 notes the seven-day solar week along with the older (i.e. pre-Caesarian republican) eight-day market weekly cycle. But the Codex-Calendar of 354 is unique in extant Roman calendars in adding to these two weekly cycles a ten-day lunar cycle. Astrology, not Christianity, probably explains these multiple ways of further subdividing the month. Indeed, while Constantine decreed Sunday a holiday in honour of Sol, and Christians saw this as a day in honour of their god, the seven-day weekly cycle had not yet taken on widespread Christian significance. That, too, would require a century or longer to infiltrate Roman notions of time.[28] But the ability of Romans to live by different weekly cycles simultaneously remains consistent with their distinctive way of structuring time within the civic as well as within the religious sphere.

---

[27] Salzman 2002, 73–83.   [28] Salzman 2004.

CONCLUSION

As the Codex-Calendar of 354 makes clear, the emperors in the fourth century were eager to maintain the ties between the political and religious institutions of the city that structured the calendars of Rome from the earliest days of the Republic. Caesar and Augustus had radically reshaped the Roman year to emphasize their roles in the state. As the imperial system continued, the emperors and their cult increasingly filled the days of the inhabitants in Rome, as we see fully developed in the fourth century. A new political/civic identity based on a new religion, Christianity, would eventually create a new public calendar that was based not on the lives, deaths, and triumphs of emperors but rather on the cycle of Christ's life and death and on the fates of the martyrs of Rome. But this would take place after the fourth century. Yet, even then, in a post-Roman world, the memory of recording such information in public did not entirely disappear; the frescoed medieval wall calendars from S. Saba and SS. Quattro Coronati in Rome attest to the longevity and vitality not only of the Roman way of structuring time, but also of projecting it on calendars for the inhabitants of the city.

FURTHER READING

Degrassi 1963 is the essential collection of Roman calendars from Rome and Italy, with extensive documentation and discussion of all aspects of the subject. It is the basic source for modern scholarship on the Roman calendar.

Feeney 2007 is a stimulating study of the changes in time and temporal management in the late republican and early Augustan ages. Hannah 2008 offers a new and lively account of how the Greeks and Romans calculated time. Michels is the fundamental work on the calendar of the Roman Republic, with extensive discussions of the calendar notations. Rosen 2004 offers a collection of essays comparing how premodern societies constructed time and space, ranging from Assyria and Babylonia to Rome, Greece and China. Rüpke 1995 is an updated and sociologically informed analysis of the Roman calendar, useful for updating Degrassi's magisterial study.

Zerubavel 2003 provides a fascinating sociological perspective on how communities use time to construct identity.

28: CEMETERIES AND CATACOMBS

Leonard V. Rutgers

I n ancient Rome, death could strike at any moment. Low life expectancy along with insalubrious living conditions in an over-populated city where infectious diseases spread all too easily made death into a reality that affected all social strata evenly: the untimely demise of nineteen-year-old Lucius, beloved grandson of the emperor Augustus, or of fourteen-year-old Romulus, the much-lamented child of Maxentius, provide us with well-known examples to show that the offspring of Rome's aristocracy was as prone to disease and early death as were those less deftly placed in society (see Chapter 3).

To cope with this harsh reality and to integrate death into their daily existence, the Romans are known to have remembered their dead regularly, first in the form of such commemorations as the *parentalia*, the *rosalia* and the *dies violae*, and later, as the Christianization of the empire progressed, in the shape of a church-sponsored cult aimed at the martyrs or special Christian dead. Inevitably, death was a major source of sorrow for the Romans. Yet, in due course, death also came to constitute a locus of power few chose to neglect as it provided those who could afford it with a means publicly to express their wealth and social status, and to engage in acts of patronage. After the Second Punic War had drawn to a close, well-to-do Romans began gradually to erect monumental and richly decorated tombs for themselves and their next-of-kin, including slaves, freedmen and freedwomen. They did so in the most visible of locations outside the city, along the consular roads that linked Rome to its empire. There, a series of densely packed yet loosely organized necropoleis arose that, from the third century AD onwards, also included the early Christian catacombs of Rome – yet another example of patronage informing Roman burial customs, this time with the early Christian church as benefactor burying the Christian poor free of charge in subterranean cemeteries excavated, at least partially, for that specific purpose.

While the sheer monumentality of Roman funerary has not failed to attract the systematic attention of researchers from the seventeenth century onwards – witness Antonio Bosio's *Roma Sotteranea* of 1632, G. B. Piranesi *Le antichità romane* of 1756 and several other Piranesi publications – it was not until the nineteenth century that a truly scholarly approach to the study of Roman funerary architecture finally materialized. Grounding our current understanding of Roman funerary practices and having produced a variety of excellent monographic and case studies as well as general histories of Roman tomb architecture, this nineteenth-century approach continues to characterize many a research agenda today. It seeks to study tombs comprehensively, placing special emphasis on questions of architectural typology, iconography and historical evolution, as well as on the study of the epigraphic materials that frequently accompany the funerary record. The latest and most exciting new insights into Roman burial customs, however, come from field archaeology as this particular methodology aims at coming to a proper understanding of the actual use of Roman funerary architecture through the application of various science-based analytical techniques including the systematic use of physical anthropology.

FUNERARY ARCHITECTURE

Just because the results of scholarly research allow us to draw such a comprehensive evolutionary picture of how Roman funerary architecture developed formally – from the time the Cornelii Scipiones had their monumental family tomb constructed off the Via Appia around 300 BC up to the time the catacombs came out of use in the early fifth century AD – it is easy to forget that the funerary arrangements of large sections of Rome's population, particularly those of the inner-city poor, largely continue to escape us even now. If we consider that during the period under study Rome's urban population ranged from somewhere between 500,000 and 1 million and if we assume that the crude death rate during this same time span must have been similar to that extrapolated recently from archaeological evidence preserved in the Jewish catacombs under the Villa Torlonia on the Via Nomentana, namely around forty per thousand, then it follows that annually 20,000 to 40,000 people died. This, then, was the number of individuals that needed to be buried around Rome, year in, year out. Some of these were laid to rest in the tombs recovered by archaeology, in necropoleis that rapidly filled to capacity, as evidenced by such jam-packed burial grounds as the recently excavated one on the Via Basiliano: consisting of a series of 545 tightly arranged and partially superimposed tombs this was a place in which, clearly, the capital offence of *violatio sepulcri* was a sore fact of life. Others ended up in *puticuli* – large communal burial pits for the destitute that were in operation on the Esquiline until the time of Augustus, remains of which appear to have survived into the late nineteenth century when they came to light in the Via Napoleone III, a few city blocks south of Rome's central railway station. Of the majority, however – including particularly children whose bones decay easily – not a single trace remains. Even the catacombs of Rome, containing an estimated 500,000 tombs in case of the Christian and some 7,000 in case of the Jewish catacombs, preserve but a fraction of the total number of interments that must have occurred throughout the period that burial was performed in these subterranean cemeteries.[1]

How did Roman funerary architecture evolve over the centuries? In the case of the graves of the poor and needy, it did not: from early republican through imperial and well into early medieval times, the underprivileged characteristically hollowed out their tombs from the surface of the earth. Although individual tombs of this kind vary slightly according to the financial means available – ranging from simple earthen pits containing the ashes of the deceased or the entire body in supine position (*fossa*) to tombs containing cinerary urns, encasings made of stone, containers consisting of amphorae (*enchytrismos*), as well as tombs covered with slanted tiles (*alla cappucina*) or carrying a marker of some sort made out of either perishable material or marble – it is evident that the poor were forced to be so utterly pragmatic in their conferring of the ultimate rites on their loved ones that their funerary architecture does not allow us to produce a neatly arranged typological history.[2]

With regard to the tombs of those who did have money to spend, we are, fortunately, in a better position to reconstruct how their architectural preferences changed over time. It is not until the final years of the Republic that monumental Roman funerary architecture came into its own, but when it finally did, it soon reached an astonishing variety, not just in terms of the tomb types developed, but also with

---

[1] Crude Death Rate Villa Torlonia: Rutgers et al. 2006, 353. Via Basiliano: Buccellato et al. 2003, 311–28. *Puticuli* of the Esquiline: Bodel 1994, 38–54.
[2] Examples of simple tombs: Taglietti in Heinzelmann 2001, 156–7, fig. 9; Spadano in Egidi et al. 2003, 23–9; Buranelli et al. 2005–6.

FIGURE 28.1 Tumulus tomb of Caecilia Metella on the Appian Way. Late first century BC.

regard to the individuality of tombs within a single type: of the twenty-seven or so tombs of the imposing tumulus type currently known, for example, not a single one copies another (Fig. 28.1). The emphasis of the monumental tombs from the late first century BC, which contain only small burial chambers (and sometimes none at all), is entirely on the outside as their outward appearance is clearly geared towards the self-display of single, powerful individuals. As such, tombs of this kind are frequently believed to reflect the excessively competitive nature of political life during the final, blood-stained days of the Roman Republic.[3]

Such a view makes sense, partly because it helps to explain the subsequent history of Roman funerary architecture: after Augustus' adoption of the imperial purple, wealthy Romans began increasingly to desist from erecting massive tombs aimed primarily at outdoing their peers, preferring smaller buildings intended for the burial of their

---

[3] Late republican funerary architecture: Eisner 1986, *passim*. Tomb types: Hesberg 1992, 22–6; 55–230.

FIGURE 28.2 Vatican necropolis, under St Peter's basilica, second–third century AD.

families and friends and decorated on the inside rather than on the outside. Roman tombs now became what inscriptions regularly call a *domus aeterna*. Having been built using bricks, they were arranged tightly next to one another, thus forming long funerary streets (Fig. 28.2). Their interior decoration could be, and habitually still was, sumptuous, as evidenced by the mausoleum of Valerius Herma in the Vatican necropolis, which was decked out with the most exquisite stucco work one could possibly imagine. A recent study of 1,550 inscriptions from *CIL* 6 specifying tomb size confirms what the archaeology of sites such the Vatican necropolis already seems to suggest, namely that two-thirds of all graves fall within a 10 × 10 to 20 × 20 m surface range. Not surprisingly and by contrast, to the emperor size continued to matter. Thus, Augustus' architects adopted the already impressive tumulus tomb type and transformed it into the largest sepulchre Rome had ever seen: the Mausoleum of Augustus on the Campus Martius. With a height of 45 m and diameter of 90 m, this elaborate monument was not just a place destined to receive the bodies of the imperial family up to Nerva (with some exceptions); it was one that, hardly accidentally, was to live on in the still more colossal Mausoleum of Hadrian, which served as the empire's main imperial crypt until the time of the Severi (again with some exceptions).[4]

From the first century AD onwards, then, and provided you were not the emperor, impressing others through one's funerary architecture occurred no longer through tomb size but by means of patronage, i.e. by providing one's dependants with a proper burial place. Patronage frequently, although not always, stands at the basis of what may rightfully be considered as the quintessential type of Roman tombs: the *columbarium*. Tombs of this kind, which contain the ashes of the deceased, normally in urns placed two-by-two in shallow niches, are essentially a phenomenon dating to the early imperial period, up to the reign of Claudius, when *columbaria* offering space to as many as 1,000 to 1,500 individuals were not unusual. Then *columbaria* disappeared, to undergo one final and brief renaissance in the decades between Trajan and Antoninus Pius. By that time, however, their appearance had changed quite dramatically as they were now transformed into small, lavishly decorated and intimate family tombs.[5]

Lack of space resulting from a second-century shift from cremation to inhumation caused further changes in the formal appearance of the Romans' funerary architecture. Not only did existing tombs now begin to receive underground extensions to accommodate additional, space-consuming dead bodies, Romans also started to build tombs constructed underground entirely and typically consisting of a network of interconnected galleries and burial chambers. Such *hypogea* were popular among pagans as well as early Christians whose funerary architecture can be traced beginning in the third century, with one important difference: where pagan *hypogea* never seem to have lost their essentially private character and are richly decorated and generally quite small, early Christian *hypogea* tend, by contrast, to be larger from the outset. They also lack visual decoration and mostly contain simple shelf-like graves or *loculi*. This suggests that early Christian *hypogea* were constructed from the very beginning with an eye to accommodating a numerically rapidly increasing community of believers rather than a narrowly circumscribed genetic group – an idea which, as recent radiocarbon dating in the Jewish catacombs of Rome reveals, Rome's early Christians are likely to have derived from the cultural matrix out of which early Christianity in Rome arose, namely the local

---

[4] Family tombs: Hesberg 1992, 37–42. Tomb size *CIL* 6: Eck in Heinzelmann 2001, 197–201.

[5] *Columbaria:* Jonckheere 2006, 73–130.

Jewish community, who also used catacombs for the burial of their dead.[6]

How *hypogea* evolved subsequently into catacombs consisting of an extensive network of underground galleries can best be illustrated by looking briefly at the so-called Area 1 in the catacombs of St Callixtus on the Appian Way, which is normally believed to be identical with the communal cemetery for the Christian poor commissioned by Pope Zepherynus in the early third century AD (Fig. 28.3). There two separate galleries (A and B) underwent various extensions in length and depth while they were also being interconnected through transversal galleries (C to I), receiving various burial chambers including the crypt of the popes (L[1]) in the process, thus increasing the total number of available tombs from a hypothesized original 180 to at least 1,500 within less than a few decades. In the second half of the third century, such developments picked up further speed, here as well as in other early Christian catacombs. Yet it was not until the fourth century, as the Christianization of the Roman empire got underway on a more substantial scale, that Rome's early Christian catacombs evolved into the massive subterranean cemeteries we know today.[7]

During this same period, especially in the first half of the fourth century, no less than eight funerary basilicas – among which St Peter's basilica is surely the most prominent – also emerged on the outskirts of the city, always near and sometimes directly over named catacombs. As the partial recent excavation of one such basilica, located between the Appian Way and Via Ardeatina, reveals, these *coemeteria subteglata* could accommodate a thousand burials or more under the nave and aisles, and still more in the mausoleums constructed against the basilica's outer walls by those who could afford it. It is in this specific Christianized architectural context that the great imperial mausoleums of old resurface one last time: Constantina's circular mausoleum on the Via Nomentana is but the most accomplished example of several such circular buildings that now emerged (Fig. 28.5). These large basilicas with annexed mausoleums, then, are the structures that bring the history of Roman funerary architecture to a definitive close: while burial in the catacombs was discontinued in the early fifth century AD, burial in the suburban funerary basilicas

---

[6] Pagan versus early Christian *hypogea*: Jonckheere 2006, 131–275. Radiocarbon dating: Rutgers et al. 2006.

[7] Area 1: Fiocchi Nicolai and Guyon 2006, 121–62. Catacombs in general: Fiocchi Nicolai 2001, 7–92.

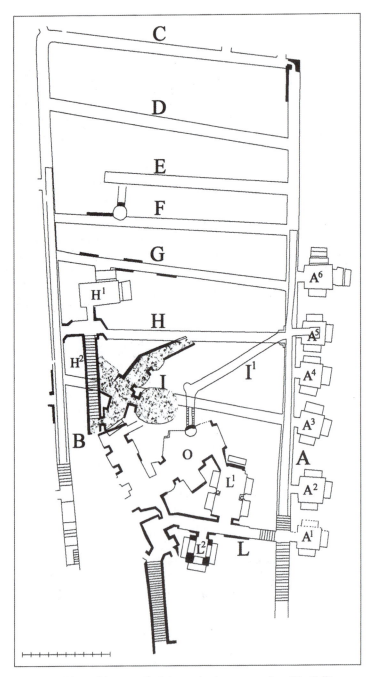

FIGURE 28.3 Plan of the so-called Area I in the catacombs of St Callixtus on the Appian Way, first half of the third century AD.

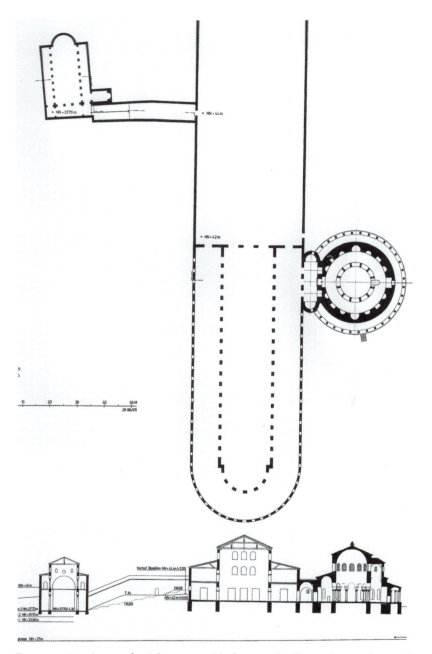

FIGURE 28.4 Agnese fuori le mura, with funerary basilica and mausoleum of Constantina (Sta. Costanza), plan and sections, first half of the fourth century AD.

FIGURE 28.5 Acrosolium with wall painting showing young Trebius Iustus, *hypogeum* of Trebius Iustus, Via Latina, first half of the fourth century AD.

continued well into the sixth century, at which time this practice fell into disuse too, and was replaced by a thoroughly un-Roman and typically Christian practice: intramural burials.[8]

ICONOGRAPHY

While many, if not most, Romans were entombed in sepulchres that lacked any visual decoration whatsoever, others were much concerned, already during their lifetimes, with the erection of tombs embellished with sculpture in the round, reliefs, mosaics, wall paintings, stucco decoration, and, from the mid second to early fifth century onwards, with richly carved and prominently displayed polychrome sarcophagi made of marble. Ever since Arthur Darby Nock's scathing critique of François Cumont's work on pagan Roman funerary symbolism, scholars have been somewhat less than confident in their interpretation of the

---

[8] Funerary basilicas: Fiocchi Nicolai 1995-6. Sta. Costanza: Rasch and Arbeiter 2007. Intramural burials: Fiocchi Nicolai 2001, 131–7.

iconographic programmes that appear with some regularity in republican and imperial Roman funerary contexts and it is surely no coincidence that we are presently still in need of an up-to-date comprehensive
monographic study on that topic.[9]

During the entire period under study here, artistic renderings of
how the respective tomb owners earned their living can be seen frequently to decorate either the exterior or the interior of the tombs
in question. That such representations enjoyed widespread popularity
among the financially secure within Rome's working classes is best evidenced by the fact that several of the key monuments in the history
of Roman funerary architecture fall precisely into this category. These
include the late first-century BC tomb of the *pistor* Marcus Vergilius
Eurysaces, recovered in 1838 during work on the Porta Maggiore –
a monument famously crowned by a set of decorative reliefs sporting various aspects of his trade. They also include an incomplete yet
magnificently sculpted set of early second-century AD marble reliefs
discovered under unclear archaeological circumstances at Centocelle
and now on display in the Vatican Museums. These plaques, which are
known as the Haterii reliefs, contain not just a miniature representation
of the funerary temple these plates are likely to have decorated, but also
a detailed rendering of an impressive crane used by an entrepreneur
(*redemptor*) who ordered these stones for the specific purpose of illustrating not merely the nature of his trade, but his keen sense of business
as well. To the same class of monuments belong, finally, several fourth-
century AD paintings preserved in Trebius Iustus' *hypogeum* on the Via
Latina, which contain pictorial representations of a *generosus magister*,
probably the tomb's owner, and of young Trebius Iustus himself, who
faces us neatly as books and various types of writing gear encircle him
(Fig. 28.5).[10] Gradual changes in the religious composition of the city's
populace in Late Antiquity did little to alter the popularity of work-
related representations such as these: visual renderings of, as well as
epigraphic references to, the world of hard physical labour were just
as popular in the artwork from the early Christian catacombs as on
pagan monuments from an earlier time, even though, as time went on,

---

[9] Nock 1946.

[10] Eurysaces: *LTUR* s.v. Sepulcrum: M. Vergilius Eurysaces; Hackworth Petersen 2006,
84–120. Reliefs of the Haterii: Sinn and Freyberger 1996, esp. 22–6, 28, and Kat. 6.
Hypogeum of Trebius Iustus: Bisconti in Rea 2004, 133–47.

such images clearly lost some of the sculptural sophistication and artistic appeal that had once inhabited them.[11]

In addition to illustrating the activities that shaped their daily lives, the Romans were particularly keen on displaying their wealth, erudition and socio-political status while ordering the iconographical programmes that graced the decorative apparel, floors, walls and ceilings of their funerary monuments. Giving visual expression to such things mattered especially to those who had reason to fear that they would be slighted by those who considered themselves to be their betters in society: people like the freedman Trimalchio – an archetypical *nouveau riche* figure who is portrayed by Petronius, the *arbiter elegantiae* who concocted him, as unpolished enough to have ordered an epitaph that specified how this self-made man had 'never listened to a philosopher' and, in spite of his humble origins, might in fact 'have been attendant on any magistrate in Rome, but refused it' (Petronius, *Satyricon* 71). The extent to which *liberti* cared about impressing others is plainly evident from the surviving epigraphic evidence but can perhaps best be illustrated by referring to a series of some 270 funerary reliefs that, in turn, contain no less than 450 portraits and that date, without exception, to the late republican and early Augustan times. They display the freedmen and their families either as full length life-size figures or, more commonly (Fig. 28.6), as life-sized busts that stiffly face the passer-by, addressing him or her through accompanying inscriptions that carry phrases such as *omnes hei mei sunt*, 'all these (i.e. the people represented here) are mine (i.e. members of my family)' (*CIL* 6, 14338). As Valentin Kockel has shown in a thorough monographic study of these reliefs, the people appearing here present themselves not just as status-conscious, but as preparing towards climbing further up the rungs of Rome's steep social ladder: dressing as true upper-class Romans, the *togati* and *matronae* that group together on these reliefs represent a two-dimensional or economical alternative to the three-dimensional statuary that decorated the funerary monuments of the Roman aristocracy – monuments that the reliefs of these *liberti* unmistakably seek to imitate. Nor is it by accident that the otherwise not very personalized faces on these sculpted plaques remind one at times of the great political leaders of the final days of the Roman Republic. Similarly and finally, nothing but conscious choice explains why some of the latest busts in the series have in fact evolved into sculpture in the round: thus was created an allusion to the portrait bust galleries famously owned by the aristocracy (*ius*

[11] Pagan: Zimmer 1982. Early Christian: Bisconti 2000.

FIGURE 28.6 Tomb facade with marble relief displaying a family of freedmen, Via Appia, late first century BC.

imaginum) and used by them to impress upon their contemporaries the venerability of their service to the state and the unassailability of their privileged societal position.[12]

While portrait busts of the type briefly referred to here characterize Roman funerary art during the later years of the Republic and the first years of the Principate, it was the large-scale production of sarcophagi, of which some 6,000 survive, that led to – or at least accompanied – the emergence of yet another artistic trend in the decoration of Roman tombs: the inclusion of representations whose subject matter was taken from Greek mythology. From a modern interpretational perspective, the mythological scenes included on these coffins are surely among the most elusive within the totality of funerary iconography under the pagan Roman empire. While some of these mythological narratives – such as the abduction of Persephone – seem appropriate enough for the funerary context in which they appear, others strike the modern observer as odd and out of place. What to make of all those

---

[12] Kockel 1993, esp. 77–9. The identification of these reliefs as belonging to the class of the *liberti* is based on a collection of seventy accompanying inscriptions.

merry-go-lucky celebrants that frolic around as part of the Dionysiac *thiasoi* and that adorn the fronts of sarcophagi on so many occasions, for example, or why include the myth of Niobe, the unfortunate mother who caused the death of all of her children, having failed miserably to gain control over her own hubris? According to the latest comprehensive study on Roman sarcophagi the Romans did not normally read too much into the myths they chose to include. Being paradigmatic in a very general sense only, such myths are now believed to express either pain and sorrow, 'visions of joy' or praise in respect to the deceased's virtues or accomplishments. On such a reading the story of Niobe comes to symbolize a more universalized kind of notion, namely the insufferable distress endured by all parents faced with losing a child. The fact that on Roman sarcophagi Niobe's children often take centre stage while she herself fades into the background, strongly supports such a reading. Along similar lines, the visual coalescence of mortal humans with immortal gods does not necessarily point towards such humans following in the footsteps of the emperors who, upon their death, were believed to enter forthwith into a divinized state. Whenever an Aphrodite-figure appears whose face has been replaced by a portrait of the deceased, for example, it is merely the celebration of past beauty rather than the production of an oncoming apotheosis that is at stake.[13]

In the years AD 230–50 the funerary iconography of the pagan Romans underwent one final thematic change: mythological pictures now largely disappeared as they were replaced by less exuberant representations that typically included pensive philosophers celebrating the ideal of the *mousikos anēr* (Fig. 28.7), shepherds in bucolic settings and renderings of the seasons. Such representations form the matrix in which the funerary art of Late Antiquity – both that of the Jews and of the early Christians – germinated. That Roman Jews ordered whatever artefacts or decorations they needed from the same workshops as their pagan and early Christian contemporaries follows particularly clearly from the fragment of a season sarcophagus on which the central *clipeus* does not carry the traditional image of the deceased or of a deceased couple united in *dextrarum iunctio*, but the sculpted image of a menorah or seven-branched candelabrum instead. Pieces such as this were not made by Roman Jews themselves in separate workshops. Rather they were customized only after they had originated from specialized

---

[13] Mythology on Roman sarcophagi: Koch and Sichtermann 1982, esp. 583–617. Latest comprehensive study: Zanker and Ewald 2004, 28–266, esp. 196–201.

FIGURE 28.7 Sarcophagus from Acilia with representation of philosophers, mid to late third century AD.

pagan workshops geared towards mass production and governed by a high degree of internal division of labour. Along with the fact that biblical scenes – which are omnipresent in early Christian art – are entirely absent in the funerary art of the Jews of ancient Rome, this phenomenon of workshop identity finally also helps to demonstrate that early Christian art in Rome does not have Jewish roots but, like Jewish art, likewise emerged in the course of the third century AD from pagan workshops capable of transforming popular iconographical types or scenes into representations Christians could infuse with a new, typically Christian meaning.[14]

While the city of Rome holds the unique distinction of being the only place in the entire Roman empire where the inception and initial development of early Christian art can still be reconstructed step by step as a result of the many early Christian wall paintings, gold glasses and pottery lamps that have survived, it is once more the 1,200 or so early Christian sarcophagi made in Rome itself that allow us to retrace the successive iconographic stages that characterize this process

[14] Jewish art in Rome and workshop identity: Rutgers 1995, 50–99.

FIGURE 28.8 Early Christian sarcophagus with reclining Jonah, praying female figure, seated philosopher, Good Shepherd and baptismal scene. Rome, S. Maria Antiqua. Later third century AD.

in a chronologically coherent fashion. Early Christian art first emerged in tetrarchic times, when the traditional pagan workshops not only continued to produce the traditional representations of bucolic figures that early Christians could easily interpret as referring to 'the Good Shepherd'. They also transformed existing iconography, such as representations of the sleeping Endymion, into biblical figures like the prophet Jonah at rest under his pergola (Fig. 28.8). Thus originated sarcophagi that stress the notion of salvation by means of loosely inserting stories inspired not only by New Testament texts on the baptism of Jesus or the raising of Lazarus, but by a number of narratives taken from the Old Testament as well, including, for example, representations of Noah alive and well in his Ark or of Daniel immersed in prayer among ferocious animals in the Lion's Den. A massive production of truly and wholly Christian sarcophagi started several years later, under Constantine: the miracles performed by Jesus and events taken from the life of Peter – evidently a figure of great ideological importance to Christians, especially in Rome – now gain particular prominence in paratactic arrangements that no longer leave any room at all for pagan subject matter. In the post-Constantinian era, early Christian sarcophagi production seems to have been somewhat on the decline again, even though renderings of the passion of Jesus now make their first appearance, documenting that for the first time in Roman history the cross is no longer considered as a token of disgrace but as a symbol that inspires pride and self-confidence instead. In Theodosian times and until AD 400 when early Christian sarcophagus production ceases definitively in Rome, early Christian iconography catches on once more to come full circle: in addition to several new scenes including that of the *traditio legis*, Jesus now appears no longer as a young man in a philosopher's garb, but as powerful sovereign set to rule over the entire universe.[15]

A full discussion of early Christian funerary art – with its exclusive emphasis on biblical imagery and its dislike for portraits and the host of other more playful iconographic motifs that had characterized pagan Roman funerary art continuously during a period of at least four hundred years – cannot detain us here. Let us merely recall, by way of conclusion, that attempts by an earlier generation of scholars to identify traces of syncretism or even heresy everywhere within early Christianity's iconographic record – as based on the unspoken assumption that heterodox Christians either had the leisure or the desire to engage in the systematic development of such an alternative iconographic language – have now been replaced with more commonsensical approaches. To give but one illustrative example, the collection of interconnected mid-fourth-century *hypogea* which are known under the erroneous name of 'catacomb' of the Via Latina (also Dino Compagni) and in which typically pagan themes taken from the life of Hercules appear contiguously with scenes that are characteristically early Christian – such as representations of Daniel in the Lion's Den or the Raising of Lazarus, amongst many others – are surely not indicative of an early Christianity gone astray totally. Instead they point towards the coexistence of Christianity and paganism among the well-to-do in fourth-century Rome, as the excavator of the site, Antonio Ferrua, has argued so cogently.[16] Such an argument is particularly convincing because it sits well with everything we know about the Christianization of Rome's upper classes during the fourth century AD on the one hand and with the sociology of conversion processes, which are known to be protracted events, on the other. The single most remarkable aspect of the interrelationship of pagan and early Christian funerary art in the later years of the Roman empire, therefore, is not so much that such art sometimes occurs side by side within one and the same archaeological context. It is rather that pagan iconographical themes disappear so rapidly from view at a time when no more than an estimated 10 per cent of all inhabitants of the Roman empire had converted to Christianity: after the early fourth century AD not only are pagan sarcophagi few and far between, painted interiors displaying pagan imagery also largely disappear from view, as evidenced by a new study of eighty-two securely dated specimens of

---

[15] Koch 2000, esp. 125–9 and 209–16. [16] Ferrua 1991, 153–65.

which no more than a trifling 3.3 per cent can be said to belong the period after AD 250.[17]

BURIAL CUSTOMS

Throughout their long history, the inhabitants of Rome are known to have practised inhumation as well as cremation. The embalming of the dead also occurred, as evidenced by isolated literary and archaeological evidence such as the Grotta Rossa mummy, but it was decidedly less popular. Scholarship has long maintained that cremation was the most popular – although not exclusive – mode of burial from later republican until Hadrianic times onwards, at which time it was being replaced gradually by inhumation as the preferred way of disposing of the dead. The huge *columbaria* of the early imperial period on the one hand and the large-scale production of sarcophagi, which began to set in under Trajan, on the other, can easily be adduced as the most tangible markers of this process, just as the Vatican necropolis can be said to contain the best archaeological evidence to illustrate the gradual nature of this transformation. Following Nock's work on this particular issue, scholars now also generally believe that the re-emergence of inhumation in the course of the second century AD should not be ascribed to oriental influences or to changes in religious affiliation or climate, let alone to the rise of Christianity. Instead, no deeper meaning is deemed to attach to the second-century change back from cremation to inhumation.[18] Be that as it may, the question of how cremation and inhumation interrelated, particularly in first-century AD Rome, is still far from settled. Recent archaeological excavations at a necropolis located along the ancient Via Triumphalis on the present-day grounds of the Vatican, for example, have revealed that throughout the first century AD, inhumation was not in the least uncommon, and other cemeteries further afield that have likewise managed to escape Rome's urban sprawl point in exactly the same direction: these necropoleis of the common folk also suggest that throughout all of Roman history the digging of a simple hole in the ground to dispose of a dead body was always more cost-effective than the erection of an elaborate funerary pyre and the subsequent burial in an urn (*olla*) that was installed in either the bright stucco niches of a

[17] Late pagan sarcophagi: Koch and Sichtermann 1982, 62, 258–9; Koch 2000, 346–53. Recent study: Feraudi-Gruénais, 2001, 164–6.

[18] Nock 1932; Koch and Sichtermann 1982, 25–30; Schrumpf 2006, 70–7.

monumental *columbarium* or in the dark and damp recesses of a plain earthen grave.[19] If anything, it was not the rise of inhumation as much as the demise of cremation that characterizes burial customs around Rome during the second century AD. The cessation of such elaborate and expensive cremation rituals, which had long been favoured by the rich and famous as an ideal way publicly to exhibit their wealth and status yet again, coincides with a previously noted general shift away from embellishing the conspicuous exteriors of tombs to decorating their more private interiors. It shows that, in any case, this era saw a major change in how Romans handled the public display of death. As for Rome's early Christians, their writers claim they never cremated their dead (e.g. Minucius Felix, *Octavius* 34.10). Whether this is really so, we will never know, since neither archaeology nor epigraphy allows us to identify the physical remains of early Christian tombs prior to the late second century AD. Obviously, the Christian preference for inhumation had biblical roots (Athanasius, *Vita Antonii* 90) and followed contemporary Jewish practice as evidenced, in Rome itself, by the Jewish community, which is known to have always favoured the inhumation over the cremation of their dead.

Of all the other burial customs that are characteristically Roman and that have left traces in the archaeological record, only two of the more salient ones will be touched upon briefly in the present context: the installation of terracotta or lead pipes directly over the graves as well as the deposition of coins into them. Archaeology confirms amply what literary and epigraphic sources also tell us, namely that the consumption of festive commemorative meals at the grave site itself was a recurrent feature of how the Romans cared to remember their dead. Architectural remains of ovens and wells that sometimes contain fragments of cooking vessels, even separate rooms as well as leftover remains of animal bone, all go to show that the custom must have been quite widespread.[20] One of the most distinctive characteristics of this Roman ritual, however, was that the dead partook of such meals regularly by means of food offerings that were introduced into the graves either through perforated grave covers, as in the case of several tombs in the Vatican necropolis,

[19] Via Triumphalis: Steinby in Heinzelmann 2001, 31–4. Further afield: Pellegrino in Heinzelmann 2001, 123–5 (Via Ostiense near Acilia); Taglietti in Heinzelmann 2001, 149–58 (Isola Sacra), esp. 157–8.
[20] Literary and epigraphic sources: Schrumpf 2006, 104–5. Separate rooms: *AE* 1977, 31. Well with cooking pottery: Messineo in Heinzelmann 2001, 138. Animal bones: Colonnelli in Buccellato et al. 2003, 359–72.

or, more commonly, through hollow tubes that could be inserted into stone and terracotta sarcophagi as well as directly into earthen graves. Recent excavations reveal how universal the practice must have been: even in cemeteries that lack graves of the more wealthy variety, the presence of tubes still seems to be a common occurrence. Thus they appear not just on top of very different types of graves, but even the preferred mode of burial – inhumation or cremation – does not seem to have affected the use of this practice in any way. According to one report, there is even evidence of such a terracotta pipe feeding directly into the mouth of the person buried under it.[21] No less interestingly, early Christian remains testify to the fact that in this particular area old habits died hard: the Lot sarcophagus from the catacombs of St Sebastian that had been prepared to receive the traditional *profusiones* (libations or pouring in of liquids to honour the dead), for example, or early Christian wall paintings that display funerary banquets as their main theme illustrate the continued pervasiveness of such practices in much the same way as does a well-known passage in the *Confessions* of Augustine – one in which Hippo's most illustrious son relates how his unsuspecting mother Monica discovered that funerary meals in honour of the 'holy' dead were considered completely out of bounds for any true Christian, precisely because such activities were deemed to be identical with the *parentalia* traditionally celebrated by her pagan contemporaries (Augustine, *Confessiones* 6.2).[22]

Something very similar holds true for the second custom to be discussed here briefly, namely that of placing a coin in the deceased's mouth. It is again archaeology that has revealed the extent to which depositing these artefacts – Charon's fare – into the oral cavity of the departed mattered to the Romans during the long years under pagan rule: in a single cemetery it is possible for several dozens of coins located in precisely that position to turn up. While such a custom has long been considered as quintessentially pagan, archaeology now tells a different, more nuanced story: in the *loculi* of the early Christian catacombs of Rome as well as in the graves of the previously mentioned funerary basilica located between the Via Appia and the Via Ardeatina – a

---

[21] Examples of tubes: Steinby in Heinzelmann 2001, 34; Cupitò in Heinzelmann 2001, 52; Taglietti in Heinzelmann 2001, 156; Spadoni in Egidi et al. 2003, 28; Buccellato et al. 2003, 325. Tube into mouth: Cupitò in Heinzelmann 2001, 52.
[22] Sarcophagus from San Sebastiano: Koch 2000, 92. Banquets on wall paintings: Bisconti 2000, 80–90. On Augustine and other early Christian evidence: Volp 2002, 214–24.

building definitely patronized by Christians and by them alone – coins are not an uncommon occurrence either.[23] Thus archaeology reveals once more what has been observed before while discussing the wall paintings preserved in the *hypogea* of the Via Latina (also Dino Compagni), namely that for large segments of Rome's population the Christianization of their world was as slow and drawn-out a process as it was a cumbersome for those trying to control it.

FUNERARY ORGANIZATION

Although the Romans were familiar with the notion of a funeral at public expense (*funus publicum*) – this was standard procedure, for example, in the event of the death of an emperor – burial was normally a private matter. As a result of the history of research on this particular aspect of Roman funerary customs, the typical Roman way of handling death is often seen as revolving around the family as the central organizational unit. During the golden years of the pagan Roman empire, it was indeed usual for families to construct *mausolea* or *hypogea* that possessed all the necessary architectural arrangements for either burying the members of the nuclear family (*fecit sibi familiaeque suae*, 'he made it for himself and his family') or, alternatively, for entombing other members of the household as well (*fecit sibi et suis et libertis libertabusque posterisque eorum*, 'he made it for himself, his next of kin, his freedmen and freedwomen and their descendants').

Considering the socio-economic composition of Rome's population at large it is evident, however, that many, if not most people were never in a position to avail themselves of such family-tomb arrangements: all they could do was hope that one day they would be able to afford as much as a single grave. To facilitate the acquisition of such single tombs and to defray further costs that attended the proper burial of one's earthly remains, *collegia* or social clubs emerged that have left a fair deal of inscriptional evidence which, in turn, has fuelled a substantial amount of scholarly attention for over a century. While Theodor Mommsen's notion to the effect that during the pagan Roman empire there existed separate *collegia funeraticia* whose sole purpose was

---

[23] Coins in pagan cemeteries in general: Ceci in Heinzelmann 2001, 87–97. Individual cemeteries: Pellegrino in Heinzelmann 2001, 125; Accurso in Egidi et al. 2003, 40; Buccellato et al. 2003, 318 and 332. Coins in catacombs: Rutgers et al. 2007. Coins in the funerary basilica: Fiocchi Nicolai 1995-6, 116.

to attend to the proper burial of their members has long been abandoned, recent work has nonetheless concluded quite uniformly that the funerary aspect was of central importance in the functioning of many an association. Such was the case, particularly, because the gatherings that surrounded the burial of individual members and the concomitant ritual commemoration of deceased ones helped to reaffirm the social cohesion that constituted the *raison d'être* of such *collegia* in the first place.[24]

Although there can be no doubt that *collegia* filled an important void in catering to the funerary needs of those who had few connections in society but at least some money to spare, it is also true that membership of a *collegium* was never a prerequisite for obtaining a decent grave. Not only was it normal for *collegia* to sell off surplus graves to outsiders who had not formally been granted membership, there also seems to have been a vibrant free market ruled by supply and demand rather than by mere social concerns, as Stefan Schrumpf has argued lately. Such a free market consisted either of enterprising individuals with sufficient means to finance the construction of a sizeable funerary monument, or of *societates monumenti*, i.e. groups of people that pursued the same goal by pooling their resources, dissolving again as soon as the projected tomb had been completed and the various sets of graves contained therein had been shared out to the collaborating payees. Graves could then be sold individually, which is precisely what happened, witness the heterogeneous provenance of those buried alongside one another in one and the same *columbarium*.[25] Whether the simple *fossa* and *cappucina* tombs that crowd so many of Rome's suburban cemeteries also entered into this regime of buying and selling is certainly a possibility, but one that escapes ascertaining, for lack of good primary evidence.

As for the organization of activities surrounding the actual burying of the dead we have reason to believe that during the first two centuries of the empire the situation described in inscriptions from Pozzuoli and Cumae applied to the city of Rome as well. Arranging for a person's last journey was a monopoly that was farmed out by the state to a *libitinarius* who did not necessarily perform such work himself but who, at any rate, directed an enterprise that in Puteoli (modern Pozzuoli) consisted of a legally required minimum number of thirty-two able-bodied employees between the ages of 20 and 50. Not surprisingly,

[24] *Collegia*: Schrumpf 2006, esp. 169–98. See also Chapter 20.
[25] Schrumpf 2006, 198–224 (arguing, furthermore, that *societates* could also operate within *collegia*).

such a monopoly came at a cost: in exchange for the exclusive right of handling the preparation of the dead body of any deceased city dweller as well as its subsequent transport and burial, funerary undertakers of the type discussed here were obliged also to remove from the city, normally within a day, any unclaimed human corpses and animal carcasses that might turn up. They finally also had to perform death penalties decreed by the magistrates and could torture slaves whenever the 'necessity' to do so arose.[26]

Did any of the habits and arrangements summarized here manage to survive into Late Antiquity? The answer to that question is manifold. The burial system based on the exclusive services of the *libitinarii* appears to have dissolved over the course of the third century AD. During this same period, the evidence for the continued existence of *collegia* involved in funerary matters likewise declined rapidly even though it did not disappear completely as suggested, perhaps, by the evidence preserved in the cubiculum of the *mensores* in the early Christian catacombs of Domitilla. Archaeology suggests that families continued to constitute a vital element in the disposal of the dead anyway – this despite the fact that the dearth of epigraphic data on the one hand and the large size of early Christian *hypogea* on the other make it usually hard to determine the exact relationship between, on the one hand, the person financing such subterranean tombs and, on the other, all those anonymous individuals buried in the simple grave recesses that generally characterize such sites. Uncertainty on matters such as these also explains the recent attempt to view *collegia* as the driving force not just behind smaller underground burial sites, but behind the much larger early Christian catacombs as well. The more traditional majority view, by contrast, sees little in such a notion, but ascribes the emergence of these catacombs to the organizational efforts of the early Church instead. While this latter view seems indeed to be the more likely one, it must be stressed that the precise nature and extent of ecclesiastical involvement – the church as the ultimate patron of all Christian believers without cash – nevertheless continues to elude us. Inscriptions suggest in any case, that, in spite of the church's policy to bury the poor free of charge, graves were typically sold rather than doled out for free. During the fourth and fifth centuries AD such sales were effectuated either by individuals or by small groups of *fossores*. Being disposers of corpses, gravediggers as well as builders of catacombs who took much pride in their work as evidenced by inscriptions and wall paintings that show

[26] Schrumpf 2006, 239–81.

them wielding the tools of their trade, these *fossores* easily remind one of the personnel employed by the *libitinarius*, except for the fact that, again, the extent to which they did or did not operate under ecclesiastical supervision remains largely unclear. The early medieval cessation of burial in the catacombs combined with a shift to inner-city burials brings these developments to a close: while the *fossores* disappear, urban priests now take on the full responsibility of burying the faithful in the respective urban churches to which these official representatives of the Roman church had been assigned.[27]

LATEST DEVELOPMENTS

The single largest idiosyncrasy characterizing the modern scholarly study of Rome's cemeteries and catacombs is that archaeologists have persisted in abstaining, until very recently, from studying the skeletal remains of those without whose patronage all these tombs would never have materialized in the first place. As for pagan Rome, while only a minute fraction of the physical anthropological work performed over the last ten to fifteen years has been published properly, this situation is now gradually starting to change, as full or partial reports on the human and animal bones from such sites as the Via Basiliano, the Osteria del Curato I–V, the necropolis of Lucrezia Romana I, as well as the *hypogeum* of Trebius Iustus have begun to appear. In addition to generating insights into questions of life expectancy, sex-ratios and into the palaeopathology of the skeletal populations under study, these publications provide us with evidence to prove definitively that a staggering 50 per cent of Rome's population did indeed not live to see their fifth birthday (as hypothesized previously by historical demographers on the basis of modern statistical proxy data such as those extracted from Coale and Demeny's Regional Model Life Tables).[28] As for the early Christian catacombs of Rome, progress in the area of physical anthropology is of even more recent date. In addition to a short preliminary report

---

[27] *Mensores* in Domitilla: Pergola 1990. *Collegia* and catacombs: Rebillard 2003. Traditional view: Fiocchi Nicolai and Guyon 2006, 158. *Fossores*: Guyon 1974. Representations of *fossores*: Bisconti 2000, 93–8.

[28] Brief synthesis: Catalano et al. 2001. Via Basiliano: Buccellato et al. 2003, 328–58. Osteria del Curato: Egidi et al. 2003. Trebius Iustus: Catalano et al. in Rea 2004, 107–31 (includes DNA). Particularly interesting also is the work of Tracy Prowse and her associates: Prowse et al. 2007 (contains references to her earlier work).

on a mass grave of uncertain date preserved in the catacombs of Marcellinus and Petrus on the Via Labicana, a recent stable isotope analysis study of an early Christian population buried in the so-called Liberian Region in the catacombs of St Callixtus indicates what possibilities the future may hold in store here too. Showing that freshwater fish must have been an important source of protein intake for the early Christian population under scrutiny, this latter study explores the historical ramifications of these results by arguing that a general absence of meat in this population's diet is indicative of a relative lack of wealth rather than of religiously motivated ascetic behaviour.[29]

FURTHER READING

On pagan funerary architecture, the articles collected in Hesberg and Zanker 1987 and in Heinzelmann 2001 provide useful introductions to recent work. For an eminently readable recent study on pagan funerary imagery as contained on sarcophagi, see Zanker and Ewald 2004. On early Christian art, Engemann 1997 is a good place to start. On the early Christian catacombs of Rome, Fiocchi Nicolai 2001 is crucial. On Jewish materials, Rutgers 1995, 2006 and Rutgers et al. 2006 have the latest.

[29] Marcellinus and Petrus catacomb: Blanchard et al. 2007. Stable isotope analysis: Rutgers et al. 2009. Further work on the Liberian region: Van der Linde 2008, 99–133.

29: WHAT DIFFERENCE DID CHRISTIANITY MAKE?

A. D. Lee

T he presence of Christians in the city of Rome from the mid-first century is attested by both classical and Christian sources, with the city's Jewish community the obvious conduit for its initial establishment.[1] However, although occasional glimpses of the development of the city's Christian community over the first three centuries can be gleaned from the surviving textual sources, it is only with the advent of Constantine as sole emperor in the west in 312 and his decision to lend his support to the church that it becomes possible to offer meaningful observations as to what difference Christianity made to the city of Rome. But assessing that impact during the fourth century and beyond is complicated by the need to take account of other significant changes which affected the city during the same period, above all the fact that Rome ceased to be an imperial capital and emperors rarely, if ever, visited the city.[2] This important development – the outcome of the empire's pressing military problems during the third century and the need for emperors to base themselves near the frontiers – shifted the dynamics of power within the city and created greater opportunities for both the senatorial aristocracy and the church to make their presences felt. At the same time, the empire's military problems eventually came to impinge directly on the city as, at various points during the fifth century, Rome found itself besieged and plundered by foreign peoples for the first time in eight centuries.

Of necessity, the following discussion limits itself to a consideration of those aspects most readily relevant to the central question: the impact of Christianity on major social groups in the life of the city – on

---

[1] Suetonius, *Claud.* 25.4; Tacitus, *Ann.* 15.44; Acts 18.2, 28.15; Rom. 16.1–16.
[2] Constantine's rival, Maxentius (306–12), was the only emperor to reside in Rome for a continuous and extended period during the fourth century. Fifth-century emperors again frequented it more regularly in the third quarter of the fifth century (Gillett 2001).

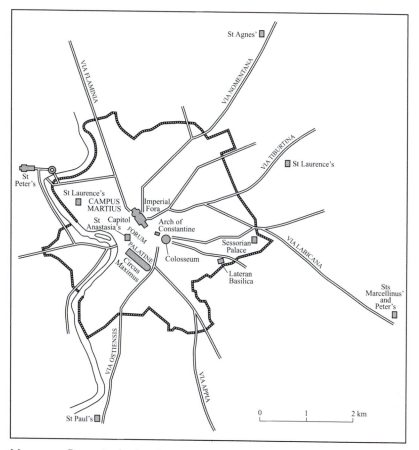

MAP 29.1 Rome in the fourth century AD.

the one hand, the senatorial aristocracy, and on the other, the urban populace – and the significance of the emergence of the bishop of Rome as a central figure in the affairs of the city. First, however, consideration is given to an aspect which might at first sight appear superficial, but which has the potential to offer important insights into more fundamental issues: how Christianity altered the physical appearance of the city.

CHRISTIANITY AND THE TOPOGRAPHY
OF THE CITY

The question of what difference Christianity made is one which was given a polemical edge by Ramsay MacMullen in the 1980s when he discussed it for the Roman world at large with reference to a range of morally charged areas such as sexuality and slavery, and concluded that its impact had mostly been minimal or for the worse.[3] Given his ideological focus, it is perhaps unsurprising that MacMullen began his paper by dismissing change in an area like 'basilica-building' as 'self-evident', without further discussion. In the intervening years, however, there has been a growing appreciation of the potential for the study of urban topography to shed light on larger issues of political and social change, especially in a city with a long and symbolically significant monumental evolution like ancient Rome, and against this background Christianity's impact on the physical cityscape of Rome during Late Antiquity undoubtedly warrants attention.

In his letter to the church in Rome, the apostle Paul referred to the Christians there as meeting in private houses (Romans 16.5) and, as elsewhere in the empire, this is likely to have remained the pattern during the first three centuries. The architectural form of these house churches ensured that, as far as its built expression was concerned, the Christian presence in the city was low profile. Although the late third and early fourth centuries probably saw the construction of some larger meeting halls, these almost certainly remained relatively nondescript.[4] Against this background, Constantine's reign marked a major change, since he sponsored the construction of a number of purpose-built churches which could not fail to be noticed by the city's inhabitants. The earliest and most impressive of these was the Lateran basilica on the Caelian Hill, followed by a number beyond the walls at the sites of martyrs' tombs – St Agnes' on the Via Nomentana to the north-east, St Laurence's on the Via Tiburtina, also to the north-east, Sts Marcellinus' and Peter's on the Via Labicana to the south-east, and, above all, St Peter's on the Vatican Hill to the west.[5]

The location of all these sites at a distance from the civic centre – the one intramural church (the Lateran) was nonetheless situated close to the city walls – has prompted the suggestion that Constantine was concerned to avoid offending pagan sentiment unnecessarily

---

[3] MacMullen 1986. See Clark 2004, 106–11 for a measured rejoinder.
[4] For the evolution of church buildings in the Roman world, see White 1996–7.
[5] For details of Constantine's churches, see Pietri 1976, 3–69; Krautheimer 1980, 20–8; Curran 2000, 90–115. Constantine built another intramural church within the Sessorian Palace complex, but its role as a palace chapel will have limited its public impact. Bowersock 2002 has suggested Constantine's son, Constans (337–50), as the more likely founder of St Peter's.

by imposing any overtly Christian structure among the temples in the heart of the city. This reading, which effectively downplays the impact of Constantine's churches, has, however, been challenged on a number of fronts. First, the location of the Lateran basilica – it was constructed on the site of the horse-guard units closely identified with the regime of Constantine's rival, Maxentius – has plausibly been seen as part of Constantine's larger scheme to eliminate all traces of Maxentius from the cityscape, while its sheer scale (100 m × 55 m) and lavish decoration marked a dramatic step-change in terms of the visibility and prestige of the city's Christian community. Second, the various churches built beyond the walls were located alongside major routes into the city and so were likely to make an impression on many visitors to the city. Third, these extramural churches gave added prominence to the regions of the city where Christian activities had long been concentrated, and so contributed significantly to the development of 'an emerging alternative topography which rivalled that of Rome's traditional landscape'[6] – a shift later highlighted at the start of the fifth century with the observation that 'the city has changed its address, as the populace hurries past the half-ruined temples and pours out to the tombs of the martyrs' (Jerome, *Epistulae* 107.1).

That shift was reinforced by the only other instance of imperially sponsored church-building in the fourth century – the major extramural basilica of St Paul's on the Via Ostiensis to the south of the city, constructed between 384 and 402/3.[7] In the intervening decades, however, successive bishops of Rome had also been active in extending the monumental expressions of the Christian presence in the city in a variety of other directions. In the first half of the century that activity appears to have focused on the hills in the eastern part of the city and the western region of Trastevere, as well as foundations beyond the walls, but without any attempt to match the scale of Constantine's churches. In the middle of the century, the bishop Liberius (352–66) further strengthened the church's physical imprint in the eastern sector of the city by constructing a basilica on the Esquiline Hill, albeit against a background of factional violence between Christians which also affected the

---

[6] For Constantine's concern to avoid offence, see Krautheimer 1980, 29–31; for alternative readings, see Curran 2000, 90–115, Hunt 2003, 115–18 (quotation at 118); for extramural Christian tombs, see Chapter 28.

[7] Pietri 1976, 514–19; Krautheimer 1980, 42–5.

election and initial years of his successor Damasus (366–84).[8] Perhaps partly in an attempt to reassert church unity, Damasus embarked on an ambitious programme of construction which marked another major step-change in Christianity's impact on the city's fabric.

Within the city walls, Damasus was responsible for the building of a distinctively Christian structure on the western edge of the Palatine, dedicated to St Anastasia, and another in the Campus Martius, dedicated to St Laurence. Both churches marked moves into new areas of the city, with the former particularly significant as the first prominent Christian structure near Rome's traditional civic and religious centre. Beyond the city walls, he undertook enhancements of buildings connected to various familiar martyrs' shrines and catacombs, but above all he seems to have organized the systematic identification of a host of less well-known sites associated with martyrs whose profile he raised through the placing of verse inscriptions. In due course this encouraged an ever greater flow of pilgrims to these suburban shrines, which in turn prompted the development of permanent settlements in the city's immediate hinterland in the form of monastic communities and 'service personnel' for the upkeep of the shrines. Damasus' tenure of office therefore marked a very significant phase in the Christianization of the city's topography.[9]

The reverse side of the topographical coin was the impact of Christianity on those structures associated with traditional religion, most obviously temples, but also buildings for entertainment, which had strong religious associations. The festivals which were their *raison d'être* were held in honour of one or other deity; the structures themselves usually incorporated a religious feature (Pompey's theatre, e.g. included a temple of Venus); events staged in them often drew inspiration from mythology and featured deities, as in pantomime; and the entertainment was preceded by religious rituals, such as the *pompa* with which each day of racing at the circus commenced – representations of the gods processing in carriages into the Circus Maximus and receiving sacrifices. The fate of these buildings and their associated activities is therefore as germane to the issue of Christianization as that of temples.

With regard to the latter, emperors did not complement their church building with the active demolition of temples. Indeed, a law

---

[8] Curran 2000, 116–42, who notes that the factional problems give the lie to any notion of a unilinear, homogeneous Christianization of the city.

[9] Curran 2000, 142–55; Trout 2003.

issued by Constantine's sons to the prefect of the city in 342 specified that temples beyond the city walls 'should remain untouched and
undamaged' (*Cod. Theod.* 16.10.3), while another prefect recorded his
repairs to a temple of Apollo in the late 350s (*CIL* 6.45 = *ILS* 3222).
The withdrawal of imperial funding for their maintenance towards the
end of the fourth century will, however, have contributed to the gradual deterioration of their fabric. Nonetheless, a law of the mid fifth
century, while making clear the problem of spoliation, also attests the
continuing concern of emperors even at this stage to preserve the city's
public buildings, including temples, albeit from aesthetic rather than
religious motives – so as to prevent 'the appearance of the venerable
city being marred' (Majorian, *Novellae* 4).[10]

The city's topography, however, was as much about its inhabitants'
use of space as about the inert structures among which they conducted
their lives,[11] and from this perspective the city's temples must have
become increasingly peripheral to the real life of the city as the fourth
century progressed. The same cannot be said, however, about buildings
for entertainment, which, despite the repeated condemnation of church
leaders, remained an important focus for communal life until the sixth
century, and whose physical integrity was therefore maintained at a
reasonable level. That continuity presupposes the willingness of wealthy
individuals to sponsor the staging of games, and it is evident that, for the
duration of the fourth century at least, there were sufficient senatorial
aristocrats with the wherewithal and motivation to fund extravagant
displays in the amphitheatre and circus, as attested in most detail by
the correspondence of Symmachus concerning the preparations for the
games to celebrate his son's magistracies in the 390s, and more succinctly
by the historian Olympiodorus when reporting the enormous sums
expended on such occasions by senators even in the early decades of
the fifth century.[12]

The most important patron of public entertainment, however,
continued to be the emperor – this despite the fact that the church
condemned the games and that, with the short-lived exception of Julian
(361–3), all emperors from Constantine onwards espoused Christianity. This apparent paradox has been explained in a number of ways.
Although emperors rarely spent time in the city during the fourth and
first half of the fifth century, Rome remained the largest city in the

---

[10] See further Ward-Perkins 1984, 85–91.   [11] As noted by Lim 1999, 265–6.
[12] Harries 2003, 129–32 (Symmachus); Olympiodorus *fr.* 43.2.

empire. Its size and symbolic significance meant that emperors could not afford to exacerbate the potential for public disorder already arising from the uncertainties of food supply by banning traditional forms of entertainment (other than those which were particularly repugnant from a Christian perspective, such as the crucifixion of condemned criminals). Moreover, such occasions were vital opportunities to promote the imperial image and reinforce public loyalty to the reigning dynasty. The official justification for imperial patronage of these events is perhaps best summed up by a phrase used in one law which sanctioned the continued staging of events on the stage and in the circus – namely that these were 'the long established amusements (*priscae voluptates*) of the Roman people' (*Codex Theodosianus* 16.10.3). On the one hand, then, it was a case of respect for tradition, and on the other, of rebranding the games as *voluptates* – a term lacking the religious connotations of older usages (*ludi* and *munera*) which has been seen as a way of 'desacralizing' these occasions and shifting them onto more religiously neutral ground. Overall, then, while Constantine's support for Christianity undoubtedly made a rapid difference topographically in terms of an explicit Christian presence in and around the city, what one might have thought would be the logical corollary – namely, the elimination or transformation of those elements of the cityscape associated with traditional religion – took much longer to happen; and when it finally did, it was not necessarily due primarily to the impact of Christianity so much as the role of other contingent factors such as war and economic decline.[13]

CHRISTIANITY AND THE SENATORIAL ARISTOCRACY

Although small in number relative to the city's total population, the senatorial aristocrats of Rome warrant special attention for a number of reasons. Their social pre-eminence and wealth gave them disproportionate influence in the city's affairs, an influence enhanced by the fact that fourth-century emperors did not reside in Rome after 312 and that imperial visits were rare. Of course the definition of senatorial status changed over the course of the fourth century as emperors who

[13] Further discussion, with differing emphases, in Ward-Perkins 1984, 92–118; Lim 1999 ('desacralization'); and Curran 2000, 218–59.

themselves had long ceased to have any roots in the traditional aristocracy honoured holders of high office in their expanding bureaucracy with senatorial status, even though such individuals might pass their lives without ever having occasion to set foot in Rome. Despite this steady expansion and dilution of the senatorial order, there remained a core of families who could trace their membership via a distinguished ancestry back before the third century, for whom the city of Rome remained an important focal point. That focus was reflected in their continuing ownership of property in the city and their monopoly of the office of prefect of the city. Their inherent interest in maintaining the city's cultural traditions meant that they had the strongest commitment to upholding the long-established cults and religious rituals of Rome, and were therefore bound to be the portion of the population most resistant to Christianity. Their response to the new religion is therefore a particularly important test of what difference the new religion made.

In the early years of the fifth century, the Christian poet Prudentius claimed, with specific reference to the city of Rome, that 'one may count hundreds of ancient noble houses who have turned to the banner of Christ' (*Contra Symmachum* 1.566–7). While the element of rhetorical embellishment may tempt one to be suspicious about such a claim, few would dispute that, by this time, the balance of religious commitment on the part of the city's traditional aristocracy had tipped inexorably in favour of Christianity. Rather, the focus of debate has been about where, over the course of the fourth century, the tipping point should be placed. That debate has been handicapped by incomplete evidence and the problem of defining what counts as conversion. For a long time the prevailing view was that the fundamental shift came late in the fourth century, but that view has been challenged. Building on evidence of the conversion of individual aristocrats as early as the first decade of Constantine's rule, a case has been made for the steady adoption of Christianity by aristocrats during the first half of the fourth century.[14] However, the most recent analysis of the available data has reasserted the final two decades of the fourth century as the critical period during which Christian aristocrats began to outnumber pagan aristocrats in the city of Rome.[15] This is paralleled by the surviving data for individuals holding pagan priesthoods in the city of Rome, for which the figures drop from sixty in 380, to thirty-one in 390, to four

---

[14] Barnes 1995.   [15] Salzman 2002, 77–8.

in 400, to zero in 410.[16] Whatever reservations one may have about the lacunose nature of the evidence, the trend is indisputable.

A range of factors has been adduced to account for this shift. While there has been disagreement about the importance of some, such as the role of aristocratic women in inducing the conversion of their male relatives, there can be no doubting the significance of imperial patronage and example.[17] It has also been recognized that the church itself had to adapt aspects of its teachings to make conversion more palatable for aristocrats, e.g. by recognizing the importance of honour, literary culture and friendship to the aristocratic ethos.[18] In other words, not only did Christianity make a difference to the religious character of Rome's aristocracy, but the aristocracy's values also made a difference to how Christianity was presented and practised in this milieu.

In a similar vein, aristocratic understanding of the implications of conversion could vary considerably. On the one hand, there is the case of Valentinus, recipient of the famous *Codex-Calendar of 354*, a luxury item whose dedication and content point strongly to his being both a senatorial aristocrat and a Christian. The codex includes lists of consuls from the early days of the city and of prefects of the city from the preceding century, alongside a cycle of the dates of Easter, and lists of the bishops of Rome, of their dates of death and of those of Roman martyrs. Yet mingled with these markers of aristocratic status and Christian allegiance are sections containing astrological material and an official calendar with traditional pagan festivals still celebrated in fourth-century Rome. It seems, then, that in the mid-fourth century, at any rate, Christian aristocrats did not necessarily see their religious commitment as entailing a definitive rejection of the city's pagan traditions.[19]

On the other hand, there is the behaviour of aristocratic women, both unmarried and widows, who dedicated themselves to an ascetic Christian life in the second half of the fourth century, sometimes even renouncing their residency in Rome to live in the Holy Land. Yet even

[16] Data in Rüpke 2005, 1.532–48. The idea of senatorial support for Eugenius' revolt stemming from concern to defend pagan traditions has proved difficult to sustain: Cameron 1999, 114.
[17] Salzman 2002, 138–99. [18] Salzman 2002, 200–20.
[19] Salzman 1990, and more briefly Chapter 27. Cf. also the famous silver casket from the late fourth-century Esquiline Treasure, with its juxtaposition of mythological scenes relating to Venus alongside its inscription, 'Secundus and Proiecta, may you live in Christ' (Shelton 1981), and Chapter 28 for this phenomenon in tomb decoration.

here, what is perhaps more significant is that this behaviour often provoked opposition from Christian members of their families, concerned
about the continuation of family lines and the dissipation of family
assets – a reaction which betrayed the limits of Christianization in some
aristocratic families. The most famous instance of ascetic dedication
involved the younger Melania, who persuaded her husband, Valerius
Pinianus, to live a life of marital celibacy and to sell all their property,
which, comprising residences in and near Rome and estates dotted
throughout Italy and the western provinces, apparently generated the
enormous annual income of 120,000 *solidi*. Family opposition to these
plans required the intervention of the emperor Honorius to allow them
to proceed.[20]

The proceeds of such momentous decisions were usually channelled into the church and its activities, and constitute the most conspicuous examples of a more general phenomenon arising from the
gradual conversion of the senatorial aristocracy – the enhancement of
the material resources at the disposal of the church in Rome. This
development in the final decades of the fourth century was fortuitous,
coinciding as it did with a decline in the imperial largesse which had
been so important in the first half of the century.[21] Aristocratic generosity took various forms. In some cases it involved direct action by
individual aristocrats to fund the building or decoration of appropriate
structures, most obviously churches. Although the long-held view that
all the so-called *tituli* – the parish churches of the city – owed their
origin to aristocratic endowment has been persuasively challenged in
recent years, there remain at least a dozen instances of *tituli* which benefited from aristocratic generosity.[22] Nor should one overlook instances
of charitable structures such as the *nosocomion* (sick-house) established
by Fabiola towards the end of the century, and her contemporary Pammachius funding the construction of a *xenodochium* (hospice) at Ostia
(Jerome, *Epist.* 77.6, 66.11).[23]

---

[20] For a valuable survey of ascetic dedication by Roman aristocrats, see Curran 2000,
260–320.

[21] Pietri 1978, 328.

[22] Pietri's view that the *tituli* were all fourth-century aristocratic foundations has been
challenged by Hillner 2006, arguing for individuals of moderate wealth from the
'sub-elite' as founders of many (while conceding aristocratic involvement in the
founding or decoration of at least a dozen *tituli*: Hillner 2007, 225 n. 3).

[23] For the significance of such charitable institutions, see Brown 2002, 33–5; Finn 2006,
82–8.

Such actions might be seen as a straightforward extension of aristocratic traditions of self-promotion through buildings, although hospices and the like were hardly grandiose constructions of the sort favoured by their pagan ancestors. Aristocratic giving was not, however, always targeted in this way and could be directed more immediately to those in need. Pammachius also spent money on feeding the poor, sick and disabled who thronged the doors of his house, and even held a banquet for the destitute in St Peter's basilica in honour of his recently deceased wife (Jerome, *Epist.* 66.5; Paulinus of Nola, *Epistulae* 13.11); Paula is said to have used a considerable portion of her fortune helping the needy on the streets of Rome (Jerome, *Epist.* 108.5); and even the staunchly pagan historian Zosimus acknowledged the generosity of Laeta through which 'many kept hunger at bay' during the Gothic siege of Rome in 409 (5.39.3). Of course even this type of activity could be distorted by ingrained habits of conspicuous display – and social prejudice – as in the notorious case reported by Jerome (*Epist.* 22.32):

> I saw just recently in St Peter's Basilica one of the noblest
> Roman women (I suppress her name in case you think this
> is a satirical attack) who, preceded by her eunuchs, was
> distributing coins one by one to the poor, handing them
> out in person so as to be thought all the more devout.
> While this was going on, a certain old woman all enveloped
> in rags and old age, ran up to take another coin. When it
> came to her turn in line, a fist shot out instead of a *denarius*,
> and blood was spilled to pay for the guilt of such a crime.[24]

More will be said below about the church's charitable enterprises, but the particular point to register here is that Christianity did gradually come to make a difference in terms of the redeployment of aristocratic resources and patronage.

A further episode which has attracted much discussion warrants brief comment – the famous controversy over the celebration of the Lupercalia. This has understandably generated interest because of the antiquity of the festival and its pagan associations, and because the controversy arose much later than the period on which this chapter is largely focused, in the final decade of the fifth century. The Lupercalia was associated with the city's early history and had traditionally involved

---

[24] Finn's translation. For further valuable discussion of this passage and of Pammachius, see Finn 2006, 105–6, 206–7, 255–7.

young aristocrats running near-naked through the city-centre striking women with goatskin strips as part of a fertility rite. However, the most recent discussion of this episode in the 490s has argued persuasively that the Lupercalia's persistence at this late date should not be seen primarily as evidence of the tenacity of pagan religious traditions ('the Lupercalia was a Roman street tradition, not a pagan challenge to Christianity'),[25] that its performance was now carried out by professional actors, and that the primary reason for its continued staging by members of an aristocracy who had for some generations now acknowledged the primacy of Christianity was their desire to exploit it as an opportunity for self-promotion.[26]

THE BISHOP OF ROME

The Lupercalia episode in the 490s is known only because of its denunciation by the bishop of Rome, Gelasius. His intervention, and willingness to criticize aristocratic members of his flock, is indicative of the way in which this office had grown in importance over the preceding two centuries. This development was consistent with a more general trend in the late Roman world whereby bishops became increasingly prominent figures in civic affairs, but the bishop of Rome was nonetheless undeniably a special case. The residual secular prestige of Rome inevitably enhanced the status of the city's bishop, further strengthened by the see of Rome being the only one in the western half of the empire which could claim to be an apostolic foundation – a detail which bishops of Rome increasingly emphasized to their advantage vis-à-vis the churches of the west. In addition to all this symbolic capital, there were the material benefits arising from Constantine's particularly generous endowment of the Roman see with property and other resources.[27]

Towards the end of the fourth century the status and perquisites of the office of bishop were sufficient to attract the attention of a pagan historian, who commented on the splendid attire of the incumbent as he was conveyed around the city in a carriage (Ammianus Marcellinus 27.3.14). Its potential lure for ambitious individuals is reflected, on the one hand, in the famous reported comment of a leading pagan senator – 'Make me bishop of the city of Rome, and I will become a Christian without delay!' (Jerome, *Contra Joannem Hierosolymitanum* 8 [*CCSL* 79A, III,2.15]) – and on the other, by the way in which competition

---

[25] North and McLynn 2008, 179.   [26] McLynn 2008.   [27] Pietri 1976, 77–96.

for the office in 366 became so fierce that it gave rise to violence which left more than 100 individuals dead (Ammianus Marcellinus 27.3.13, *Collectio Avellana* 1). The material resources at the disposal of the bishop of Rome in the fourth century should not, however, be overestimated; by one calculation, they remained modest relative to those of many senatorial aristocrats.[28] This perhaps is part of the explanation for the first known bishop of aristocratic origin not emerging until the late fifth century (Felix III [483–92]).

The bloodshed of 366 is one indication of the problems which the existence of an increasingly prominent episcopate in Rome could create for imperial officials, above all the prefect of the city. When Liberius refused to endorse the emperor Constantius II's condemnation of Athanasius, bishop of Alexandria, in 355, it fell to the prefect of the city to arrest him and remove him from the city to Milan under cover of darkness; then, when Liberius subsequently retracted his refusal and was allowed to return in 357, the prefect had to deal with the resulting turmoil between Liberius' supporters and those of Liberius' replacement, Felix. The conflict of 366 was in a sense a continuation of this earlier division since the eventual victor Damasus was alleged to have supported Felix. Although the prefect refrained from intervening in the violence of 366, he nevertheless had to deal with the ongoing fall-out as the supporters of Damasus' defeated rival Ursinus successfully lobbied the imperial court for the latter's return to the city, and continued to engage in disruptive activities even after Ursinus had been expelled for good. Another disputed episcopal election between Eulalius and Bonifatius in 418 required the intervention of the prefect as appeals from both parties to the emperor in Ravenna and his indecisive responses generated unrest and violence in Rome.[29] It is worth adding that these contested elections understandably attracted disproportionate attention in the ancient sources, and that there were many more during the fourth and fifth centuries which were settled without recourse to violence.

Another way in which the prefect found himself having to engage with the bishop was in the context of church construction. While this might sound reassuringly mundane alongside the problems of street violence surrounding some episcopal elections, it too could generate its own headaches, notably in the case of the extramural church of St Paul's,

---

[28] Pietri 1976, 90.
[29] For each of these three episodes, see Pietri 1976, 237–68, 407–18, 452–60, with Curran 2000, 129–42 for the first two, and Lizzi Testa 2004, 129–70 for Damasus and Ursinus.

begun in the mid-380s on imperial initiative. Surviving documents show one prefect being asked by the imperial court to liaise with the bishop concerning the siting and layout of the building, while another had to deal with accusations and counter-accusations of overspending by the builders (*Collectio Avellana* 3; Symmachus, *Relationes* 25–6).

But if the existence of the bishop of Rome caused problems for the prefect in the second half of the fourth century, the fifth century provided opportunities for the bishop to make more constructive contributions in times of crisis. The most high-profile type of such activity was the role of the bishop as envoy in the context of barbarian threats to the city. In 409 Innocentius (401–17) participated in a senatorial embassy to Ravenna with a view to avoiding another Gothic blockade of Rome by facilitating negotiations between the imperial court and Alaric (Olympiodorus *fr.* 8,1; Zosimus 5.45.5); in 452, Leo (440–61) joined two eminent civilians in an embassy to Attila hoping to forestall any further Hunnic advance into the Italian peninsula (Prosper *Chron.* *s.a.* 452); and in 455 Leo negotiated with the Vandal leader Geiseric outside the gates of the city (Prosper of Aquitaine, *Epitoma Chronicon s.a.* 455). The bishop's involvement did not of course guarantee success – the forces of both Alaric and Geiseric ended up plundering Rome – but Innocentius' mission was undoubtedly overtaken by circumstances beyond his control, while Leo is credited with having persuaded Geiseric to place some limits on the depredations of his troops. As for Leo's encounter with Attila, there is no doubt that later accounts amplified the bishop's role in the Hunnic retreat, possibly at the expense of more practical constraints on Attila (e.g. logistics), but this should not obscure the fundamental point to emerge from contemporary evidence for this and the other episodes – the prominence of the bishop in Roman society, and his participation in embassies with civilians of high standing.[30]

Alongside these newsworthy episodes should be placed the more mundane but vital activities of the bishop relating to the charitable endeavours of the church (which of course assumed heightened importance in times of crisis): oversight of the distribution of relief to the needier sectors of the population, but also the preaching which helped to elicit contributions from the better-off members of Roman society.[31] This is a subject which leads naturally into a consideration of what difference Christianity made to the ordinary inhabitants of Rome.

---

[30] Cf. Gillett 2003, 114–15.

[31] For this as a major theme in nearly half of Leo's extant sermons, see Lepelley 1962, and more generally Finn 2006, 116–75.

CHRISTIANITY AND THE ROMAN
POPULACE

The withdrawal of fourth-century emperors from residency in Rome might have been expected to lessen their concern to continue the traditional imperial responsibility for free handouts of bread (supplemented during the third century by free allowances of oil and pork, and a subsidized quota of wine). However, throughout the fourth century and beyond, one of the most important duties delegated to the prefect of the city was the maintenance of these arrangements – with all the attendant risks of dealing with mob violence when supplies were interrupted.[32] In the light of this, one might wonder what need there was for the charitable activities of the church. A major part of the answer is that imperial distributions were restricted.[33] Figures in a law of 419 concerning the pork allowance (*Cod. Theod.* 14.4.10) imply a total of 120,000 recipients, which is usually assumed to be the number also eligible for the other handouts during Late Antiquity; even on the more pessimistic estimates of the city's population during the fourth century of under half a million inhabitants, this still leaves at least two-thirds of the populace without this sort of assistance.[34]

As early as the mid-third century the church in Rome is reported to have been supporting more than 1,500 widows and poor (Eusebius, *Historia Ecclesiastica* 6.43.11), a number which must have expanded dramatically over the course of the fourth century. The fact that such a figure was known at the time – it is preserved in the text of a bishop's letter – implies the maintenance of records relating to such matters (presumably an early version of the poor-registers (*matricula*) attested in later periods),[35] which in turn implies some degree of organizational infrastructure. The same letter also refers to the personnel of the church as including seven deacons and seven subdeacons, whose primary responsibility will have been the practical administration of that support – an undertaking facilitated by the decision of the bishop Fabianus (236–50) in the years just before this to 'divide the regions of the city amongst

---

[32] Chastagnol 1960, 296–334; Jones 1964, 695–705; Durliat 1989, 41–90, with Purcell 1999 for much thought-provoking comment on the late Roman populace more generally.

[33] Brown 2002, 52.

[34] Jones 1964, 702, 1289 n. 35 for the calculation, with 696, 1285 n. 19 for the generalization, and Barnish 1987, 161–4 for the problems of determining the city's population in this period.

[35] Brown 2002, 65; Finn 2006, 74–6.

the deacons' (*Liber Pontificalis* 21.2). Since New Testament times, the diaconate had had responsibility for ministering to the material needs of church members; the clearest evidence for this continued role is a fifth-century source recording the death of a deacon of the church in Rome while 'distributing money to the poor' (Prosper of Aquitaine, *Epit. Chron. s.a.* 426).[36]

The growing numbers of Christian aristocrats towards the end of the fourth century, and the increasing flow of resources into episcopal coffers, will undoubtedly have enhanced the ability of the church to meet the needs of the poor in Rome.[37] A major component of those resources was property in the city's hinterland and beyond bequeathed to the church in Rome which, with the passage of time, came to be referred to as the *patrimonia* of the church and which generated both revenues and foodstuffs for consumption in the city.[38] The growing level of organization required in church finances by the late fifth century is reflected in the church's income being formally divided four ways between the bishop's needs, maintenance of the clergy, repair and lighting of churches, and charity to the poor.[39]

The bishop's responsibility for the poor was also another way of promoting his position and authority in the city, since the recipients of his largesse could generally be relied upon to back him in a crisis. This is certainly a plausible interpretation of the behaviour of the crowds in the Circus Maximus in 357 who heckled the visiting emperor Constantius II until he agreed to recall the exiled bishop Liberius.[40] Despite the enhanced resources at his disposal, however, he would never be in a position to eliminate poverty in the city. Jesus' famous aphorism – 'The poor you have with you always' (Mark 14.7) – was bound to be particularly relevant in a metropolis like Rome, which was always attracting (and consuming) immigrants. Nonetheless, as emphasized by a number of eminent scholars, such charity directed towards individuals with no real prospect of reciprocating represented a fundamental shift in outlook from the euergetistic assumptions of the classical city, reflected in the fact that Christian establishments such as hospices and orphanages bore names for which there were no classical precedents.[41] This was

---

[36] Pietri 1976, 134–6, 645–59.

[37] For the usual content of episcopal charity to the poor (food, coins, clothing), see Finn 2006, 78–82.

[38] Marazzi 1998, 17–79, with Costambeys 2000.   [39] Jones 1964, 902.

[40] Theodoret, *Hist. eccl.* 2.17, with Finn 2006, 209.

[41] Veyne 1990, 19–34 (nomenclature at 33); Brown 2002; Clark 2004, 107–11; cf. also Finn 2006, 32–3, 258–68.

perhaps the most significant difference Christianity made, not just in the city of Rome, but in the empire as a whole.

FURTHER READING

The single most important contributor to understanding the transition to a Christianized Rome has been Charles Pietri, through his massive monograph (1976) and numerous articles (collected in Pietri 1997). Also influential has been Richard Krautheimer's work on the church buildings of Rome, as distilled in his 1980 study of the city's evolution from Constantine to the late medieval period. More recently, John Curran's 2000 monograph on the religious history of the city during the fourth century offers a valuable survey of earlier scholarship alongside his own judicious insights on a number of central issues; this is the best place to start. Also important is the 1999 collection of conference papers edited by William Harris; the focus is broader than the religious history of the period, but there are few contributions which do not have some relevance to the themes of this chapter. More recently still, there has appeared the 2007 volume edited by Kate Cooper and Julia Hillner, which does have a religious focus. The beautifully illustrated 2000 exhibition catalogue edited by Serena Ensoli and Eugenio La Rocca provides an excellent overview of the archaeological evidence for Rome's development in Late Antiquity.

EPILOGUE

30: The city in Ruins

Text, Image and Imagination

Catharine Edwards

For Petrarch in the fourteenth century Rome's ruins are a spur to contemplation and philosophical conversation (*Epistolae familiares* 6.2). Poggio Bracciolini's characters muse on the significance of the ruins of Rome in the context of his fifteenth-century treatise on the vagaries of fortune (*De varietate fortunae* book 1).[1] The celebration of ruins, their capacity to evoke melancholy and offer consolation is often characterized as a specifically modern phenomenon, not widely attested until the Renaissance (even for Hildebert of Lavardin in the twelfth century the prime significance of ruined pagan Rome is as a marker of the triumph of Christianity[2]) – and one particularly associated with Rome. In recent centuries, ancient ruins themselves have been deliberately preserved in Rome from a variety of motives, as symbols of identity, assertions of control or instruments of legitimation by the occupying forces of Napoleon, by nineteenth-century popes, by Mussolini's fascist regime, as well as by post-war governments.

In the aftermath of the Second World War, when so many European cities lay in ruins, a number of governments elsewhere in Europe were persuaded to preserve selected ruins as memorials to the loss and suffering brought by the conflict. The communist authorities in East Germany, for instance, opted to preserve the ruins of Die Frauenkirche in Dresden as a monument to the effects of capitalist warmongering.[3] Ruined churches still stand as war memorials in London (and other British cities), among them Christ Church in Newgate Street in the City. Other media could also play a part in sustaining the memory of what was lost, as well as the violence of its destruction. War artists such as John Piper forged works of terrifying beauty from scenes of devastation. His painting of Coventry Cathedral in flames (*Coventry Cathedral, 15 November 1940*) according to a recent critic 'became for Britons what Picasso's *Guernica* had been for loyalist Spaniards: an expression of

---

[1] Woodward 2001, ch. 1.   [2] Krautheimer 1980, 199–202.   [3] Woodward 2001, 210.

British resilience'.[4] Here the focus is on the moment of destruction, the horror of conflagration, rather than its aftermath.

After the Persian war, the Athenians, we are told, chose to leave in ruins the Acropolis, the sacred heart of their city, for thirty years as a reminder of all they had suffered. The oath sworn by the Greek forces before the battle of Plataea is said by some sources to have contained the clause: 'I shall in no way rebuild any of the temples that have been burned and demolished by the barbarians, but I shall allow them to be left as a reminder (*hypomnema*) to future generations of the barbarians' impiety' (Diodorus Siculus 11.29.3).[5] There is no indication that the ancient city of Rome included deliberately preserved ruins (there was a hut supposed to have belonged to Romulus but it was regularly renewed rather than left to decay).[6] Yet scenes of ruins in Rome and of Rome in ruins haunt the literature of Roman antiquity. This chapter aims to explore the significance of the ruined city as imagined by a number of Roman (and Greek) writers, Virgil and Tacitus in particular. Such ruins often serve as traces of violent ruptures in the history of a city whose literary presences more usually work to emphasize continuity and durability.

These Roman ruins need to be considered in relation to the ruins of other great cities, most obviously Troy and Carthage. Contemplating the once flourishing city of Carthage in flames, Scipio, its destroyer, is said to have shed tears, as he quoted Hector's prophecy on the future of Troy from the *Iliad* (6.448–9): 'A day will come when holy Troy will perish, and Priam and the people of Priam'. Scipio likens the fall of the city before him to that of Troy but his thoughts also turn to his own city. 'When Polybius . . . asked him what he meant by the words, they say that without any concealment he named his own country, for which he feared when he reflected on the nature of all things human' (according to Appian, *Bellum Punicum* 19.132, citing Polybius).[7] A tradition of Hellenistic epigrams savoured the melancholy evoked by the ruin of once great cities such as Mycenae; the mighty Scipio, then, seems to combine Roman military achievement with a Hellenistic sensibility (as well as a concern to avoid affronting the gods).[8] For Polybius, it was the combination of such qualities in at least some Romans which made them fit to govern an empire.

---

[4] Woodward 2001, 218. [5] See Meiggs 1972, 504–7. [6] Edwards 1996, 32–42.
[7] O'Gorman 2000, 172–3; Astin 1967, 182–7.
[8] Gow and Page (1968, 2.428–9) discuss Greek epigrams dating from the first century BC and first century AD.

The ruins of Carthage have a somewhat different significance in a story Plutarch relates centuries later about another great republican general, Gaius Marius. According to Plutarch, Marius, in exile following his defeat in the conflict with Sulla in 88 BC, was on the Roman governor's orders forbidden entry to the province of Africa. When he was asked what reply he wanted relayed to the governor: 'he answered with a deep groan: "Tell him then, that you have seen Gaius Marius, a fugitive, seated amid the ruins of Carthage." And the parallel he drew between the fortune of the city and his own was a telling one' (Plutarch, *Marius* 40). In Plutarch's account, Marius sees the ruins of Carthage as standing for his own future: once a great man, now destroyed by Rome.[9] Yet in drawing the comparison, Marius, familiar as he no doubt was with the story of Scipio's tears, may perhaps also have been hinting at the possible future of Rome itself.

The visual images paraded in Roman triumphal processions sometimes seem to have included pictures (or models) of enemy cities destroyed. Appian relates that Scipio Africanus' triumphal display of 201 BC boasted paintings showing the events of the war (*Bell. Pun.* 66).[10] In a highly fictionalized account of the Punic Wars, Silius Italicus' Flavian epic has Scipio's great opponent Hannibal looking around the Italian town of Liternum as he relishes his recent success at the battle of Lake Trasimene. At Liternum he is confronted with a series of images of Romans vanquishing his own city and celebrating their victory. Angered he conjures up in his own imagination a vision of the blazing ruins of Rome. Not only will he destroy the city, he will also put on display in Carthage images immortalizing the moment of Rome's destruction. 'O Carthage, you will depict Rome blazing with Libyan torches and Jupiter the Thunderer thrown down from the Tarpeian rock' (*Punica* 6.712–13).[11] Silius himself, the last of the Neronian consulars (as Pliny describes him, *Epistulae* 3.7.10), will very likely have witnessed in his own time Rome in flames not once but twice, in the great fire of AD 64 (to which we shall return) – and again in 69, in the course of the civil wars following Nero's downfall.

The analogy between the life-cycle of a city and that of a human being evoked in Plutarch's account of Marius recurs also in a letter from Servius Sulpicius Rufus to Cicero, following the death of Cicero's beloved daughter Tullia (45 BC). Sulpicius asserts the consoling power of ruins:

---

[9] On Carthage in the Roman imaginary, see O'Gorman 2004.
[10] Beard 2007, 178–86. [11] Discussed in Fowler 2000, 93–107.

I want to tell of something that has brought me no slight
comfort (*consolationem*), in the hope that perhaps it may
have some power to lighten your sorrow, too. As I was on
my way back from Asia, sailing from Aegina towards
Megara, I began to gaze at the landscape around me. There
behind me was Aegina, in front of me Megara, to the right
Piraeus, to the left Corinth; once flourishing towns, now
lying low in ruins (*prostrata et diruta*) before one's eyes.
(*Epistulae ad familiares* 4.5.4; SB 248)

In terming the towns a little later as *cadavera* ('corpses'), Sulpicius reinforces the analogy with the human life-cycle; a living being cannot last
forever. The contemplation of these ruins leads Sulpicius to see the
death of any human individual as trivial in comparison with the end of
a whole community. Already in the late Republic, then, we can trace a
sense of the potency of ruins in Roman culture. The ruin of one city
inevitably evokes the ruin of others. Ruins function as both warning
and consolation. Memorialized in literature – the letter of Sulpicius, for
instance, mobilizes the *thought* of ruins – they have the power to move
those who do not actually see them.

It is Troy – as well as Rome – Scipio thinks of as he looks
at the burning ruins of Carthage, according to Polybius. In Graeco-
Roman antiquity, Troy was of course the paradigmatic ruined city.[12]
Troy's ruin looms as a prospect over the *Iliad* (even though the action
of the poem concludes before Troy actually falls) and figures in the
opening lines of the *Odyssey*; Odysseus' protracted homeward journey
unfolds in the wake of Troy's destruction. Its ruins loom or smoulder
in the background in numerous tragedies, Euripides' *Trojan Women*, his
Hecuba, Naevius' *Equos Troianus*, Livius Andronicus' play of the same
title, Seneca's *Troades*. In a sense Troy's fame lies in its ruin – as Lucan
would memorably observe (*Phars.* 9.964).

At the start of Virgil's Roman epic, too, Troy, as Rome's mother
city, lies in smoking ruins. Aeneas, impelled by destiny to travel far
to found what will be Rome, flees the burning wreck of his homeland. 'The ancient city falls, for many years a queen' (*Aeneid* 2.363)
he laments.[13] Concluding his account to Dido at the start of Book 3,
he sums up: 'Proud Ilium fell and all Neptune's Troy smokes from the
ground' (*Aen.* 3.2–3). His mother Venus later swears by the smouldering
remains of Troy, as she begs Jupiter to spare Aeneas' son (10.45–6). It

[12] Scully 1990, 23; Kahane 2011.   [13] Cf. also *Aen.* 2.324–7.

is notable that, as in Scipio's contemplation of the fall of Carthage, the opening of the *Aeneid* shifts between the three cities of Troy, Carthage and Rome. 'There was an ancient city' – *urbs antiqua fuit* – introduces not Troy, as the reader might expect (particularly given that the place is presented as a cause Juno's anger), but Carthage (*Aen.*1.12). Virgil calls it *antiqua*. Yet Carthage is a new city, still under construction. Should we read this as a proleptic allusion to the perspective of the time in which he is writing, a time when Carthage is not only ancient but also ruined? Its ruin indeed is already determined by Juno at the very start of the poem (1.22). This seems one strategy among many to assimilate Carthage and Troy in the *Aeneid*. When Troy itself is later termed *urbs antiqua* (2.363), *ruit* glosses *fuit* in the opening of book 1.[14] With regard to both Carthage and Troy, the perfect tense of the positive *fuit* has the force of a present negative.[15] That city is no longer.

The description of Troy's fall, which Virgil has Aeneas offer Dido, draws extensively on a literary tradition of narrating not only the fall of Troy but the fate of many other captured cities at the hands of enemy forces. Such descriptions figure in earlier epic and particularly in tragedy, as well as in history writing, while Quintilian enumerates the features of the *urbs capta* as they may be treated by the orator (*De institutione oratoria* 8.3.67–8).[16] Rossi traces striking similarities between Virgil's fall of Troy and Livy's account in Book 1 of the fall of Alba (which may well have drawn on Ennius' version of the fall of Alba). Indeed a resemblance between accounts of the fall of Alba and Virgil's treatment of the fall of Troy was already noted in Servius' commentary on the *Aeneid*.[17] Livy comments on Alba's destruction: 'A single hour gave over to destruction and ruin [*excidio ac ruinis*] all that had been achieved in the four hundred years during which Alba stood' (1.29.6). An awareness of Alba's passing adds an additional poignancy to Anchises' prophecy in *Aeneid* 6. He shows Aeneas his descendants who will be founders of the towns of Alba (6.776). For Aeneas these will be famous names for territories that in his own time are nameless. For Virgil's contemporaries, though, these places have again become nothing more than pieces of land, known only for the reputation they once had.[18]

[14] On Troy, Carthage and Rome see Reed 2007, ch. 5.
[15] Cf. *Aen.* 2.324–7. Labate 1991, 173.
[16] On the *urbs capta* see Paul 1982 and Kraus 1994.   [17] Rossi 2002, 237–8.
[18] See Feeney 1986, 6–8.

Virgil's Rome, then, springs (indirectly via the foundation and destruction of Alba) from the ruins of Troy. Troy is already a ruin. Carthage, too, and Alba, not yet founded in the time of Aeneas, are destined to become ruins. In Virgil's epic, however, there would appear to be no explicit thought of Rome's ruin. Intriguingly, Rome's own end is perhaps evoked in Virgil's earlier *Georgics*: 'the power of Rome, the kingdoms doomed to fall' (2.498), at least as it is interpreted centuries later by the Christian Augustine, in a sermon probably delivered after Rome's sack in AD 410 (*Sermones* 105.7.10).

Yet the *Aeneid* itself does offer a disconcerting vignette of ruins in Rome. Though Rome will not be founded for a couple of generations, Aeneas pays a visit to its future site. The Arcadian refugee Evander guides Aeneas around what will one day be Rome. The passage shuttles suggestively between the rustic landscape of Aeneas' day and the golden city of the Augustan future: 'Hence to the Tarpeian citadel he leads him and the Capitol, Golden now, then covered with woodland thickets' (*Aen.* 8.347–8). Cattle are lowing in what will one day be the Roman Forum. Yet already in the time of Aeneas there are ruins on the hills of Rome. As Evander relates: 'Moreover in these towns with walls o'erthrown, thou seest the relics and memorials of men of old. This fort father Janus built, that Saturn; Janiculum was this called, that Saturnia' (355–8). Even before its foundation, ruins are part of Rome.[19] They are surely a destabilizing presence in this poem, in tension with the urge to celebrate the golden city of the Augustan present, the eternal city of an empire without limit.

Ovid's great anti-epic *Metamorphoses*, written a few years after the *Aeneid* and in response to it, perhaps offers a more assertive hint that Rome, too, may be subject to the same processes of decay as other once great cities. In the speech of Pythagoras in the final book of the poem, a pronouncement on the shifting fate of cities serves as the climax to a discourse on change more generally. Troy appears as the first of many cities, once great, which are now only ruins:

So was Troy great in wealth and men, and for ten years was able to give so freely of her blood; but now, humbled to earth, she has nought to show but ancient ruins, no wealth but ancestral tombs.

(15.422–5)

[19] On later appropriations of this passage with an emphasis on Rome's reversion to ruin see Hardie 1992; Edwards 1996.

Pythagoras goes on to note the rise and fall of Sparta, Mycenae, Thebes and Athens (15.431–52). Next comes Rome, destined to be capital of the world, he proclaims. Yet this city's flourishing too must surely be followed in its turn by decline; in this poem *everything* is subject to change (15.165).[20]

The parallel between once flourishing, now ruined, Troy and Rome is pressed further by the Neronian poet Lucan. In his epic poem on the civil war between Pompey and Julius Caesar, Caesar, visiting the site of Troy, tramples insensitively over the ground on which Hector and Achilles once fought. 'He wanders around Troy, famous only as the name of a city now destroyed' (*Phars.* 9.964). Even ruins – all that survived of Troy, according to Ovid's Pythagoras – have been worn away: *etiam periere ruinae* (9.969). The model for Caesar's tour of the site of Troy is Aeneas' tour of the landmarks past and future of Rome in *Aeneid* 8; the same thorns, *dumetis*, grow among their ruins.[21] Caesar himself is a ruin-maker par excellence. Lucan figures him early on as a devastator: 'by destruction he delights to make his way' (*Phars.* 1.150).[22] Earlier Caesar is implicitly compared to Hannibal (1.30–2), whose desire to destroy Rome haunted the Roman imagination for centuries after his death, as we saw earlier. The self-destructive conflict of Rome's civil war is all too likely to obliterate in turn Rome itself.

Lucan here evokes a concern felt urgently by many Romans in the time of the civil war he describes. A number of late republican texts disclose a strong sense of Rome's fragility.[23] The author of the Sallustian *Epistulae ad Caesarem* (1.5.2) anticipates the imminent ruin of Rome itself. Cicero, in a letter to Servius Sulpicius Rufus of (probably) September 46 BC, tries to console his friend: 'in such dark times, when the Republic lies in ruins' (*Epist. ad fam.* 4.3.2 = SB 202). Cicero uses the same term *parietinae* for the ruins of Corinth (destroyed following its defeat by the Romans themselves a century earlier), whose power to move the Roman visitor is briefly evoked in his *Tusculan Disputations* (3.58). It is striking that Servius Sulpicius chooses visions of ruins as a strategy to console Cicero himself, devastated a few months later by the loss of his beloved daughter. Indeed Sulpicius shifts between consoling Cicero for the loss of Tullia and commiserating with him over the loss of *libertas* in the collapse of the Roman republic.

---

[20] See e.g. Hardie 1992, 61; Labate 1991, 171–2.
[21] Labate 1991, 183–4; Hardie 1992, 59; Martindale 1993, 49–51.
[22] See Spencer 2005, 53.   [23] As Labate 1991 has emphasized.

Horace, too, writing just a few years later, while civil war raged on, imagines Rome itself ruined: 'Another generation is worn down by civil wars. Rome falls by her own force (*suis et ipsa Roma viribus ruit*)' (*Epodes* 16.1–2). Civil war, in this vision, so weakens Rome that foreign invaders take over and destroy the city, digging up and scattering the remains of Romulus. This apocalyptic vision of the city in ruins seems to echo the Sibylline oracle, a text which Lactantius at least interpreted as prophesying the ruin of Rome (*Divinae institutiones* 7.25.7).[24]

The idea of the eternal city, the golden city of the emperor Augustus, gains a poignant significance against this background. The eternal city seems predicted by Jupiter in the first book of Virgil's *Aeneid* (1.278–9). It is celebrated by his younger contemporary Tibullus: 'Romulus had not yet shaped the walls of the eternal city' (2.5.23).[25] It is invoked by Ovid in the *Fasti* who terms Romulus the father of the eternal city, *aeternae . . . pater urbis* (3.72). This idea, at least initially, serves in part as a vehicle for the expression of relief that the dangers posed by the civil war have receded.[26]

Yet for a number of Augustan writers the apparent durability of the city and its monuments under the new regime also posed something of a challenge, giving a new edge to comparisons between the power to withstand time of monuments on the one hand and of texts on the other. Horace claimed to have created a literary monument more lasting than bronze, superior to the pyramids (*Carmina* 3.30).[27] The final lines of Ovid's *Metamorphoses* (15.871–9) lay claim to a different order of longevity for his poem, which, impervious to fire, iron and the anger of Jupiter himself, will last as long and spread as far as Rome's own dominion. Yet Ovid's *Fasti* (probably written around the same time between AD 5 and 8) makes a bid for durability by insinuating itself into the fabric of the city (as well as its calendar). Propertius, too, in his fourth book of elegies (published after 16 BC), also with considerable ambivalence, attaches his poetic project to the city past and present.[28] The Rome he constructs seems pitted against the Rome being constructed around him by Augustus. His elegies evoke a Virgilian contrast between the rustic Rome of earliest times and the monumental city of the present: 'Whatever you see here, stranger, where great Rome

---

[24] Macleod 1983, 218–19.
[25] Koch 1952; Mellor 1981; Hardie 1992; Edwards 1996, 86–8.   [26] Labate 1991,171.
[27] The metaphorical *monumentum* may be more durable but the use of the term carries the implication that metaphorical monuments may also be subject to decay, as the fine discussion by Fowler emphasizes (Fowler 2000, 193–217).
[28] See Edwards 1996, 52–63. On Propertius see also Fantham 1997; Welch 2005.

is, before Trojan Aeneas was hill and grass' (4.1.1–2). The present day visitor must summon up the vision of Aeneas on the green hills where Rome would be, must imagine the once simple and plain buildings of early Rome, its rustic past contrasted with its splendid present.

At the same time, for Propertius, Rome's rise is balanced by the decline of other Italian towns. The time of flourishing is now over for Alba and Gabii, he observes: 'And Alba stood and was strong, brought forth from the omen of the white sow, and Gabii, which now is nothing, was then thronged with people' (4.1.34–5). Within Italy, also, then, Rome's transformative energy powers both its own rise and the collapse of other places.[29] As well as Troy, Carthage and Corinth, Rome has subsumed many of the small towns of Italy too. Rome feeds on the ruins of all these other places. Poem 4.10 offers a lament for Veii, an Etruscan centre a few miles from Rome, conquered by the Romans in the early fourth century BC and now largely deserted.[30]

> Alas for ancient Veii! You too ruled widely then and a
> golden throne stood in your forum. Now within your walls
> the lazy shepherd sounds his pipe and harvests are gathered
> among your bones.
>
> (4.10.27–30)

This poignant scene confirms the lethal superiority of Rome's power but may also have implications for Rome's future. Rome and Veii were once equals. May they not be so again? Rome is different. Or is it?

Rome itself was of course destroyed by the Gauls in the early fourth century BC (Livy's account of this is suggestively analysed by Kraus); the city rose again to become still greater. Yet it continued to suffer significant damage in periodic fires and floods. In the time of Nero, most notoriously, a huge swathe of the city was devastated by a terrible fire. In the aftermath of this disaster, Seneca wrote Letter 91 of the *Epistulae morales* addressing the grief of his friend Liberalis at the destruction by fire not of Rome but of the city of Lugdunum in Gaul, Liberalis' place of origin. Many of his comments might apply to Rome also: 'How many beautiful works, any one of which would give lustre to a city, one night destroyed' (91.2). The would-be wise man, Seneca advises, must prepare himself against the possibility of losses such as these: 'We should bear with untroubled minds the destruction

---

[29] As Labate 1991, 177 stresses. Cf. Feeney 1986, 7–8.
[30] On Livy's version see Kraus 1994, 270–3.

of cities. They stand only to fall' (91.11–12). Seneca here echoes the line of thought articulated in Sulpicius' letter of consolation to Cicero (discussed above), that cities, like human individuals, cannot last forever. Yet Rome, partially destroyed only recently and with considerable loss of life, is a conspicuous absence in this letter.

Though it would be rather more obtrusive in Lucan's *Bellum civile*, the idea of the destruction of Rome is generally well beneath the surface of the Augustan texts considered above. However, their explorations of Rome and its changing appearance are key influences on Tacitus' later accounts of the city's actual (albeit temporary) destruction in the great fire. Though Rome is at the centre of his history writing (the first words of the *Annales* are *urbem Romam*), Tacitus is in general curiously reticent about the physical fabric of the city of Rome.[31] In relation to the opening of the year 57, he articulates his objection to describing new monuments:

> With Nero (for the second time) and L. Piso as consuls, there were few events worth recalling – unless one likes to fill volumes with praising the foundations and beams with which Caesar had set up a massive amphitheatre on the Field of Mars, despite the finding that what accords with the worthiness of the Roman people is that illustrious matters should be entrusted to annals.
>
> (*Ann.* 13.31.1)

If itemizing the particulars of construction is unsuitable for annals, the same is not, it seems, true of ruin. Tacitus' account of the conflagration of the Capitol in AD 69, in the course of the civil war conflict (*Historiae* 3.71–2), evokes in detail the dense historical associations of the hill and its monuments, the dire significance of their destruction.[32]

The fate of the city as a whole, devastated by the fire of AD 64, similarly calls for considerable comment in the *Annals* (15.38–41; the fire is also described by Suetonius, *Nero* 38.2, and Cassius Dio, 62.16–18). For Tacitus, this is more damaging than any other fire ever to have befallen the city. Streaking through the Circus Maximus, where it had its beginning, the fire roams up hill and down again into the plain. The inhabitants are stricken with terror and struggle to escape, many failing. Only after six days is the fire brought under control through the demolition of buildings at the foot of the Esquiline. Even then it breaks

[31] Rouveret 1991, 3056.   [32] Edwards 1996, 74–82; and see now Ash 2007.

out again taking a heavy toll on porticos and shrines to the gods. 'Rome is divided into fourteen districts of which only four remained untouched and three were levelled to the ground; in the other seven there survived a few traces of housing, mauled and charred' (*Ann.*15.40.4). Rome is a smoking ruin.

The individual buildings lost are too numerous to be counted. But the historian does itemize the most venerable of the religious structures destroyed by the fire (15.41). The temple of the Moon attributed to King Servius Tullius comes first, then the great altar and holy place dedicated by Evander to Hercules (both of whom figure prominently in Virgil's treatment of the site of Rome in *Aeneid* 8). The temple vowed by Romulus to Jupiter Stator, too, was destroyed (a monument also attributed to Romulus by Livy, 1.12.6). The Regia, Numa's sacred residence, and Vesta's shrine containing the *penates* and the Palladium were also consumed by the fire – these objects were believed critically important to the future of Rome itself. The first century BC antiquarian Varro, in the dedication of his *Antiquitates rerum divinarum*, had identified as critical moments in the history of Roman religion Aeneas' saving of the Penates from Troy and, in the third century, the rescue of the *sacra* (including the Pompeian Palladium) from the burning temple of Vesta by the *pontifex maximus* Metellus (1, fr.2a Cardauns = Augustine *De civitate dei* 6.2). Each religious foundation referred to here marks a stage in the life of the city, as Rouveret emphasizes, evoking Evander, Romulus, Numa, with implicit links back even to Aeneas.

Also lost were the precious spoils – of so many great Roman victories (*opes tot victoriis quaesitae*), as well as Greek artistic masterpieces (*Graecarum artium decora*). The reference to ancient and unspoiled monuments to Roman greatness (*monumenta ingeniorum antiqua et incorrupta*) could be interpreted as referring to literary works (perhaps those kept in the Palatine library associated with the temple of Apollo), but its lack of precision also evokes a more general category of lost treasures. So that despite all the splendour of the newly reconstructed city, older people remembered much which could not be replaced (15.41.2). Here, as in his account of the destruction of the Capitol in the *Historiae*, Tacitus mourns lost memorials to the Rome of earlier times, while at the same time offering his own text as a kind of substitute for them. We might see this as a new take on the well-worn topos of Rome then and now. Where poets of the Augustan age had evoked the humble rustic settlement of the distant past as a point of contrast with the splendour of the urban present, Tacitus offers a fleeting vision of the rich and venerable accumulation of buildings and objects, a vast nexus of tangible links to Rome's history. But these are described at the very moment that they are consumed by fire, to survive only in the memories of the older generation – and the historian's text.[33]

Tacitus' account of the fire has recently been read as the culmination of a tragic plot.[34] Certainly the motif of the destruction of a once great and ancient city is a familiar feature of tragedy, as we have seen. The episode is immediately preceded by his account of Nero's plans for a Grand Tour (plans which do not come to fruition) and his life of excess in Rome, culminating in the description of a party, after which Nero takes part in a mock marriage and publicly enacted 'wedding night' with Pythagoras. Tacitus presents the fire as a consequence of this: *sequitur clades* (15.38.1). The possibility that Nero himself is directly responsible for the fire is raised at the outset and again later (15.38.7).[35]

Tacitus repeatedly invites his reader to compare this catastrophe with the destruction of Troy by the Greeks, particularly as it is described by Virgil.[36] The fire spreads through Rome because of the character of the city, its narrow, twisting streets (*Ann.* 15.38.4), evoking the labyrinthine ways of Virgil's burning Troy (*Aen.* 2.736–7). The city is filled with the laments of terrified women (15.38.5), as is Troy in its last hours (*Aen.* 2.487–8). When the people of Nero's Rome become refugees, *populo . . . profugo* (15.39.2), the adjective echoes the situation of Aeneas, who in the opening lines of the *Aeneid* is also *profugus* following the destruction of his native city (*Aen.*1.2). The temple of Vesta, one of the most important monuments destroyed by the Neronian fire, has its counterpart in Troy's temple to Vesta where Aeneas meets (and is tempted to kill) Helen (*Aen.* 2.567). The Greek artistic masterpieces *Graecarum artium decora* lost in Rome's fire invite comparison with the heaped up spoils taken from burning Troy: 'Here from all over the treasures of Troy, snatched from burning shrines, tables of the gods, bowls of solid gold, and plundered garments, are heaped up' (*Aen.* 2.763–6). For while some rich and beautiful objects are destroyed by the fire that rages through Rome, others are stolen. In Rome, those who are looting and preventing residents from putting out the flames are not, however, foreign enemies, like the Greek soldiers of the *Aeneid*, but Romans who claimed to be acting on orders from above. 'Nor did anyone dare

33 Cf. Ash 2007, 236, on Tacitus' account of the destruction of the Capitol in AD 69.
34 See Santoro L'Hoir 2006, 248–50.   35 O'Gorman 2000, 171–2.
36 Feeney 2007, 107.

to fight back the fire, given the frequency of threats from the numbers who prevented its quenching, and because others openly threw torches and shouted that they had authorization – whether to conduct their looting more licentiously or by order' (15.38.6–7).

Tacitus recounts that Nero returned to the city (though only when the fire threatened his own residence) and initiated numerous measures to benefit the fire's victims. But, says Tacitus, such measures were overshadowed by the potent rumour that, when Rome was in flames, Nero chose to sing of the destruction of Troy:

> The story had spread widely that even while the city was
> burning he had gone onto his private stage and given a
> performance of 'The fall of Troy', likening the current
> crisis to the ancient one.
>
> (15.39.3)

Nero, too, then perceives, reinforces and perverts the parallels between Rome in flames and burning Troy. Feeney comments: 'With the monarchy of Nero, the last of the Aeneadae, as Cassius Dio calls him (62.18.3–4), Roman history reverts to the Trojan fairy stories peddled by the Julii.'[37] In his first public speech Nero had discoursed eloquently 'on the Romans' descent from Troy and how Aeneas was the ancestor of his family and other matters not far removed from fairy stories' (12.58.1). Indeed Nero first appears in the *Annals* (at least as they survive) as a participant in the Game of Troy (11.11.2), again evoking the *Aeneid*, where the Troy Game forms part of the funeral rituals of Anchises. The regressive nature of this repetition traps not only Nero himself but also the people of Rome, who, as the fire rages, are prevented from escaping by the city itself (15.38.3). Above all in relation to the fire, Nero subverts the distinction between myth and history.[38] Troy and Rome collapse into one another (it is interesting to speculate how Lucan might have handled Nero singing of Troy while Rome burned in the – now lost – *De incendio urbis*, referred to by Statius, *Silvae* 2.7.60–1).

Yet unlike Troy, Rome is not permanently reduced to a heap of charred ruins. Instead it will rise again. The city has of course done this before, most notably after its sack by the Gauls in 390 BC. Indeed Tacitus observes that some were struck by the date. The fire began on 19 July, exactly 418 years, 418 months and 418 days since the traditional date of the burning of Rome by the Gauls in 390 BC (15.41.2). A little

---

[37] Feeney 2007, 105.   [38] Feeney 2007, 105–7.

later Tacitus himself goes on to draw a contrast with the situation *ut post Gallica incendia* (15.43.1). Tacitus' account of the fire and subsequent rebuilding of the city has much in common with Livy's (5.43–50) and indeed, as Kraus argues, engages closely with it. Livy himself compared the destruction of Rome by the Gauls to the fall of Troy, even if only implicitly. 'In this case, as often, Tacitus proves one of Livy's best readers', Kraus comments.[39] Rather curiously, Livy's rebuilt Rome is all crooked. The layout of Rome resembles that of an occupied city (5.55.5). Livy's Rome, however, is clearly marked out as destined for a different future from that of Troy; in the time of Camillus, at least, there is progress as well as repetition.[40]

So what is at stake in Tacitus' evocation of Livy's account of Rome devastated by the Gauls? Might Nero aspire to be a new Camillus (who in Livy's history seems to serve as model for Augustus, Nero's great-grandfather)? Certainly he seeks the glory of refounding and indeed renaming the city. Indeed Feeney comments: 'Nero transfers the epithet and wants the glory of being the founder of a *new city*.'[41] Suetonius reports that he wanted to rename the city Neropolis (*Nero* 55). Nero will be a new Aeneas abandoning the smouldering remains of his fatherland to found another settlement. But in Nero's case, it will be on the same site and he must, it seems, first himself play the part of the city's destroyer in order to make this possible.

Nero himself then is figured here as Rome's attacker. Tacitus had already portrayed his predecessor Tiberius as engaging in a kind of warfare with his own city, shedding the blood of citizens through *maiestas* trials; the city became a battleground littered with corpses (*Ann.*6.19.2). This civil war imagery is suggestively explored by Keitel who observes, stressing in particular the characterization of Rome in flames as a captured city: 'Nero makes war on his own city much more directly'.[42] Nero notoriously takes advantage of the ruin of his fatherland, *patriae ruinis* (15.42.1), to make space for his splendid new residence; a later chapter characterizes the house as 'hated and built of the spoils taken from citizens' (15.52.1). His Golden House astonished not so much with the splendour of its materials, long made familiar through luxury, as Tacitus observes, but rather through its 'fields and lakes and the air of solitude given by woodland alternating with open spaces and prospects' (15.42.1).[43] Within the confines of the Golden House, at least, we seem to have returned to the rustic origins of

---

[39] Kraus 1994, 274.   [40] Kraus 1994, 282–5.   [41] Feeney 2007, 106.
[42] Keitel 1984, 307.   [43] On rusticity as luxury see Edwards 1993, 143–9.

Rome. Tacitus' account of the project has it figure as a spectacular instance of the gulf between whimsical Neronian fantasy on the one hand and, on the other, the weighty achievements, military, political and religious, of Roman history, as embodied in the fabric of the now vanished buildings, whose place has been taken by the new imperial residence.

In the aftermath of the fire, attempts are made to placate Rome's gods (15.44). Nero singles out the Christians, members of a sect that had recently manifested itself in the city, as scapegoats for the fire. In relation to the spread of Christianity to Rome, Tacitus observes that this is the city 'to which from all places everything vile and shameful converges and there is celebrated' (15.44.3). We might compare the characterization of Neronian Rome Tacitus puts in the mouths of the emperor's critics, some time earlier, as they attack:

> imported laxity which causes everything potentially
> corrupting or corruptible to be on show in the capital –
> foreign influence demoralizes our young men, making
> them pursuers of idleness, gymnastics and shameful love
> affairs.
>
> (*Ann.* 14.20.5)

In earlier periods, by contrast, Rome had attracted all that was finest, as Tacitus implies with regard to the treasures the city had amassed in the course of its conquests, treasures lost forever in the great fire.

These observations engage with an established discourse on cities and their moral character, which makes Tacitus' comments all the more pointed. Cicero (in an echo of Plato's *Laws* 704d–e) offers a stern account of the dangers of selecting a maritime situation for a city:

> Cities on the coast experience a corruption and
> degeneration of morals. Strange languages and customs mix
> with their own, . . . so that their ancestral institutions
> cannot remain unaffected.
>
> (*De re publica* 2.4.7)

He goes on to offer the examples of Carthage and Corinth as cities devoted to pleasure and luxury, habits which stimulate and are stimulated by trade. Hence they abandoned agriculture and warfare and left themselves vulnerable to destruction (both were reduced to ruins by

Roman armies in 146 BC, a key moment in the city's rise to domination). In the *De re publica* Romulus' choice of site for Rome at a safe distance from the coast is sharply contrasted with the situation of these now conquered cities. But the Rome of Nero, as Tacitus describes it, a point of confluence for luxury and vice from all over the empire, seems much more to resemble the doomed cities of Carthage and Corinth than the Rome of Romulus.

In the wake of the fire, Rome is rebuilt, though Tacitus is characteristically ambivalent about the new version. Even the ruins of the beautiful and ancient monuments destroyed by the fire can no longer be seen. They have been obliterated by Rome's latest Caesar. Here, the agent of destruction is the ruler and his building projects rather than the passage of time or enemy action. Nero's Golden House, with its faux rusticity, offers a perverse return to Rome's rustic origins. But Tacitus' writing preserves from oblivion the smoking ruins alongside the new palace (itself destined to be short-lived). Indeed, this *imago* has the potential to last longer than any material monument. At last Hannibal's desire (at least as Silius imagined it) for an immortal image of Rome in flames is fulfilled.

The fire of 64 (and that of 69) occurred in Tacitus' own lifetime (he was born in AD 56 or 57). Of provincial origin, he may not have been directly familiar with the old city. But his parents' generation, the distinguished orators from whom he learned his formidable rhetorical skills, would have been able to recall the buildings of Rome as it was, variously quaint, monumental, picturesque, austere, but all freighted with the memories of centuries past, tangible connections to an earlier, perhaps better, Rome. The ruins of Rome preserved in the *Annals* (and the *Histories*) provoke none of the sweet melancholy, the nostalgia of the ruins in Petrarch or Poggio. They signify rather a bitter and raw sense of loss. Romans have been dispossessed of their city through their own collusive folly and cowardice as much as through the deluded self-aggrandizement and incompetence of their emperor. We should not forget, of course, that Tacitus' own outrage and sorrow are licensed by the change of dynasty which followed Nero's reign. The Flavians could share in the anger provoked by Nero's Golden House even as they took advantage of the opportunity it offered for their own spectacular construction projects; the Colosseum was to occupy a key part of the site. We do not know how, if at all, Tacitus chose to notice in his own work the construction of this other amphitheatre, still greater than the one he ruthlessly disparages as outside the proper purview of annals in the passage from Book 13 quoted earlier.

The end of the *Annals* is lost (as is the end of the *Histories*). But the conclusion to Tacitus' earlier work, his biography of his father-in-law Agricola, returns to the comparison between texts and material objects explored by his Augustan predecessors.

> Men's statues, like men themselves, are fragile and
> vulnerable to decay. The mind's essence, however, is
> eternal, something which you can preserve and reproduce
> not by the material form of another's artistry but only in
> your own character.
>
> *(Agricola* 46.3)

Agricola's memory, if it is not to be lost like that of so many other great men, if it is to aspire to eternal *fama*, requires of course the agency of the historian to transmit to future generations. The text will ensure his survival in a way that no statue ever could. Through texts, the city of Rome, too, could aspire to an eternity which might preserve all the nuances of its complex history. Like John Piper's image of Coventry ablaze, Tacitus' *Annals* preserves the memory both of the ancient and beautiful monuments of the city and also of the devastation Nero brought to Rome, while his readers give Tacitus' ruined Rome a kind of longevity to which even Nero's rebuilt capital could not aspire.

31: ROMA AETERNA

Ingrid Rowland

THE END OF ANTIQUITY

It is hard to put a decisive date to the end of ancient Rome. Long after the active capitals of the empire had moved to Ravenna and Constantinople, long after Goths and Vandals had entered Rome itself, after Christian churches had supplanted ancient temples, the aqueducts lay in ruins, and dense neighbourhoods had turned to pastureland, the city still survived as an enduring symbol. Roman rituals of civic pride and imperial triumph infused the ceremony of the Christian Church. Ancient Roman symbols, traditions, art and literature inspired not only the residents of the ancient capital, fewer and poorer though they may have been, but also the regions that had once formed part of the former empire in northern Europe and the Mediterranean. In Constantinople and the eastern realms of the empire, Roman imperial government lived on uninterrupted until the Ottoman conquest in 1453, and in a sense the Roman tradition of Byzantium lives on to this day in the modern Greek term for Greekness, *Romiosyne*, which derives from the Byzantine word for patriotism, and really means 'Romanness'.

But by the time that Byzantine Constantinople began to face a serious threat from the Sultan in the fifteenth century, Rome itself was once again prepared to take up the cultural heritage of the ancient empire, east and west. And thus, in the early days of the Italian Renaissance, Rome became the Eternal City, the seemingly timeless place we know today, a Rome that is in fact a carefully constructed, ingeniously preserved creation of human ingenuity. Rome's longest history is a history of inspiration rather than military conquest, of persuasion and education rather than coercion, of civilization in its most civil sense.

When Alaric and the Visigoths sacked Rome in AD 410 the city had already been physically vulnerable for centuries; between AD 271 and 274, Emperor Aurelian had raised the first fortifications since republican times to protect the metropolis and its 1 million people.

Nonetheless, the sack's symbolic charge was as devastating as its brutality. Signs of the violence are still evident today, in details like the floor of the Basilica Aemilia in the Roman Forum, its coloured marble speckled with raised greenish dots: these are the melted remains of coins that spilled from the stalls and purses of fleeing moneychangers and liquefied when the building's huge timber roof beams collapsed in flames. News of the devastation spread outward along the roads that led to Rome, by then not only the capital of a political empire, but also of the Christian Church. Terrified Christians turned for comfort to one of their living sages, the North African bishop Augustine of Hippo. Augustine replied with a huge book, *The City of God*, in which, with relentless energy, he reminded his readers that Rome was only a human city, subject to mortal cycles of birth, growth, decline and decay; the eternal City of God existed only in Heaven.

As if to bear Augustine out, over the next two centuries, Ostrogoths, Vandals and Lombards would follow the Visigoths to Rome, cutting the great aqueducts, devastating fields and destroying the complex networks – human, animal and technological – that had forged the imperial city's infrastructure. Yet even as the invaders ran wild through the streets of Rome, they fell captive to the city's power of suggestion; they had come to Rome, after all, because the capital symbolized supreme power on earth.

By early medieval times, power within what remained of the Roman empire had shifted away from Rome itself to places like Constantinople, Ravenna and Trier. The greatest minds and the greatest artistic talents had long since moved north and east. Only the Church held firm, in its massive basilicas and the sprawling labyrinth of the Lateran Palace, a former imperial property transformed into the residence of Popes. The remaining population thinned and shifted; modest farms and vineyards began to sprout among the looming ruins of ancient temples, tombs, houses and baths. The gigantic early Christian basilicas stood in ever-greater isolation, huge islands of masonry in a sea of green fields. The people who ruled Rome, whether local barons, immigrant churchmen, the few surviving tradesmen or humble workers, lived in buildings that looked more like fortresses than houses. Natural disasters seemed to underline the destruction wrought by human malevolence: the Tiber continued its regular pattern of floods, burying the Circus Maximus and Campus Martius in layer upon layer of mud. Periodic earthquakes shook down ancient vaults, cornices and columns, upsetting the delicate interplay of stresses that had kept baths and basilicas in place. A new disease, malaria, infested the low-lying areas of the city, but it positively raged just to the south of Rome, in the watery wastelands of the Pomptine Marshes.

Still, the symbolic power of Rome continued to transcend any of its difficulties in the real world. An astute Roman-born Pope, Gregory I (r. 590–604) – Gregory the Great – assumed political power alongside his spiritual duties, reclaiming many of the same temporal rights as Roman emperors in addition to ceremonial trappings like a throne and red shoes.

Nor were Popes the only rulers to adapt ancient Roman signs and ceremonies to enhance their authority. In 800, Pope Leo III crowned the Frankish king Charlemagne 'Emperor of the Romans', and the king's coins appropriately portray him wreathed in Roman laurels. Charlemagne probably commissioned the earliest surviving manuscript of Vitruvius, as if he were a new Augustus, and he certainly ordered the construction of a magnificent rotunda in Aachen as his own version of the Pantheon. A similar ceremonial transfer of Roman *imperium*, *translatio imperii*, would play an especially important role in German-speaking lands, for 900 years, from 962 to 1806, when an unruly group of small states united as a single political ideal, the Holy Roman Empire (though Voltaire, confident that the true *translatio imperii* had occurred between Rome and Paris, dismissed the German invention as 'neither holy, nor Roman, nor an empire').[1]

For Rome's eastern capital, the *translatio imperii* took place in 330, when the emperor Constantine moved his court from Rome to Byzantium, which he rechristened 'Constantinople'. Constantine's New Rome was firmly Greek in its language, Orthodox in its Christianity, and devoted, with truly Roman *gravitas*, to tradition, although tradition, as in ancient Rome itself, could transform itself with astounding ingenuity.

MEDIEVAL ROME: THE LION CITY

As Constantinople carried on its duties as the New Rome, Old Rome, dependent on the new capital politically, clung stubbornly to its ancient civic traditions. The senate, now a city council for a settlement of 50,000 souls rather than the governing body for a world empire, was revived in the sixth century, and was still meeting centuries later in a fortress-like palazzo on the Capitoline – renamed Monte Caprino,

[1] *Essai sur l'histoire générale et sur les mœurs et l'esprit des nations* (1756), ch. 70.

'Goat Hill' – rather than the Curia in the Forum, better known as the 'Cow Pasture', Campo Vaccino. The privilege of wearing scarlet had passed long ago from this Senate to the 'Sacred Senate', the College of Cardinals, just as the red shoes that had marked out Roman patricians were now reserved for the Pope. As Byzantine control over Rome weakened in the ninth century, a handful of wealthy families took over the city. These local clans would produce most of the medieval popes, however loudly the Roman Church continued to proclaim its universality.

One ritual in particular reinforced that universal ideal: pilgrimage. Jesus himself had never set foot in Rome, but few cities preserved clearer evidence of Christianity's transformation from a persecuted Jewish sect to Europe's dominant religion. Undaunted by treacherous roads, tiny ships and shifting politics, the faithful came to Rome to retrace the Apostles' footsteps. Like many modern tourists, medieval pilgrims left their graffiti everywhere in Rome (including some Scandinavian runes scratched into a tenth-century fresco). Like modern tourists, they returned home with tales of the marvellous sights they had seen: the standing wonders of Colosseum and Pantheon, both largely intact; ruined baths; ancient churches with their seamless connection between classical beauty and Christian piety. Large sections of the imperial palace on the Palatine stood until 1084, when Holy Roman Emperor Henry IV invaded Rome, driving Pope Gregory VII into the fortress of Castel Sant'Angelo, the former mausoleum of the emperor Hadrian. When Gregory, in turn, called in reinforcements from southern Italy, an army of 36,000 Norman warriors, under Robert Guiscard, put large tracts of the city to flame; some ruined neighbourhoods would not be resettled until after the unification of Italy in 1870.

Faced with such devastation, Gregory's protégé, Pope Paschal II (r. 1099–1118), began a rebuilding campaign that continued with the popes of the twelfth and thirteenth centuries; their efforts survive in Romanesque church towers, some graceful porticos and some of the city's most dazzling mosaics.

In 1300, pilgrimage took on an official form: the Jubilee of Indulgence. Pope Boniface VIII called the first recorded Jubilee in 1300, but the practice is recorded at least a century earlier, and can plausibly be connected not only to the Jewish ritual of Jubilee, a recurring festival when debts were forgiven, but also to ancient Roman (and Etruscan) calendrical festivals like the *ludi saeculares*. Jubilee pilgrims received indulgences, reprieves from time spent in Purgatory, in return for having made their pious journey. The poet Dante, who loathed Boniface VIII, set his *Divine Comedy* in this same Jubilee Year of 1300 in order to contrast his own pilgrimage through the cosmos with more common pilgrims' quest for a worldly Rome, ruled by a worldly Pope.[2]

By the later Middle Ages, however, Rome offered more than an image of Christian empire. Many visitors came looking instead for traces of the ancient empire, especially those who came from the ranks of the new merchant and professional class that began to develop in European cities from the eleventh century onward. Universities in Italy and elsewhere began to prepare students for careers in law, in medicine, as notaries; these students read Cicero and began to identify their own conditions with those of the Roman Republic, admiring the stern republican virtues of frugality and probity that had once built a tiny village into an international power. Rome's symbolic significance would always be twofold: for monarchs, the divinely ordained individual rule of imperial Rome; for communities, the Roman Republic's superior claims of the civic body over any individual, a guarantee of individual freedom within the rule of law.

Renaissance Popes would contrast the misery of medieval Rome with their own epic ambitions, but to the Romans themselves, and to many of the pilgrims who flocked to the Jubilee, those rumours of decline and fall were greatly exaggerated. Art and architecture continued in a tradition that never truly departed from classical ideals of harmony and proportion, for the most ambitious buildings in medieval Rome used stone, especially columns and floors, taken directly from ancient structures. Medieval artists drew their inspiration from the ancient city in all its cosmopolitan glory: thus a pair of sphinxes with Egyptian *nemes* (headdresses) guards one entrance to Pietro Vassalletto's thirteenth-century cloister at St John Lateran, where Egyptian influence also shows along the frieze in the head of a house cat, peering out nonchalantly from a row of lion heads. The radiant angels of the thirteenth-century painter Pietro Cavallini, with their monumental bodies and shimmering wings, still show their descent from the winged genius figures of ancient Rome (and of the Etruscans). New mosaics glittered in the twelfth century from the facades and interiors of the city's most important churches, like Santa Maria Maggiore and Santa Maria in Trastevere, but mosaic technique itself derived from antiquity; we can still compare the fifth-century mosaics in the

---

[2] Julia Bolton Holloway, 'Dante Alighieri and the 1300 Jubilee', <www.florin.ms/dantejubilee.html>.

nave of Santa Maria Maggiore with the mosaics of its twelfth-century apse.

Politically, in the meantime, the endless conflict between Rome's baronial families and their lock on the papacy eventually took their toll. In 1306, a cabal of French cardinals succeeded in moving Pope and Curia (College of Cardinals) to Avignon, along with the necessary bankers and bureaucrats, and their families. An uprooted child of one such papal bureaucrat, Tuscan-born, French-educated Petrarch (Francesco Petrarca, 1304–74), compared this voluntary exile in Provence to that of the Jews in the court of Nebuchadnezzar, calling it the 'Babylonian Captivity'. By the waters of his French Babylon, Petrarch would conceive the ideas that led directly to Rome's self-conscious rebirth as the Eternal City in the fifteenth century.

First, however, Rome itself endured a series of cataclysms, both natural and human. With the Popes gone, and the city shaken and once again depopulated, a sharp-witted local official decided that the only solution to Rome's woes was a new Republic. Cola di Rienzo (1313–54) was a self-made man, so fascinated by ancient Rome that he learned to read ancient inscriptions. Shrewd and eloquent, he was sent as an ambassador to the papal court in France, and returned in 1344 as an administrator for the Curia. In 1347, he mounted the Capitoline with one hundred men-at-arms and declared Rome an independent commune, and himself its Tribune. His revolt lasted only seven months, for the portly Tribune of Rome quickly proved to be as tyrannical as any Pope or baron.

In 1348 the Black Death swept Rome in its rampage through Europe. The year 1349 marked one of the most devastating earthquakes in the city's history; the outer wall of the Colosseum crashed to the ground. Local legend still says that when the Colosseum falls, Rome shall fall, and with Rome, the world. In 1349, that possibility looked all too real. As Tribune, Cola di Rienzo commissioned a fresco showing a personification of the Church dressed in mourning and pleading 'Holy Father, what will become of me if Rome perishes?'

Cola's second term as Tribune in 1353 ended with his assassination a year later, but his basic political insight transcended his own personal limitations: the romance of the Roman Republic took on a new life that would one day rival the romance of the imperial papacy. His was only the first in a recurring series of republican revolts in Rome, the most recent as late as 1946, when Italy rejected its monarchy in a national plebiscite and laid the foundations for the present Italian Republic.

RENAISSANCE ROME

Crowded together in the swampy plain of the Campus Martius, enclosed within a bend of the Tiber at the mercy of the river's floods, fourteenth-century Romans had seen their *imperium*, the divinely ordained right of command, 'translated' to the Greek Orthodox lords of Constantinople as well as to several dynasties of French and German kings. With the Popes at home in Avignon, Rome, despite its busy river traffic, could no longer compete economically with seafaring powers like Amalfi, Salerno, Naples, Pisa, Venice or Genoa, or even with the river port of Florence. When Petrarch visited the city for the second time in 1367–8, he was despondent:

> Although when I first . . . went to Rome, almost nothing was left of that old Rome but an outline or an image, and only the ruins bore witness to its bygone greatness, nonetheless, among those ashes there were still some noble sparks; but now the ash is long extinguished and grown cold.[3]

But noble sparks still survived, chief among them Petrarch himself and his strange contemporary, Caterina Benincasa, St Catherine of Siena (1347–80), the eloquent young mystic who in 1376 begged Pope Gregory XI (r. 1370–8) – as her 'dear *babbo* (Daddy)' – to return to his rightful home among the traces of the Apostles and martyrs. Both Petrarch and Catherine experienced Rome as outsiders, longing for the city as pilgrims did. In powerful language, Petrarch in a revolutionary new Latin modelled on the ancients, and Catherine in Sienese vernacular, demanded that their contemporaries revive Rome as a real capital, political and religious, a New Jerusalem for their own time.

But the man who returned the papacy to Rome was a real *Romano*, from one of the baronial families who had held the medieval city in their grasp: Martin V, born in Rome as Oddone Colonna (r. 1417–31). Martin did not actually enter his dilapidated native city until 1420, but events on the margins of Europe would soon conspire to reinforce Rome's real as well as symbolic centrality: in Asia, the Ottoman Turks were on the march. Rome's survival as an idea could no longer depend on the physical survival of its eastern capital and the power of *Romiosyne*. Twenty years after the Popes' return from Avignon healed the Great

---

[3] Francesco Petrarca, Letter to Guido Sette, *c.* 1367–8. Cited from Petrarch 1979, 952.

Schism among the cardinals, the Byzantine emperor John VIII Palaiolo-
gos encouraged western Christians to heal a still older breach, calling on
Pope Eugenius IV (1431–47) to reconcile eastern and western churches
(and supply him with a combined army against the Sultan). Two years
of meetings in Florence and Ferrara succeeded only in converting two
influential members of John's entourage to Catholicism. Greek refugees
began trickling into Italy, bringing icons, manuscripts and hopes that
Christian Rome, like ancient Rome, would embrace Greek culture as
an essential part of its heritage.

The cataclysm came in 1453. Islam became the New Rome's
dominant religion, and Old Rome took on the symbolism of New
Athens and New Jerusalem as well as the Eternal City. Inspired by the
challenge, fifteenth-century Popes began to rebuild Rome as a modern
cultural and religious capital, combining reverence for ancient tradition
with an appetite for new ideas, new technology and new exploration.
From the old Lateran Palace, they shifted to St Peter's and the Vatican,
close to Rome's new financial heart.

The best-educated citizens of this revived Rome, like the ancient
Romans before them, studied Greek and Latin, as well as the new
vernacular. When Pope Nicholas V established a Vatican Library in
the 1450s, its holdings included manuscripts in the classical languages,
but also Hebrew texts, the works of Arab writers, mostly in Latin
translation, and vernacular writers from Dante and Petrarch up to his
own exuberantly creative era. Whatever Europe's political and religious
divisions in the next few centuries, classical culture would provide a
single shared tradition, modelled on the cosmopolitan society of imperial Rome. However many ways this classical heritage was adapted and
fictionalized, it continued, like the idea of ancient Rome itself, to bind
widely differing people together in common projects and common
ideals.

Nicholas was the first fifteenth-century pope to reside permanently in Rome. He staffed the Curia with classically educated scholars,
most notably Leone Battista Alberti, writer, painter, sculptor, athlete,
archaeologist and, like so many of the figures who transformed Rome in
this period, a self-made man. The projects initiated by Nicholas V and
Alberti set the pattern for subsequent Renaissance Popes: a new lead
roof on the dome of the Pantheon, a new porch on the early Christian
church of Santo Stefano Rotondo, straightening the streets that led to
the Vatican from the bankers' quarter, putting a basin under the Trevi
fountain, establishing the Vatican Library, reinforcing the Vatican's fortification walls and the bastion at Castel Sant'Angelo, and broaching the

project of remodelling Saint Peter's Basilica, by then a building with more than a thousand years behind it. Art and architecture consciously adopted classical standards of beauty, drawing inspiration from surviving texts of ancient authors like Vitruvius and Pliny, but also from physical remnants of architecture, sculpture and painting.

Rome's revival was also, necessarily, an economic revival, and this meant reviving the finances of the Church. Cardinals brought in their own incomes: curial officials, bankers and tax collectors paid for their positions, buying and selling them in an early version of the stock market. Taxes, tithes and pilgrims poured into the Vatican from the whole Christian world, from churches in Ireland, Sweden, Poland and Germany, Franciscan missions in Alexandria, Venetian colonists on Crete, Franciscans in China. Money could buy masses, indulgences and curial positions, spiritual goods and services whose marketing observed the same economic principles as gold, grain or cloth. The fifteenth century, in Italy especially, was an age of expansive capitalism, and Rome was not the only place where religion mixed candidly with finance. In Rome, however, the mixture was consistent and ingenious.

For the next 400 years, Roman popes, from Nicholas V to his nineteenth-century successor Pius IX, would undertake the same series of duties as an essential part of their pontificate: restoring the city's ancient monuments, preserving the written heritage of Greece and Rome, encouraging acts of Christian piety, improving the city's physical conditions, commissioning new public works like bastions, churches, streets and buildings, calling Jubilees, assuming their temporal responsibilities as an integral part of their sacred priesthood. Papal rhetoric began to speak of Rome as a city reborn; the French term 'Renaissance' may date back to the nineteenth century, but the language of rebirth, like the vision of Rome as an Eternal City, belongs to the mid-fifteenth century.

The revival of ancient Rome also sparked new scholarly disciplines: philology and archaeology. In the second half of the fifteenth century, the University of Rome, originally founded to train lawyers for the curial court, began offering classes in Latin grammar and rhetoric, but both the Professor of Grammar, Giovanni Sulpizio da Veroli, and the Professor of Rhetoric, Giulio Pomponio Leto, supplemented their courses in Latin language with direct experience on the ground in Rome. Sulpizio edited the first printed edition of the ancient Roman architect Vitruvius in 1486 and sponsored the first public performance since antiquity of a Latin drama, Seneca's *Hippolytus*, with his students providing both cast and stage crew. Meanwhile, Pomponio Leto and his students subjected ancient manuscripts and ancient monuments to the same kinds of careful comparative study. At the same time, professional artists and architects honed their skills by drawing the ancient monuments and often compared notes and sketches with the scholars. Ancient Rome breathed life into modern Rome, and modern Rome breathed life into the ancient city.

As a universal religious capital, Rome could repay its visitors and benefactors with spiritual as well as monetary rewards. Renaissance popes understood that a more beautiful and more comfortable city would attract more pilgrims by offering a more vivid foretaste of Heaven. Generations of Popes invoked a great Crusade to win back lost terrain from the Ottomans, but they put their real trust, and their real money, in the arts of sublime persuasion.

Sixtus IV, an eminent Franciscan theologian, was the first Pope to make changes to the city that are still easily visible today. He reorganized the Vatican Library, throwing the collection open to scholars and commissioning an extensive series of new manuscripts to round out its holdings. In 1472, he opened the world's first public museum on the Capitoline Hill, seat of Rome's city council and what remained of the Roman senate, inviting artists, scholars and distinguished visitors to draw inspiration from his collection of ancient monuments. At the same time, Sixtus also tended Rome's infrastructure, repairing walls, roads and aqueducts and constructing the gracefully arcaded Ponte Sisto bridge just in time for the Jubilee of 1475. He commissioned a new chapel, the Sistine, to house papal ceremonies and chose the theme for its frescoed walls: a comparison between the life of Moses and the life of Christ.

Pope Alexander VI, Rodrigo Borgia (reigned 1492–1503), was the first Pope to contend with the entry of the New World into European trading networks. Over the next two centuries, Christian missionaries would encourage all nations to acknowledge Rome as their spiritual capital, beginning with the Franciscans in Asia and the New World, and culminating in the worldwide expansion of the Jesuits in the sixteenth and seventeenth centuries. Christianity's spiritual Roman empire consciously strove, then, to push far beyond the boundaries of its ancient predecessor.

The city's status as a universal cultural and religious capital crystallized in its definitive form under Alexander's successor and bitter adversary, Julius II (r. 1503–13). Many of his interventions forever changed Rome's standards for painting, sculpture, architecture and city planning. In a remarkable move, the Pope also decided to restore St Peter's Basilica. His initial plan may have envisioned no more than reinforcing the foundations, but the cornerstone that Julius and his architect, Donato Bramante, laid in 1506 was quickly incorporated into a whole new building. By this massive project, Julius meant to send a signal to the newly expanded Christian world: sixteenth-century Rome was a new Rome, not a city revived or remodelled, but a city recreated, the modern capital of a truly universal church.

Julius applied the same combination of bold insight and relentless bullying to improving the rest of Rome. For a Pope who reigned only ten years, the list of Julius's interventions in Rome is astounding: Michelangelo's Sistine Chapel ceiling, Raphael's paintings for Julius's apartments, new streets like the Via Giulia, widened streets, paved piazzas, new libraries. Projects that looked reckless proved not to be, driven to completion by his fierce will and backed by a solvent treasury.

At the same time, the Pope took it upon himself to enforce his temporal as well as his spiritual power, twice leading military expeditions against rebellious vassal states. He resolved to drive the French from Italy and succeeded by 1512. He engaged a troop of Swiss mercenaries as his papal guard, the same Swiss Guards who protect the Vatican today. But Julius also called an ecumenical council, the Fifth Lateran Council, to address charges of corruption within the Church. By the time it convened in 1512, however, his health, never good, had begun to collapse. By March 1513, Julius was dead. In a dialogue penned for the occasion, Erasmus caricatured him stomping up to Heaven in a clanking suit of armour to berate St Peter at the Pearly Gates. The title 'Julius Excluded from Heaven' gives away the outcome of this bitingly funny pamphlet.

Julius II was the last Pope to preside over an undivided western Church. His successor, Leo X, found himself ineffectually caught between the machinations of France, Spain and the Holy Roman Emperor. Although the Lateran Council continued under Leo, its initiatives for reforming the Church came too late: in 1517, an Augustinian friar from Wittenberg in northern Germany, Martin Luther, advertised ninety-five theses disputing papal authority, and it fell to Leo to excommunicate the German renegade in 1521. Rome's stature as cultural capital would have to contend ever afterward with its northern European counter-image as a new Babylon, mired in corruption.

The Protestant Reformation quickly became a political as well as a religious question. When Holy Roman Emperor Charles V released a troop of German Protestant mercenaries from service in central Italy in the spring of 1527, they descended on Rome, sacking the city repeatedly over the course of six months. To classically minded contemporaries, the sack of 1527 seemed to recall the disaster of AD 410, though in fact it was far less cataclysmic in its real effects. Both the physical city of Rome and its image as an eternal capital rebounded fairly quickly from the brief, terrifying setback.

Protestant pressures did, however, convince the Roman Church that it should undertake its own internal reforms. In 1539, Pope Paul III called a general council of the Church, but rather than meeting in Rome again, it eventually settled in the northern Italian city of Trent in order to make at least a physical approach towards the German reformers. Contentious and politicized, the Council of Trent issued its final decrees only in 1563, and these acknowledged a permanent rift with the Protestant world. Although some Popes took the Council's reforms to mean that the Vatican should sell off its collection of classical statues – like the saintly Pius V – in general, the papacy understood its mission in the same terms as Julius II: Rome was the eternal capital of a confluence of cultures that transcended every difference of time, place and language, and a Pope's responsibilities to the city, like an ancient emperor's, ranged from spiritual guidance to city planning, construction and attention to infrastructure. Hence an intellectual pope like Gregory XIII (r. 1572–85) established colleges for the study of Greek and Hebrew, sponsored a new building for the Jesuits' Roman College, appointed the Jesuit mathematician Christoph Clavius to oversee the first reformation of the calendar since Julius Caesar, and put that revised Gregorian calendar into effect. A militant pope like Sixtus V (r. 1585–90), Gregory's successor, created long, straight ancient-style streets to accommodate the new fashion of transportation by carriage, and re-erected four Egyptian obelisks – after duly exorcizing them, baptizing them and topping them with bronze crosses – to guide pilgrims on their way through Rome. But Sixtus also installed a new aqueduct to bring water to the heights of the Quirinal Hill and set up a silk factory inside the Colosseum. Every move these Popes made was marked by statues, inscriptions, pamphlets and parades, in which classical allegories continued to provide the chief means of communicating their goals. The buildings and urban schemes they commissioned, and their relationships with their architects, continued to follow the example set by Julius II and Bramante, from Sixtus V with Domenico Fontana (a brilliantly ingenious engineer but a thoroughly conventional architect) to the great papal patrons of the seventeenth century.

BAROQUE ROME: THE POWER OF BEAUTY

It took many decades for the popes to grasp the truth of Renaissance rhetoric: as its political influence continued to wane, Rome's most powerful asset as a Christian capital was, in fact, its beauty, put on special display for Jubilee years. Burning heretics could not compete with cooling fountains, and the papal armies never obtained anywhere near the success of the papal artists, architects and city planners; it is these who have best conveyed the essence, and the long history, of Rome to the world.

Three Popes, Urban VIII Barberini, Innocent X Pamphili and Alexander VII Chigi, were the greatest patrons, and the real creators, of Baroque Rome. Urban may be best known now for supervising the trial of Galileo in 1633 and for stripping the porch of the Pantheon of its bronze to create the Baldacchino that stands over the tomb of St Peter in St Peter's Basilica. He was also, however, a tireless sponsor of art, architecture, literature and music, who attracted a glittering court in Rome as he curried favour with his allies in France. Long before Louis XIV, who imitated his imagery, Urban cast himself as a Sun King. The great sculptor Gian Lorenzo Bernini, the painter-architect Pietro da Cortona and the architect Francesco Borromini all began their careers under Urban, and these are only the three best-known names in a legion of creators.

The most urgent political problem to face Urban VIII was the brutal war between Catholics and Protestants that had ravaged Germany since 1618; it would eventually be known as the Thirty Years War, for it ended by parley in 1648, under the papacy of Urban's successor, Innocent X. Innocent was quick to realize the potential impact of peace on Rome as a lure for pilgrims, especially in the Jubilee of 1650. Bernini's Fountain of the Four Rivers in Piazza Navona, Borromini's remodelling of the Basilica of St John Lateran and marble wall revetments for the interior of St Peter's still proclaim this Pope's emphasis on Rome as a welcoming destination for tourists and pilgrims alike, capitalizing on the growing northern European custom of the Grand Tour.

The most concerted Baroque interventions in Rome's physical fabric came, however, with Innocent's successor (and former secretary of state), Fabio Chigi, elected in 1655 as Alexander VII. Alexander combined continuing patronage of Bernini, Borromini and Cortona with penetrating attention to city planning, placing artistic and architectural signposts along all the major routes for pilgrims and visitors, culminating in Bernini's grand oval piazza in front of St Peter's, which transformed a formless square into an open-air Colosseum, with a company of hundreds of statues of saints ranged along its cornice. The Rome we experience today, from its northern entrance at Piazza del Popolo to the colonnade of St Peter's, is the Rome conceived, and to an amazing extent realized, by Alexander VII. Subsequent Popes, like Clement XI (r. 1700–21), followed the lines laid down by these three great patrons of the Baroque, all of them following the lead of the emperor Augustus in transforming Rome ever more completely into a city of marble.

MODERN ROME

In 1798, Corsican-born Napoleon Bonaparte invaded Italy with a French army, driving Pope Pius VII Braschi into exile. With 1,000 years of Frankish and then French *translatio imperii* behind him, Napoleon had no qualms about assuming ancient Roman titles, from Consul to Emperor. Neither did he hesitate, like triumphing Roman generals, to loot the places he had conquered. Documents, manuscripts and works of art made their way from the Vatican to Paris, the new capital of the new European empire, and as always there were great artists ready to commemorate the ruler in all his imperial glory, from Jacques-Louis David to Jean-Auguste-Dominique Ingres, both of them profoundly steeped in the traditions of classical art. By 1814, Napoleon's adventure was largely over, and Rome was able to recover most, but by no means all, of its looted treasures. Important Inquisitorial records were destroyed in transit, notably the trial transcripts of the heretic Giordano Bruno, burned at the stake in 1600, and several Vatican manuscripts have remained in France because of French claims to their importance for the development of French literature. Napoleon's experience shows how central Rome remained to the European imagery of empire. In Rome itself, however, his advent broke the tradition of the Papa-Re, the 'Pope-King' who had carried on the combined religious and political roles of ancient emperors, and Enlightenment ideas about democracy and republics did the rest. Nineteenth-century popes would never muster the same degree of temporal power as their Baroque predecessors, and in 1849 they temporarily lost power altogether.

In 1849, 500 years after Cola di Rienzo, Rome once again became a republic, this time in connection with a surge of revolutionary movements throughout Europe. An uprising in the city, backed by the troops of the gifted general Giuseppe Garibaldi, set up the radical republican political theorist Giulio Mazzini as President of the Roman Republic, and sent the new Pope Pius IX (r. 1848–78) into exile in the port of Gaeta. Pius appealed to France for help, and in the summer of 1849 a French army under General Nicolas Charles Victor Oudinot attacked Rome from the Janiculum hill, finally taking it after days of savage battle.

Pius IX retaliated, characteristically, with weapons both artistic and religious. In his long reign he would build and restore churches, convents, schools and the Ministry of Tobacco (a commodity he put, like salt, under papal jurisdiction) in a consciously Renaissance classical style inspired by Bramante and Raphael, modelling himself on his forceful Renaissance predecessor, Julius II. He established the Immaculate Conception of the Virgin Mary as dogma, and the infallibility of the papacy *ex cathedra*. His personal army, the papal Zouaves, enlisted Catholic troops from all over Europe and the Americas.

For a group of American artists, ironically, the authoritarian Rome of Pius IX remained a sanctuary for freedom. Many of these American expatriates were abolitionists, like the sculptor William Wetmore Story and a group of women sculptors, including Harriet Hosmer and Edmonia Lewis, who moved to Rome to pursue art and to escape the constraints put on them by society at home, not only as women, but as lesbians.

For Italians, too, the defeat of Mazzini and Garibaldi in 1849 did nothing to stop the movement for national unification. By 1860, most of Italy had joined forces under Victor Emanuel II, the King of Sardinia and Savoy, with Florence as the capital. Ultimately, however, there could be only one capital on the Italian peninsula, and that, for all its millennial reasons, was Rome. In 1870, a contingent of black-plumed Bersaglieri (light-armed marksmen) breached the walls of Rome at Porta Pia, somehow sparing Michelangelo's decorations, and turned Pope Pius IX from the leader of armies into the proverbial 'Prisoner of the Vatican'. Victor Emanuel II now reigned as King of Italy and Sicily, with only the tiny Republic of San Marino abstaining.

The movement for Italian unification once again drew on ancient Rome for its inspiration in a mix of republican and imperial symbolism, although its most conspicuous monument, the Altare della Patria dedicated to King Victor Emmanuel II on the Capitoline Hill (designed in the 1880s, completed in 1911), is more imperial than republican in its gleaming expanses of white Carrara marble. Long vilified, the 'Vittoriano' began to rise in the Romans' esteem once it, too, had reached a certain age, and, precisely for its scale, its eclecticism, its strong political message and its grandiosity, it must certainly be the modern building that most resembles the grandiose structures of imperial Rome as they looked in their heyday.

Italy's entry into the First World War proved a disastrous mistake, and post-war instability fostered the rise of a movement that began to exchange its socialist principles for a return to the militarism of imperial Rome. The Fascists adopted the same insignia as the Roman consuls: the *fasces*, the bundle of rods and axe that denoted consular power over life and limb, but favoured the bold use of force and dictatorial rule rather than republican institutions. Taking the Roman title of Dux, Italianized as Duce, their leader, Benito Mussolini, used the new mass media of radio and film reel to revive the idea of a renewed Roman empire, blazing broad new streets through the centre of Rome, down which he paraded soldiers, trucks and tanks as they marched down to the sea and off to Abyssinia, Somalia and Libya, symbolically reclaiming North Africa for Scipio. Mussolini saw the ruins of ancient Rome as an ideal repertory of themes and symbols for contemporary Italy, and devoted tremendous efforts to archaeological excavation and restoration, although the work was often hasty and the restorations, like the 'Area Sacra' of Largo Argentina, mixed together material from various sites in order to make a more impressive display. Consciously adopting the Renaissance as a model, Fascist art and architecture took the ancient world as inspiration for new creativity, but in a streamlined, hard-edged, consciously modern style, best seen today in the areas of the Foro Italico, Termini train station (designed before the Second World War, and completed in 1950) and the unfinished site for a Fascist World's Fair, the Esposizione Universale Romana (EUR). Like Julius II, Sixtus V and Urban VIII, Mussolini was a great builder and an equally great destroyer.

In one of his lasting achievements, Mussolini formalized relations with the Catholic Church in the Lateran Accords of 1929, which restored properties to the Church that had been confiscated at the time of unification. Collaboration between Church, state and civic authorities is essential for the smooth running of sacred events like the Jubilees and canonizations, so that in many respects contemporary Rome may seem to preserve an unbroken line of ancient tradition. That continuity, however, has been hard won, sometimes by violent conflict, largely by patient negotiation over the millennia.

The Duce's greatest tactical error was allying himself with Adolf Hitler, whose ideology of a Third Reich preferred Celtic and

Indo-European elements (the swastika) to those of Rome. As a result, self-consciously barbarian elements persist in the symbolic repertory of Italian neo-fascism, leaving the symbols of ancient Rome free for further appropriation by the Italian state and the Comune di Roma, the civic authorities of Rome. Manhole covers and public buses are still embossed with the initials SPQR, *Senatus Populusque Romanus*. Eagles and laurel wreaths still proclaim Rome's glory and fame respectively.

If the Fascist hierarchs, like Renaissance Popes, looked back to imperial Rome in order to look forward to their own new era, it is no surprise to discover that their opponents drew inspiration from the Roman Republic. When Italy deposed Mussolini and switched to the Allied side in 1943, the United States and the Soviet Union became the two major poles of Italian political identification; ultimately the prevailing ideal would be that of the Roman Republic, the same ideal that inspired the constitution of the United States. In 1946, Italy rejected, and indeed exiled, its king, instead establishing a parliamentary democracy with a Senate and a Chamber of Deputies, a prime minister (the President of the Council of Ministers) and a president. The Italian Republic and the Pope continue to wrestle with one another over the true legacy of Rome, as they have for nearly two millennia. In a real sense, they are both rightful heirs to Roman tradition, for only together have they been able to make the Eternal City eternal.

FURTHER READING

In general see, Hibbert 1988. On late antique and medieval Rome, see Edward Gibbon, *History of the Decline and Fall of the Roman Empire*. First published 1776–88, it is still valuable. Furthermore, see Krautheimer 1980 [2000] and Gardiner 2008. On Renaissance Rome, see Stinger 1995 and Hall 2005. On baroque Rome, see Magnuson 1982-6 and Metzger Habel 2002. On eighteenth-century Rome, see Johns 1993 and Collins 2004. On Napoleonic Rome, see Vandiver Nicassio 2009. On Risorgimento Rome, see Kertzer 2006. On fascist Rome, see Painter Jr 2007.

BIBLIOGRAPHY

Aberson, M. 1994. *Temples votifs et butin de guerre dans la Rome républicaine*. Geneva.

Adam, J. P. 1994. *Roman Building: Materials and Techniques*. London.

Adams, G. W. 2008. *Rome and the Social Role of Elite Villas in its Suburbs*, British Archaeological Reports. Oxford.

Adams, J. N. 1983. 'Words for "prostitute" in Latin'. *Rheinisches Museum* 126: 321–58.

    2003. *Bilingualism and the Latin Language*. Cambridge.

Africa, T. 1971. 'Urban violence in imperial Rome'. *The Journal of Interdisciplinary History* 2: 3–21.

Agostini, S., and W. Pellegrini. 1996. 'Altre risorse della Maiella: Testimonianze di archaeologia industriale'. In *La presenza dell' uomo sulla Maiella: Archeologia e paesaggio storico: Guida alla Sezione Archeologica del Museo Paolo Barrasso Centro Visitatori della Riserva naturale Valle dell'Orfento*, ed. A. R. Staffa. Chieti.

Aicher, P. 1995. *Guide to the Aqueducts of Ancient Rome*. Wauconda, Il.

Aldrete, G. 1999. *Gestures and Acclamations in Ancient Rome*. Baltimore.

    2007. *Floods of the Tiber in Ancient Rome*. Baltimore.

    and D. J. Mattingly. 1999. 'Feeding the city: the organization, operation, and scale of the supply system for Rome'. In *Life, Death, and Entertainment in the Roman Empire*, ed. D. S. Potter and D. J. Mattingly. Ann Arbor, 171–204.

Alföldy, G. 1988. *Antike Sklaverei: Widersprüche, Sonderformen, Grundstrukturen*. Bamberg.

Allison, P. M. 2004. *Pompeian Households: An Analysis of Material Culture*. Los Angeles.

Amelotti, M. 1955. 'La posizione degli atleti di fronte al diritto romano'. *Studia et Documenta Historiae et Iuris* 21: 123–56.

Ampolo, C. 1988. 'La nascità della città'. In *Storia di Roma*, I, ed. A. Momigliano and A. Schiavone. Turin, 153–80.

Anderson Jr, J. C. 1984. *The Historical Topography of the Imperial Fora*. Brussels.

    1997. *Roman Architecture and Society*. Baltimore.

Andreau, J. 1987. 'L'espace de la vie financière à Rome'. In *L'Urbs: espace urbain et histoire (Ier siècle av. J.-C.–IIIe siècle ap. J.-C.)*. Rome, 157–74.

    1999. *Banking and Business in the Roman World*. Cambridge.

    and R. Descat. 2007. *Esclave en Grèce et à Rome*. Paris.

Andreussi, M. 1999. 'Pomerium'. In *LTUR* 4.96–105.

Arce, J. 1999. 'El inventario de Roma: Curiosum y Notitia'. In *The Transformations of Urbs Roma in Late Antiquity*, ed. W. V. Harris. Portsmouth, RI, 15–22.

Ascensi, A. et al. 1996. 'The Roman mummy of Grottarossa'. In *Human Mummies*, ed. K. Spindler et al. Vienna, 205–18.

Ash, R. 2007. 'Victim and voyeur: Rome as a character in Tacitus' *Histories* 3'. In *The Sites of Rome: Time, Space, Memory*, ed. D. H. J. Larmour and D. Spencer. Oxford, 211–37.

Ashby, Th. 1935. *The Aqueducts of Ancient Rome*. Oxford (Italian translation: Rome 1992).

Astin, A. E. 1967. *Scipio Aemilianus*. Oxford.

Ausbüttel, F. M. 1982. *Untersuchungen zu den Vereinen im Westen des römischen Reiches*. Kallmünz.

Baccari, M. P. 1996. *Cittadini, popoli e communione nella legislazione dei secoli IV–VI*. Turin.

Bakker, J. T. 2001. 'Les boulangeries à moulin et les distributions de blé gratuites'. In *Ostia, port et porte de la Rome antique*, ed. J.-P. Descœudres. Geneva, 179–85.

Balty, J. et al. eds. 2004–6. *Thesaurus cultus et rituum antiquorum*. Los Angeles.

Balzaretti, R. 2004. 'The history of the countryside in sixteenth-century Varese Ligure'. In *Ligurian Landscapes: Studies in Archaeology, Geography and History*, ed. R. Balzaretti, M. Pearce and C. Watkins. London, 105–12.

Barabàsi, A.-L. 2002. *Linked: The New Science of Networks*. Cambridge.

Barnes, T. D. 1995. 'Statistics and the conversion of the Roman aristocracy'. *Journal of Roman Studies* 85: 135–47.

Barnish, S. J. B. 1987. 'Pigs, plebeians and *potentes*: Rome's economic hinterland, *c*.350–600 A.D.'. *Papers of the British School at Rome* 55: 157–85.

Barry, W. 1993. 'Popular violence and the stability of Roman Alexandria, 30 BC–AD 215'. *Bulletin de la Société Archéologique d'Alexandrie* 45: 19–34.

Barton, I. M. 1996. *Roman Domestic Buildings*. Exeter.

Bauer, H. 1993. 'Cloaca, Cloaca Maxima'. *LTUR* 1.288–90.

Beard, M. 1987. 'A complex of times: no more sheep on Romulus' birthday'. *Proceedings of the Cambridge Philological Society* 33: 1–15.

2007. *The Roman Triumph*. New Haven.

Beard, M., J. North and S. Price. 1998. *Religions of Rome*. Cambridge.

Beare, R. 1978. 'Were bailiffs ever free born?'. *Classical Quarterly* 28: 398–401.

Bell III, M. 1994. 'An imperial flour mill on the Janiculum'. In *Le ravitaillement en blé de Rome et des centres urbains des débuts de la République jusqu'au Haut empire: Actes du colloque international de Naples 1991*. Naples, 73–89.

Bendlin, A. 2006. 'Nicht der Eine, nicht die Vielen: zur Pragmatik religiösen Verhaltens in einer polytheistischen Gesellschaft am Beispiel Roms'. In *Götterbilder – Gottesbilder – Weltbilder*, ed. R. G. Kratz and H. Spieckermann. Tübingen, vol. 2, 279–311.

Bennett, C. 2003. 'The early Augustan calendars in Rome and Egypt'. *Zeitschrift für Papyrologie und Epigraphik* 142: 221–40.

Bergmann, B. and Kondoleon, C. eds. 1999. *The Art of Ancient Spectacle*. Washington D.C.

Bernstein, F. H. 1997. *Ludi Publici: Untersuchungen zur Entstehung und Entwicklung der öffentlichen Spiele im republikanischen Rom*. Stuttgart.

Bickermann, E. 1980. *Chronology of the Ancient World*. 2nd edn. London.

Bisconti, F. 2000. *Mestieri nelle catacombe romane: Appunti sul declino dell'iconografia del reale nei cimiteri cristiani di Roma*. Vatican City.

Black, S., Browning, J. L., Laurence, R. 2009. 'From quarry to road: towards an economic model for the supply of basalt for road paving in the Tiber Valley'.

In *Mercator placidissimus: The Tiber Valley in Antiquity*, ed. F. Coarelli and H. Patterson. Rome.

Blanchard, Ph. et al. 2007. 'A mass grave from the catacomb of Saints Peter and Marcellinus in Rome, second–third century AD'. *Antiquity* 81: 898–998.

Blastenbrei, P. 2006. 'Violence, arms and criminal justice in Papal Rome, 1560–1600'. *Renaissance Studies* 20: 68–87.

Bloch, H. 1959. 'The Serapeum of Ostia and the brick-stamp of 123: new landmark in the history of Roman architecture'. *American Journal of Archaeology* 63: 225–40.

Boatwright, M. T. 1986. 'The pomerial extension of Augustus'. *Historia* 35: 13–27.

1987. *Hadrian and the City of Rome*. Princeton.

Bodel, J. 1994. *Graveyards and Groves: A Study of the Lex Lucerina*. Cambridge, Mass.

2005. '*Caveat emptor*. Towards a study of the Roman slave-trade'. *Journal of Roman Archaeology* 18: 181–95.

2008. '*Genii loci* ed i mercati di Roma'. In *Epigrafia 2006: atti della XIVe rencontre sur l'épigraphie* (Tituli 9), ed. M. L. Caldelli et al. Rome, 209–36.

Bodson, L. 2000. 'Motivations for pet-keeping in ancient Greece and Rome: a preliminary survey'. In *Companion Animals and Us*, ed. A. L. Podberscek, E. S. Paul and J. A. Serpell. Cambridge, 27–41.

Bollmann, B. 1998. *Römische Vereinshäuser: Untersuchungen zu den Scholae der römischen Berufs-, Kult- und Augustalen-Kollegien in Italien*. Mainz.

Bowersock, G. 2002. 'Peter and Constantine'. In '*Humana sapit*': *Études d'antiquité tardive offertes à Lellia Cracco Ruggini*, ed. J.-M. Carrié and R. Lizzi Testa. Turnhout, 209–17.

Bradley, K. R. 1991. *Discovering the Roman Family*. Oxford.

1994. *Slavery and Society at Rome*. Cambridge.

Bradley, M. A. 2002. 'It all comes out in the wash: looking harder at the Roman *fullonica*'. *Journal of Roman Archaeology* 15: 21–44.

Brandenburg, H. 2005. *Ancient Churches of Rome from the Fourth to the Seventh Century*. Turnhout.

Brélaz, C. 2005. *La sécurité publique en Asie Mineure sous le Principat (Ier-IIIème s. ap. J.-C.)*. Basle.

Brigham, T. et al. 1996. 'Current archaeological work at Regis House in the City of London (Part I)'. *London Archaeologist* 82: 31–8.

Brilliant, R. 1967. *The Arch of Septimius Severus in the Roman Forum*. Rome.

Broadhead, W. 2004. 'Rome and the mobility of the Latins: problems of control'. In *La mobilité des personnes en Méditerranée, de l'Antiquité à l'époque moderne: Procédures de contrôle et documents d'identification*, ed. C. Moatti. Rome, 315–35.

Broekaert, W. 2008. 'Roman economic policies during the third century AD: the evidence of the *tituli picti* on oil amphorae'. *Ancient Society* 38: 197–219.

2010. 'Navicularii et negotiantes: a prosopographical study of Roman traders and the commercial organisation during the empire'. Unpublished PhD dissertation. Ghent.

Broughton, T. R. S. 1951–86. *The Magistrates of the Roman Republic*. New York.

Brown, P. 2002. *Poverty and Leadership in the Later Roman Empire*. Hanover.

Browning, R. 1952. 'The riot of A.D. 387 in Antioch: the role of the theatrical claques in the later empire'. *Journal of Roman Studies* 42: 13–20.

Brunt, P. A. 1971. *Italian Manpower 225 B.C.–A.D. 14*. Oxford.

1980. 'Free labour and public works at Rome'. *Journal of Roman Studies* 70: 81–100.

1988. *The Fall of the Roman Republic and Related Essays*. Oxford.

Bruun, C. 1991. *The Water Supply of Ancient Rome: A Study of Roman Imperial Administration*. Helsinki.

1997. 'A city of temples and squares, emperors, horses and houses'. *Journal of Roman Archaeology* 10: 389–98.

2000. 'Water shortage and surplus in the ancient world'. In *Cura aquarum in Sicilia*, ed. G. Jansen. Leiden, 215–24.

2003a. '*Medius fidius . . . tantam pecuniam Nicomedenses perdiderunt!*': Roman water supply, public administration, and private contractors'. In *Tâches publiques et entreprise privée dans le monde romain*, ed. J.-J. Aubert. Neuchâtel, 305–25.

2003b. 'Velia, Quirinale, Pincio: note su proprietari di *domus* e su *plumbarii*'. *Arctos* 37: 27–48.

2004. 'The impossibility of reaching an exact value for the Roman *quinaria* measure'. In Rodgers 2004, 342–6.

2006. 'Der Kaiser und die stadtrömischen *curae*: Geschichte und Bedeutung'. In *Herrschaftsstrukturen und Herrschaftspraxis*, ed. A. Kolb. Berlin, 89–114.

2007. 'Why did Frontinus write the *De Aquaeductu*?'. *Journal of Roman Archaeology* 20: 460–6.

2010. 'Cognomina plurubariorum', *Epigraphica* 72: 297–331.

Buccellato, A. et al. 2003. 'Il comprensorio della necropolis di Via Basiliano (Roma): un'indagine multidisciplinare'. *Mélanges d'archéologie et d'histoire de l'École française de Rome. Antiquité* 115: 311–76.

2008. 'La nécropole de Collatina'. *Dossiers d'Archéologie* 330: 22–31.

Buchner, E. 1982. *Die Sonnenuhr des Augustus*. Mainz.

Buranelli, F. et al. 2005–6. 'I nuovi scavi della necropolis della Via Trionfale in Vaticano'. *Rendiconti della pontificia accademia di archeologia* 78: 451–72.

Caldelli, M. L. 1993. *L'Agon Capitolinus: storia e protagonisti dall'istituzione Domizianea al IV secolo*. Rome.

Cameron, A. 1976. *Circus Factions: Blues and Greens at Rome and Byzantium*. Oxford.

1999. 'The last pagans of Rome'. In *The Transformations of Urbs Roma in Late Antiquity*, ed. W. V. Harris. Portsmouth, RI, 109–21.

Campbell, J. B. 1984. *The Emperor and the Roman Army: 31 BC–AD 235*. Oxford.

Canci, A. et al. 2005. 'A case of healing spinal infection from classical Rome'. *International Journal of Osteoarchaeology* 15: 77–83.

Cancik, H. 2008. *Römische Religion im Kontext: Gesammelte Aufsätze I*, Tübingen.

Capasso, L. 2000. 'Indoor pollution and respiratory diseases in ancient Rome'. *Lancet* 356: 1774.

2007. 'Infectious diseases and eating habits at Herculaneum (1st century AD, southern Italy)'. *International Journal of Osteoarchaeology* 17: 350–7.

Carandini, A. 1997. *La nascita di Roma: Dèi, lari, eroi e uomini all'alba di una civiltà*, 2 vols. Turin.

2006a. *Remo e Romolo: Dai rioni dei Quiriti all città dei Romani (775/750–700/675 a. C.)*. Turin.

ed. 2006b. *La fattoria e la villa dell'Auditorium nel quartiere Flaminio di Roma*. Rome.

Carandini, A. and E. Papi, eds. 2005. *Palatium e Sacra Via II. L'età tardo-repubblicana e la prima età imperiale*. Rome.

Carrettoni, G. et al. 1960. *La pianta marmorea di Roma antica (Forma Urbis Romae)*. Rome.

Cascione, C. 1999. *Tresviri capitales: Storia di una magistratura minore*. Naples.

Casson, L. 1965. 'Harbour and river boats of Ancient Rome'. *Journal of Roman Studies* 55: 31–9.

    1971. *Ships and Seamanship in the Ancient World*. Princeton.

    1994. *Ships and Seafaring in Ancient Times*. Austin.

Catalano, P. 1978. 'Aspetti spaziali del sistema giuridico-religioso romano'. *Aufstieg und Niedergang der römischen Welt* II.16.1, 440–553.

    et al. 2001. 'Vivere e morire a Roma tra il primo ed il terzo secolo'. *Mitteilungen des deutschen archäologischen Instituts, Römische Abteilung* 108: 355–63.

    2008. 'Les ensembles funéraires de l'époque impériale à Rome'. *Dossiers d'Archéologie* 330: 10–13.

Cecamore, C. 2002. *Palatium: Topografia storica del Palatino tra III Sec. a.c. e I Sec d.c.* Rome.

Champlin, E. 1982. 'The *suburbium* of Rome'. *American Journal of Ancient History* 7: 97–117.

    1991. *Final Judgments: Duty and Emotion in Roman Wills*. Berkeley.

    2003. *Nero*. Cambridge, Mass.

Chastagnol, A. 1960. *La préfecture urbaine à Rome sous le bas-empire*. Paris.

Childe, V. Gordon. 1950. 'The urban revolution'. *Town Planning Review* 21: 3–17.

Chini, P. 1995. 'Forica romana in Via Garibaldi'. *Archeologia laziale* 12.1: 207–12.

Chioffi, L. 1999. *Caro: Il mercato della carne nell'occidente romano*. Rome.

    2008. 'A proposito di confini nella città di Roma: la Regio XIV da *pagus* ad *urbs*'. In *Epigrafia 2006: atti della XIVe rencontre sur l'épigraphie (Tituli 9)*, ed. M. L. Caldelli et al. Rome, 239–69.

Cifani, G. 2008. *Architettura romana arcaica: edilizia e società tra monarchia e repubblica*. Rome.

Cima, M. and E. La Rocca. 1998. *Horti romani*. Rome.

Claridge, A. 2010. *Rome: An Oxford Archaeological Guide*. Oxford.

    2007. 'Hadrian's lost temple of Trajan'. *Journal of Roman Archaeology* 20: 54–92.

Clark, A. J. 2007. *Divine Qualities: Cult and Community in Republican Rome*, Oxford.

Clark, G. 2004. *Christianity and Roman Society*. Cambridge.

Clark, P. 1983. *The English Alehouse: A Social History, 1200–1830*. London.

Clarke, J. R. 2003. *Art in the Lives of Ordinary Romans: Visual Representation and Non-elite Viewers in Italy, 100 BC–AD 315*. Berkeley.

Clasen, T. F. and A. Bastable. 2003. 'Faecal contamination of drinking water during collection and household storage: the need to extend protection to the point of use'. *Journal of Water and Health* 1.2: 1–7.

Clauss, M. 1973. 'Probleme der Lebensalterstatistik aufgrund römischer Grabinschriften'. *Chiron* 3: 395–417.

Clavel-Lévêque, M. 1984. *L'Empire en jeux: Espace symbolique et pratique sociale dans le monde romain*. Paris.

Coarelli, F. 1972. *Rome*. London.

    1983. *Il Foro Romano. I. Periodo arcaico*. Rome.

    1985. *Il Foro romano: Periodo repubblicano e augusteo*. Rome.

    1988. *Il Foro Boario dalle origini alla fine della Repubblica*. Rome.

    1989. 'Rediscovering the Roman forum'. *Journal of Roman Archaeology* 2: 157–66.

    1997. *Il Campo Marzio dalle origini alla fine della Repubblica*. Rome.

    2001. *The Colosseum*. Los Angeles.

    2007. *Rome and its Environs: An Archaeological Guide*. Berkeley.

Coates-Stephens, R. 2003. 'The water-supply of early medieval Rome'. In *Technology, Ideology, Water: From Frontinus to the Renaissance and Beyond*, ed. C. Bruun and A. Saastamoinen. Rome, 81–113.

    2004. *Porta Maggiore. Monument and Landscape. Archaeology and Topography of the Southern Esquiline from the Late Republican Period to the Present*. Rome.

Cohen, W. B. 1998. *Urban Government and the Rise of the French City*. New York.

Coleman, K. M. 2006. *Martial: Liber spectaculorum*. Oxford.

Collins, J. L. 2004. *Papacy and Politics in Eighteenth-Century Rome: Pius VI and the Arts*. Cambridge.

Colonnelli, G., M. Carpaneto and M. Cristaldi. 2000. 'Uso alimentare e allevamento del ghiro Myoxus glis presso gli antichi romani: materiale e documenti'. In *Atti del 2° Convegno Nazionale di Archeozoologia*, ed. G. Malerba, C. Cilli and G. Giacobini. Forlì, 315–25.

Cooper, K. 2007. *The Fall of the Roman Household*. Cambridge.

    and J. Hillner, eds. 2007. *Religion, Dynasty, and Patronage in Early Christian Rome, 300–900*. Cambridge.

Corbier, M. 1989. 'The ambiguous status of meat in ancient Rome'. *Food and Foodways* 3: 223–64.

    1999. 'The broad bean and the moray: social hierarchies and food in Rome'. In *Food: A Culinary History from Antiquity to the Present*, ed. J.-L. Flandrin. New York, 128–40.

Cornell, T. J. 1995. *The Beginnings of Rome: Italy and Rome from the Bronze Age to the Punic Wars (c. 1000–264 BC)*. London.

Costambeys, M. 2000. 'Property, ideology and the territorial power of the papacy in the early Middle Ages'. *Early Medieval Europe* 9: 367–96.

Coulston, J. 2000. 'Armed and belted men: the soldiery in imperial Rome'. In *Ancient Rome: the Archaeology of the Eternal City*, ed. J. Coulston and H. Dodge. Oxford, 76–118.

Cracco Ruggini, L. 1976. '"Fame laborasse Italiam": una nuova testimonianza sulla carestia del 383 d. C'. *Athenaeum, vol. spec. in onore di P. Fraccaro*. Pavia, 83–98.

Crawford, M. 1996. *Roman Statutes*. London.

Cristofani, M., ed. 1990. *La grande Roma dei Tarquini*. Rome.

Crook, J. 1967. *Law and Life of Rome*. London.

Cucchi, T. and J.-D. Vigne. 2006. 'Origins and diffusion of the house mouse in the Mediterranean'. *Human Evolution* 21: 95–106.

Cucina, A. et al. 2006. 'The necropolis of Vallerano (Rome, 2nd–3rd century AD): an anthropological perspective on the ancient Romans in the *suburbium*'. *International Journal of Osteoarchaeology* 16: 104–17.

Cullhed, M. 1994. *Conservator Urbis Suae: Studies in the Politics and Propaganda of the Emperor Maxentius*. Stockholm.

Curran, J. 2000. *Pagan City and Christian Capital: Rome in the Fourth Century*. Oxford.

Dalby, A. 2002. *Empire of Pleasures: Luxury and Indulgence in the Roman World*. London.

Darvill, T. and A. McWhirr. 1984. 'Roman brick production and the environment'. In *The Romano-British Countryside: Studies in Rural Settlement and Economy*, ed. D. Miles. Oxford, 137–50.

Darwall-Smith, R. 1996. *Emperors and Architecture: A Study of Flavian Rome*. Brussels.

Dasen, V. and T. Späth, eds. forthcoming. *Children, Memory and Family: Identity in Roman Culture*. Oxford.

Davies, J. K. 2005. 'Linear and non-linear flow models for the ancient economy'. In *The Ancient Economy: Evidence and Models*, ed. J. G. Manning and I. Morris. Stanford, 127–56.

Davies, P., D. Hemsoll and M. Wilson Jones. 1987. 'The Pantheon: triumph of Rome or triumph of compromise?'. *Art History* 10.2: 133–53.

Davis, D. B. 1966. *The Problem of Slavery in Western Culture*. Oxford.

DeFelice, J. 2007. 'Inns and taverns'. In *The World of Pompeii*, ed. J. J. Dobbins and P. W. Foss. London, 474–86.

De Grossi Mazzorin, J. 1995. 'La fauna rinvenuta nell'area della Meta Sudans nel quadro evolutivo degli animali domestici in Italia'. In *Atti del 1° Convegno Nazionale di Archeozoologia*, ed. R. Peretto and O. De Curtis. Rovigo, 309–18.

2004. 'I resti animali del mitreo della Crypta Balbi: testimonianze di pratiche cultuali'. In *Roman Mithraism: The Evidence of the Small Finds*, ed. M. Martens and G. De Boe. Brussels, 179–81.

2005. 'Introduzione e diffusione del pollame in Italia ed evoluzione delle sue forme di allevamento fino al Medioevo'. In *Atti del 3° Convegno Nazionale di Archeozoologia*. Rome, 351–61.

De Grossi Mazzorin, J. and C. Minniti. 2001. 'Reperti ossei'. In *Roma dall'antichità al medioevo: archeologia e storia nel Museo Nazionale Romano. Crypta Balbi*, ed. M. S. Area et al. Rome, 328–30.

De Grossi Mazzorin, J., A. Reidel, and A. Tagliacozzo. 1998. 'Horse remains in Italy from the Eneolithic to the Roman period'. In *International Union of Prehistoric and Protohistoric Sciences: Proceedings of the XIII Congress: Vol. VI–Tome I*. Forli, 87–92.

De Grossi Mazzorin, J. and A. Tagliacozzo. 1997. 'Dog remains in Italy from the Neolithic to the Roman period'. *Anthropozoologica* 25/26: 429–40.

DeLaine, J. 1997. *The Baths of Caracalla: A Study in the Design, Construction, and Economics of Large Scale Building Projects in Imperial Rome*. Portsmouth, RI.

2000a. 'Bricks and mortar: exploring the economics of building techniques at Rome and Ostia'. In *Economies beyond Agriculture in the Classical World*, ed. D. J. Mattingly and J. Salmon. London, 230–68.

2000b. 'Building the Eternal City: the building industry of imperial Rome'. In *Ancient Rome: the Archaeology of the Eternal City*, ed. J. Coulston and H. Dodge. Oxford, 119–41.

2005. 'The commercial landscape of Ostia'. In *Roman Working Lives and Urban Living*, ed. A. MacMahon and J. Price. Oxford, 29–47.

De Ligt, L., and S. Northwood, eds. 2008. *People, Land and Politics: Demographic Developments and the Transformation of Roman Italy, 300 BC–AD 14*. Leiden.

De Maria, S. 1988. *Gli archi onorari di Roma e dell'Italia romana*. Rome.

De Neeve, P. W. 1984. *Colonus: Private Farm Tenancy in Roman Italy during the Republic and the Early Principate*. Amsterdam.

De Robertis, F. M. 1935. 'La *cura regionum urbis* nel periodo imperiale'. *Athenaeum* 13: 184–6.

Degrassi, A. 1963. *Inscriptiones Italiae, vol. 13: Fasti et Elogia, fasc. 2: Fasti Anni Numani et Iuliani*. Rome.

Del Chicca, F., ed. and comm. 2004. *Frontino: De aquae ductu urbis Rome*. Rome.

Dixon, S. 1988. *The Roman Mother*. London.

1992. *The Roman Family*. Baltimore.

Donoghue, H. D. and M. Spigelman. 2006. 'Pathogenic microbial ancient DNA: a problem or an opportunity?'. *Proceedings of the Royal Society: Biological Sciences* 272: 641–2.

Drogula, F. K. 2007. 'Imperium, potestas, and the pomerium in the Roman Republic'. *Historia* 56: 419–52.

Dudley, D. R. 1967. *Urbs Roma: A Source Book of Classical Texts on the City and its Monuments*. London.

Dumser, E. 2005. 'The architecture of Maxentius'. PhD dissertation. University of Pennsylvania.

Duncan-Jones, R. 1996. 'The impact of the Antonine plague'. *Journal of Roman Archaeology* 9: 108–36.

Dupré Raventós, X., and J.-A. Remolà, eds. 2000. '*Sordes Urbis*': *La eliminición de residuos en la ciudad romana*. Rome.

Durliat, J. 1989. *De la ville antique à la ville byzantine: Le problème des subsistences*. Paris.

Durry, M. 1938. *Les cohortes prétoriennes*. Paris.

Dyson, S. L. 2010. *Rome: A living portrait of an ancient city*. Baltimore.

Echols, E. 1958. 'The Roman city police: origin and development'. *Classical Journal* 53: 377–85.

Eck, W. 1984. 'Senatorial self-representation: developments in the Augustan period'. In *Caesar Augustus: Seven Aspects*, ed. F. Millar and E. Segal. Oxford, 129–67.

——— 1995–8. *Die Verwaltung des römischen Reiches in der hohen Kaiserzeit: Ausgewählte und erweiterte Beiträge*. 2 vols. Basle.

Edwards, C. 1993. *The Politics of Immorality in Ancient Rome*. Cambridge.

——— 1996. *Writing Rome: Textual Approaches to the City*. Cambridge.

Edwards, C. and G. Woolf, eds. 2003. *Rome the Cosmopolis*. Cambridge.

Egelhaaf-Gaiser, U. 2000. *Kulträume im römischen Alltag: Das Isisbuch des Apuleius und der Ort von Religion im kaiserzeitlichen Rom*. Stuttgart.

Egidi, R. et al. eds. 2003. *Aspetti di vita quotidiana dalle necropoli della Via Latina: Località Osteria del Curato*. Rome.

Eisner, M. 1986. *Zur Typologie der Grabbauten im Suburbium Roms*. Mainz.

Ellis, S. J. R. 2004. 'The distribution of bars at Pompeii: archaeological, spatial, and viewshed analyses'. *Journal of Roman Archaeology* 17: 371–84.

Ellis, S. P. 1988. 'The end of the Roman house'. *American Journal of Archaeology* 92: 565–76.

——— 2000. *Roman Housing*. London.

Engels, D. 1999. *Classical Cats: The Rise and Fall of the Sacred Cat*. New York.

Engemann, J. 1997. *Deutung und Bedeutung frühchristlicher Bildwerke*. Darmstadt.

Ensoli, S., and E. La Rocca, eds. 2000. *Aurea Roma: Dalla città pagana alla città cristiana*. Rome.

Erdkamp, P. 2000. 'Feeding Rome or feeding Mars? A long-term approach to C. Gracchus' lex frumentaria'. *Ancient Society* 30: 53–70.

——— 2002. 'A starving mob has no respect: urban markets and food riots in the Roman world, 100 BC–400 AD'. In *The Transformation of Economic Life under the Roman Empire*, ed. L. de Blois and J. Rich. Amsterdam, 93–115.

——— 2005. *The Grain Market in the Roman Empire: A Social, Political and Economic Study*. Cambridge.

——— 2008. 'Mobility and migration in Italy in the second century BC'. In *People, Land, and Politics: Demographic Developments and the Transformation of Roman Italy*, ed. L. de Ligt and S. J. Northwood. Leiden, 417–49.

Evans, H. B. 1994. *Water Distribution in Ancient Rome: The Evidence of Frontinus*. Ann Arbor.

Evans Grubbs, J. 2002. *Women and the Law in the Roman Empire*. London.

Fabre, G. 1981. *Libertus: Recherches sur les rapports patron–affranchi à la fin de la République romaine*. Rome.

Fagan, G. 1999. *Bathing in Public in the Roman World*. Ann Arbor.

2006. 'Bathing for health with Celsus and Pliny the Elder'. *Classical Quarterly* 56: 190–207.

Fant, J. C. 1993. 'Ideology, gift, and trade: a distribution model for the Roman imperial marbles'. In *The Inscribed Economy: Production and Distribution in the Roman Empire in the Light of Instrumentum Domesticum*, ed. W. V. Harris. Portsmouth, RI, 145–70.

Fantham, E. 1997. 'Images of the city: Propertius' new-old Rome'. In *The Roman Cultural Revolution*, ed. T. Habinek and A. Schiesaro. Cambridge, 122–35.

Favro, D. 1992. '*Pater urbis*: Augustus as city father of Rome'. *Journal of the Society of Architectural Historians* 51: 61–84.

1996. *The Urban Image of Augustan Rome*. New York.

Feeney, D. 1986. 'History and revelation in Virgil's underworld'. *Proceedings of the Cambridge Philological Society* 212: 1–24.

2007. *Caesar's Calendar: Ancient Time and the Beginnings of History*. Berkeley.

Fentress, E. 2005. 'On the block: *Catastae, chalcidica*, and *cryptae* in early imperial Italy'. *Journal of Roman Archaeology* 18: 220–34.

Feraudi-Gruénais, F. 2001. '*Ubi diutius nobis habitandum est*': Die Dekoration der kaiserzeitlichen Gräber Roms. Wiesbaden.

Ferrua, A. 1991. *The Unknown Catacomb: A Unique Discovery of Early Christian Art*. New Lanark.

Finley, M. I. 1980. *Ancient Slavery and Modern Ideology*. London; expanded edition by B. C. Shaw, Princeton, 1998.

Finn, R. D. 2006. *Almsgiving in the Later Roman Empire: Christian Promotion and Practice, 313–450*. Oxford.

Fiocchi Nicolai, V. 1995–6. 'La nuova basilica circiforme della Via Ardeatina', *Rendiconti della pontificia accademia di archeologia* 68: 69–233.

2001. *Strutture funerarie ed edifici di culto paleocristiani di Roma dal IV al VI secolo*. Vatican City.

Fiocchi Nicolai, V. and J. Guyon, eds. 2006. *Origine delle catacombe romane*. Vatican City.

FitzGerald, C. et al. 2006. 'Health of infants in an imperial Roman skeletal sample: perspective from dental microstructure'. *American Journal of Physical Anthropology* 130: 179–89.

Flohr, M. 2003. '*Fullones* and Roman society: a reconsideration'. *Journal of Roman Archaeology* 16: 447–50.

Flower, H. L. 2004. 'Spectacle and political culture'. In *Companion to the Roman Republic*, ed. H. L. Flower. Cambridge, 322–43.

Forsythe, G. 2005. *A Critical History of Early Rome from Prehistory to the First Punic War*. Berkeley.

Fowler, D. 2000. 'The ruin of time: monuments and survival at Rome'. In *Roman Constructions: Readings in Postmodern Latin*. Oxford, 193–217.

Foxhall, L. 1990. 'The dependent tenant: leasing and labour in Italy and Greece'. *Journal of Roman Studies* 80: 97–114.

Foxhall, L. and H. A. Forbes. 1982. 'Sitometreia: the role of grain as a staple food in classical antiquity'. *Chiron* 12: 41–90.

Frank, T. 1940. *An Economic Survey of Ancient Rome, vol. 5: Rome and Italy of the Empire.* Baltimore.

Fraschetti, A. 1990. *Roma e il principe.* Rome.

Frayn, J. M. 1993 *Markets and Fairs in Roman Italy.* Oxford.

Fredrick, D., ed. 2002. *The Roman Gaze: Vision, Power, and the Body.* Baltimore.

Freis, H. 1967. *Die Cohortes Urbanae.* Cologne.

Frézouls, E. 1987. 'Rome ville ouverte: réflexions sur les problèmes de l'expansion urbaine d'Auguste à Aurélien'. In *L'Urbs: espace urbain et histoire (Ier siècle av. J.-C.–IIIe siècle ap. J.-C.).* Rome, 373–92.

Frier, B. 1985. *The Rise of the Roman Jurists: Studies in Cicero's Pro Caecina.* Princeton.

Fuhrmann, C. J. 2012. *Policing the Roman Empire: Soldiers, Administration, and Public Order.* New York.

Funiciello, R., G. Heiken and D. De Rita. 2006. *The Seven Hills of Rome: A Geological Tour of the Eternal City.* Princeton.

Gabba, E. 1984. 'The *Collegia* of Numa: problems of method and political ideas'. *Journal of Roman Studies* 74: 81–6.

Galinsky, K. 1996. *Augustan Culture: An Interpretive Introduction.* Princeton.

García Morcillo, M. 2005. *Las ventas por subasta en el mundo romano: la esfera privada.* Barcelona.

Gardiner, E. ed. 2008. *The Marvels of Rome: Mirabilia Urbis Romae,* New York.

Gardiner, R. ed. 1995. *The Age of the Galley: Mediterranean Oared Vessels since Pre-classical Times.* London.

Gardner, J. 1998. *Family and Familia in Roman Law and Life.* Oxford.

Garnsey, P. 1983. 'Grain for Rome'. In *Trade in the Ancient Economy,* ed. P. Garnsey, K. Hopkins and C. R. Whittaker. London, 118–30.

    1988. *Famine and Food-Supply in the Graeco-Roman World: Responses to Risk and Crisis.* Cambridge.

    1991. 'Mass diet and nutrition in the city of Rome'. In *Nourrir la plèbe,* ed. A. Giovannini. Basle, 67–101.

    1999. *Food and Society in Classical Antiquity.* Cambridge.

Garnsey, P. and D. Rathbone. 1985. 'The background to the grain law of Gaius Gracchus'. *Journal of Roman Studies* 75: 20–5.

George, M. 1997. *The Roman Domestic Architecture of Northern Italy.* Oxford.

    ed. 2005. *The Roman Family in the Empire: Rome, Italy, and Beyond.* Oxford.

Gilhus, I. S. 2006. *Animals, Gods and Humans: Changing Attitudes to Animals in Greek, Roman and Early Christian Ideas.* London.

Gillett, A. 2001. 'Rome, Ravenna and the last western emperors'. *Papers of the British School at Rome* 69: 131–67.

    2003. *Envoys and Political Communication in the Late Antique West, 411–533.* Cambridge.

Giovannini, A., ed. 1991. *Nourrir la plèbe: Actes du colloque . . . en hommage à Denis van Berchem.* Basle.

Girri, G. 1954. *La taberna nel quadro urbanistico e sociale di Ostia.* Rome.

Giuliani, C. F. and P. Verduchi. 1987. *L'area centrale del Foro Romano.* Florence.

Gjerstadt, E. 1953–73. *Early Rome.* 6 vols. Lund.

Glazebrook, A., and M. Henry. 2011. *Greek Prostitutes in the Ancient Mediterranean, 800 BCE–200 CE*. Madison, Wis.

Gonzales, A. 2007. 'Peur des affranchis impériaux et compassion envers les affranchis privés dans l'oeuvre de Pline le Jeune'. In *Fear of Slaves – Fear of Enslavement in the Ancient Mediterranean*, ed. A. Serghidou. Athens, 307–24.

Goodman, P. 2007. *The Roman City and its Periphery: From Rome to Gaul*. London.

Gordon, R. 2008. '*Superstitio*, superstition and religious repression in the late Roman Republic and Principate (100 BCE–300 CE)'. *Past & Present* 199: 72–94.

Gow, A. S. F. and D. L. Page. 1968. *The Garland of Philip*. Cambridge.

Graham, E.-J. 2006. *The Burial of the Urban Poor in Italy in the Late Roman Republic and Early Empire*. Oxford.

Graham, S. 2005. 'Of lumberjacks and brick stamps: working with the Tiber as infrastructure'. In *Roman Urban Living*, ed. A. MacMahon and J. Price. Oxford, 106–24.

   2006. *Ex Figlinis: The Network Dynamics of the Tiber Valley Brick Industry in the Hinterland of Rome*. Oxford.

   2009. 'The space between: places and connections in the Tiber Valley'. In *Mercator Placidissimus: The Tiber Valley in Antiquity. New Research in the Upper and Middle River Valley*, ed. F. Coarelli and H. Patterson. Rome, 671–86.

Graham, S. and G. Ruffini. 2007. 'Network analysis and Greco-Roman prosopography'. In *Prosopography Approaches and Applications: a Handbook*, ed. K. S. B. Keats-Rohan. Oxford, 325–36.

Grandazzi, A. 1997. *The Foundation of Rome: Myth and History*. Ithaca, NY.

   2007. 'Penser les origines de Rome'. *Bulletin de l'Association Guillaume Budé* 2: 21–70.

   2008. *Alba Longa, histoire d'une légende: recherches sur l'archéologie, la religion, les traditions de l'ancien Latium*. 2 vols. Rome.

Grey, C. and A. Parkin. 2003. 'Controlling the urban mob: the *colonatus perpetuus* of *CTh* 14.18.1'. *Phoenix* 57: 284–99.

Grieser, H. 1997. *Sklaverei im spätantiken und frühmittelalterlichen Gallien (5.–7. Jh.)*. Stuttgart.

Griffin, M. 1991. 'Urbs Roma, plebs and princeps'. In *Images of Empire*, ed. L. Alexander. Sheffield, 19–46.

Groag, E. and A. Stein. 1933–. *Prosopographia Imperii Romani 2*. Berlin.

Gruen, E. S. 1990. 'Plautus and the public stage'. In *Studies in Greek Culture and Roman Policy*. Berkeley, 124–57.

   1992. 'The theatre and aristocratic culture'. In *Culture and National Identity in Republican Rome*. Ithaca, 183–222.

Gülzow, H. 1969. *Christentum und Sklaverei in den ersten drei Jahrhunderten*. Bonn. (New edition: Münster, ed. B. Dauber with an epilogue by G. Theißen 1999.)

Günther, L.-M. 1989. 'Gladiatoren beim Fest Antiochus IV. zu Daphne (166 v. Chr.)?'. *Hermes* 117: 250–2.

Gundry, S. W. et al. 2006. 'Contamination of drinking water between source and point-of-use in rural households of South Africa and Zimbabwe: implications for monitoring the Millennium Development Goal for water'. *Water Practice and Technology* 1.2: 1–9.

Gustafsson, G. 2000. *Evocatio Deorum: Historical and Mythical Interpretations of Ritualised Conquest in the Expansion of Ancient Rome*. Uppsala.

Guzzo, P. G., and V. Scarano Ussani. 2009. 'Ex corpore lucrum facere': La prostituzione nell'antica Pompei. Rome.

Guyon, J. 1974. 'La vente des tombes à travers l'épigraphie de la Rome chrétienne (IIIe–VIIe siècles): le rôle des fossores, mansionarii, praepositi et prêtres'. Mélanges d'archéologie et d'histoire de l'École française de Rome: Antiquité 86: 549–96.

Hackworth Petersen, L. 2006. The Freedman in Roman Art and History. Cambridge.

Hales, S. 2003. The Roman House and Social Identity. Cambridge.

Hall, M. ed. 2005. Rome: Artistic Centers of the Italian Renaissance. Cambridge.

Halsberghe, G. 1972. The Cult of Sol Invictus. Leiden.

Hanes, C. 1996. 'Turnover costs and the distribution of slave labor in Anglo-America'. Journal of Economic History 56: 307–29.

Hannah, R. 2008. Time in Antiquity. London.

Hardie, P. 1992. 'Augustan poets and the mutability of Rome'. In Roman Poetry and Propaganda in the Age of Augustus, ed. A. Powell. Bristol, 59–82.

Harries, J. 2003. 'Pagans, Christians and public entertainment in late antique Italy'. In Lomas and Cornell 2003, 125–41.

　2007. Law and Crime in the Roman World. Cambridge.

Harrill, J. A. 1995. The Manumission of Slaves in Early Christianity. Tübingen.

Harris, W. V. 1979. War and Imperialism in Republican Rome. Oxford.

　1993. The Inscribed Economy: Production and Distribution in the Roman Empire in the Light of Instrumentum Domesticum. Portsmouth, RI.

　1999a. 'Demography, geography and the sources of Roman slaves'. Journal of Roman Studies 89: 62–75.

　ed. 1999b. The Transformations of Vrbs Roma in Late Antiquity. Portsmouth, RI.

Haselberger, L. 2007. 'Urbem adornare': Rome's Urban Metamorphosis under Augustus. Portsmouth, RI.

Haselberger, L., D. G. Romano, E. A. Dumser et al. 2008. Mapping Augustan Rome. 2nd edn. Portsmouth, RI.

Hasenohr, C. 2003. 'Les compitalia à Délos'. Bulletin de Correspondance Hellénique 127: 167–249.

Hawkins, C. 2006. 'Work in the city: Roman artisans and the urban economy'. Unpublished dissertation. The University of Chicago.

Heinz, W. 1983. Römische Thermen: Badewesen und Badeluxus im römischen Reich. Munich.

Heinzelmann, M. 2001. Römischer Bestattungsbrauch und Beigabensitten in Rom, Norditalien und den Nordwestprovinzen von der späten Republik bis in die Kaiserzeit. Wiesbaden.

Hekster, O. 2005. 'Captured in the gaze of power: visibility, games and Roman imperial representation', in Imaginary Kings: Royal Images in the Ancient Near East, Greece and Rome, ed. O. Heksterand and R. Fowler. Stuttgart, 157–76.

Hemphill, P. 1987. 'Report on fieldwork on Roman forestry in Italy'. American Journal of Archaeology 91: 304.

Hermansen, G. 1973. 'Domus and insula in the city of Rome'. In Classica et mediaevalia. Diss. 9. Francisco Blatt septuagenario dedicata, ed. O. S. Due, H. F. Johansen and B. D. Larsen. Copenhagen, 333–41.

　1978. 'The population of imperial Rome: the Regionaries'. Historia 27: 129–68.

　1982. Ostia: Aspects of Roman City Life. Edmonton.

Herrmann-Otto, E. 1994. Ex ancilla natus: Untersuchungen zu den 'hausgeborenen' Sklaven und Sklavinnen im Westen des römischen Kaiserreiches. Stuttgart.

2001. 'Soziale Mobilität in der römischen Gesellschaft: persönliche Freiheit im Spiegel von Statusprozessen'. In *Fünfzig Jahre Forschungen zur antiken Sklaverei an der Mainzer Akademie 1950–2000*, ed. H. Bellen and H. Heinen. Stuttgart, 171–84.

2006. 'Sklaven und Frauen unter Konstantin'. In *Konstantin der Große. Geschichte – Archäologie – Rezeption*, ed. A. Demandt and J. Engemann. Trier, 83–95.

2008. 'Konstantin, die Sklaven und die Kirche'. In *Antike Lebenswelten. Konstanz – Wandel – Wirkungsmacht*, ed. P. Mauritsch. Wiesbaden, 353–66.

2009. *Sklaverei und Freilassung in der griechisch-römischen Welt*. Hildesheim.

Herz, P. 1988. *Studien zur römischen Wirtschaftsgesetzgebung: Die Lebensmittelversorgung*. Stuttgart.

Hesberg, H. von. 1992. *Römische Grabbauten*. Darmstadt.

Hesberg, H. von and P. Zanker, eds. 1987. *Römische Gräberstraßen: Selbstdarstellung – Status – Standard*. Munich.

Hetland, L. M. 2007. 'Dating the Pantheon'. *Journal of Roman Archaeology* 20: 95–112.

Hibbert, C. 1988. *Rome: The Biography of a City*. Harmondsworth.

Hillner, J. 2006. 'Clerics, property and patronage: the case of the Roman titular churches'. *Antiquité Tardive* 14: 59–68.

2007. 'Families, patronage and the titular churches of Rome'. In *Religion, Dynasty, and Patronage in Early Christian Rome, 300–900*, ed. K. Cooper and J. Hillner. Cambridge, 225–61.

Hirschfeld, O. 1913 [1891]. 'Die Sicherheitspolizei im römischen Kaiserreich'. In *Kleine Schriften*. Berlin, 576–612.

Höbenreich, E. 1997. *Annona: juristische Aspekte der stadtrömischen Lebensmittelversorgung im Prinzipat*. Graz.

Hodge, A. T. 1992. *Roman Aqueducts and Water Supply*. London.

Hohlfelder, R. L., ed. 2008. *The Maritime World of Ancient Rome*. Ann Arbor.

Holleran, C. 2005. 'The retail trade in the city of Rome'. Unpublished dissertation. University of Manchester.

2011. 'Migration and the urban economy of Rome'. In *Demography and the Graeco-Roman World: New Insights and Approaches*, ed. C. Holleran and A. Pudsey. Cambridge, 155–80.

2012. *Shopping in Ancient Rome: The Retail Trade in the Late Republic and the Principate*. Oxford.

Holliday, P. J. 1997. 'Roman triumphal painting: its function, development, and reception'. *The Art Bulletin* 79: 130–47.

Hollnsteiner-Racelis, M. 1988. 'Becoming an urbanite: the neighbourhood as a learning environment'. In *The Urbanization of the Third World*, ed. J. Gugler. New York, 230–41.

Holloway, R. R. 1994. *The Archeology of Early Rome and Latium*. London.

2004. *Constantine and Rome*. New Haven.

Hopkins, K. 1978a. *Conquerors and Slaves: Sociological Studies in Roman History I*. Cambridge.

1978b. 'Economic growth and towns in classical antiquity'. In *Towns in Societies: Essays in Economic History and Historical Sociology*, ed. P. Abrams and E. A. Wrigley. Cambridge, 35–77.

1999. *A World Full of Gods: The Strange Triumph of Christianity*, London.

Hopkins, K. and M. Beard. 2005. *The Colosseum*. Cambridge, Mass.

Horden, P. and N. Purcell. 2000. *The Corrupting Sea: A Study of Mediterranean History*. Oxford.

Houston, G. W. 2002. 'The slave and freedman personnel of public libraries in ancient Rome'. *Transactions of the American Philological Association* 132: 139–76.

Hübner, S. R. and D. M. Ratzan, eds. 2009. *Growing up Fatherless in Antiquity*. Cambridge.

Hughes, J. D., and J. V. Thirgood. 1982. 'Deforestation in ancient Greece and Rome: a cause of collapse'. *The Ecologist* 12: 196–208.

Humphrey, J. H. 1986. *Roman Circuses: Arenas for Chariot Racing*. London.

Hunt, E. D. 2003. 'Imperial building at Rome: the role of Constantine'. In Lomas and Cornell 2003, 105–24.

Hyland, A. 1990. *Equus: The Horse in the Roman World*. London.

Isaac, B. 2004. *The Invention of Racism in Classical Antiquity*. Princeton.

Jashemski, W. 2008. 'Gardens'. In *The World of Pompeii*, ed. J. J. Dobbins and P. W. Foss. London, 487–98.

Jennison, G. 1937. *Animals for Show and Pleasure in Ancient Rome*. Manchester (reprinted 1995, Philadelphia).

Johnstone, C. 2004. 'A biometric study of equids in the Roman world'. PhD dissertation. University of Bradford.

Jonckheere, R. 2006. *Christenen en de dood: Een studie naar het ontstaan van de christelijke catacomben te Rome*. Utrecht.

Jones, A. H. M. 1960. *Studies in Roman Government and Law*. Oxford.

　1964. *The Later Roman Empire, 284–602: A Social, Economic, and Administrative Survey*. Oxford.

Jones, A. H. M., J. R. Martindale and J. Morris. 1971. *The Prosopography of the Later Roman Empire. Vol. I: A.D. 260–395*. Cambridge.

Jones, P. J. 2005. *Reading Rivers in Roman Literature and Culture*. Lanham, Md.

Jongman, W. 1991. *The Economy and Society of Pompeii*. Amsterdam.

　2000. 'Wool and the textile industry of Roman Italy: a working hypothesis'. In *Mercati permanenti e mercati periodici nel mondo romano*, ed. E. Lo Cascio. Bari, 187–97.

　2001. *Lemma* 'Roma II: Bevölkerung und Wirtschaft der Stadt Rom, B Wirtschaft.' In *Der Neue Pauly. Enzyklopädie der Antike* X, ed. H. Cancik and H. Schneider. Stuttgart and Weimar, 1079–81.

　2007. 'The early Roman empire: consumption'. In *The Cambridge Economic History of the Greco-Roman World*, ed. W. Scheidel, I. Morris and R. Saller. Cambridge, 592–618.

Johns, C. M. S. 1993. *Papal Art and Cultural Politics: Rome in the Age of Clement XI*. Cambridge.

Johnson, M. J. 2006. 'Architecture of empire'. In *The Cambridge Companion to the Age of Constantine*, ed. N. Lenski. Cambridge, 278–97.

Jory, E. J. 1984. 'The early pantomime riots'. In *Maistor: Classical, Byzantine and Renaissance Studies for Robert Browning*, ed. A. Moffatt. Canberra, 57–66.

Joshel, S. R. 1992. *Work, Identity, and Legal Status at Rome: A Study of the Occupational Inscriptions*. Norman, Okla.

Kadletz, E. 1976. 'Animal sacrifice in Greek and Roman religion'. PhD dissertation. University of Washington.

Kahane, A. 2011. 'Image, word and the antiquity of ruins'. *European Review of History* 18: 829–50.

Keene, D. J. 1982. 'Rubbish in medieval towns'. In *Environmental Archaeology in the Urban Context*, ed. A. R. Hall and H. K. Kenward. London, 26–30.

Keitel, E. 1984. 'Principate and civil war in the *Annals* of Tacitus'. *American Journal of Philology* 105: 306–25.

Keller, O. 1909/13. *Die antike Tierwelt Band 1–2*. Leipzig.

Kelly, B. 2007. 'Riot control and imperial ideology in the Roman empire'. *Phoenix* 61: 150–76.

Kelly, G. 2008. *Ammianus Marcellinus: The Allusive Historian*. Cambridge.

Kertzer, D. 2006. *Prisoner of the Vatican: The Popes, the Kings, and Garibaldi's Rebels in the Struggle to Rule Modern Italy*. New York.

Killgrove, K. 2010. 'Identifying immigrants to imperial Rome using strontium isotope analysis'. In *Roman Diasporas: Archaeological Approaches to Mobility and Diversity in the Roman Empire*, ed. H. Eckardt. Portsmouth, RI, 157–74.

King, A. 1999. 'Diet in the Roman world: a regional inter-site comparison of the mammal bones'. *Journal of Roman Archaeology* 12: 168–202.

Klees, H. 2002. 'Die römische Einbürgerung der Freigelassenen und ihre naturrechtliche Begründung bei Dionysios von Halikarnassos'. *Laverna* 13: 91–117.

Kleiner, F. S. 1985. *The Arch of Nero in Rome: A Study of the Roman Honorary Arch in Rome before and under Nero*. Rome.

Knigge, U. 2005. *Der Bau Z*. 2 vols. Munich.

Knoch, St. 2005. *Sklavenfürsorge im Römischen Reich*. Hildesheim.

Koch, C. 1952. 'Roma Aeterna', *Gymnasium* 58: 128–43, 196–20.

Koch, G. 2000. *Frühchristliche Sarkophage*. Munich.

Koch, G., and H. Sichtermann. 1982. *Römische Sarkophage*. Munich.

Kockel, V. 1993. *Porträtreliefs stadtrömischer Grabbauten: Ein Beitrag zur Geschichte und zum Verständnis des spätrepublikanisch-frühkaiserzeitlichen Privatporträts*. Mainz.

Kolb, F. 1995. *Rom: die Geschichte der Stadt in der Antike*. Munich.

Koller, D. et al. 2006. 'Fragments of the city: Stanford's digital *Forma Urbis Romae* Project'. In *Imaging Ancient Rome: Documentation, Visualization, Imagination*, ed. L. Haselberger and J. Humphrey, *Journal of Roman Archaeology Supplementary Series*, 61. Portsmouth, RI, 237–52.

Koolhaas, R. et al. 2000. *Mutations*. New York.

Kraus, C. 1994. 'No second Troy: *topoi* and refoundation in Livy book V'. *Transactions of the American Philological Association* 124: 267–89.

Krause, J.-U. 1994–5. *Witwen und Waisen im römischen Reich*. Stuttgart.
 2004. *Kriminalgeschichte der Antike*. Munich.

Krautheimer, R. 1980. *Rome: Profile of a City, 312–1308*. Princeton (revised by Marvin Trachtenberg, Princeton 2000).

Kron, G. 2005. 'Anthropometry, physical anthropology, and the reconstruction of ancient health, nutrition, and living standards'. *Historia* 54: 68–83.

La Rocca, E. 2001. 'La nuova imagine dei fori imperiali: Appunti in margine agli scavi'. *Römische Mitteilungen* 108: 171–213.

Labate, M. 1991. 'Città morte, città future: un tema della poesia augustea'. *Maia* 43: 167–84.

Lahusen, G. 1983. *Untersuchungen zur Ehrenstatue in Rom*. Rome.

Lampe, P. 2003. *From Paul to Valentinus: Christians at Rome in the First Two Centuries.* Minneapolis.

Lancaster, L. 1998. 'Building Trajan's markets'. *American Journal of Archaeology* 102: 283–308.

2005. *Concrete Vaulted Construction in Imperial Rome: Innovations in Context.* Cambridge.

2007. 'The Colosseum for the general public'. *Journal of Roman Archaeology* 20: 454–9.

Lançon, B. 2000. *Rome in Late Antiquity: Everyday Life and Urban Change AD 312–609*, trans. A. Nevill. Edinburgh.

Larmour, D. H. J. 2007. 'Holes in the body: sites of abjection in Juvenal's Rome'. In *The Sites of Rome: Time, Space, Memory*, ed. D. H. J. Larmour and D. Spencer. Oxford, 168–210.

Laurence, R. 1991. 'The urban *Vicus*: the spatial organization of power in the Roman city'. In *Papers of the Fourth Conference of Italian Archaeology*, ed. E. Herring, R. Whitehouse and J. B. Wilkins. London, 145–51.

1997. 'Writing the Roman metropolis'. In *Roman Urbanism: Beyond the Consumer City*, ed. H. Parkin. London, 1–20.

1999. *The Roads of Roman Italy: Mobility and Cultural Change.* London.

2001. 'The creation of geography: an interpretation of Roman Britain'. In *Travel and Geography in the Roman Empire*, ed. C. Adams and R. Laurence. London, 67–94.

2004. 'The economic exploitation of geological resources in the Tiber valley: road building', in *Bridging the Tiber: Approaches to Regional Archaeology in the Middle Tiber Valley*, ed. H. Patterson. London, 285–96.

2007. *Roman Pompeii: Space and Society.* 2nd edn. London.

2008. 'City traffic and the archaeology of Roman streets'. In *Stadtverkehr in der Antiken Welt / Traffico Urbano nel Mondo Antico (Palilia 13)*, ed. D. Mertens. Rome, 87–106.

Le Houerou, H. N. 1981. 'Impact of man and his animals on Mediterranean vegetation'. In *Mediterranean-type Shrublands*, ed. F. Di Castri, D. W. Goodall and R. L. Specht. Amsterdam, 479–521.

Leon, H. 1960. *The Jews of Ancient Rome.* Philadelphia (updated edition 1995).

Lepelley, C. 1962. 'Léon le Grand et la cité romaine'. *Revue des sciences religieuses* 35: 130–50.

Lepper, F. A. and S. S. Frere. 1988. *Trajan's Column: A New Edition of the Cichorius Plates.* Gloucester.

Lim, R. 1999. 'People as power: games, munificence, and contested topography'. In *The Transformations of Urbs Roma in Late Antiquity*, ed. W. V. Harris. Portsmouth, RI, 265–81.

Linderski, J. 1986. 'The augural law'. *Aufstieg und Niedergang der römischen Welt* II.16.3, 2146–312.

Lintott, A. W. 1999. *Violence in Republican Rome*, 2nd edn. Oxford.

Liu, J. 2008. 'The economy of endowments: the case of Roman associations'. In *'Pistoi dia tèn technèn': Bankers, Loans and Archives in the Ancient World*, ed. K. Verboven et al. Leuven, 231–56.

Lizzi Testa, R. 2004. *Senatori, populi, papi: il governo di Roma al tempo dei Valentiniani.* Bari.

Lo Cascio, E. 1997. 'Le procedure di recensus dalla tarda repubblica al tardo antico e il calcolo della popolazione di Roma'. In *La Rome impériale. Démographie et logistique.* Rome, 3–76.

2001a. 'Condizioni igienico-sanitarie e dinamica della popolazione della città di Roma dall'età tardorepubblicana al tardoantico'. In *Thérapies, médicine et démographie antiques*, ed. J.-N. Corvisier, C. Didier and M. Valdher. Arras, 37–70.

2001b. 'Recruitment and the size of the Roman population from the third to the first century BCE', in *Debating Roman Demography*, ed. W. Scheidel. Leiden, 111–38.

2003. 'La population'. In *La Ville de Rome sous le Haut-Empire.* Toulouse, 179–98.

2006. 'Did the population of imperial Rome reproduce itself?'. In Storey 2006, 52–68.

Loane, H. J. 1938. *Industry and Commerce of the City of Rome (50 B.C.–200 A.D.).* Baltimore.

Lomas, K., and T. Cornell, eds. 2003. *Bread and Circuses: Euergetism and Municipal Patronage in Roman Italy.* London.

Lott, J. B. 2004. *The Neighborhoods of Augustan Rome.* Cambridge.

Lucassen, J. 1987. *Migrant Labour in Europe 1600–1900: The Drift to the North Sea.* London.

Lugli, G. 1947. *Monumenti minori del Foro Romano.* Rome.

Lyding Will, E. 1983. 'Exportation of olive oil from Baetica to the eastern Mediterranean'. In *Producción y comercio del aceite en la Antigüedad: Segundo Congreso Internacional (Sevilla 1982).* Madrid, 391–440.

McClelland, J. S. 1989. *The Crowd and the Mob: From Plato to Canetti.* Boston.

McCormick, M. 2003. 'Rats, communications, and plague: towards an ecological history'. *Journal of Interdisciplinary History* 34: 1–25.

MacDonald, W. L. 1982. *The Architecture of the Roman Empire: An Introductory Study.* New Haven.

McGinn, T. A. J. 1998. *Prostitution, Sexuality, and the Law in Ancient Rome.* New York.

2002. 'Pompeian brothels and social history'. In *Pompeian Brothels, Pompeii's Ancient History, Mirrors and Mysteries, Art and Nature at Oplontis and the Herculaneum 'Basilica'*, ed. T. McGinn, P. Carafa, N. de Grummond, B. Bergmann, and T. Najbjerg. Portsmouth, RI, 7–46.

2004. *The Economy of Prostitution in the Roman World: A Study of Social History and the Brothel.* Ann Arbor.

2011. 'Roman prostitutes and marginalization'. In *Oxford Handbook on Social Relations in the Roman World*, ed. M. Peachin. Oxford.

McKay, A. G. 1975 [1998]. *Houses, Villas and Palaces in the Roman World.* Ithaca.

McKeown, N. 2007. *The Invention of Ancient Slavery?* London.

MacKinnon, M. 2001. 'High on the hog: linking zooarchaeological, literary, and artistic data for pig breeds in Roman Italy'. *American Journal of Archaeology* 105: 649–73.

2004. *Production and Consumption of Animals in Roman Italy: Integrating the Zooarchaeological and Ancient Textual Evidence.* Ann Arbor.

2006. 'Supplying exotic animals for the Roman amphitheatre games: new reconstructions combining archaeological, ancient textual, historical and ethnographic data'. *Mouseion* 6: 137–61.

2007. 'State of the discipline: osteological research in classical archaeology'. *American Journal of Archaeology* 111: 473–504.

Macleod, C. W. 1983. *Collected Essays.* Oxford.

McLynn, N. 2008. 'Crying wolf: the pope and the Lupercalia'. *Journal of Roman Studies* 98: 161–75.

MacMahon, A. 2005a. 'The shops and workshops of Roman Britain'. In MacMahon and Price 2005, 48–69.

2005b. 'The *taberna* counters of Pompeii and Herculaneum'. In MacMahon and Price 2005, 70–87.

MacMahon, A. and J. Price, eds. 2005. *Roman Working Lives and Urban Living*. Oxford.

MacMullen, R. 1986. 'What difference did Christianity make?'. *Historia* 35: 322–43.

1990. 'Late Roman slavery'. *Historia* 36: 359–82.

1993. 'The unromanized in Rome'. In *Diasporas in Antiquity*, ed. S. H. D. Cohen and E. S. Frerichs. Atlanta, 47–64.

Magnuson, T. 1982–6. *Rome in the Age of Bernini*. 2 vols. Atlantic Highlands, NJ.

Mantovani, D. 1988. 'Sulla competenza penale del *praefectus urbi* attraverso il *Liber Singularis* di Ulpiano'. In *Idee vecchie e nuove sul diritto criminale romano*, ed. A. Burdese. Padua, 171–223.

Manuwald, G. 2011. *Roman Republican Theatre*. Cambridge.

Manzi, G. et al. 1999. 'Discontinuity of life conditions at the transition from the Roman imperial age to the early Middle Ages: example from central Italy evaluated by pathological dento-alveolar lesions'. *American Journal of Human Biology* 11: 327–41.

Marazzi, F. 1998. *I 'Patrimonia Sanctae Romanae Ecclesiae' nel Lazio (secoli IV–X): Struttura amministrativa e prassi gestionali*. Rome.

Mari, Z. 1991. 'Nuovi cippi degli acquedotti aniensi: considerazioni sull'uso dei cippi acquari'. *Papers of the British School at Rome* 59: 151–75.

Martin, S. D. 1989. *The Roman Jurists and the Organization of Private Building in the Late Republic and Early Empire*. Brussels.

Martindale, C. 1993. *Redeeming the Text: Latin Poetry and the Hermeneutics of Reception*. Cambridge.

Marx, G., and D. McAdam. 1994. *Collective Behavior and Social Movements: Process and Structure*. Upper Saddle River, NJ.

Marzano, A. 2007. *Roman Villas in Central Italy: A Social and Economic History*. Leiden.

Massey, D., J. Allen and S. Pile. 1999. *City Worlds: Understanding Cities 1*. London.

Mattern, S. P. 2008. *Galen and the Rhetoric of Healing*. Baltimore.

Matthews, J. 1989. 'Hostages, philosophers, pilgrims and the diffusion of ideas in the late Roman Mediterranean and Near East'. In *Tradition and Innovation in Late Antiquity*, ed. F. M. Clover and R. S. Humphreys. Madison, WI, 29–49.

Mattingly, D. J. 1996. 'First fruit? The olive in the Roman world'. In *Human Landscapes in Classical Antiquity: Environment and Culture*, ed. G. Shipley and J. Salmon. London, 213–53.

Meiggs, R. 1972. *The Athenian Empire*. Oxford.

1973. *Roman Ostia*. Oxford.

1982. *Trees and Timber in the Ancient Mediterranean World*. Oxford.

Mellor, R. 1981. 'The goddess Roma'. *Aufstieg und Niedergang der römischen Welt* II.17.2, 950–1030.

Ménard, H. 2001. 'L'insécurité de la Rome impériale: entre réalité et imaginaire'. In *Rome, ville et capitale de Jules César à la fin des Antonins*, ed. S. Lefebvre. Paris, 390–407.

2004. *Maintenir l'ordre à Rome: IIe–IVe siècles ap. J.-C.* Seyssel.

Merlen, R. H. A. 1971. *De canibus: Dog and Hound in Antiquity*. London.

Messineo, G. 1991. *La Via Flaminia: Da Porta del Popolo a Malborghetto*. Rome.

Metzger Habel, D. 2002. *The Urban Development of Rome in the Age of Alexander VII*. Cambridge.

Michels, A. K. 1967. *The Calendar of the Roman Republic*. Princeton.

Millar, F. 1977. *The Emperor in the Roman World (31 BC–AD 69)*. London.

    1984. 'The political character of the classical Roman republic, 200–151 BC'. *Journal of Roman Studies* 74: 1–19.

    1986. 'Politics, persuasion, and the people before the Social War (150–90 B.C.)'. *Journal of Roman Studies* 76: 1–11.

    1989. 'Political power in mid-republican Rome: curia or *comitium*?'. *Journal of Roman Studies* 79: 138–50.

    1998. *The Crowd in Rome in the Late Republic*, Ann Arbor.

Miller, D. L. 2000. *Introduction to Collective Behavior and Collective Action*. 2nd edn. Prospect Heights, IL.

Miller, P. A. 2007. 'I get around: sadism, desire and metonymy on the streets of Rome with Horace, Ovid, and Juvenal'. In *The Sites of Rome: Time, Space, Memory*, ed. D. H. J. Larmour and D. Spencer. Oxford, 138–67.

Moatti, C. 1993. *In Search of Ancient Rome*. London.

    ed. 2004. *La mobilité des personnes en Méditerranée, de l'Antiquité à l'époque moderne: Procédures de contrôle et documents d'identification*. Rome.

    2006. 'Translation, communication and mobility in the Roman empire'. *Classical Antiquity* 25: 141–80.

    2007. 'Le contrôle des gens de passage à Rome aux trois premières siècles de L'Empire', in *Gens de passage en Méditerranée, de l'antiquité à l'époque moderne*, ed. C. Moatti and W. Kaiser. Paris, 79–116.

Mollenkopf, J. H. 1992. *A Phoenix in the Ashes: The Rise and Fall of the Koch Coalition in New York City Politics*. Princeton, 23–43.

Mommsen, Th. 1887–8. *Römisches Staatsrecht*. 3rd edn. Leipzig.

Morgan, T. 1998. *Literate Education in the Hellenistic and Roman Worlds*. Cambridge.

Morley, N. 1996. *Metropolis and Hinterland: The City of Rome and the Italian Economy, 200 BC–AD 200*. Cambridge.

    2005. 'The salubriousness of the Roman city'. In *Health in Antiquity*, ed. H. King. London, 192–204.

    2006. 'The poor in the city of Rome'. In *Poverty in the Roman World*, ed. R. Osborne and M. Atkins. Cambridge, 21–39.

    2007. 'The early Roman empire: distribution'. In *The Cambridge Economic History of the Greco-Roman World*, ed. W. Scheidel, I. Morris and R. Saller. Cambridge, 570–91.

Mouritsen, H. 2001. *Plebs and Politics in the Late Roman Republic*. New York.

Muccigrosso, J. 2006. 'Religion and politics: did the Romans scruple about the placement of their temples?'. In *Religion in Republican Italy*, ed. C. E. Schultz and P. B. Harvey Jr, Cambridge, 181–206.

Müller-Karpe, H. 1956. *Vom Anfang Roms*. Heidelberg.

    1962. *Zur Stadtwerdung Roms*. Heidelberg.

Münzer, F. 1920. *Römische Adelsparteien und Adelsfamilien*. Stuttgart (trans. T. Ridley, *Roman Aristocratic Parties and Families*. Baltimore, 1999).

Narducci, P. 1889. *Sulle fognature della città di Roma*. Rome.

Nash, E. 1961–2. *A Pictorial Dictionary of Ancient Rome*. 2 vols. London.

Nelis-Clément, J., and J.-M. Roddaz, eds. 2008. *Le cirque romain et son image*. Bordeaux.

Nencioni, L., A. Canci and P. Catalano. 2001. 'Caratterizzazione antropologica preliminare'. In *Ad Deverticulum: scavi archaeologici Lungo la Bretella Nomentana-GRA*, ed. P. Di Manzano. Rome, 73–80.

Newbold, R. F. 1974. 'Some social and economic consequences of the AD 64 fire at Rome'. *Latomus* 33: 858–69.

Newsome, D. 2009. 'Centrality in its place: representations and definitions of urban space in the city of Rome'. In *Proceedings of the Eighteenth Annual Theoretical Roman Archaeology Conference, Amsterdam 2008*, ed. M. Driessen et al. Oxford, 25–38.

Nicolet, C. 1987. 'La table d'Héraclée et les origines du cadastre romain'. In *L'Urbs: espace urbain et histoire (Ier siècle av. J.-C.–IIIe siècle ap. J.-C.)*. Rome, 1–25.

Nielsen, I. 1990. *'Thermae et balnea': The Architecture and Cultural History of Roman Public Baths*. Aarhus.

Nippel, W. 1984. 'Policing Rome'. *Journal of Roman Studies* 74: 20–9.

1988. *Aufruhr und 'Polizei' in der römischen Republik*. Stuttgart.

1995. *Public Order in Ancient Rome*. Cambridge.

Nock, A. D. 1932. 'Cremation and burial in the Roman empire'. *Harvard Theological Review* 25: 321–59.

1946. 'Sarcophagi and symbolism'. *American Journal of Archaeology* 50: 140–70.

Nörr, D. 2007. 'Osservazioni in tema di terminologia giuridica predecemvirale e di *ius mercatorium* mediterraneo: il primo trattato cartaginese–romano'. In *Le Dodici Tavole: dai decemviri agli umanisti*, ed. M. Humbert. Pavia, 147–89.

Nordh, C. A. 1949. *Libellus de Regionibus Urbis Romae*. Lund.

North, J. A. and N. McLynn. 2008. 'Postscript to the Lupercalia: from Caesar to Andromachus'. *Journal of Roman Studies* 98: 176–81.

Noy, D. 2000a. *Foreigners in Rome, Citizens and Strangers*. London.

2000b. 'Immigrants in late imperial Rome'. In *Ethnicity and Culture in Late Antiquity*, ed. S. Mitchell and G. Greatrex. London.

O'Gorman, E. 2000. *Irony and Misreading in the Annals of Tacitus*. Cambridge.

2004. 'Cato the Elder and the destruction of Carthage'. *Helios* 31: 97–125.

Oates, W. J. 1934. 'The population of Rome'. *Classical Philology* 29: 101–16.

Oleson, J. P., ed. 2008. *The Oxford Handbook of Engineering and Technology in the Classical World*. Oxford.

Orlin, E. M. 1997. *Temples, Religion and Politics in the Roman Republic*. Leiden.

2002. 'Foreign cults in republican Rome: rethinking the Pomerial rule'. *Memoirs of the American Academy at Rome* 47: 1–18.

Osiek, C. and D. L. Balch. 1997. *Families in the New Testament World: Households and House Churches*. Louisville.

Ottini, L. et al. (2001) 'Le condizioni di vita nella popolazione di età imperiale: indicatori paleopatologici da necropolis nel territorio di Roma'. *Mitteilungen des deutschen archäologischen Instituts, Römische Abteilung* 108: 364–6.

Packer, J. E. 1971. *The Insulae of Imperial Ostia*. Rome.

1997. *The Forum of Trajan in Rome: A Study of the Monuments*. Berkeley.

2001. *The Forum of Trajan in Rome: A Study of the Monuments in Brief*. London.

Paine, R. R. and G. R. Storey. 2006. 'Epidemics, age at death, and mortality in ancient Rome'. In Storey 2006, 69–85.

Painter Jr, B. W. 2007. *Mussolini's Rome: Rebuilding the Eternal City*. New York.

Palmer, R. E. A. 1974. 'The *excusatio magisteri* and the administration of Rome under Commodus'. *Athenaeum* 52: 266–88.

1978–80. 'C. Verres' legacy of charm and love to the city of Rome: a new document'. *Rendiconti della Pontificia Accademia di Archeologia* 51–52: 111–36.

1980. 'Customs on market goods imported into the city of Rome'. In *The Seaborne Commerce of Ancient Rome: Studies in Archaeology and History*, ed. E. C. Kopff and J. H. D'Arms. Rome, 217–33.

1981. 'The topography and social history of Rome's Trastevere southern sector'. *Proceedings of the American Philosophical Society* 125.5: 368–97.

Panciera, S. 1970. 'Tra topografia e epigrafia'. *Archeologia classica* 22: 131–63.

1993. 'Soldati e civili a Roma nei primi tre secoli dell'impero'. In *Prosopographie und Sozialgeschichte*, ed. W. Eck. Cologne, 261–76.

2000. 'Nettezza urbana a Roma: organizzazione e responsabili'. In *'Sordes urbis': la eliminación de residuos en la ciudad romana*, ed. X. Dupré Raventós and J. A. Remolà. Rome, 95–105.

Panella, C., ed. 1996. *Meta Sudans. 1. Un' area sacra in Palatio e la valle del Colosseo prima e dopo Nerone*. Rome.

Papi, E., ed. 2007. *Supplying Rome and the Empire*. Portsmouth, RI.

Parkin, T. G. 1992. *Demography and Roman Society*. Baltimore.

2003. *Old Age in the Roman World*. Baltimore.

Passerini, A. 1939. *Le coorti pretorie*. Rome.

Patterson, J. 1992. 'The city of Rome: from Republic to empire'. *Journal of Roman Studies*, 82: 186–215.

2000. 'On the margins of the city of Rome'. In *Death and Disease in the Ancient City*, ed. V. M. Hope and E. Marshall. London, 85–103.

2006. *Landscapes and Cities: Rural Settlement and Civic Transformation in Early Imperial Italy*. Oxford.

2010. 'The city of Rome revisited: from mid-Republic to mid-empire', *Journal of Roman Studies*, 100: 210–32.

Patterson, O. 1982. *Slavery and Social Death: A Comparative Study*. London.

Paul, G. M. 1982. '*Urbs capta*: sketch of an ancient literary motif'. *Phoenix* 36: 144–55.

Pearse, J. D. L. 1974. 'The organization of Roman building during the late Republic and early empire'. Unpublished dissertation. University of Cambridge.

1976–7. 'Three Alba of the *Collegium Fabrum Tignariorum* at Rome'. *Bullettino della Commissione Archeologica Comunale di Roma* 85: 163–76.

Pedroni, L. 1992. 'Per una lettura verticale della Forma Urbis marmorea'. *Ostraka* 1: 223–30.

Peña, J. T. 1998. 'The mobilization of state olive oil in Roman Africa: the evidence of late 4th-c. *ostraca* from Carthage'. In *Carthage Papers: The Early Colony's Economy, Water Supply, a Public Bath and the Mobilization of State Olive Oil*, ed. J. T. Peña et al. Portsmouth, RI, 117–238.

1999. *The Urban Economy during the Early Dominate: Pottery Evidence from the Palatine Hill*. Oxford.

Pensabene, P., and S. Falzone, eds. 2001. *Scavi del Palatino. I*. Rome.

Pensabene, P., and A. D'Alessio. 2006. 'L'immaginario urbano: spazio sacro sul Palatino tardo-repubblicano'. In *Imaging Ancient Rome: Documentation – Visualization – Imagination*, ed. L. Haselberger and J. Humphrey. Portsmouth, RI, 30–49.

Pergola, P. 1990. '*Mensores, frumentarii christiani* et annone à la fin de l'Antiquité (relecture d'un cycle des peintures)'. *Rivista di Archeologia Cristiana* 66: 167–84.

Perry, J. S. 2006. *The Roman Collegia: The Modern Evolution of an Ancient Concept.* Leiden.

Petrarch. 1979. *Opere di Francesco Petrarca*, ed. Emilio Bigi. Milan.

Pietri, C. 1976. *Roma Christiana: Recherches sur l'église de Rome, son organisation, sa politique, son idéologie de Miltiade à Sixte III (311–440).* 2 vols. Rome.

    1978. 'Evergétisme et richesses ecclésiastiques dans l'Italie du IVe à la fin du Ve s.: l'exemple romain'. *Ktema* 3: 317–37 (= Pietri 1997, 813–33).

    1997. *Christiana Respublica: Éléments d'une enquête sur le christianisme antique.* 3 vols. Rome.

Piranomonte, M., ed. 2002. *Il santuario della musica e il bosco sacro di Anna Perenna.* Milan.

Pirson, F. 2008. 'Shops and industries'. In *The World of Pompeii*, ed. J. J. Dobbins and P. W. Foss. London, 457–73.

Platner, S. B. and T. Ashby. 1926. *A Topographical Dictionary of Ancient Rome.* Oxford.

Pollitt, J. J. 1983. *The Art of Rome, c. 753 BC–AD 337: Sources and Documents.* Cambridge.

Potter, D. S. 2006. 'Spectacle'. In *A Companion to the Roman Empire*, ed. D. S. Potter. Oxford, 385–408.

Pottier, B. 2009. 'Contrôle et répression des vagabonds et des mendiants dans l'empire romain au IVe siècle'. In *Le monde de l'itinérance en Méditerranée, de l'Antiquité à l'époque moderne*, ed. C. Moatti and W. Kaiser. Bordeaux, 203–40.

Poucet, J. 2000. *Les rois de Rome: tradition et histoire.* Brussels.

Poulson, B. et al. 1992–2008. *The Temple of Castor and Pollux.* 3 vols. Rome.

Price, S. 2000. 'Religions of Rome'. In *Ancient Rome: The Archaeology of the Eternal City*, ed. H. Dodge and J. Coulston. Oxford, 290–305.

Priester, S. 2002. *Ad summas tegulas: Untersuchungen zu vielgeschossigen Gebäudeblöcken mit Wohneinheiten und Insulae im kaiserzeitlichen Rom.* Rome.

Prowse, T. L. et al. 2007. 'Isotopic evidence for age-related immigration to imperial Rome'. *American Journal of Physical Anthropology* 132: 510–19.

    2008. 'Isotopic and dental evidence for infant and young child feeding practices in an imperial Roman skeletal sample'. *American Journal of Physical Anthropology* 137: 294–308.

Purcell, N. 1983. 'The *apparitores*: a study of social mobility'. *Papers of the British School at Rome* 51: 125–73.

    1985. 'Wine and wealth in ancient Italy'. *Journal of Roman Studies* 75: 1–19.

    1987a. 'Tomb and suburb'. In *Römische Gräberstraßen Selbstdarstellung – Status – Standard*, ed. H. von Hesberg and P. Zanker. Munich, 25–41.

    1987b. 'Town in country and country in town'. In *Ancient Roman Villa Gardens*, ed. E. B. MacDougall. Washington, D.C., 187–203.

    1994. 'The city of Rome and the *plebs urbana* in the late Republic'. In *The Cambridge Ancient History*, vol. 9. 2nd edn. Cambridge, 644–88.

    1995a. 'The Roman villa and the landscape of production'. In *Urban Society in Roman Italy*, ed. T. Cornell and K. Lomas. London, 151–79.

    1995b. 'Literate games: Roman society and the game of *alea*'. *Past and Present* 147: 3–37. Reprinted in *Studies in Ancient Greek and Roman Society*, ed. R. G. Osborne, Cambridge 2004, 177–205.

    1996. 'Rome and its development under Augustus and his successors'. In *Cambridge Ancient History*, vol. 10. 2nd edn. Cambridge, 782–811.

1999. 'The populace of Rome in Late Antiquity: problems of classification and historical description'. In *The Transformations of Urbs Roma in Late Antiquity*, ed. W. V. Harris. Portsmouth, RI, 135–61.

2007. 'The *horti* of Rome and the landscape of property'. In *Res bene gestae: ricerche di storia urbana su Roma antica in onore di Eva Margareta Steinby*, ed. A. Leone et al. Rome, 361–74.

Raaflaub, K. A., ed. 2005. *Social Struggles in Archaic Rome: New Perspectives on the Conflict of the Orders*. 2nd edn. Berkeley.

Raepsaet, G. 2008. 'Land transport, Part 2: riding, harnesses, and vehicles'. In *The Oxford Handbook of Engineering and Technology in the Classical World*, ed. J. P. Oleson. Oxford, 580–605.

Rainbird, J. S. 1986. 'The fire stations of imperial Rome'. *Papers of the British School at Rome* 54: 147–69.

Ramage, E. S. 1984. 'Urban problems in ancient Rome'. In *Aspects of Graeco-Roman Urbanism: Essays on the Classical City*, ed. R. T. Marchese. Oxford, 61–92.

Ramage, N. H. and A. Ramage. 2008. *Roman Art: Romulus to Constantine*. London.

Rasch, J. J. and A. Arbeiter. 2007. *Das Mausoleum der Constantina in Rom*. Mainz.

Rauh, N. K. 1989. 'Finance and estate sales in republican Rome'. *Aevum* 63: 45–76.

Rawson, B. 1974. 'Roman concubinage and other *de facto* marriages'. *Transactions and Proceedings of the American Philological Association* 104: 279–305.

1981. 'Chariot-racing in the Roman Republic'. *Papers of the British School at Rome* 49: 1–16. Reprinted in Rawson 1991, 389–407.

1985. 'Theatrical life in republican Rome and Italy'. *Papers of the British School at Rome* 53: 97–113. Reprinted in Rawson 1991, 468–87.

1987. '*Discrimina ordinum*. The *lex Iulia theatralis*'. *Papers of the British School at Rome* 55: 83–114. Reprinted in Rawson 1991, 508–45.

1989. '*Spurii* and the Roman view of illegitimacy'. *Antichthon* 23: 10–41.

1991. *Roman Culture and Society*. Oxford.

2003. *Children and Childhood in Roman Italy*. Oxford.

2011. 'Degrees of freedom: *vernae* and Junian Latins in the Roman *familia*'. In *Children, Memory and Family: Identity in Roman Culture*, ed. V. Dasen and T. Späth. Oxford.

Rea, R. ed. 2004. *L'ipogeo di Trebio Giusto sulla Via Latina: scavi e restauri*. Vatican City.

Rebillard, E. 2003. *Religion et sépulture: L'Église, les vivants et les morts dans l'Antiquité tardive*. Paris.

Reed, J. D. 2007. *Virgil's Gaze: Nation and Poetry in the 'Aeneid'*. Princeton.

Reimers, P. 1989. '*Opus omnium dictu maximum*: literary sources for the knowledge of Roman city drainage'. *Opuscula Romana* 17: 137–41.

Reynolds, D. W. 1996. 'Forma Urbis Romae: the Severan marble plan and the urban form of ancient Rome'. Unpublished PhD dissertation. University of Michigan.

Ricci, G. 2002. 'Un laboratorio tessile a ponte Milvio: indagini 2001–2002'. In *Il Santuario della Musica e il Bosco Sacro di Anna Perenna*, ed. M. Piramonte. Milan, 89–95.

Richardson Jr, L. 1992. *A New Topographical Dictionary of Ancient Rome*. Baltimore.

Rickman, G. 1971. *Roman Granaries and Store Buildings*. Oxford.

1980a. *The Corn Supply of Ancient Rome*. Oxford.

1980b. 'The grain trade under the Roman empire'. *Memoirs of the American Academy in Rome* 36: 261–75.

Rico, C. 1995. 'La diffusion par mer des matériaux de construction en terre cuite: un aspect mal connu du commerce antique en Méditerranée occidentale'. *Mélanges de l'École Française de Rome* 107: 767–800.

Rinkewitz, W. 1984. *'Pastio villatica': Untersuchungen zur intensiven Hoftierhaltung in der römischen Landwirtschaft*. Frankfurt.

Rives, J. B. 2002. 'Magic in the XII Tables revisited'. *Classical Quarterly* 52: 270–90.

Robert, J. 1888. *Le chien d'appartement et d'utilité: Education, dressage, hygiène, maladies*. Paris.

Robinson, O. F. 1992. *Ancient Rome: City Planning and Organization*. London.

Rodgers, R. H., ed. 2004. *Frontinus, De aquaeductu urbis Romae*. Cambridge.

  2005. 'Translation of Sextus Julius Frontinus, *De aquaeductu urbis Romae*'. *Journal of Roman Archaeology* 18: 514–34.

Rodriguez-Almeida, E. 1981. *Forma Urbis marmorea: Aggiornamento*. Rome.

Rosen, R. M. ed. 2004. *Time and Temporality in the Ancient World*. Philadelphia, PA.

Rosen, R. M. and I. Sluiter, eds. 2006. *City, Countryside, and the Spatial Organization of Value in Classical Antiquity*. Leiden.

Rossi, A. 2002. 'The fall of Troy: between tradition and genre'. In *Clio and the Poets: Augustan Poetry and the Traditions of Roman Historiography*, ed. D. Levene and D. P. Nelis. Leiden, 231–51.

Rouveret, A. 1991. 'Tacite et les monuments'. *Aufstieg und Niedergang der römischen Welt* II.33.4, 3051–99.

Royden, H. L. 1988. *The Magistrates of the Roman Professional Collegia in Italy from the First to the Third Century AD*. Pisa.

Rüpke, J. 1990. *Domi militiae: Die religiöse Konstruktion des Krieges in Rom*. Stuttgart.

  1995. *Kalendar und Öffentlichkeit: Die Geschichte der Repräsentation und religiösen Qualification von Zeit in Rom*. Berlin.

  2005. *Fasti sacerdotum: Die Mitglieder der Priesterschaften und das sakrale Funktionspersonal römischer, griechischer, orientalischer und jüdisch-christlicher Kulte in der Stadt Rom von 300 v. Chr. bis 499 n. Chr.* 3 vols. Wiesbaden.

  ed. 2007a. *A Companion to Roman Religion*. Oxford.

  2007b. *The Religion of the Romans*. Cambridge.

Rutgers, L. V. 1995. *The Jews in Late Ancient Rome: Evidence of Cultural Interaction in the Roman Diaspora*. Leiden.

  2006. 'Reflections on the demography of the Jewish community of ancient Rome'. In *Les cités de l'Italie tardo-antique (IVe–VIe siècle)*, ed. M. Ghilardi et al. Rome, 345–66.

  et al. 2006. 'Sul problema di come datare le catacombe ebraiche di Roma'. *Babesch* 81: 169–78.

  et al. 2007. 'Further radiocarbon dates from the catacombs of St. Callixtus in Rome'. *Radiocarbon* 49: 1221–9.

  et al. 2009. 'Stable isotope data from the early Christian catacombs of ancient Rome: new insights into the dietary habits of Rome's early Christians'. *Journal of Archaeological Science* 36: 1127–34.

Saastamoinen, A. 2003. 'The literary character of Frontinus' *De aquaeductu*'. In *Technology, Ideology, Water: From Frontinus to the Renaissance and Beyond*, ed. C. Bruun and A. Saastamoinen. Rome, 15–39.

Sablayrolles, R. 1996. *Libertinus miles: Les cohortes de vigiles*. Rome.

    1997. '*Sparteoli*, les vigiles dans Rome'. In *La rue, lieu de sociabilité?*, ed. A. Lemémorel. Rouen, 97–104.

    2001. 'La rue, le soldat et le pouvoir: la garnison de Rome de César à Pertinax'. *Pallas* 55: 127–53.

Säflund, G. 1932. *Le Mura di Roma repubblicana, saggio di archeologia romana*. Paris.

Sallares, R. 2002. *Malaria and Rome: A History of Malaria in Ancient Italy*. Oxford.

Saller, R. 1994. *Patriarchy, Property and Death in the Roman Family*. Cambridge.

    2003. 'Women, slaves, and the economy of the Roman household'. In *Early Christian Families in Context: An Interdisciplinary Dialogue*, ed. D. L. Balch and C. Osiek. Cambridge, 185–204.

Saller, R. and B. Shaw. 1984. 'Tombstones and Roman family relations in the Principate: civilians, soldiers and slaves'. *Journal of Roman Studies* 74: 124–56.

Salvadei, L., F. Ricci and G. Manzi. 2001. 'Porotic hyperostosis as a marker of health and nutritional conditions during childhood: studies at the transition between imperial Rome and the early Middle Ages'. *American Journal of Human Biology* 13: 709–17.

Salzman, M. R. 1981. 'New evidence for the dating of the calendar at Santa Maria Maggiore in Rome'. *Transactions and Proceedings of the American Philological Association* 111: 215–27.

    1990. *On Roman Time: The Codex-calendar of 354 and the Rhythms of Urban Life in Late Antiquity*. Berkeley.

    2002. *The Making of a Christian Aristocracy: Social and Religious Change in the Western Roman Empire*. Cambridge, Mass.

    2004. 'Pagan and Christian notions for the week in the 4th century CE western Roman empire'. In *Time and Temporality in the Ancient World*, ed. R. Rosen. Philadelphia, Pa., 185–212.

Santoro L'Hoir, F. 2006. *Tragedy, Rhetoric and the Historiography of Tacitus' Annales*. Ann Arbor.

Scheid, J. 2003. *An Introduction to Roman Religion*. Bloomington.

    ed. 2009. 'Les biens des temples à Rome et dans le monde romain'. *Archiv für Religionsgeschichte* 11: 1–120.

Scheidel, W. 1994. 'Libitina's bitter gains: seasonal mortality and endemic disease in the ancient city of Rome'. *Ancient Society* 25: 151–75.

    1996. 'The most silent women of Greece and Rome: rural labour and women's life in the ancient world (II)'. *Greece & Rome* 43: 1–10.

    1997. 'Quantifying the sources of slaves in the early Roman Empire'. *Journal of Roman Studies* 87: 156–169.

    2001. 'Progress and problems in Roman demography'. In *Debating Roman demography*, ed. W. Scheidel. Leiden, 1–81.

    2002. 'The hireling and the slave: a transatlantic perspective'. In *Money, Labour and Land: Approaches to the Economies of Ancient Greece*, ed. P. Cartledge et al. London, 175–84.

    2003. 'Germs for Rome'. In *Rome the Cosmopolis*, ed. C. Edwards and G. Woolf. Cambridge, 158–76.

    2004. 'Human mobility in Roman Italy, I: the free population'. *Journal of Roman Studies* 94: 1–26.

2005. 'Human mobility in Roman Italy, II: the slave population'. *Journal of Roman Studies* 95: 64–79.

2007. 'Demography'. In *The Cambridge Economic History of the Greco-Roman World*, ed. W. Scheidel, I. Morris and R. Saller. Cambridge, 38–86.

2008. 'The comparative economics of slavery in the Greco-Roman world'. In *Slave Systems: Ancient and Modern*, ed. E. Dal Largo. Cambridge, 105–26.

Schnegg-Köhler, B. 2002. *Die augusteischen Säkularspiele*. Munich.

Schollmeyer, P. 2008. *Römische Tempel: Kult und Architektur im Imperium Romanum*. Mainz.

Schrumpf, S. 2006. *Bestattung und Bestattungswesen im Römischen Reich*. Bonn.

Schumacher, L. 2001. *Sklaverei in der Antike: Alltag und Schicksal der Unfreien*. Munich.

Schwarz, L. D. 1992. *London in the Age of Industrialisation: Entrepreneurs, Labour Force, and Living Conditions, 1700–1850*. Cambridge.

Scobie, A. 1986. 'Slums, sanitation, and mortality in the Roman world'. *Klio* 68: 399–433.

Scullard, H. H. 1981. *Festivals and Ceremonies of the Roman Republic*. London.

Scully, S. 1990. *Homer and the Sacred City*. Ithaca.

Sear, F. 2004. *Roman Theatres: An Architectural Study*. Rome.

Shaw, B. D. 1991. 'The cultural meaning of death: age and gender in the Roman family'. In *The Family in Italy from Antiquity to the Present*, ed. D. I. Kertzer and R. P. Saller. New Haven, 66–90.

1996a. 'Seasons of death: aspects of mortality in imperial Rome'. *Journal of Roman Studies* 86: 100–38.

1996b. 'Agrarian economy and the marriage cycle of Roman women'. *Journal of Roman Archaeology* 10: 57–76.

2000. 'Rebels and outsiders'. In *The Cambridge Ancient History*, vol. 11. Cambridge, 361–403.

2001. 'Raising and killing children: two Roman myths'. *Mnemosyne* 54: 31–77.

2006. 'Seasonal mortality in imperial Rome and the Mediterranean: three problem cases'. In Storey 2006, 86–109.

Shelton, K. J. 1981. *The Esquiline Treasure*. London.

Sinn, F., and K. Freyberger. 1996. *Die Grabdenkmäler*, vol. 2: *Die Ausstattung des Haterier-grabes*. Mainz.

Sirks, A. J. B. 1983. 'The Lex Iunia and the effects of informal manumission and iteration'. *Revue internationale des droits de l'antiquité* 28: 211–92.

1991. *Food for Rome: The Legal Structure of the Transportation and Processing of Supplies for the Imperial Distributions in Rome and Constantinople*. Amsterdam.

Smith, C. 1996. *Early Rome and Latium: Economy and Society c. 1000–500 BC*. Oxford.

Smith, J. T. 1997. *Roman Villas: A Study in Social Structure*. New York.

Smith, R. 1974. 'Multi-storey building in Scotland 1750–1970'. In *Multi-Storey Living: The British Working Class Experience*, ed. A. Sutcliffe. London, 207–43.

Smits, W., and T. Stromback. 2001. *The Economics of the Apprenticeship System*. Cheltenham.

Solin, H. 1983. 'Juden und Syrer im westlichen Teil der römischen Welt'. *Aufstieg und Niedergang der römischen Welt* II.29.2, 770–9.

Sonenscher, M. 1989. *Work and Wages: Natural Law, Politics, and the Eighteenth-Century French Trades*. Cambridge.

Speidel, M. P. 1994. *Riding for Caesar: The Roman Emperors' Horse Guards*. London.

Spencer, D. 2005. 'Lucan's follies: memory and ruin in a civil war landscape'. *Greece & Rome* 52: 46–69.

Sperduti, A. 1995. 'I resti scheletrici umani della necropoli di età romano-imperiale di Isola Sacra (I–III sec. d. C.): analisi paleodemografica'. PhD dissertation. University of Rome 'La Sapienza'.

Stambaugh, J. E. 1978. 'The functions of Roman temples'. *Aufstieg und Niedergang der römischen Welt* II.16.1, 554–608.

1988. *The Ancient Roman City*. Baltimore.

Stamper, J. W. 2005. *The Architecture of Roman Temples: The Republic to the Middle Empire*. Cambridge.

Stathakopoulos, D. C. 2004. *Famine and Pestilence in the Late Roman and Early Byzantine Empire: A Systematic Survey of Subsistence Crises and Epidemics*. Aldershot.

Stedman Jones, G. 1971. *Outcast London: A Study in the Relationship between Classes in Victorian Society*. Oxford.

Stevens, S. 2005. 'Reconstructing the garden houses at Ostia: exploring water supply, and building height'. *Babesch* 80: 113–23.

Stewart, P. 2003. *Statues in Roman Society: Representation and Response*. New York.

Stinger, C. 1995. *The Renaissance in Rome*. Bloomington.

Storey, G. R. 1997. 'The population of ancient Rome'. *Antiquity* 71: 966–78.

2001. 'Regionaries-type *insulae* 1: architectural/residential units at Ostia'. *American Journal of Archaeology* 105: 389–401.

2002. 'Regionaries-type *insulae* 2: architectural/residential units at Rome'. *American Journal of Archaeology* 106: 411–34.

2003. 'The "skyscrapers" of the ancient Roman world'. *Latomus* 62: 3–26.

2004. 'The meaning of *insula* in Roman residential terminology'. *Memoirs of the American Academy at Rome* 49: 47–84.

ed. 2006. *Urbanism in the Preindustrial World: Cross-Cultural Approaches*. Tuscaloosa.

Sumi, G. 2005. *Ceremony and Power: Performing Politics in Rome between Republic and Empire*. Ann Arbor.

Syme, R. 1960. 'Bastards in the Roman aristocracy'. *Proceedings of the American Philosophical Society* 104: 323–7.

Talbert, R. J. A. 1984. *The Senate of Imperial Rome*. Princeton.

Taylor, L. R. 1937. 'The opportunities for dramatic performances in the time of Plautus and Terence'. *Transactions of the American Philological Association* 68: 284–304.

1966. *Roman Voting Assemblies: From the Hannibalic War to the Dictatorship of Caesar*. Ann Arbor.

Taylor, L. R. and L. A. Holland. 1952. 'Janus and the *Fasti*'. *Classical Philology* 47: 137–42.

Tengström, E. 1974. *Bread for the People: Studies of the Corn-Supply of Rome during the Late Empire*. Stockholm.

Thomas, Y. 1996. *Origine et commune patrie: Études de droit public romain*. Rome.

Thompson, E. P. 1971. 'The moral economy of the English crowd in the eighteenth century'. *Past and Present* 50: 76–136.

Timms, D. 1971. *The Urban Mosaic: Towards a Theory of Residential Differentiation*. Cambridge.

Tomber, R. 1987. 'Evidence for long-distance commerce: imported bricks and tiles at Carthage'. *Rei Cretariae Romanae Fautores* 25/26: 161–74.

Tomei, M. A. 1995. 'Domus oppure lupanar? I materiali dallo scavo boni della "Casa Repubblicana" a ovest dell'Arco di Tito'. Mélanges de l'École Française de Rome (Antiquité) 107: 549–619.

Toynbee, J. M. C. 1973. Animals in Roman Life and Art. Baltimore.

Tran, N. 2006. Les membres des associations romaines: Le rang social des collegiati en Italie et en Gaules sous le haut-empire. Rome.

Treggiari, S. 1975a. 'Family life among the staff of the Volusii'. Transactions of the American Philological Association 105: 393–401.

1975b. 'Jobs in the household of Livia'. Papers of the British School at Rome 43: 48–77.

1979. 'Lower class women in the Roman economy'. Florilegium 1: 65–86.

1980. 'Urban labour in Rome: mercennarii and tabernarii'. In Non-slave Labour in the Greco-Roman World, ed. P. Garnsey. Cambridge.

1986. Il trionfo dell'acqua: acque e acquedotti a Roma: IVsec.a.c.–XX sec.: Mostra, 31 ottobre 1986–15 gennaio 1987. Rome.

1991. Roman Marriage: Iusti Coniuges from the Time of Cicero to the Time of Ulpian. Oxford.

Trout, D. E. 2003. 'Damasus and the invention of early Christian Rome'. Journal of Medieval and Early Modern Studies 33: 517–36.

Turcan, R. 1996. The Cults of the Roman Empire, trans. A. Nevill. London.

Ulrich, R. B. 1996. Contignatio, Vitruvius and the Campanian builder. American Journal of Archaeology 100: 137–51.

Usener, H. 1913 [1900]. 'Italische Volksjustiz'. In Kleine Schriften, vol. 4. Leipzig, 356–82.

Valentini, R. and G. Zucchetti. 1940–53. Codice topografico della città di Roma. Rome.

Van Berchem, D. 1939. Les distributions de blé et d'argent à la plèbe romaine sous l'empire. Geneva.

Van Deman, E. B. 1934. The Building of the Roman Aqueducts. Washington, D.C.

Van der Linde, C. 2009. 'Roman Catacombs and Demography: A Case Study of the Liberian Region in the Catacombs of St. Callixtus in Rome'. PhD dissertation. University of Utrecht.

Van Nijf, O. M. 1997. The Civic World of Professional Associations in the Roman East. Amsterdam.

Van Tilburg, C. 2007. Traffic and Congestion in the Roman Empire. London.

Vanderbroeck, P. 1987. Popular Leadership and Collective Behavior in the Late Roman Republic. Amsterdam.

Vandiver Nicassio, S. 2009. Imperial City: Rome under Napoleon. Chicago.

Varone, A. 2005. 'Nella Pompei a luci rosse: Castrensis e l'organizzazione della prostituzione e dei suoi spazi'. Rivista di Studi Pompeiani 16: 93–109.

Verboven, K. 2004. 'Mentalité et commerce: le cas des negotiatores et de ceux qui negotia habent: une enquête préliminaire'. In Mentalités et choix économiques, ed. J. Andreau, J. France and S. Pittia. Bordeaux, 179–97.

2007. 'The associative order: status and ethos among Roman businessmen in late Republic and early empire'. Athenaeum 95: 861–93.

Veyne, P. 1983. 'Le folklore à Rome et les droits de la conscience publique sur la conduite individuelle'. Latomus 42: 3–30.

1990. Bread and Circuses: Historical Sociology and Religious Pluralism. London.

Virlouvet, C. 1991. 'La plèbe frumentaire à l'époque d'Auguste: une tentative de définition'. In *Nourrir la plèbe*, ed. A. Giovannini. Basel, 43–62.

Volp, U. 2002. *Tod und Ritual in den christlichen Gemeinden der Antike*. Leiden.

Von Petrikovits, H. 1981. 'Die Spezialisierung des römischen Handwerks'. In *Das Handwerk in vor- und frühgeschichtlicher Zeit. Teil I: Historische und rechtshistorische Beiträge und Untersuchungen zur Frühgeschichte der Gilde*, ed. Herbert Jankuhn, Walter Janssen, Ruth Schmidt-Wiegand und Heinrich Tiefenbach. Göttingen, 64–132.

Wacke, A. 2001. '*Manumissio matrimonii causa*: die Freilassung zwecks Heirat nach den Ehegesetzen des Augustus'. In *Fünfzig Jahre Forschungen zur antiken Sklaverei an der Mainzer Akademie 1950–2000: Miscellanea zum Jubiläum*, ed. H. Bellen and H. Heinen. Stuttgart, 133–58.

Waddington, D., K. Jones and C. Critcher. 1989. *Flashpoints: Studies in Public Disorder*. New York.

Waldstein, W. 1986. *Operae libertorum: Untersuchungen zur Dienstpflicht freigelassener Sklaven*. Stuttgart.

Wallace-Hadrill, A. 1991. 'Elites and trade in the Roman town'. In *City and Country in the Roman World*, ed. J. Rich and A. Wallace-Hadrill. London, 143–81.

1994. *Houses and Society in Pompeii and Herculaneum*. Princeton.

2003. 'The streets of Rome as a representation of imperial power'. In *The Representation and Perception of Imperial Power*, ed. L. de Blois et al. Amsterdam, 189–206.

2008. *Rome's Cultural Revolution*. Cambridge.

Waltzing, J.-P. (1895–1900) *Étude historique sur les corporations professionnelles chez les Romains depuis les origines jusqu'à la chute de l'empire d'Occident*. 4 vols. Louvain.

Ward-Perkins, B. 1984. *From Classical Antiquity to the Middle Ages: Urban Public Building in Northern and Central Italy, AD 300–850*. Oxford.

Watts, D. 1999. *Small Worlds: The Dynamics of Networks between Order and Randomness*. Princeton.

Weiler, I. 2003. *Die Beendigung des Sklavenstatus im Altertum: Ein Beitrag zur vergleichenden Sozialgeschichte*. Stuttgart.

Welch, K. E. 2007. *The Roman Amphitheatre: From its Origins to the Colosseum*. Cambridge.

Welch, T. 2005. *The Elegiac Cityscape: Propertius and the Meaning of Roman Monuments*. Columbus, O.

Welwei, K.-W. 2000. *Sub corona vendere: Quellenkritische Studien zu Kriegsgefangenschaft und Sklaverei in Rom bis zum Ende des Hannibalkrieges, unter Berücksichtigung des Nachlasses von G. Prachner*. Stuttgart.

White, K. D. 1970. *Roman Farming*. London.

White, L. M. 1996–7. *The Social Origins of Christian Architecture*. 2 vols. Valley Forge, Pa.

Whittaker, C. R. 1993. 'The poor in the city of Rome'. In *Land, City and Trade in the Roman Empire*. Aldershot, 1–25.

Wiedemann, T. E. J. 1981. *Greek and Roman Slavery*. London.

1985. 'The regularity of manumission at Rome'. *Classical Quarterly* 35: 162–75.

1992. *Emperors and Gladiators*. London.

1997. *Slavery*. 3rd edn. Oxford.

Wikander, Ö. 1979. 'Water-mills in ancient Rome'. *Opuscula Romana* 12: 13–36.

Williams, M. 1994. 'The organisation of Jewish burials in ancient Rome in the light of evidence from Palestine and the Diaspora'. *Zeitschrift für Papyrologie und Epigraphik* 101: 165–82.

Wilson, A. 2000. 'The water-mills on the Janiculum'. *Memoirs of the American Academy of Rome* 45: 219–46.

2003. 'Late-antique water mills on the Palatine'. *Papers of the British School at Rome* 71: 85–109.

2007. 'The *castra* of Frontinus'. In *'Res bene gestae': ricerche di storia urbana su Roma antica in onore di E. M. Steinby*, ed. A. Leone et al. Rome, 439–44.

Wiseman, T. P. 1998. 'A stroll on the rampart'. In *Horti romani*, ed. M. Cima and E. La Rocca. Rome, 13–22.

2008. *Remembering the Roman People*. Oxford.

Wissemann, M. 1984. 'Die Spezialisierung des römischen Handels'. *Münstersche Beiträge zur Antiken Handelsgeschichte* 3: 116–24.

Witcher, R. 2005. 'The extended metropolis: *urbs, suburbium*, and population'. *Journal of Roman Archaeology* 18: 120–38.

2006. 'Settlement and society in early imperial Etruria'. *Journal of Roman Studies* 96: 88–123.

Woods, R. 2003. 'Urban–rural mortality differentials: an unresolved debate'. *Population and Development Review* 29: 29–46.

Woodward, C. 2001. *In Ruins: A Journey through History, Art, and Literature*. London.

Wright, J. A., S. W. Gundry and R. Conroy. 2004. 'Household drinking water in developing countries: a systematic review of micobiological contamination between source and point-of-use'. *Tropical Medicine and International Health* 9: 106–17.

Wrigley, E. A. 1987. *People, Cities and Wealth: The Transformation of Traditional Society*. Oxford.

Yavetz, Z. 1965. '*Plebs sordida*'. *Athenaeum* 43: 295–311.

1987. 'The urban plebs in the days of the Flavians, Nerva and Trajan'. In *Opposition et résistances à l'empire d'Auguste à Trajan*, ed. A. Giovannini. Geneva, 135–86.

1988. *Plebs and Princeps*, 2nd edn. Oxford.

Zanker, P. 1988. *The Power of Images in the Age of Augustus*. Ann Arbor.

Zanker, P., and B. J. Ewald. 2004. *Mit Mythen leben: Die Bilderwelt der römischen Sarkophage*. Munich.

Zerubavel, E. 2003. *Time Maps: Collective Memory and the Social Shape of the Past*. Chicago.

Zimmer, G. 1982. *Römische Berufsdarstellungen*. Berlin.

Zink, S., and H. Piening. 2009. '*Haec aurea templa*: the Palatine temple of Apollo and its polychromy'. *Journal of Roman Archaeology* 22: 109–22.

Ziolkowski, A. 1992. *The Temples of Mid-republican Rome and their Historical and Topographical Context*. Rome.

1999. 'Ritual cleaning-up of the city: from the Lupercalia to the Argei'. *Ancient Society* 29: 191–218.

2008. 'Le origini di Roma e la società romana arcaica'. In *Storia d'Europa e del Mediterraneo. IV, Grecia e Mediterraneo dalle guerre persiane all'ellenismo*, ed. A. Barbero. Rome, 103–35.

INDEX

❧